GUY DELISLE

HOSTAGE

GUY DELISLE

HOSTAGE

Translated by Helge Dascher

Jonathan Cape
London

1 3 5 7 9 10 8 6 4 2

Jonathan Cape, an imprint of Vintage Publishing,
20 Vauxhall Bridge Road,
London SW1V 2SA

Jonathan Cape is part of the Penguin Random House group of companies whose
addresses can be found at global.penguinrandomhouse.com.

Penguin
Random House
UK

First published as Senfuir: Récit d'un otage by Dargaud, Paris in 2016

First published in the United Kingdom by Jonathan Cape in 2017

penguin.co.uk/vintage

A CIP catalogue record for this book is available from the British Library

ISBN 9781911214441

Printed and bound in India by Replika Press Pvt Ltd

Penguin Random House is committed to a sustainable future for our business,
our readers and our planet. This book is made from Forest Stewardship Council® certified paper.

MIX
Paper from
responsible sources
FSC   FSC® C018179
www.fsc.org

The events reported here occurred in 1997, when Christophe André was working for a humanitarian NGO in the Caucasus.

This book recounts his story as he told it to me.

Guy Delisle

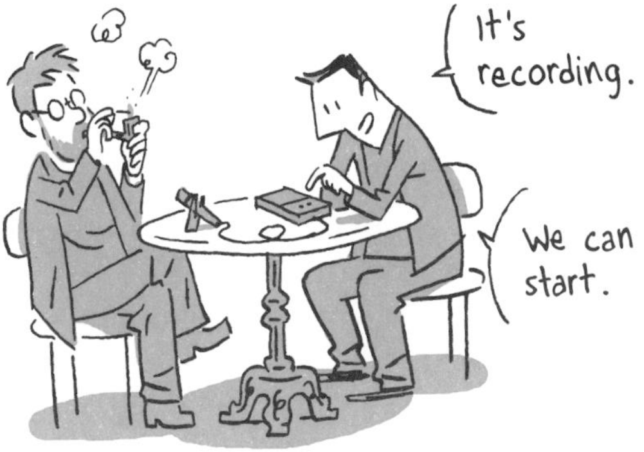
It's recording.
We can start.

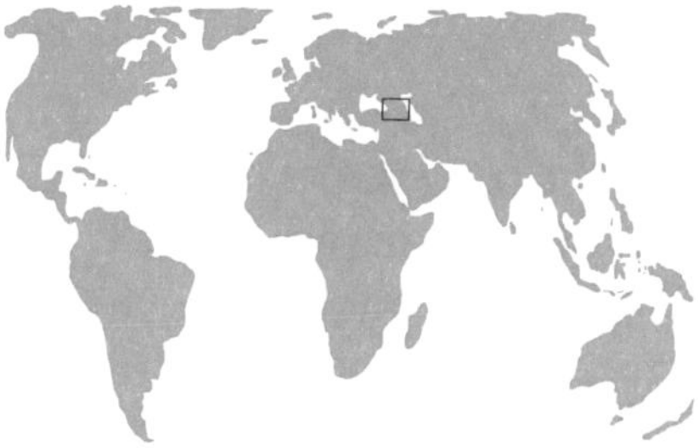

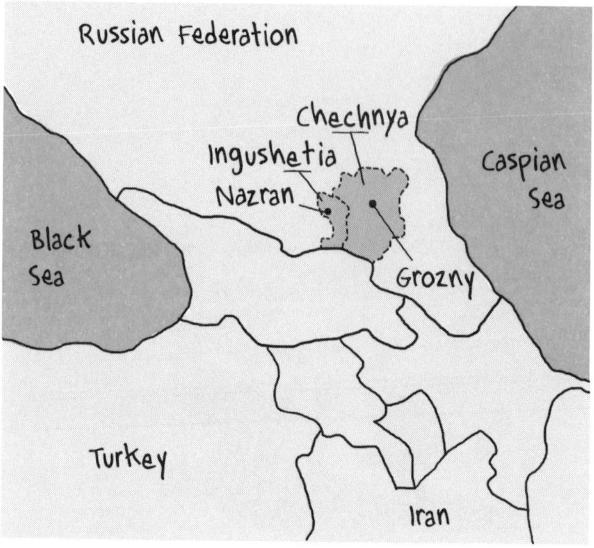
Russian Federation
Chechnya
Ingushetia
Nazran
Caspian Sea
Black Sea
Grozny
Turkey
Iran

I

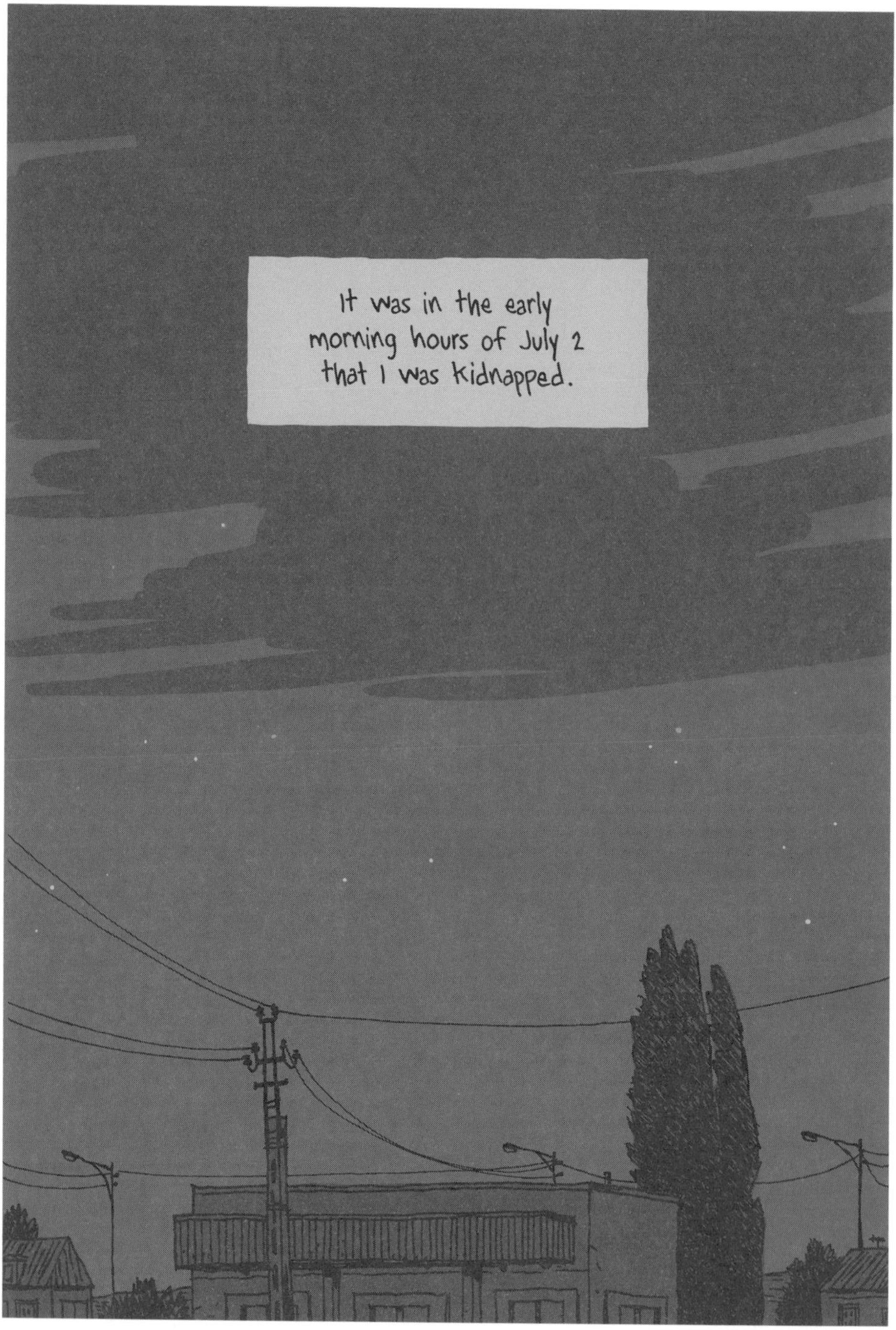
It was in the early morning hours of July 2 that I was kidnapped.

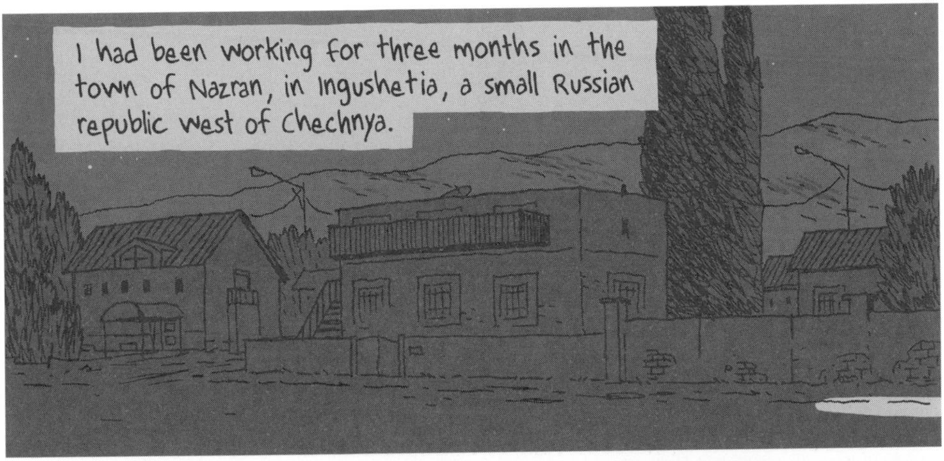
I had been working for three months in the town of Nazran, in Ingushetia, a small Russian republic west of Chechnya.

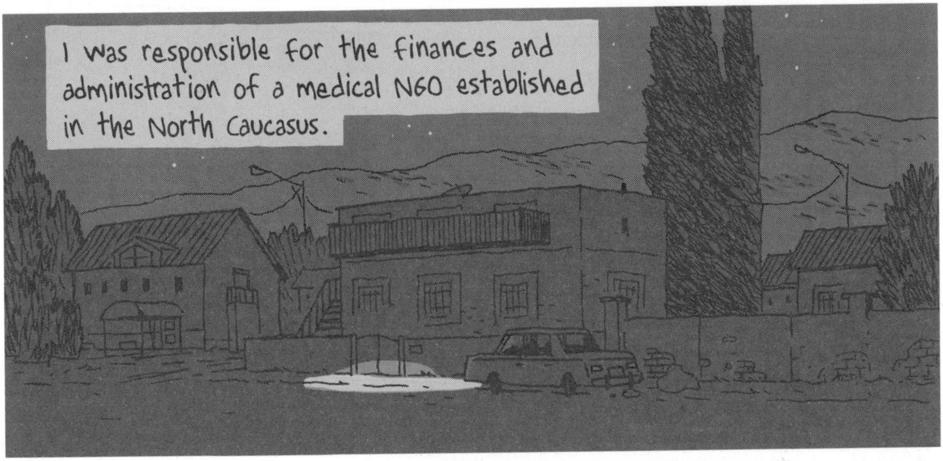
I was responsible for the finances and administration of a medical NGO established in the North Caucasus.

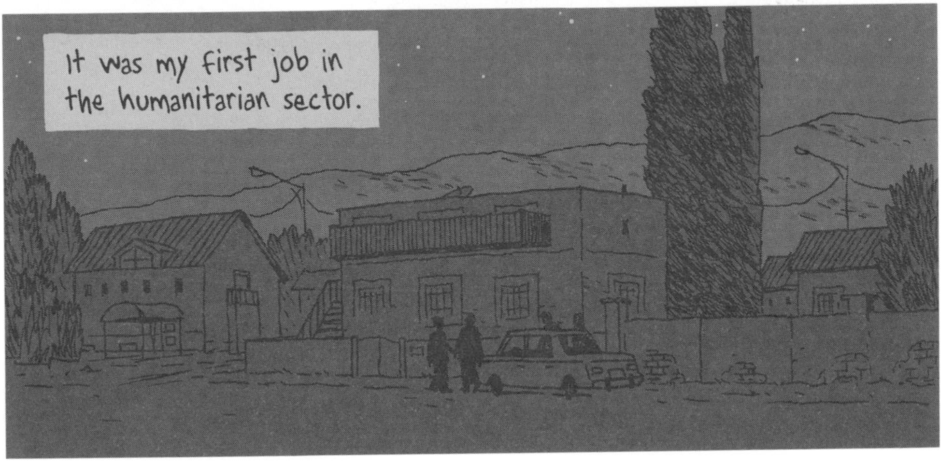
It was my first job in the humanitarian sector.

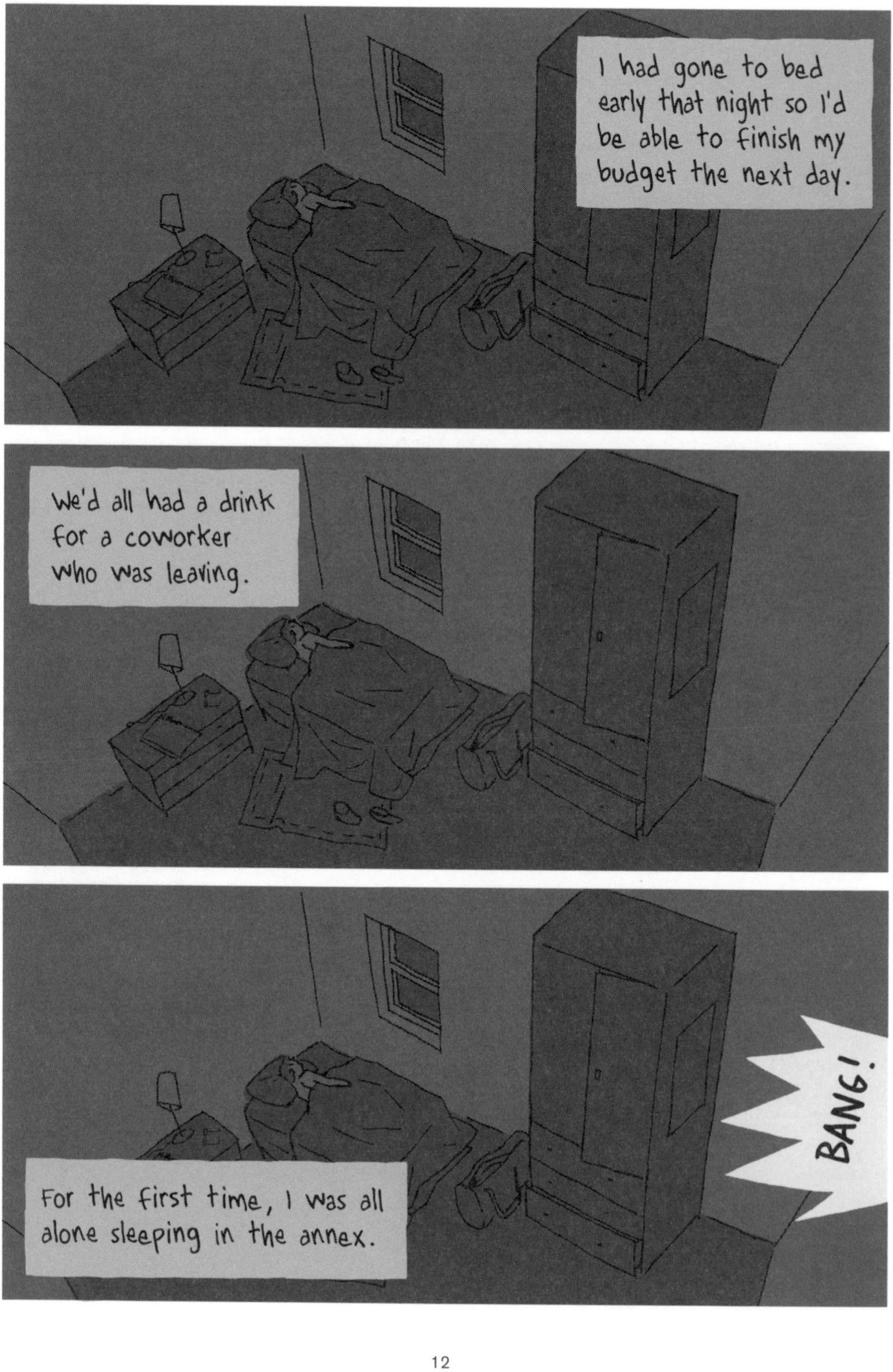
I had gone to bed early that night so I'd be able to finish my budget the next day.
We'd all had a drink for a coworker who was leaving.
For the first time, I was all alone sleeping in the annex.
BANG!

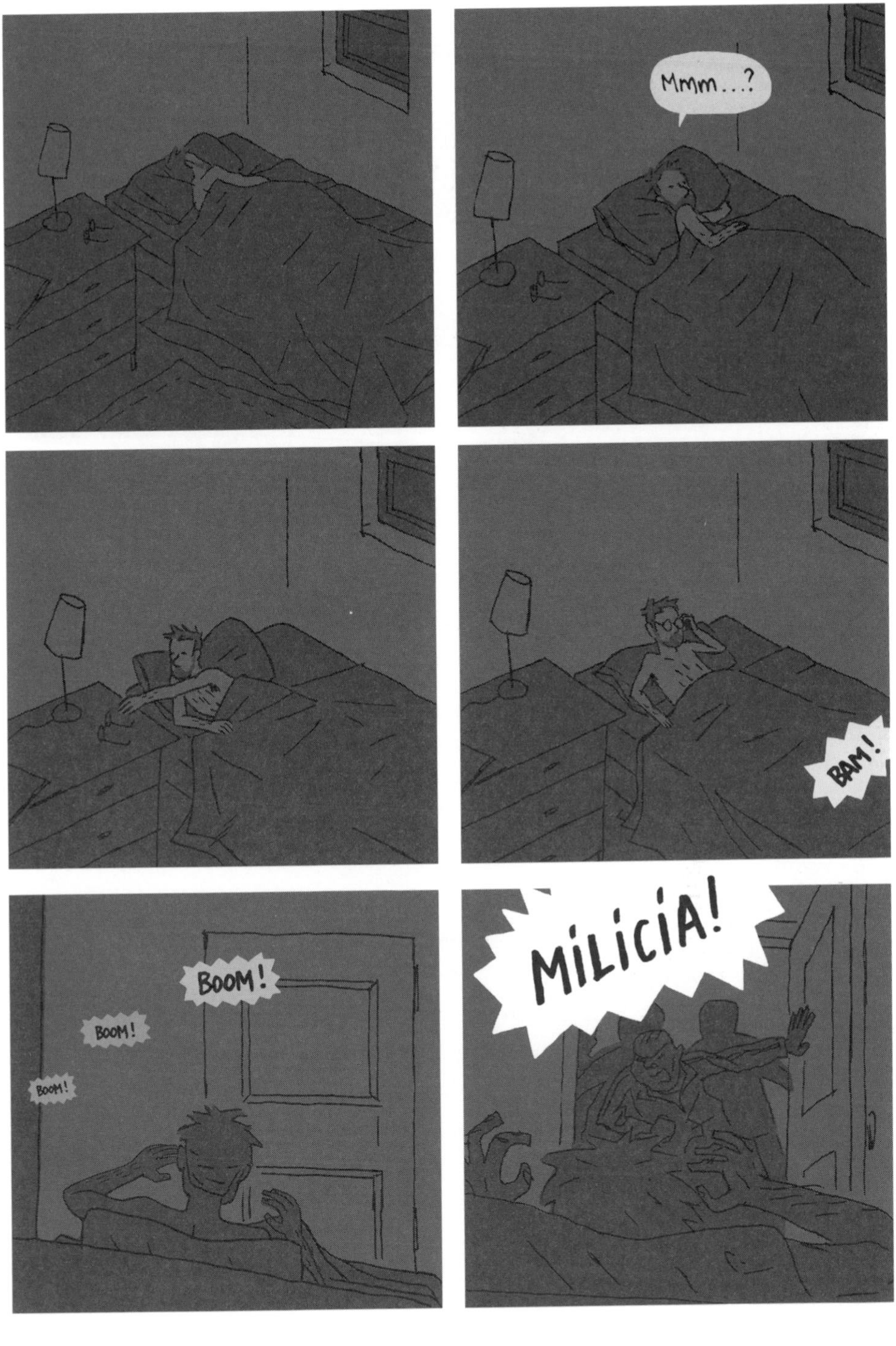
Mmm...?
BAM!
BOOM!
BOOM!
BOOM!
MILICIA!

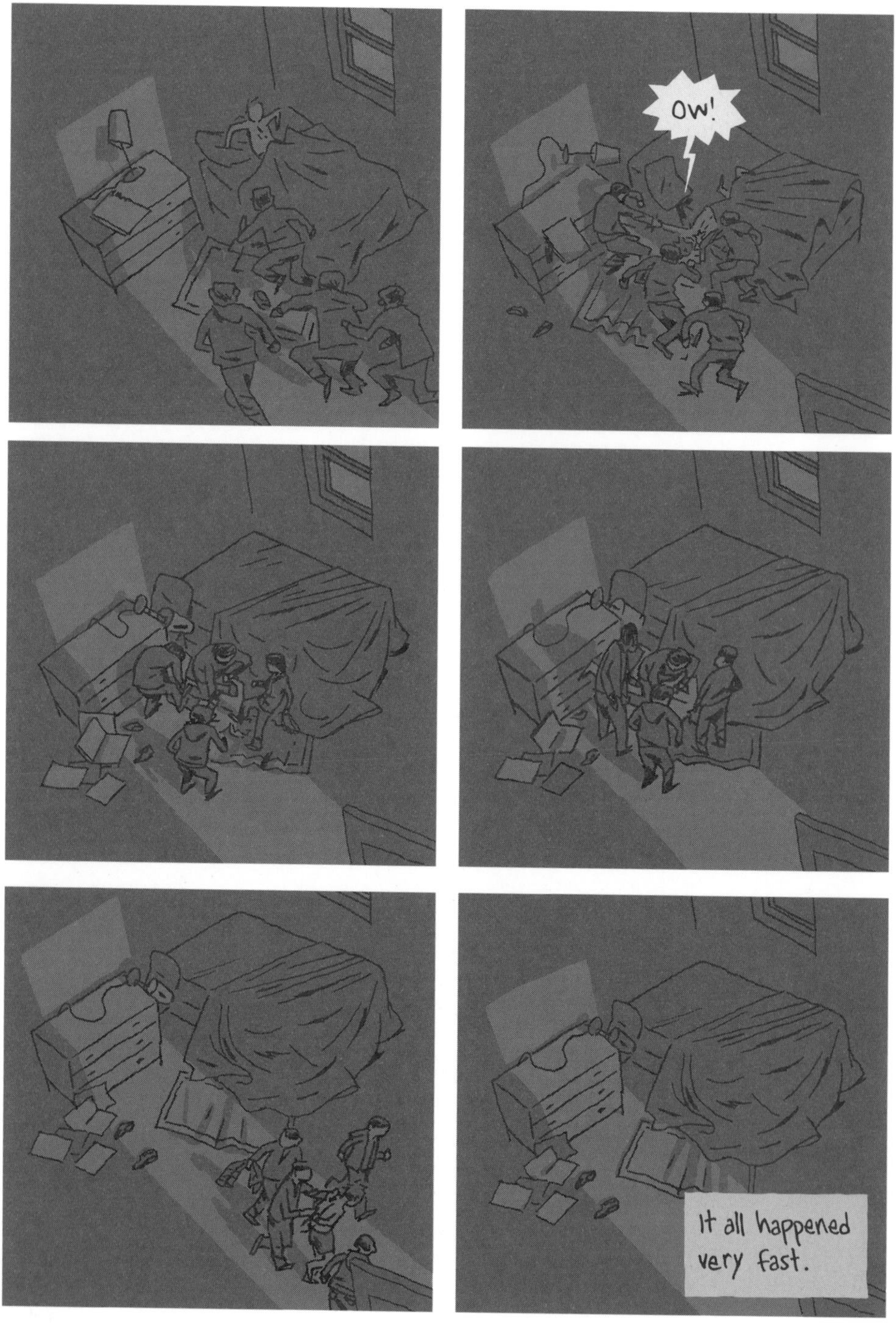
OW!
It all happened very fast.

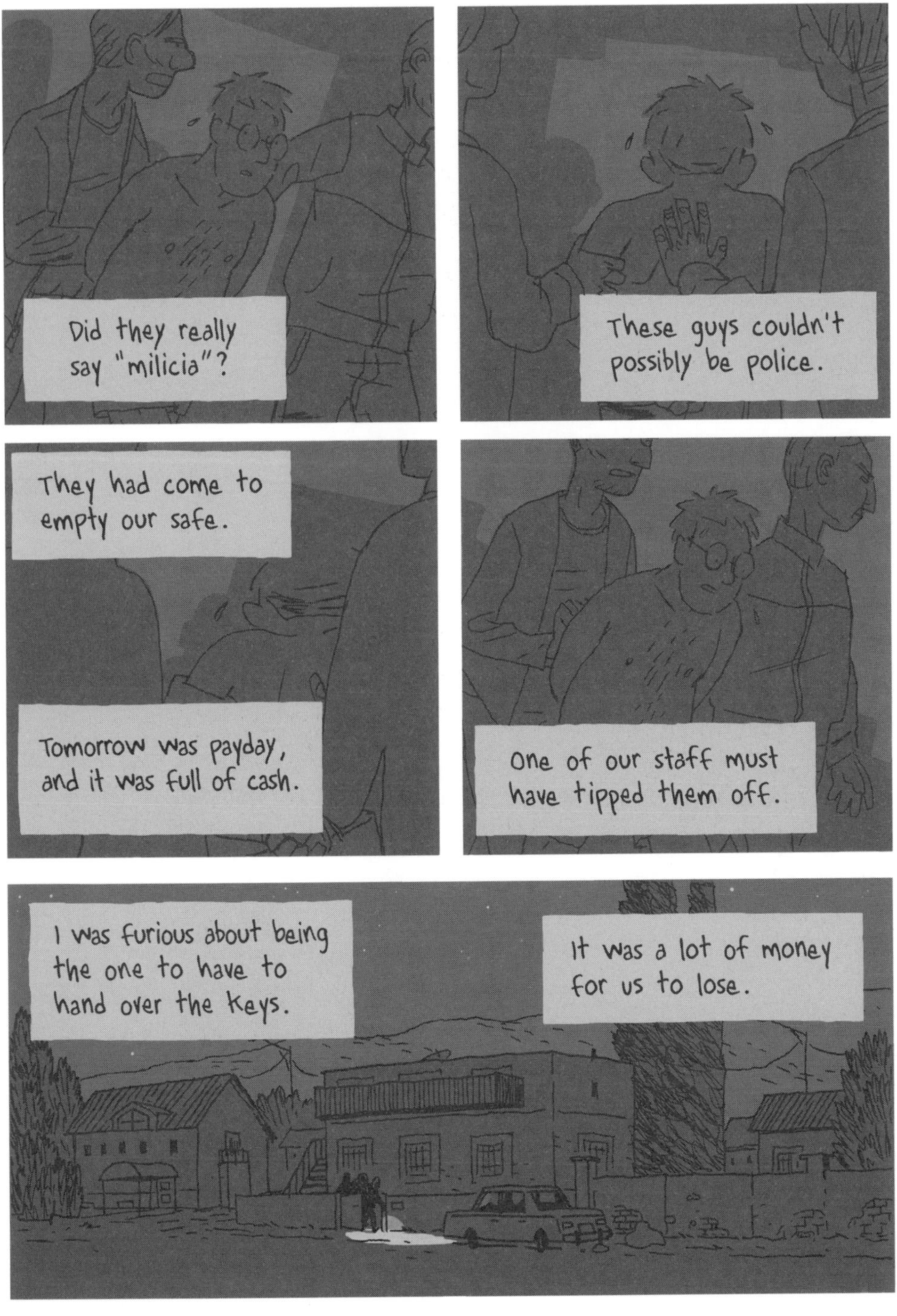
Did they really say "milicia"?
These guys couldn't possibly be police.
They had come to empty our safe.
Tomorrow was payday, and it was full of cash.
One of our staff must have tipped them off.
I was furious about being the one to have to hand over the keys.
It was a lot of money for us to lose.

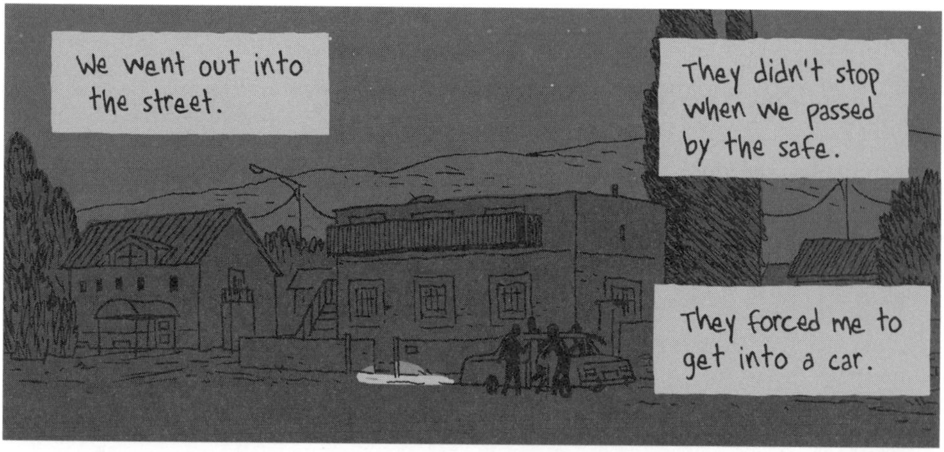
We went out into the street.
They didn't stop when we passed by the safe.
They forced me to get into a car.

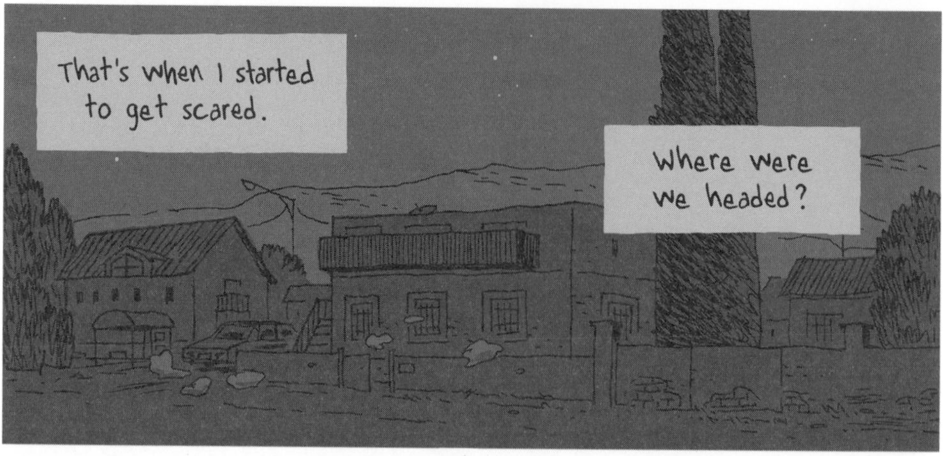
That's when I started to get scared.
Where were we headed?

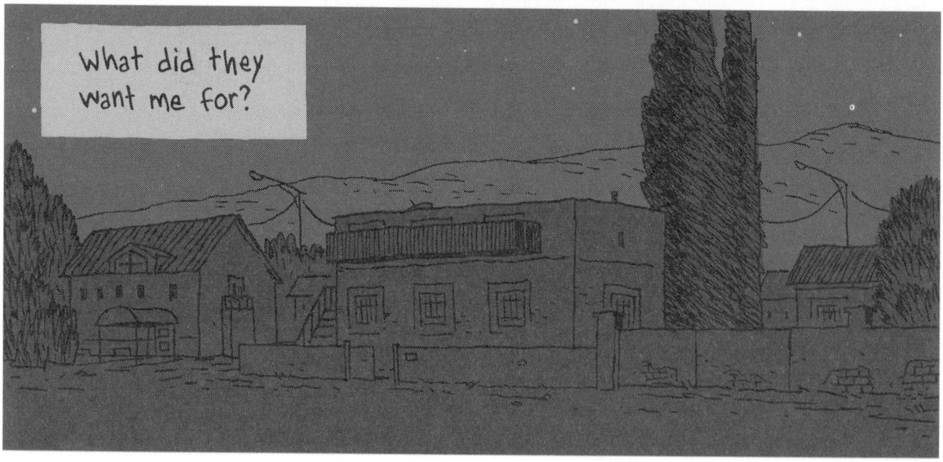
What did they want me for?

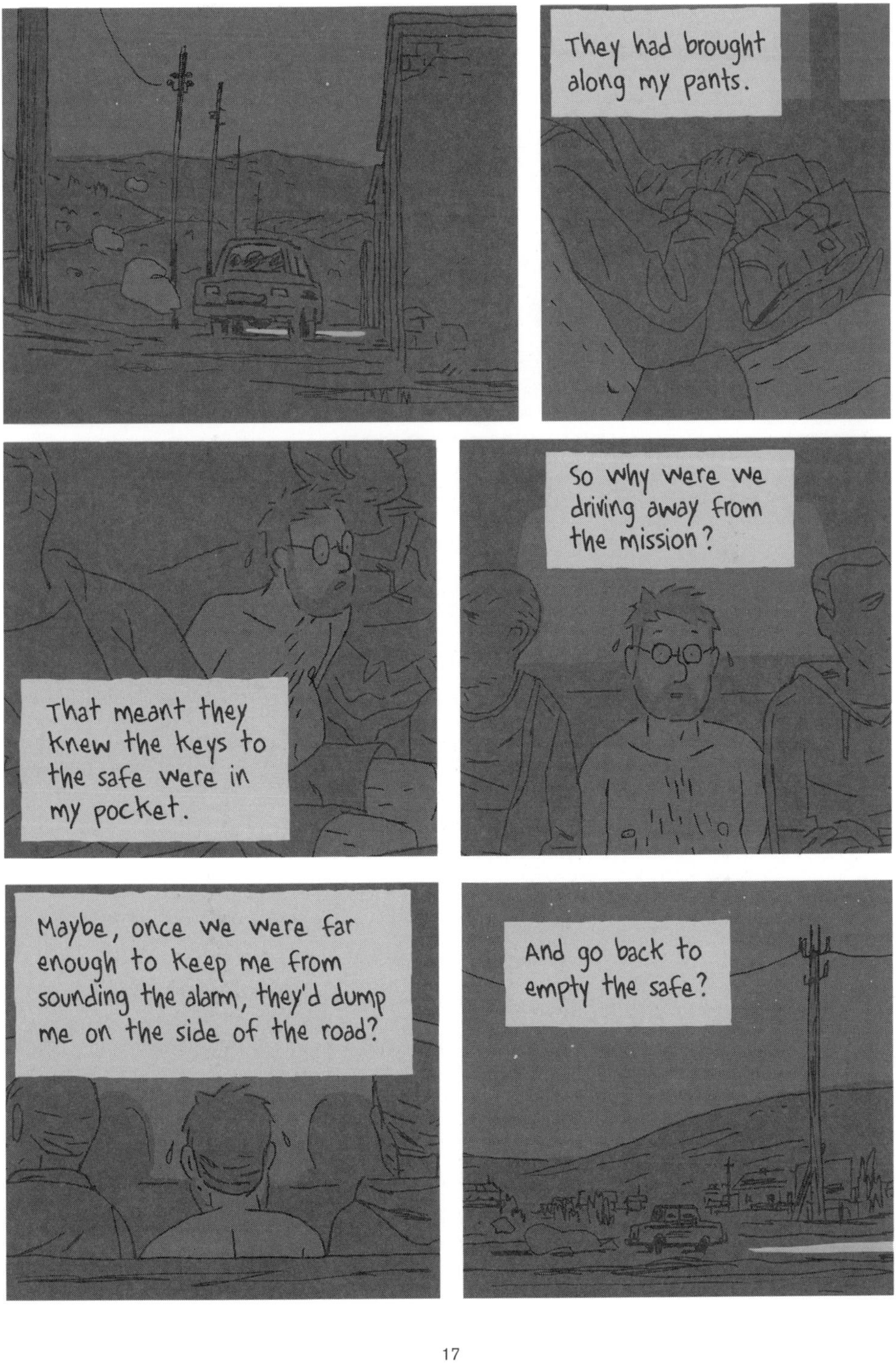
They had brought along my pants.
That meant they knew the keys to the safe were in my pocket.
So why were we driving away from the mission?
Maybe, once we were far enough to keep me from sounding the alarm, they'd dump me on the side of the road?
And go back to empty the safe?

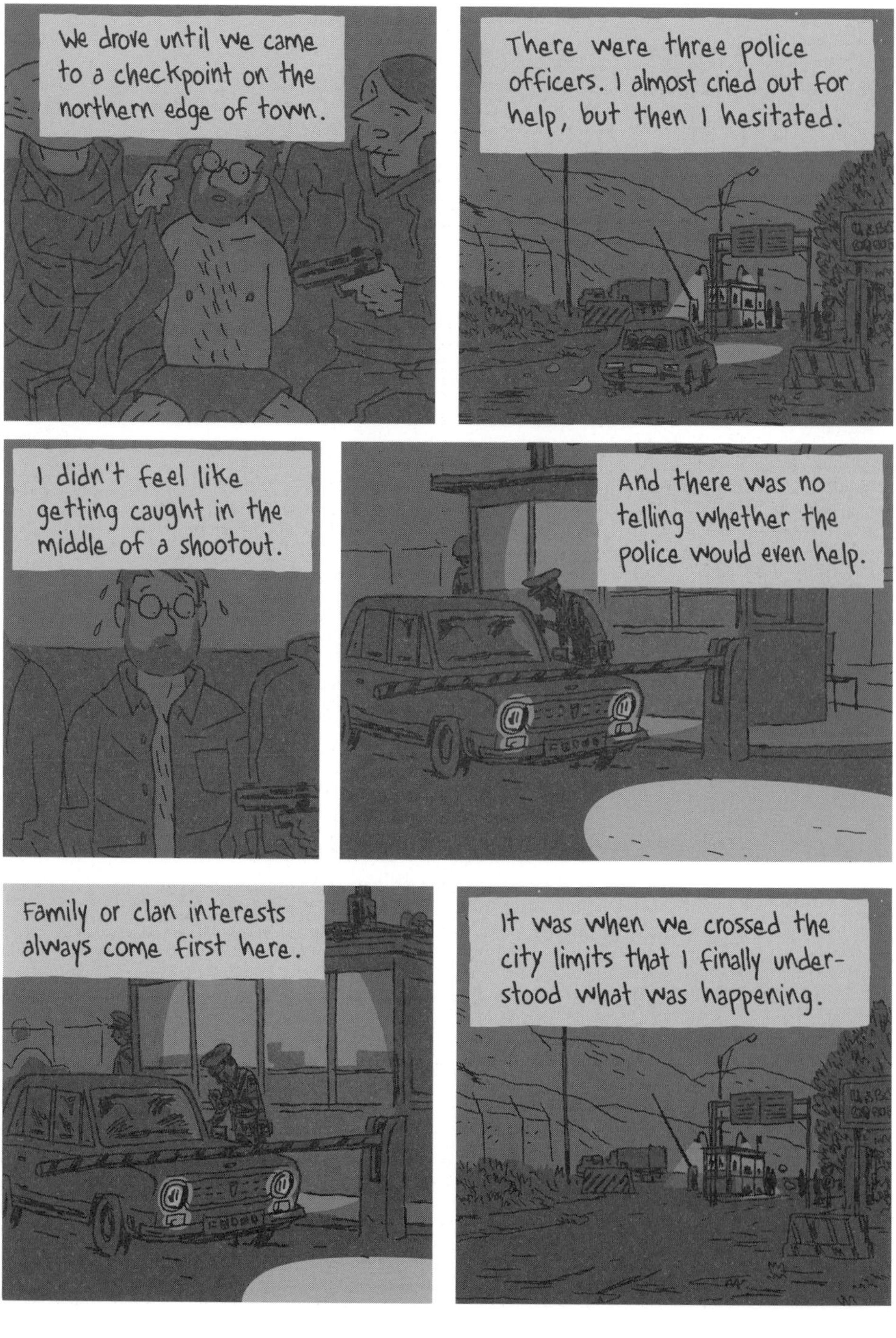
We drove until we came to a checkpoint on the northern edge of town.
There were three police officers. I almost cried out for help, but then I hesitated.
I didn't feel like getting caught in the middle of a shootout.
And there was no telling whether the police would even help.
Family or clan interests always come first here.
It was when we crossed the city limits that I finally understood what was happening.

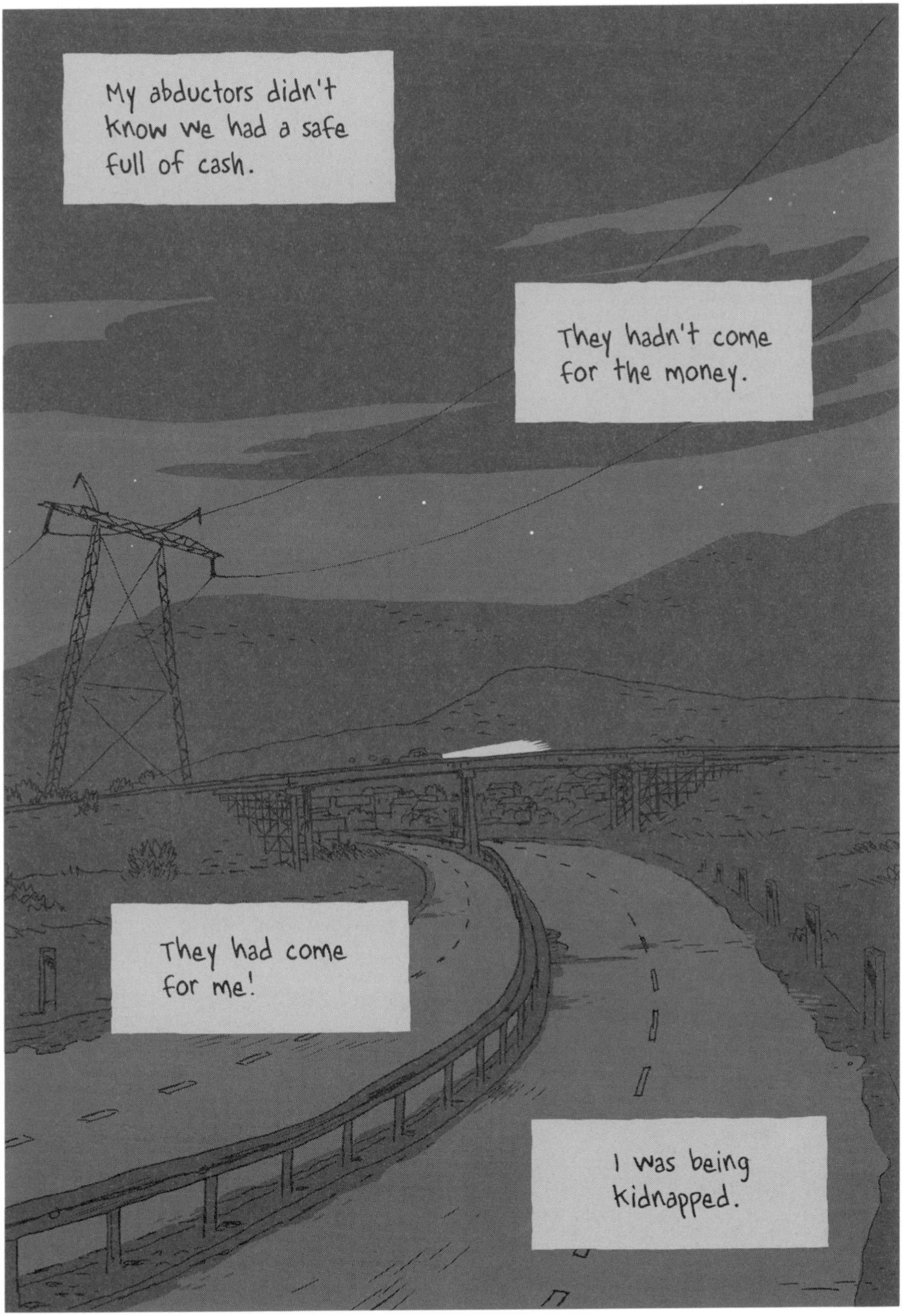
My abductors didn't know we had a safe full of cash.
They hadn't come for the money.
They had come for me!
I was being kidnapped.

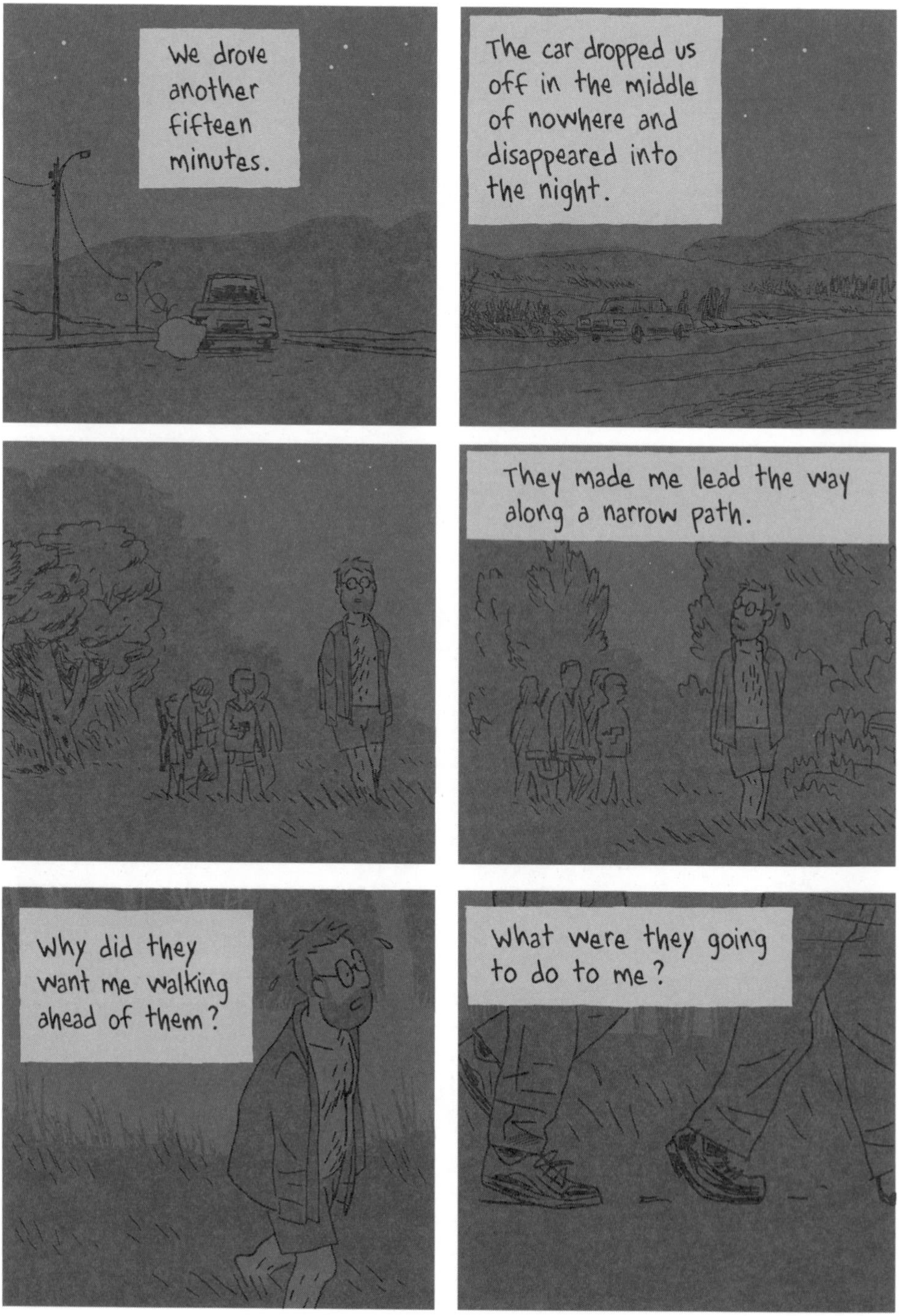
We drove another fifteen minutes.
The car dropped us off in the middle of nowhere and disappeared into the night.
They made me lead the way along a narrow path.
Why did they want me walking ahead of them?
What were they going to do to me?

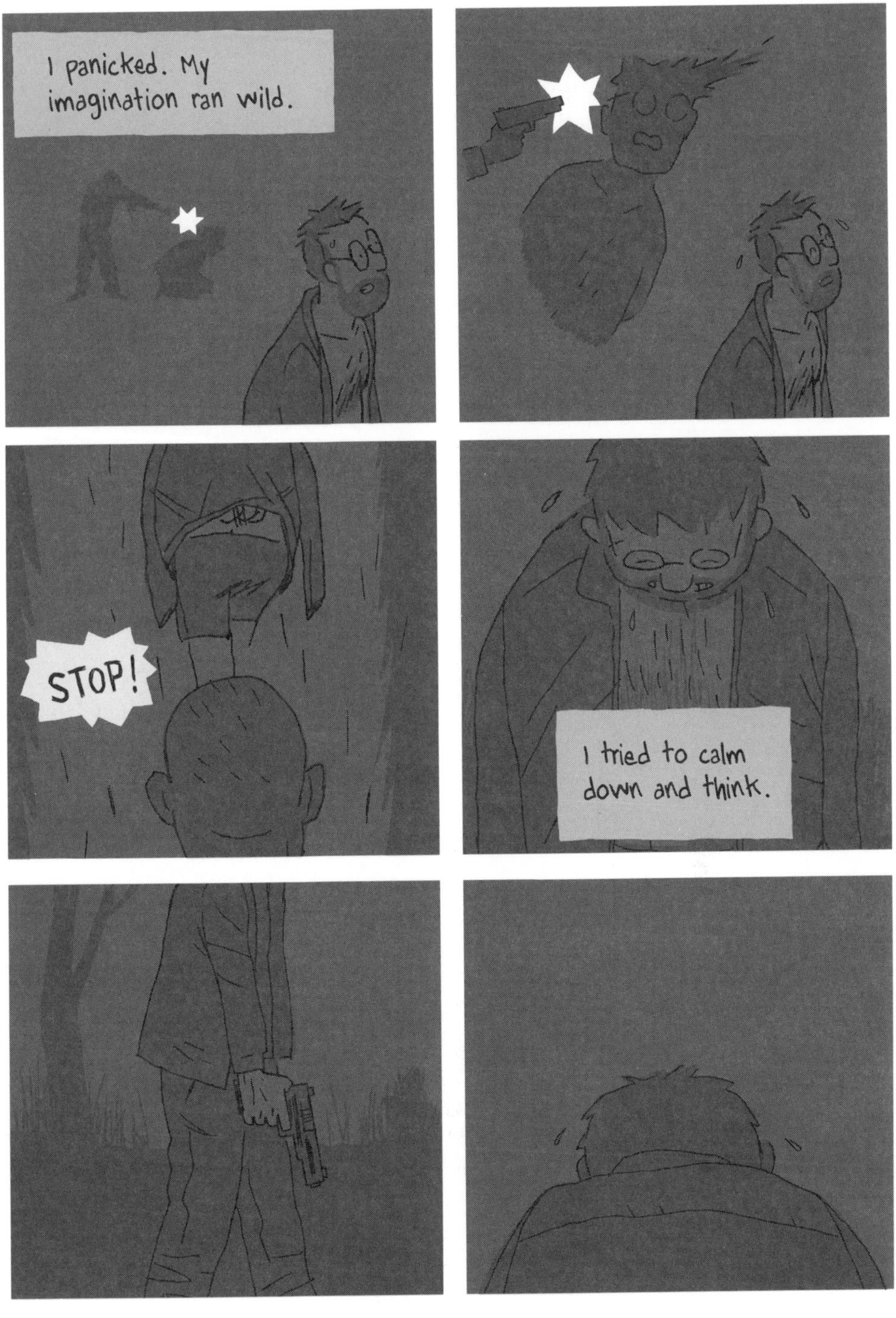
I panicked. My imagination ran wild.
STOP!
I tried to calm down and think.

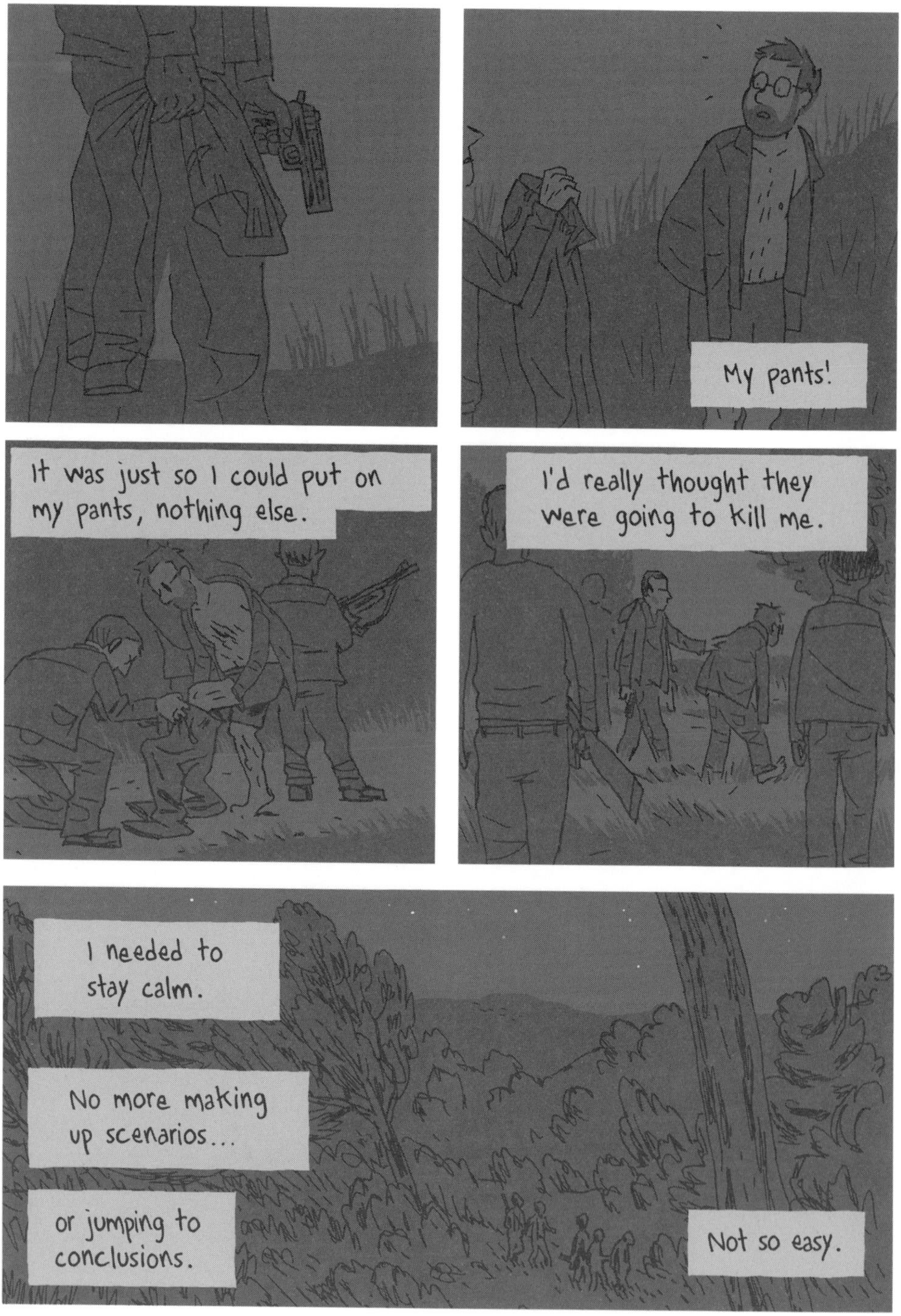
My pants!
It was just so I could put on my pants, nothing else.
I'd really thought they were going to kill me.
I needed to stay calm.
No more making up scenarios...
or jumping to conclusions.
Not so easy.

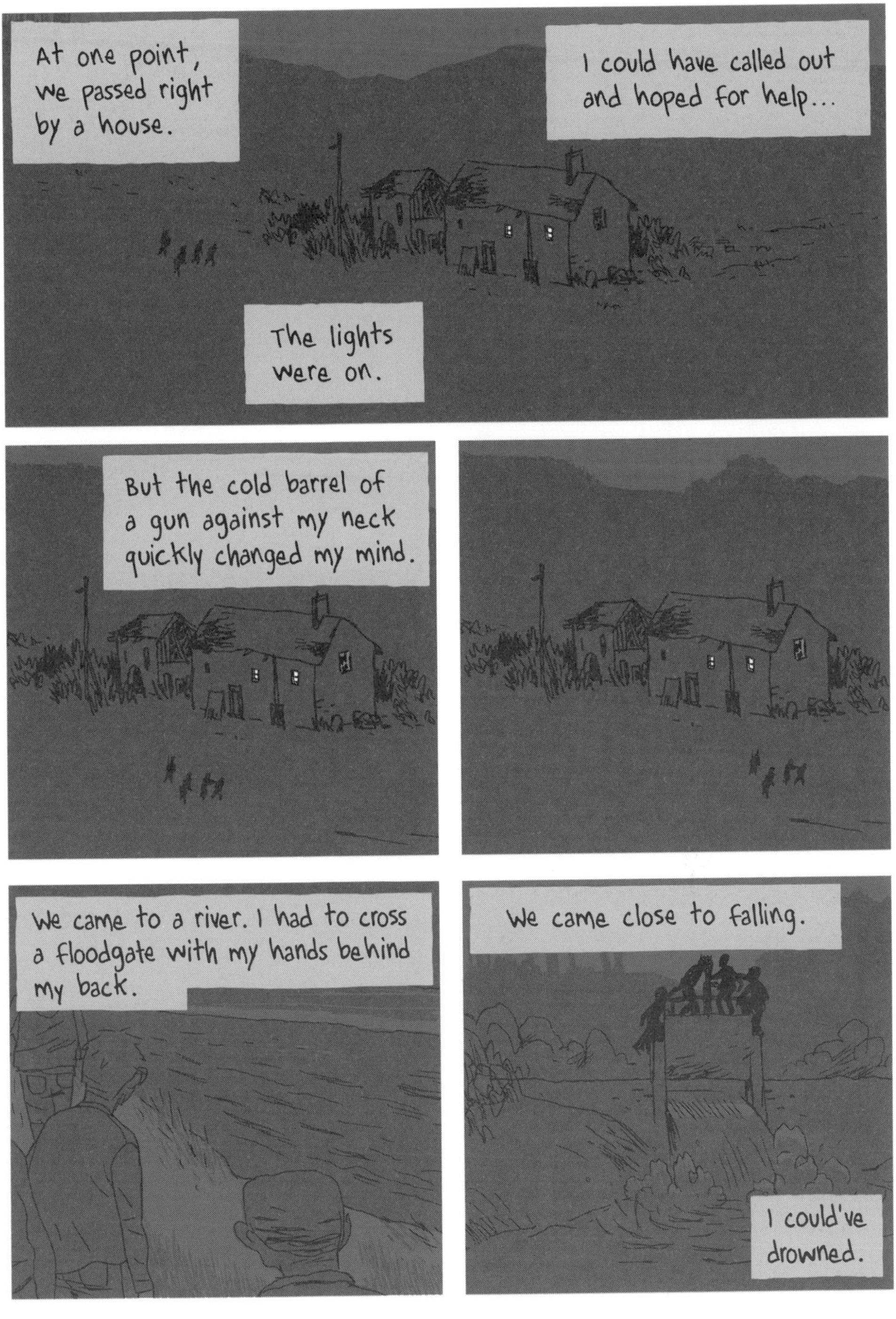
At one point, we passed right by a house.
I could have called out and hoped for help...
The lights were on.
But the cold barrel of a gun against my neck quickly changed my mind.
We came to a river. I had to cross a floodgate with my hands behind my back.
We came close to falling.
I could've drowned.

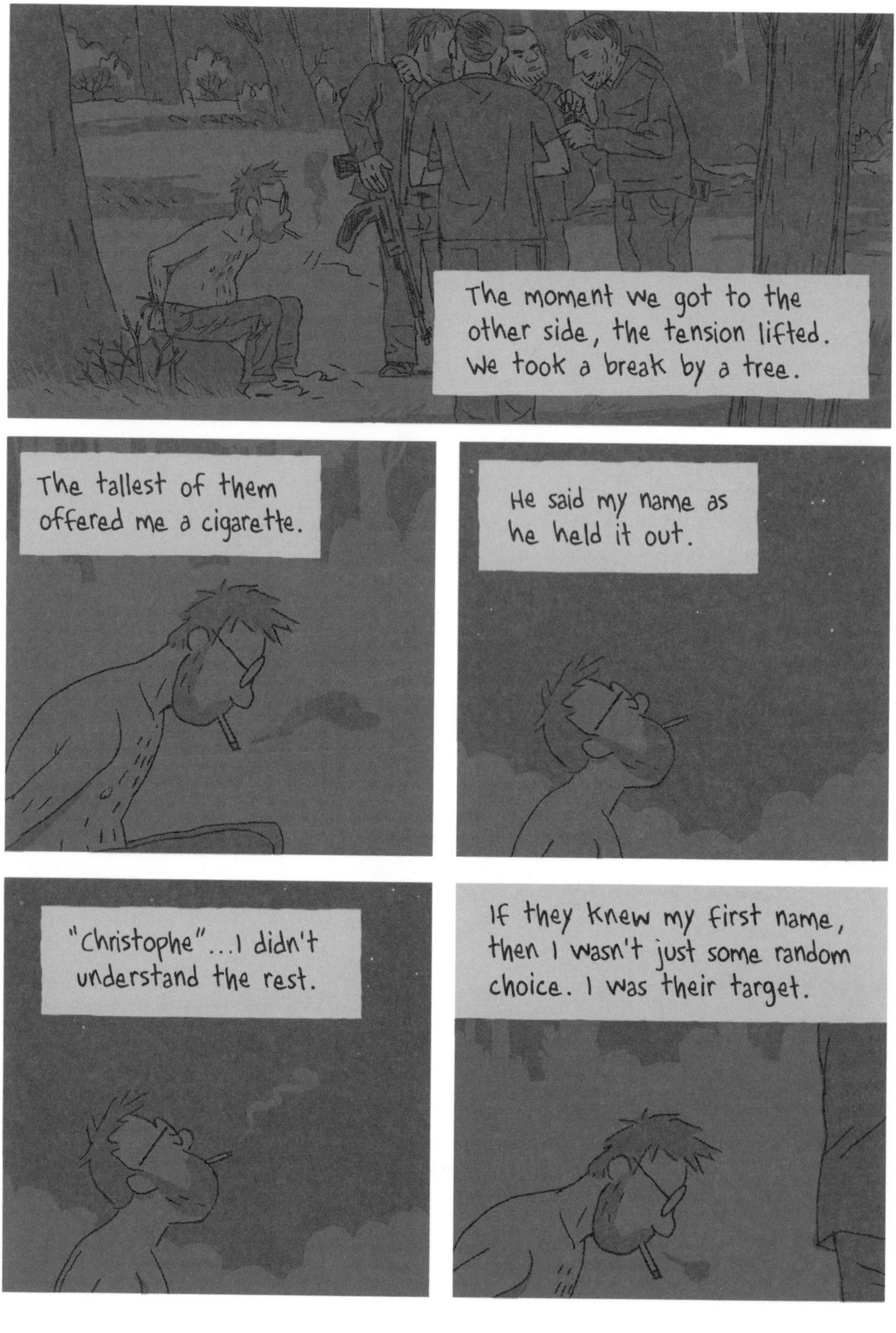
The moment we got to the other side, the tension lifted. We took a break by a tree.
The tallest of them offered me a cigarette.
He said my name as he held it out.
"Christophe"...I didn't understand the rest.
If they knew my first name, then I wasn't just some random choice. I was their target.

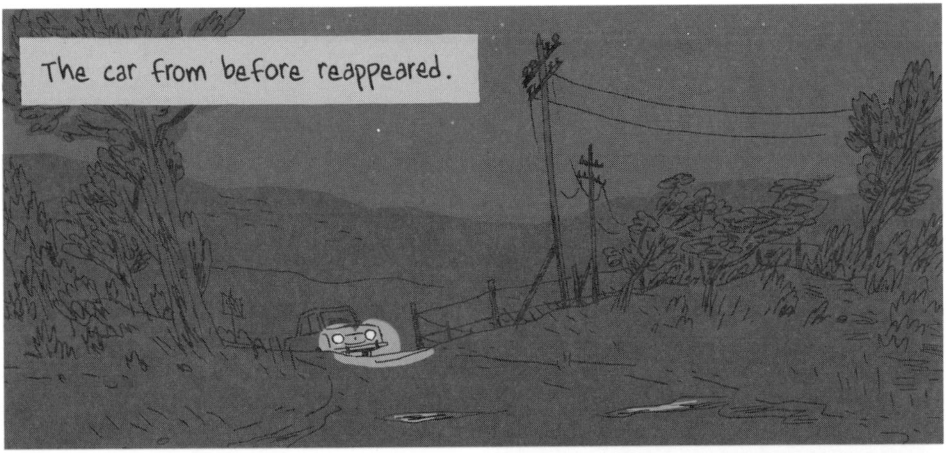
The car from before reappeared.

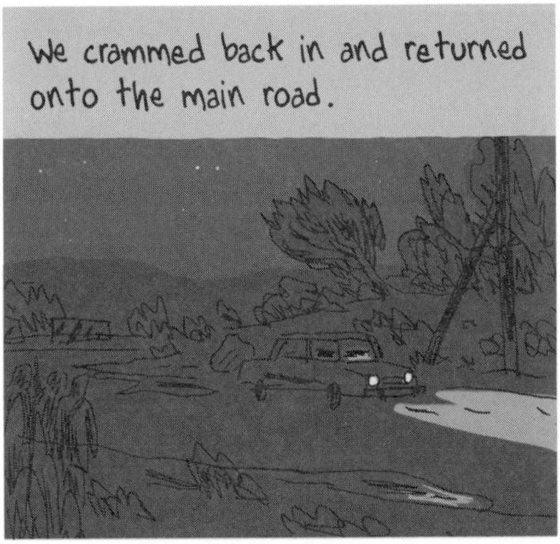
We crammed back in and returned onto the main road.

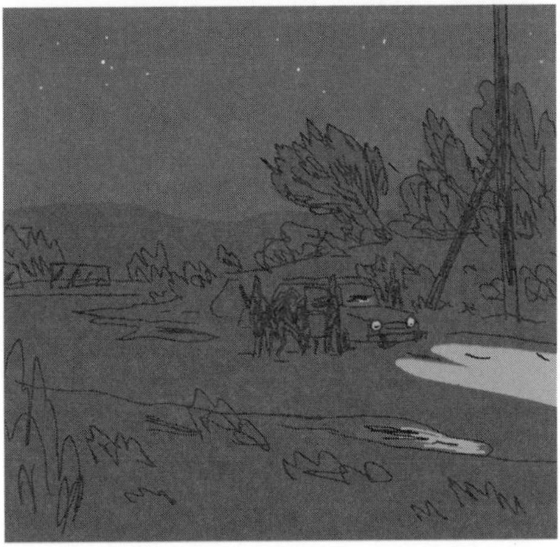

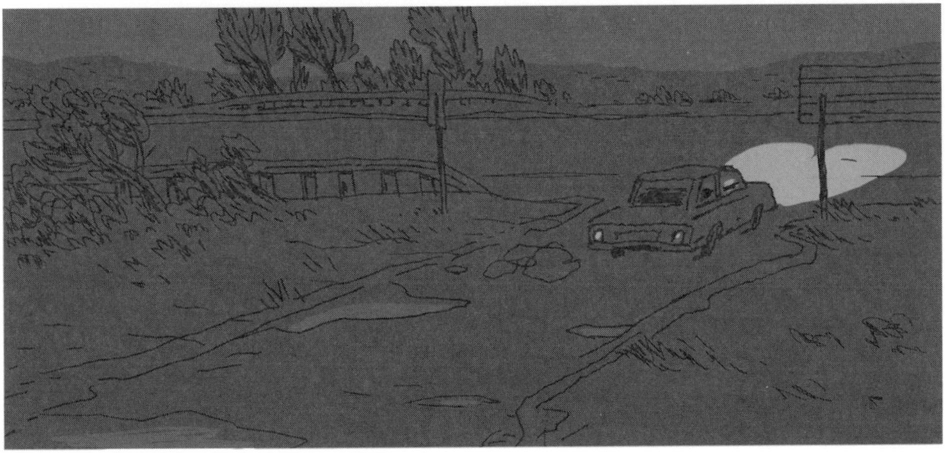

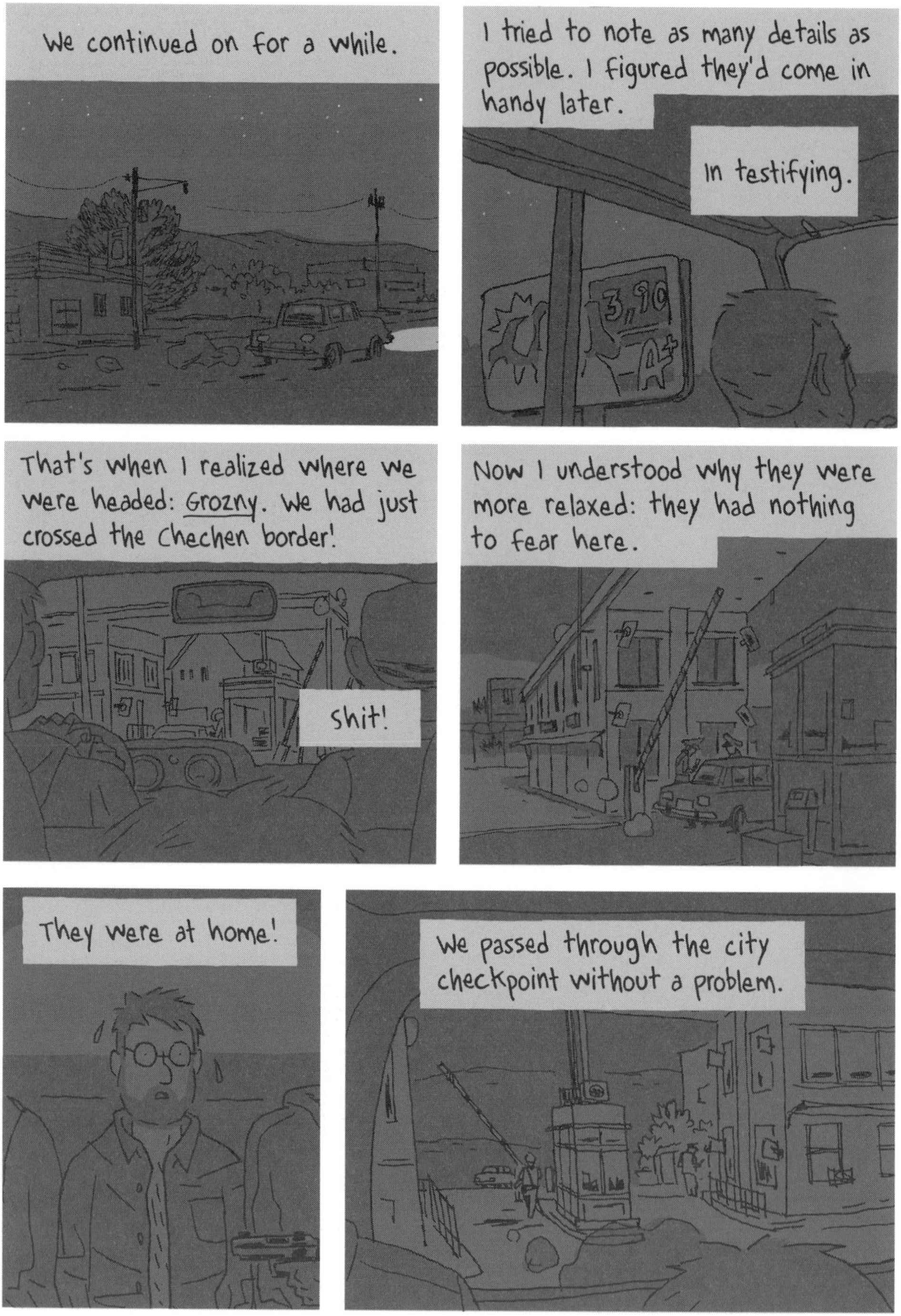
We continued on for a while.
I tried to note as many details as possible. I figured they'd come in handy later.
In testifying.
3,10
A+
That's when I realized where we were headed: Grozny. We had just crossed the Chechen border!
Shit!
Now I understood why they were more relaxed: they had nothing to fear here.
They were at home!
We passed through the city checkpoint without a problem.

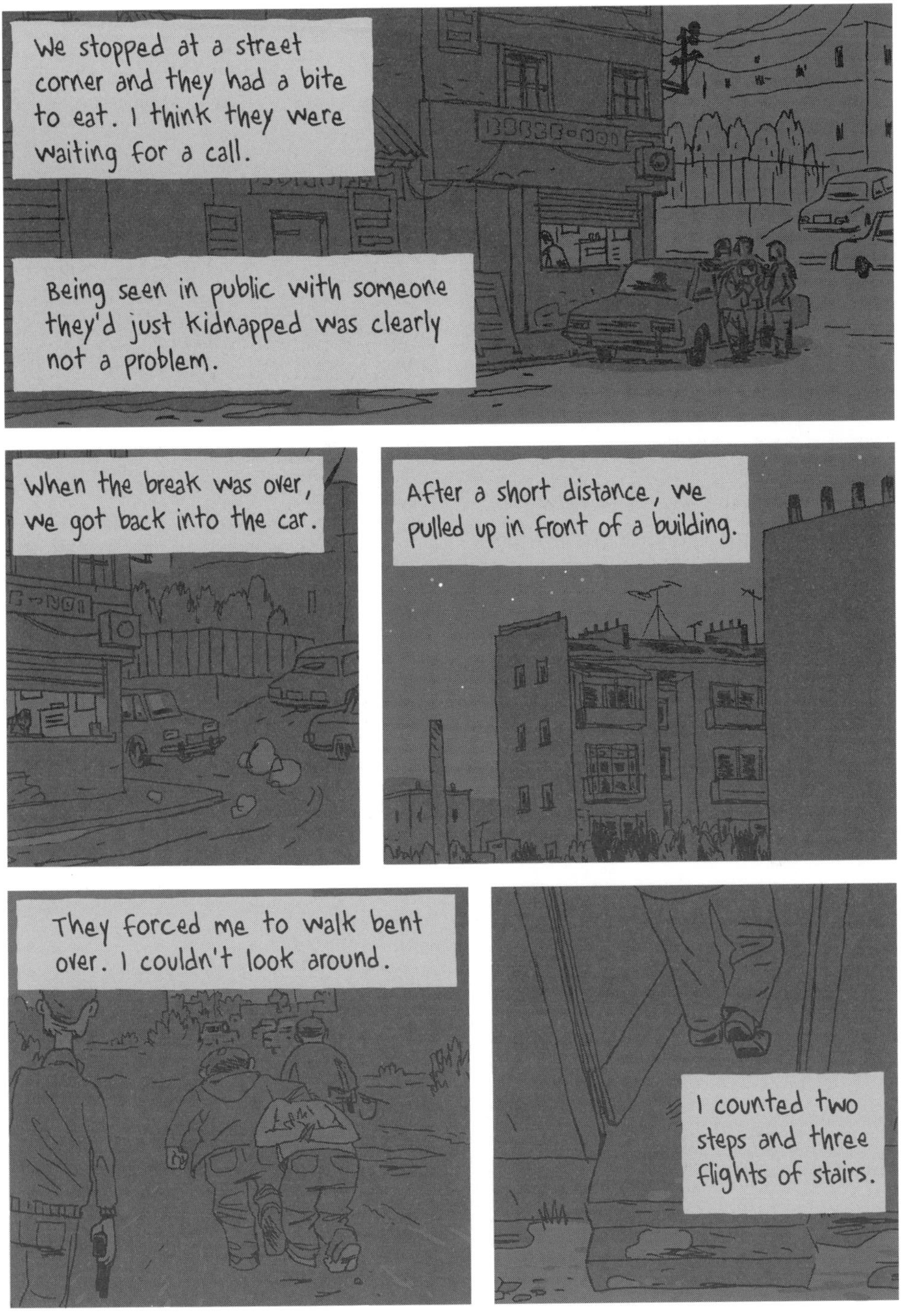
We stopped at a street corner and they had a bite to eat. I think they were waiting for a call.
Being seen in public with someone they'd just kidnapped was clearly not a problem.
When the break was over, we got back into the car.
After a short distance, we pulled up in front of a building.
They forced me to walk bent over. I couldn't look around.
I counted two steps and three flights of stairs.

They finally freed my hands.

My abductors left the room.

There was a mattress in one corner.

Some furniture.

And a window on the far side.

I could have opened it, but it was much too high to jump.

A back court-yard was visible.

The door had no lock, but I could hear the guys talking down the hall.

Bla blap blbla.

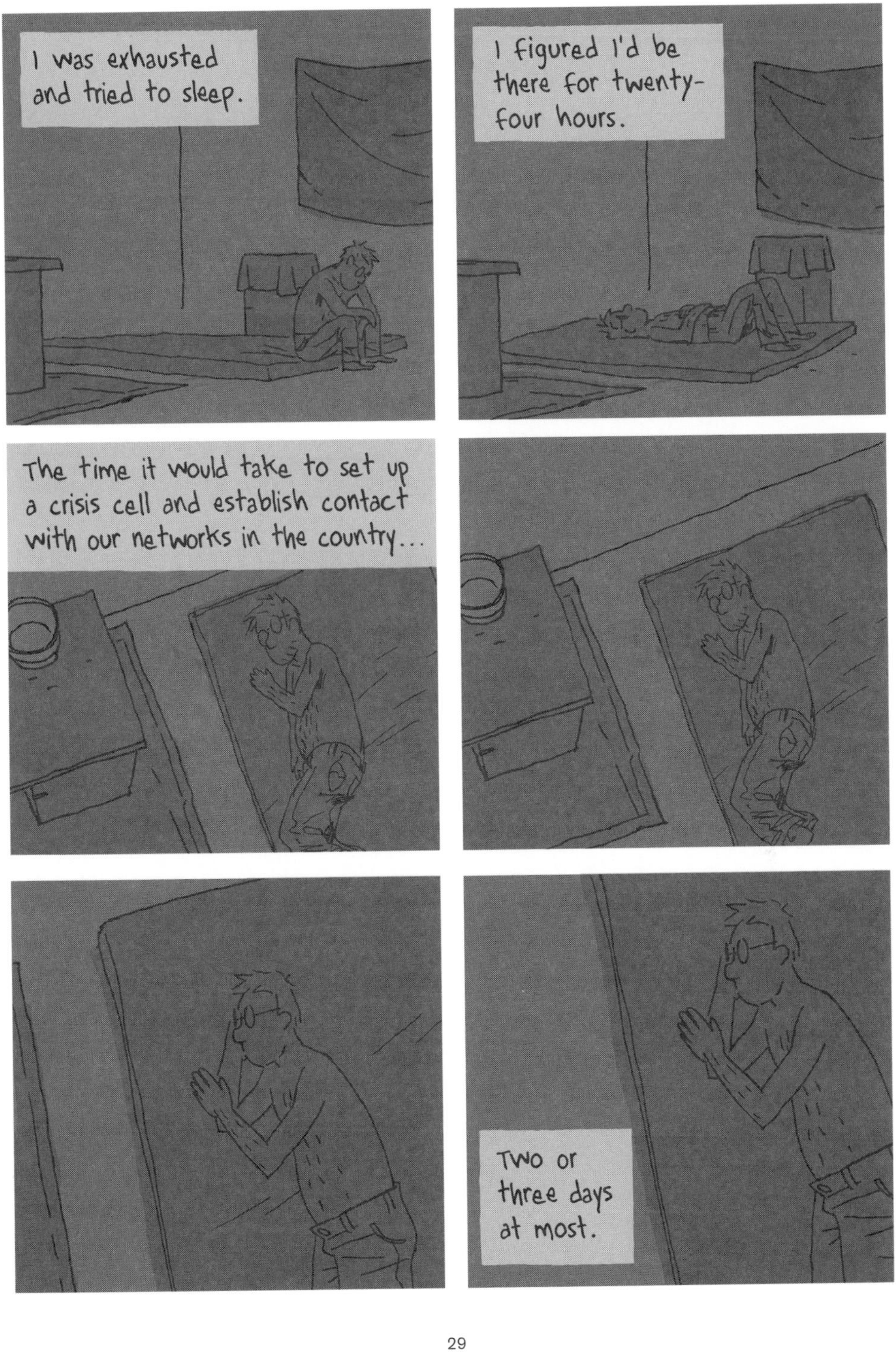
I was exhausted and tried to sleep.
I figured I'd be there for twenty-four hours.
The time it would take to set up a crisis cell and establish contact with our networks in the country...
Two or three days at most.

2

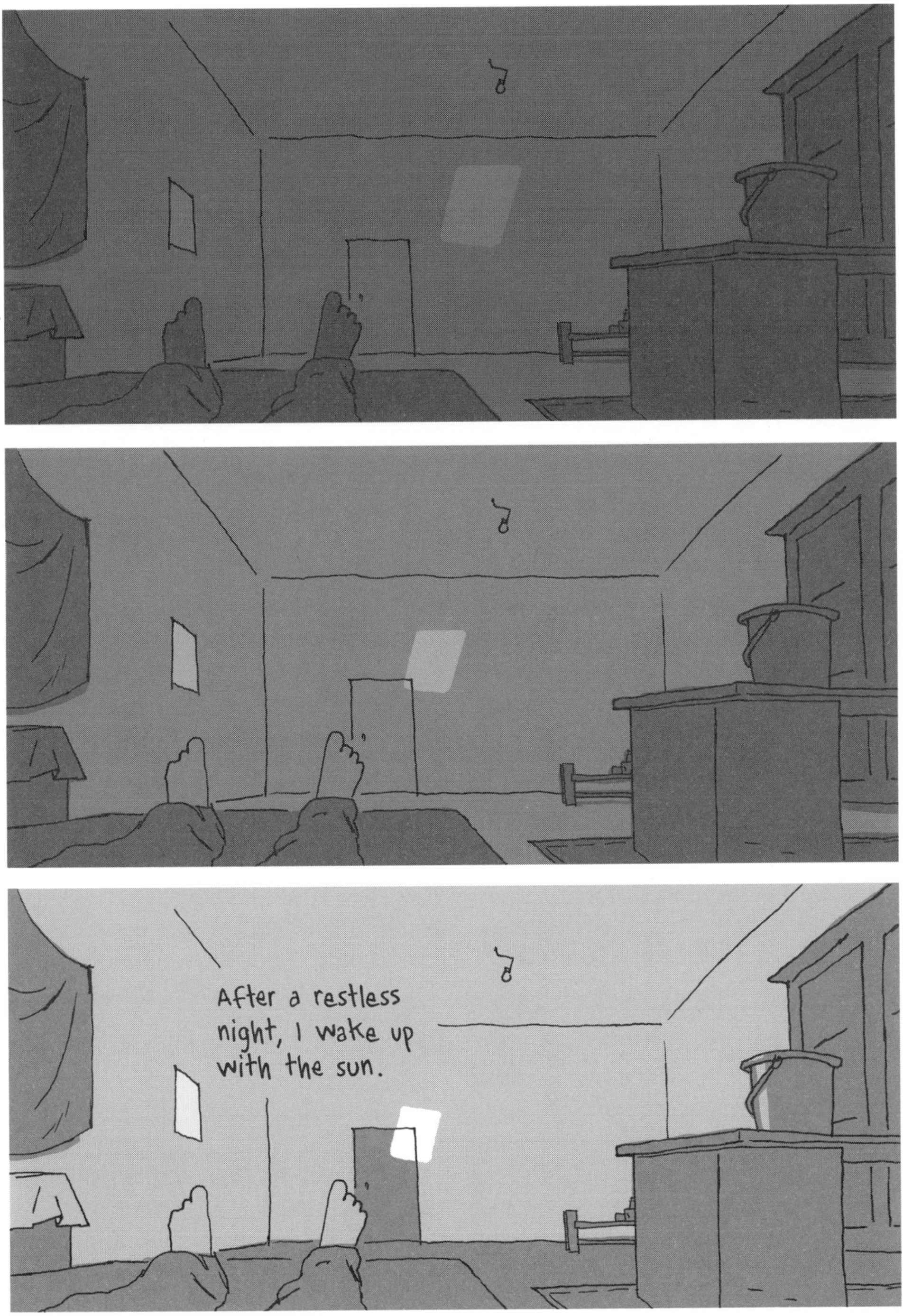
After a restless night, I wake up with the sun.

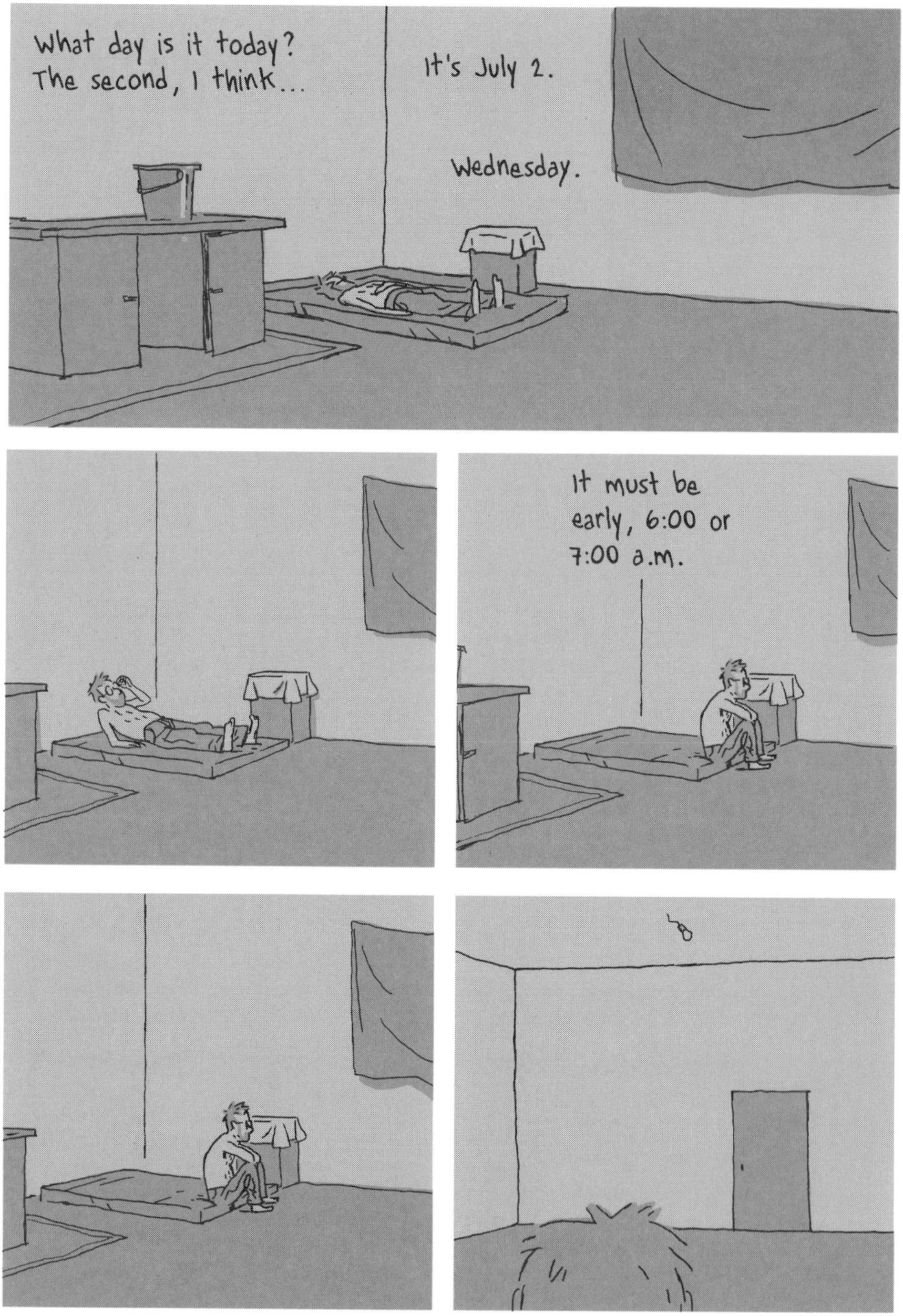
What day is it today?
The second, I think...
It's July 2.
Wednesday.
It must be early, 6:00 or 7:00 a.m.

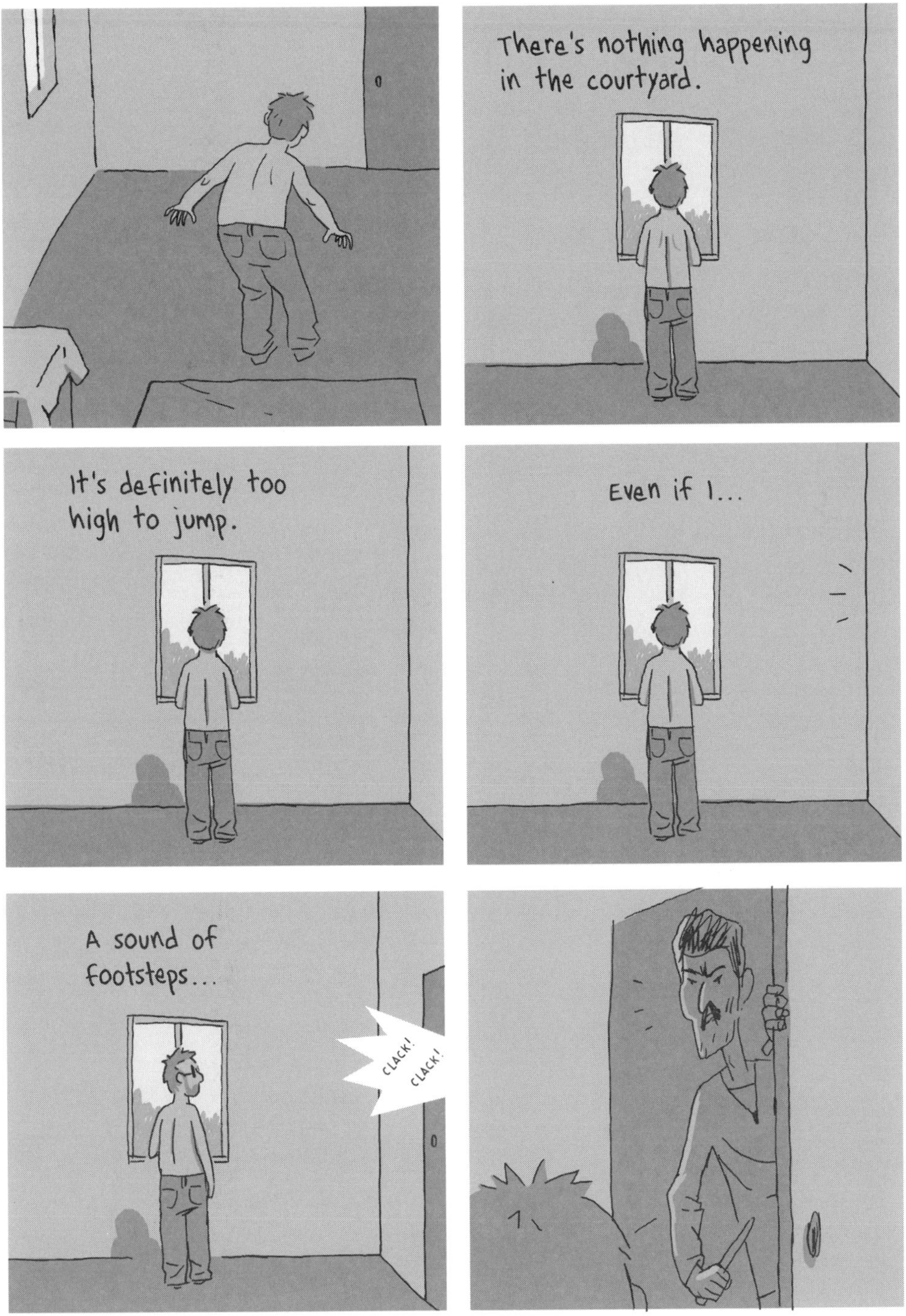
There's nothing happening in the courtyard.
It's definitely too high to jump.
Even if I...
A sound of footsteps...
CLACK! CLACK!

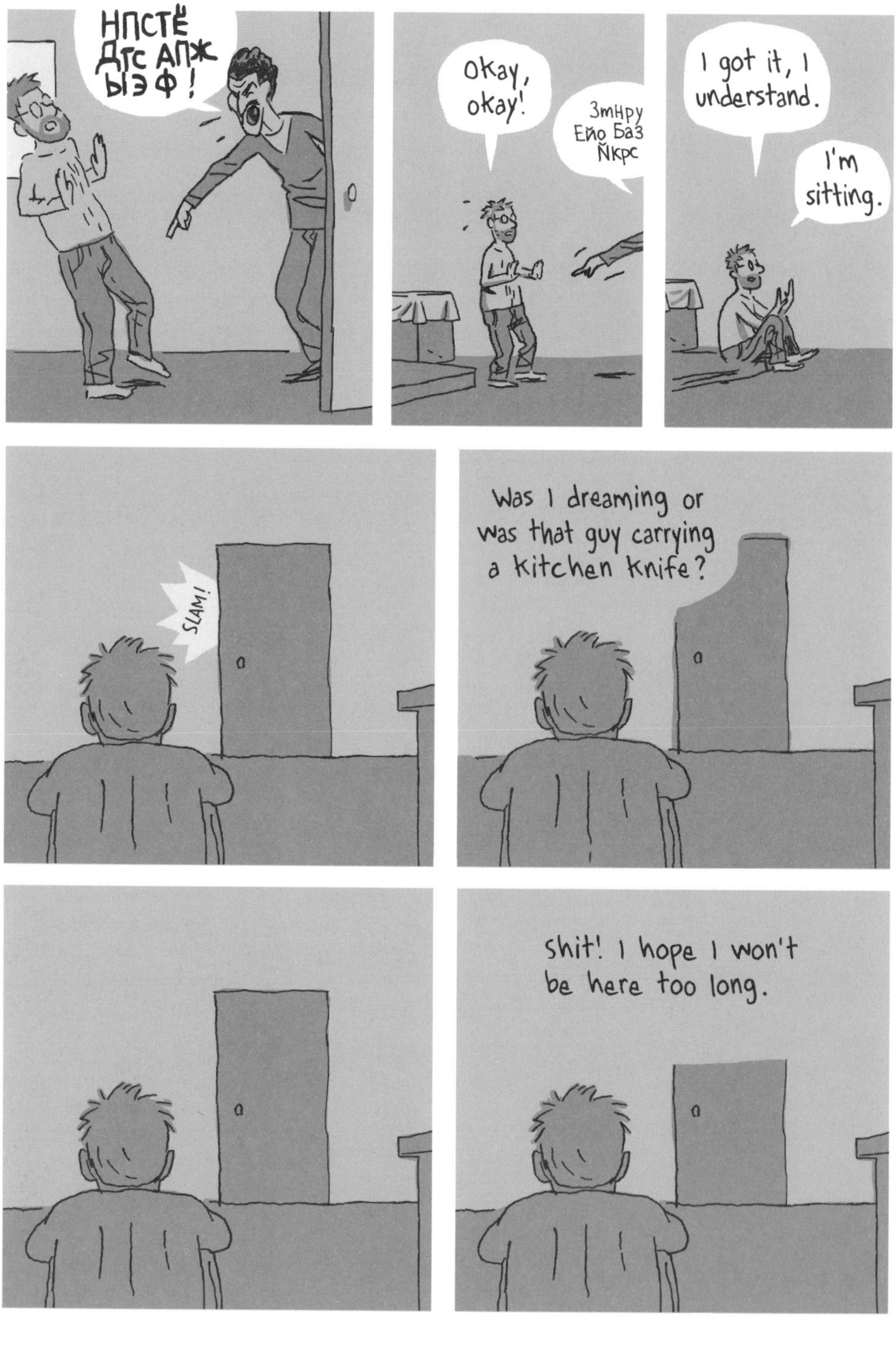
НПСТЁ ДГС АПЖ ЫЭ Ф!
Okay, okay!
Зтнру Ейо Баз Ñкрс
I got it, I understand.
I'm sitting.
SLAM!
Was I dreaming or was that guy carrying a kitchen knife?
Shit! I hope I won't be here too long.

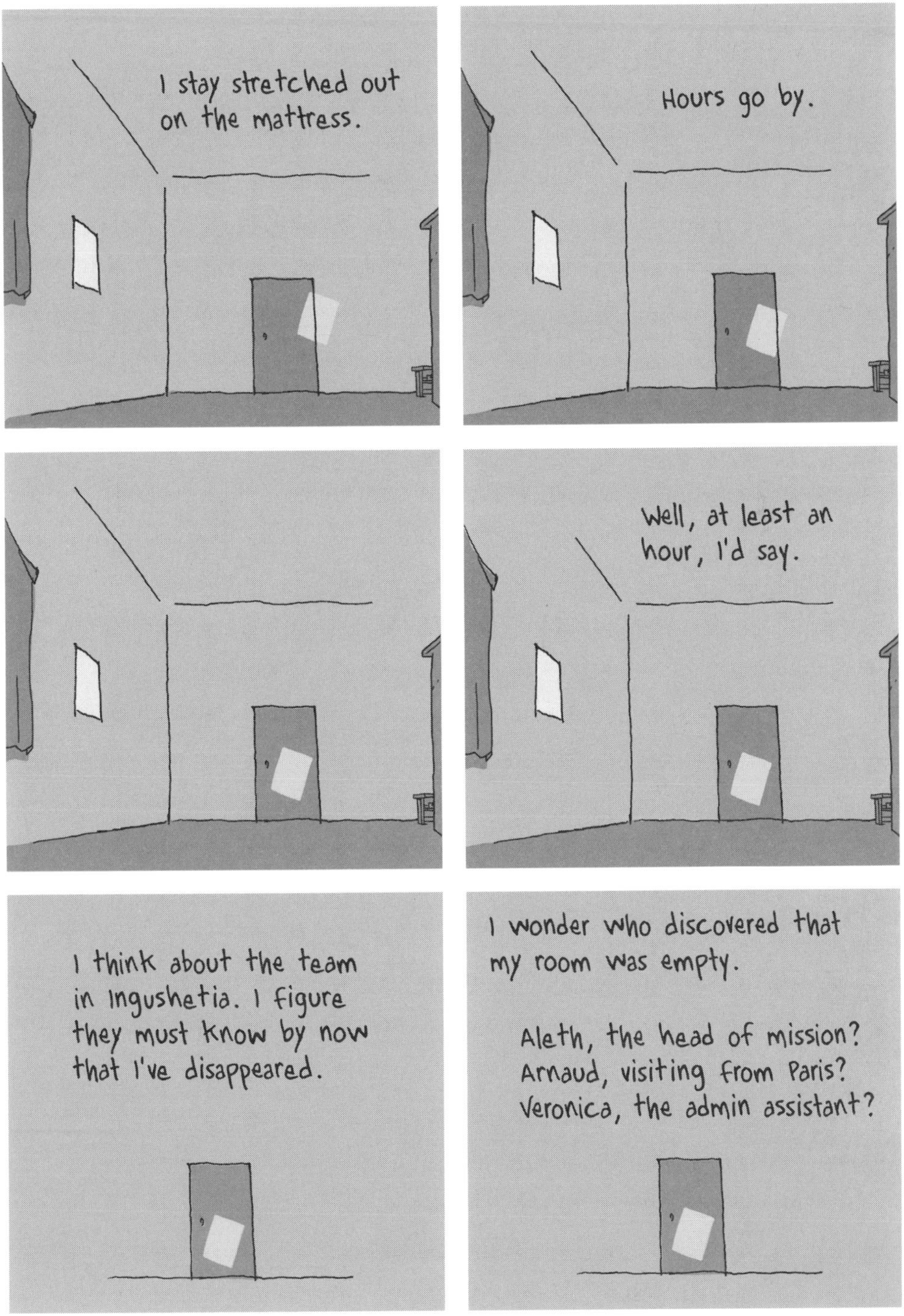
I stay stretched out on the mattress.
Hours go by.
Well, at least an hour, I'd say.
I think about the team in Ingushetia. I figure they must know by now that I've disappeared.
I wonder who discovered that my room was empty.
Aleth, the head of mission? Arnaud, visiting from Paris? Veronica, the admin assistant?

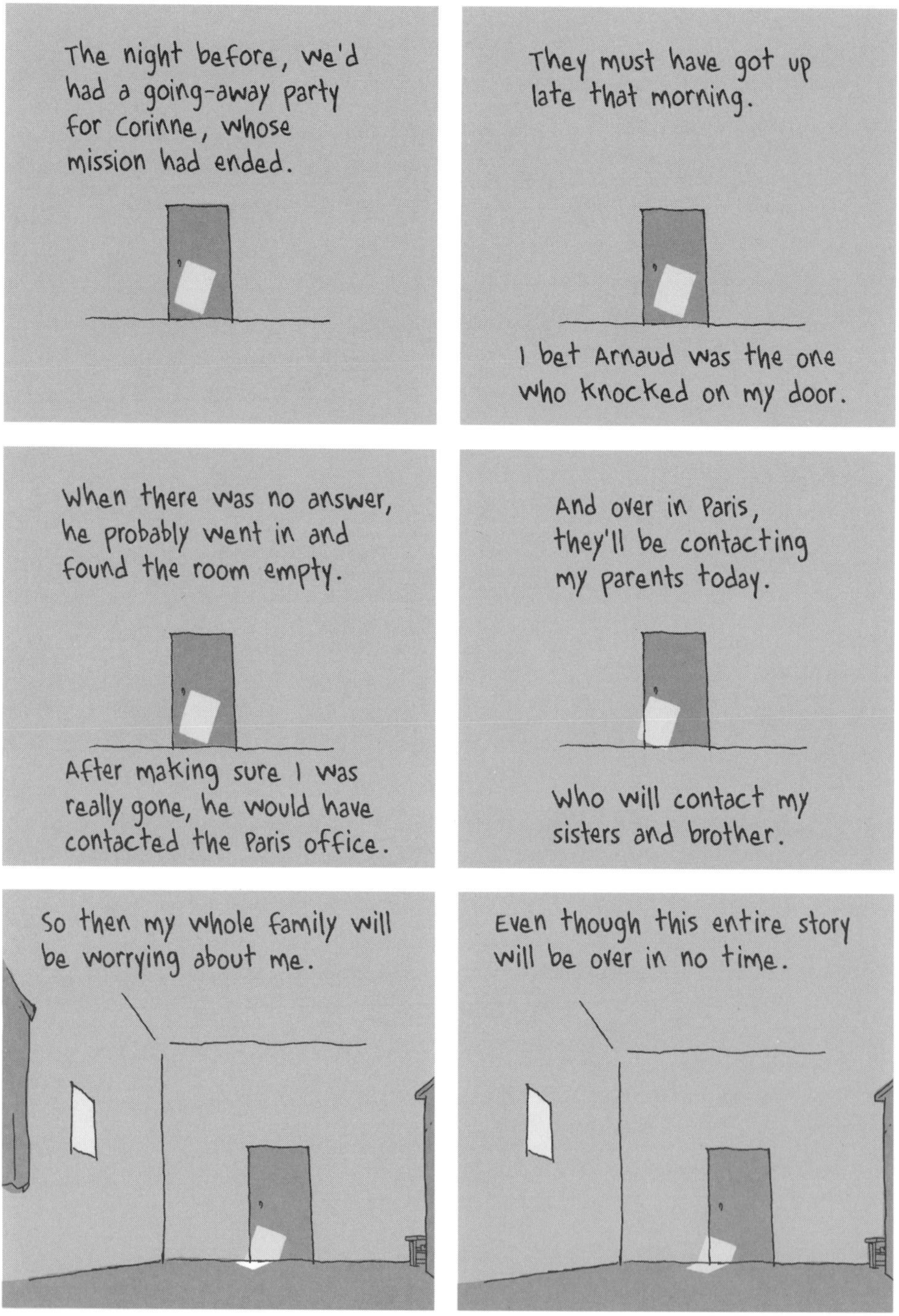
The night before, we'd had a going-away party for Corinne, whose mission had ended.
They must have got up late that morning.
I bet Arnaud was the one who knocked on my door.
When there was no answer, he probably went in and found the room empty.
After making sure I was really gone, he would have contacted the Paris office.
And over in Paris, they'll be contacting my parents today.
Who will contact my sisters and brother.
So then my whole family will be worrying about me.
Even though this entire story will be over in no time.

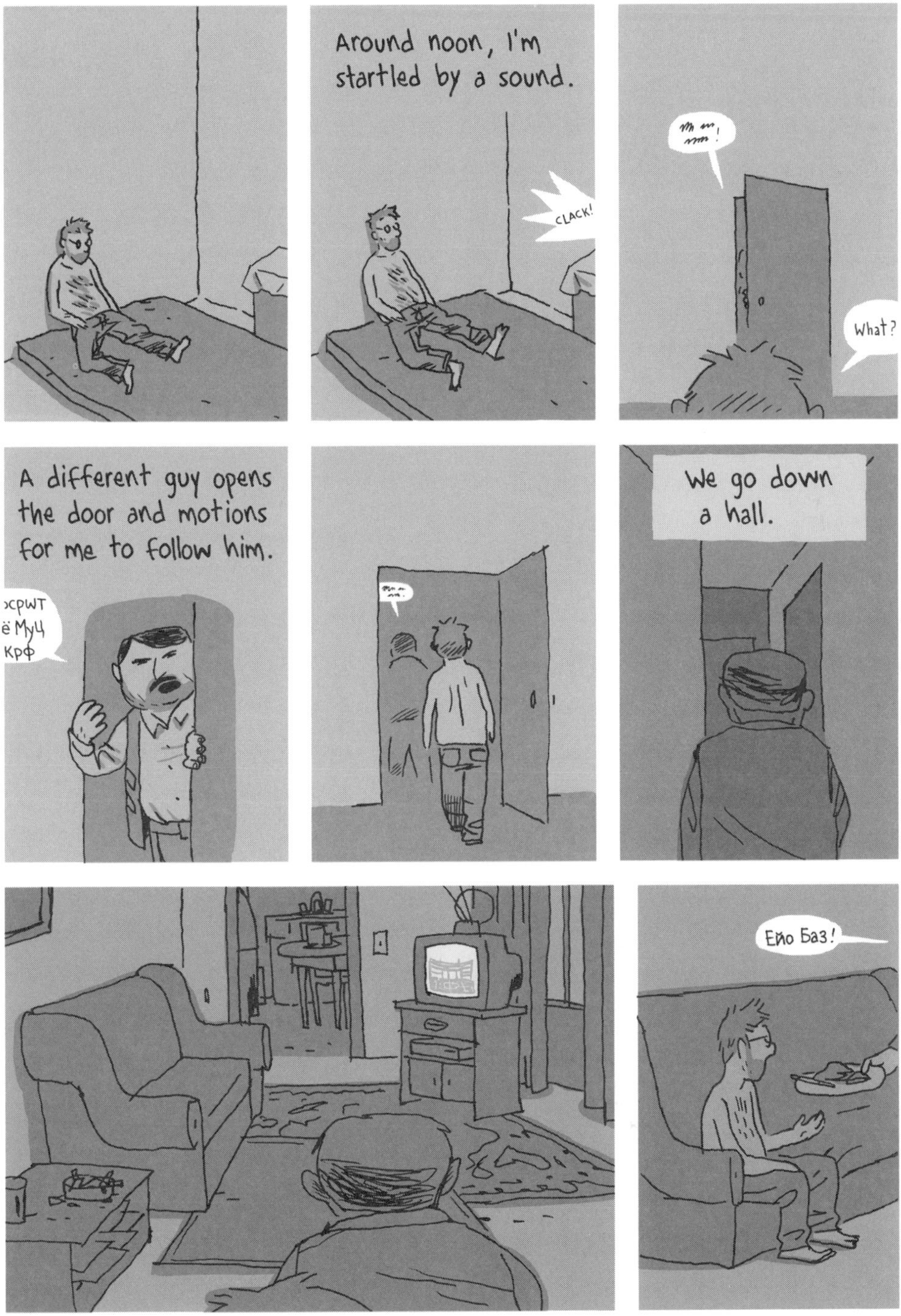

Around noon, I'm startled by a sound.
CLACK!
What?
A different guy opens the door and motions for me to follow him.
ɔcpWT ё Муц Крф
We go down a hall.
Ейо Баз!

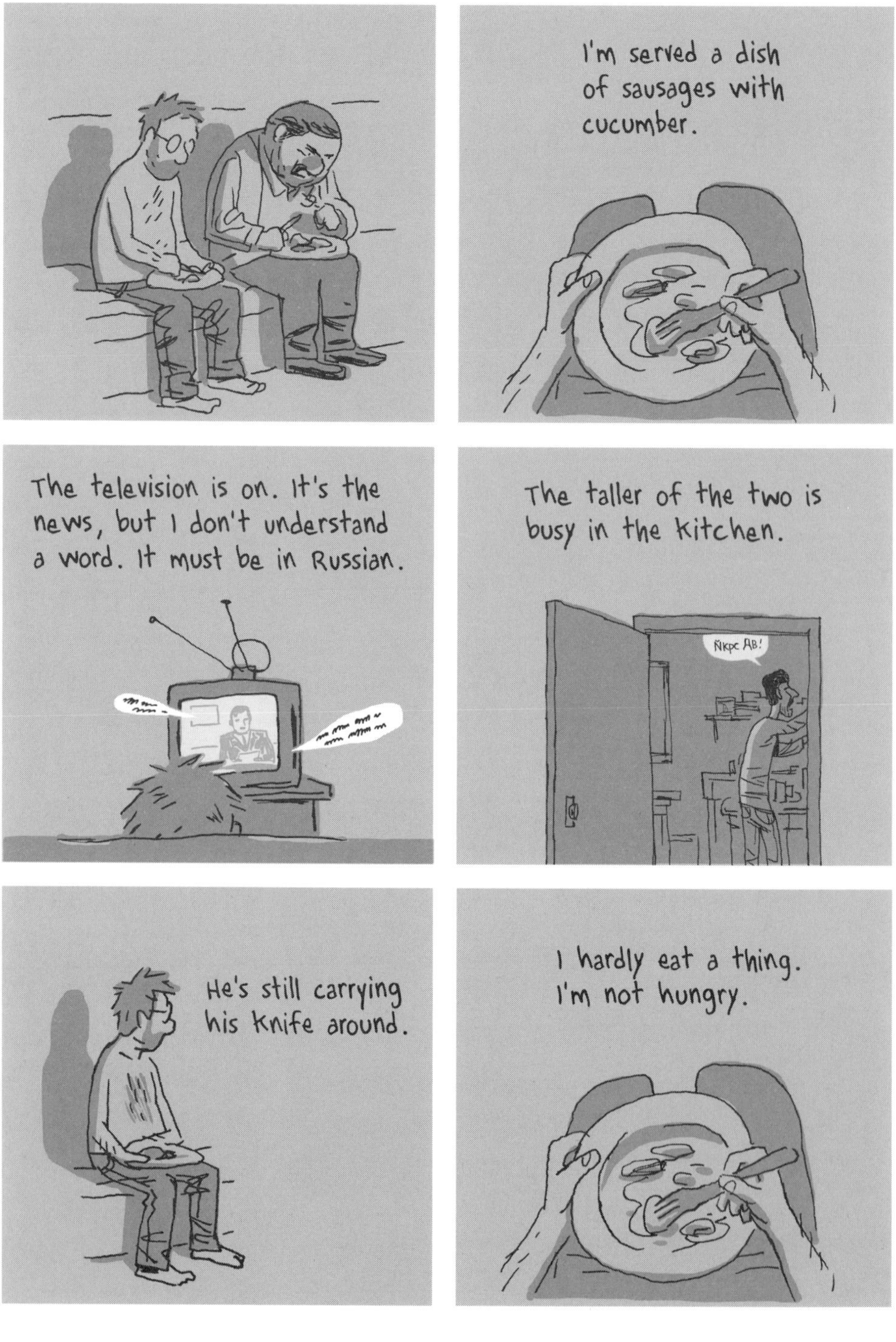
I'm served a dish of sausages with cucumber.
The television is on. It's the news, but I don't understand a word. It must be in Russian.
The taller of the two is busy in the kitchen.
Йкрс ДВ!
He's still carrying his knife around.
I hardly eat a thing. I'm not hungry.

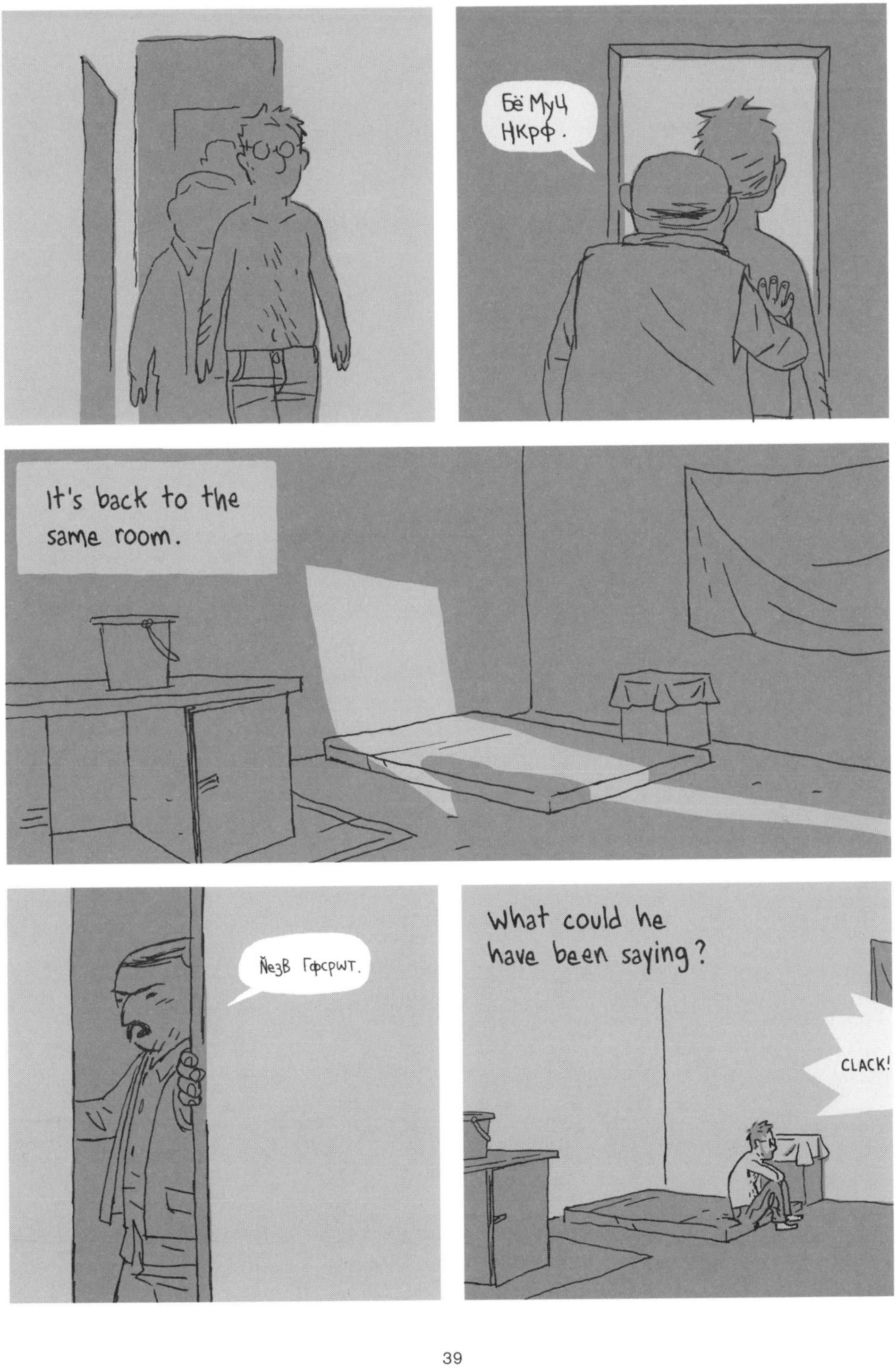
Бё Муц Нкрф.
It's back to the same room.
Йезв Гфсрwт.
What could he have been saying?
CLACK!

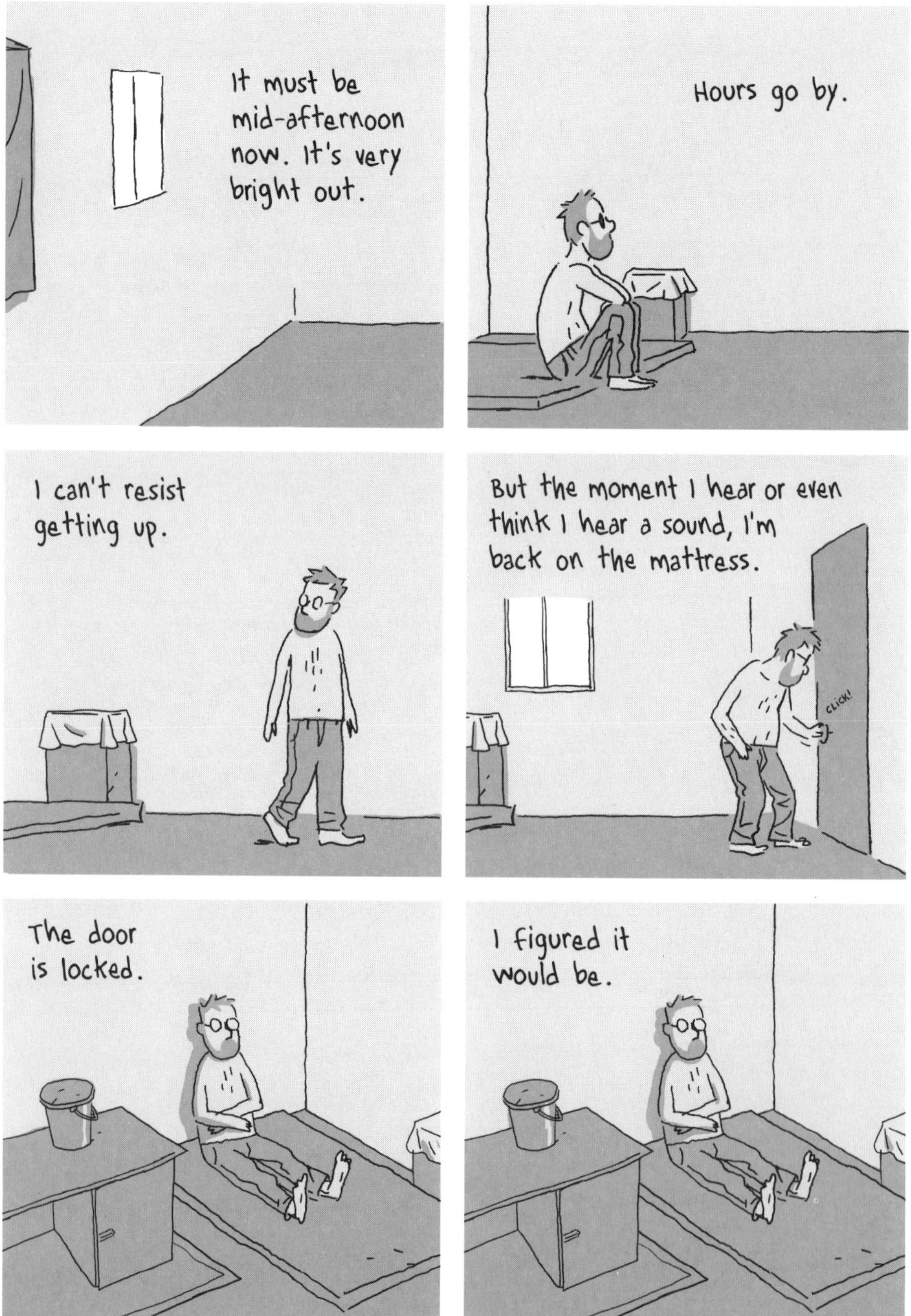
It must be mid-afternoon now. It's very bright out.
Hours go by.
I can't resist getting up.
But the moment I hear or even think I hear a sound, I'm back on the mattress.
CLICK!
The door is locked.
I figured it would be.

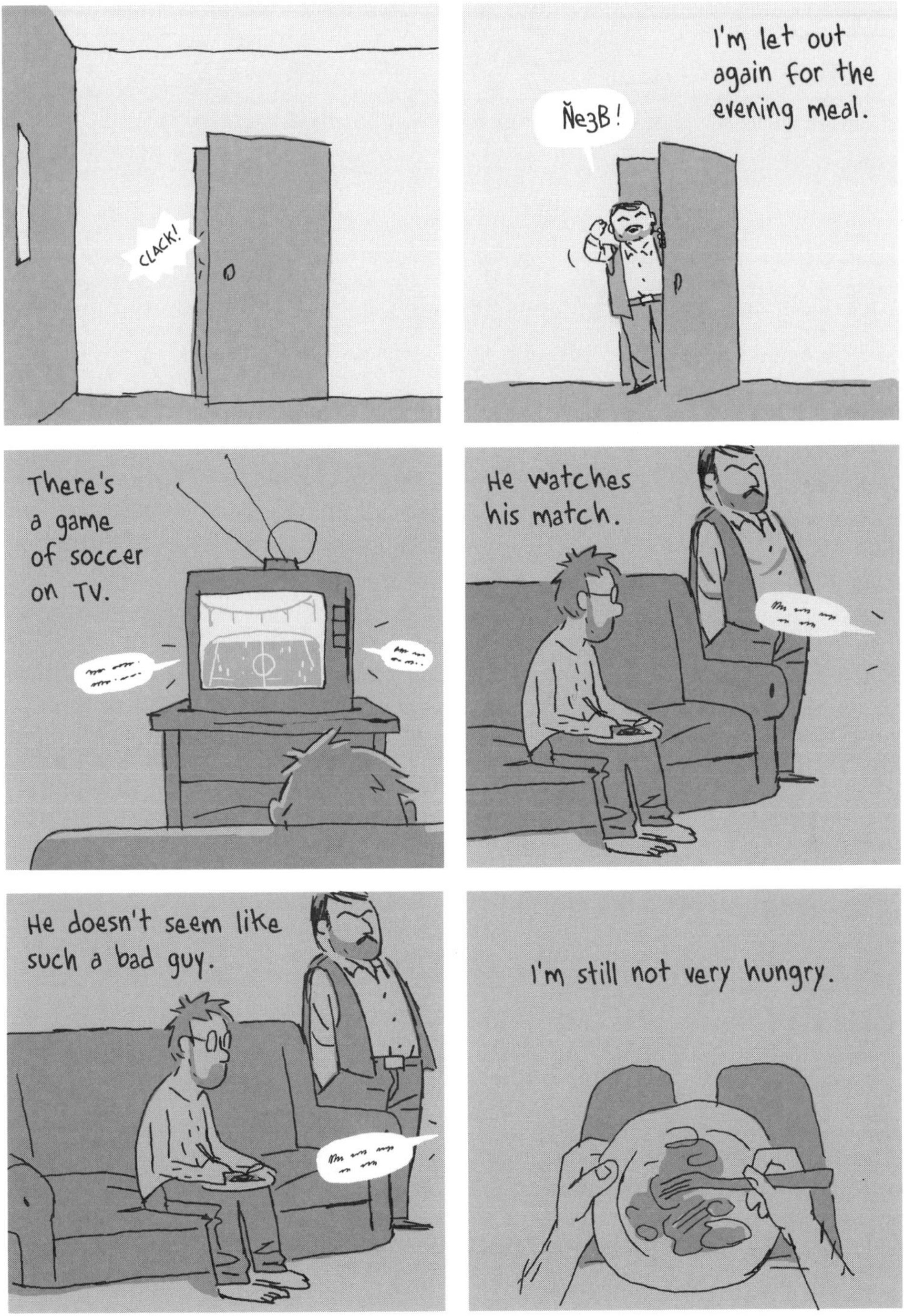
CLACK!
I'm let out again for the evening meal.
Ňe3B!
There's a game of soccer on TV.
He watches his match.
He doesn't seem like such a bad guy.
I'm still not very hungry.

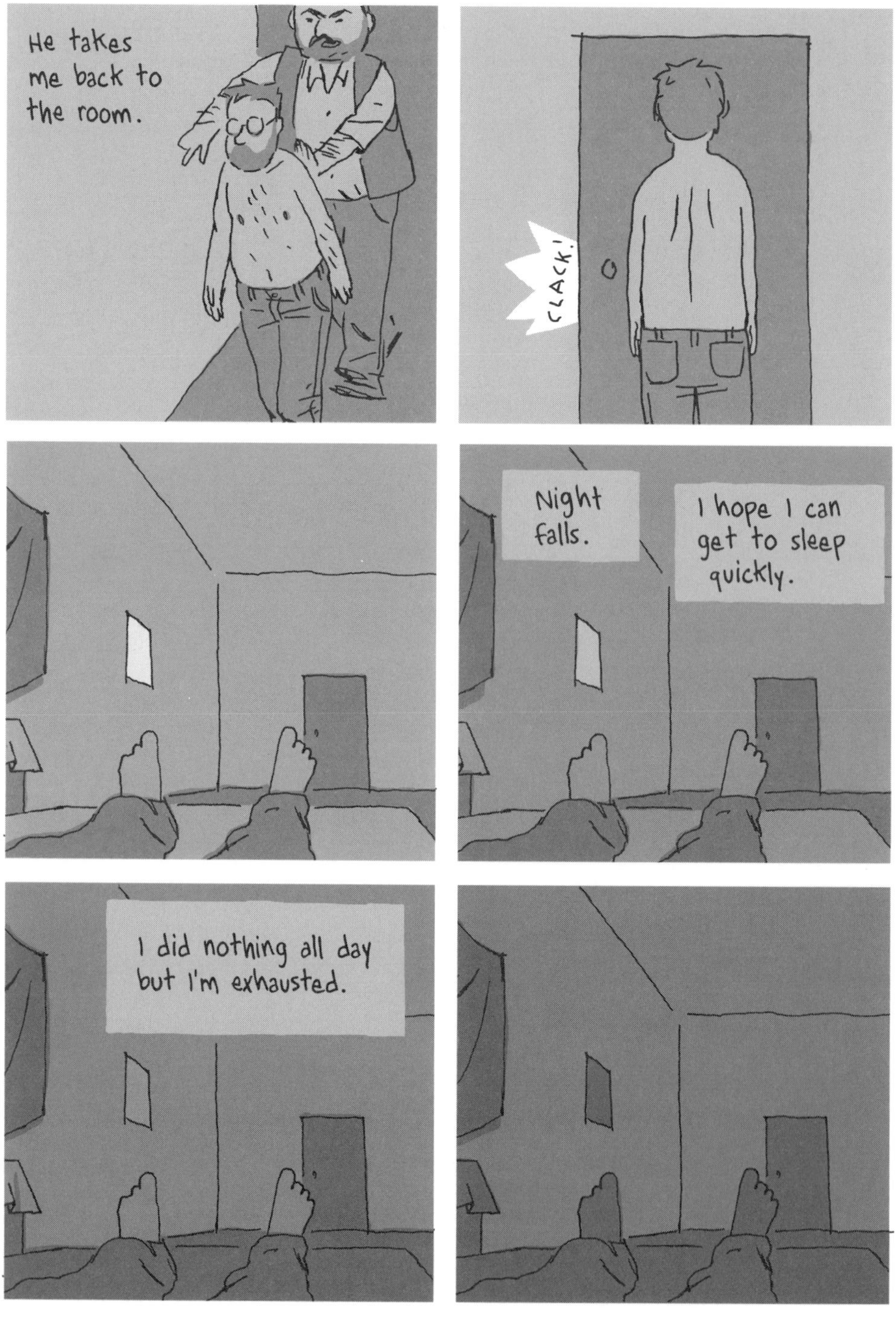
He takes me back to the room.
CLACK!
Night falls.
I hope I can get to sleep quickly.
I did nothing all day but I'm exhausted.

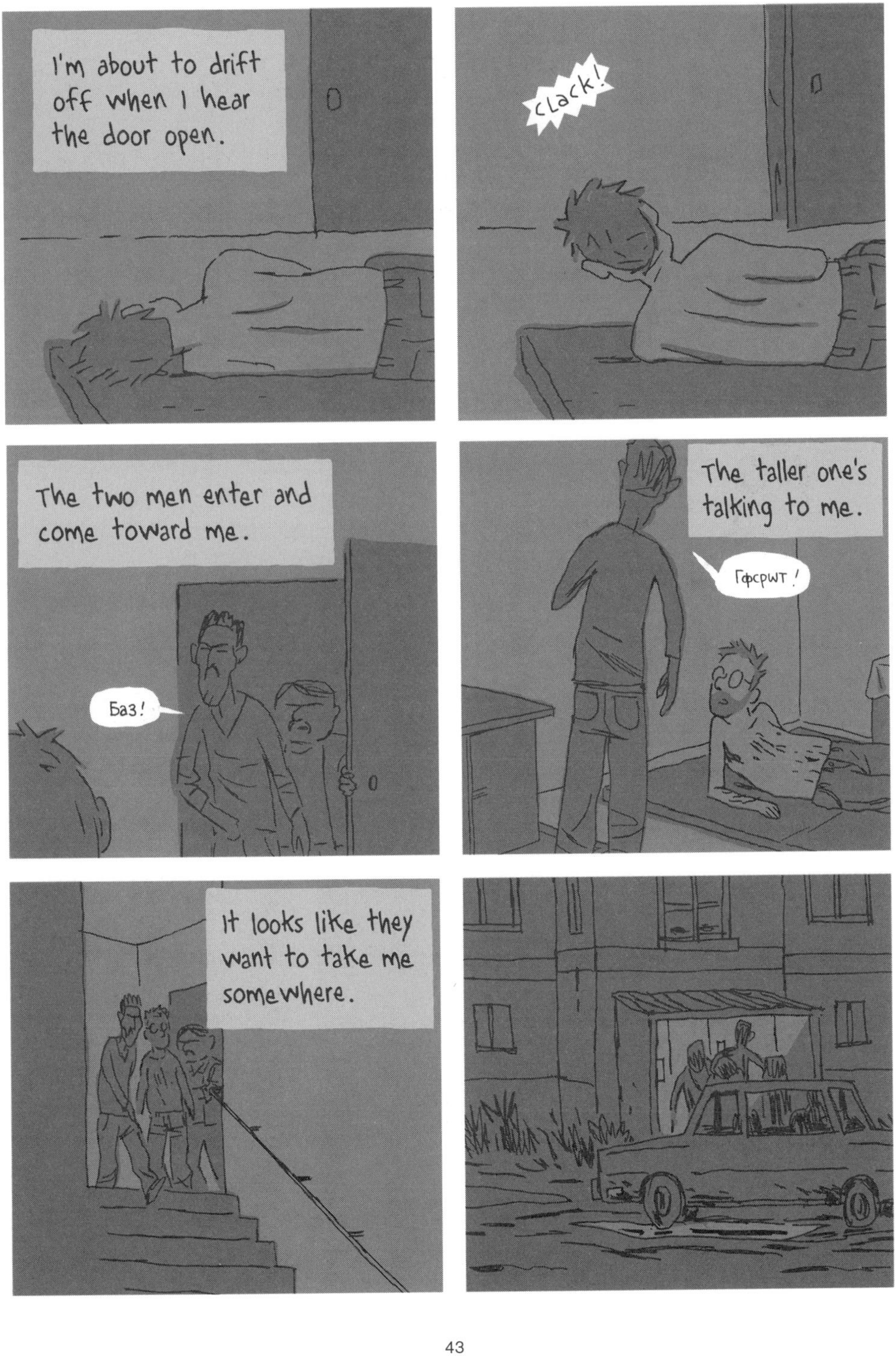
I'm about to drift off when I hear the door open.
CLACK!
The two men enter and come toward me.
Баз!
The taller one's talking to me.
Гфсрwт!
It looks like they want to take me somewhere.

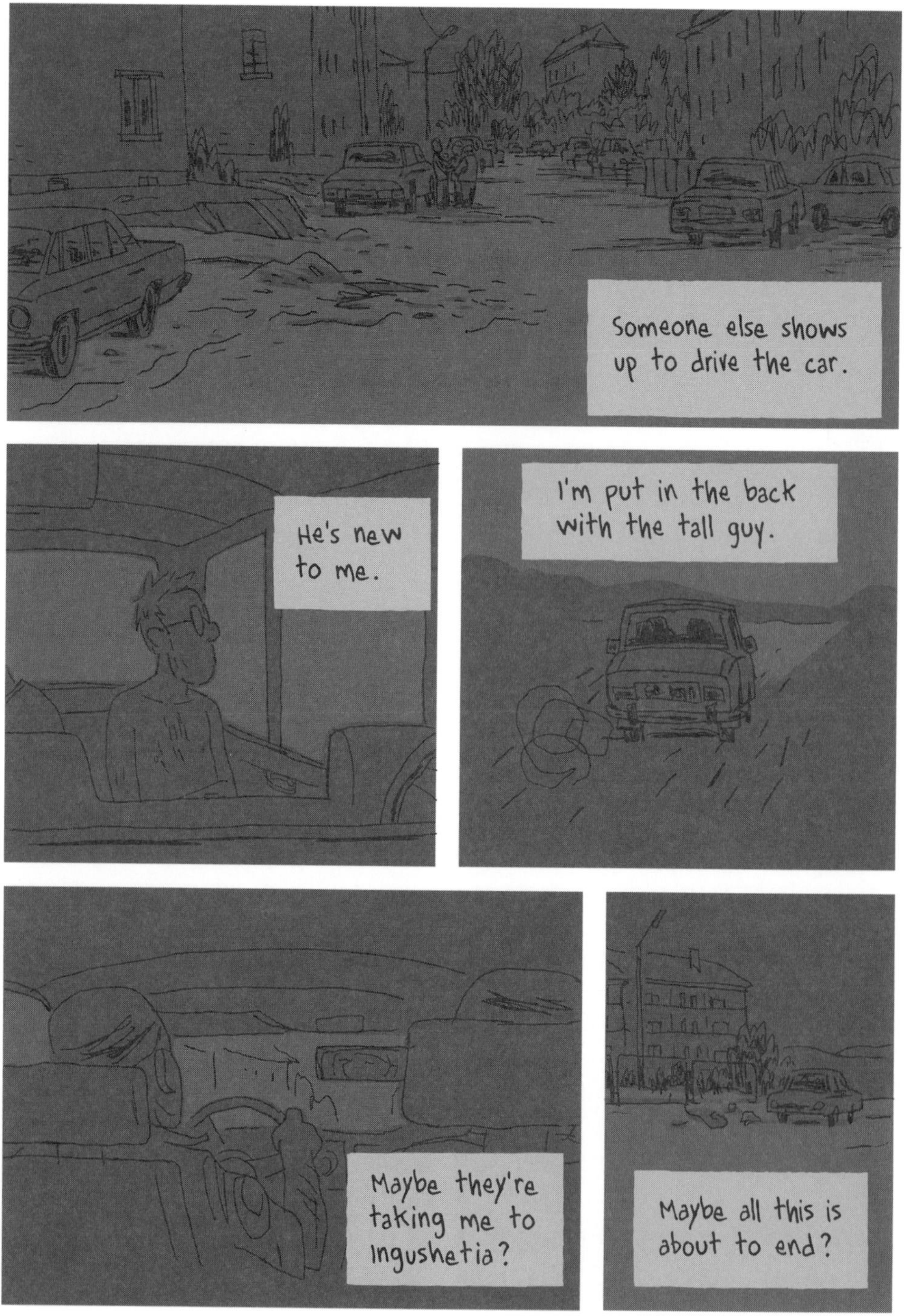
Someone else shows up to drive the car.
He's new to me.
I'm put in the back with the tall guy.
Maybe they're taking me to Ingushetia?
Maybe all this is about to end?

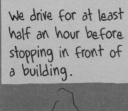We drive for at least half an hour before stopping in front of a building.

We go up to the third floor, into an apartment.

One of them leads me into an empty room.

Then takes out a pair of handcuffs...

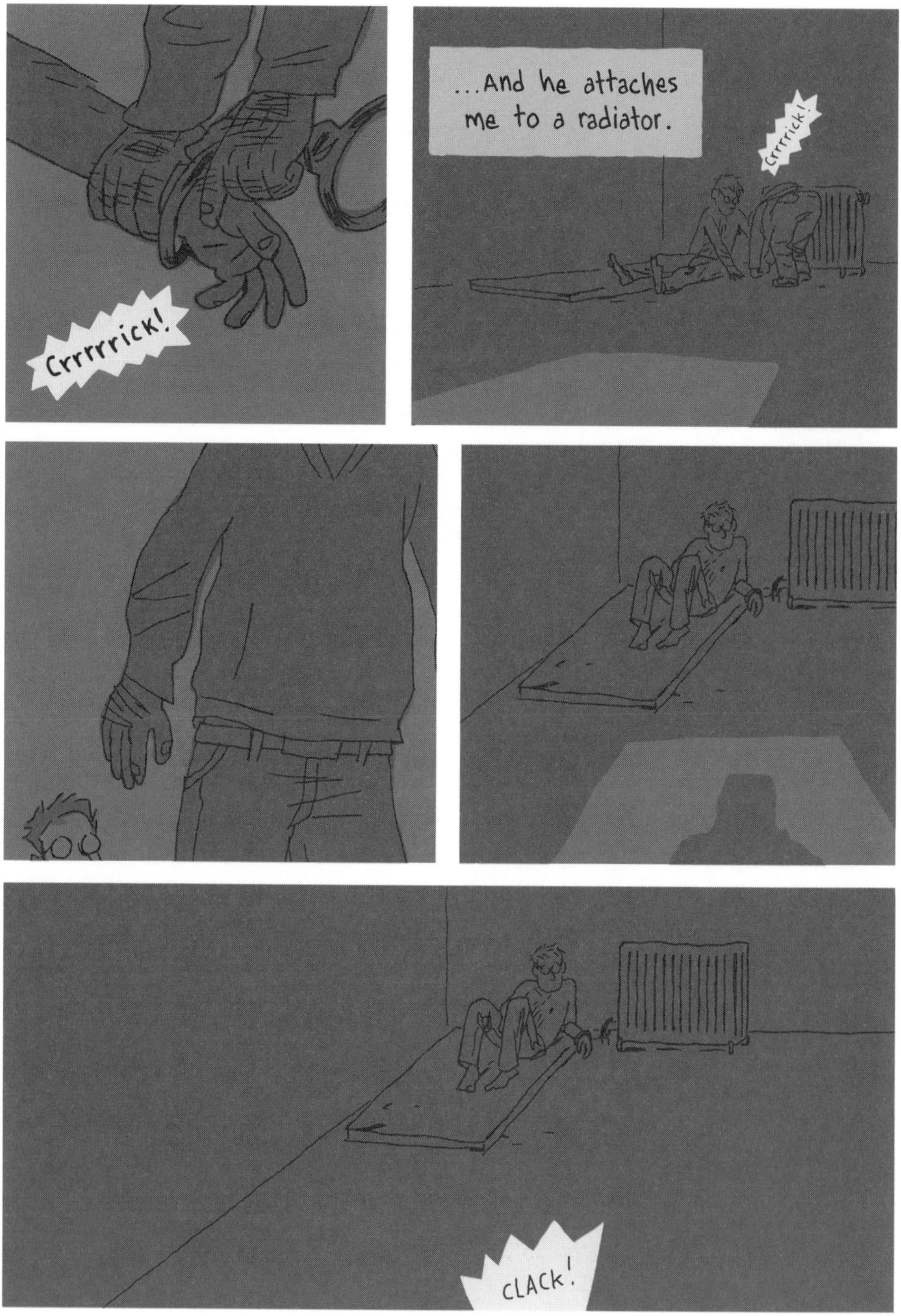
Crrrrrick!
...And he attaches me to a radiator.
Crrrrick!
CLACK!

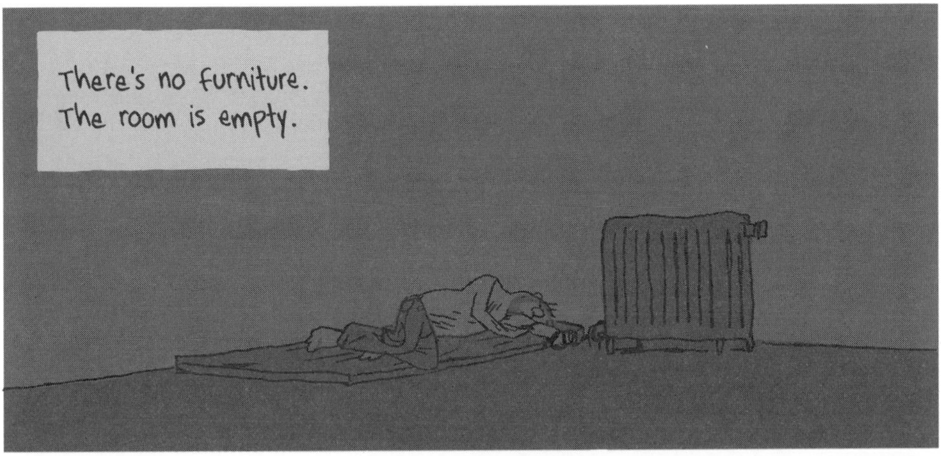
There's no furniture.
The room is empty.

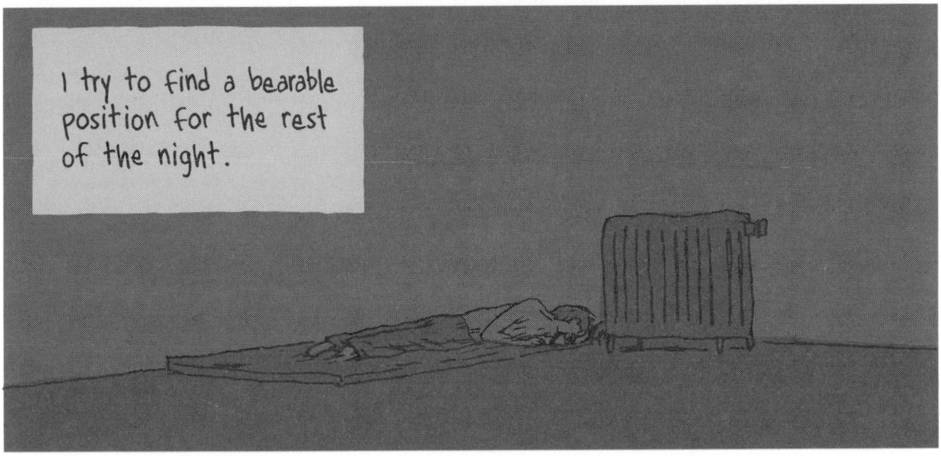
I try to find a bearable position for the rest of the night.

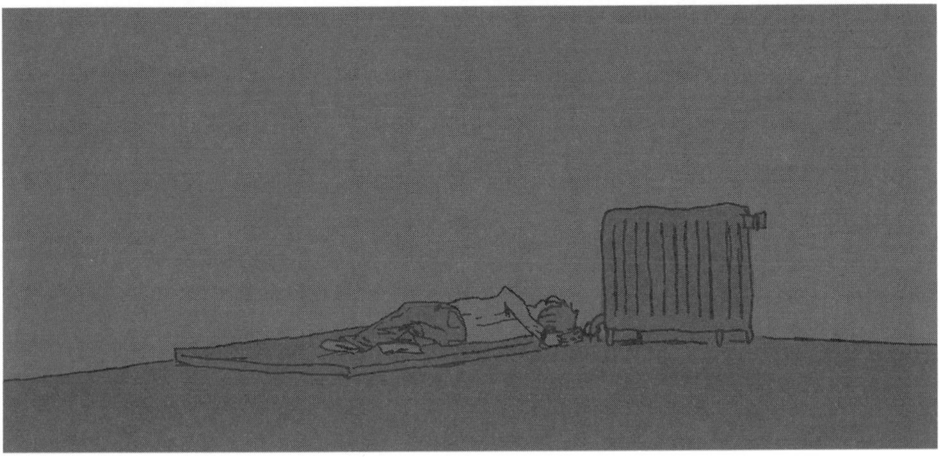

3

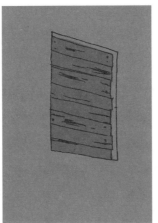

The sun finally comes up...

...but it's hard to tell with the window boarded over.

Ouch! My arm!

I must have pulled something in my sleep.

Aaah!

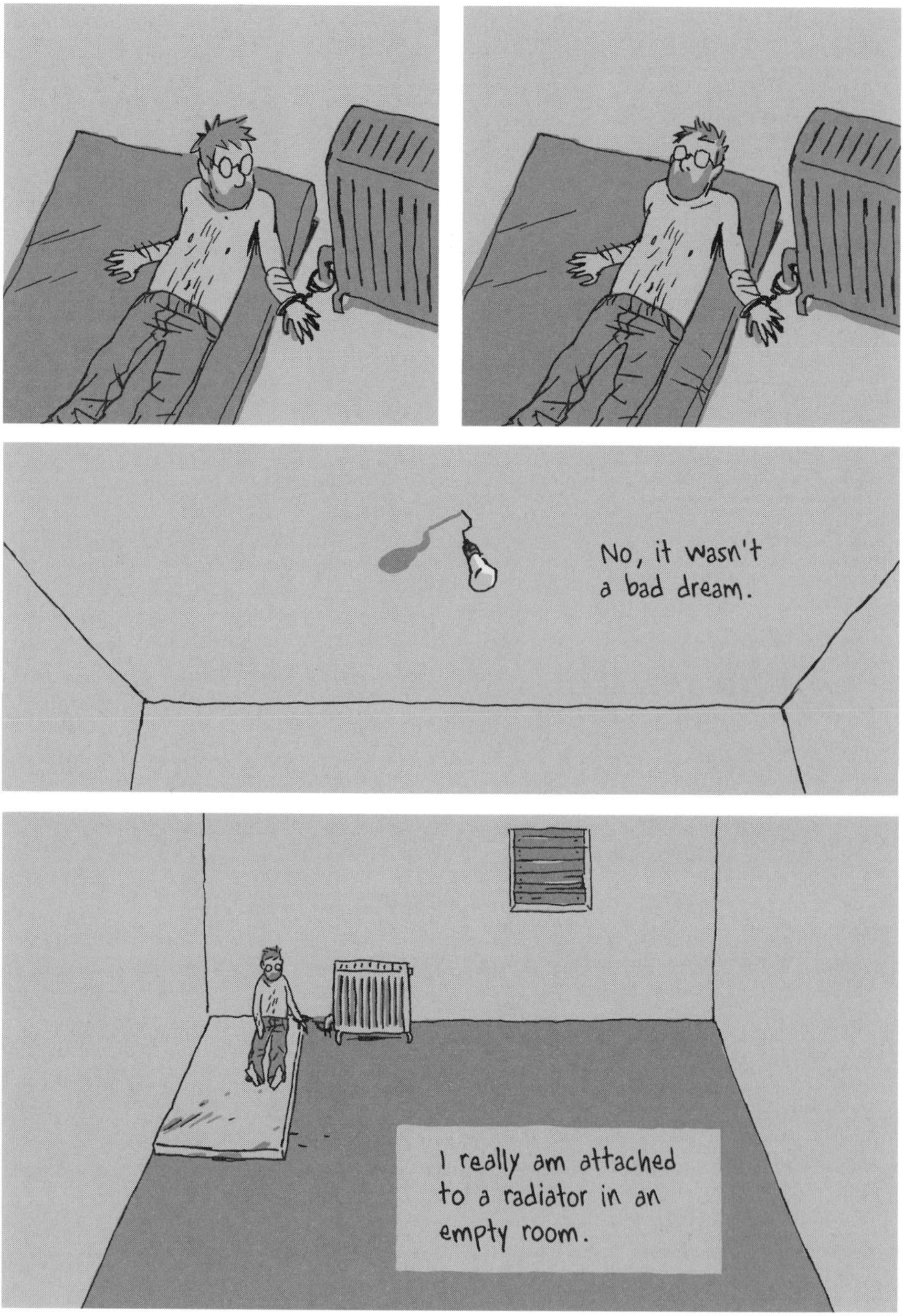
No, it wasn't a bad dream.
I really am attached to a radiator in an empty room.

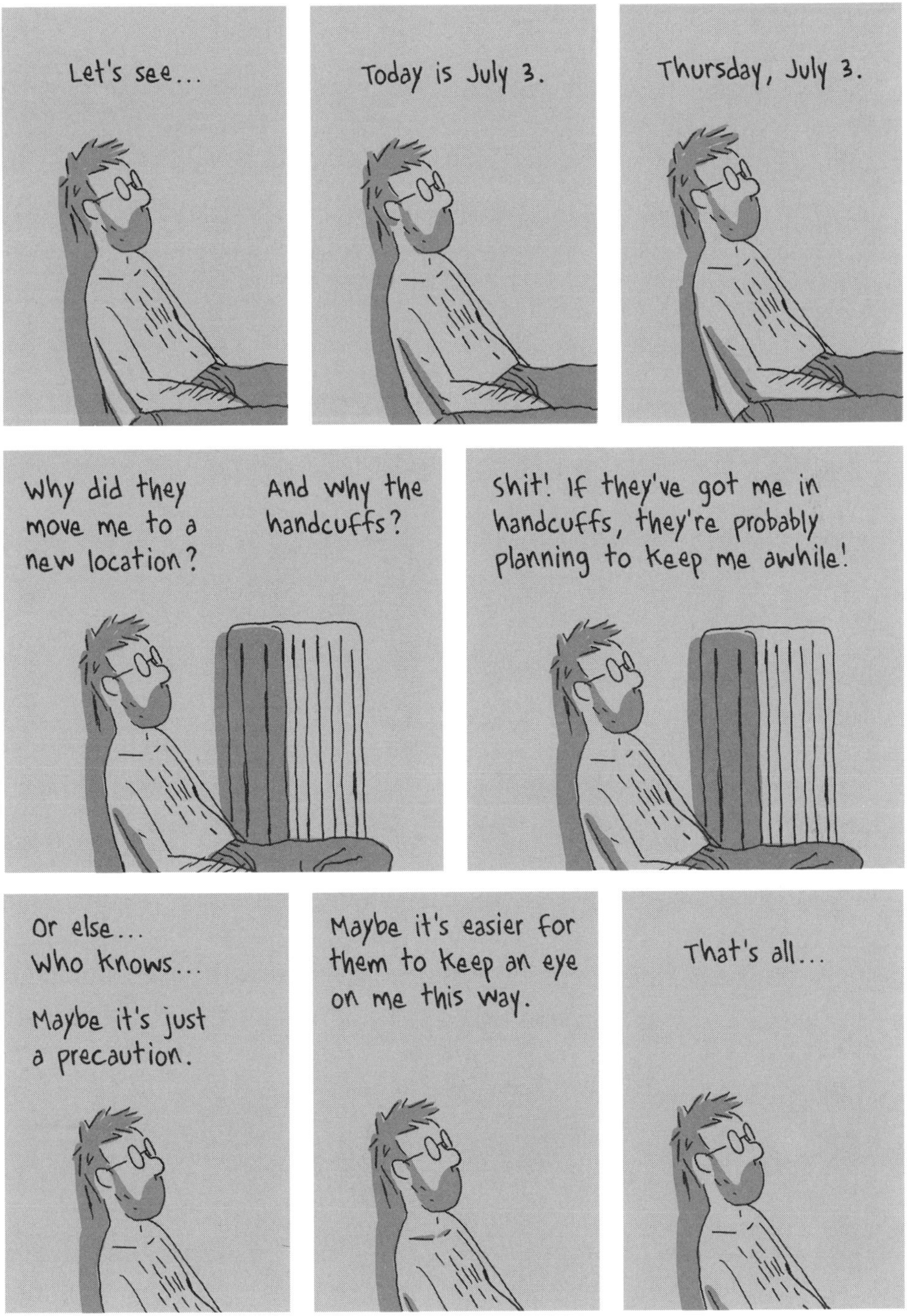
Let's see...
Today is July 3.
Thursday, July 3.
Why did they move me to a new location?
And why the handcuffs?
Shit! If they've got me in handcuffs, they're probably planning to keep me awhile!
Or else... Who knows...
Maybe it's just a precaution.
Maybe it's easier for them to keep an eye on me this way.
That's all...

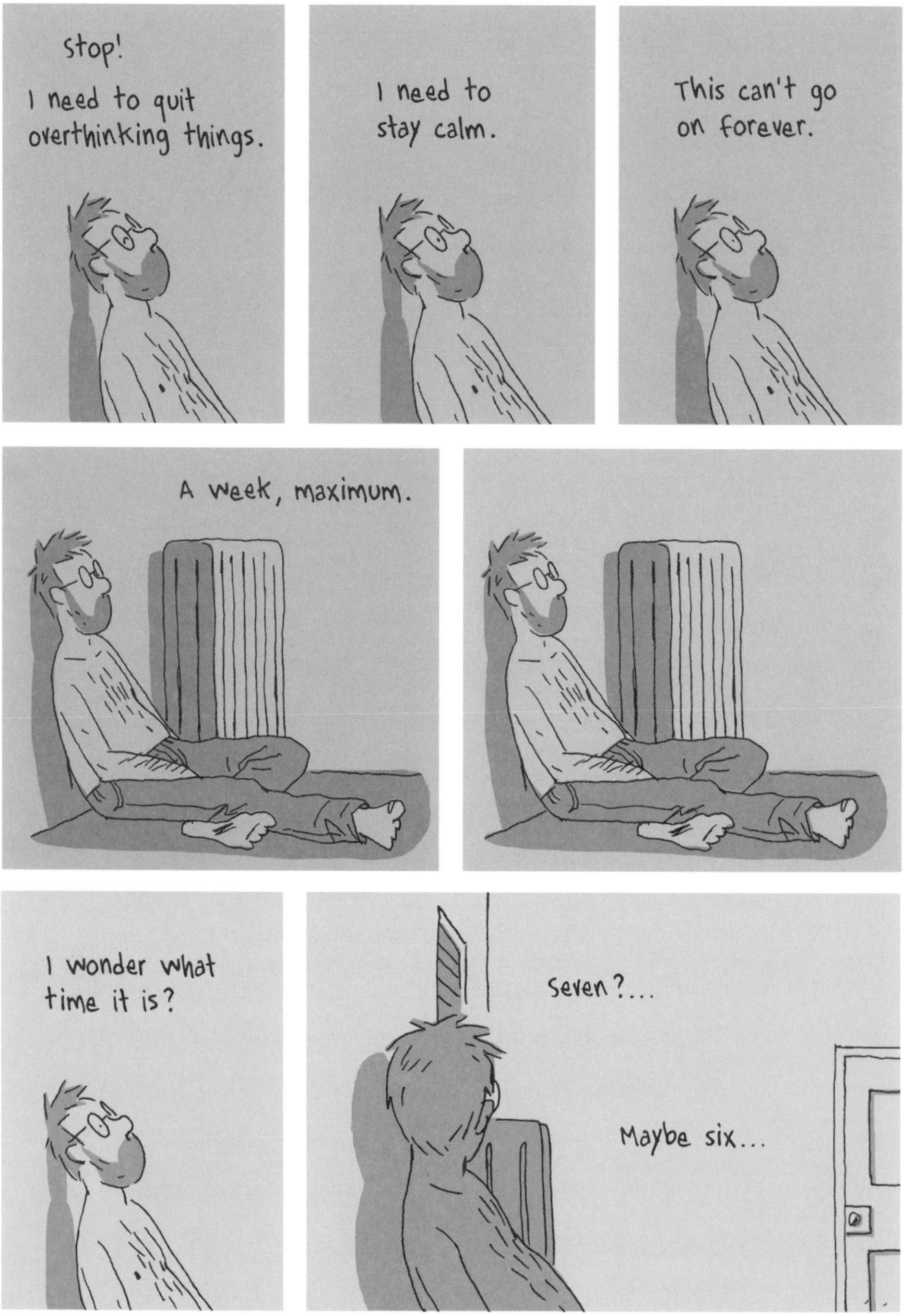
Stop!
I need to quit overthinking things.
I need to stay calm.
This can't go on forever.
A week, maximum.
I wonder what time it is?
Seven?...
Maybe six...

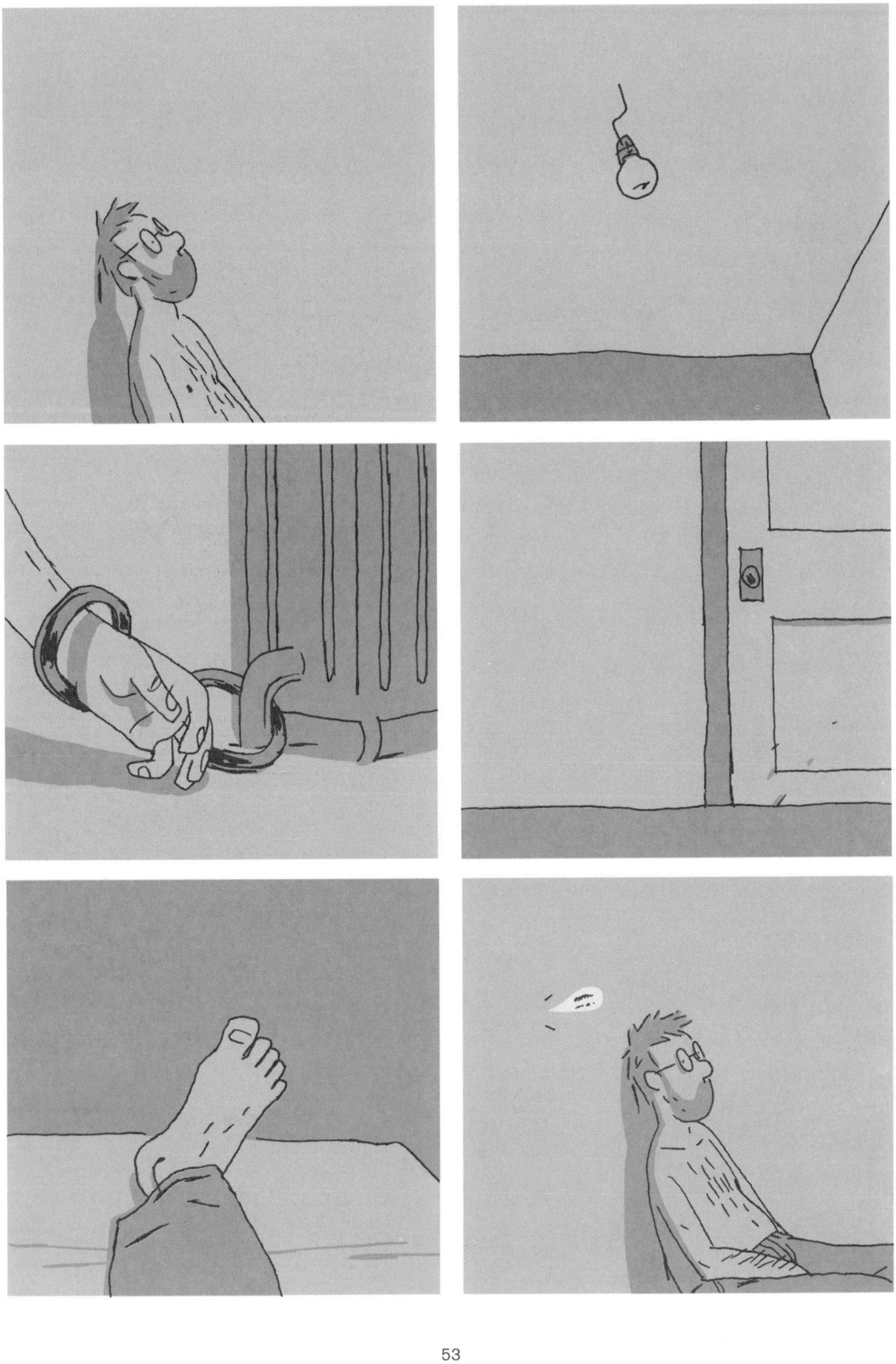

I hear sounds coming from the next room.
There are at least three people.
Including one woman.
I get the feeling people live here... I'm in somebody's apartment.
The door!
CLICK!
CLACK!
ФхНёгВ
This guy again.
His friend can't be far.

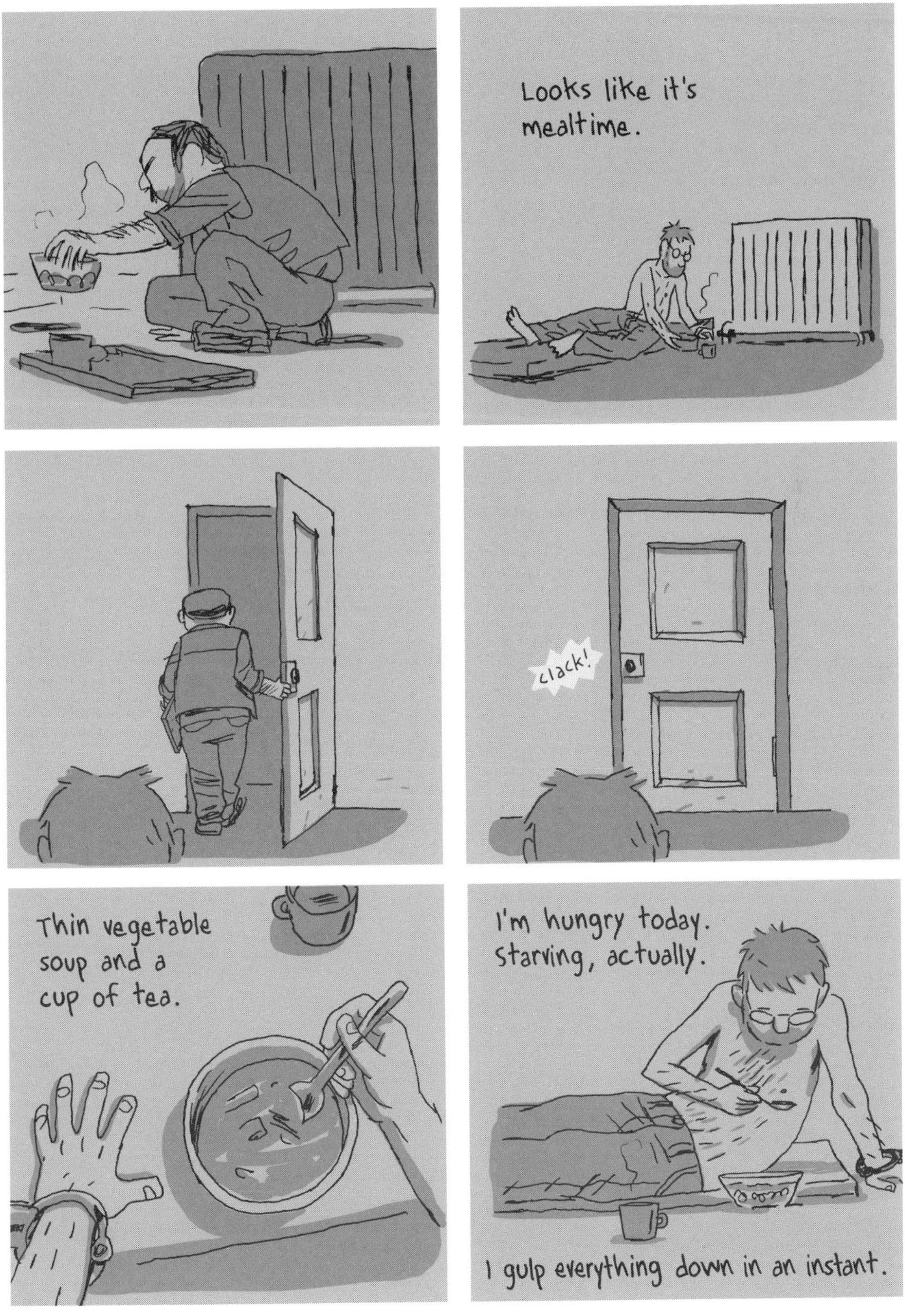
Looks like it's mealtime.
CLACK!
Thin vegetable soup and a cup of tea.
I'm hungry today. Starving, actually.
I gulp everything down in an instant.

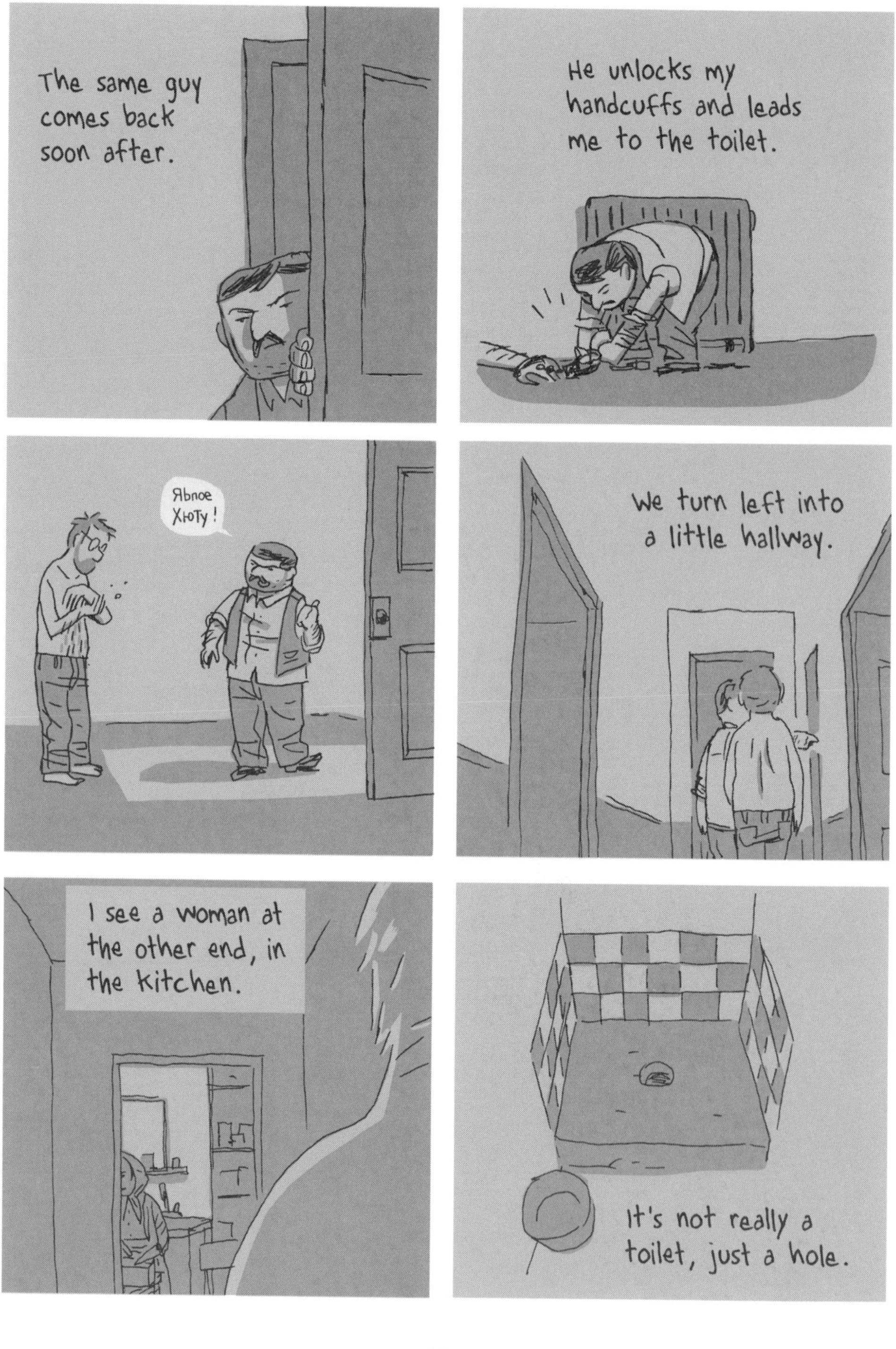
The same guy comes back soon after.
He unlocks my handcuffs and leads me to the toilet.
Яьпое
Хюту !
We turn left into a little hallway.
I see a woman at the other end, in the kitchen.
It's not really a toilet, just a hole.

Is there toilet paper? Tissue paper? Anything?

He points at the bucket and I figure it out.

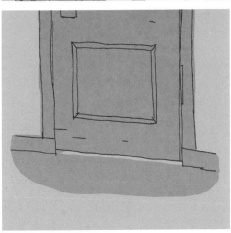

CRRICK

He takes me back to the room.

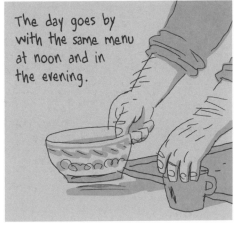

The day goes by with the same menu at noon and in the evening.

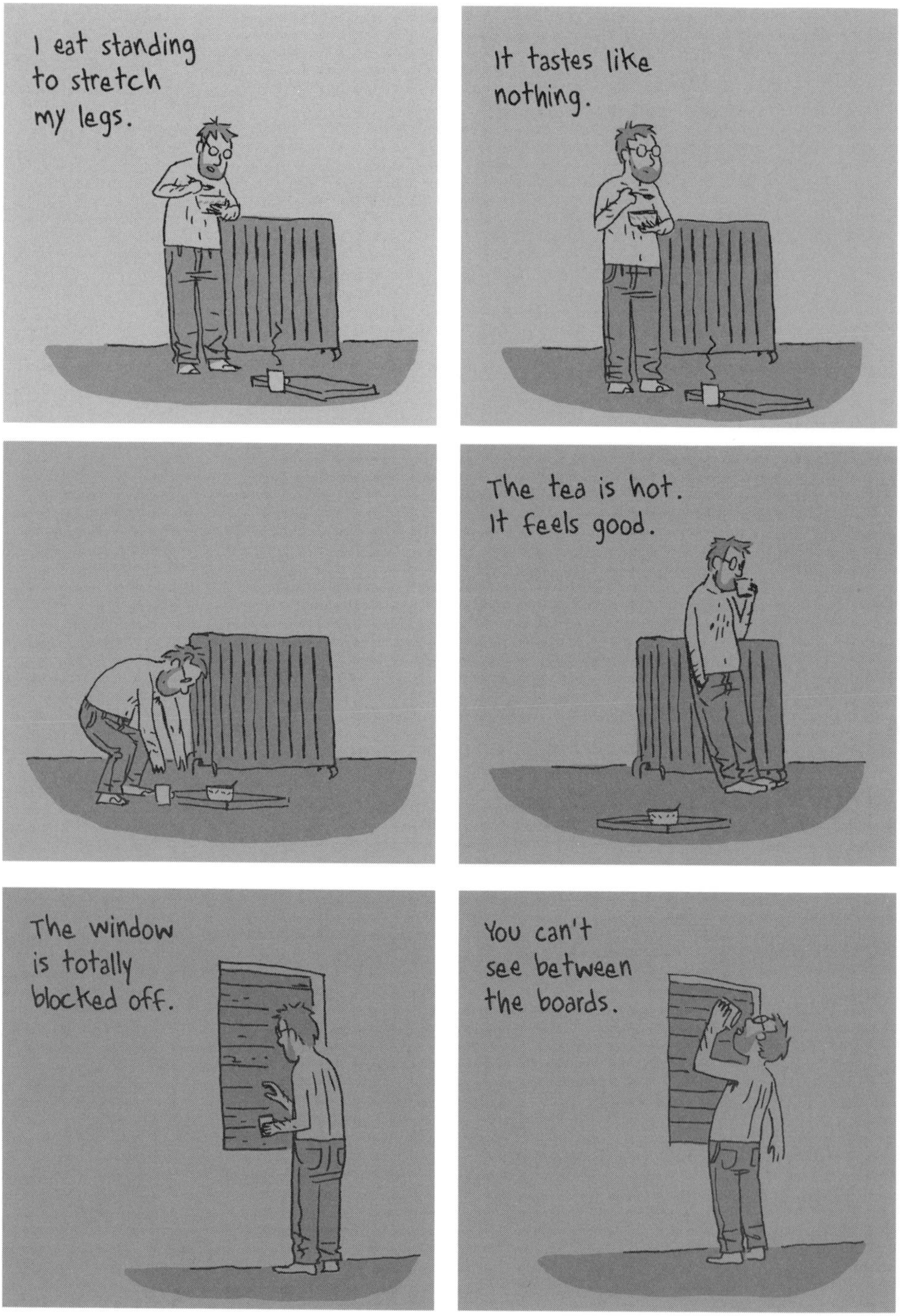
I eat standing to stretch my legs.
It tastes like nothing.
The tea is hot. It feels good.
The window is totally blocked off.
You can't see between the boards.

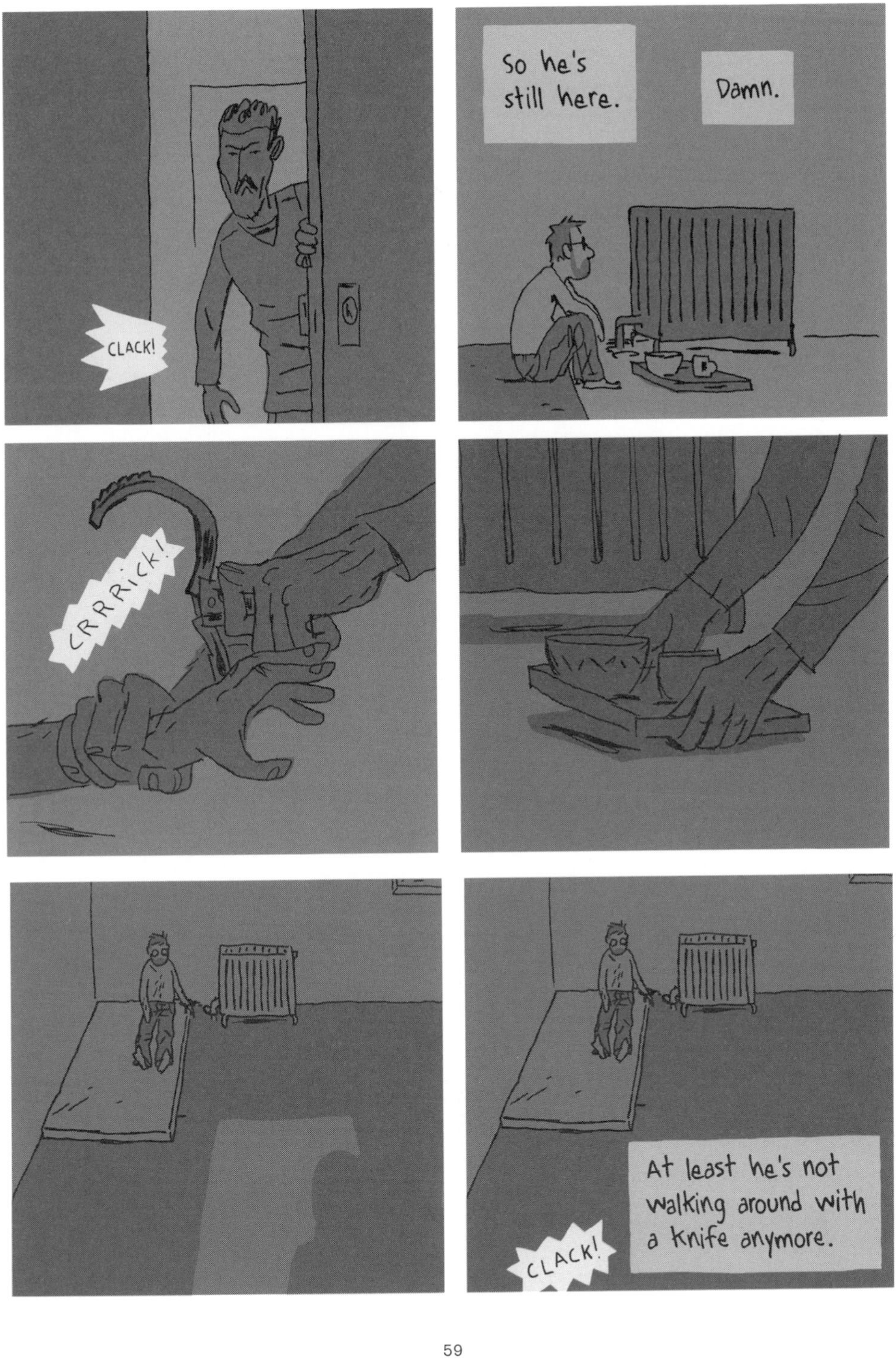
CLACK!
So he's still here.
Damn.
CRRRICK!
At least he's not walking around with a knife anymore.
CLACK!

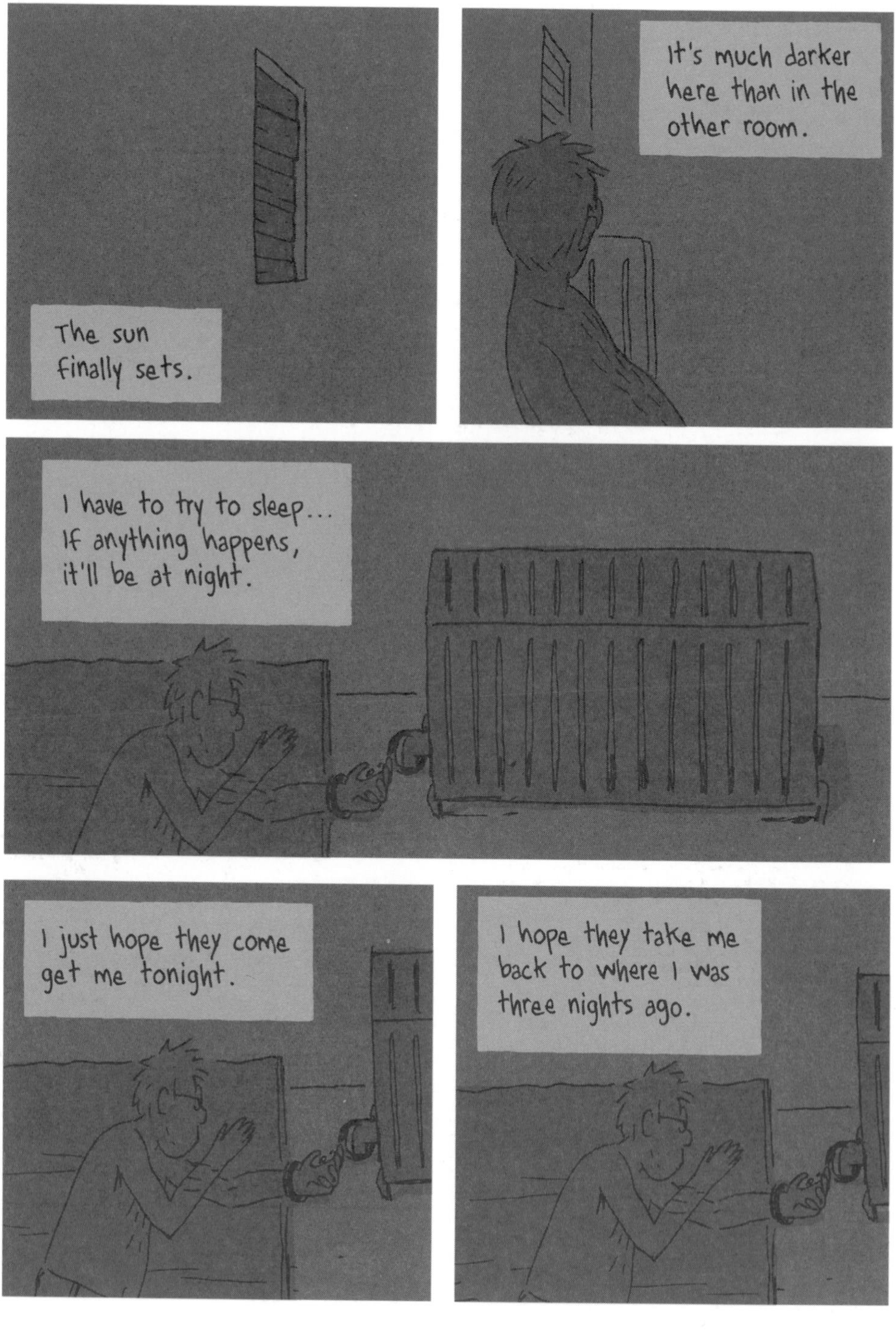
The sun finally sets.
It's much darker here than in the other room.
I have to try to sleep... If anything happens, it'll be at night.
I just hope they come get me tonight.
I hope they take me back to where I was three nights ago.

4

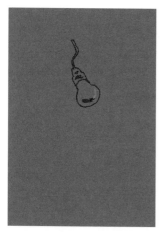
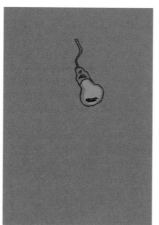

Today is July 4.

Friday, July 4.

Nothing happened
last night.

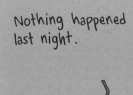

Nobody came to get
me out of here.

Maybe they'll
come tonight?

In the meantime, I'll
be spending another day
attached to this radiator.

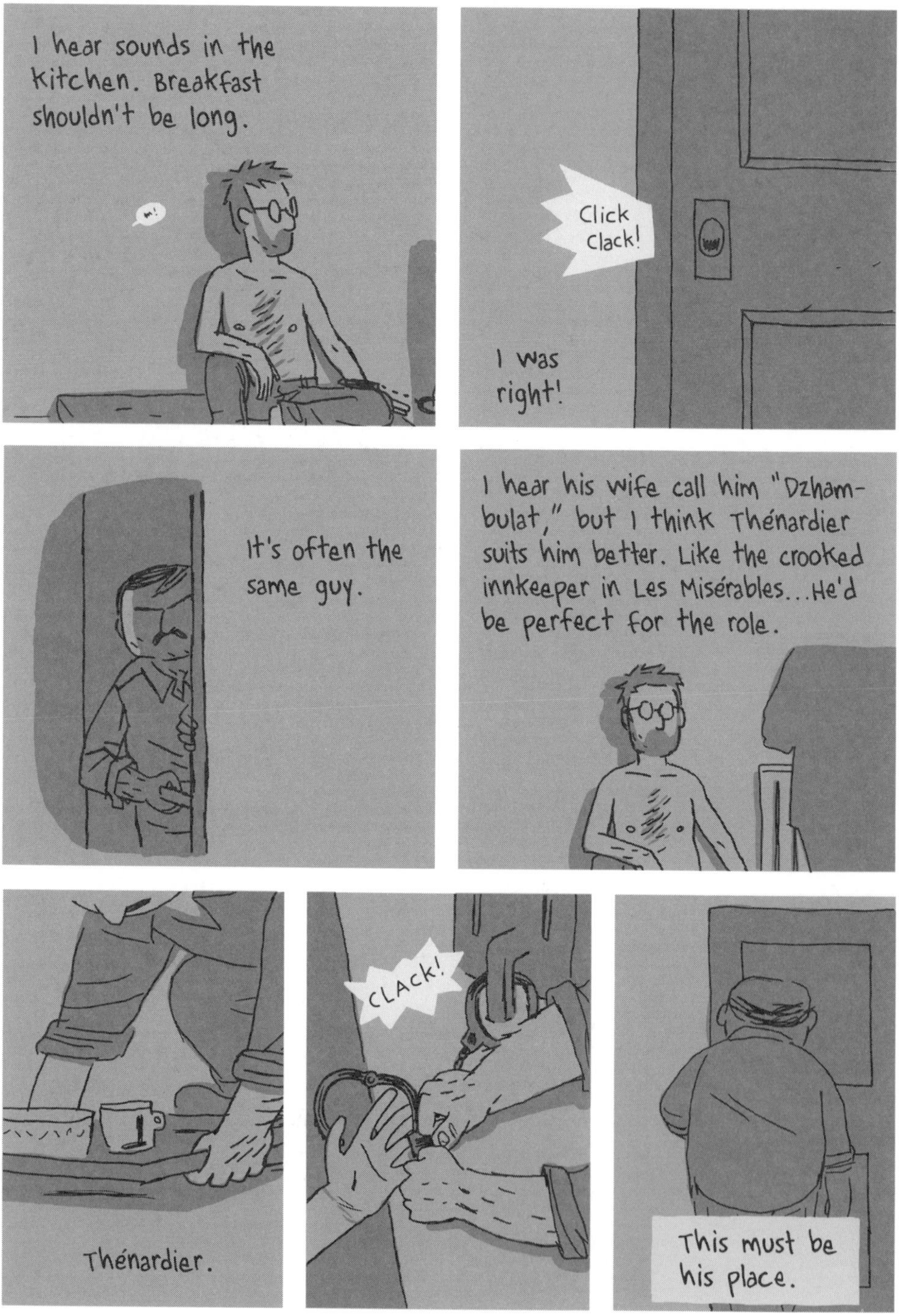
I hear sounds in the kitchen. Breakfast shouldn't be long.
Click Clack!
I was right!
It's often the same guy.
I hear his wife call him "Dzhambulat," but I think Thénardier suits him better. Like the crooked innkeeper in Les Misérables...He'd be perfect for the role.
Thénardier.
CLACK!
This must be his place.

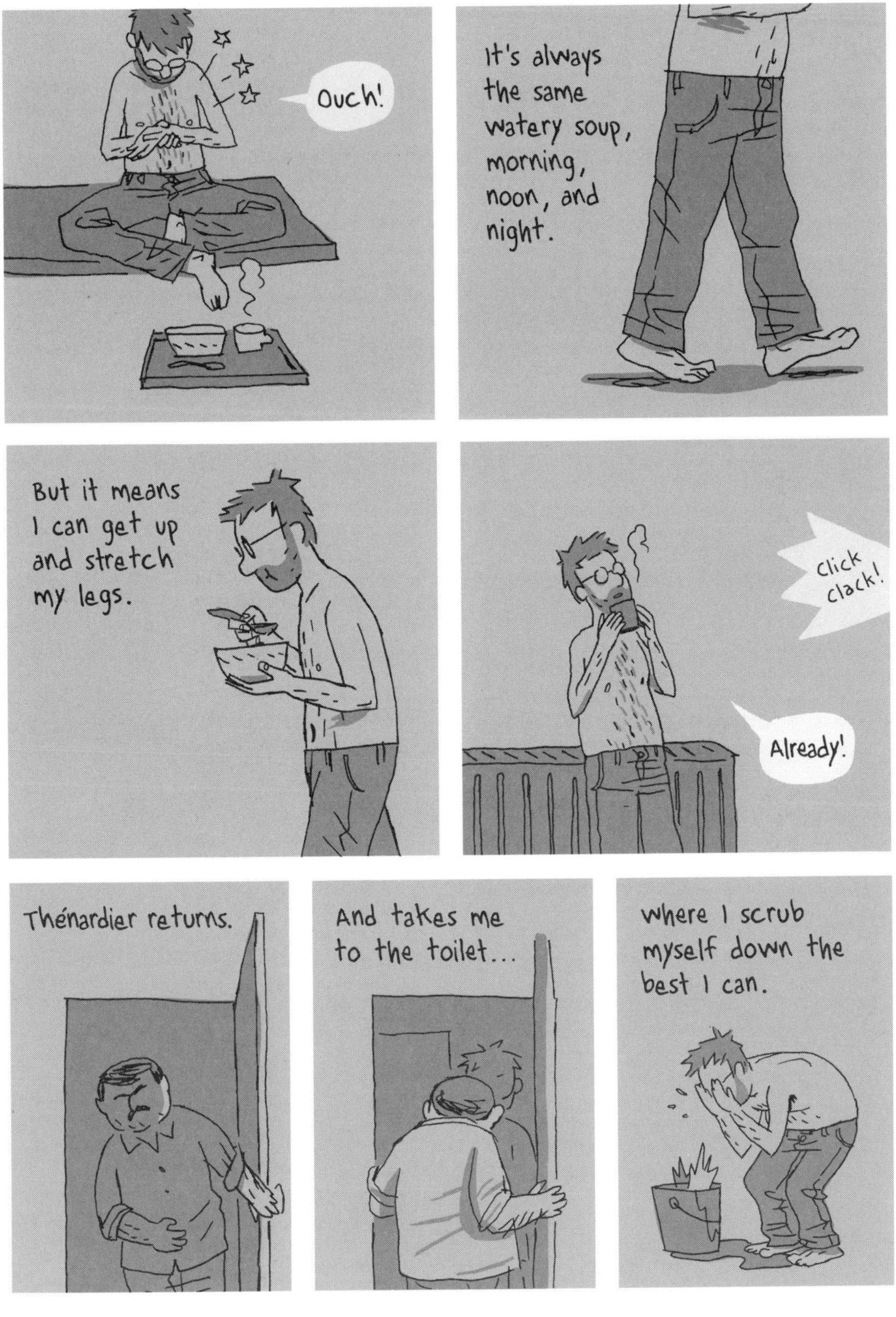
Ouch!
It's always the same watery soup, morning, noon, and night.
But it means I can get up and stretch my legs.
Click clack!
Already!
Thénardier returns.
And takes me to the toilet...
where I scrub myself down the best I can.

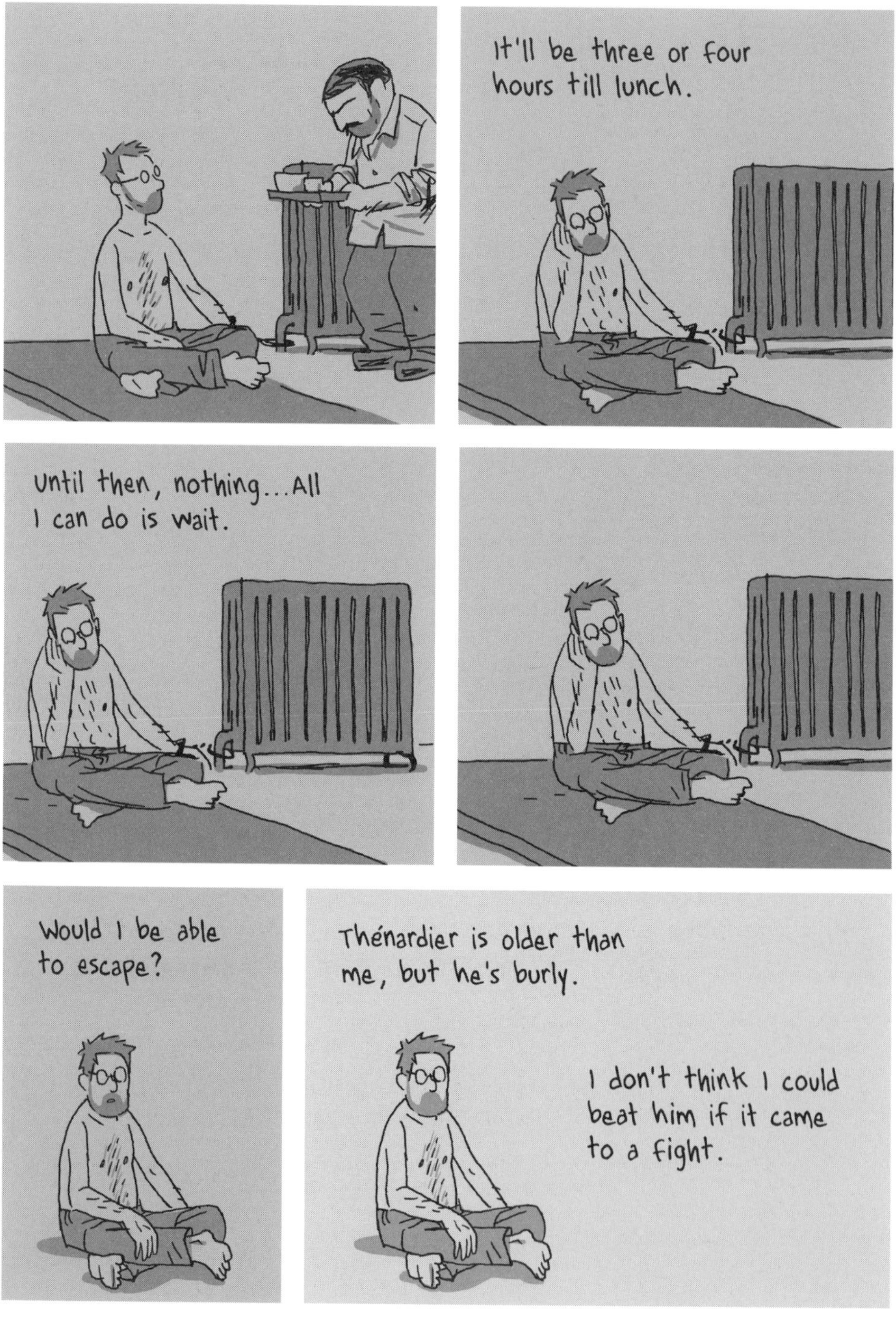
It'll be three or four hours till lunch.
Until then, nothing...All I can do is wait.
Would I be able to escape?
Thénardier is older than me, but he's burly.
I don't think I could beat him if it came to a fight.

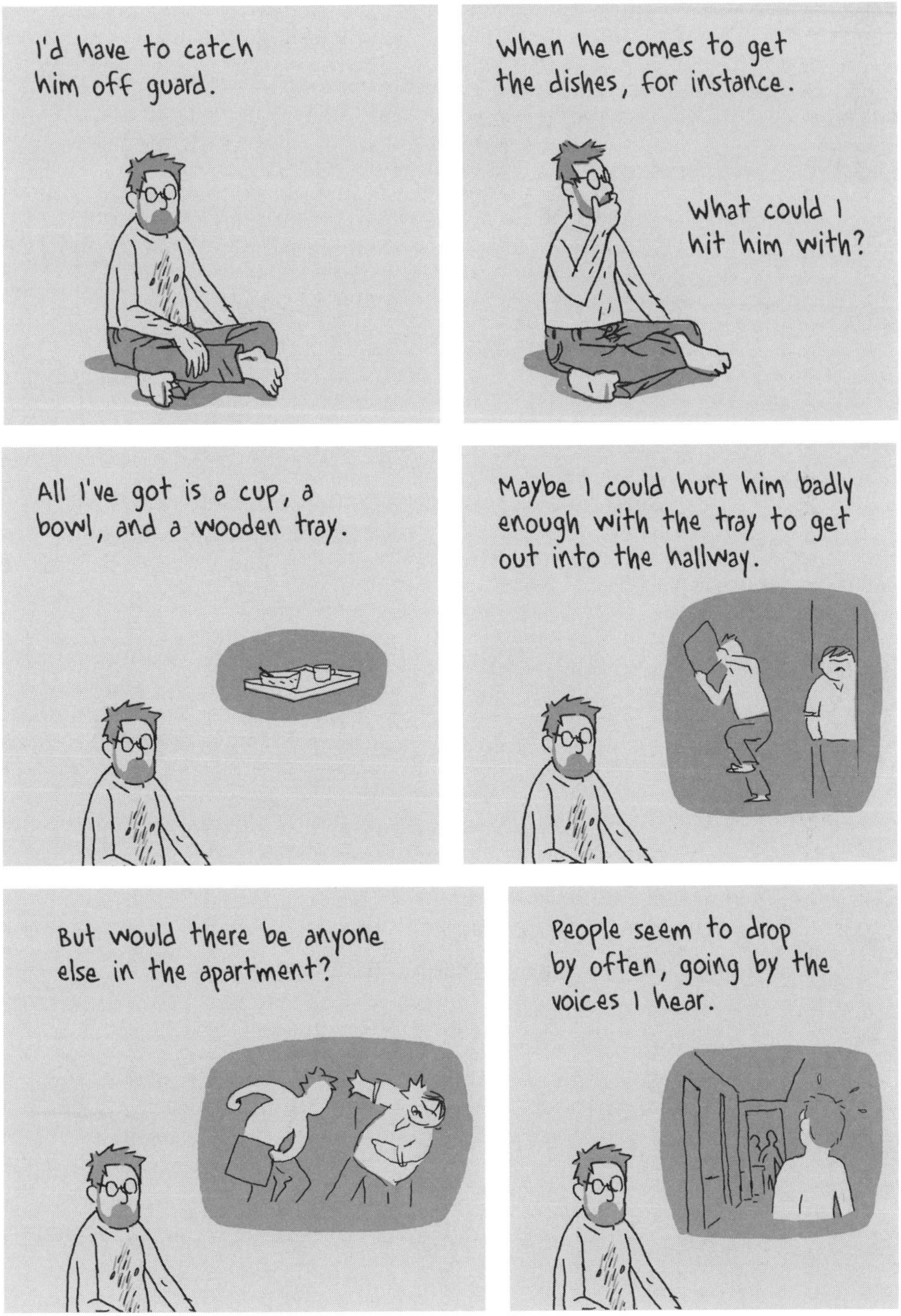
I'd have to catch him off guard.
When he comes to get the dishes, for instance.
What could I hit him with?
All I've got is a cup, a bowl, and a wooden tray.
Maybe I could hurt him badly enough with the tray to get out into the hallway.
But would there be anyone else in the apartment?
People seem to drop by often, going by the voices I hear.

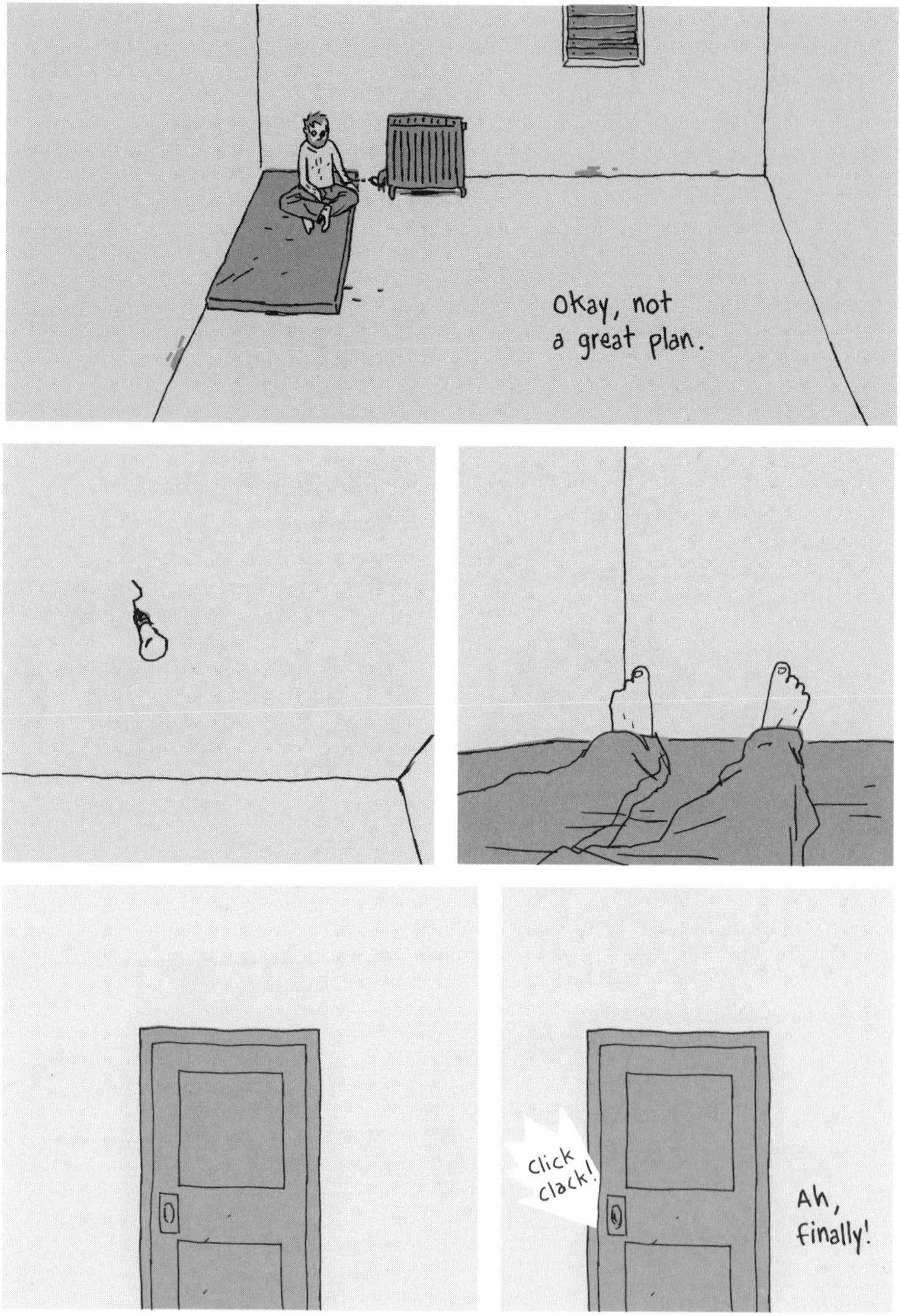
Okay, not a great plan.
Click clack!
Ah, finally!

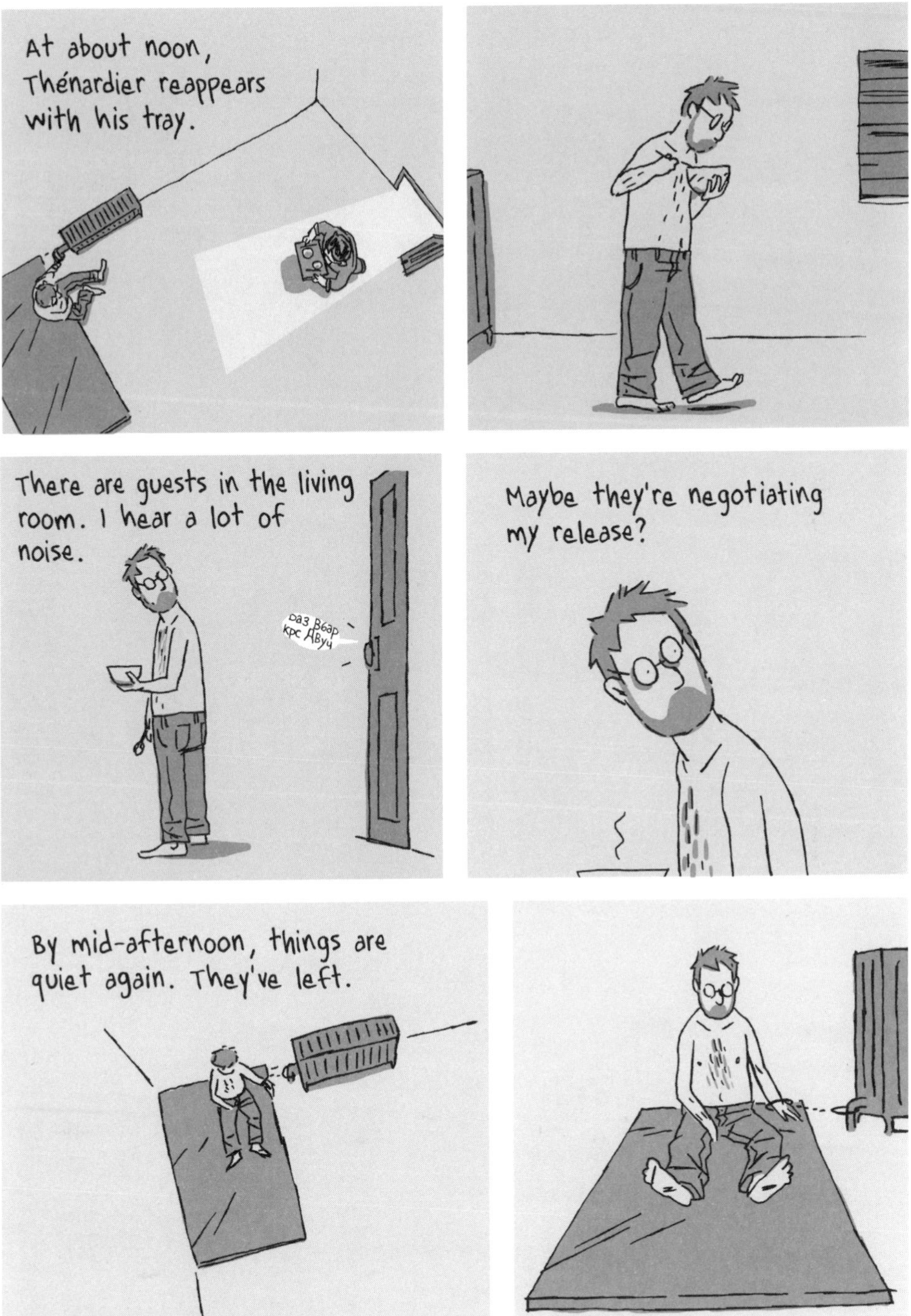
At about noon, Thénardier reappears with his tray.
There are guests in the living room. I hear a lot of noise.
Баз Вбар крс Двуч
Maybe they're negotiating my release?
By mid-afternoon, things are quiet again. They've left.

In the evening, Thénardier comes in empty-handed. He unlocks the cuffs.
Баз Вбар Двуч!
I don't understand what he wants.
Ейо Баз!
What?
He motions for me to follow him.
We enter a small living room. The tall guy is there.
I don't know what to expect, but they seem to be in a good mood and that's reassuring.
Ñкрс.
They offer me a drink.
Thanks!
Ñкрс Двуч.
In my situation, there's no refusing. Distractions are hard to come by.

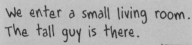

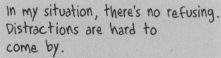

We spend part of the evening sitting on the couch, watching a video.

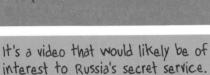

It shows footage of a Chechen training camp.

They seem proud to show it to me.

It's a video that would likely be of interest to Russia's secret service.

Basayer!

They point at someone. It must be Basayer, the Chechen commander.

Russia's most wanted man.

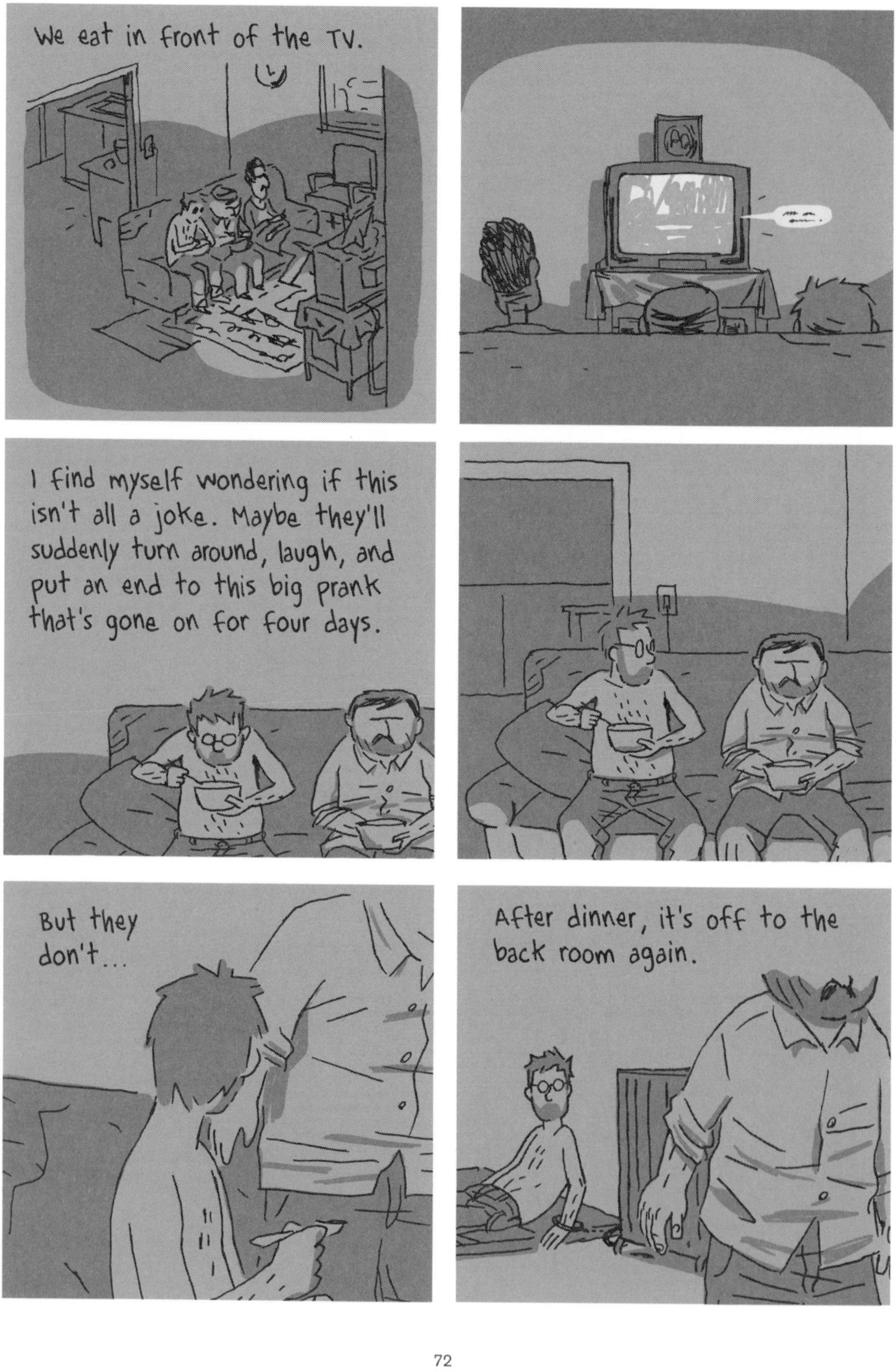
We eat in front of the TV.
I find myself wondering if this isn't all a joke. Maybe they'll suddenly turn around, laugh, and put an end to this big prank that's gone on for four days.
But they don't...
After dinner, it's off to the back room again.

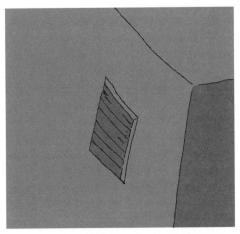

The sun has set.

It's been, what, four nights since I left?

They must have contacted my abductors by now to discuss my release.

Maybe it'll happen tonight?

5

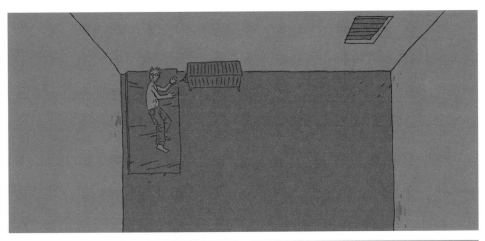

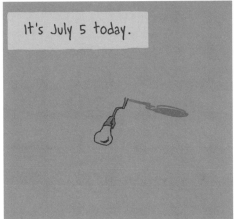

It's July 5 today.

Saturday, July 5.

Saturday... The first day of the weekend.

Which means what? That the office in Nazran is closed and it'll be Monday before anything happens?

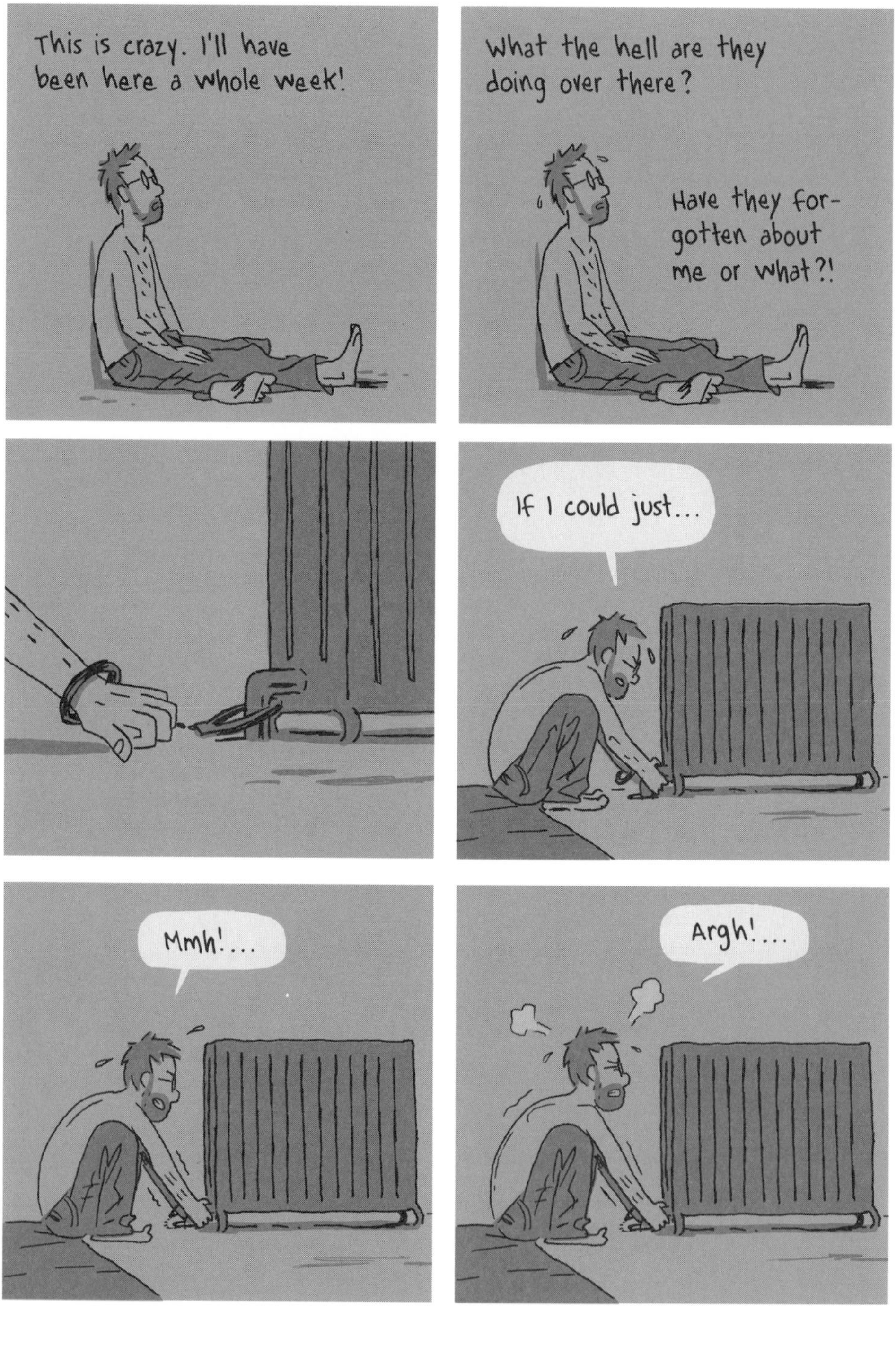
This is crazy. I'll have been here a whole week!
What the hell are they doing over there?
Have they for-gotten about me or what?!
If I could just...
Mmh!...
Argh!...

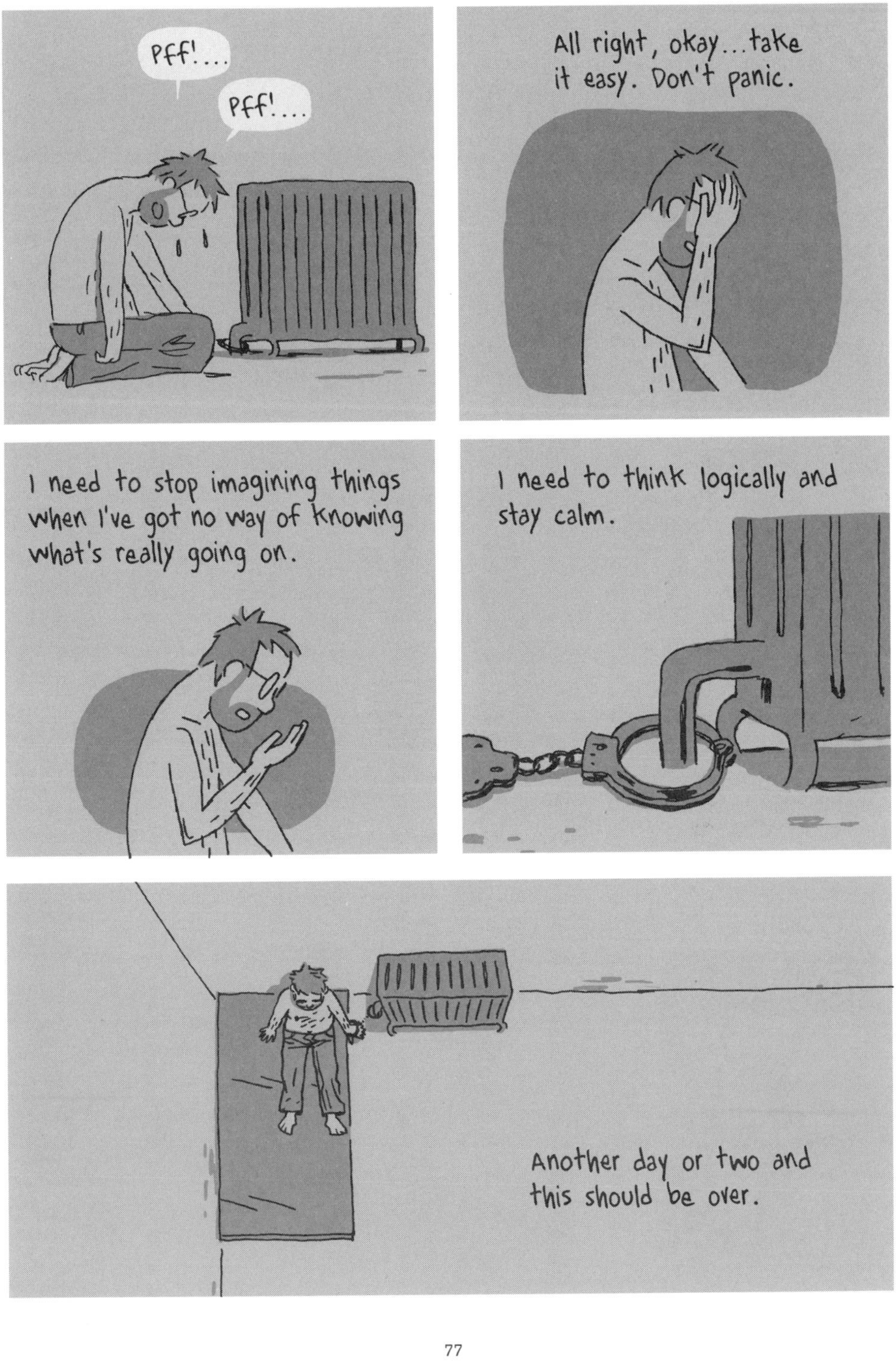

Pff!...
Pff!...
All right, okay...take it easy. Don't panic.
I need to stop imagining things when I've got no way of knowing what's really going on.
I need to think logically and stay calm.
Another day or two and this should be over.

Click
clack!

Thénardier comes to unlock
my cuffs for breakfast.

Вбар Лтоб
АВуч.

CLACK!

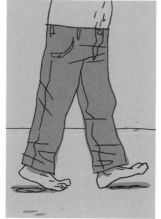

And again for lunch.

Змнру
ио Баз.

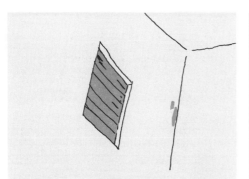

It's the brightest time of day.
It must be 2:00 p.m.

Thénardier's wife is talking to someone.

Another woman.

A friend, I suppose.

BANG!

What the hell was that?

A door being broken down?

BANG!

BANG!

Gunfire? No.

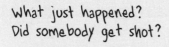
What just happened?
Did somebody get shot?

No, I don't think
so. I don't hear
anything anymore.

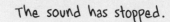
The sound has stopped.

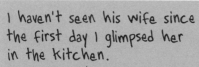

I haven't seen his wife since
the first day I glimpsed her
in the kitchen.

He's probably ordered her to stay
out of sight whenever I leave
the room.

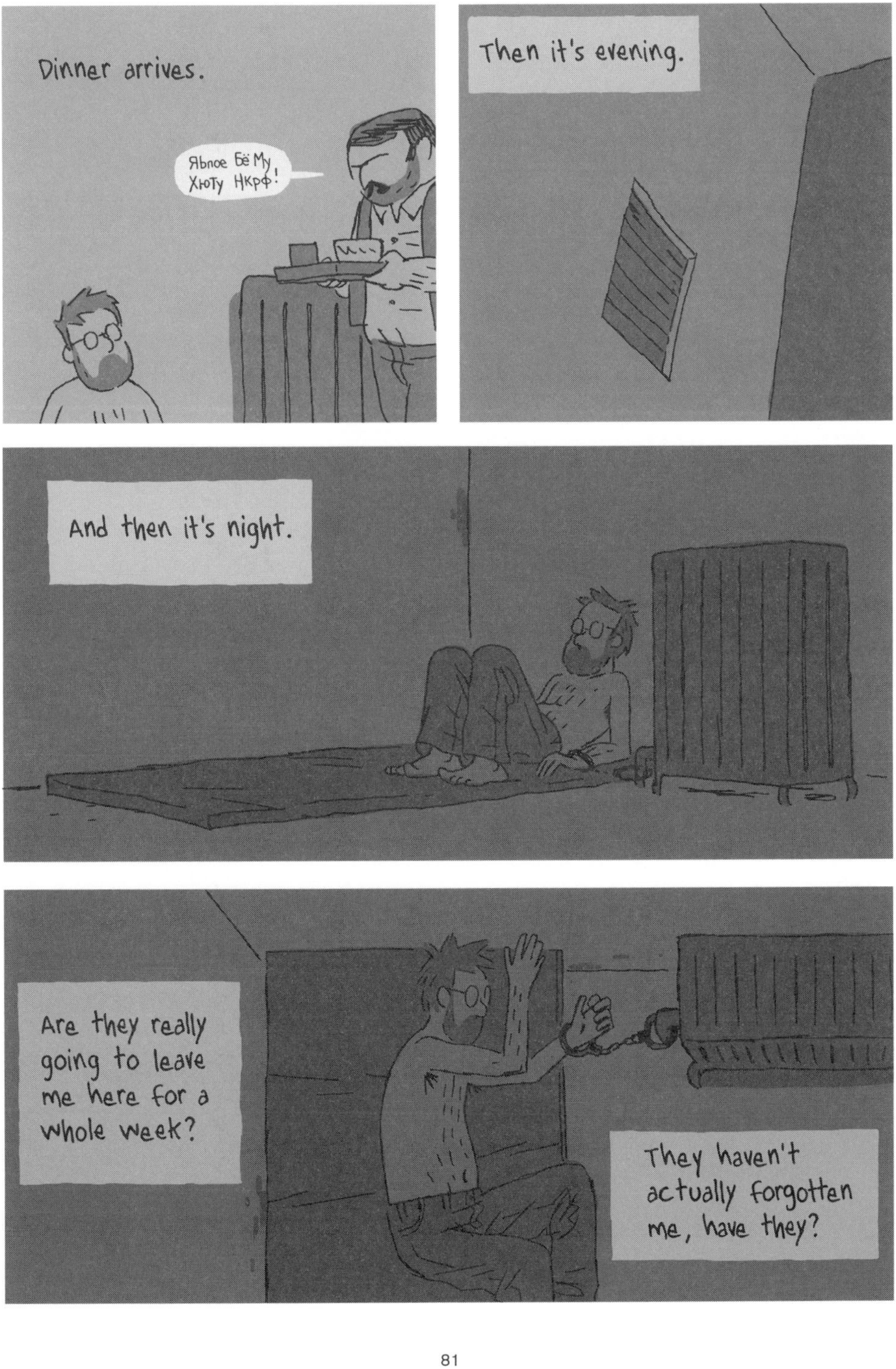
Dinner arrives.
Яbпое Бё Му,
Хюту Нкрф!
Then it's evening.
And then it's night.
Are they really going to leave me here for a whole week?
They haven't actually forgotten me, have they?

9

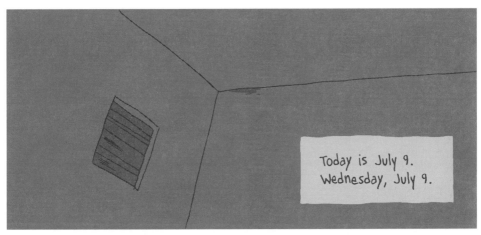

Today is July 9.
Wednesday, July 9.

One week...

I've been locked up for a week now.

They better hurry and come get me because I don't think I can hold out like this for another week.

I'll go crazy.

Maybe during a meal...

spoon

I could pry a board off the window...

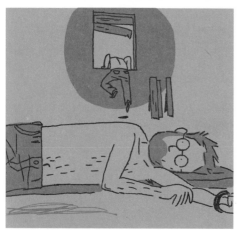

and jump...

A bit risky, from the third floor...

Fuck.

CLACK!

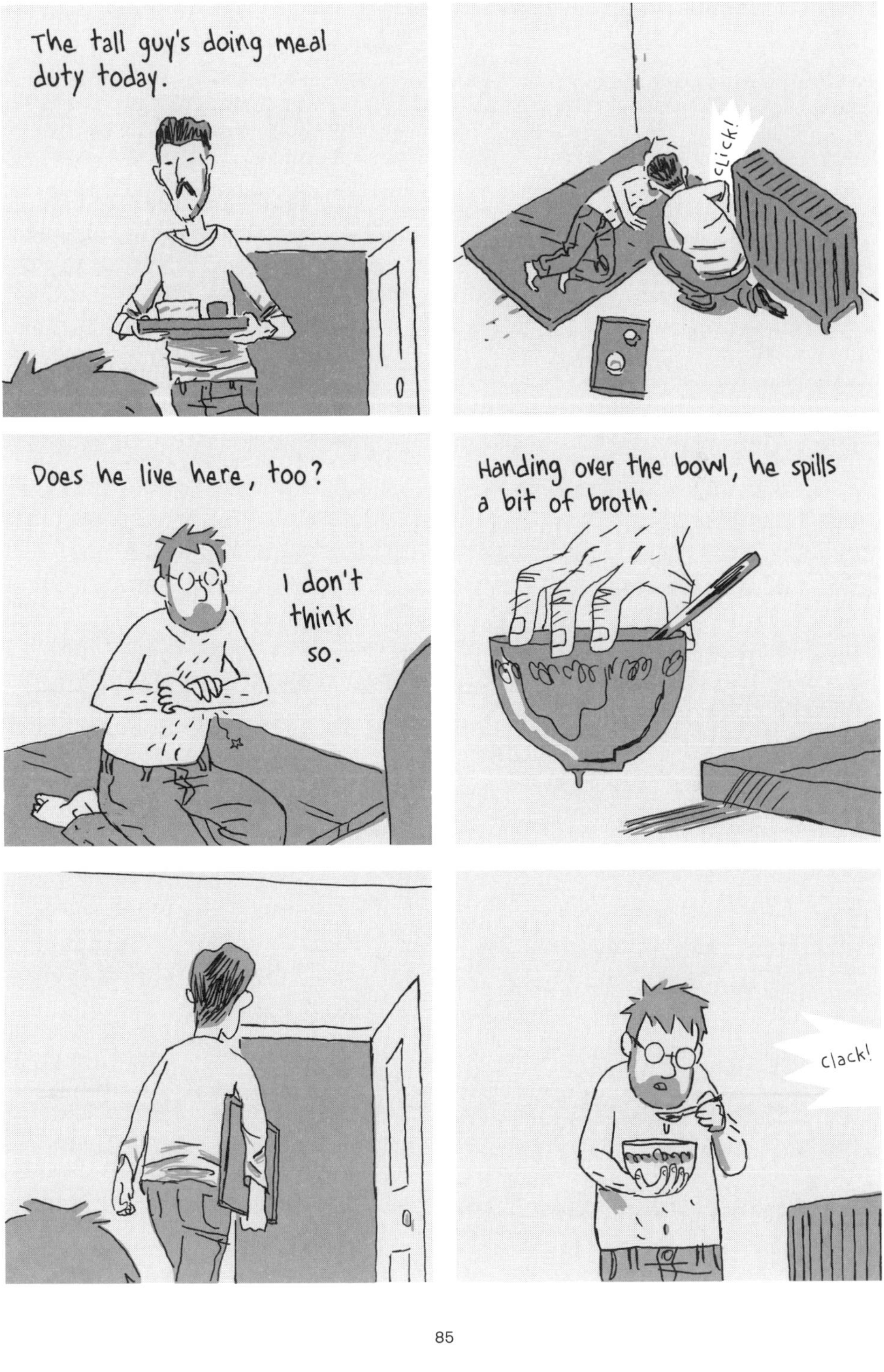
The tall guy's doing meal duty today.
Click!
Does he live here, too?
I don't think so.
Handing over the bowl, he spills a bit of broth.
Clack!

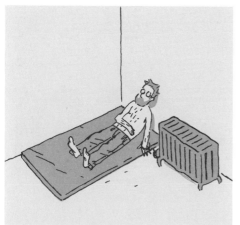

Not much noise today.

There was some chanting at one point.

A radio or something.

I think they were praying.

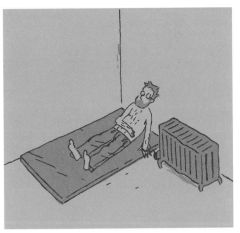

clack!

After dinner, the tall guy offers me a cigarette.

Thanks.

A bit of spilled broth and a smoke... The two big events of my day.

10

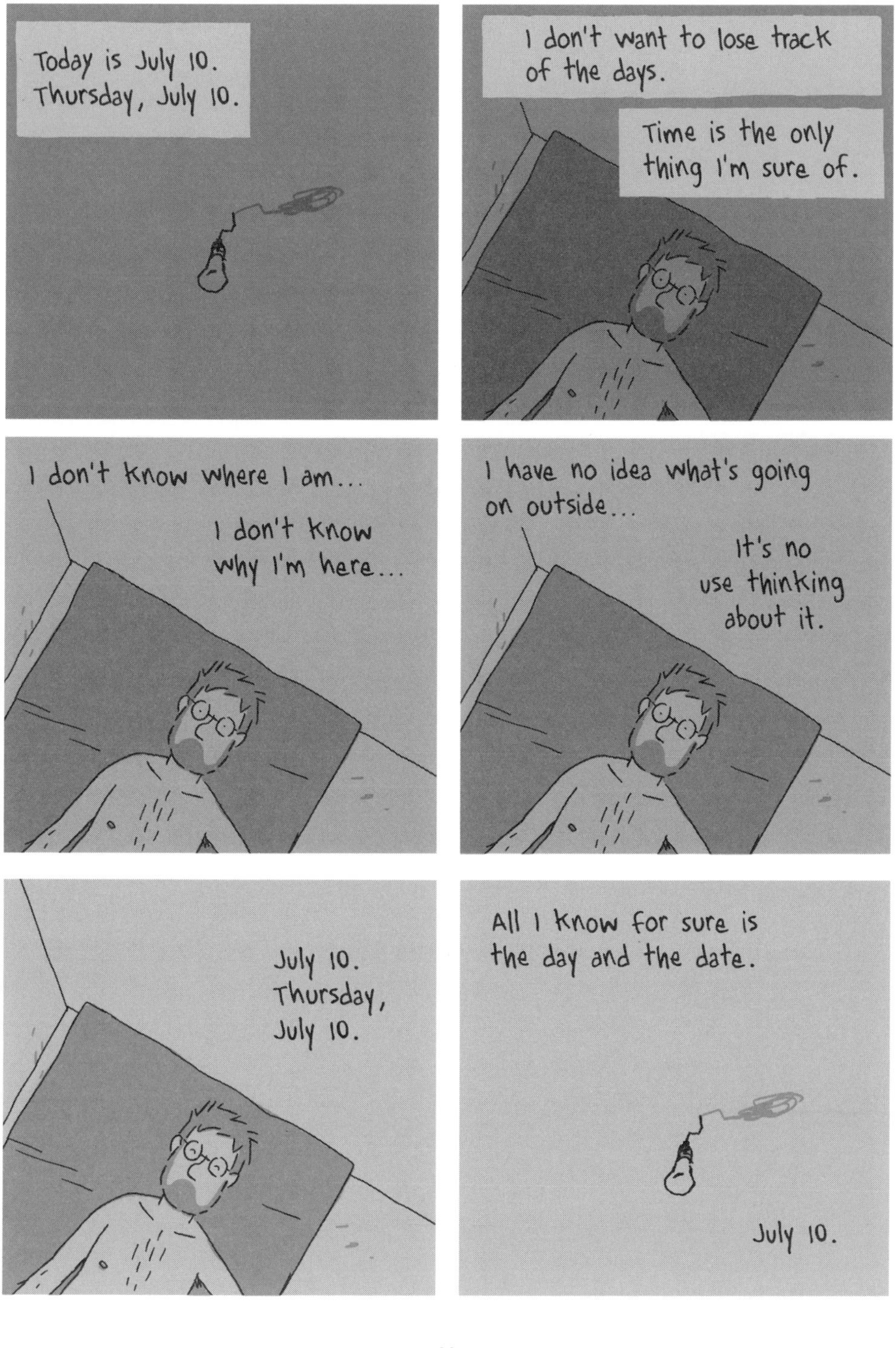
Today is July 10. Thursday, July 10.
I don't want to lose track of the days.
Time is the only thing I'm sure of.
I don't know where I am...
I don't know why I'm here...
I have no idea what's going on outside...
It's no use thinking about it.
July 10. Thursday, July 10.
All I know for sure is the day and the date.
July 10.

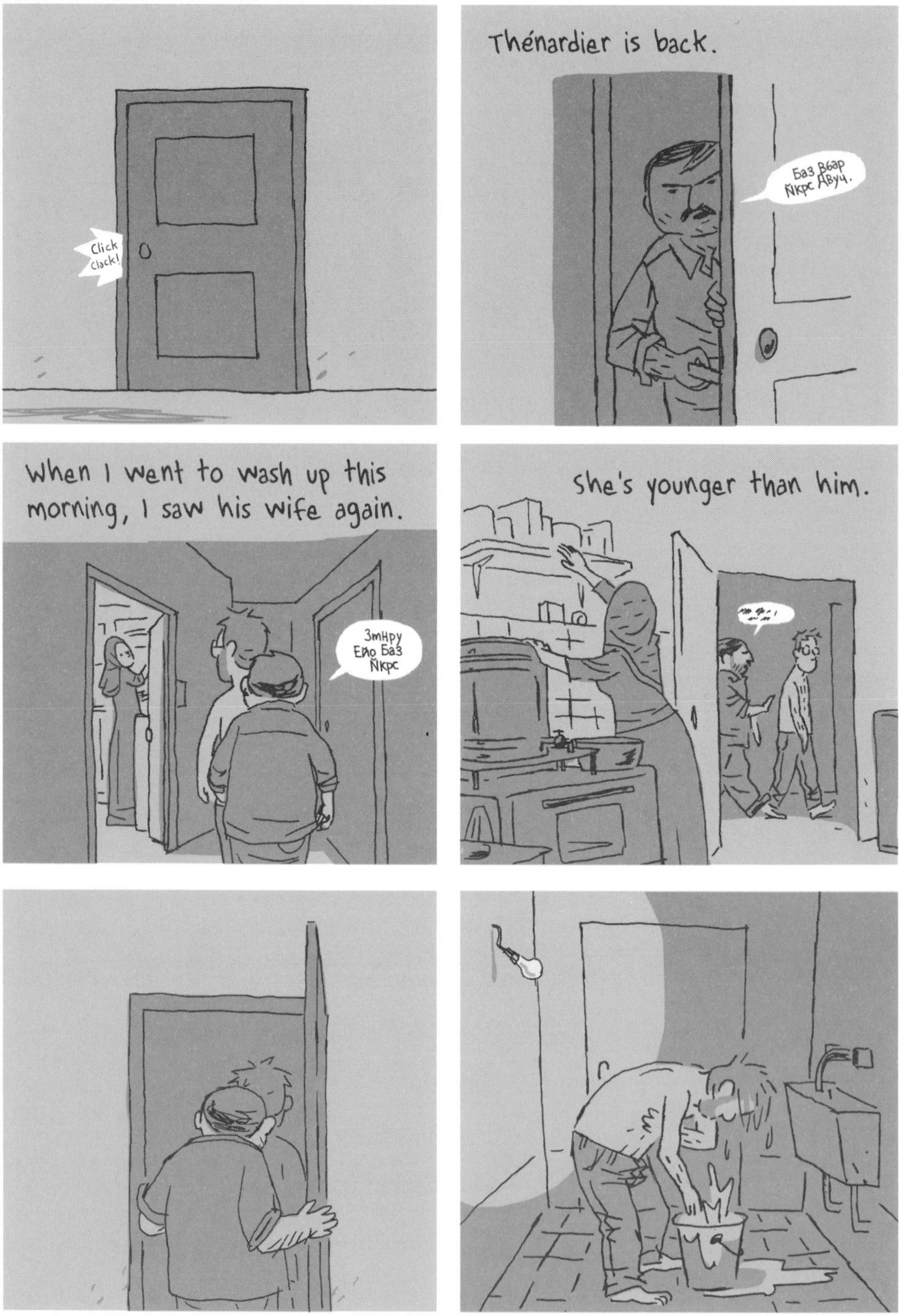
Click clack!
Thénardier is back.
Баз Вбар Ñкрс Авуч.
When I went to wash up this morning, I saw his wife again.
Зтнру Ейо Баз Ñкрс
She's younger than him.

On my way back, she was in the hall.

Thénardier snapped at her.

НПСТЁ ДГС АПЖ ЫЭ Ф!

He seemed on edge.

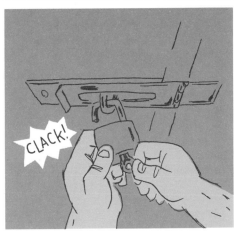

CLACK!

She'd just finished sweeping the back room.

CLICK!

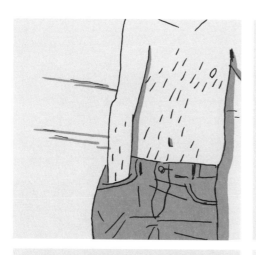

If I still had the keys to the safe in my pocket, I could pick the lock on my handcuffs.

They took everything.

It looks easy in the movies.

But even with a free hand, I'd still have to open the door.

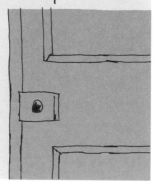

And since it's bolted on the other side, there's no way I'd be able.

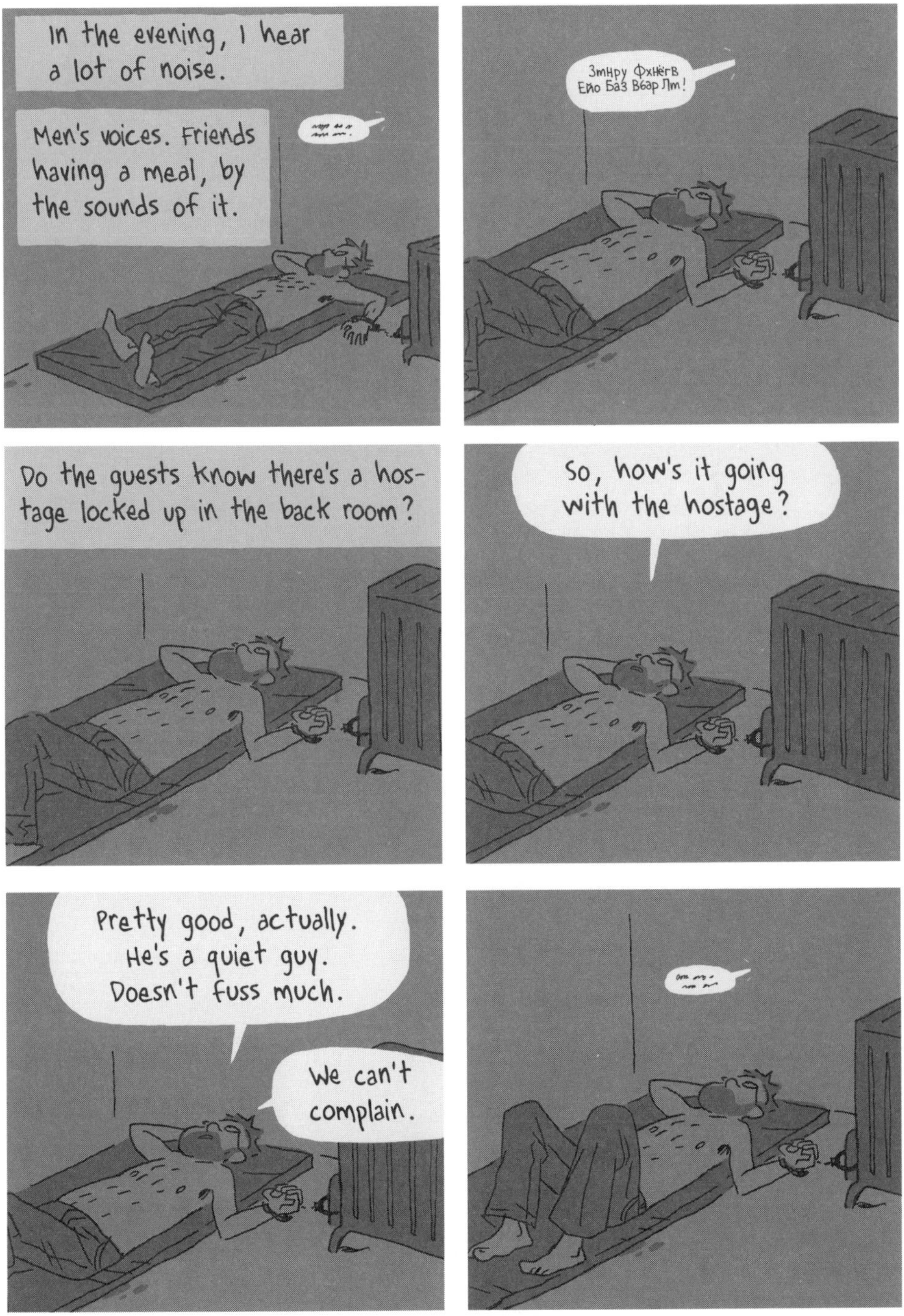
In the evening, I hear a lot of noise.
Men's voices. Friends having a meal, by the sounds of it.
Змнру Фхнёгв Ейо Баз Вбар Лм!
Do the guests know there's a hostage locked up in the back room?
So, how's it going with the hostage?
Pretty good, actually. He's a quiet guy. Doesn't fuss much.
We can't complain.

I'm about to drift off when I hear the door open.

CLACK!

BÑKpc!

Бáap Лmos ABy4.

I have a brief moment of joy at the thought that something's about to happen...

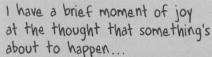

that contact has been established with the outside...

I'm going to be released...I'll see the team in Nazran again.

I'll get back to work and forget about this nightmare!

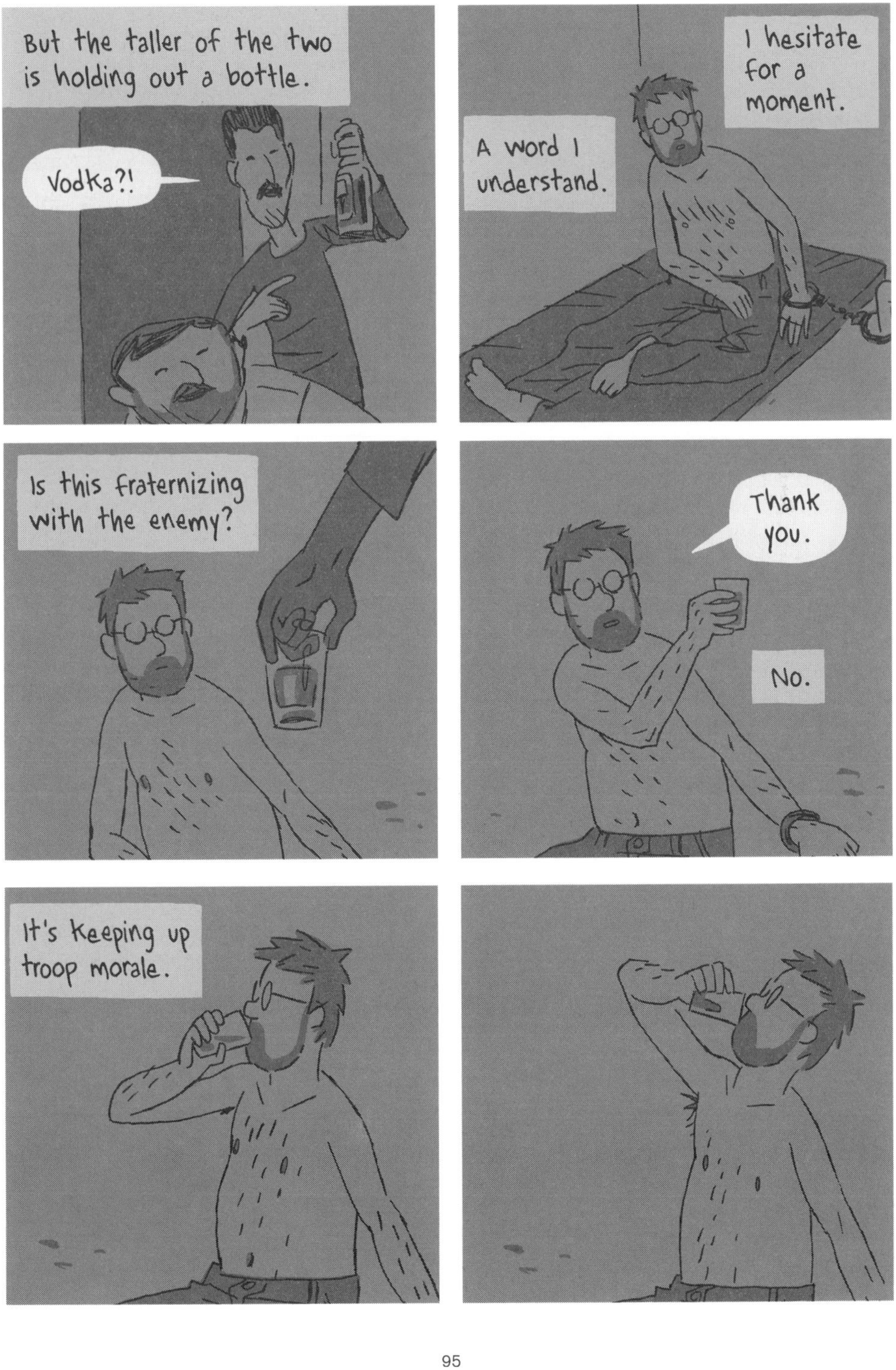
But the taller of the two is holding out a bottle.
Vodka?!
I hesitate for a moment.
A word I understand.
Is this fraternizing with the enemy?
Thank you.
No.
It's keeping up troop morale.

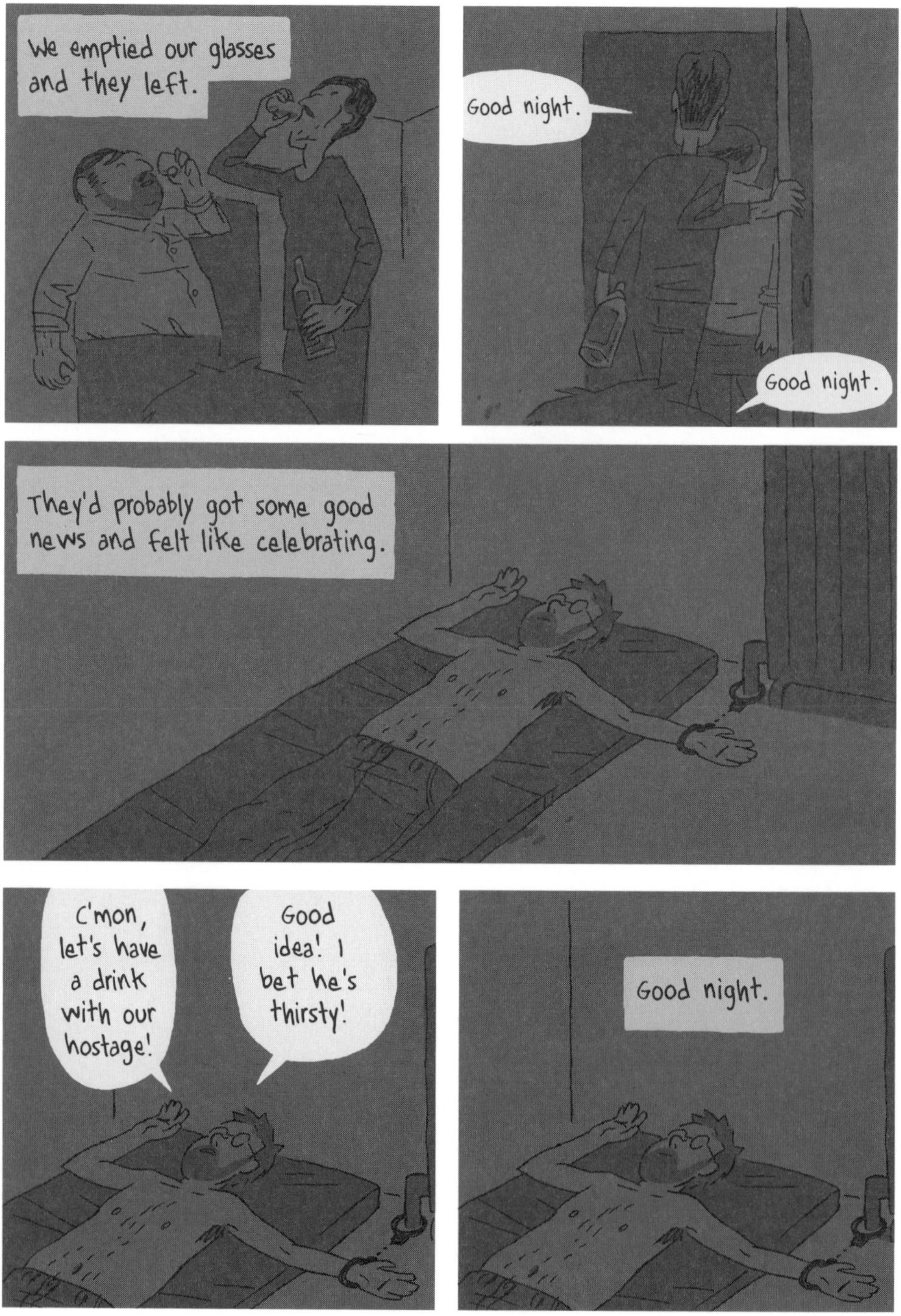
We emptied our glasses and they left.
Good night.
Good night.
They'd probably got some good news and felt like celebrating.
C'mon, let's have a drink with our hostage!
Good idea! I bet he's thirsty!
Good night.

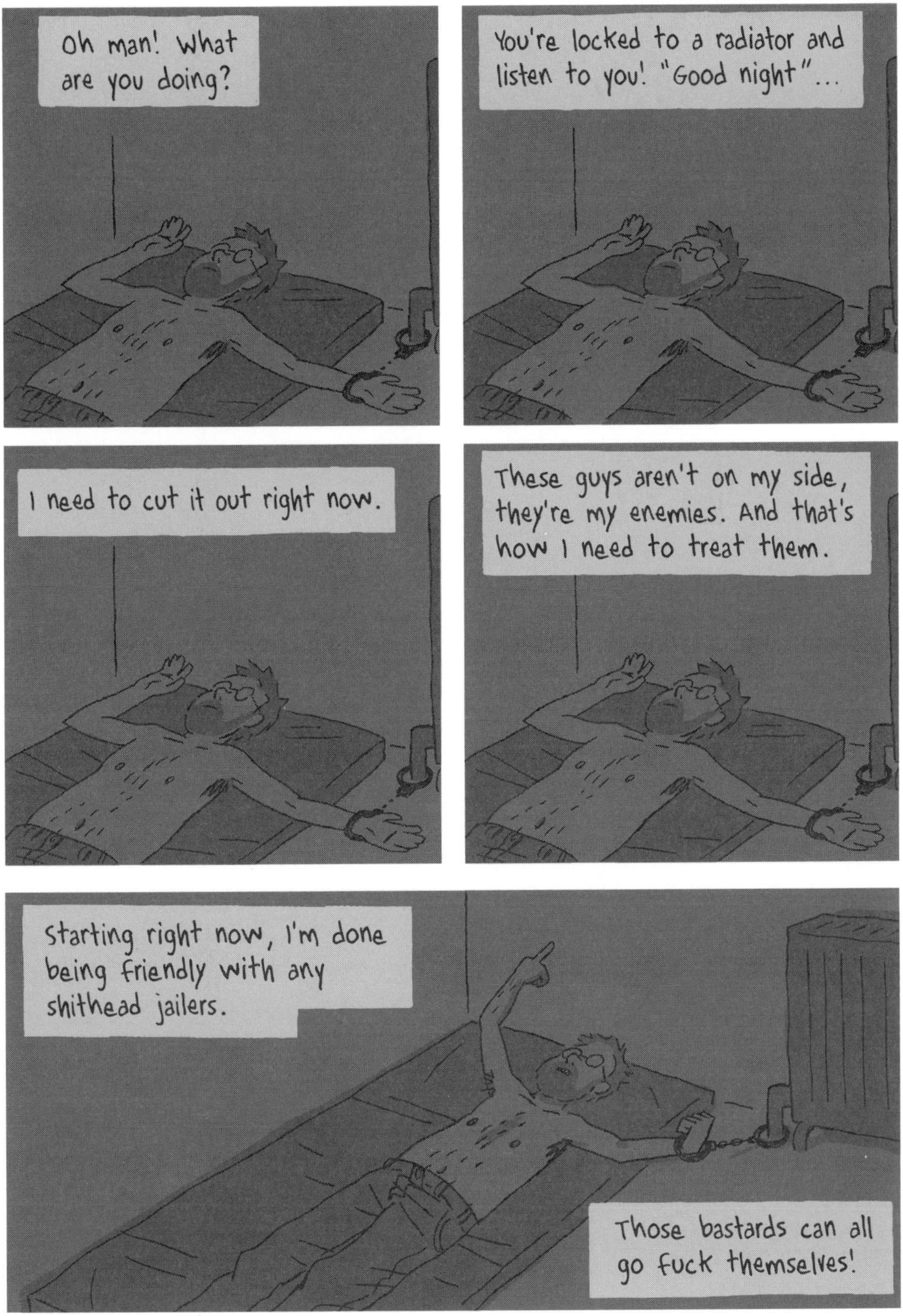
Oh man! What are you doing?
You're locked to a radiator and listen to you! "Good night"...
I need to cut it out right now.
These guys aren't on my side, they're my enemies. And that's how I need to treat them.
Starting right now, I'm done being friendly with any shithead jailers.
Those bastards can all go fuck themselves!

13

Today is July 13.
Sunday, July 13.

It's been almost two weeks now.

I don't get it...

According to the emergency plan, communication should have been established in the first forty-eight hours.

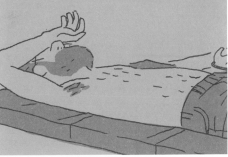

And we already have contacts with many of the clan leaders in the region.

So what's wrong?
This makes no sense at all...
Two weeks!
Maybe they've left Nazran?
Maybe they're not even looking for me?

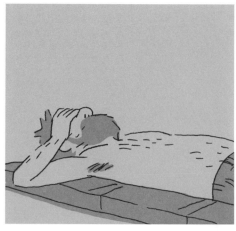

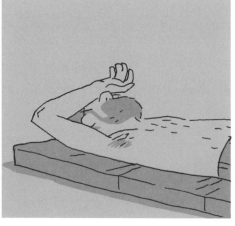

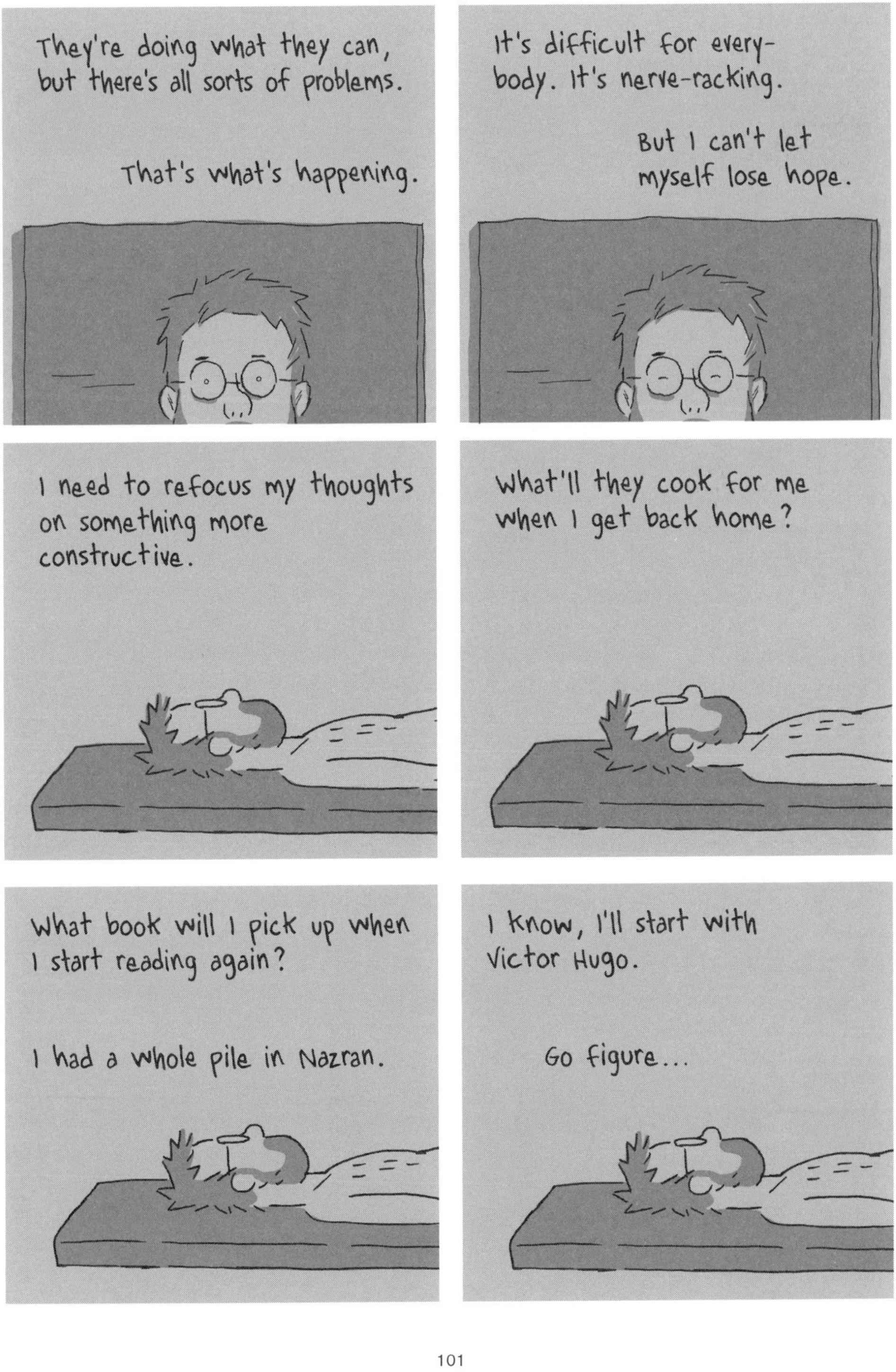
They're doing what they can, but there's all sorts of problems.
That's what's happening.
It's difficult for everybody. It's nerve-racking.
But I can't let myself lose hope.
I need to refocus my thoughts on something more constructive.
What'll they cook for me when I get back home?
What book will I pick up when I start reading again?
I had a whole pile in Nazran.
I know, I'll start with Victor Hugo.
Go figure...

ЯxHёsB Cεap Лmos!

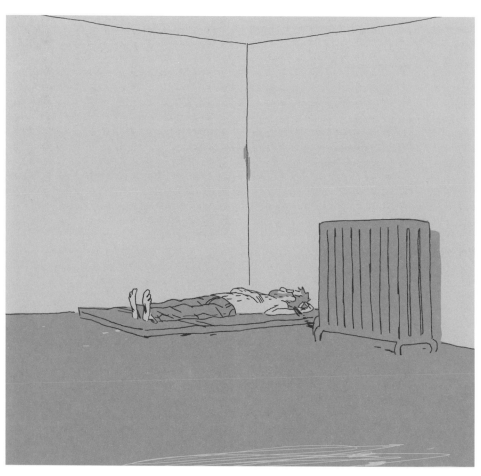

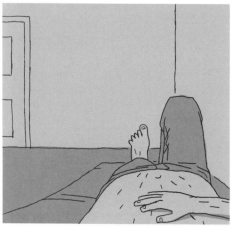

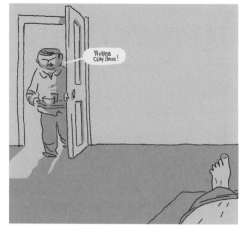

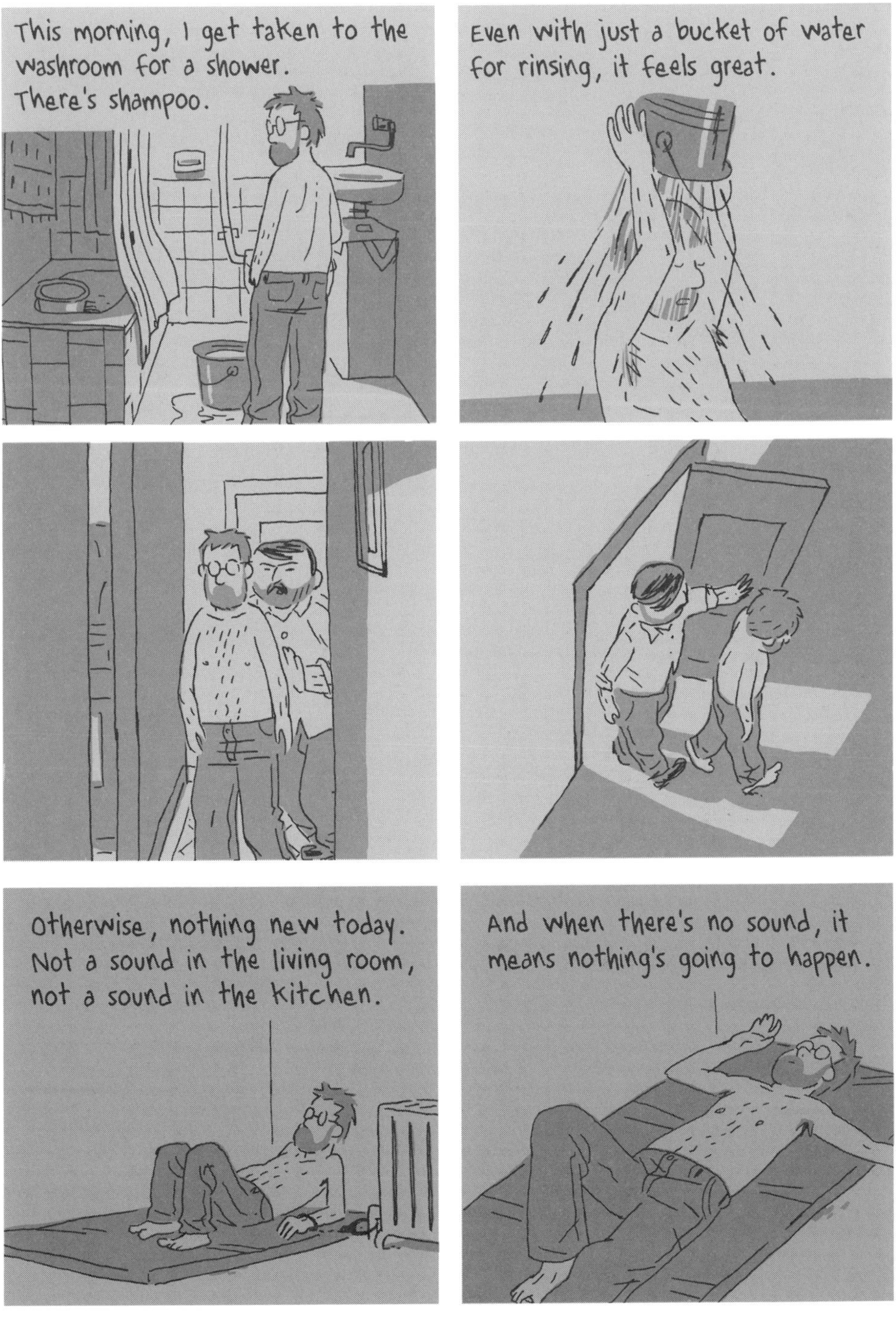
This morning, I get taken to the washroom for a shower. There's shampoo.
Even with just a bucket of water for rinsing, it feels great.
Otherwise, nothing new today. Not a sound in the living room, not a sound in the kitchen.
And when there's no sound, it means nothing's going to happen.

Being a hostage is worse than being in prison.

In prison, you know why you've been locked up.

There's a reason. Whether it's right or wrong, at least there's a reason.

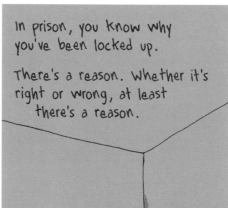

But being a hostage is just bad luck.

Wrong place, wrong time.

In prison, you know when you'll get out. You know the exact date...

So you can count down the days to your release.

The only thing I can count here are the days that go by, and I have no idea when this is all going to end.

Click Clack!

The tall guy brought dinner this evening.

Before leaving, he offered me a cigarette. I didn't refuse.

Баз Вбар.

Except this time, I skipped the niceties.

Instead, I thought to myself: Fuck you. Fuck your cigarette, your bowl of soup, and your handcuffs.

One of these days...

I'm going to get out of here.

CLACK!

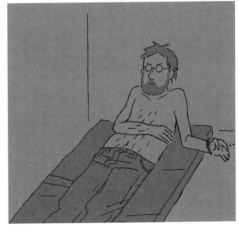

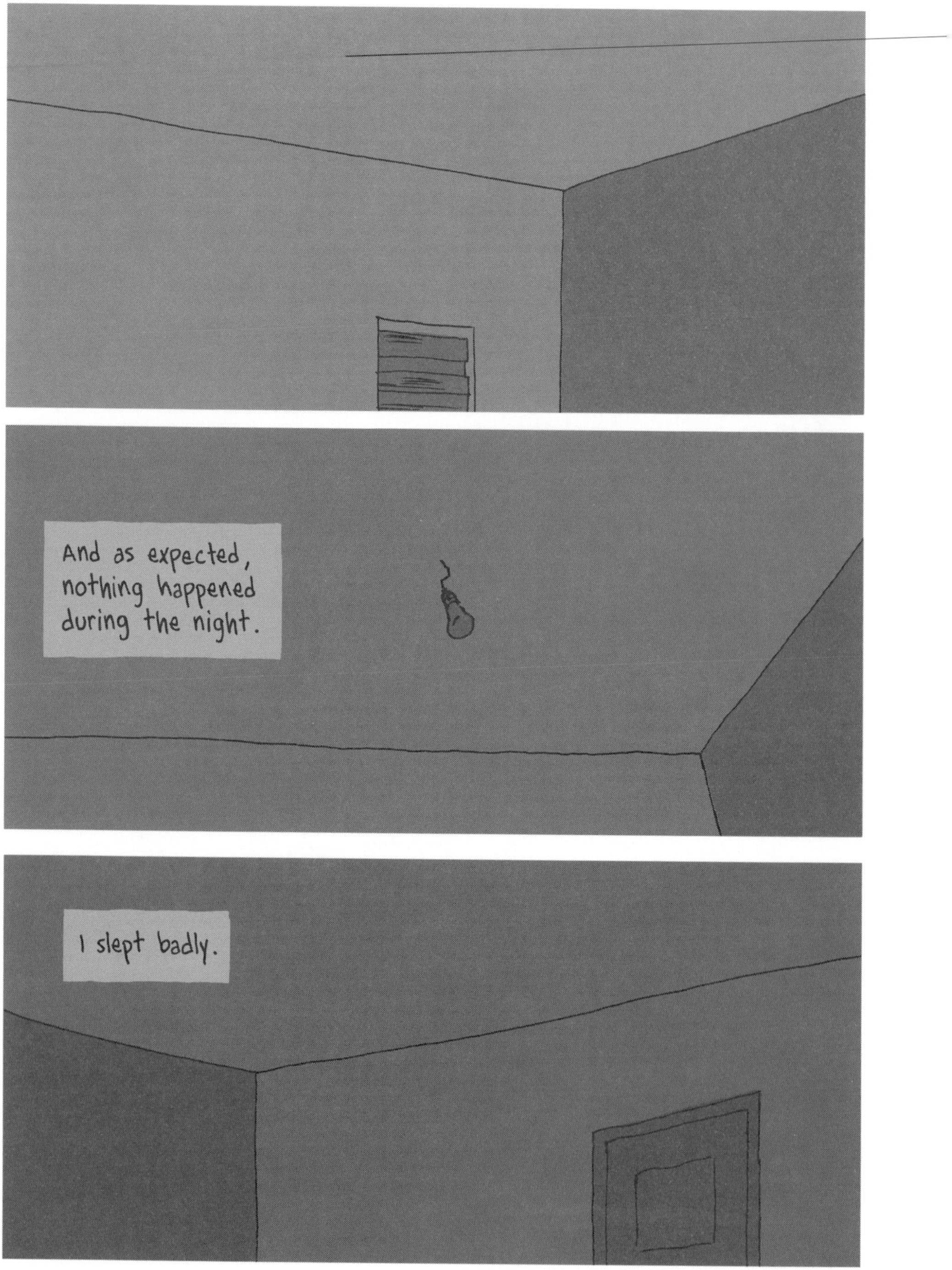
And as expected, nothing happened during the night.
I slept badly.

15

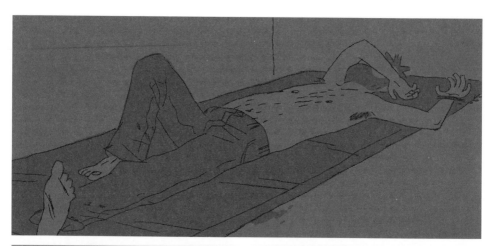

Today is July 15.
Monday, July 15.

No, yesterday was Monday. Today is Tuesday. Tuesday, July 15.

I need to keep the days straight!

I heard sounds this morning. People were talking in the living room.

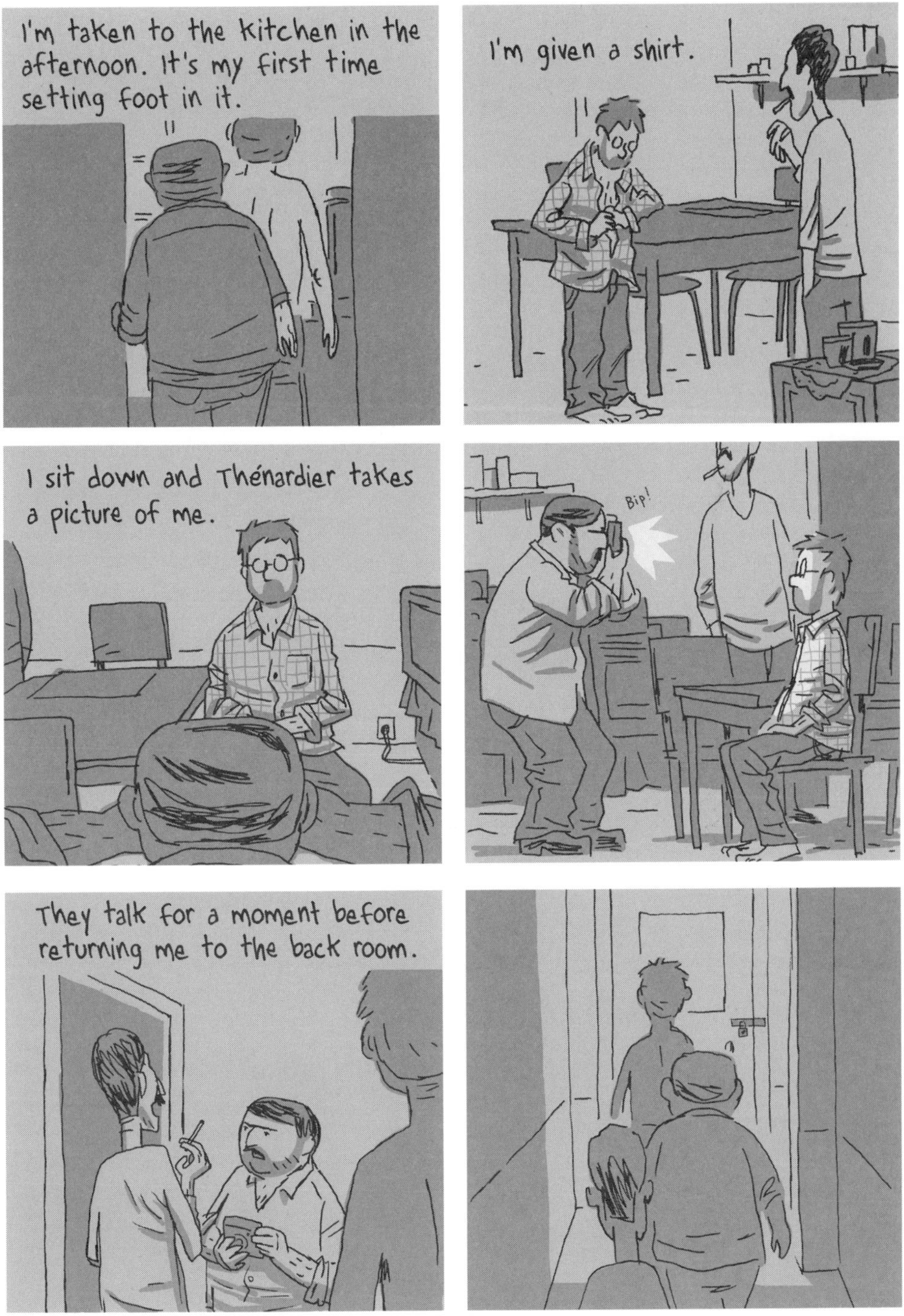
I'm taken to the kitchen in the afternoon. It's my first time setting foot in it.
I'm given a shirt.
I sit down and Thénardier takes a picture of me.
Bip!
They talk for a moment before returning me to the back room.

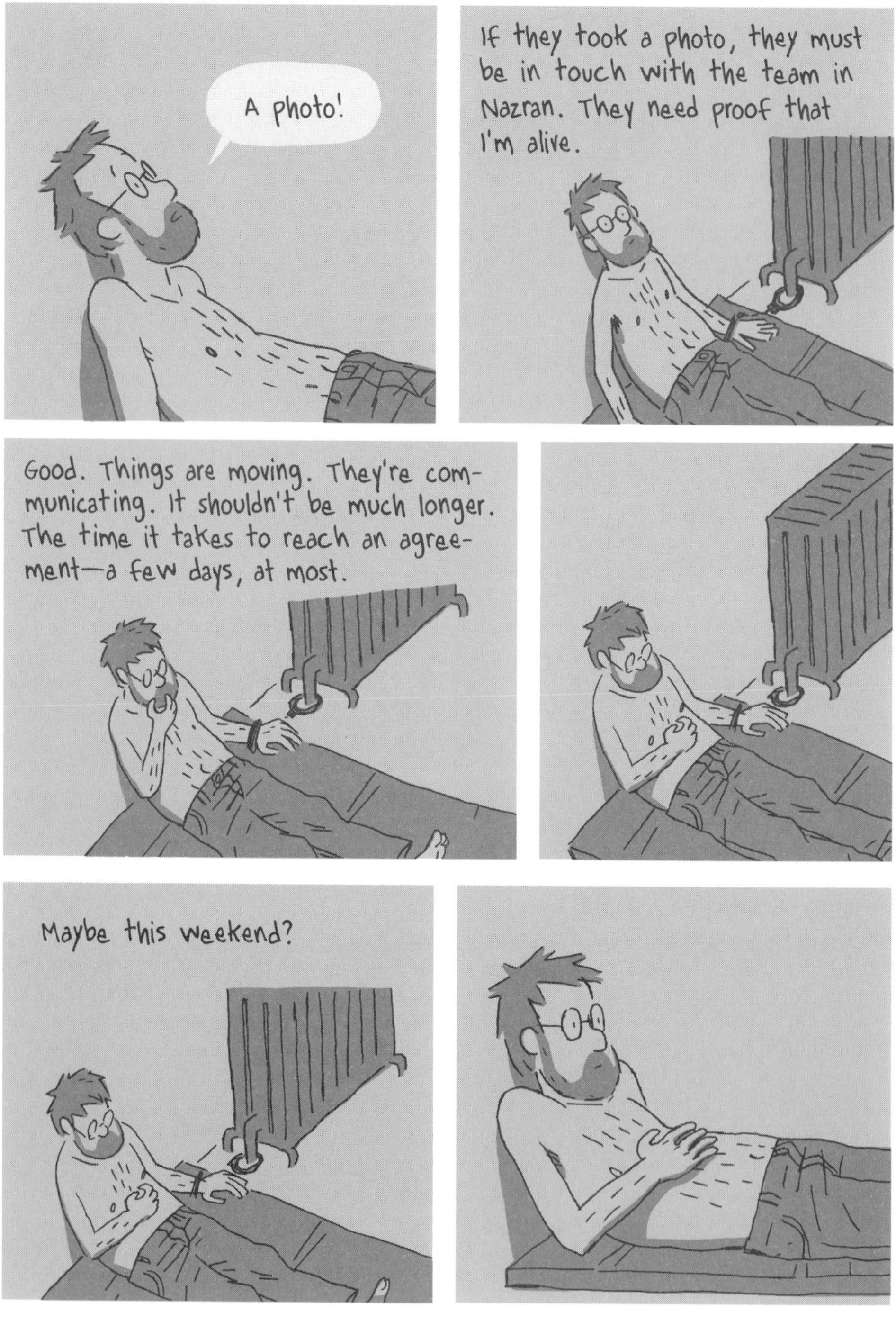
A photo!
If they took a photo, they must be in touch with the team in Nazran. They need proof that I'm alive.
Good. Things are moving. They're communicating. It shouldn't be much longer. The time it takes to reach an agreement—a few days, at most.
Maybe this weekend?

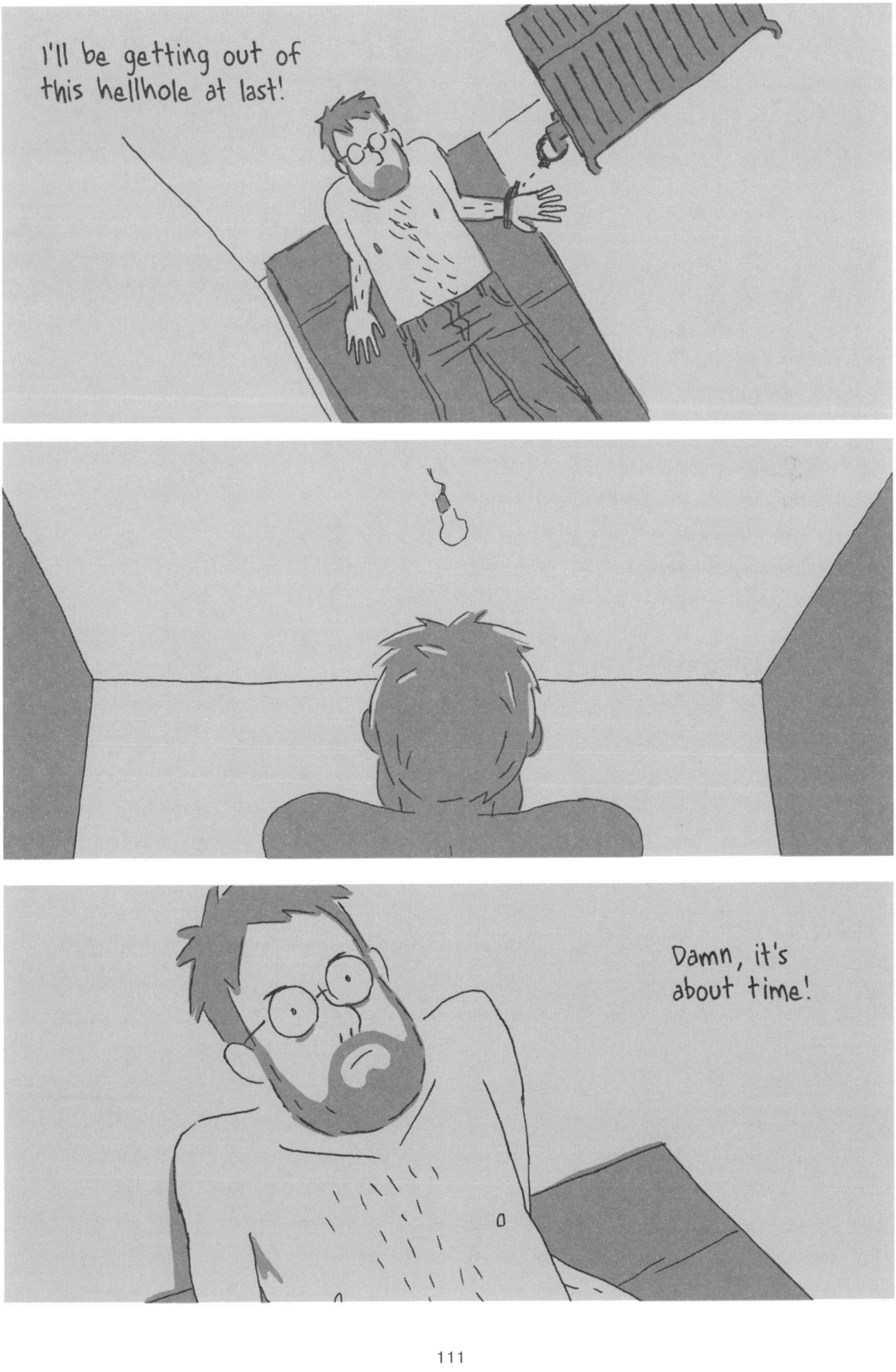
I'll be getting out of this hellhole at last!
Damn, it's about time!

19

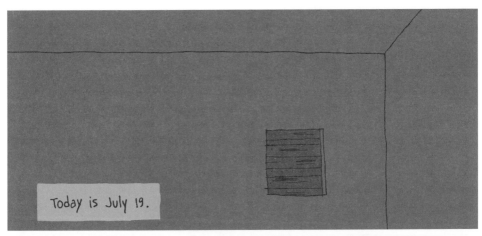

Today is July 19.

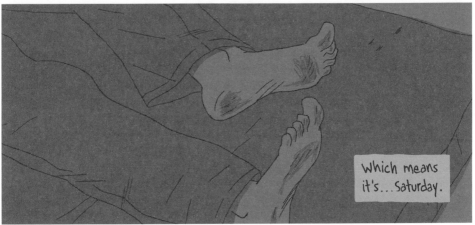

Which means it's... Saturday.

Saturday, July 19.

Six days!

Almost a week!

It's been six days since they took the photo.

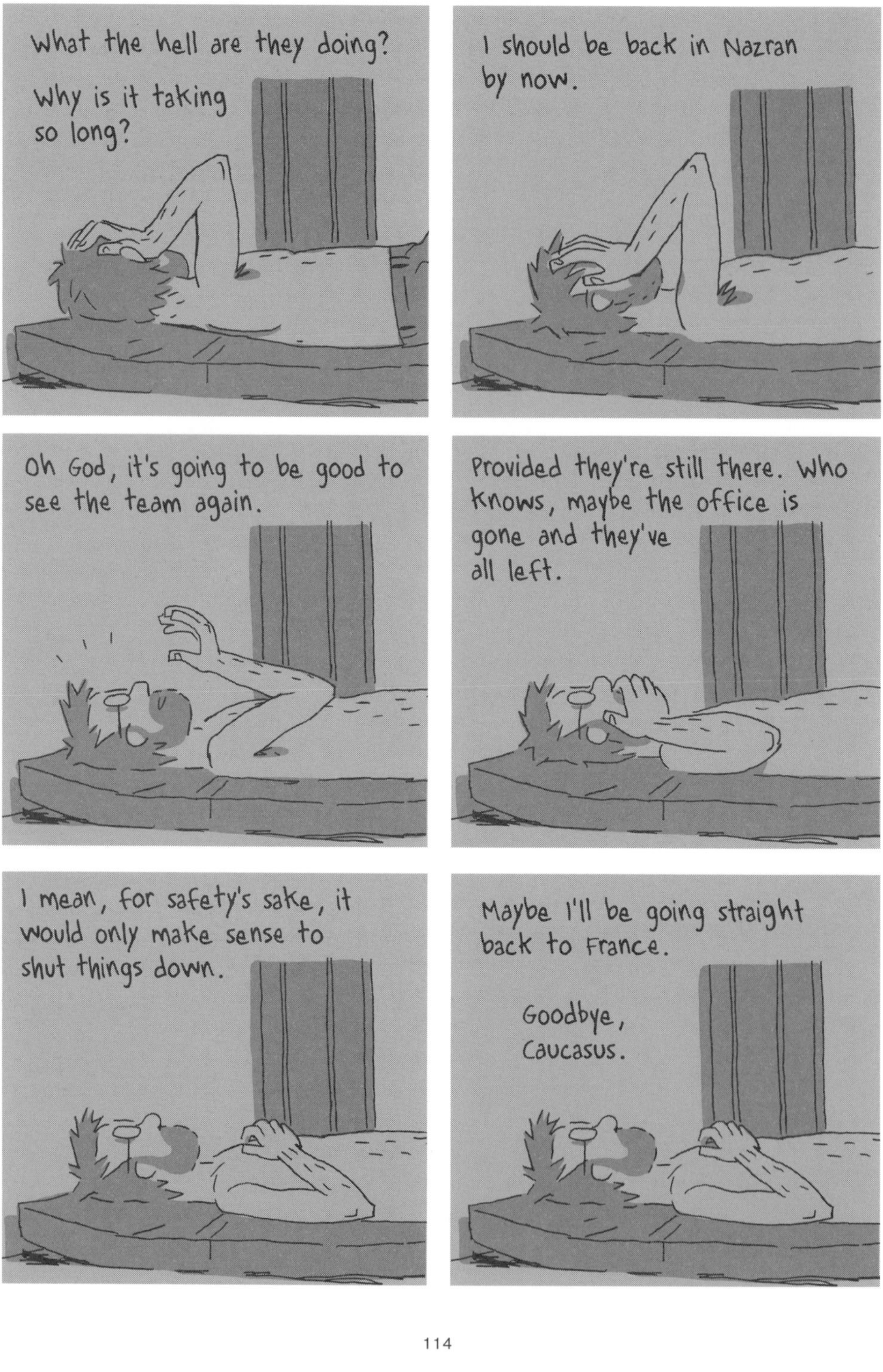

What the hell are they doing?
Why is it taking so long?
I should be back in Nazran by now.
Oh God, it's going to be good to see the team again.
Provided they're still there. Who knows, maybe the office is gone and they've all left.
I mean, for safety's sake, it would only make sense to shut things down.
Maybe I'll be going straight back to France.
Goodbye, Caucasus.

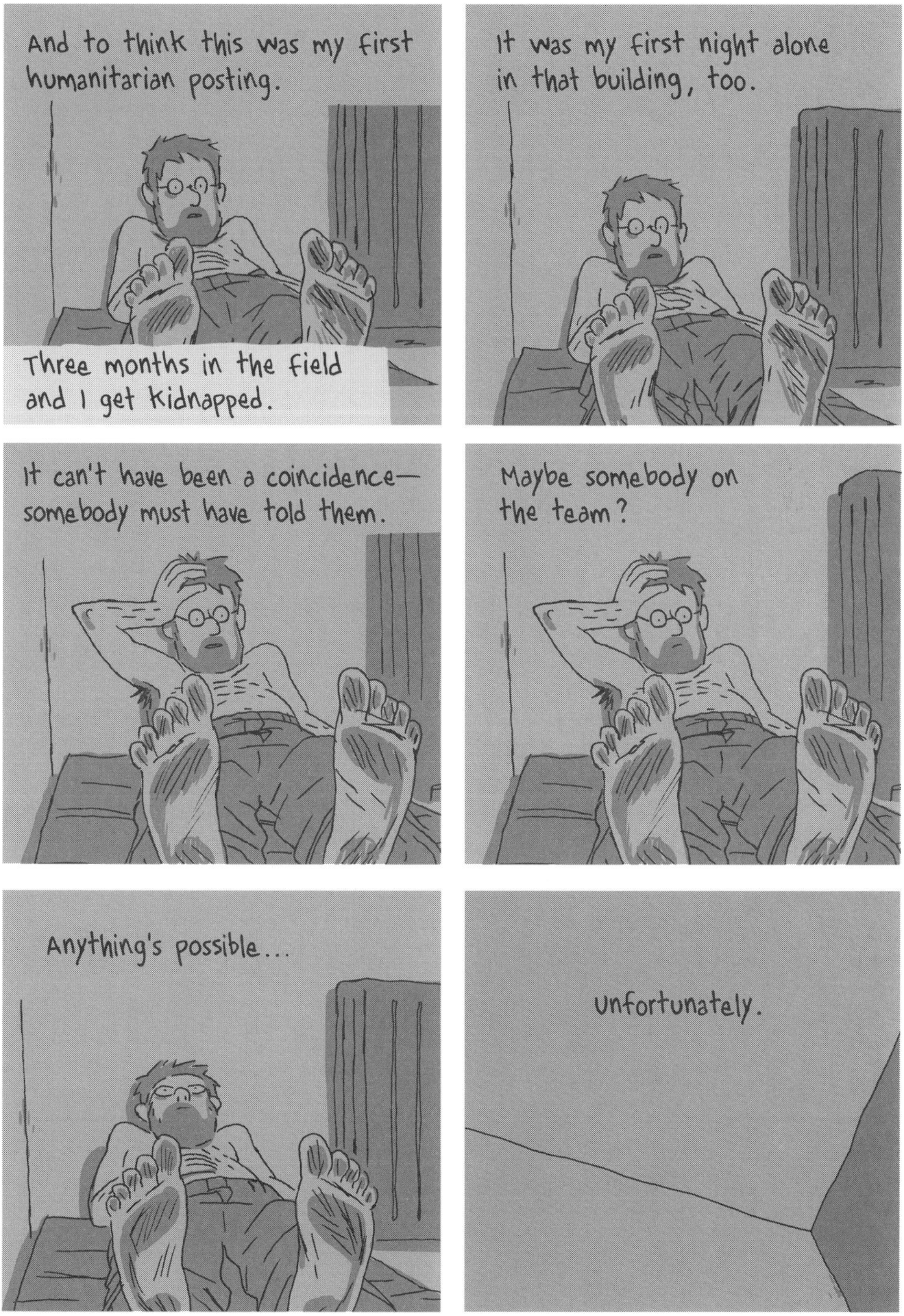
And to think this was my first humanitarian posting.
Three months in the field and I get kidnapped.
It was my first night alone in that building, too.
It can't have been a coincidence— somebody must have told them.
Maybe somebody on the team?
Anything's possible...
Unfortunately.

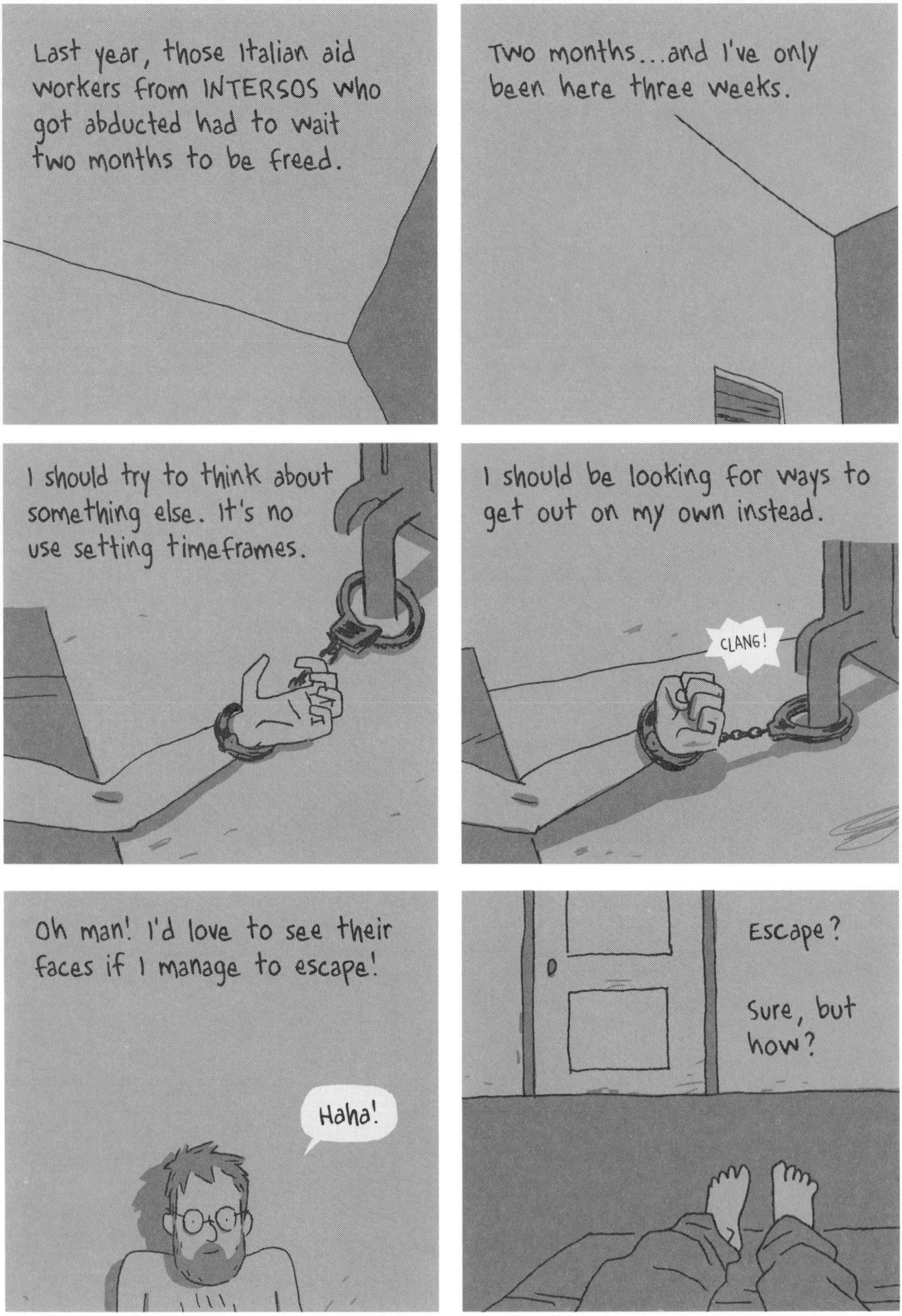

Last year, those Italian aid workers from INTERSOS who got abducted had to wait two months to be freed.
Two months...and I've only been here three weeks.
I should try to think about something else. It's no use setting timeframes.
I should be looking for ways to get out on my own instead.
CLANG!
Oh man! I'd love to see their faces if I manage to escape!
Haha!
Escape?
Sure, but how?

I doze a bit in the afternoon.

Even though I do nothing all day, I'm sometimes very tired.

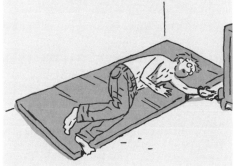

Maybe it's because I don't get enough to eat and it's wearing me down.

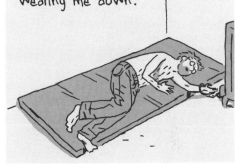

Or maybe it's because I keep going over and over the same thoughts in my head.

BANG!

BANG!

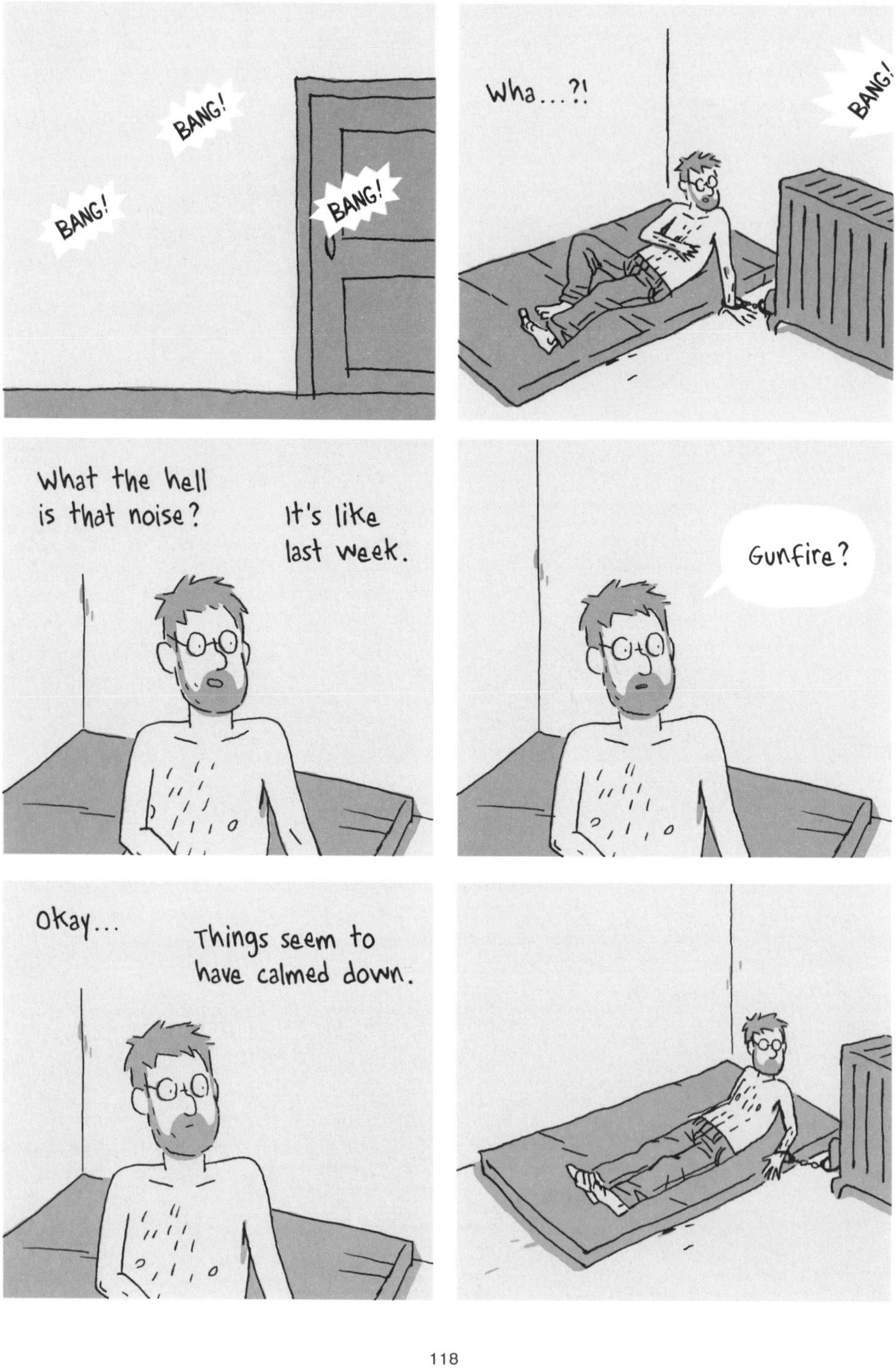
BANG!
BANG!
BANG!
Wha...?!
BANG!
What the hell is that noise?
It's like last week.
Gunfire?
Okay...
Things seem to have calmed down.

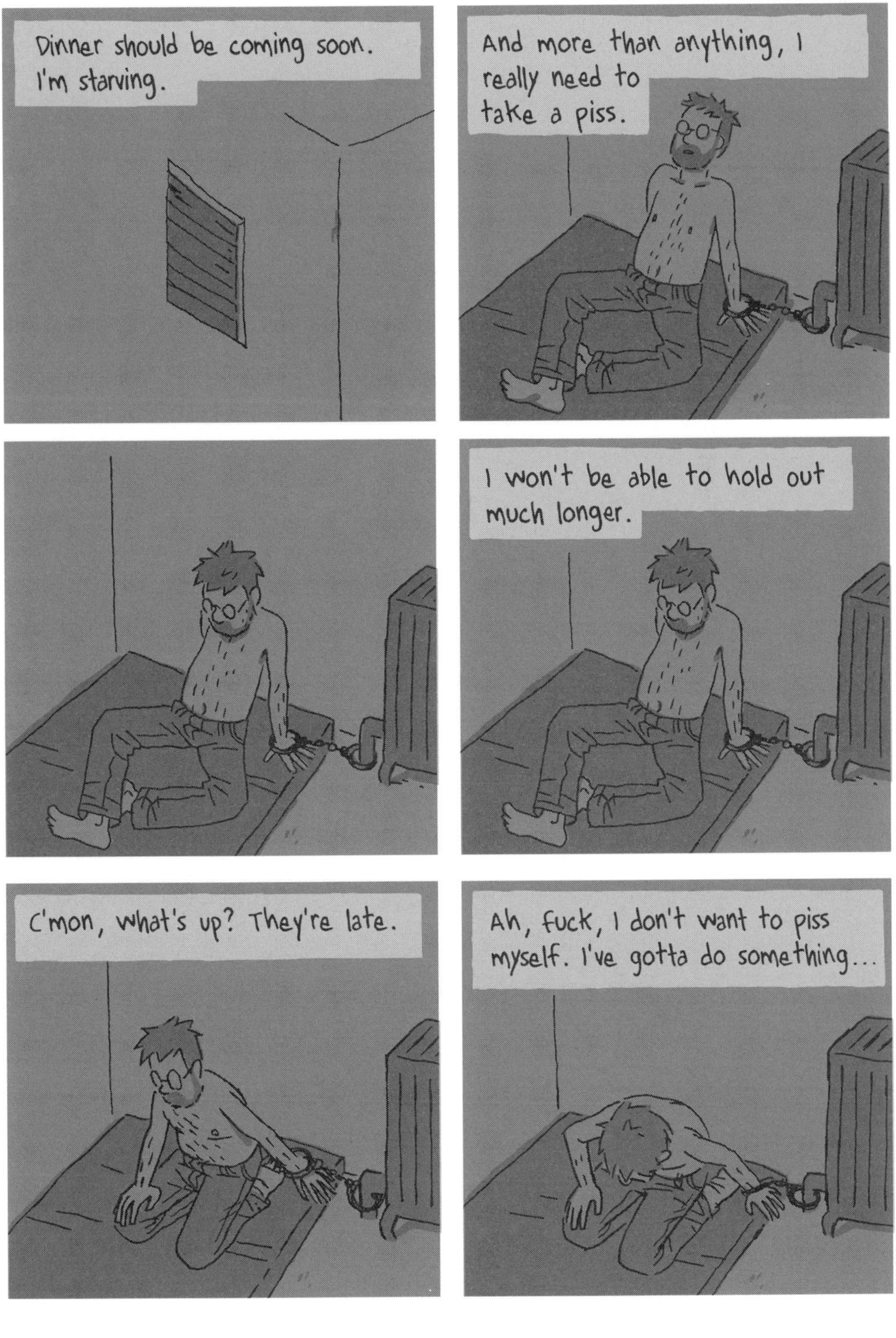
Dinner should be coming soon. I'm starving.
And more than anything, I really need to take a piss.
I won't be able to hold out much longer.
C'mon, what's up? They're late.
Ah, fuck, I don't want to piss myself. I've gotta do something...

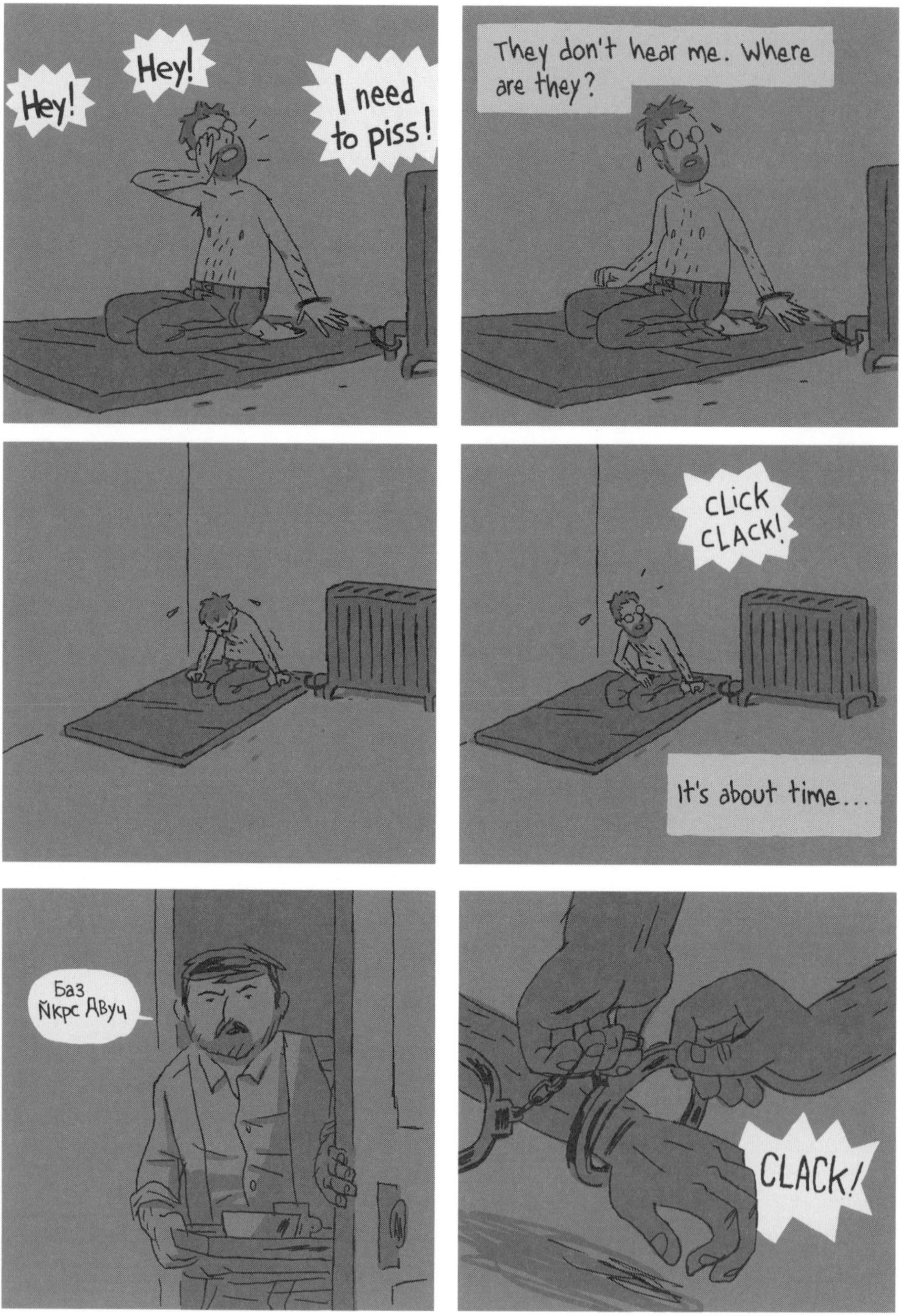
Hey!
Hey!
I need to piss!
They don't hear me. Where are they?
CLick CLACK!
It's about time...
Баз Ñкрс Двуч
CLACK!

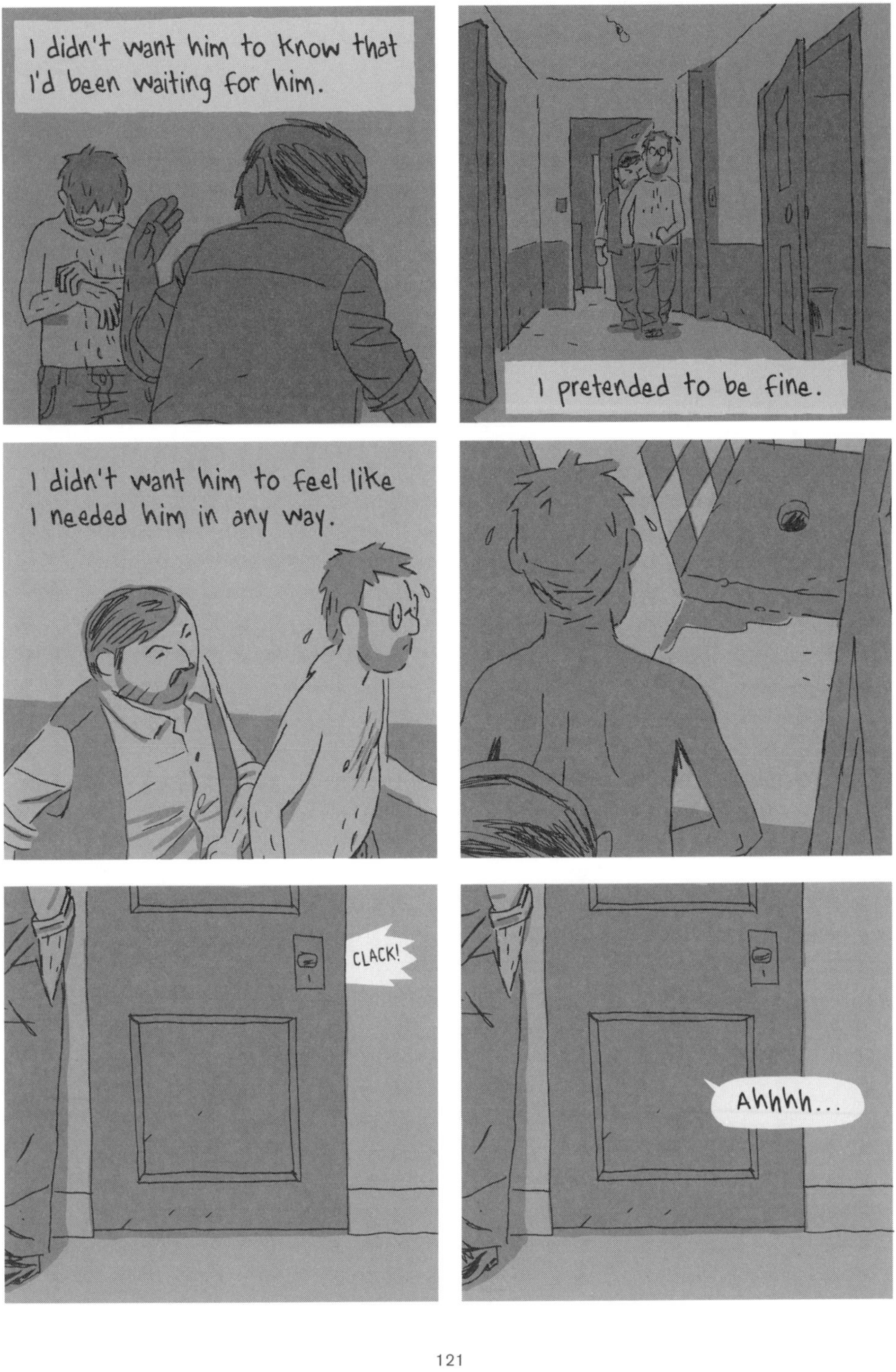
I didn't want him to know that I'd been waiting for him.
I pretended to be fine.
I didn't want him to feel like I needed him in any way.
CLACK!
Ahhhh...

21

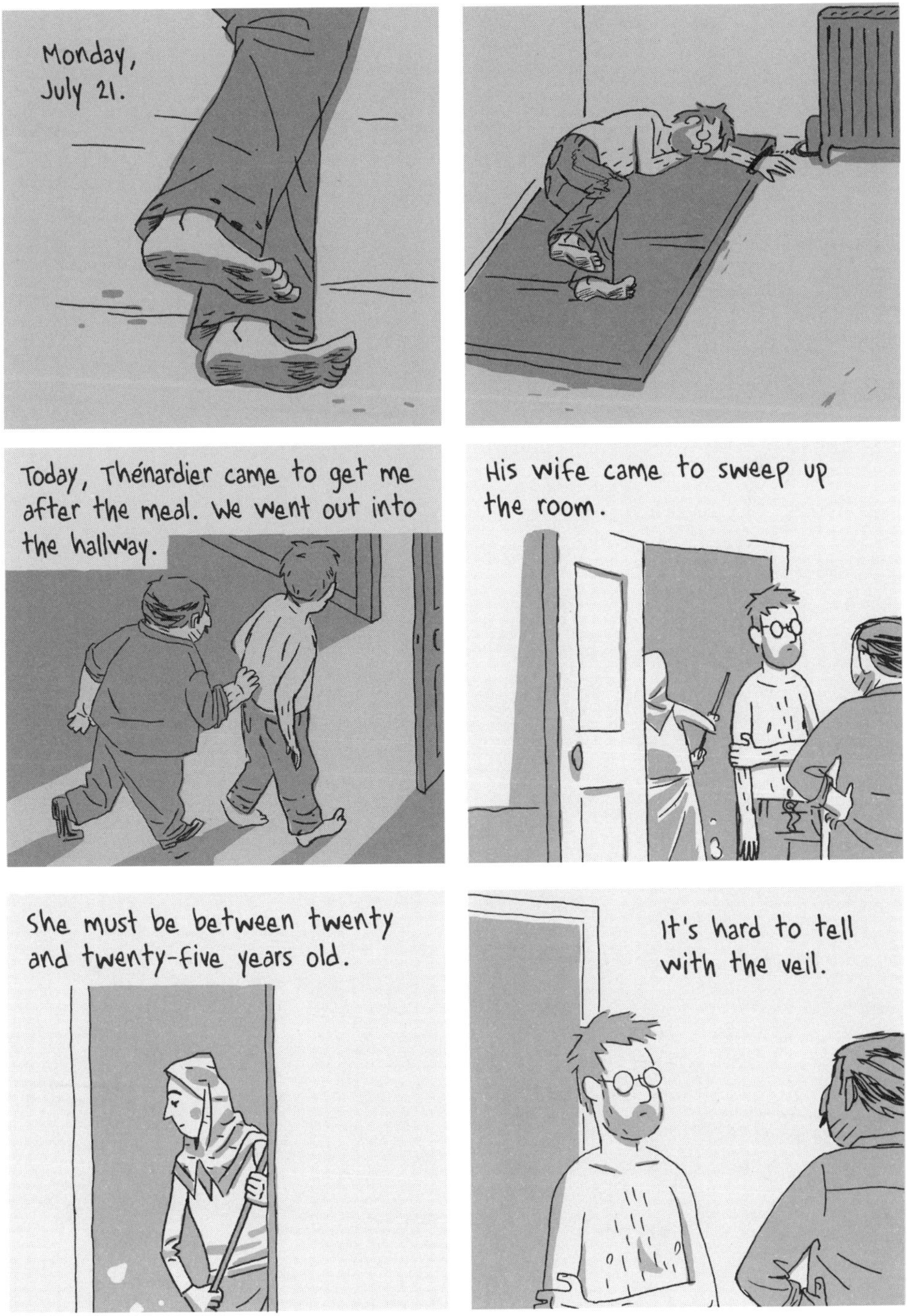
Monday, July 21.
Today, Thénardier came to get me after the meal. We went out into the hallway.
His wife came to sweep up the room.
She must be between twenty and twenty-five years old.
It's hard to tell with the veil.

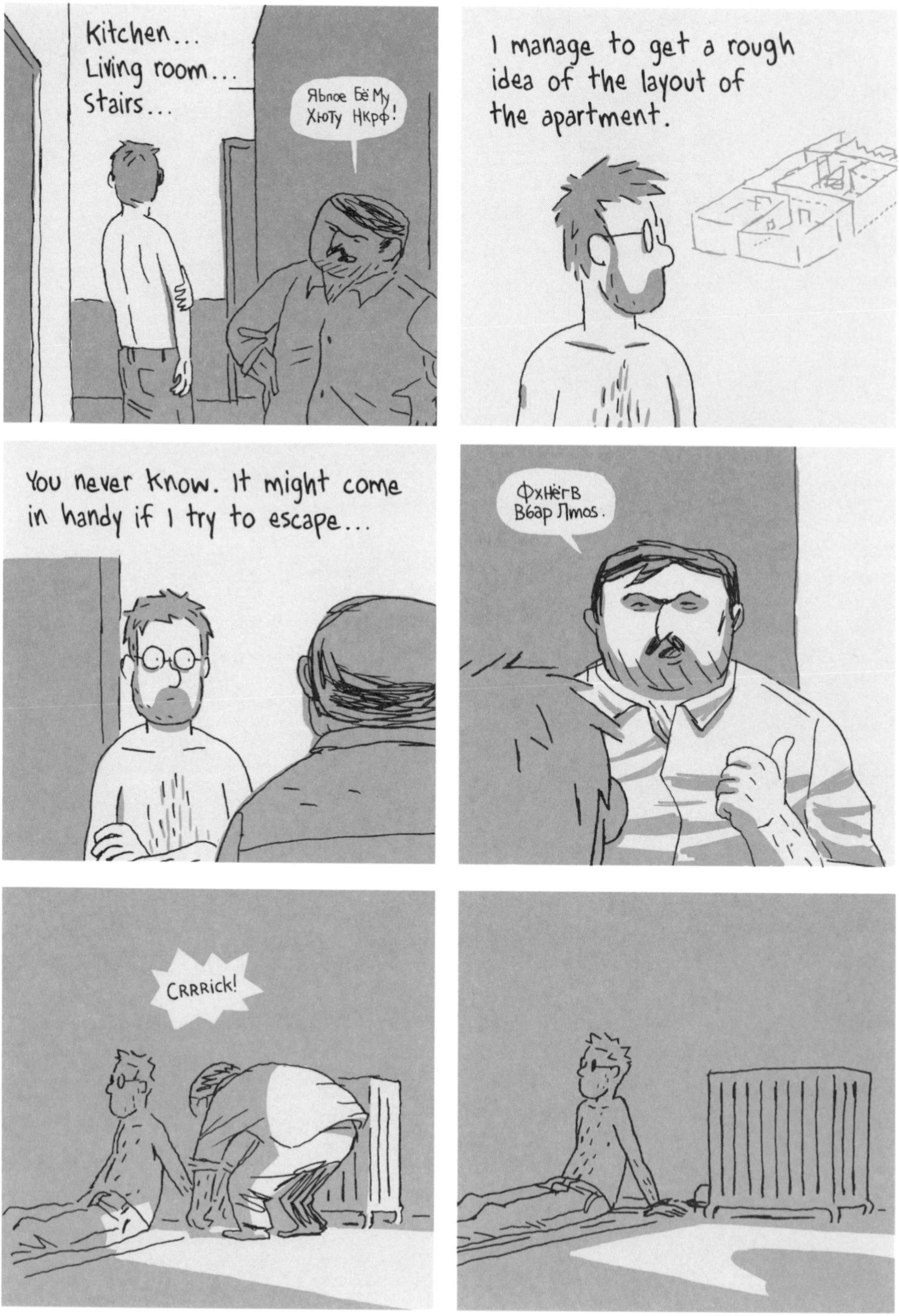
Kitchen... Living room... stairs...
Яьпое Бё Му Хюту Нкрф!
I manage to get a rough idea of the layout of the apartment.
You never know. It might come in handy if I try to escape...
Фхнёгв Вбар Лmos.
CRRRick!

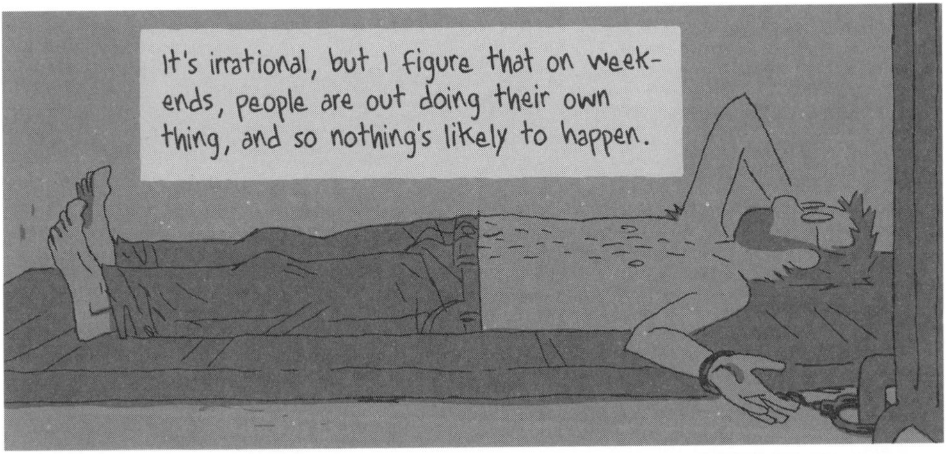
It's irrational, but I figure that on week-ends, people are out doing their own thing, and so nothing's likely to happen.

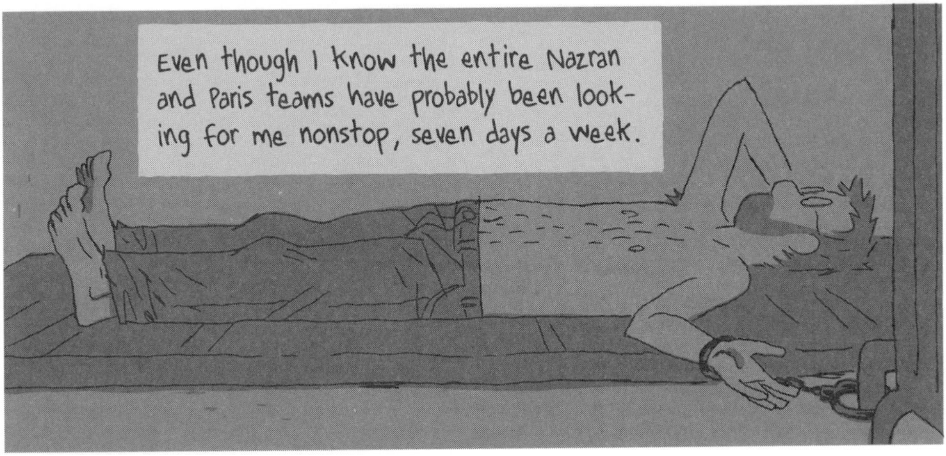
Even though I know the entire Nazran and Paris teams have probably been look-ing for me nonstop, seven days a week.

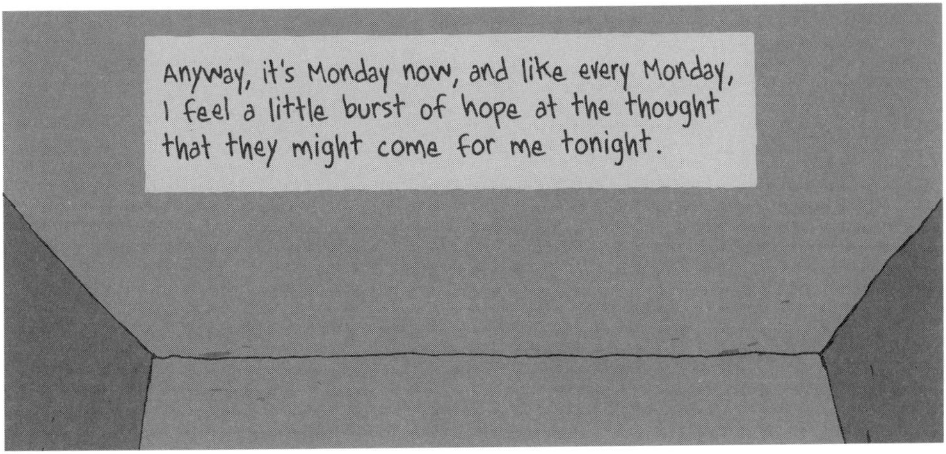
Anyway, it's Monday now, and like every Monday, I feel a little burst of hope at the thought that they might come for me tonight.

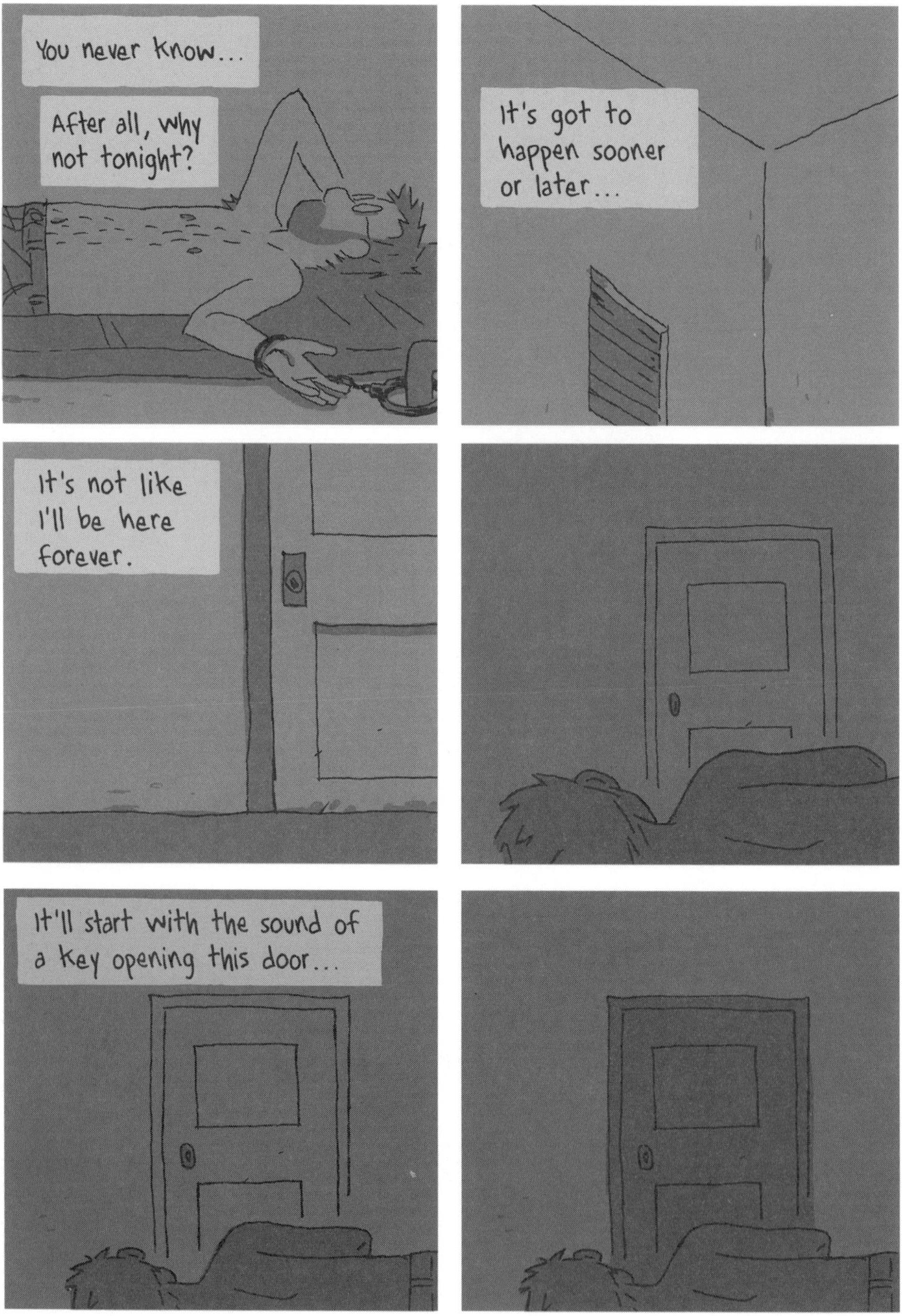
You never know...
After all, why not tonight?
It's got to happen sooner or later...
It's not like I'll be here forever.
It'll start with the sound of a key opening this door...

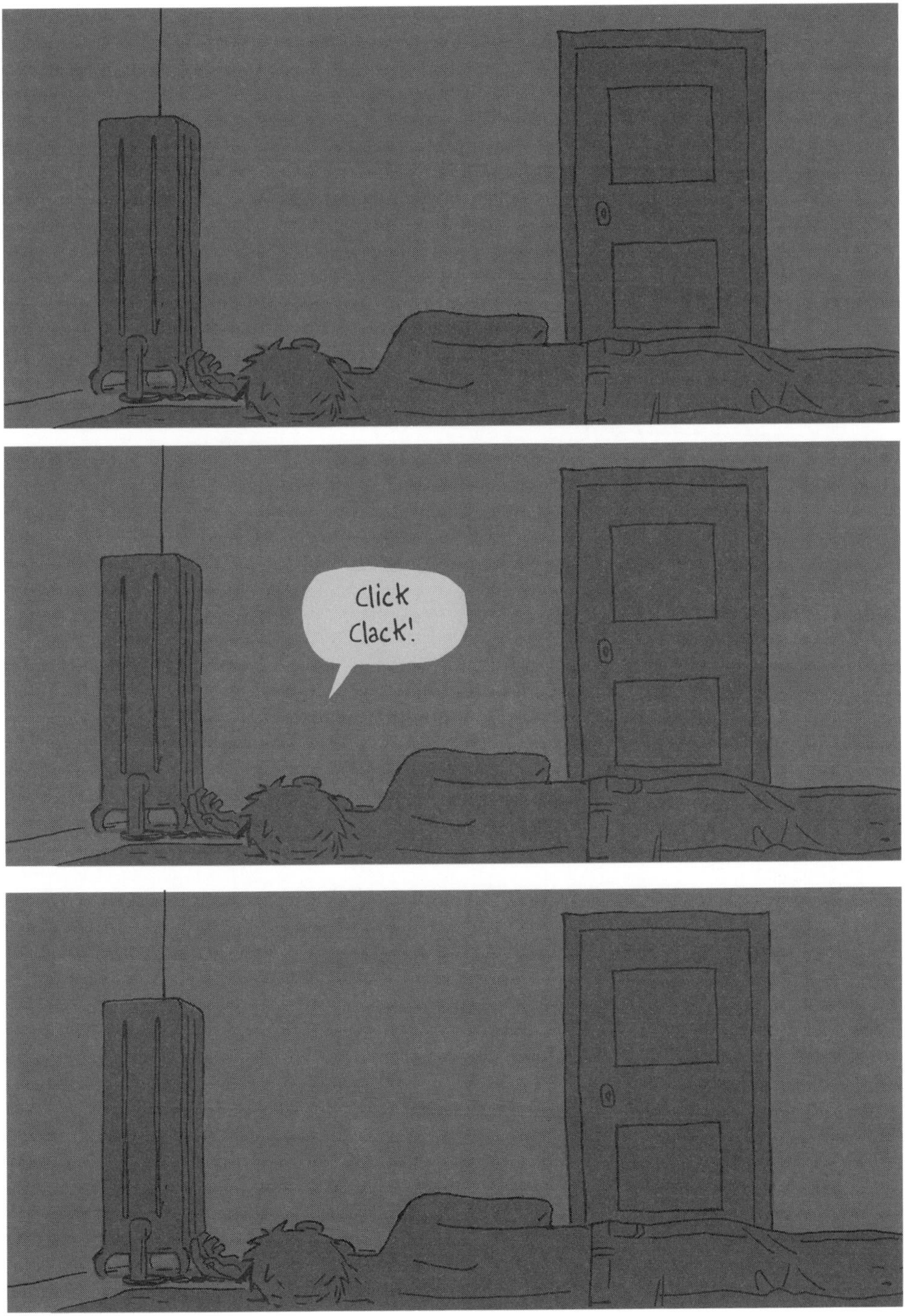
Click Clack!

23

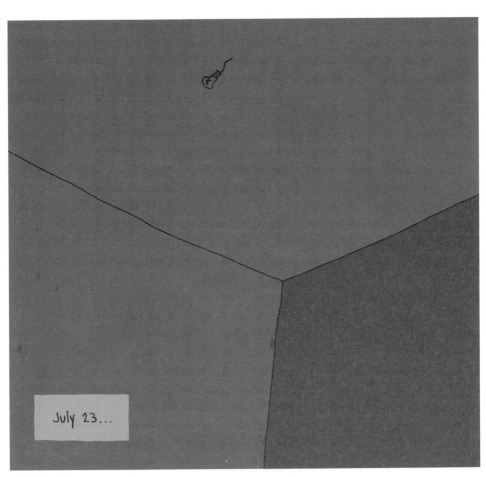

July 23...

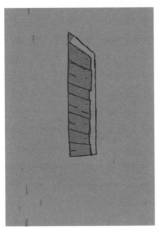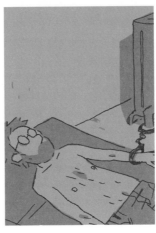

Wednesday, July 23.

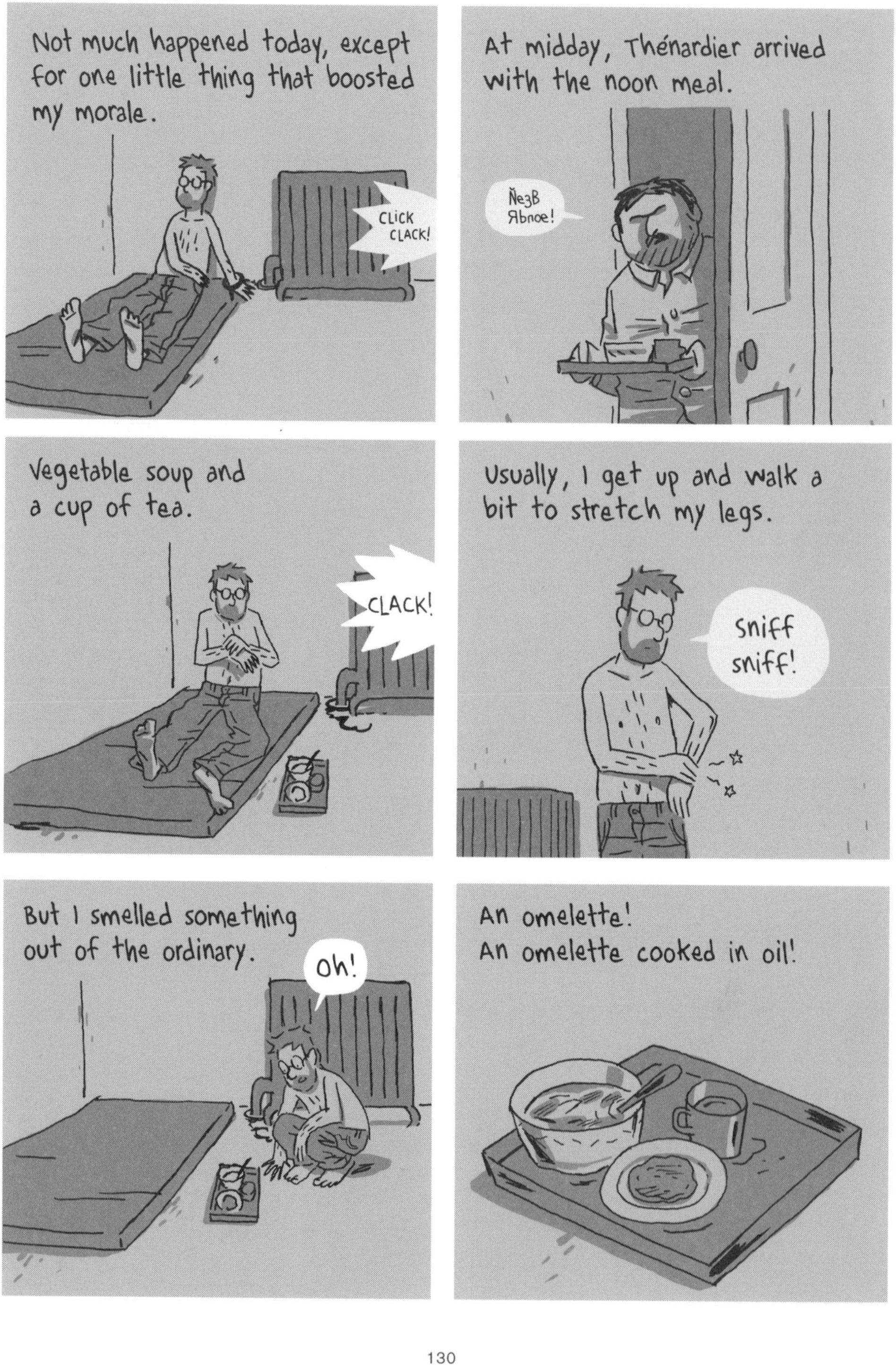

Not much happened today, except for one little thing that boosted my morale.
CLICK CLACK!
At midday, Thénardier arrived with the noon meal.
Ñeзв Ябпое!
Vegetable soup and a cup of tea.
CLACK!
Usually, I get up and walk a bit to stretch my legs.
Sniff sniff!
But I smelled something out of the ordinary.
Oh!
An omelette!
An omelette cooked in oil!

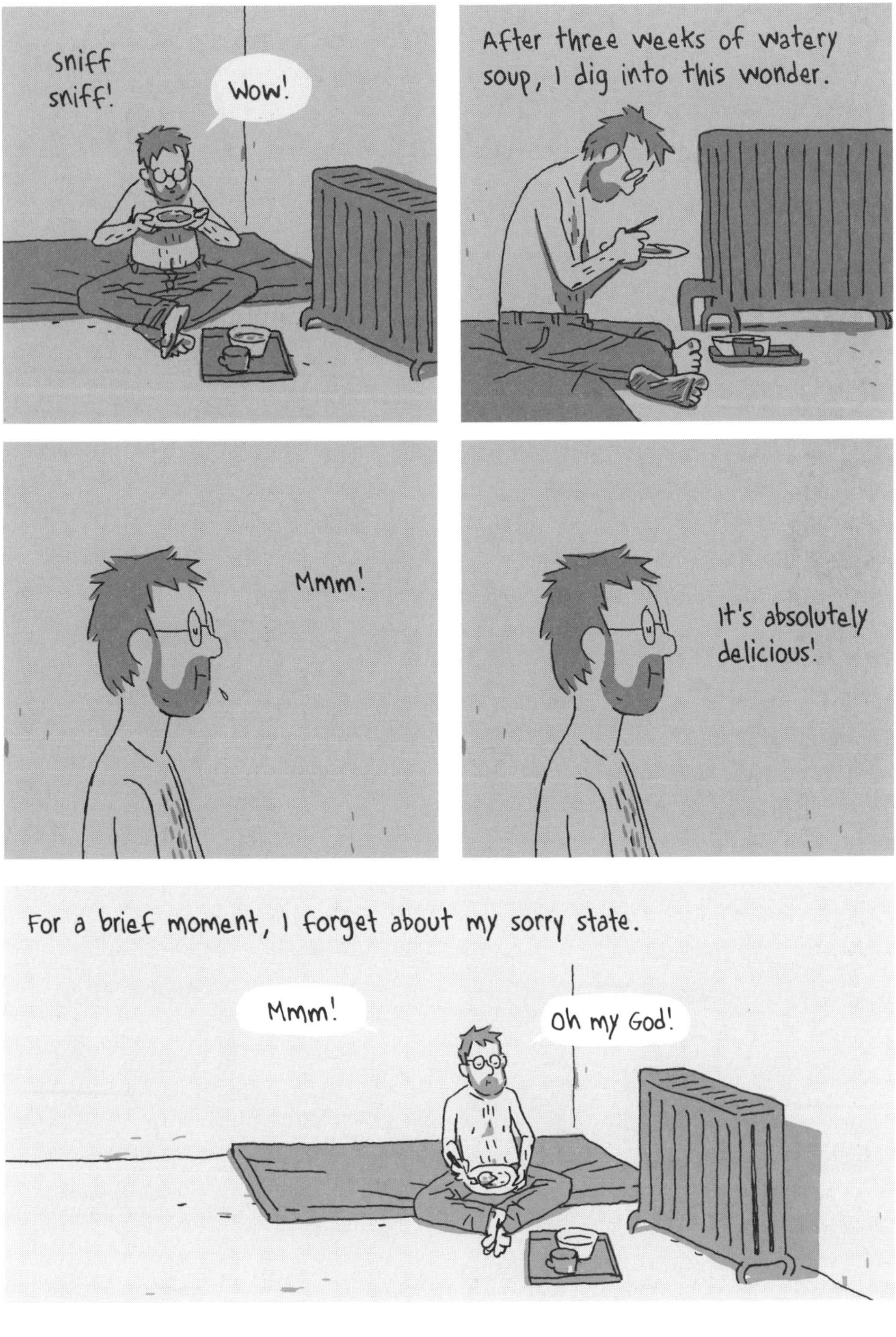
Sniff sniff!
Wow!
After three weeks of watery soup, I dig into this wonder.
Mmm!
It's absolutely delicious!
For a brief moment, I forget about my sorry state.
Mmm!
Oh my God!

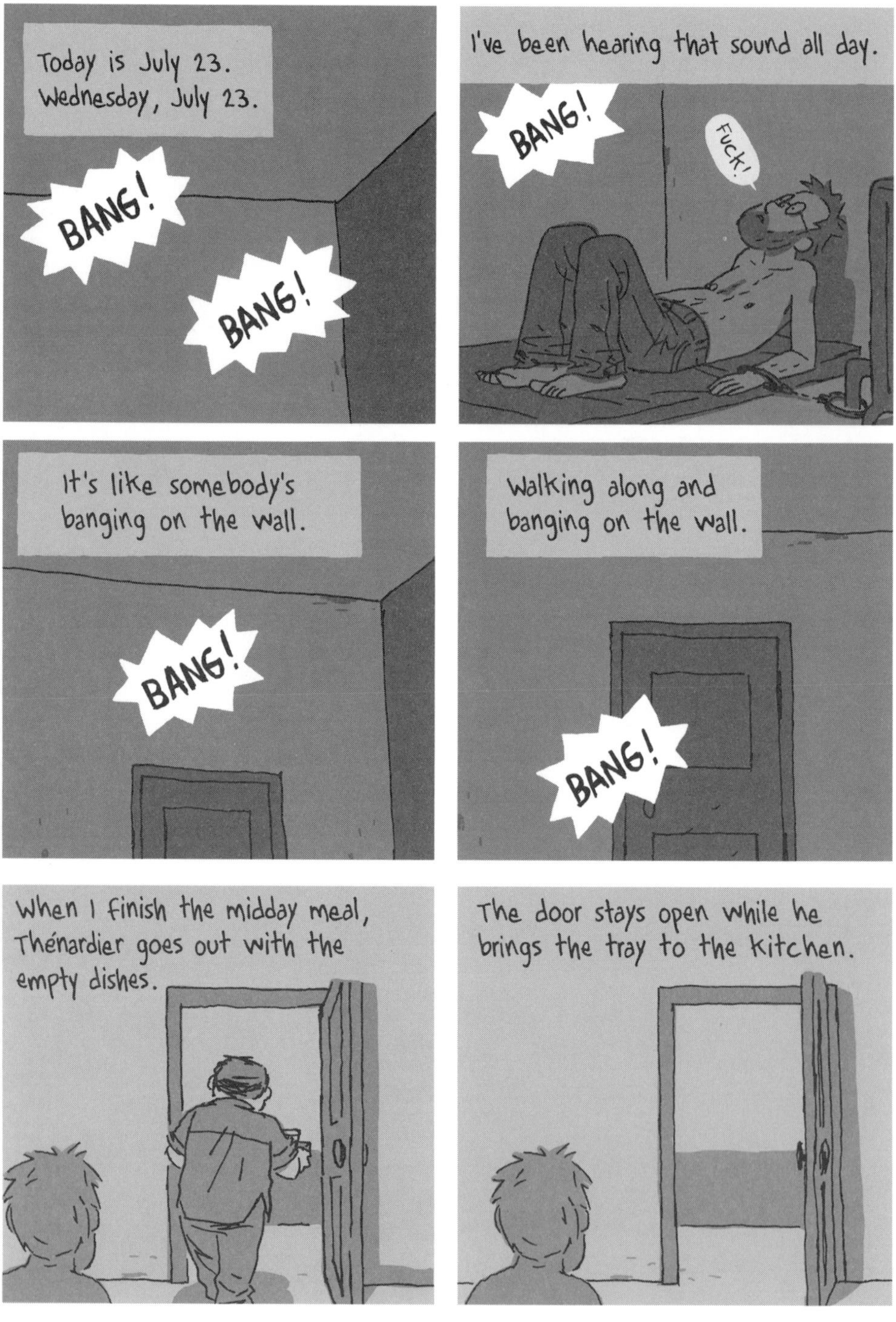
Today is July 23.
Wednesday, July 23.
BANG!
BANG!
I've been hearing that sound all day.
BANG!
Fuck!
It's like somebody's banging on the wall.
BANG!
Walking along and banging on the wall.
BANG!
When I finish the midday meal, Thénardier goes out with the empty dishes.
The door stays open while he brings the tray to the kitchen.

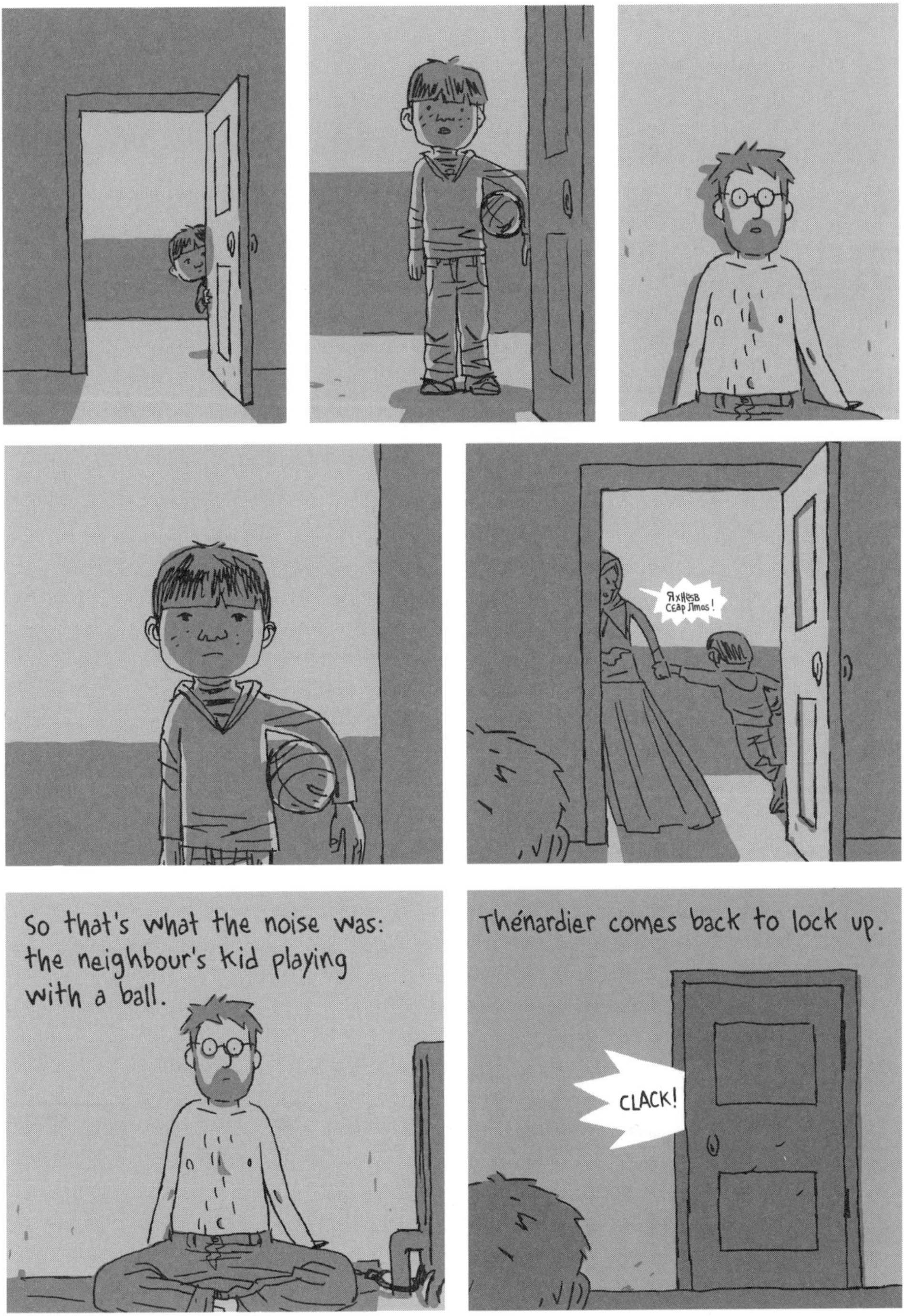
So that's what the noise was: the neighbour's kid playing with a ball.
Thénardier comes back to lock up.
CLACK!

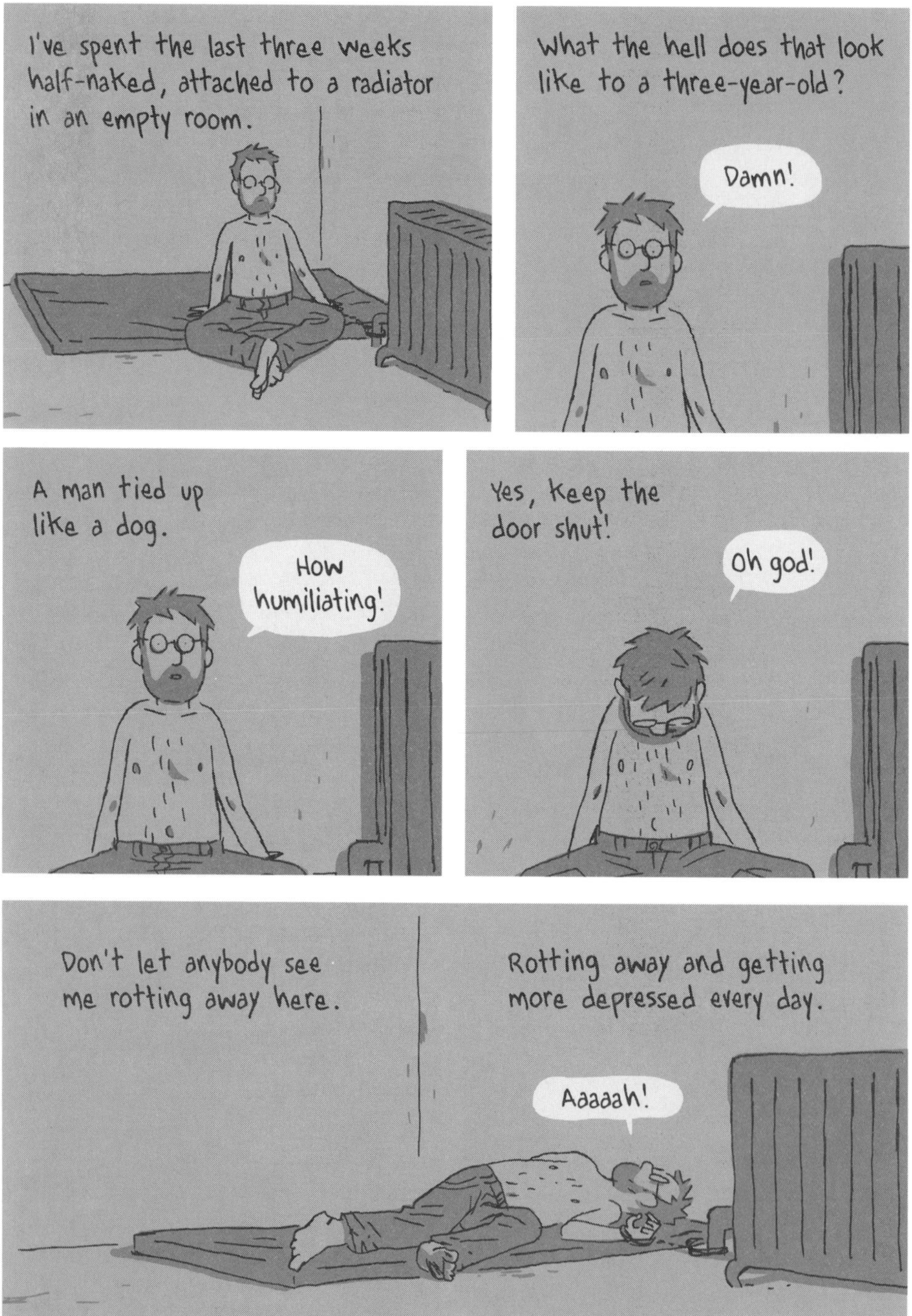
I've spent the last three weeks half-naked, attached to a radiator in an empty room.
What the hell does that look like to a three-year-old?
Damn!
A man tied up like a dog.
How humiliating!
Yes, keep the door shut!
Oh god!
Don't let anybody see me rotting away here.
Rotting away and getting more depressed every day.
Aaaaah!

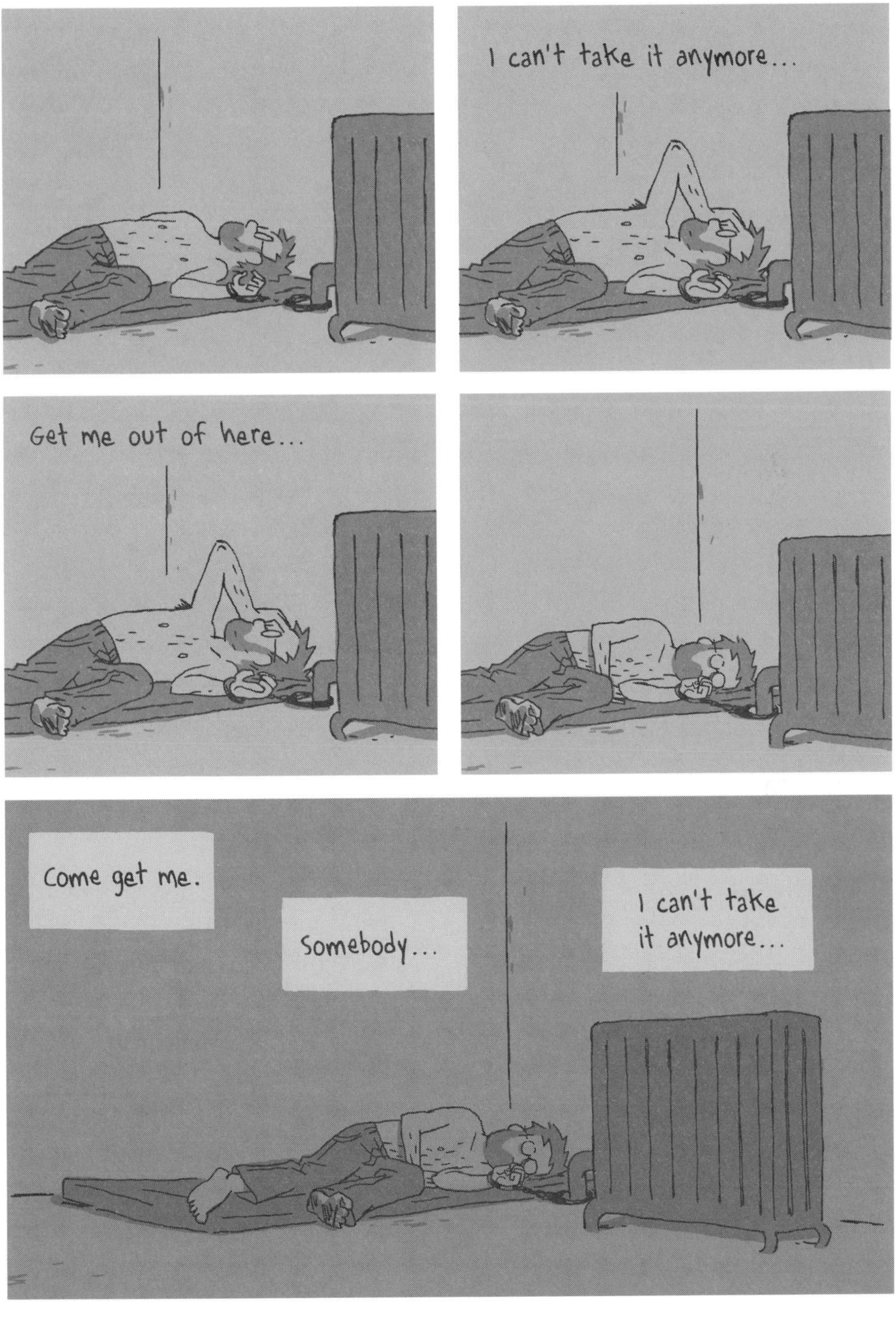

I can't take it anymore...
Get me out of here...
Come get me.
Somebody...
I can't take it anymore...

31

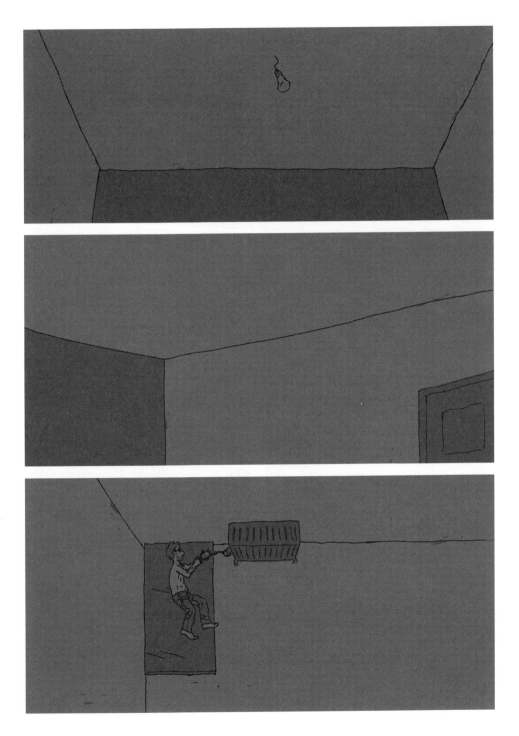

Today is the last day of July. It's July 31.

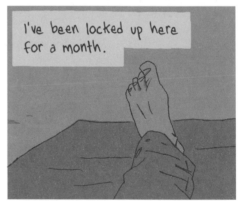

I've been locked up here for a month.

A month...

It feels like it's been a year.

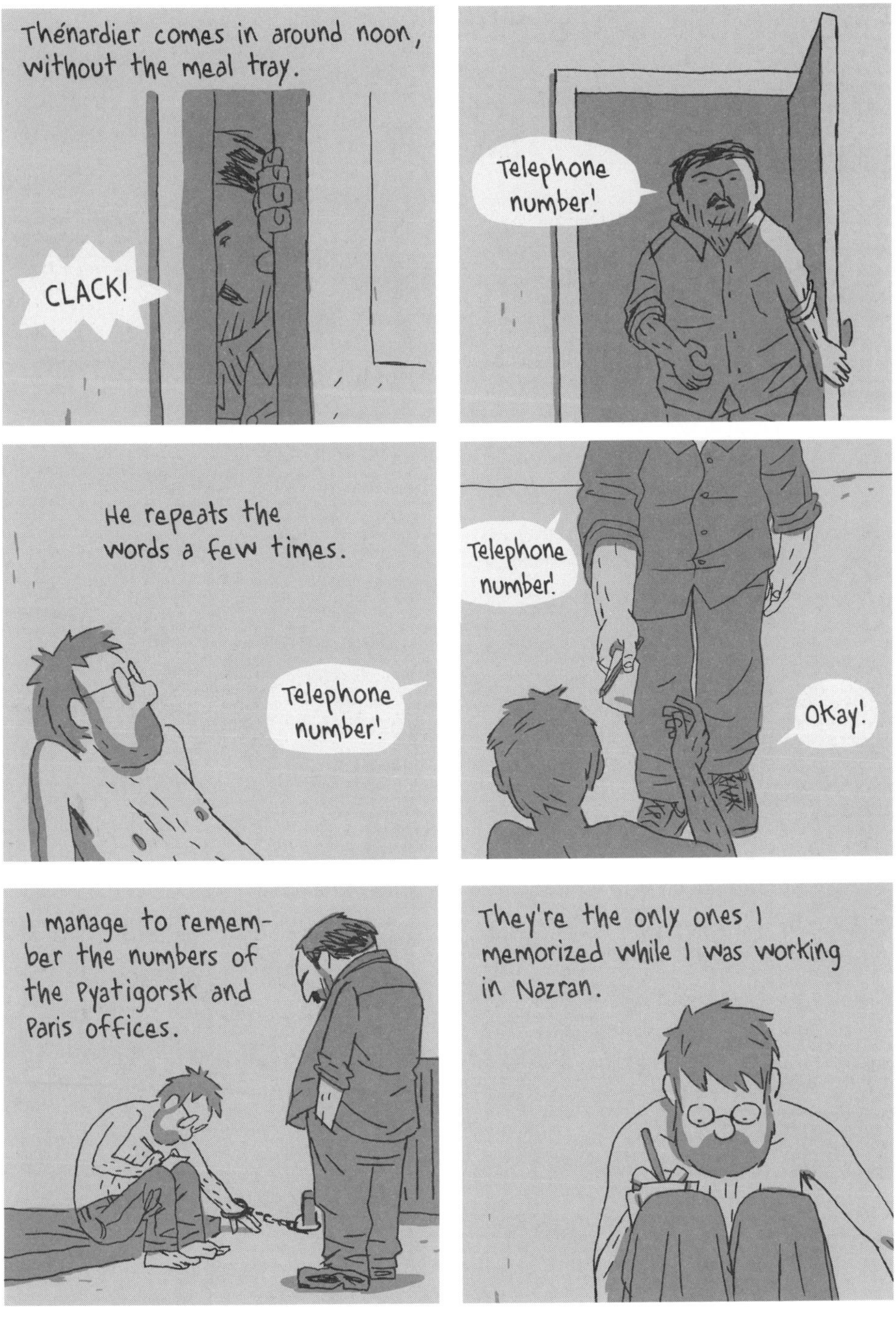
Thénardier comes in around noon, without the meal tray.
CLACK!
Telephone number!
He repeats the words a few times.
Telephone number!
Telephone number!
Okay!
I manage to remember the numbers of the Pyatigorsk and Paris offices.
They're the only ones I memorized while I was working in Nazran.

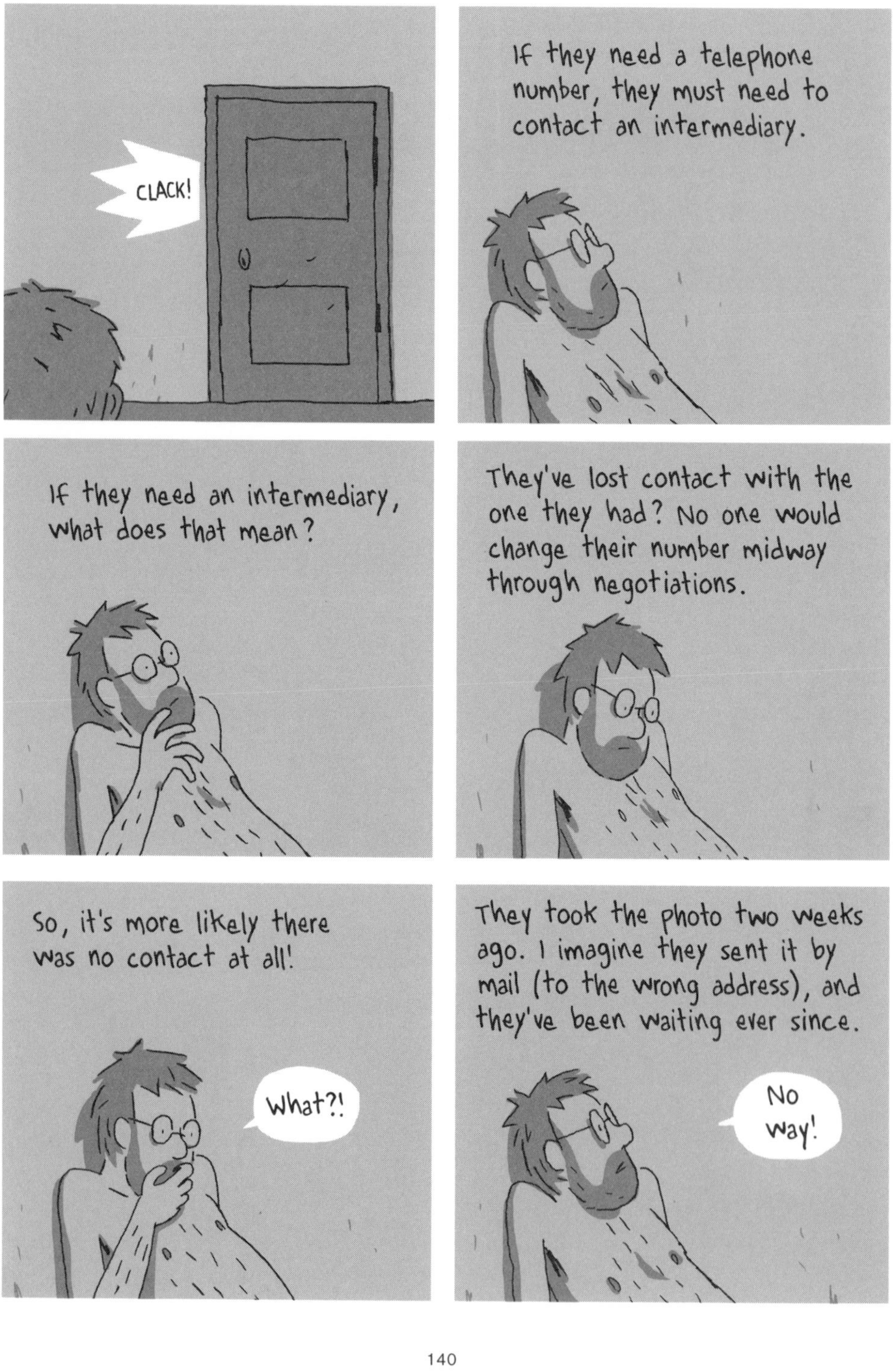
CLACK!
If they need a telephone number, they must need to contact an intermediary.
If they need an intermediary, what does that mean?
They've lost contact with the one they had? No one would change their number midway through negotiations.
So, it's more likely there was no contact at all!
What?!
They took the photo two weeks ago. I imagine they sent it by mail (to the wrong address), and they've been waiting ever since.
No way!

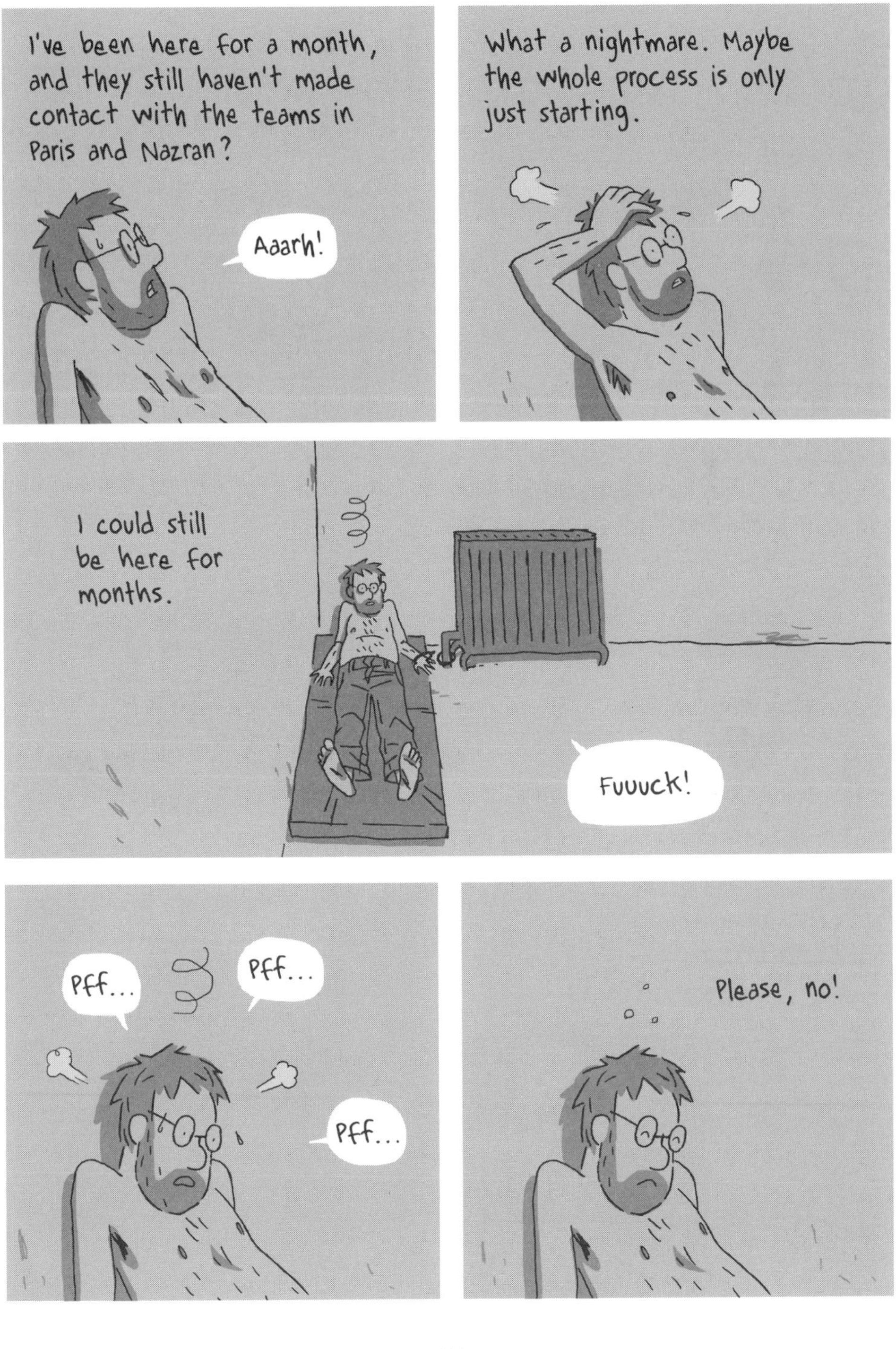
I've been here for a month, and they still haven't made contact with the teams in Paris and Nazran?
Aaarh!
What a nightmare. Maybe the whole process is only just starting.
I could still be here for months.
Fuuuck!
Pff...
Pff...
Pff...
Please, no!

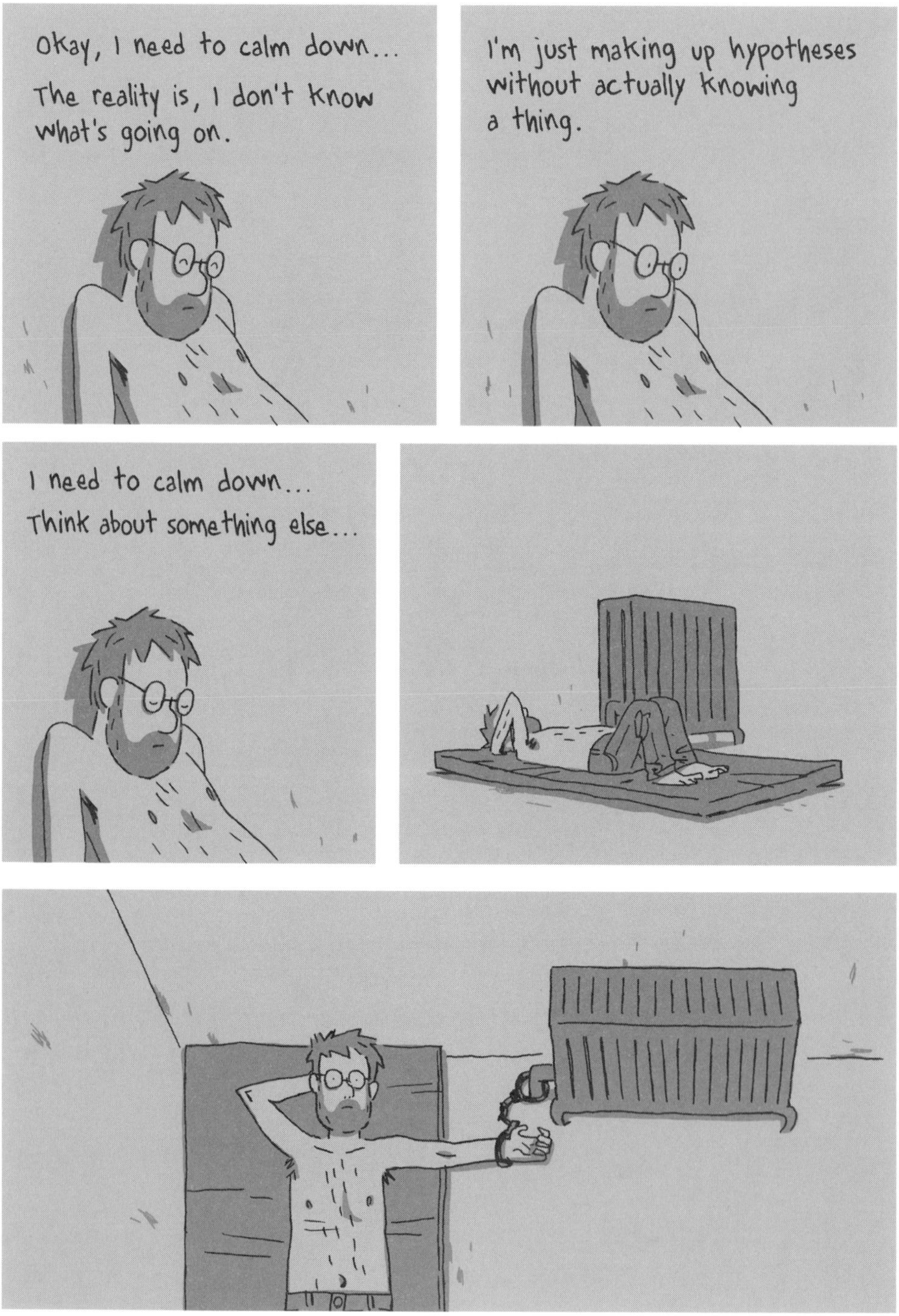
Okay, I need to calm down...
The reality is, I don't know what's going on.
I'm just making up hypotheses without actually knowing a thing.
I need to calm down...
Think about something else...

32

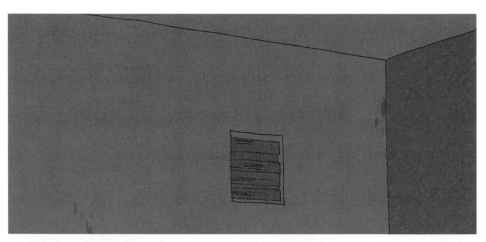

It's August 2.

Saturday, August 2.

I've been here for over a month.

My beard has grown a few millimetres.

Thanks to all their vegetable soup, I've probably lost a kilo or two.

I manage to sleep a few hours at night and I often doze during the day.

I have a pretty good sense of what time of day it is, despite the constant darkness in this room.

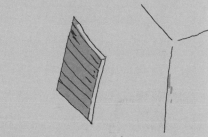

Right now, it must be 4:00 p.m.

Next meal's in two hours...

I'm hungry.

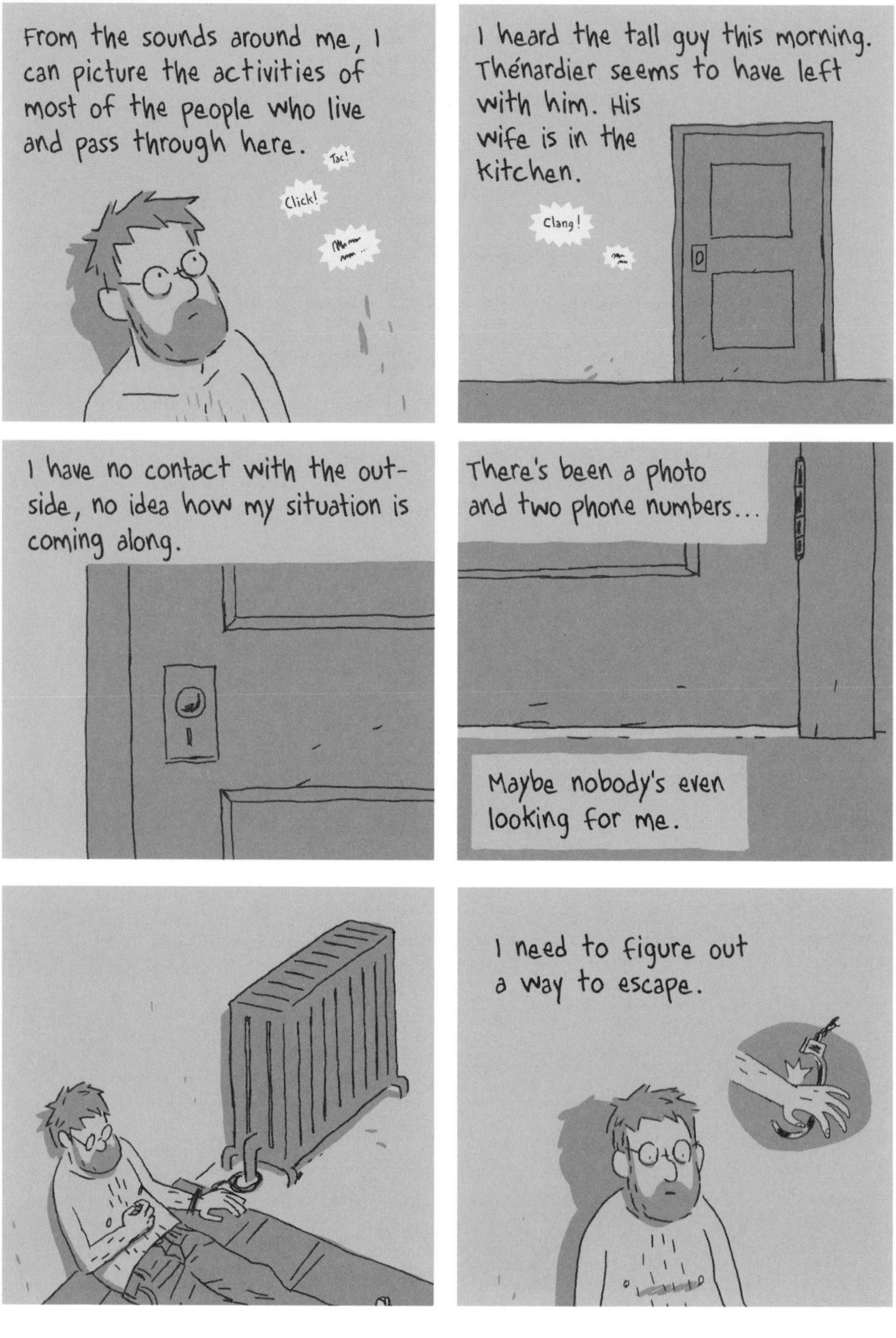
From the sounds around me, I can picture the activities of most of the people who live and pass through here.
Tac!
Click!
I heard the tall guy this morning. Thénardier seems to have left with him. His wife is in the kitchen.
Clang!
I have no contact with the out-side, no idea how my situation is coming along.
There's been a photo and two phone numbers...
Maybe nobody's even looking for me.
I need to figure out a way to escape.

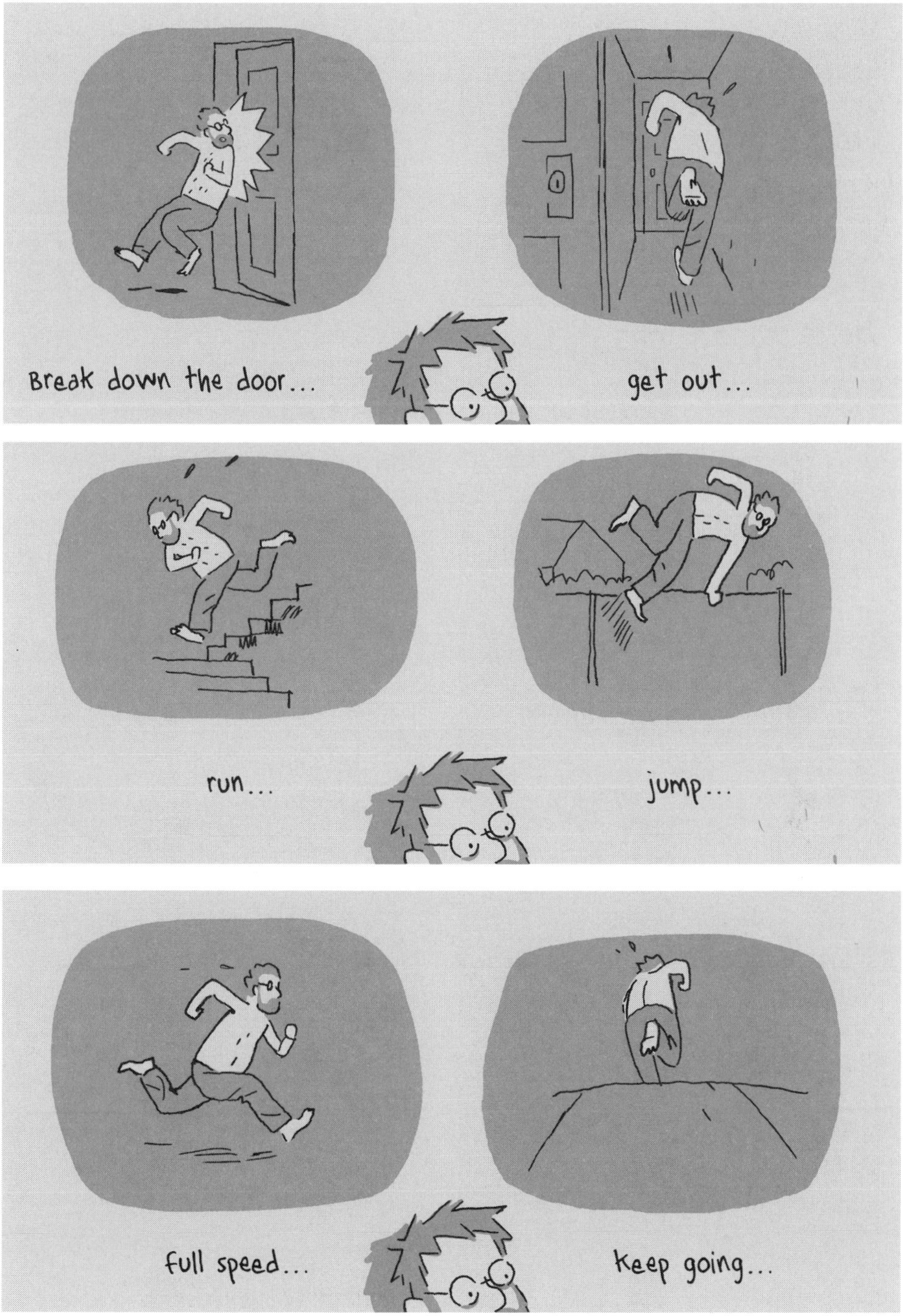
Break down the door...
get out...
run...
jump...
full speed...
keep going...

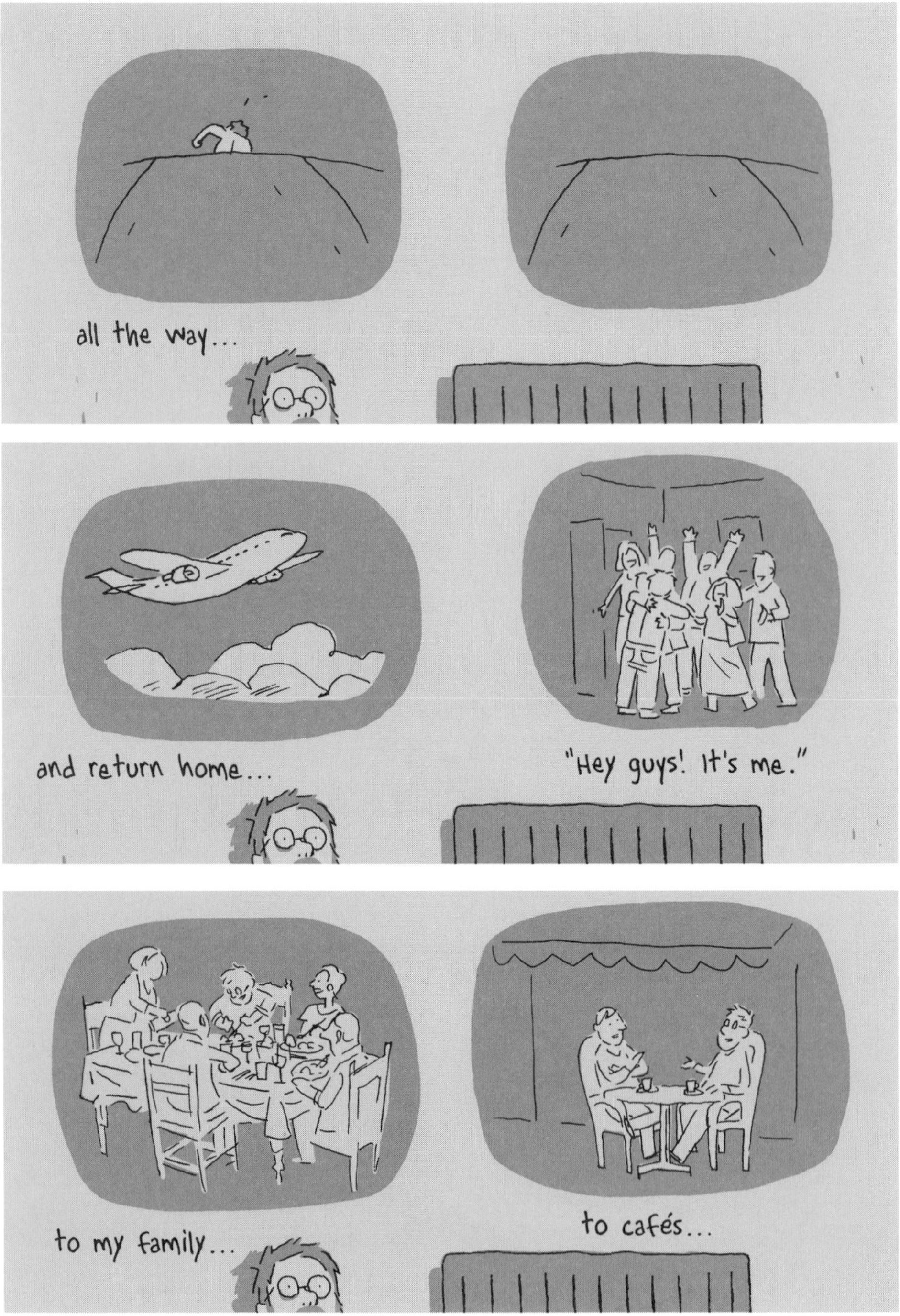
all the way...
and return home...
"Hey guys! It's me."
to my family...
to cafés...

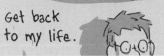
Get back
to my life.

Movies...

Walks...

Books...

Music...

Pff!....

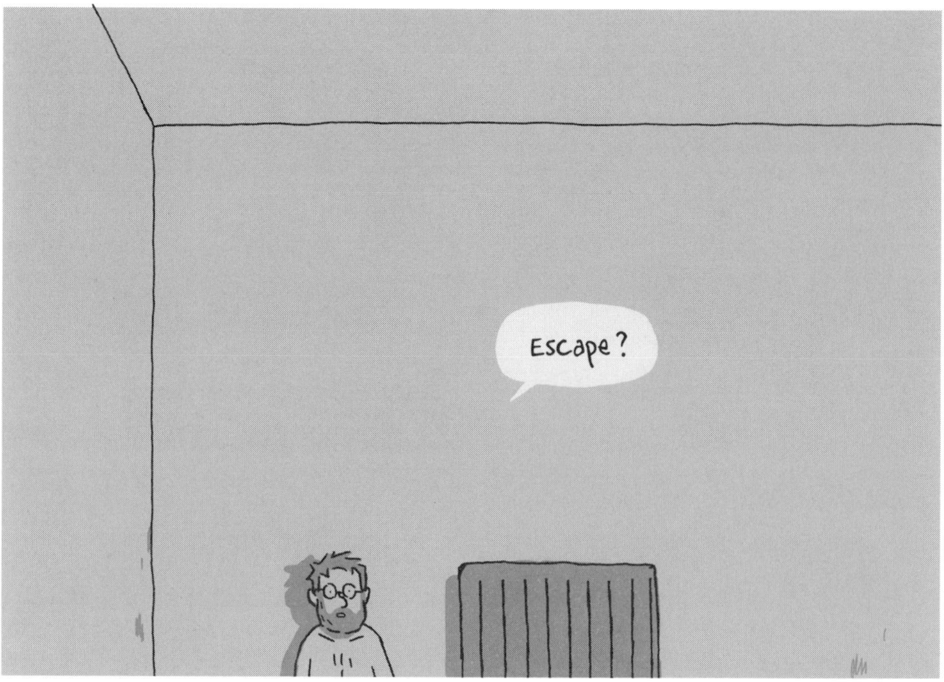
Escape?

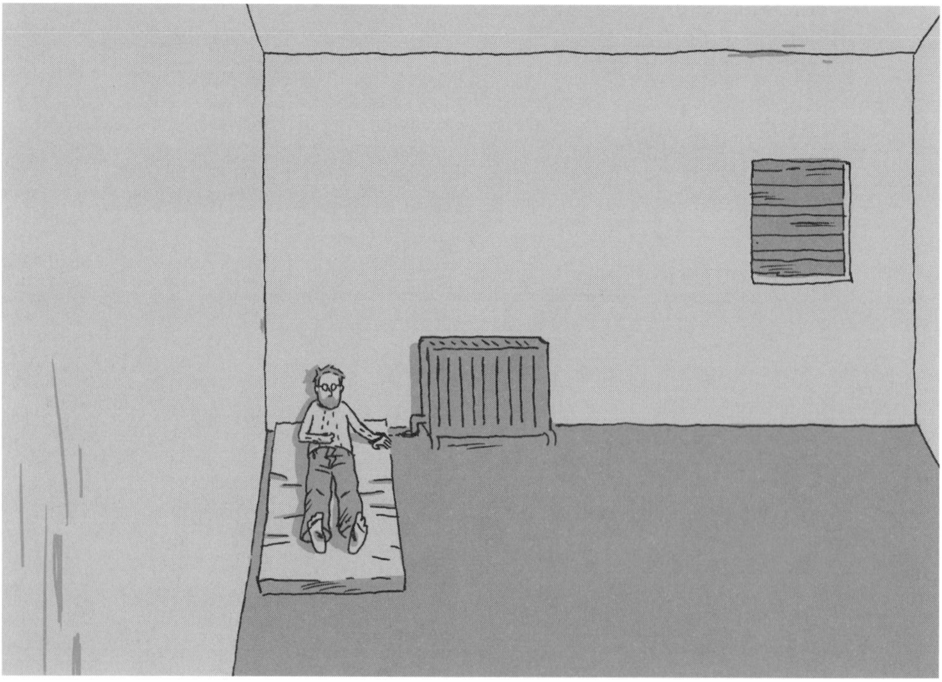

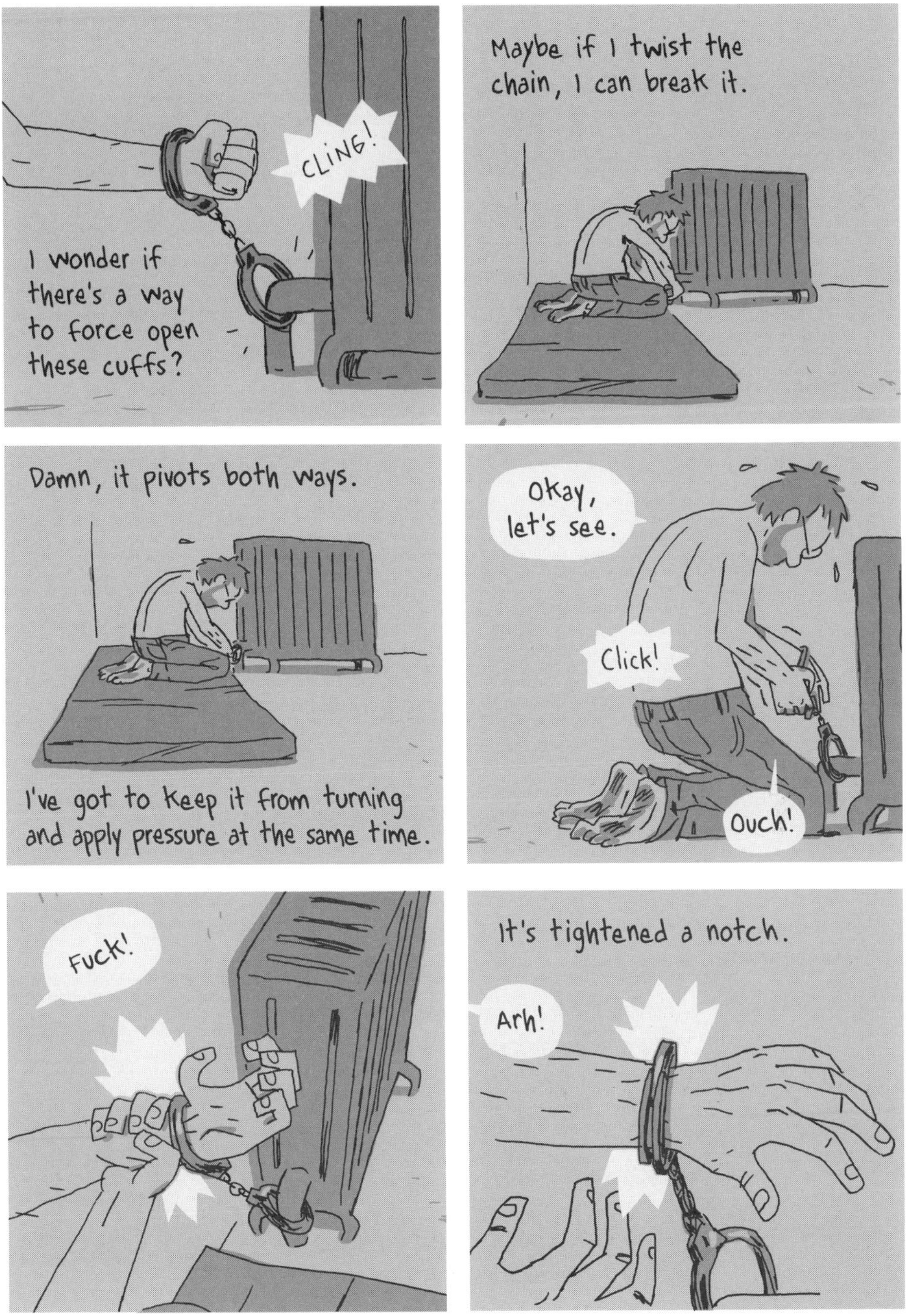
CLING!
I wonder if there's a way to force open these cuffs?
Maybe if I twist the chain, I can break it.
Damn, it pivots both ways.
I've got to keep it from turning and apply pressure at the same time.
Okay, let's see.
Click!
Ouch!
FUCK!
It's tightened a notch.
Arh!

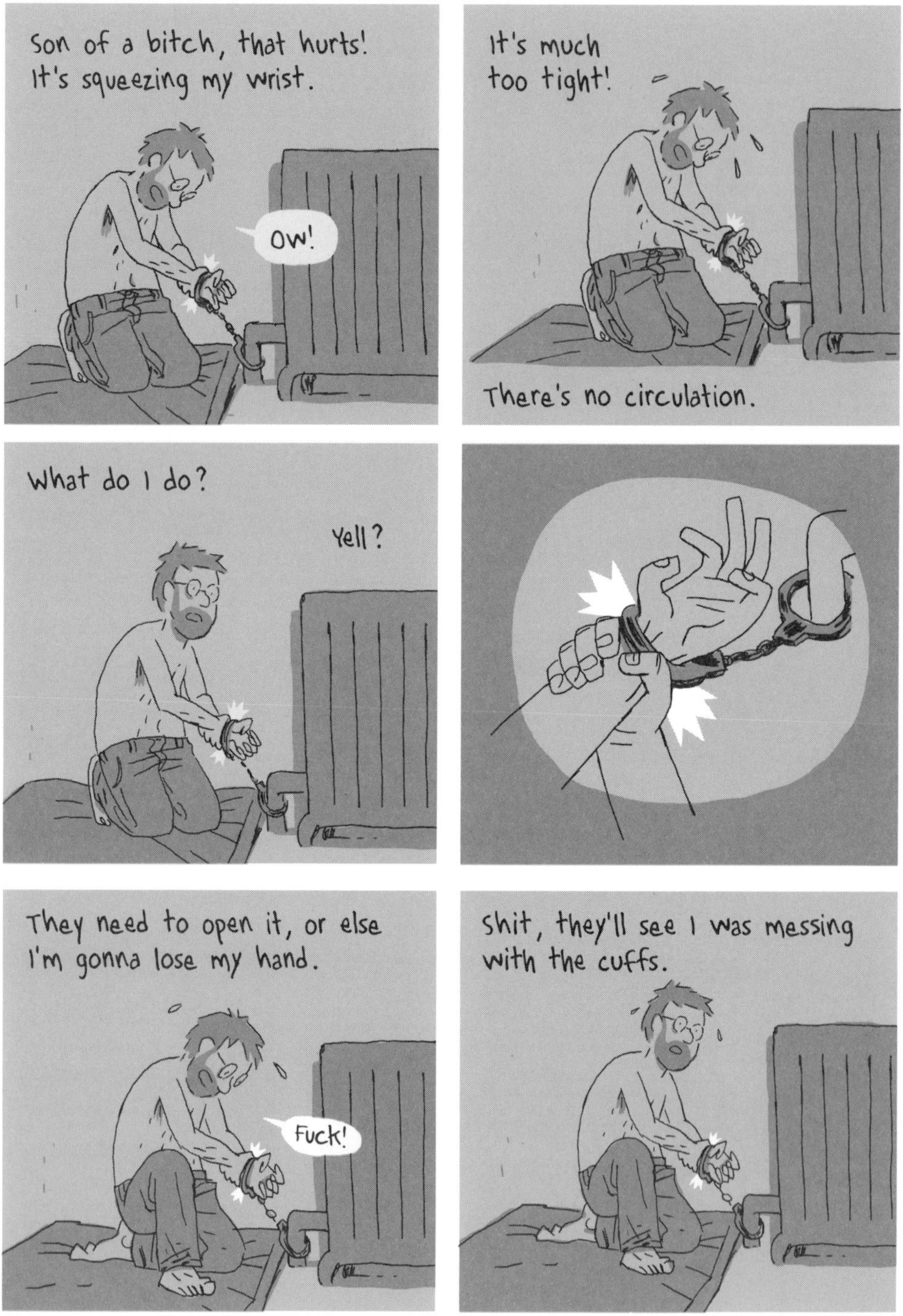
Son of a bitch, that hurts! It's squeezing my wrist.
Ow!
It's much too tight!
There's no circulation.
What do I do?
Yell?
They need to open it, or else I'm gonna lose my hand.
Fuck!
Shit, they'll see I was messing with the cuffs.

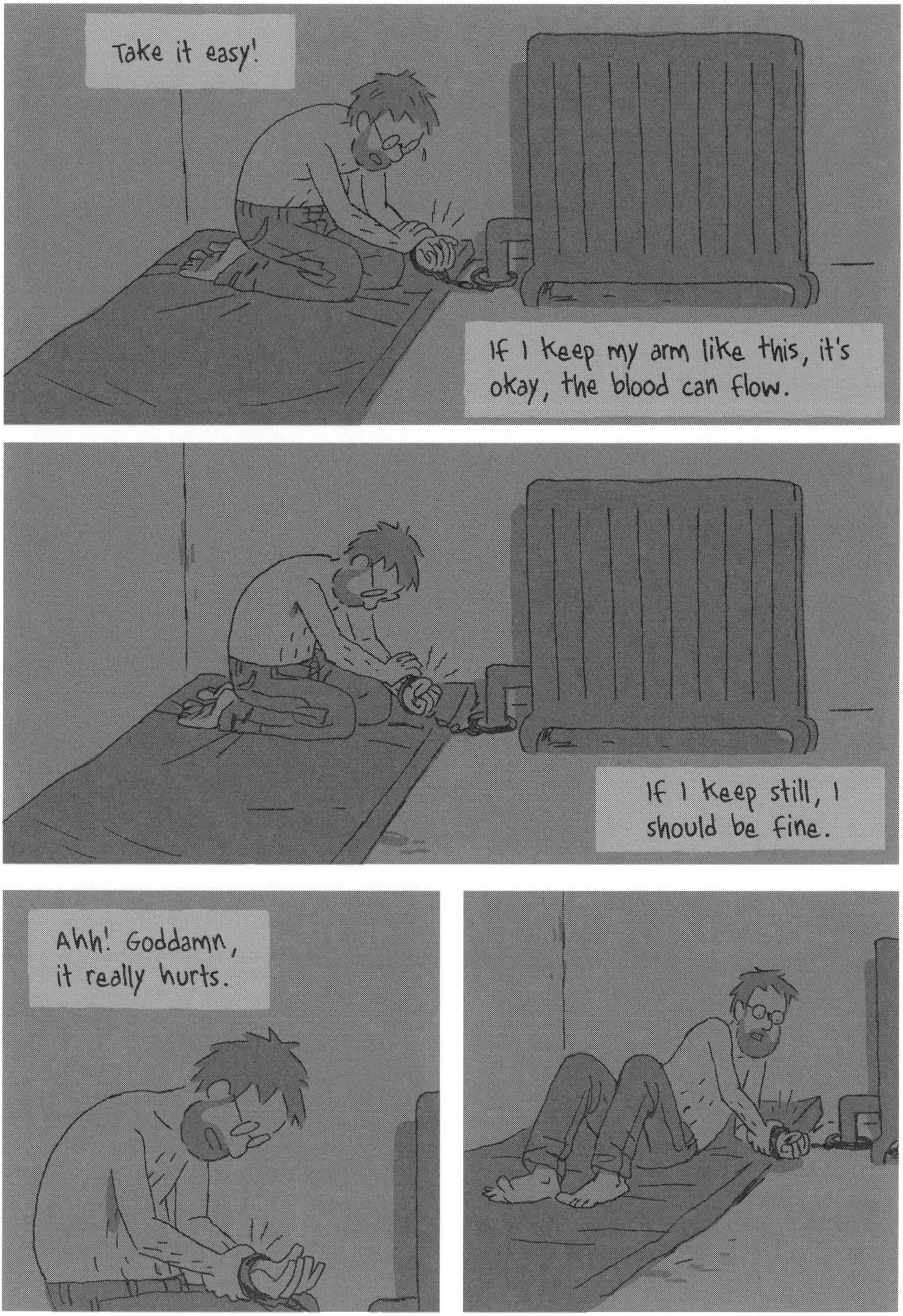
Take it easy!
If I keep my arm like this, it's okay, the blood can flow.
If I keep still, I should be fine.
Ahh! Goddamn, it really hurts.

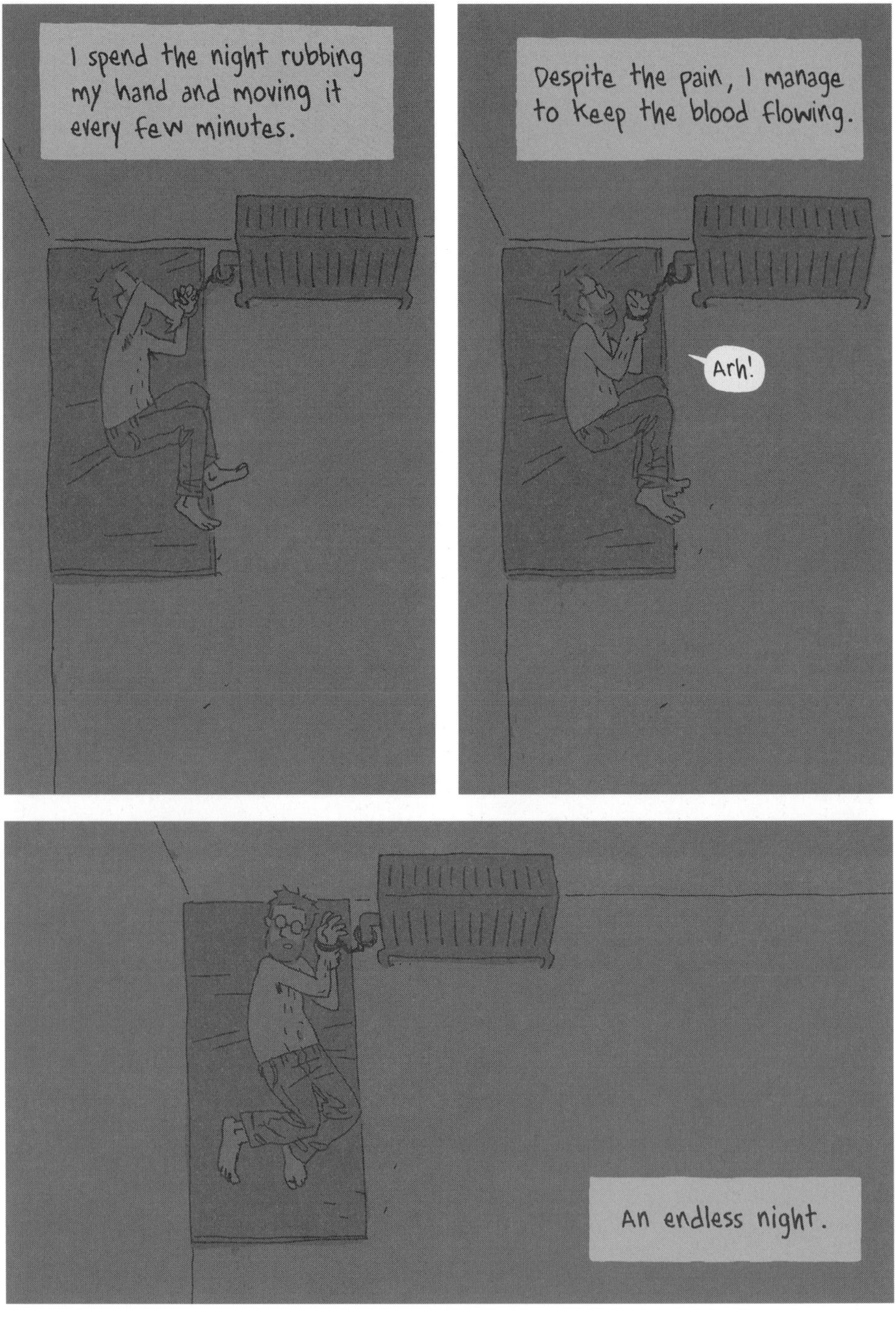
I spend the night rubbing my hand and moving it every few minutes.
Despite the pain, I manage to keep the blood flowing.
Arh!
An endless night.

By morning, I can hardly wait for breakfast to arrive.

CLACK!

Thénardier comes in, I pretend to be asleep.

CLICK!

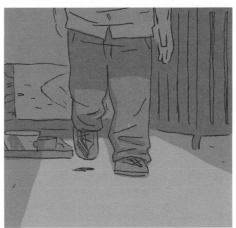

SLAM!

Ow! Ow! Ouch!

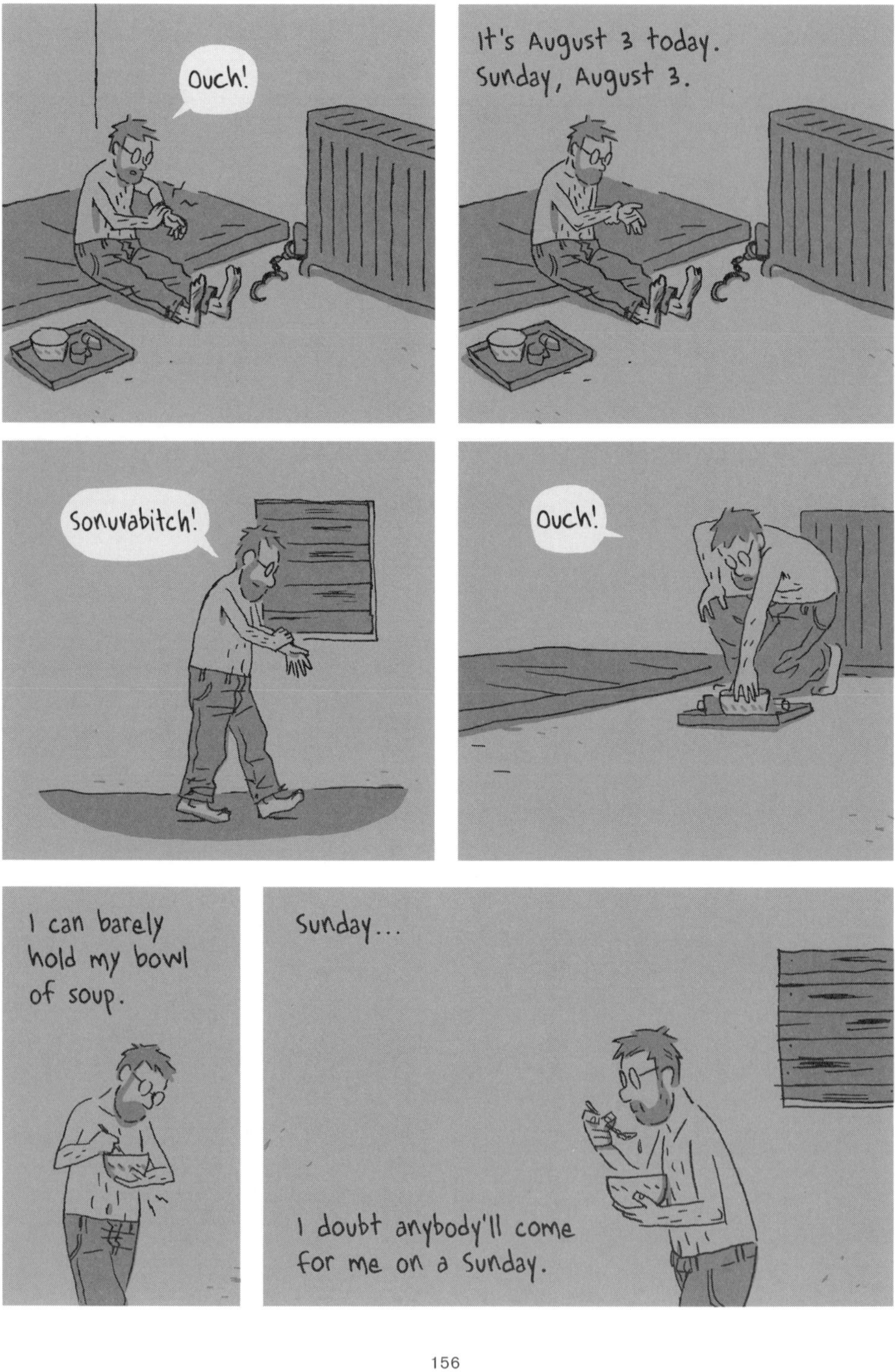
Ouch!
It's August 3 today. Sunday, August 3.
Sonuvabitch!
Ouch!
I can barely hold my bowl of soup.
Sunday...
I doubt anybody'll come for me on a Sunday.

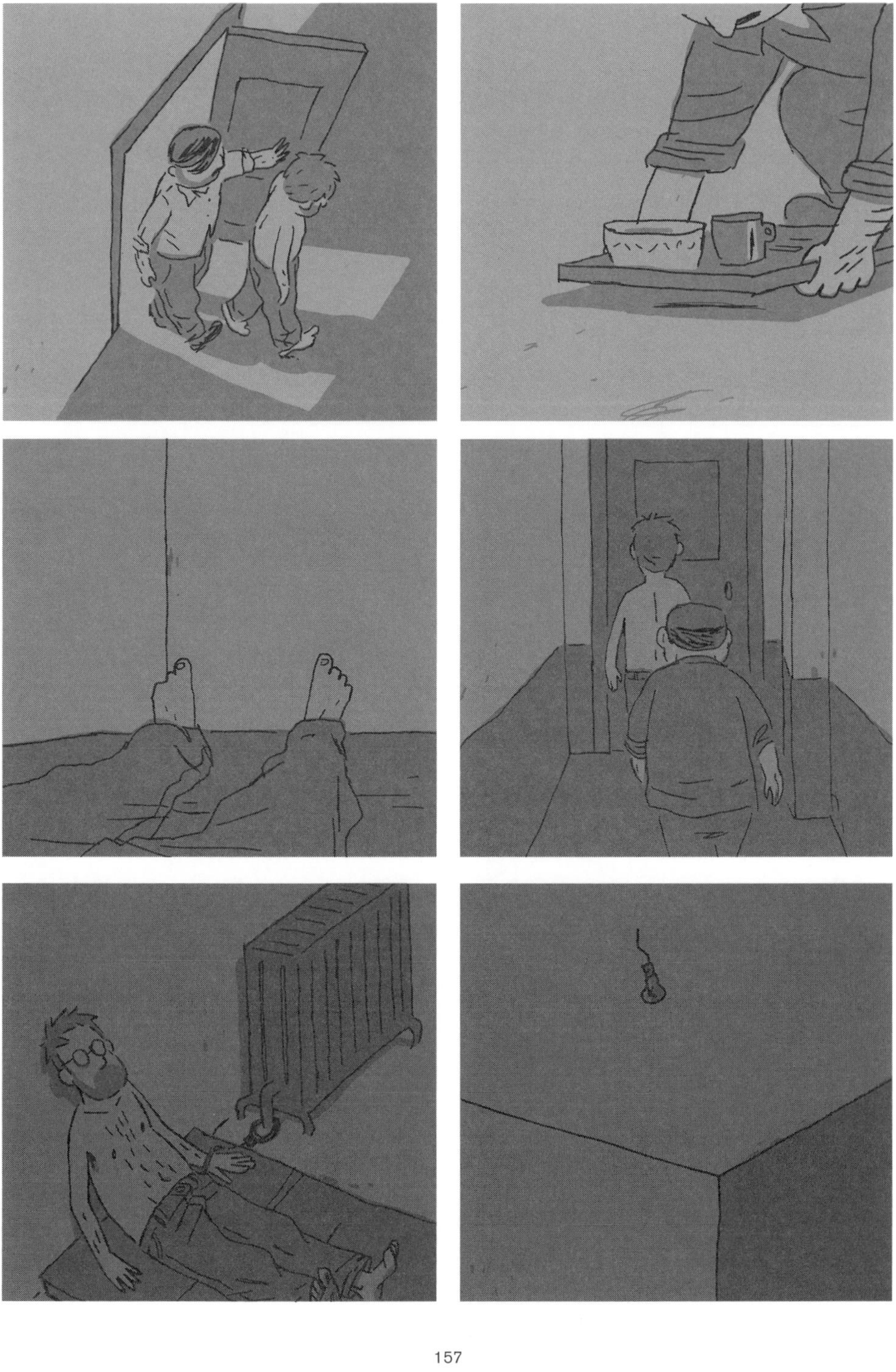

34

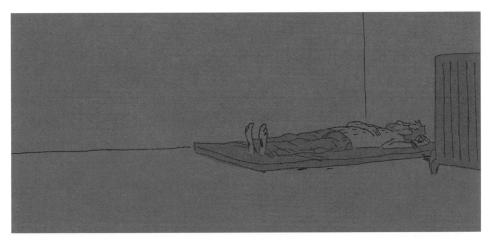

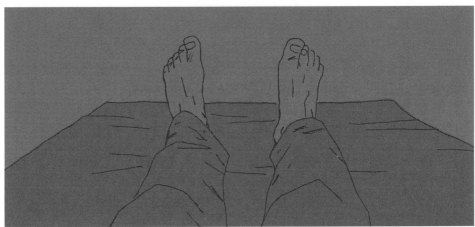

Today is August 5. Tuesday, August 5.

I think that's right...

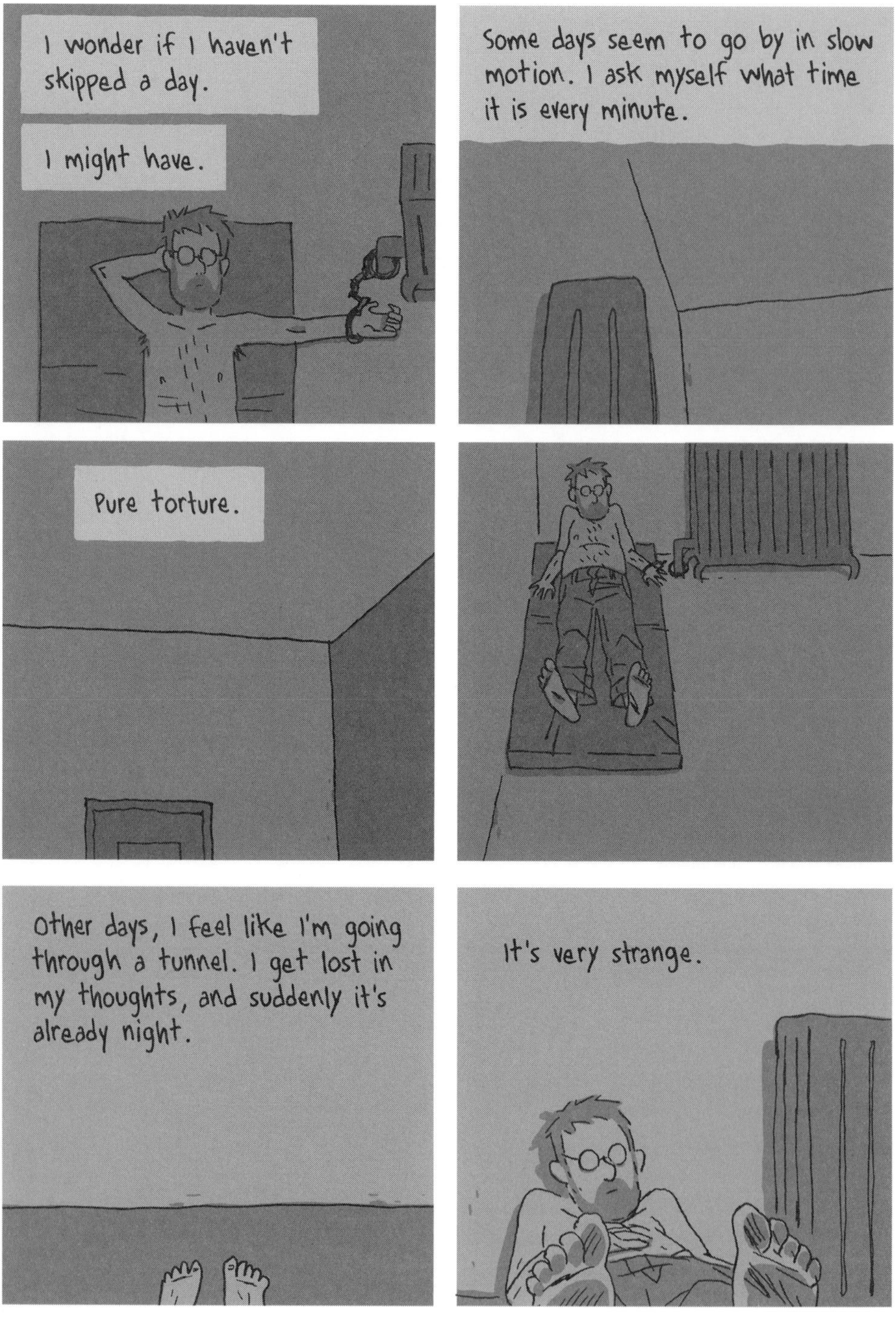
I wonder if I haven't skipped a day.
I might have.
Some days seem to go by in slow motion. I ask myself what time it is every minute.
Pure torture.
Other days, I feel like I'm going through a tunnel. I get lost in my thoughts, and suddenly it's already night.
It's very strange.

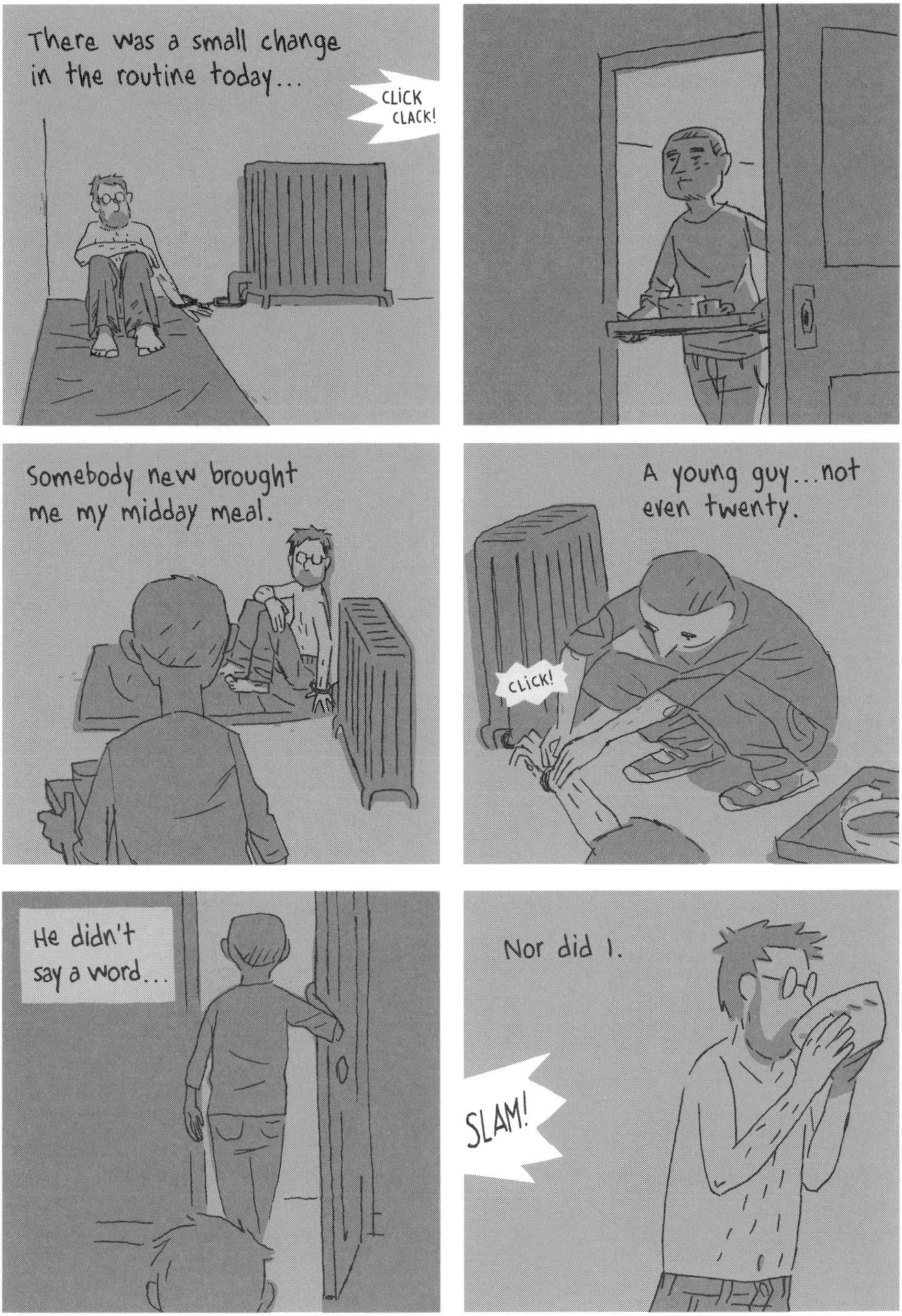
There was a small change in the routine today...
CLICK CLACK!
Somebody new brought me my midday meal.
A young guy...not even twenty.
CLICK!
He didn't say a word...
Nor did I.
SLAM!

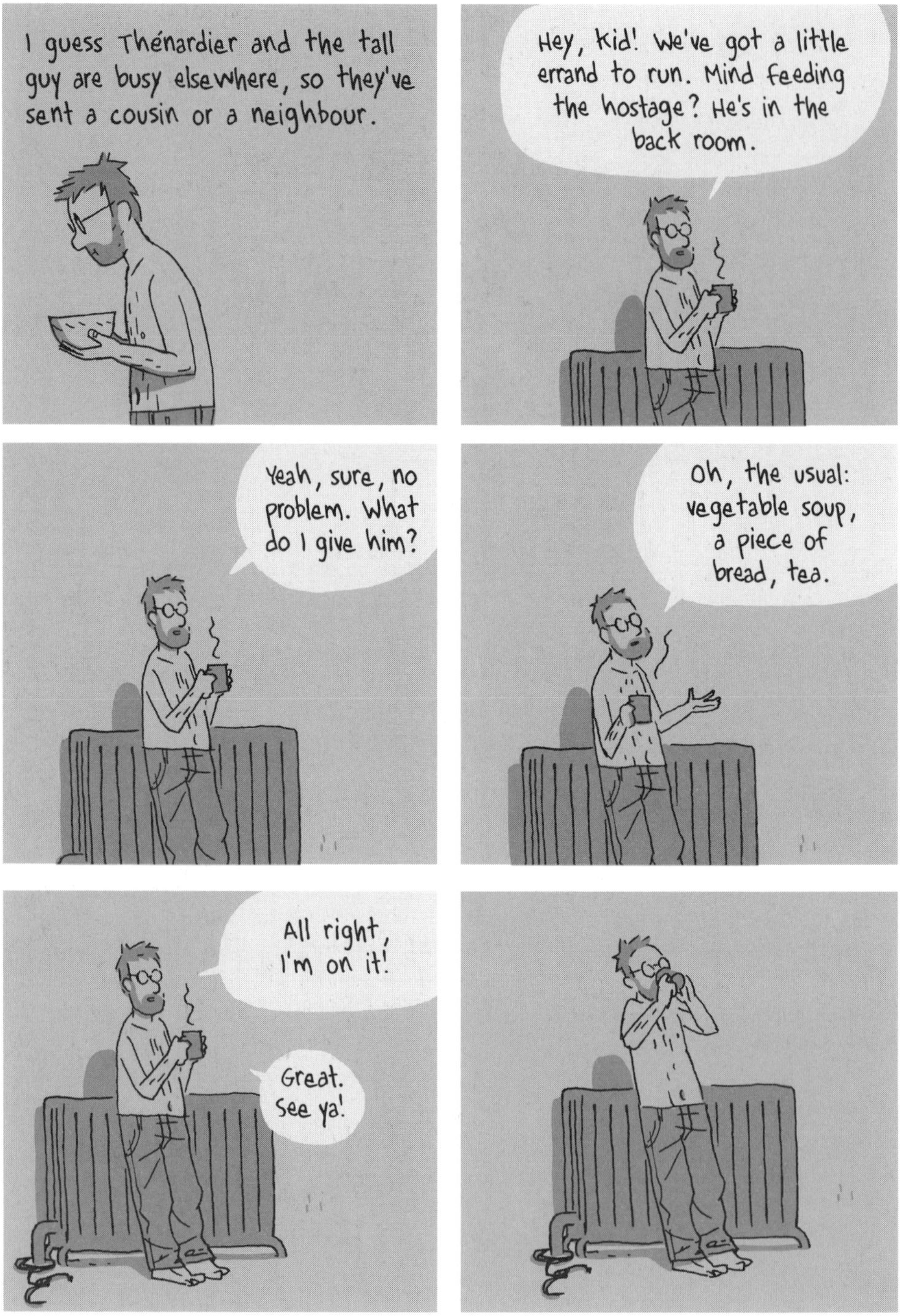
I guess Thénardier and the tall guy are busy elsewhere, so they've sent a cousin or a neighbour.
Hey, kid! We've got a little errand to run. Mind feeding the hostage? He's in the back room.
Yeah, sure, no problem. What do I give him?
Oh, the usual: vegetable soup, a piece of bread, tea.
All right, I'm on it!
Great. See ya!

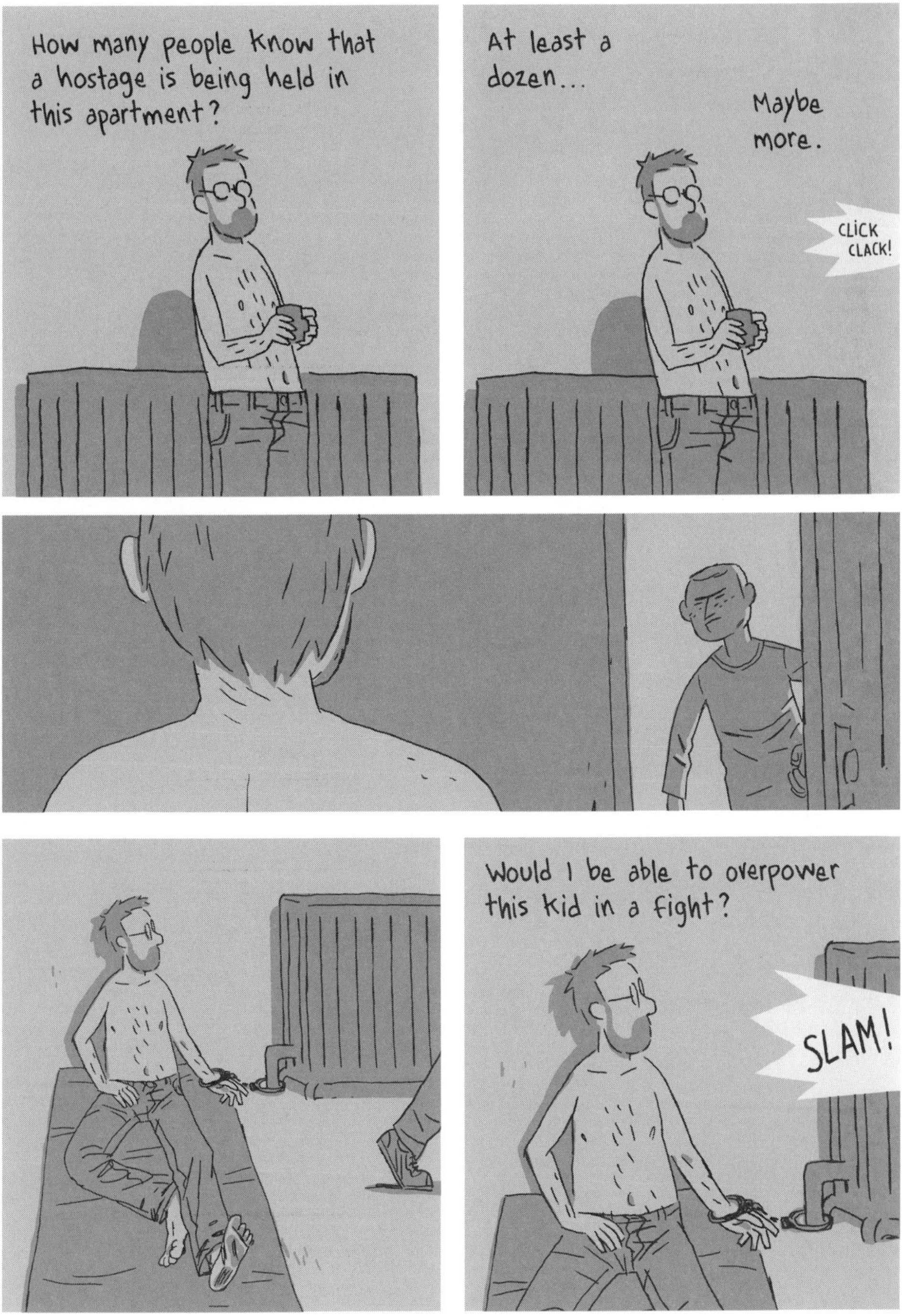

How many people know that a hostage is being held in this apartment?
At least a dozen...
Maybe more.
CLICK CLACK!
Would I be able to overpower this kid in a fight?
SLAM!

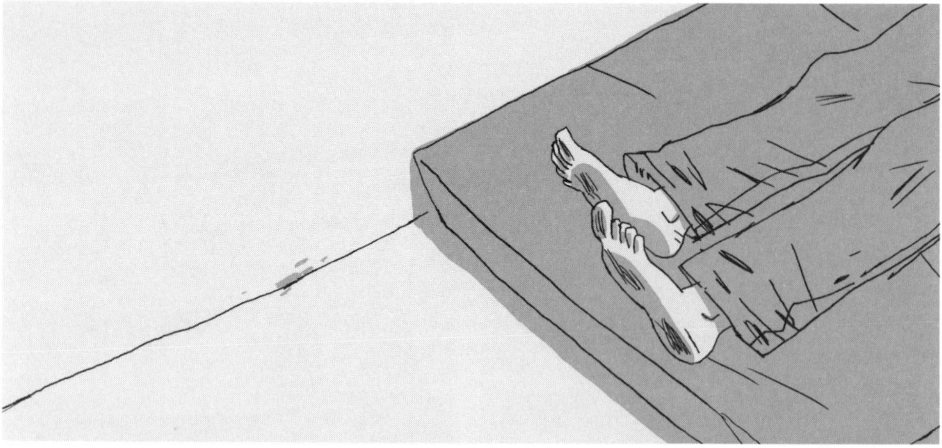

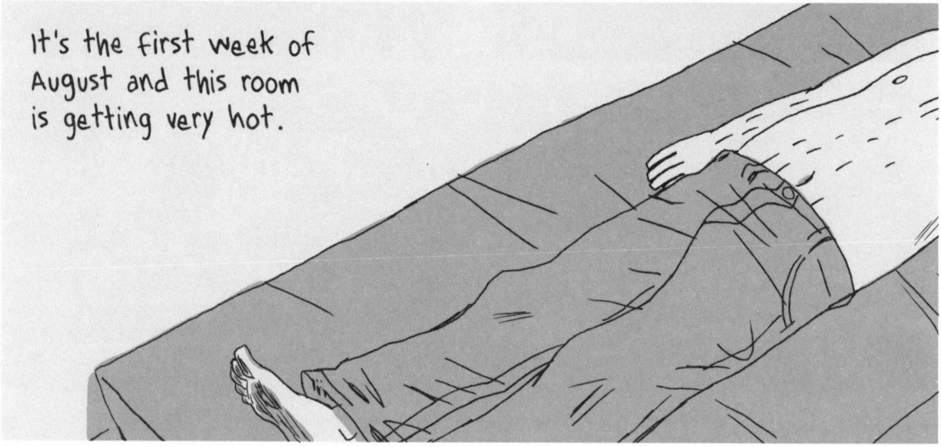
It's the first week of August and this room is getting very hot.

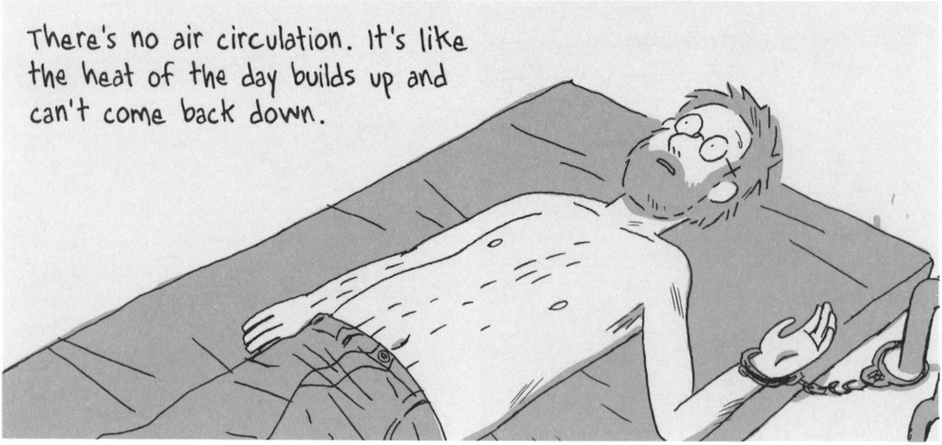
There's no air circulation. It's like the heat of the day builds up and can't come back down.

I'm suffocating.

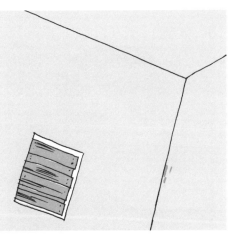

If Thénardier and the tall guy are gone...

maybe it's because they're busy making contact with the team in Nazran.

Or even directly with Paris.

Paris...

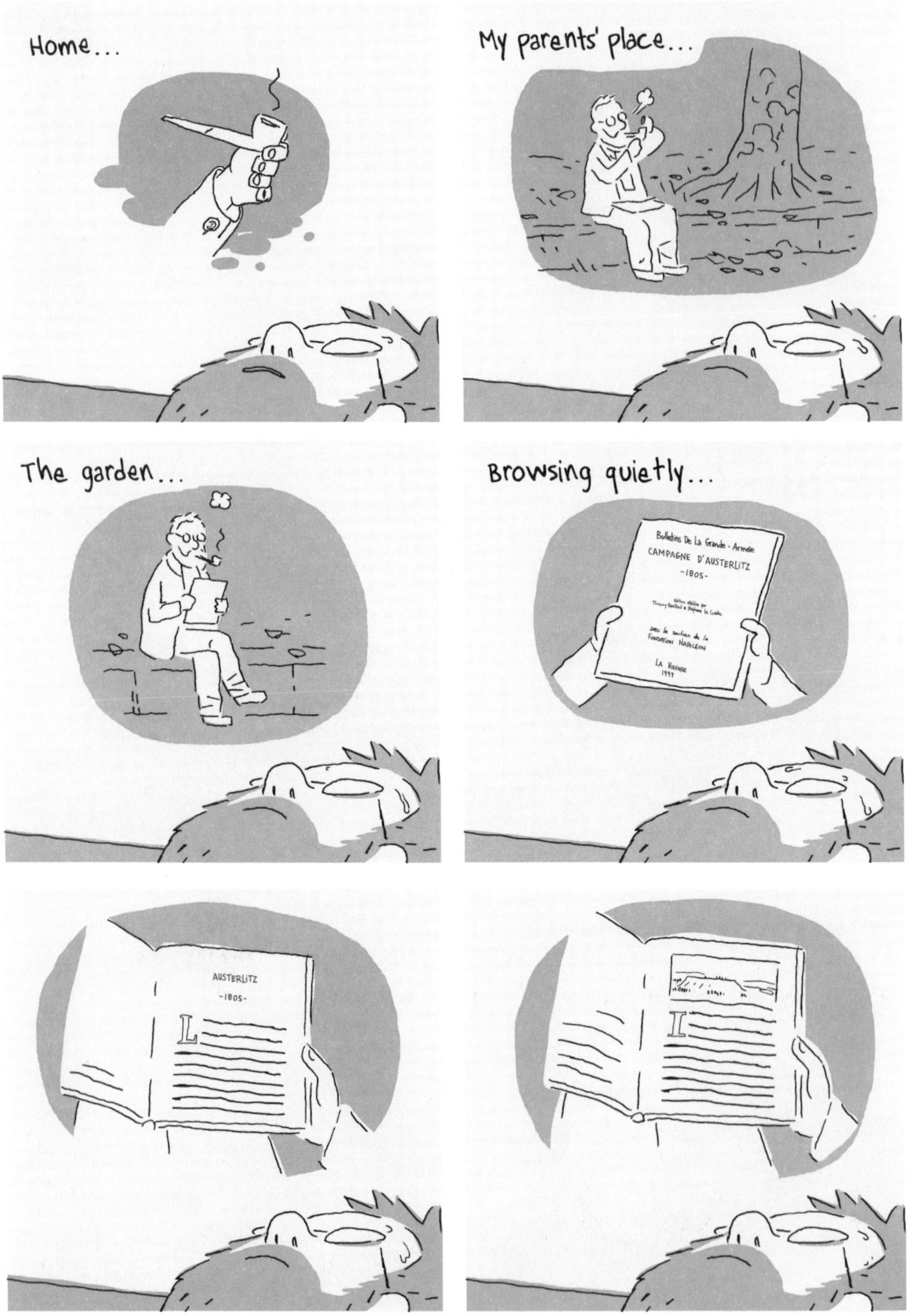

Home...
My parents' place...
The garden...
Browsing quietly...
Bulletins De La Grande - Armée
CAMPAGNE D'AUSTERLITZ
-1805-
avec le soutien de la
FONDATION NAPOLEON
LA VOUIVRE
1999
AUSTERLITZ
-1805-

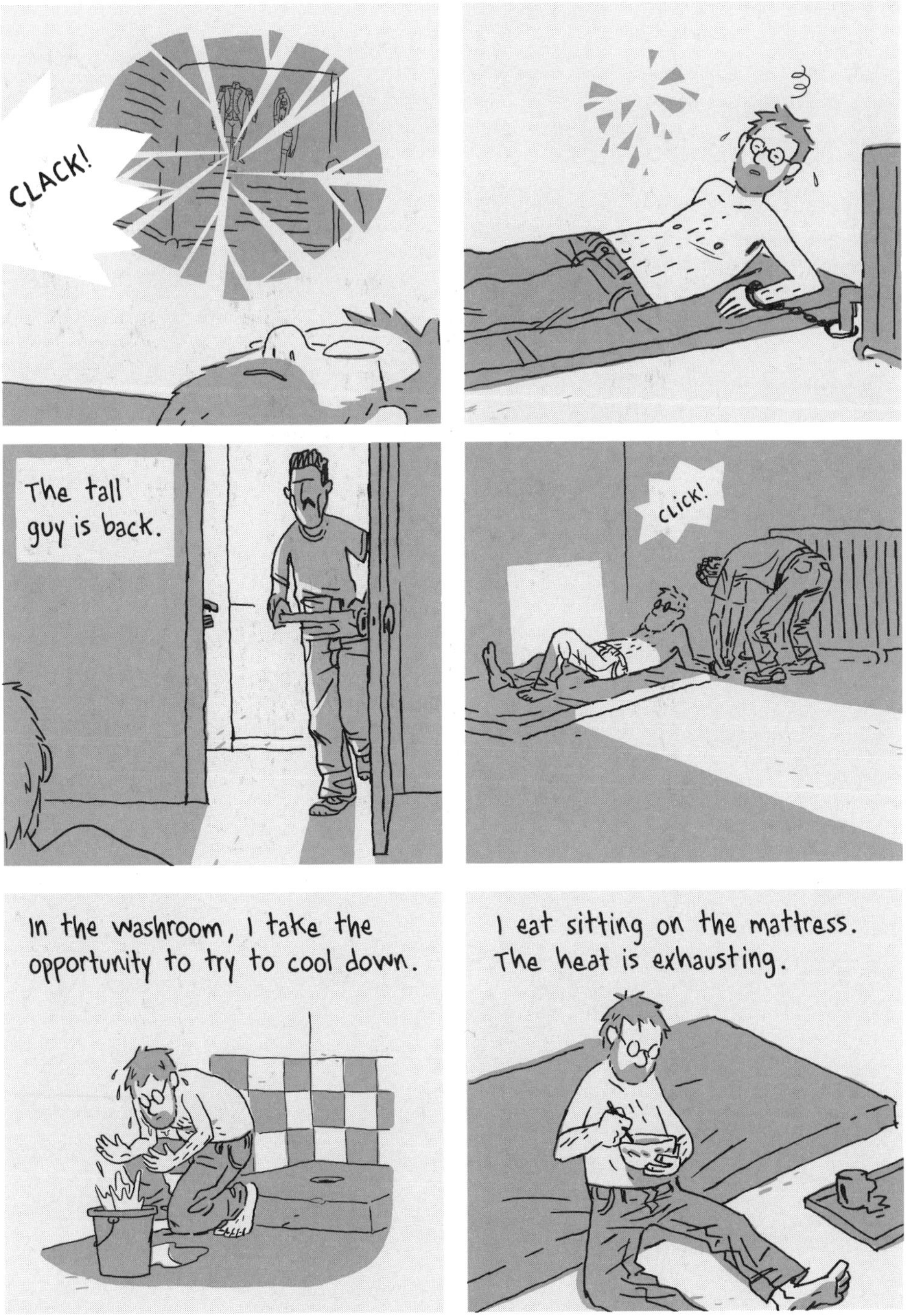
CLACK!
The tall guy is back.
CLICK!
In the washroom, I take the opportunity to try to cool down.
I eat sitting on the mattress. The heat is exhausting.

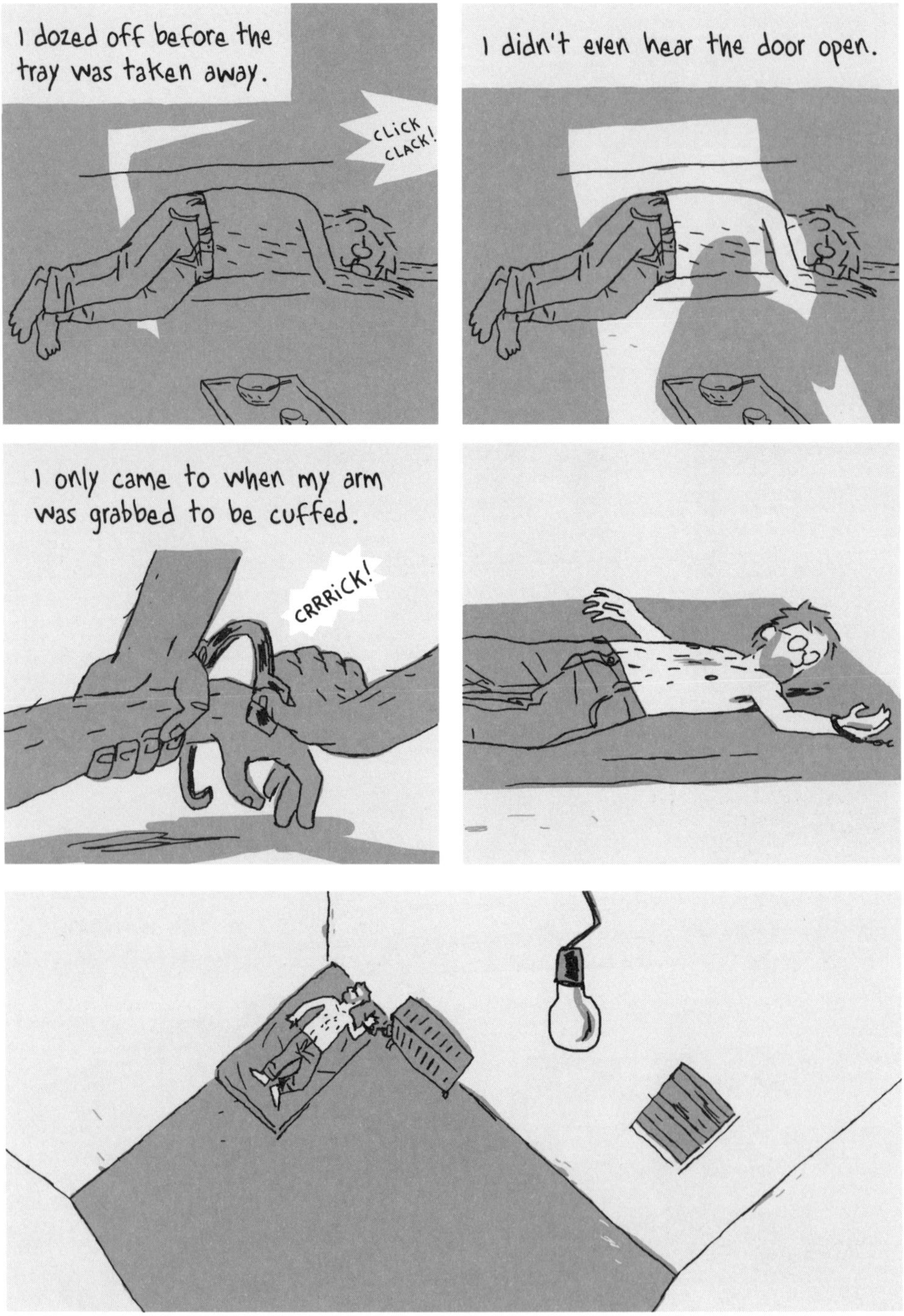
I dozed off before the tray was taken away.
CLICK CLACK!
I didn't even hear the door open.
I only came to when my arm was grabbed to be cuffed.
CRRRICK!

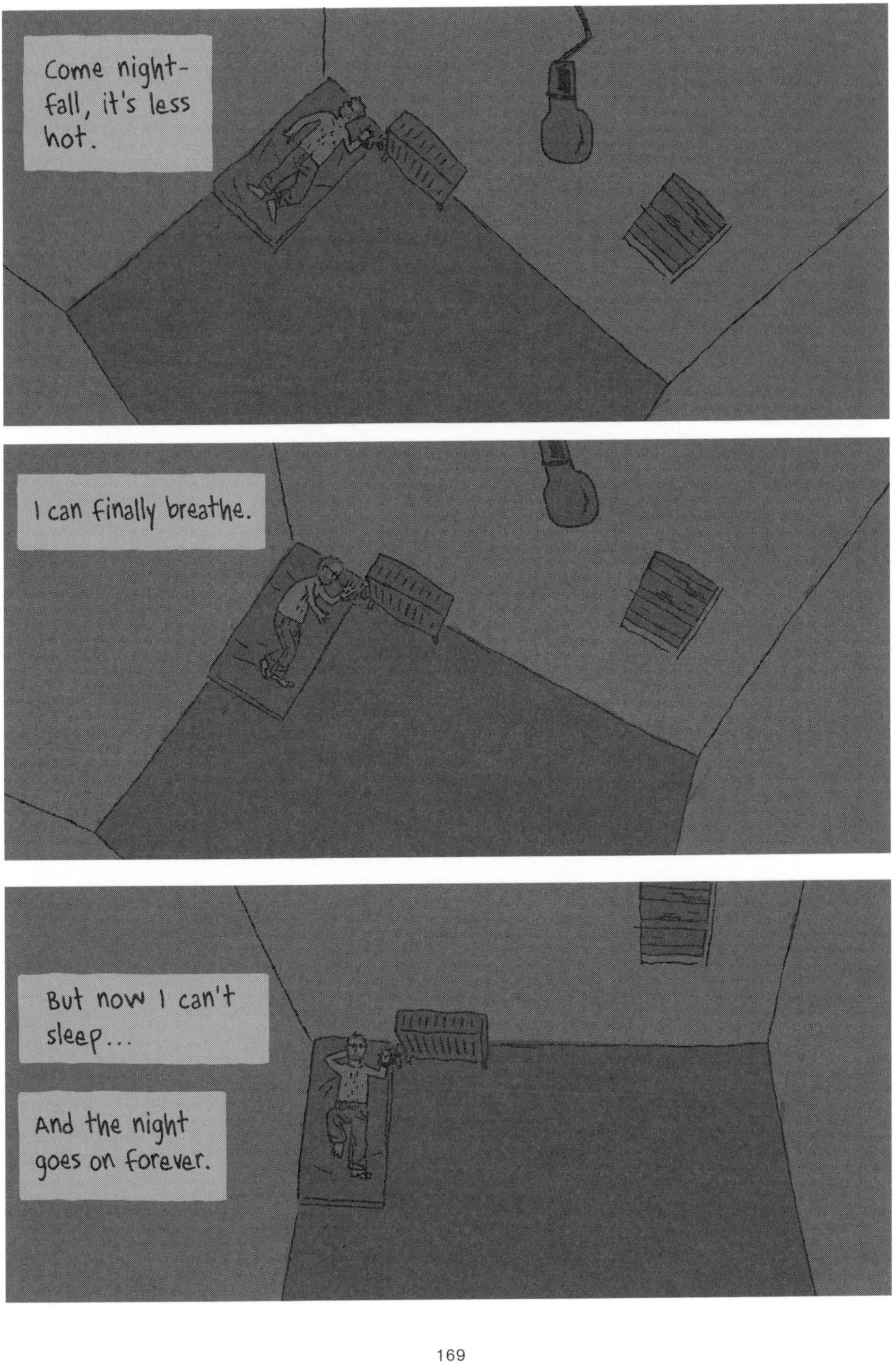
Come night-fall, it's less hot.
I can finally breathe.
But now I can't sleep...
And the night goes on forever.

38

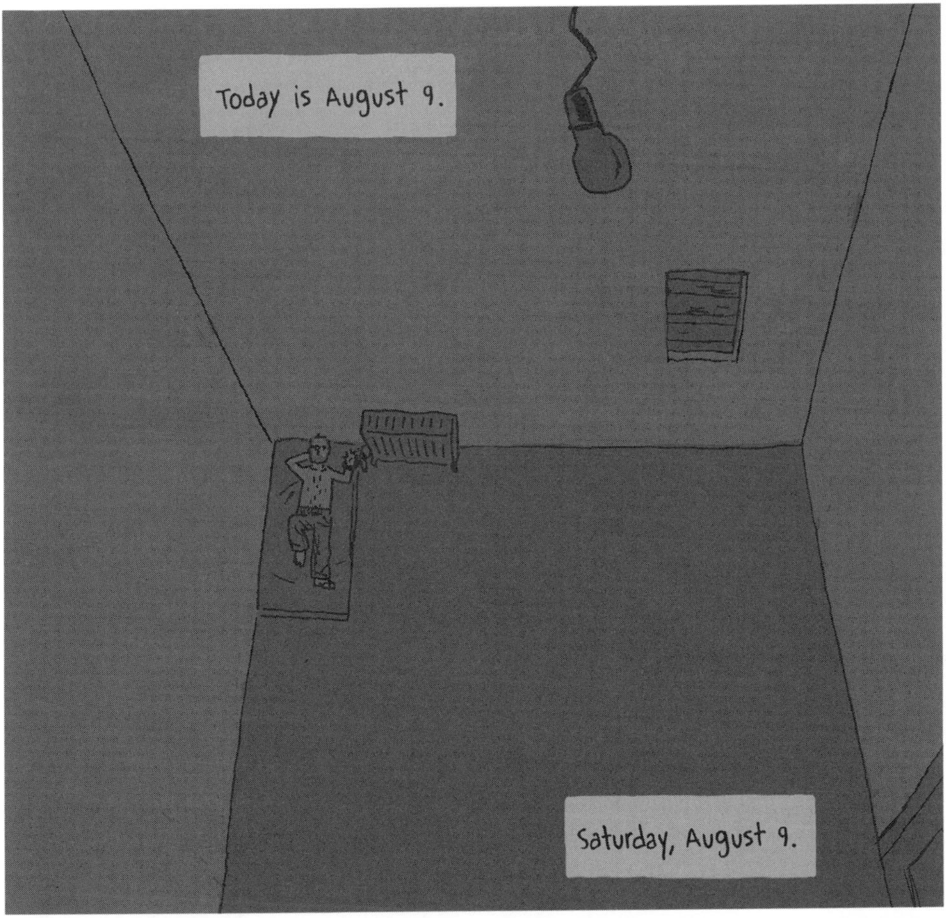
Today is August 9.
Saturday, August 9.

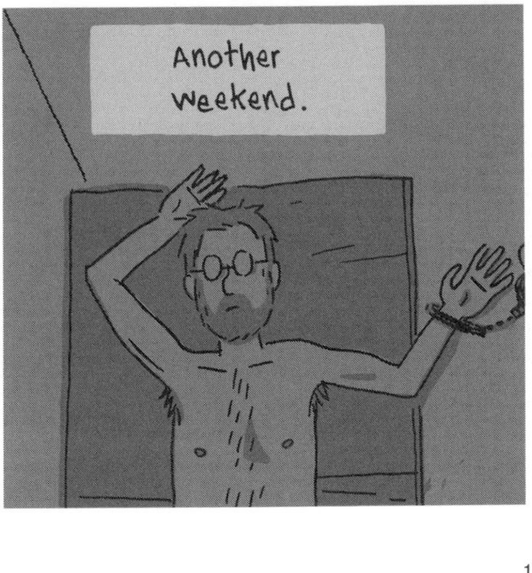
Another weekend.

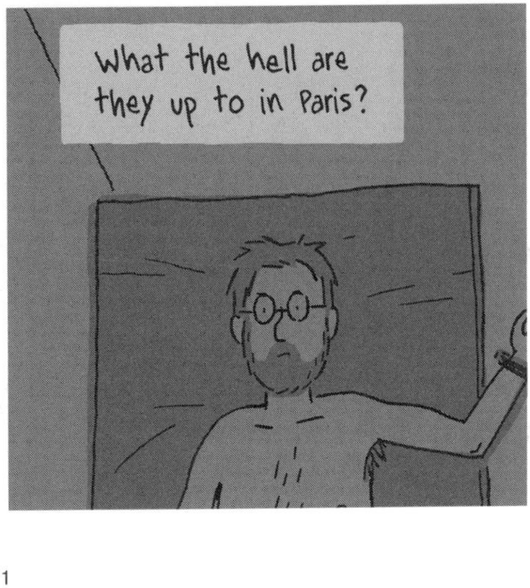
What the hell are they up to in Paris?

Nothing, no news since I was abducted.

Has contact been established at least?

Maybe they think I'm dead and they're not even looking for me anymore.

Maybe I'll never see my family again...

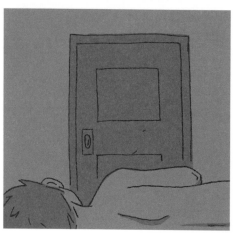

And there's my sister's wedding in September...

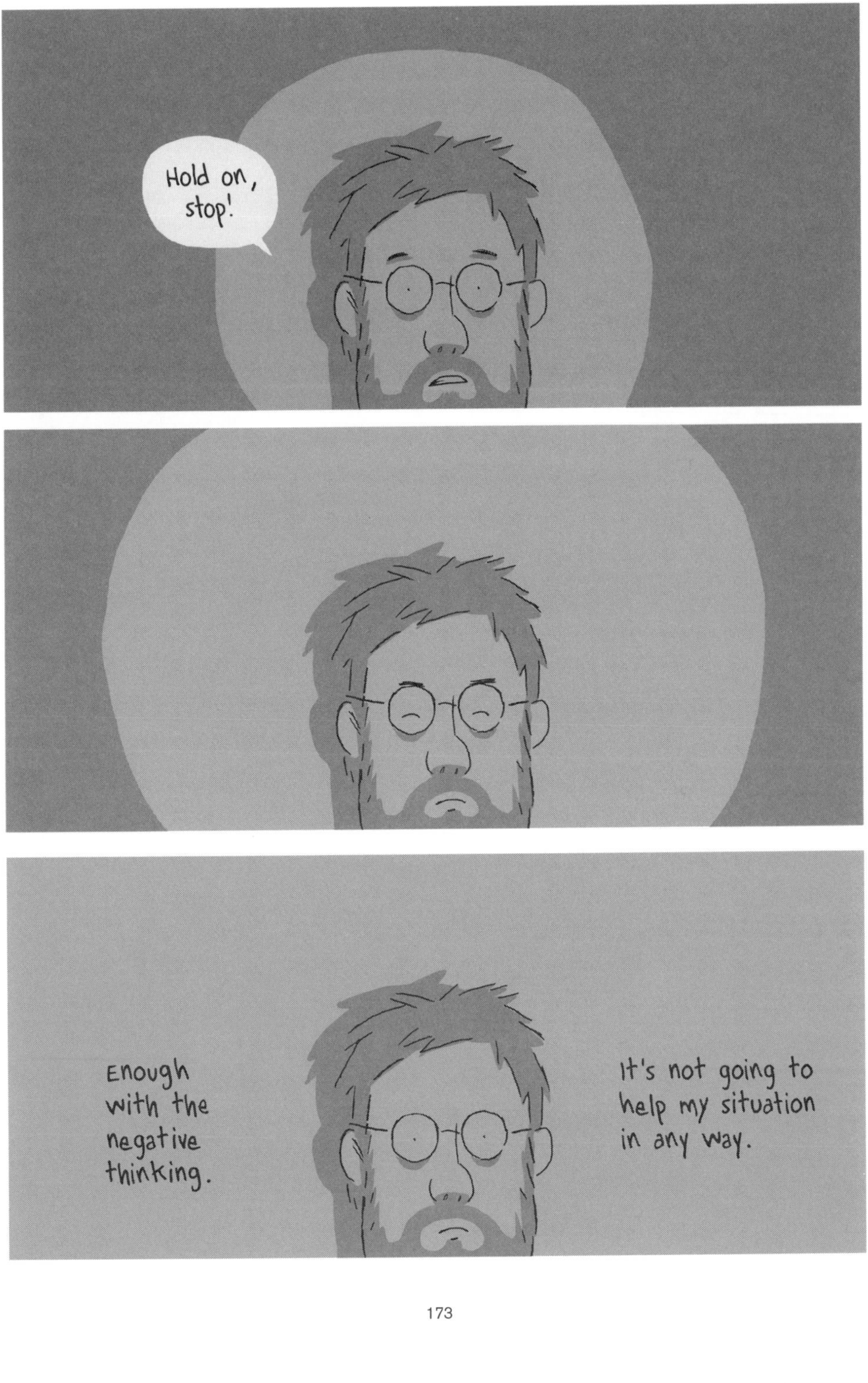
Hold on, stop!
Enough with the negative thinking.
It's not going to help my situation in any way.

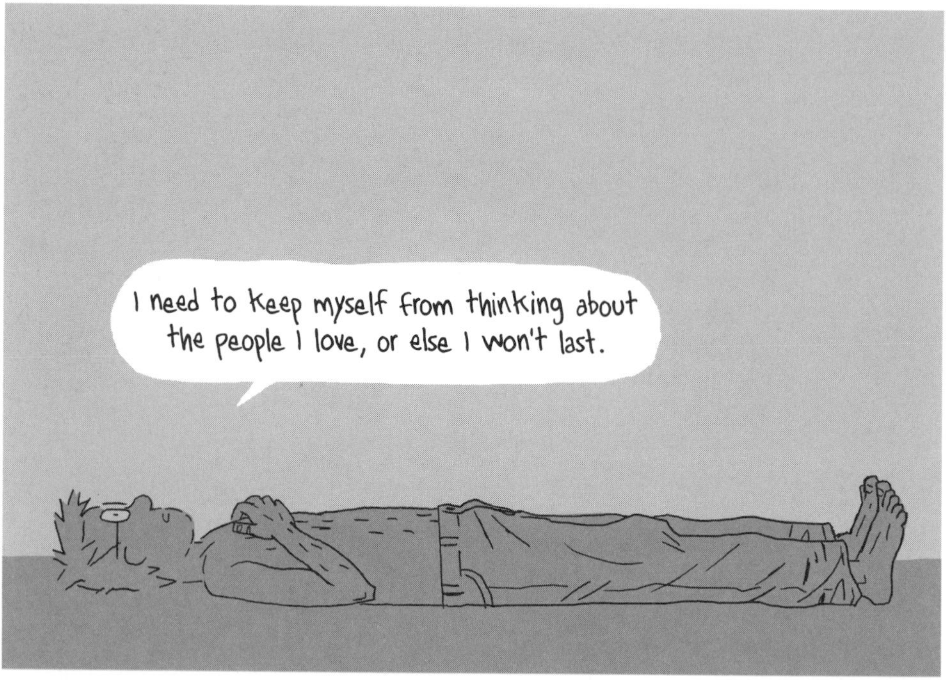
I need to keep myself from thinking about the people I love, or else I won't last.

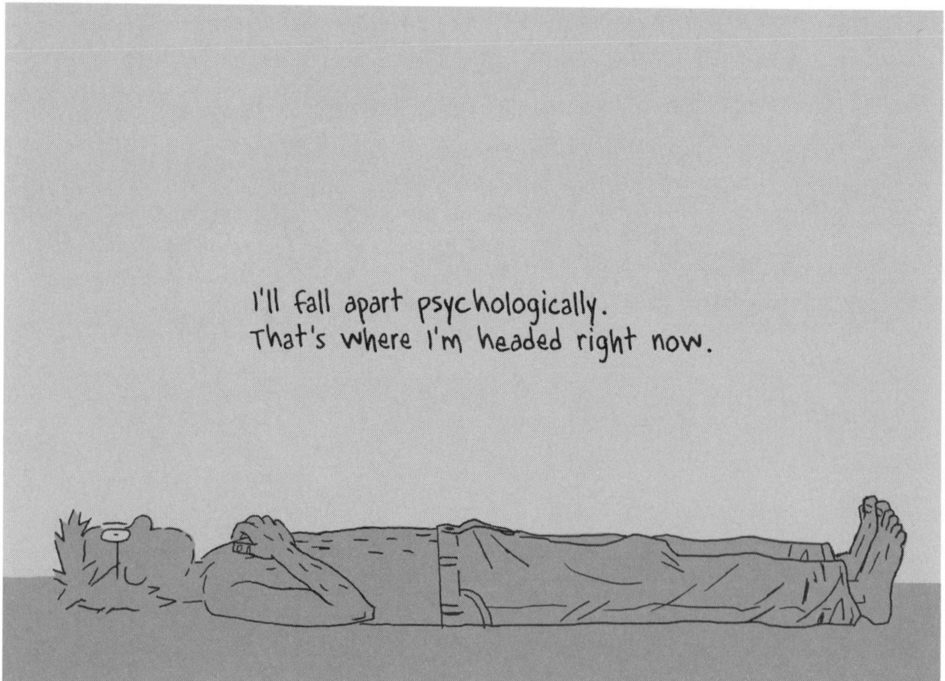
I'll fall apart psychologically.
That's where I'm headed right now.

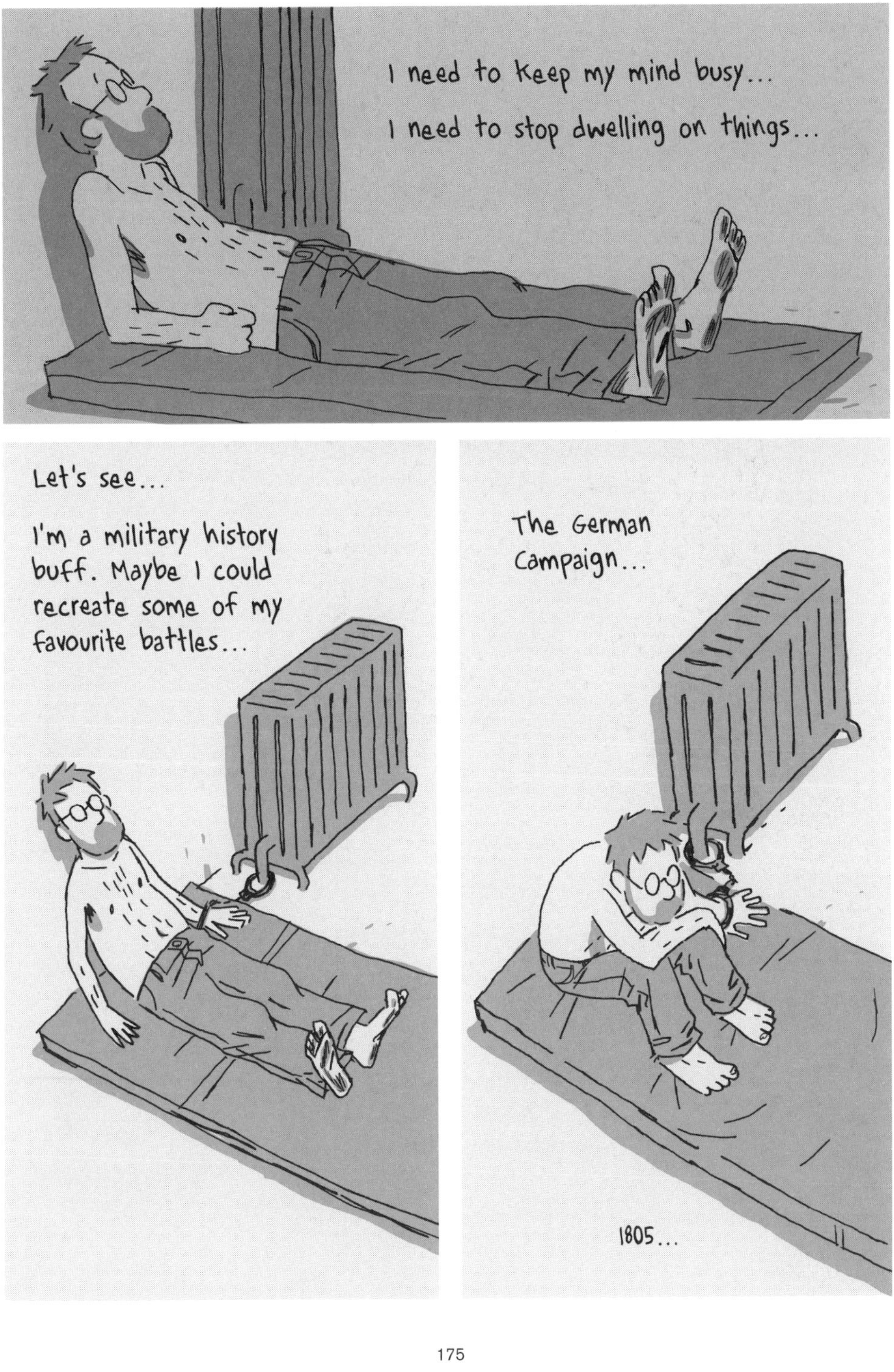
I need to keep my mind busy...
I need to stop dwelling on things...
Let's see...
I'm a military history buff. Maybe I could recreate some of my favourite battles...
The German Campaign...
1805...

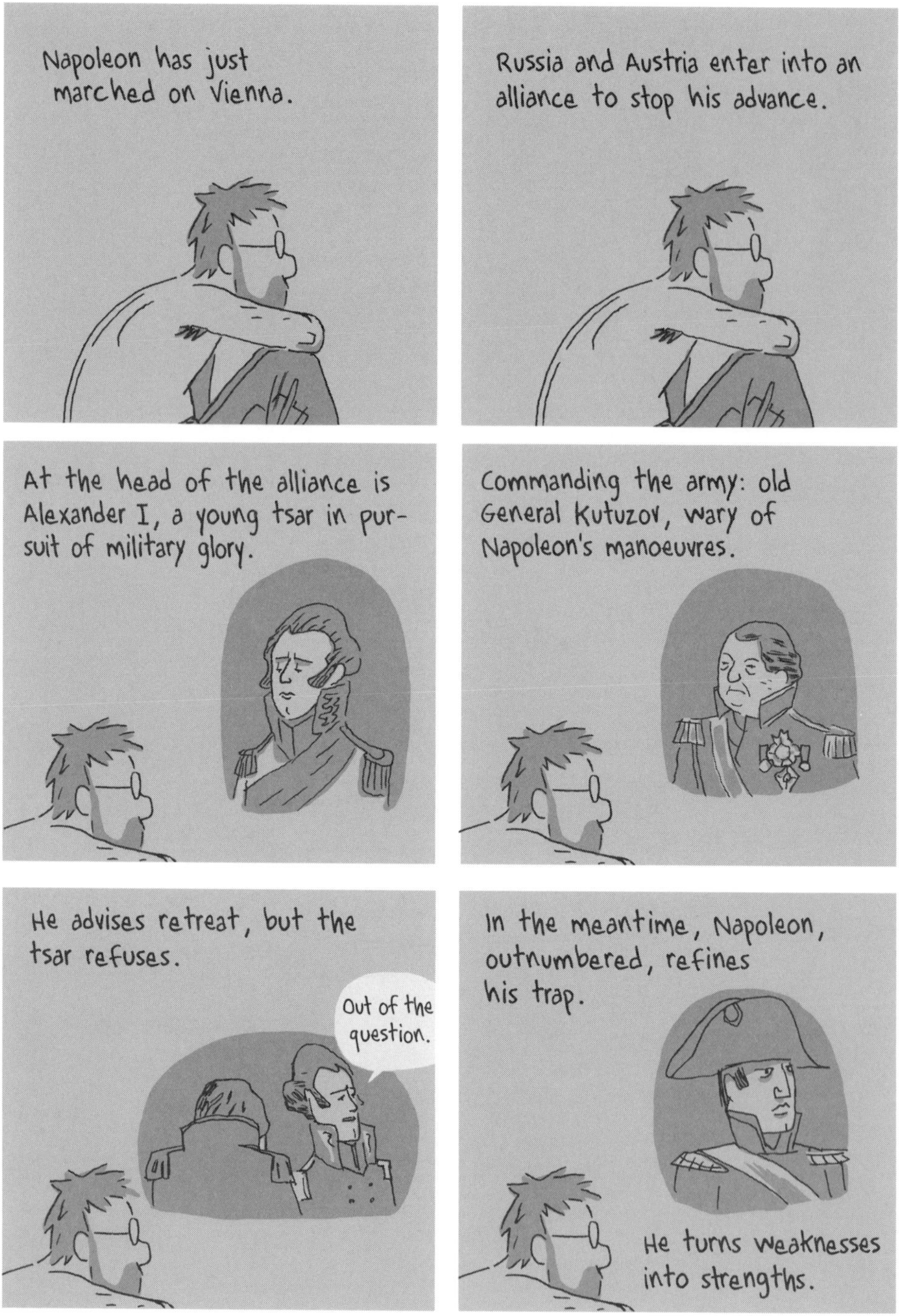
Napoleon has just marched on Vienna.
Russia and Austria enter into an alliance to stop his advance.
At the head of the alliance is Alexander I, a young tsar in pursuit of military glory.
Commanding the army: old General Kutuzov, wary of Napoleon's manoeuvres.
He advises retreat, but the tsar refuses.
Out of the question.
In the meantime, Napoleon, outnumbered, refines his trap.
He turns weaknesses into strengths.

On November 28, he pulls out his advance guard, strategically positioned on the Pratzen Heights.

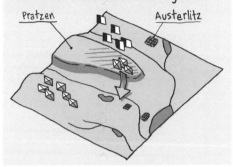

Pratzen   Austerlitz

Feigning retreat, Napoleon sends his aide-de-camp with a request for a truce. The tsar refuses.

Out of the question.

The ruse is a success. On December 2, the Russians attack the French right flank, which Bonaparte had deliberately weakened.

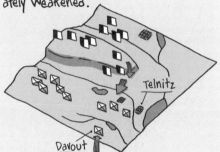

Telnitz

Davout

At dawn, Buxhoeveden descends toward Telnitz, where Davout arrives with reinforcements. Napoleon gives the signal to attack.

Let's go.

Liechtenstein deploys to the wrong location, creating confusion among the Austro-Russian troops.

Johann I, tenth prince of Liechtenstein

Davout holds firm one side of the Goldbach, while a majority of the Russian troops mass on the other.

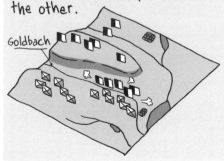

Goldbach

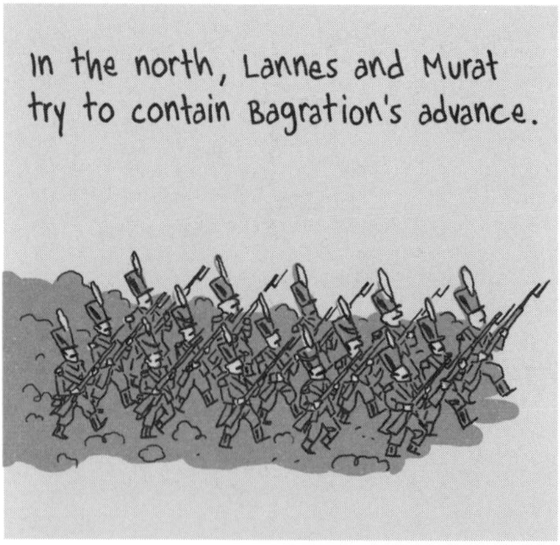
In the north, Lannes and Murat try to contain Bagration's advance.

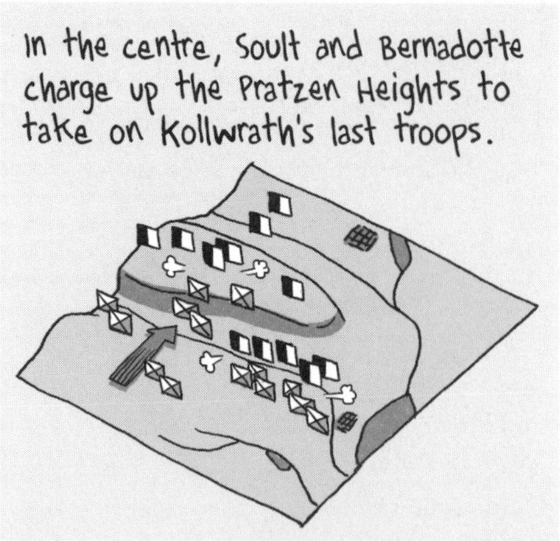
In the centre, Soult and Bernadotte charge up the Pratzen Heights to take on Kollwrath's last troops.

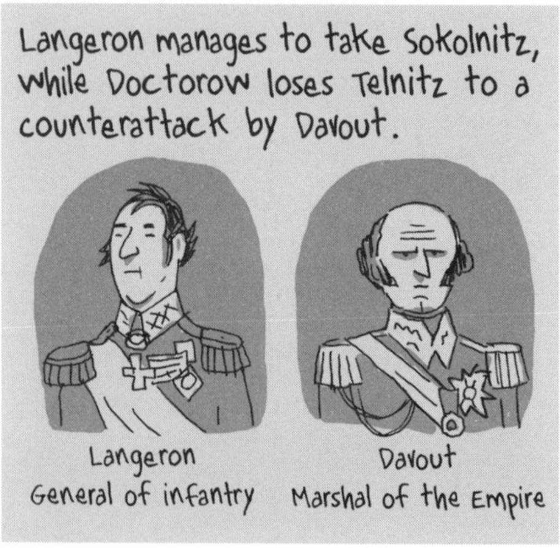
Langeron manages to take Sokolnitz, while Doctorow loses Telnitz to a counterattack by Davout.
Langeron
General of infantry
Davout
Marshal of the Empire

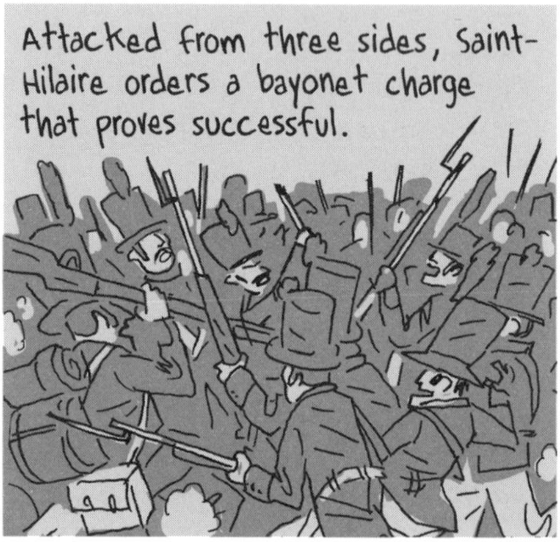
Attacked from three sides, Saint-Hilaire orders a bayonet charge that proves successful.

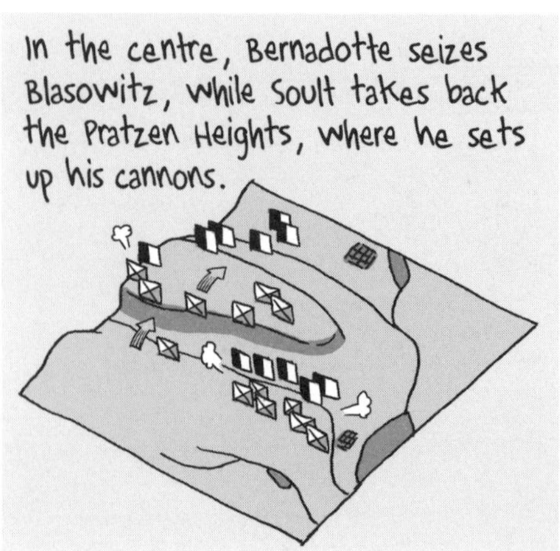
In the centre, Bernadotte seizes Blasowitz, while Soult takes back the Pratzen Heights, where he sets up his cannons.

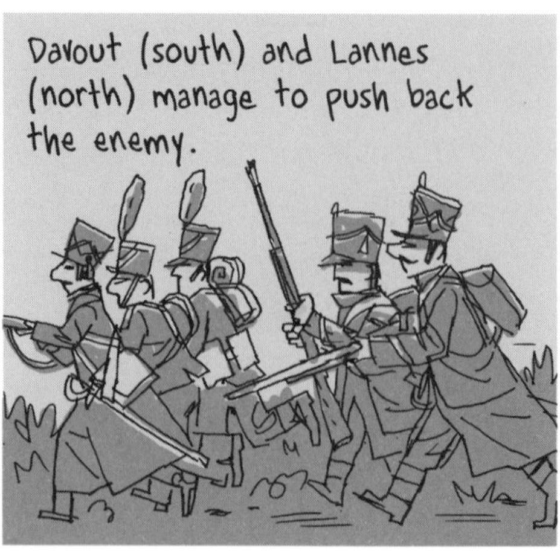
Davout (south) and Lannes (north) manage to push back the enemy.

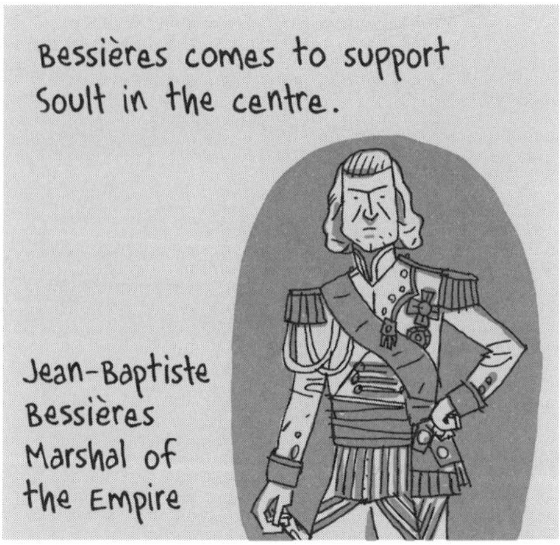
Bessières comes to support Soult in the centre.
Jean-Baptiste Bessières Marshal of the Empire

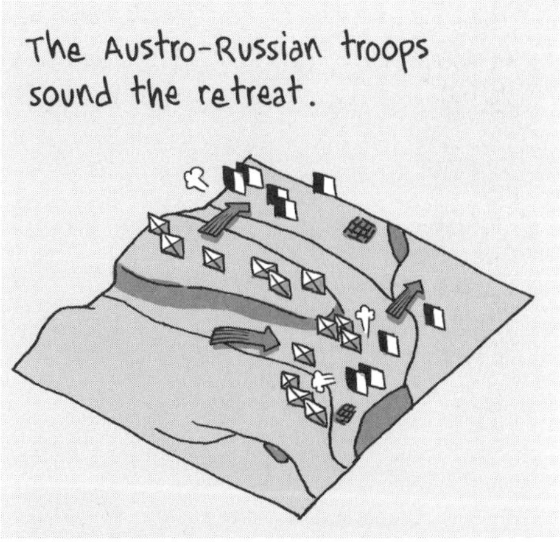
The Austro-Russian troops sound the retreat.

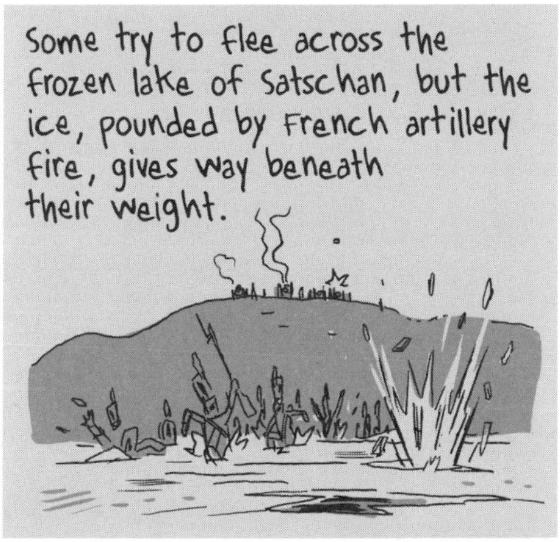
Some try to flee across the frozen lake of Satschan, but the ice, pounded by French artillery fire, gives way beneath their weight.

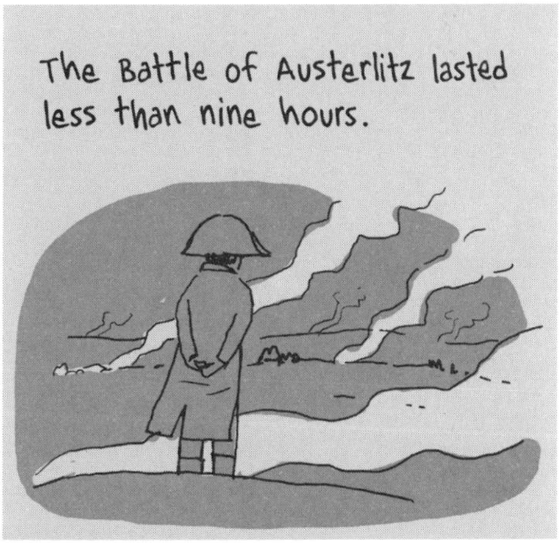
The Battle of Austerlitz lasted less than nine hours.

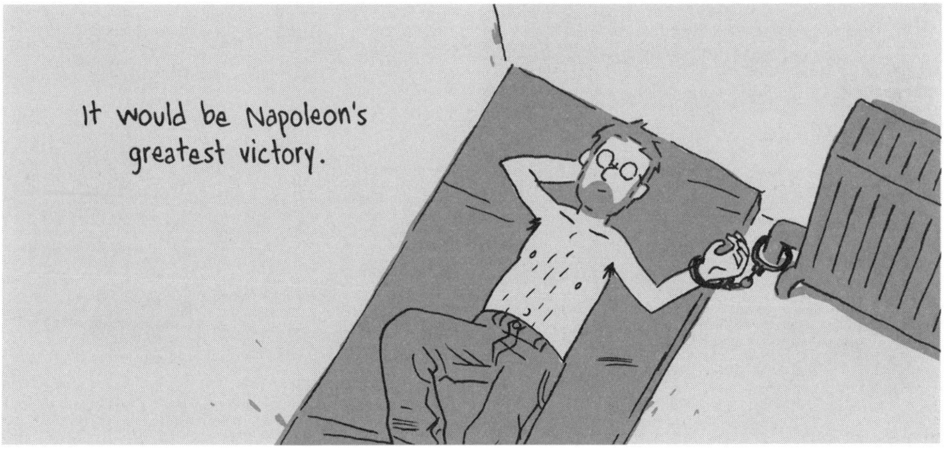
It would be Napoleon's greatest victory.

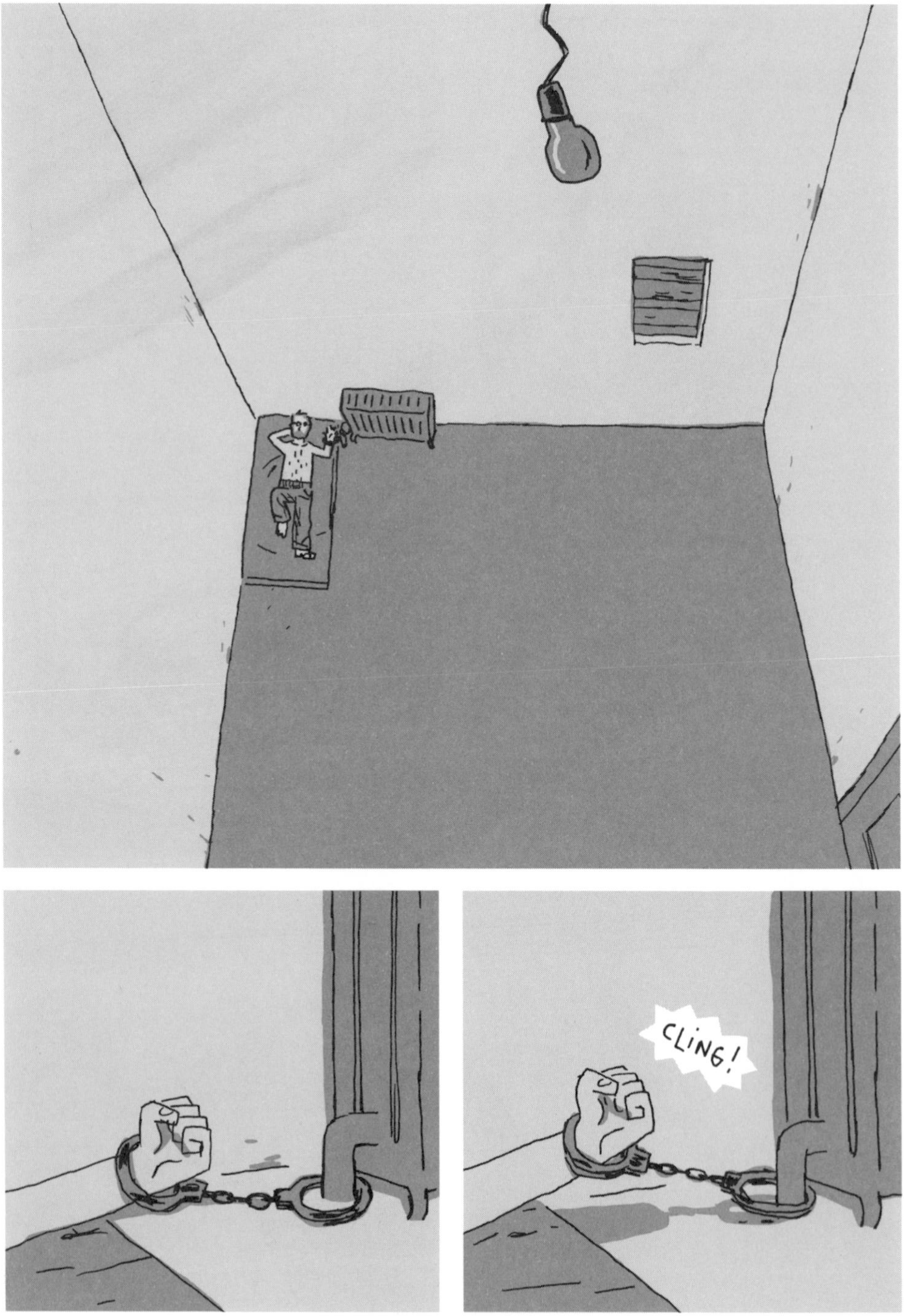
CLING!

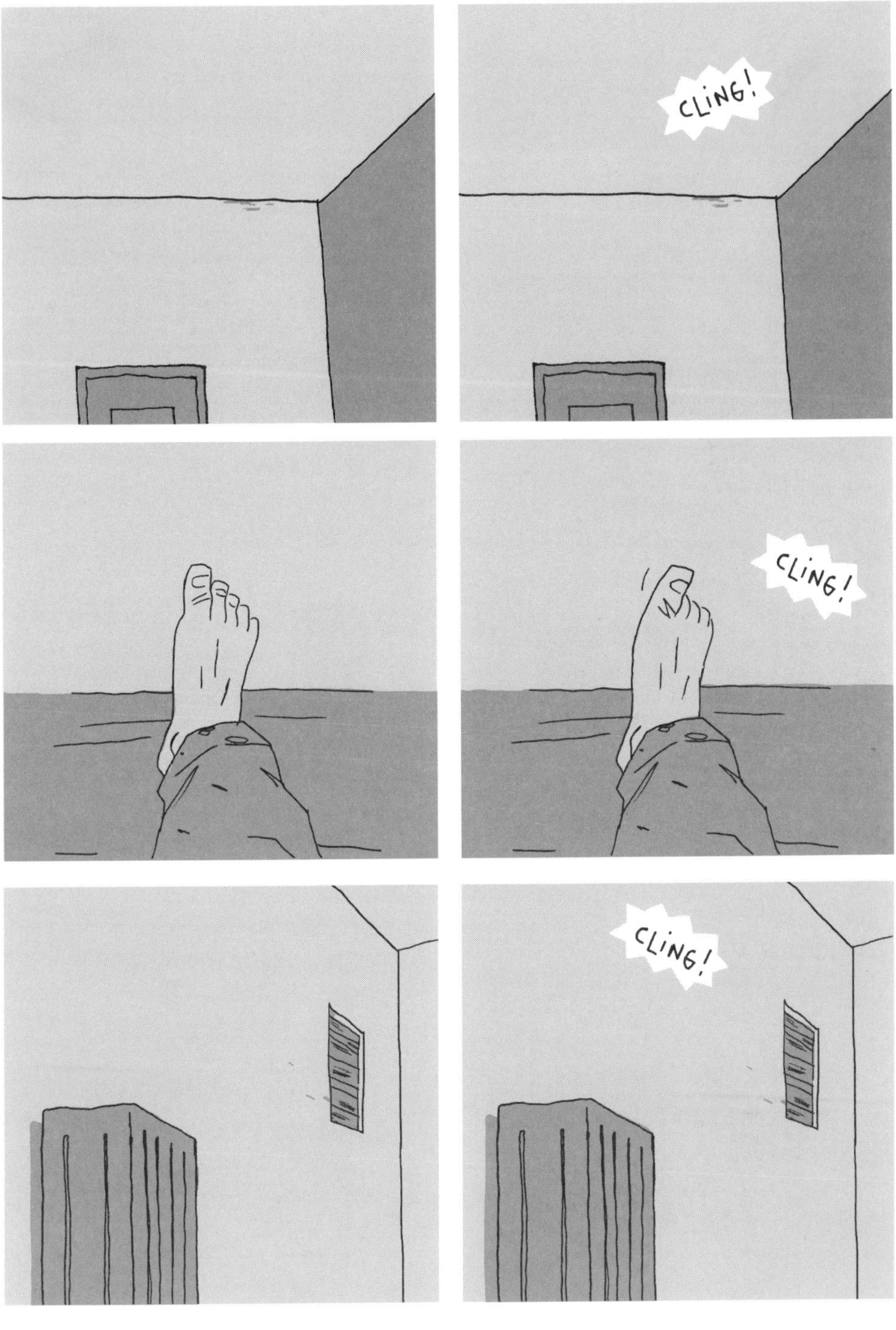
CLING!
CLING!
CLING!

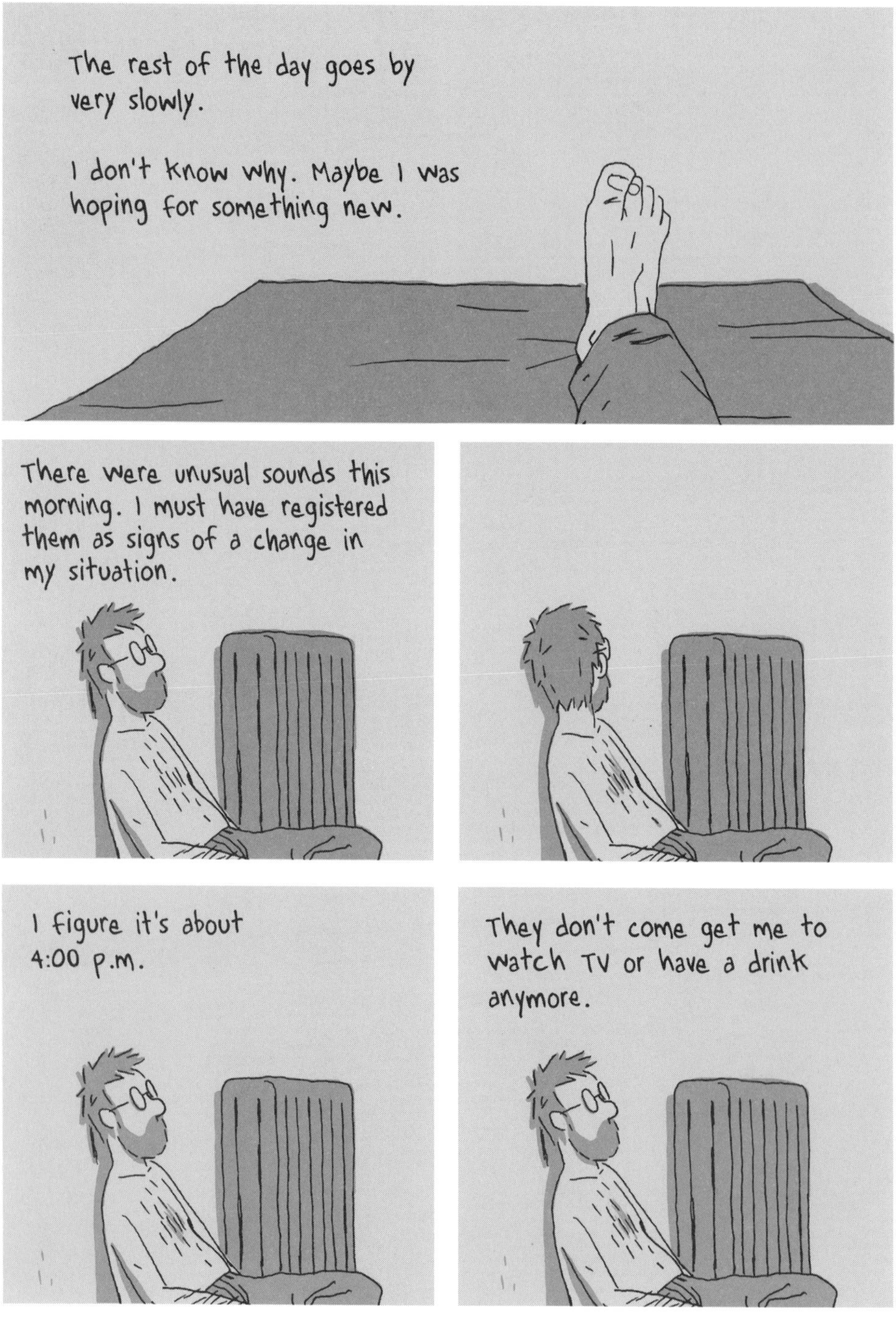
The rest of the day goes by very slowly.
I don't know why. Maybe I was hoping for something new.
There were unusual sounds this morning. I must have registered them as signs of a change in my situation.
I figure it's about 4:00 p.m.
They don't come get me to watch TV or have a drink anymore.

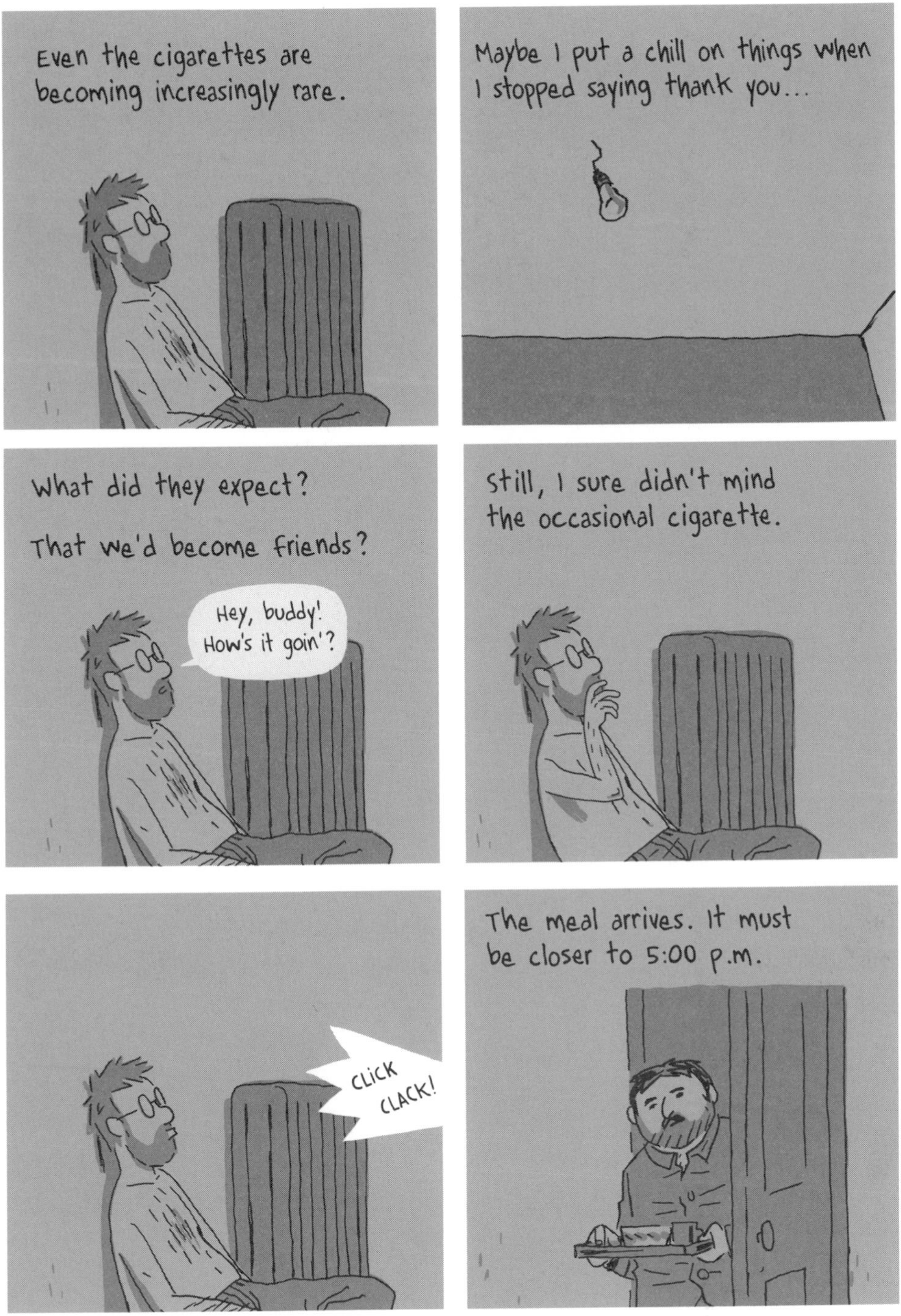
Even the cigarettes are becoming increasingly rare.
Maybe I put a chill on things when I stopped saying thank you...
What did they expect?
That we'd become friends?
Hey, buddy! How's it goin'?
Still, I sure didn't mind the occasional cigarette.
CLICK CLACK!
The meal arrives. It must be closer to 5:00 p.m.

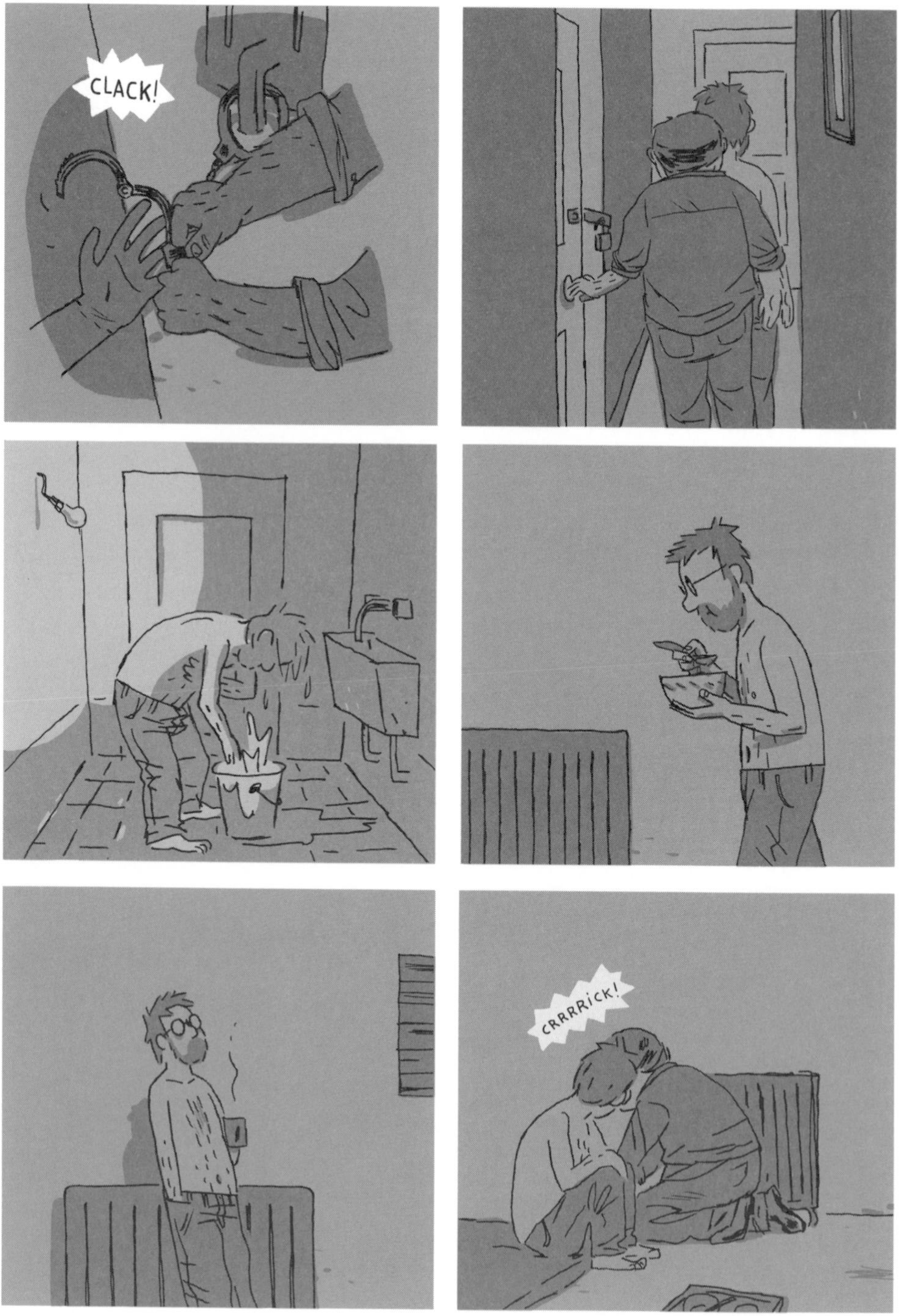
CLACK!
CRRRRICK!

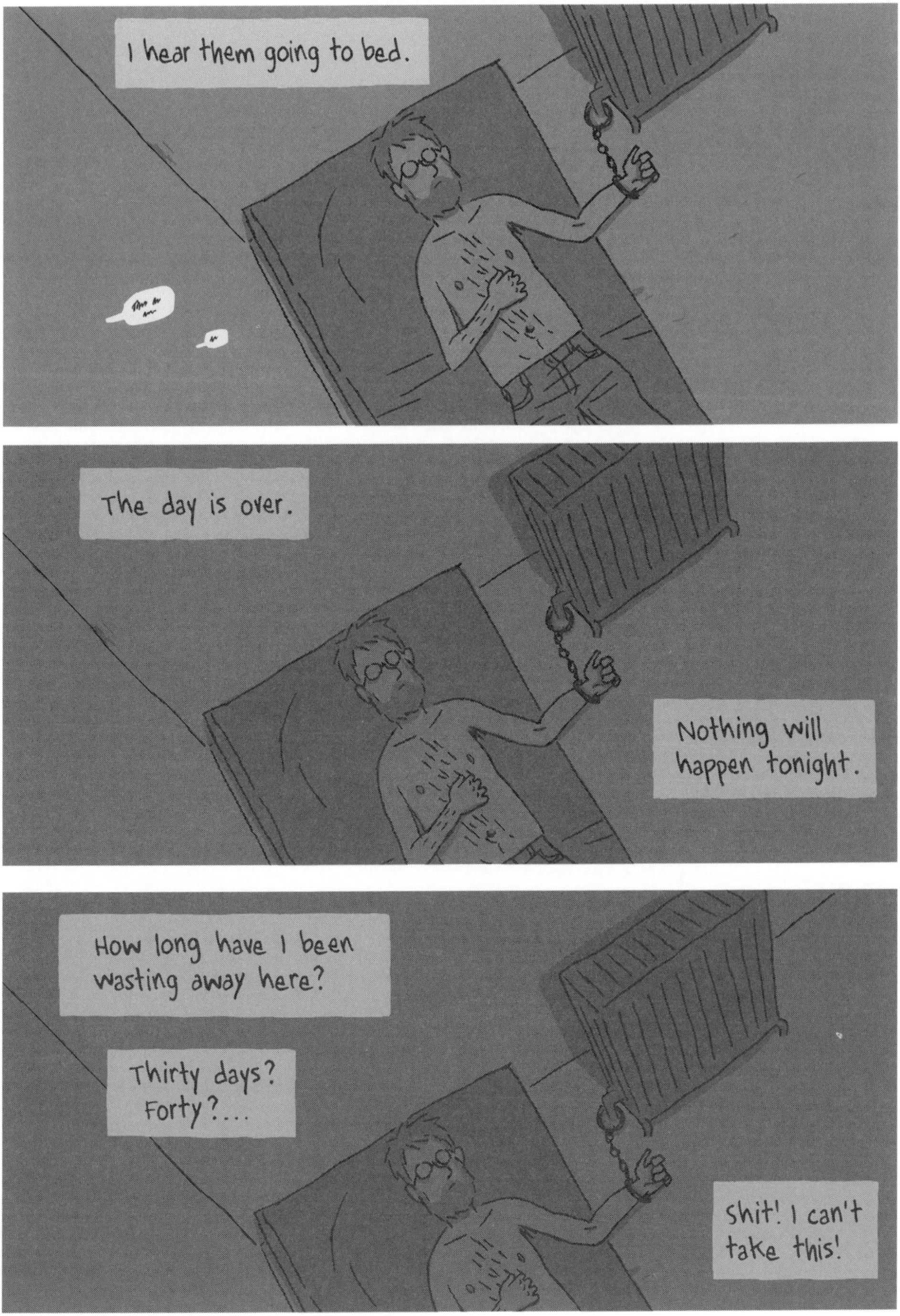
I hear them going to bed.
The day is over.
Nothing will happen tonight.
How long have I been wasting away here?
Thirty days? Forty?...
Shit! I can't take this!

44

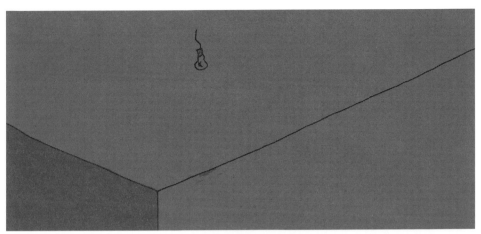

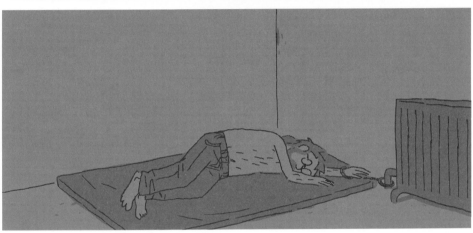

Today is August 15.

Friday, August 15.

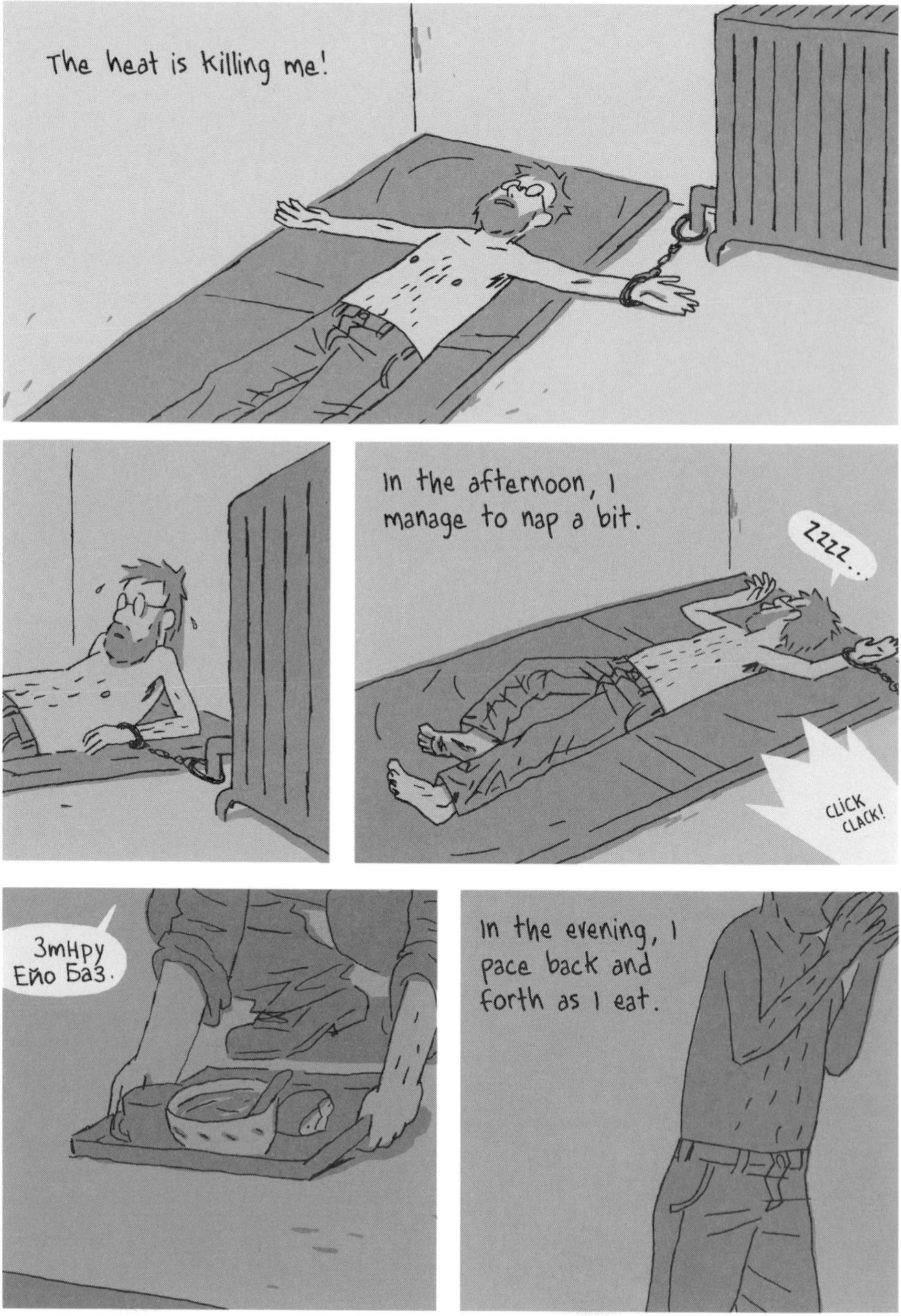
The heat is killing me!
In the afternoon, I manage to nap a bit.
Zzzz...
CLICK CLACK!
ЗмНру Ейо Баз.
In the evening, I pace back and forth as I eat.

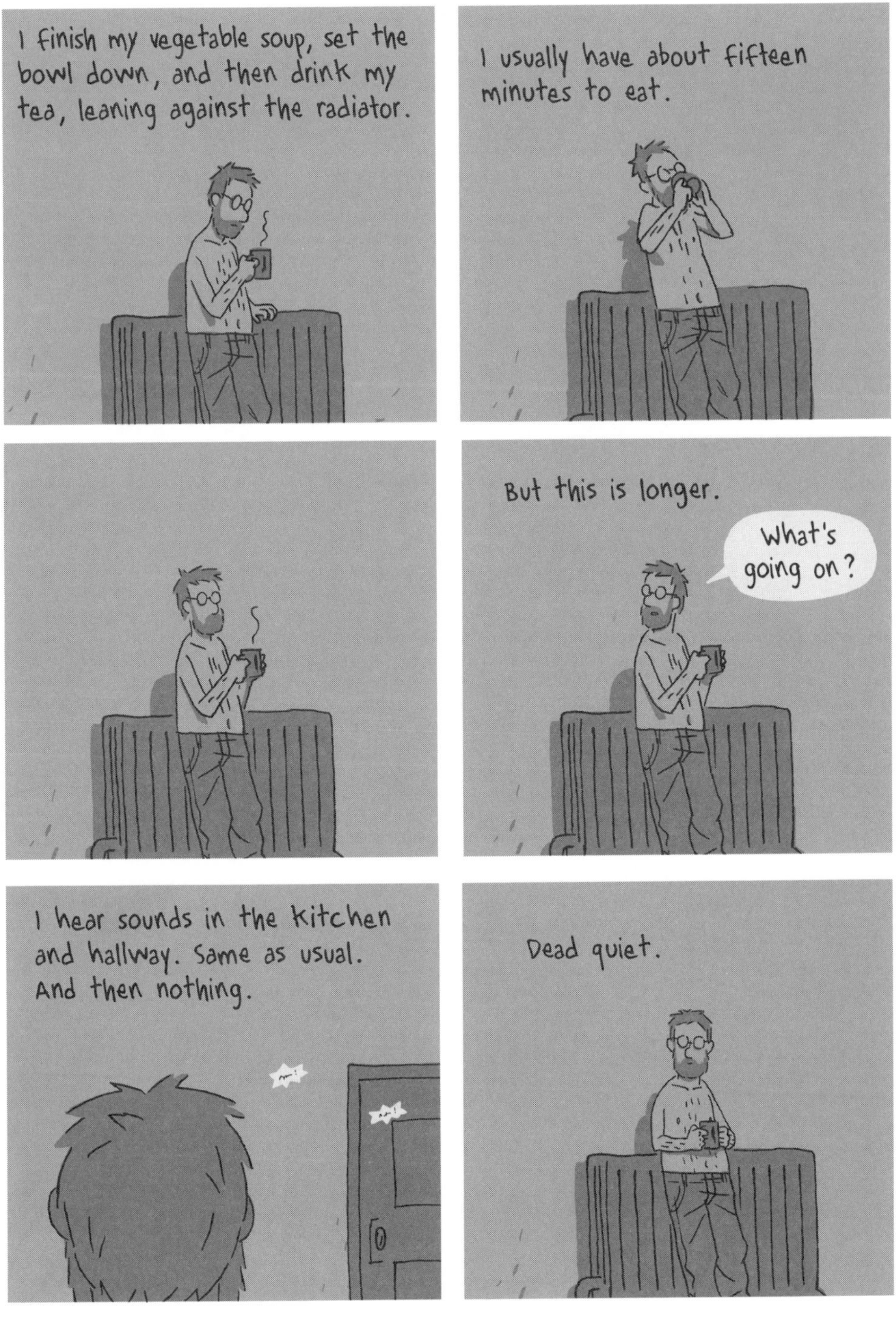
I finish my vegetable soup, set the bowl down, and then drink my tea, leaning against the radiator.
I usually have about fifteen minutes to eat.
But this is longer.
What's going on?
I hear sounds in the kitchen and hallway. Same as usual. And then nothing.
Dead quiet.

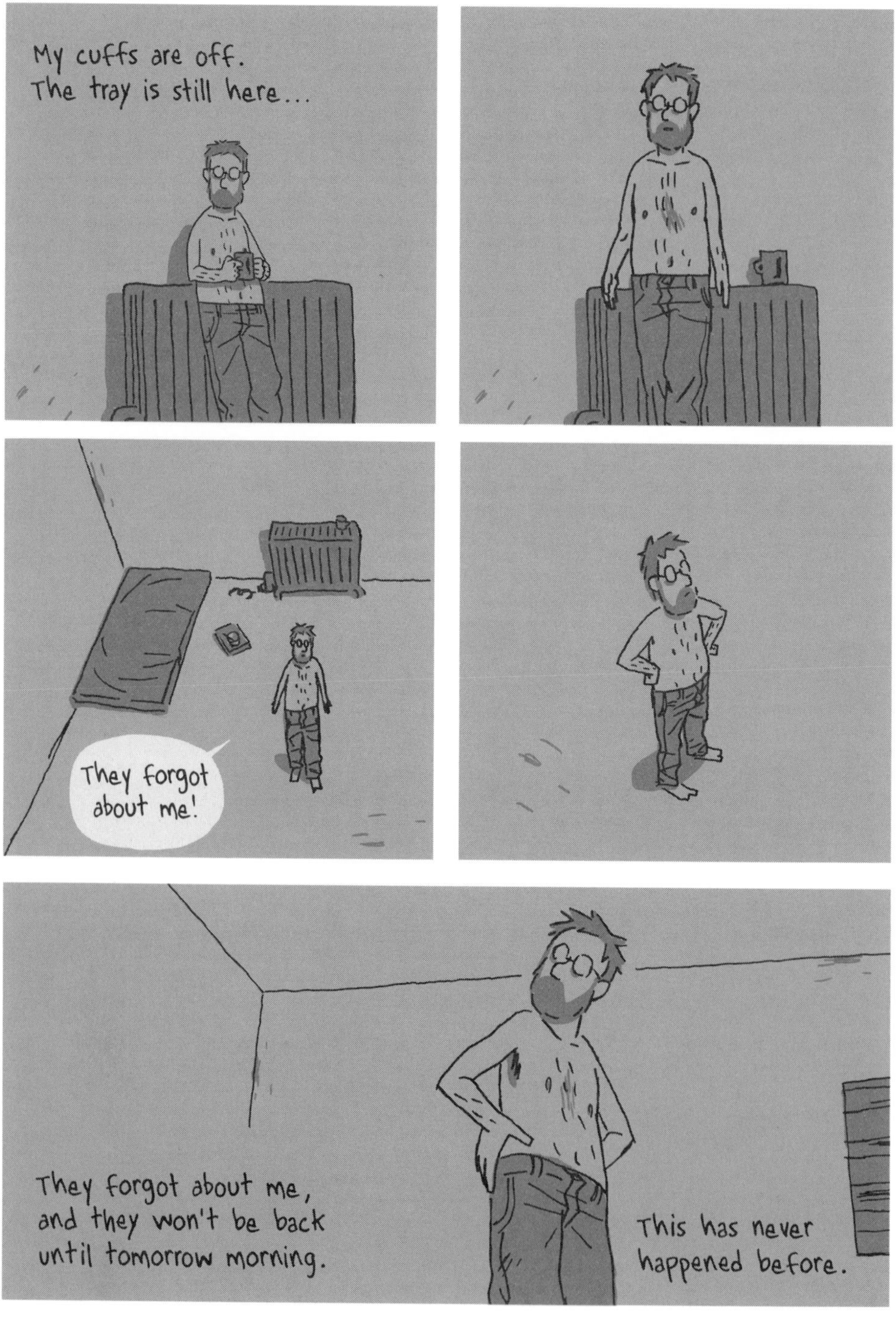
My cuffs are off.
The tray is still here...
They forgot about me!
They forgot about me, and they won't be back until tomorrow morning.
This has never happened before.

For the first time, I can walk around the room for more than fifteen minutes.

Without being under anybody's control.

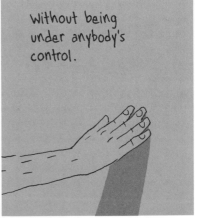

Wow!

I touch the back wall.

I feel like a kid breaking a rule.

The back wall.

An ounce of freedom suddenly reappears.

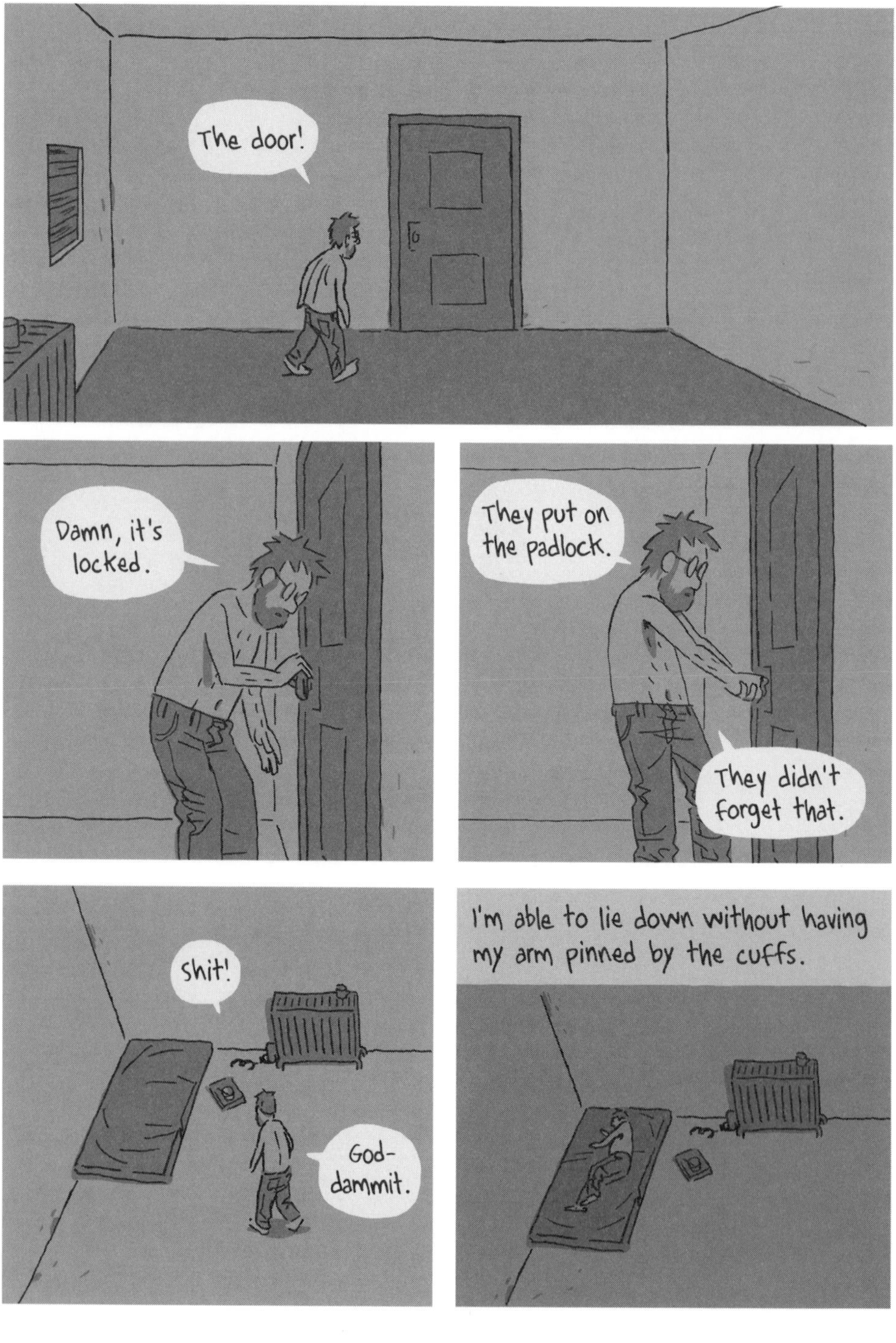
The door!
Damn, it's locked.
They put on the padlock.
They didn't forget that.
Shit!
God-dammit.
I'm able to lie down without having my arm pinned by the cuffs.

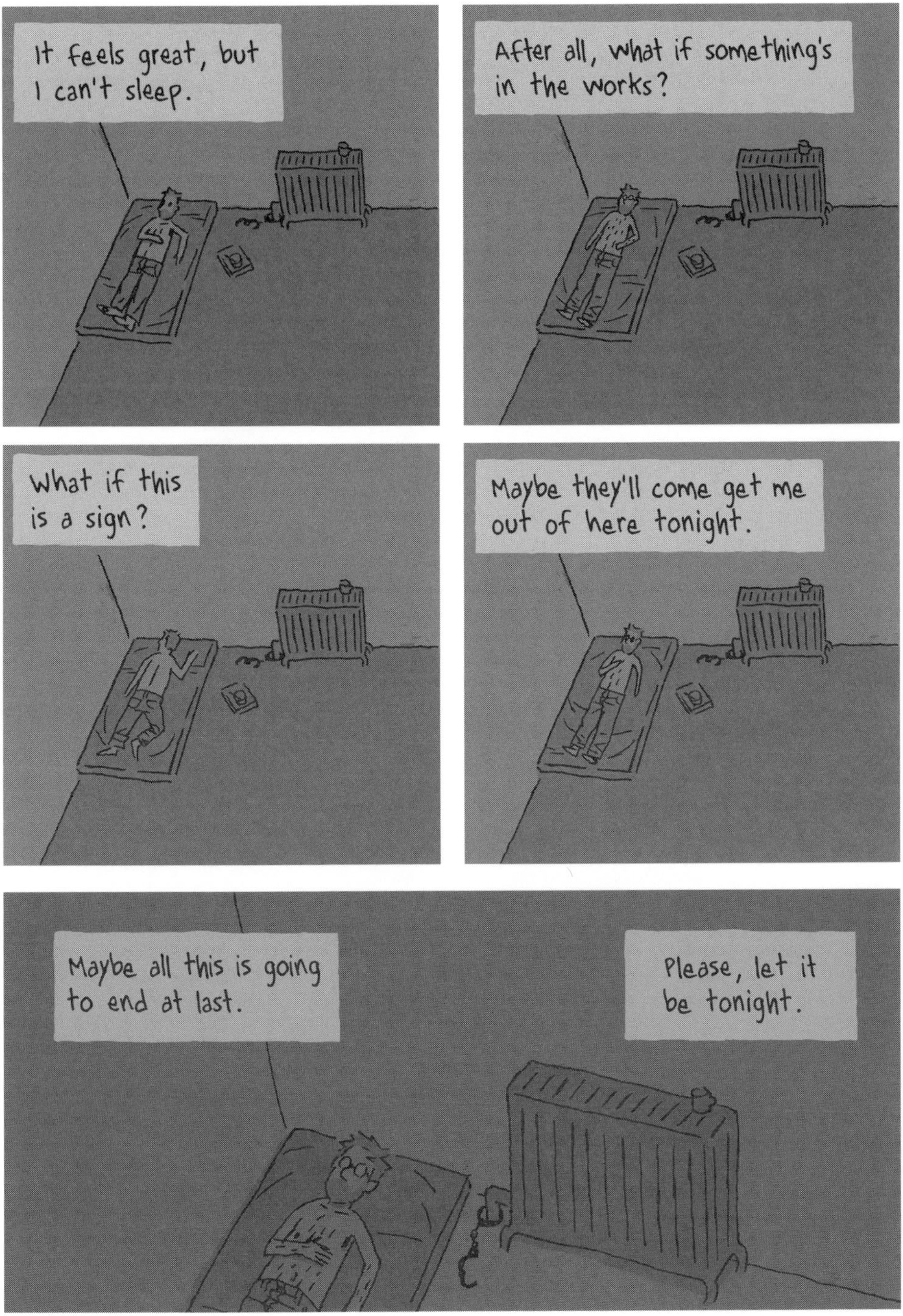
It feels great, but I can't sleep.
After all, what if something's in the works?
What if this is a sign?
Maybe they'll come get me out of here tonight.
Maybe all this is going to end at last.
Please, let it be tonight.

45

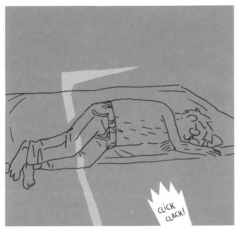

CLICK
CLACK!

The next day, it's the tall guy bringing the morning meal.

When he sees that I'm not attached, he smiles.

ФтнРУ
ЕЙЅ БЕЗ!

I get the feeling he's laughing at me. One more bit of humiliation.

He sets down the meal, takes the other tray, and we head for the toilet.

I eat, he comes back, and he cuffs me. My moment of freedom is over.

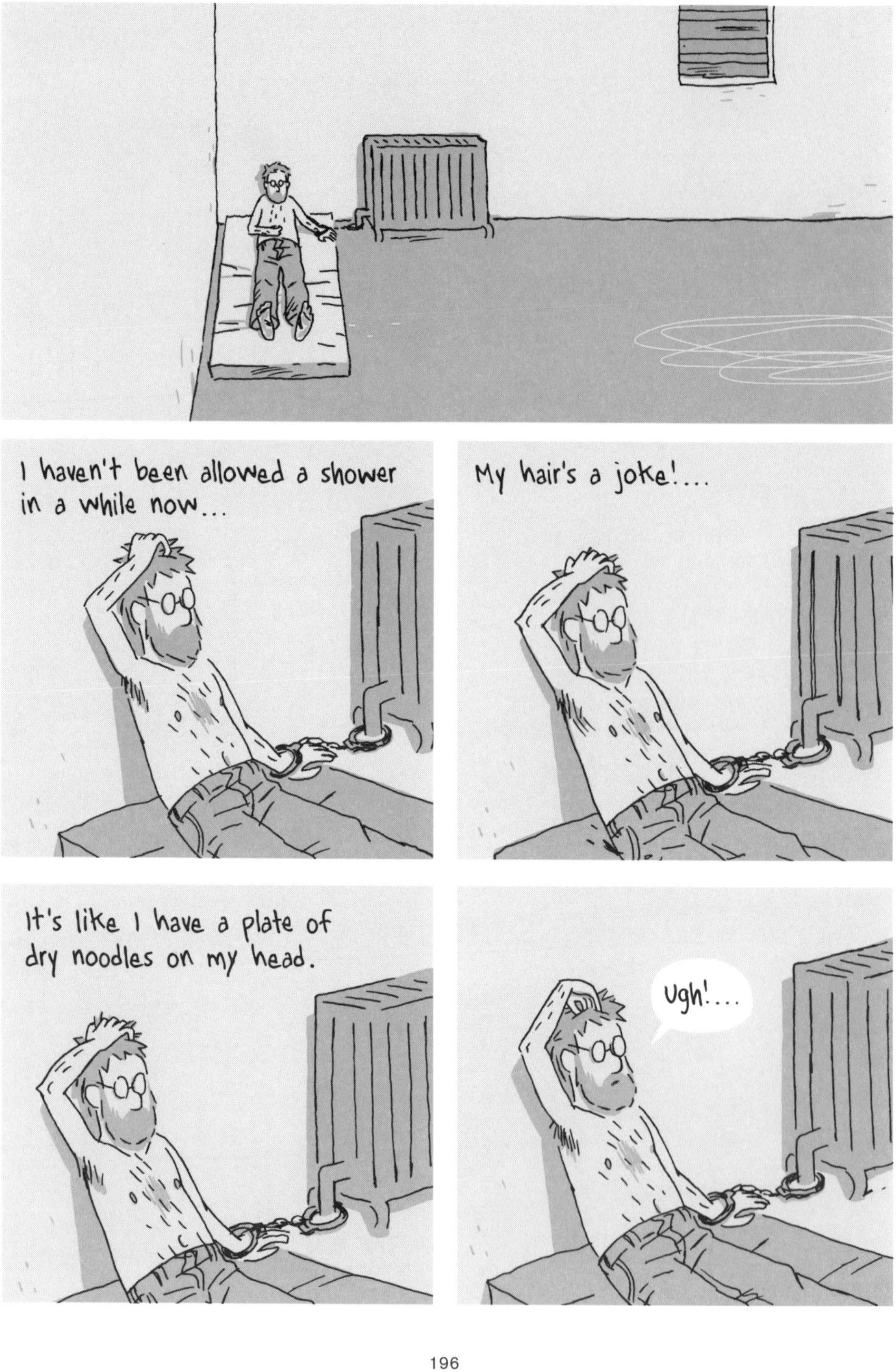
I haven't been allowed a shower in a while now...
My hair's a joke!...
It's like I have a plate of dry noodles on my head.
Ugh!...

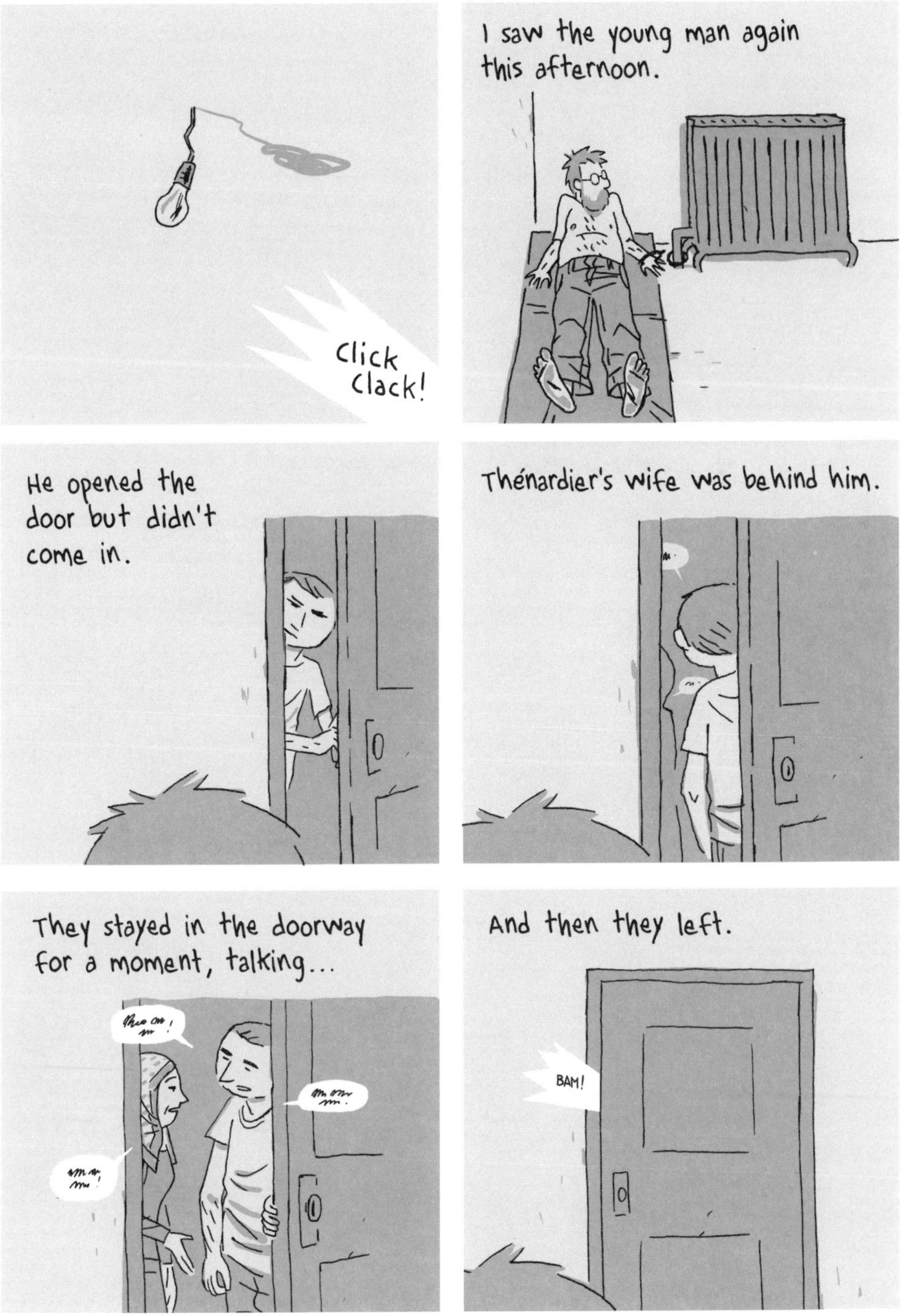

Click
Clack!
I saw the young man again this afternoon.
He opened the door but didn't come in.
Thénardier's wife was behind him.
They stayed in the doorway for a moment, talking...
And then they left.
BAM!

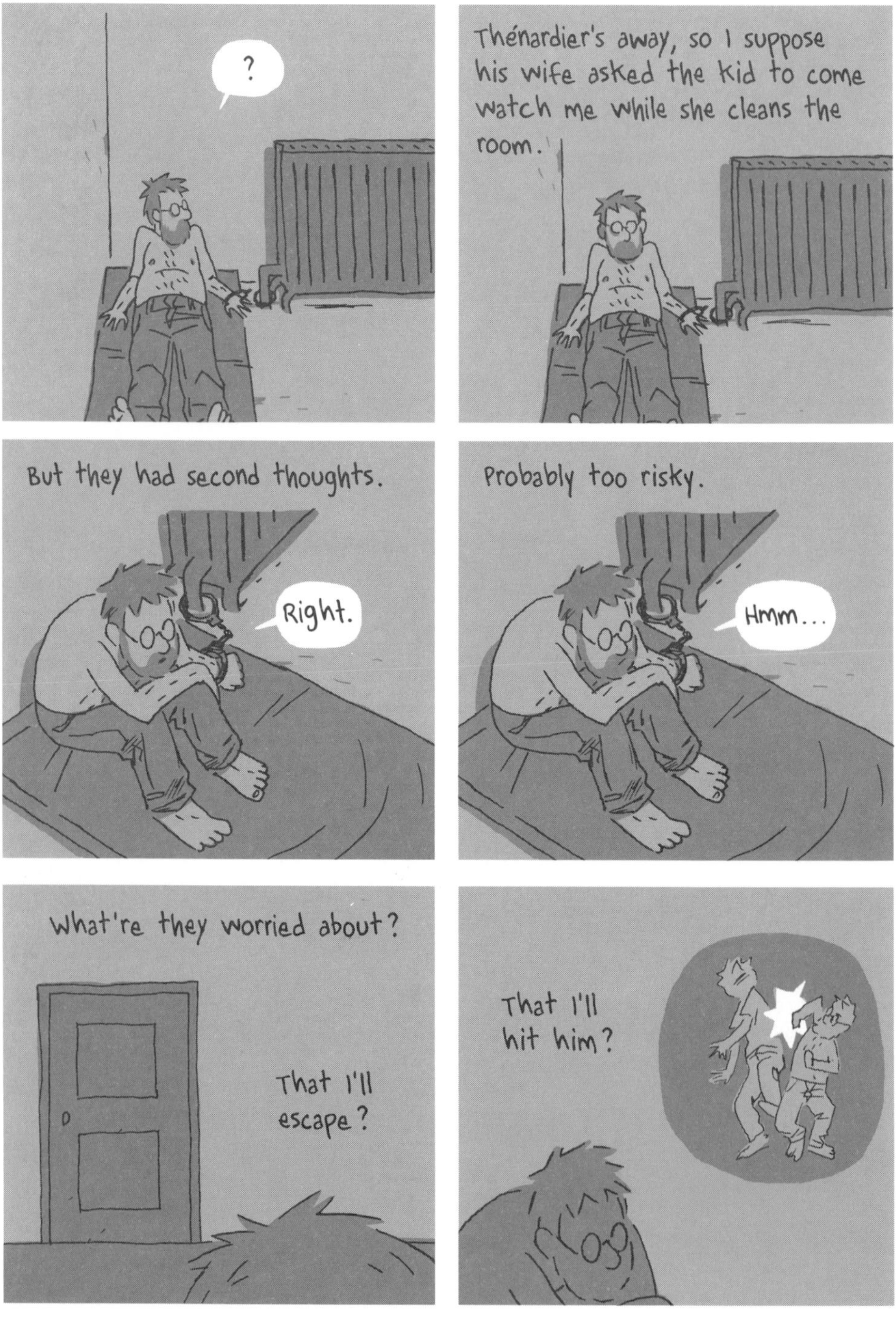
?
Thénardier's away, so I suppose his wife asked the kid to come watch me while she cleans the room.
But they had second thoughts.
Right.
Probably too risky.
Hmm...
What're they worried about?
That I'll escape?
That I'll hit him?

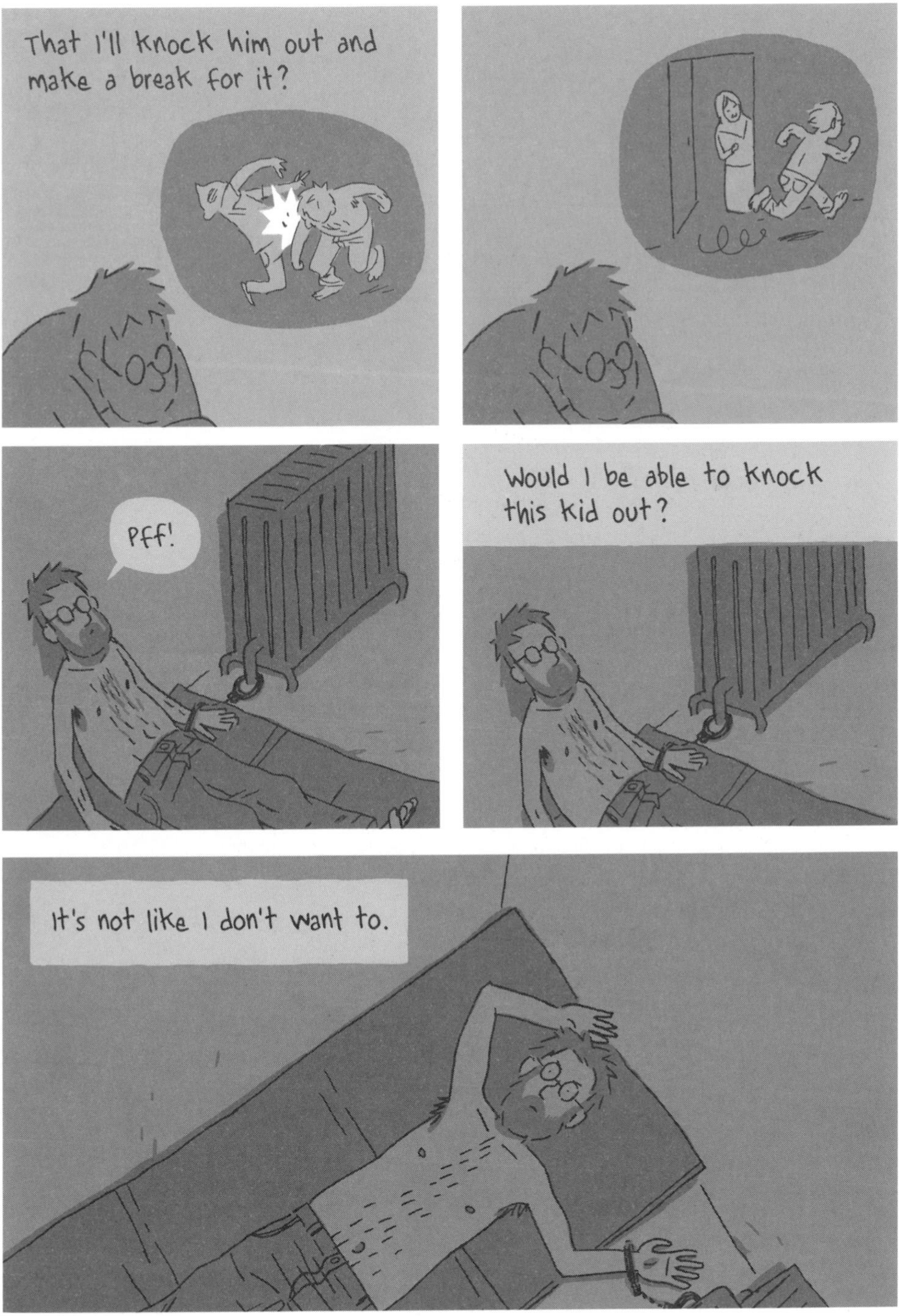
That I'll knock him out and make a break for it?
PFF!
Would I be able to knock this kid out?
It's not like I don't want to.

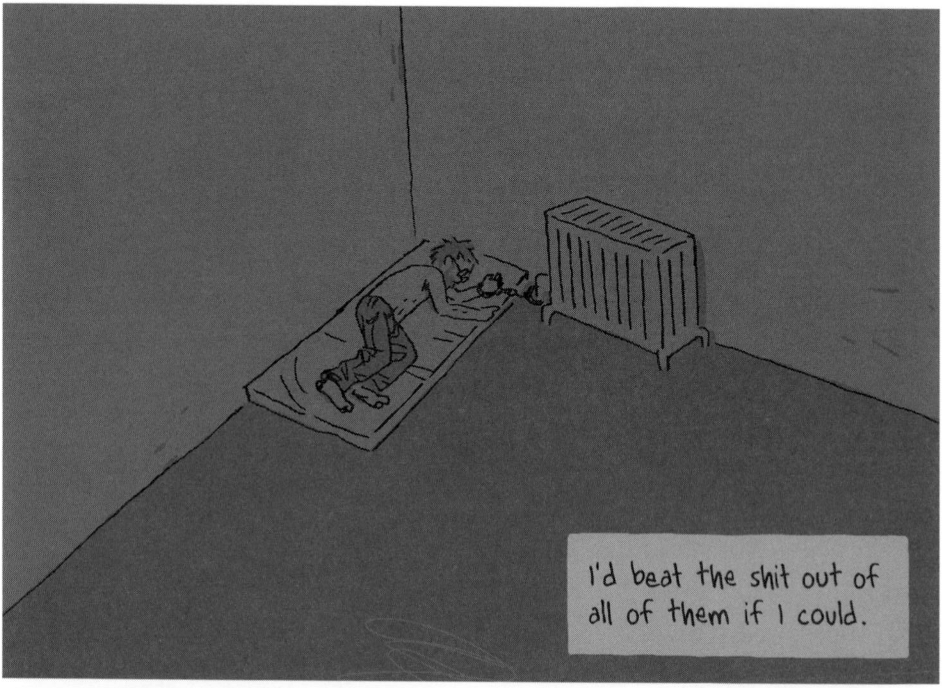
I'd beat the shit out of all of them if I could.

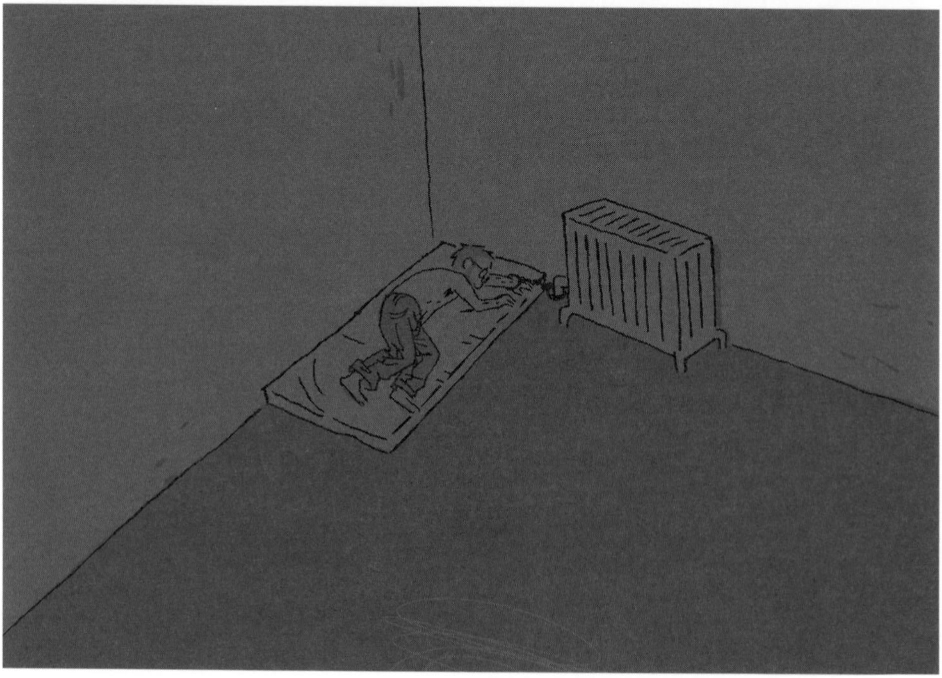

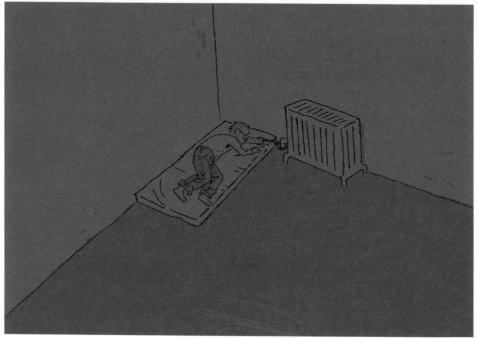

51

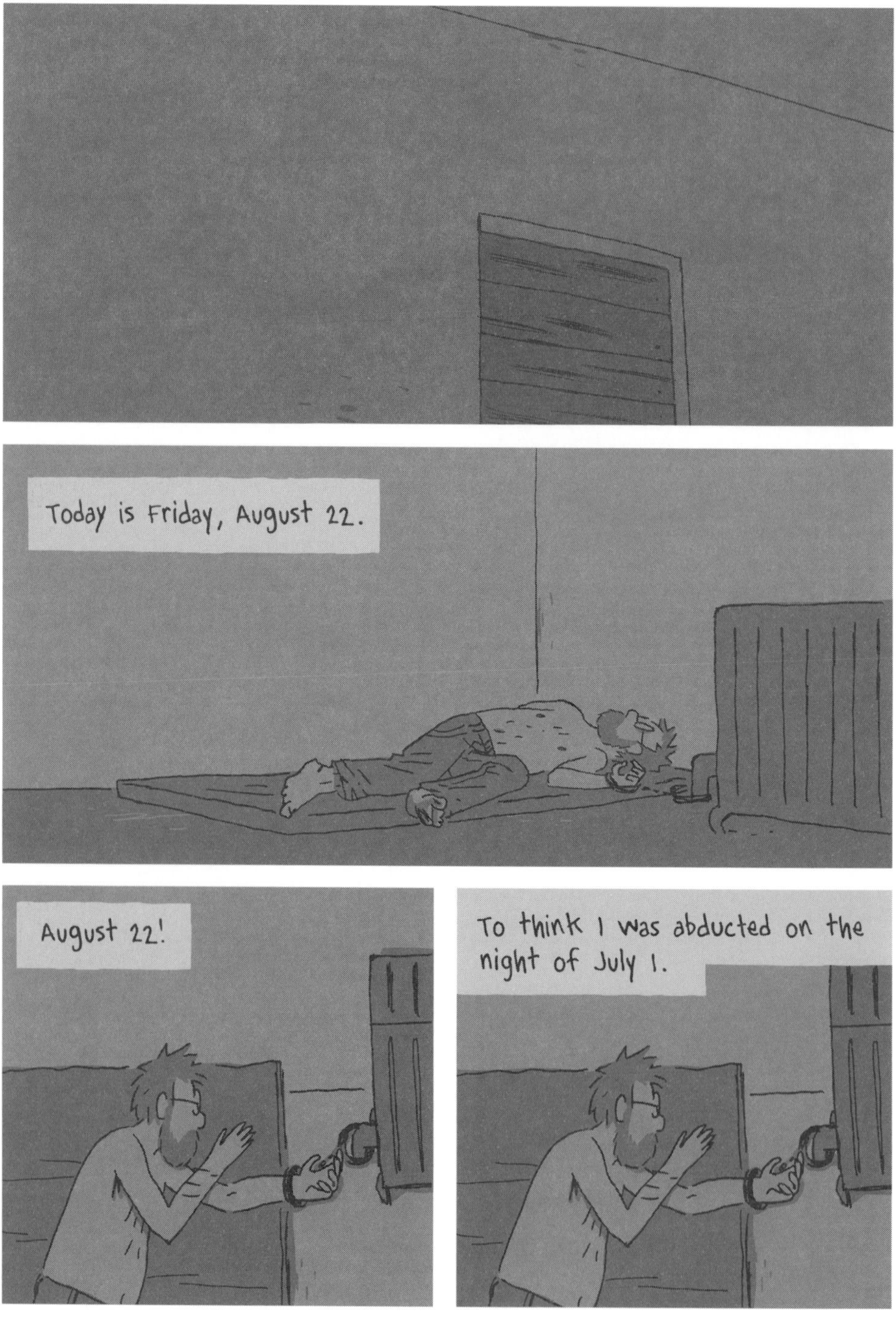
Today is Friday, August 22.
August 22!
To think I was abducted on the night of July 1.

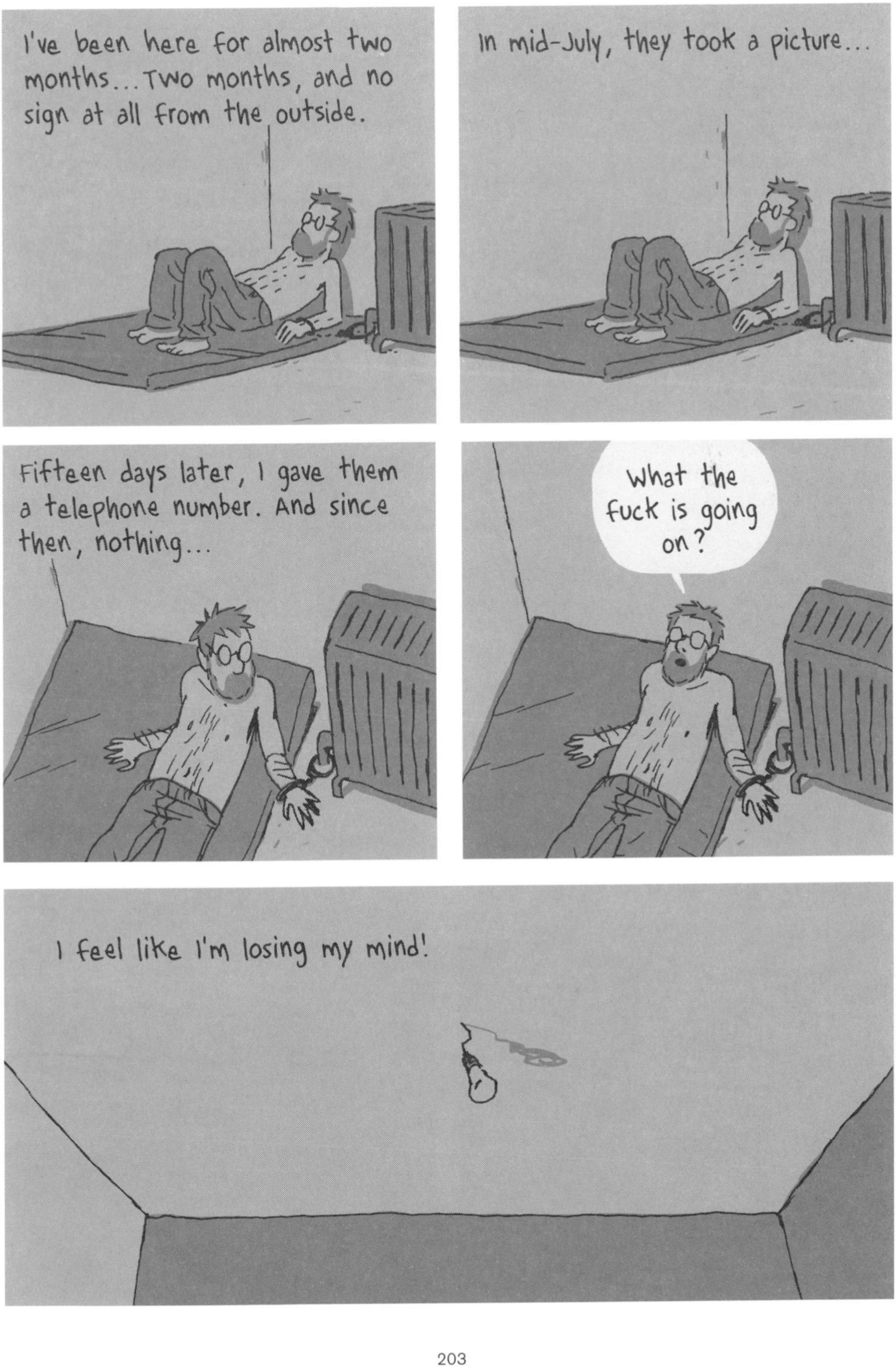
I've been here for almost two months... Two months, and no sign at all from the outside.
In mid-July, they took a picture...
Fifteen days later, I gave them a telephone number. And since then, nothing...
What the fuck is going on?
I feel like I'm losing my mind!

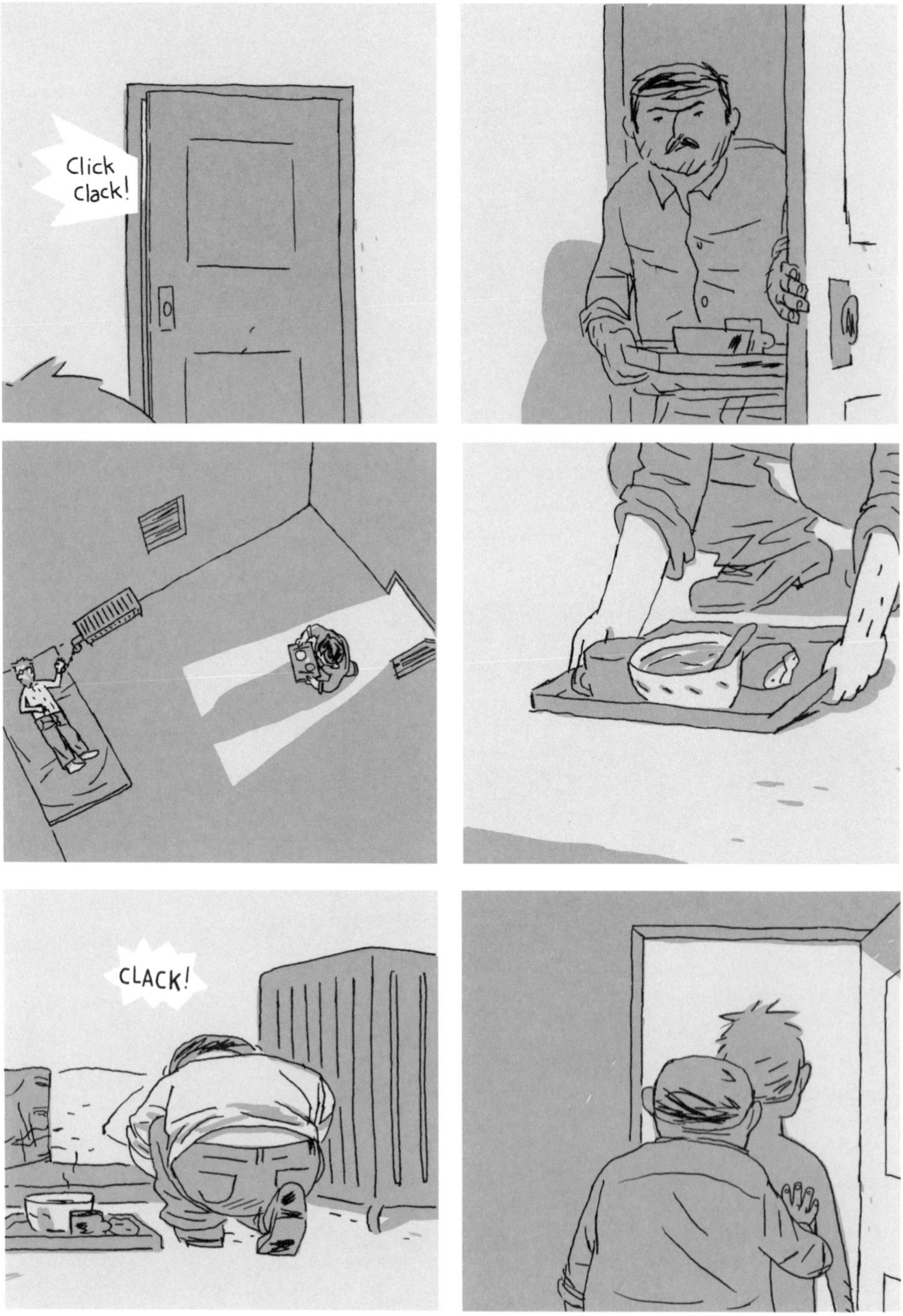
Click
Clack!
CLACK!

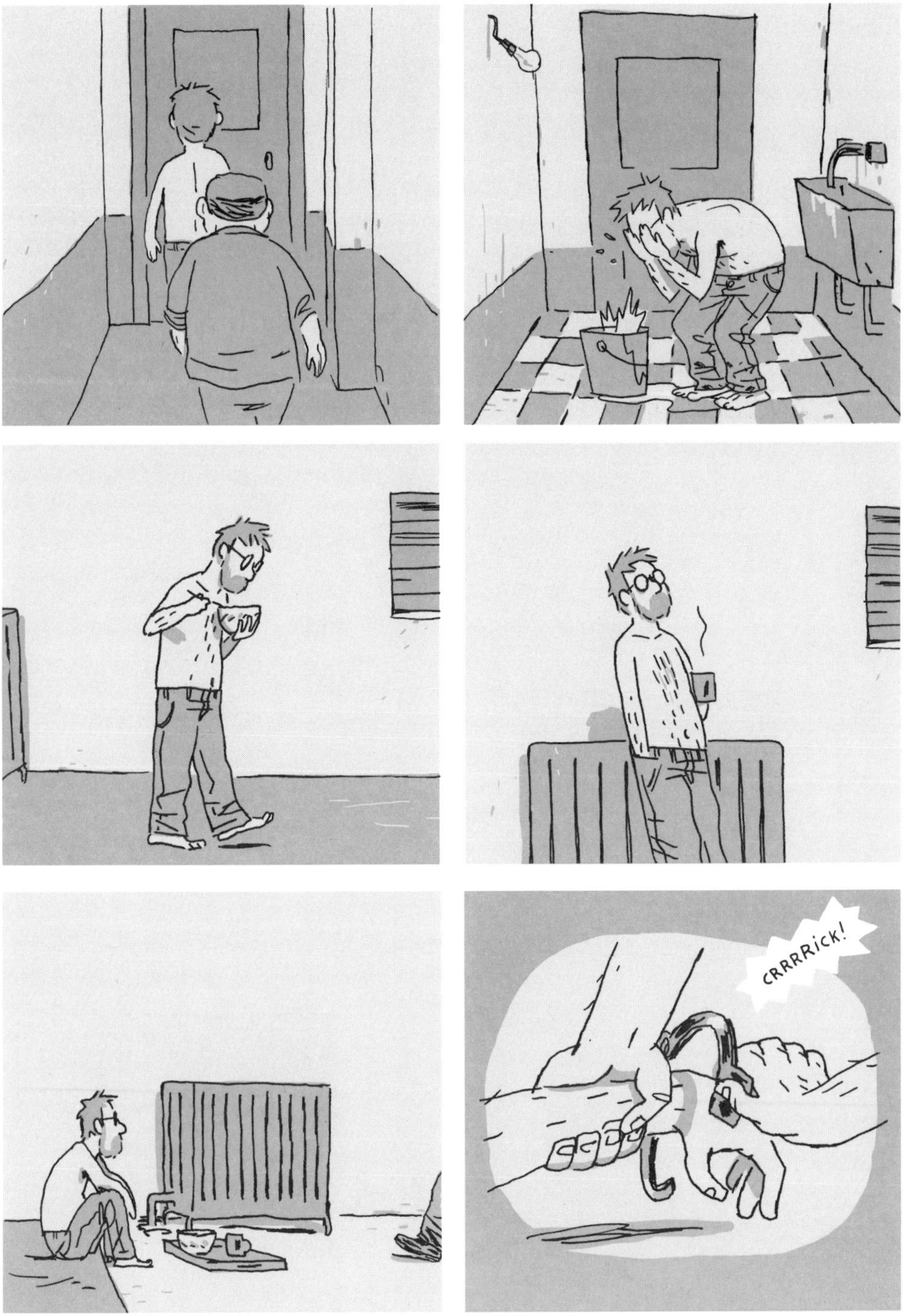
CRRRRICK!

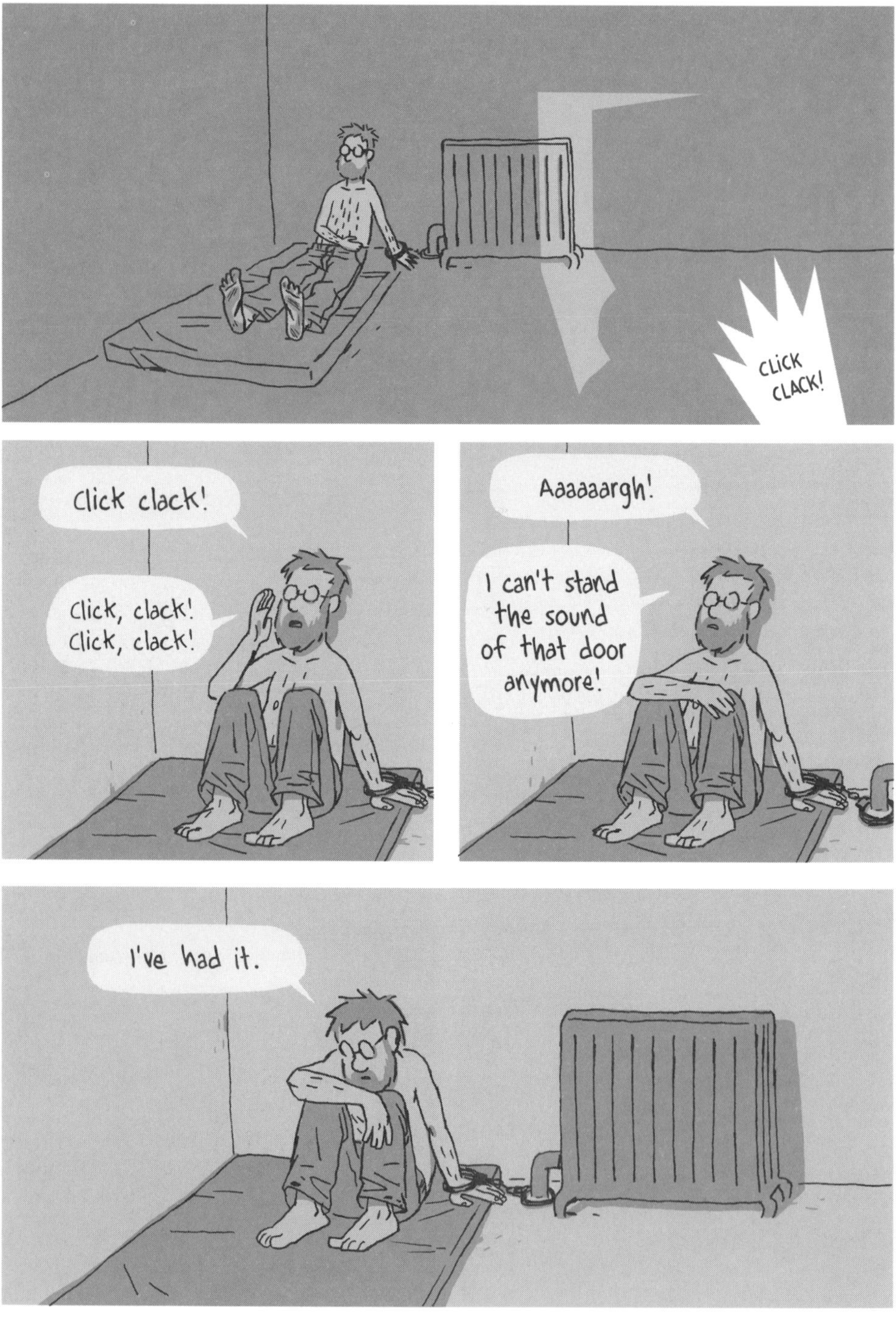
CLICK CLACK!
Click clack!
Click, clack! Click, clack!
Aaaaaargh!
I can't stand the sound of that door anymore!
I've had it.

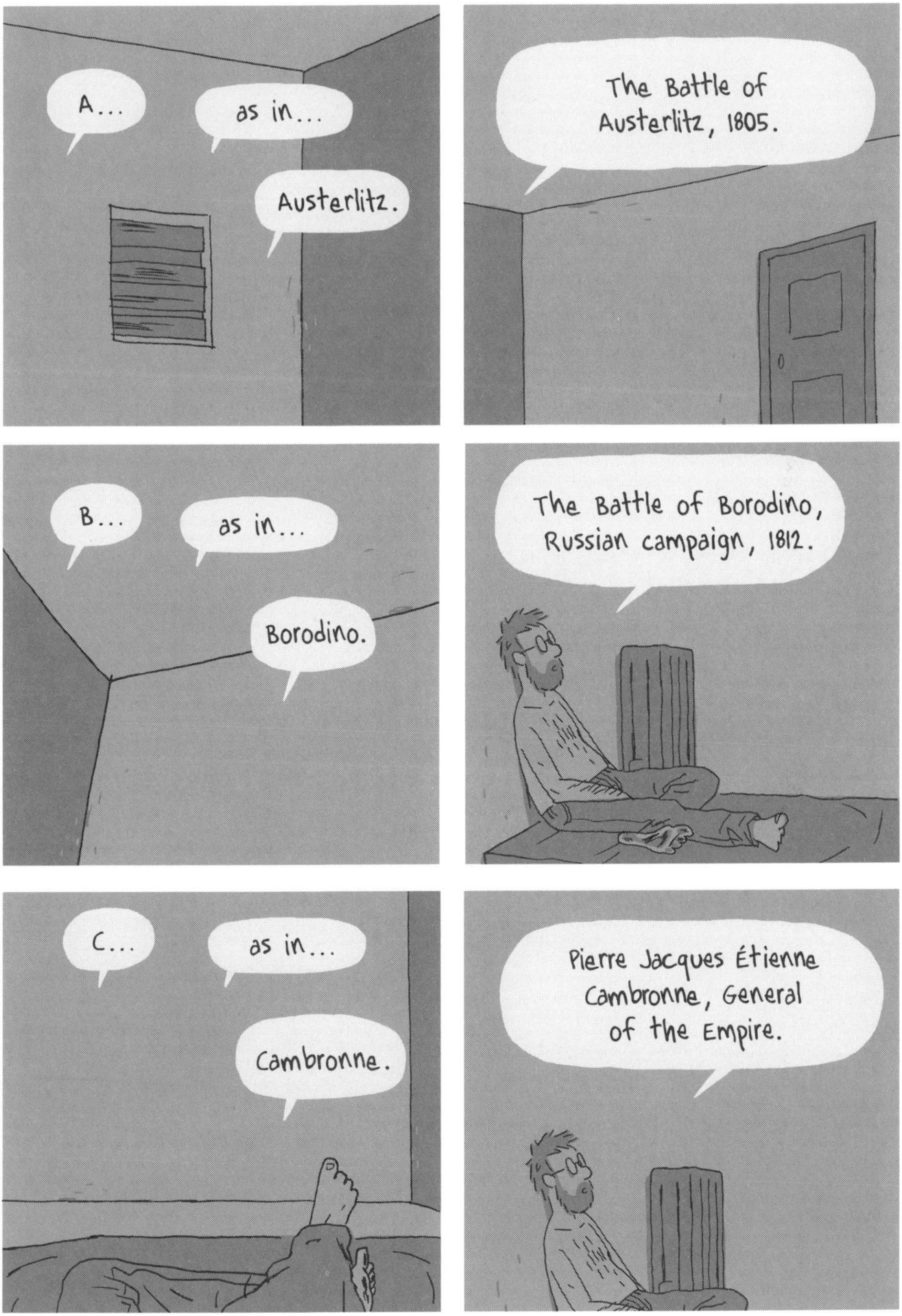
A...
as in...
Austerlitz.
The Battle of Austerlitz, 1805.
B...
as in...
Borodino.
The Battle of Borodino, Russian campaign, 1812.
C...
as in...
Cambronne.
Pierre Jacques Étienne Cambronne, General of the Empire.

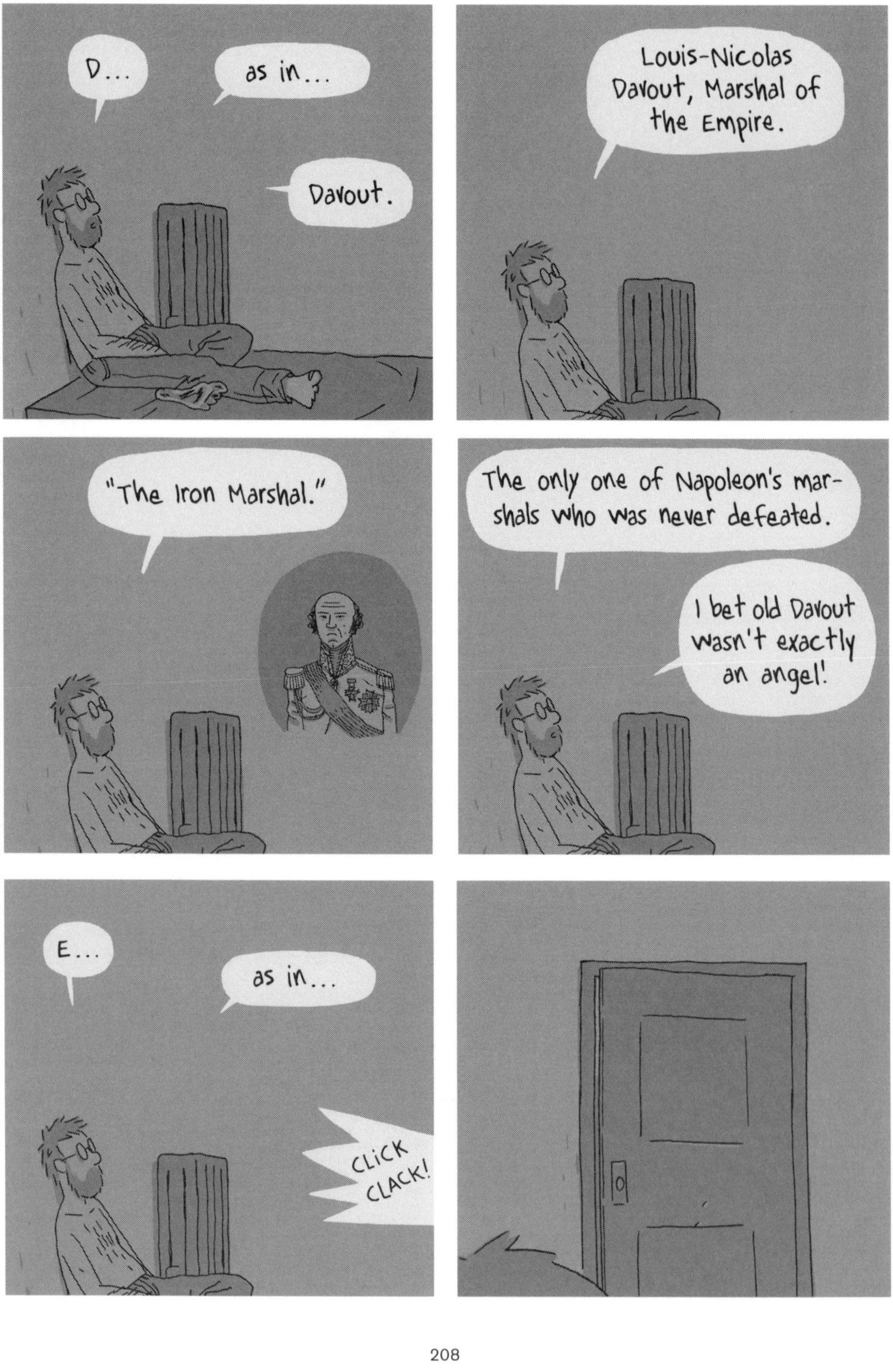
D...
as in...
Davout.
Louis-Nicolas Davout, Marshal of the Empire.
"The Iron Marshal."
The only one of Napoleon's marshals who was never defeated.
I bet old Davout wasn't exactly an angel!
E...
as in...
CLICK CLACK!

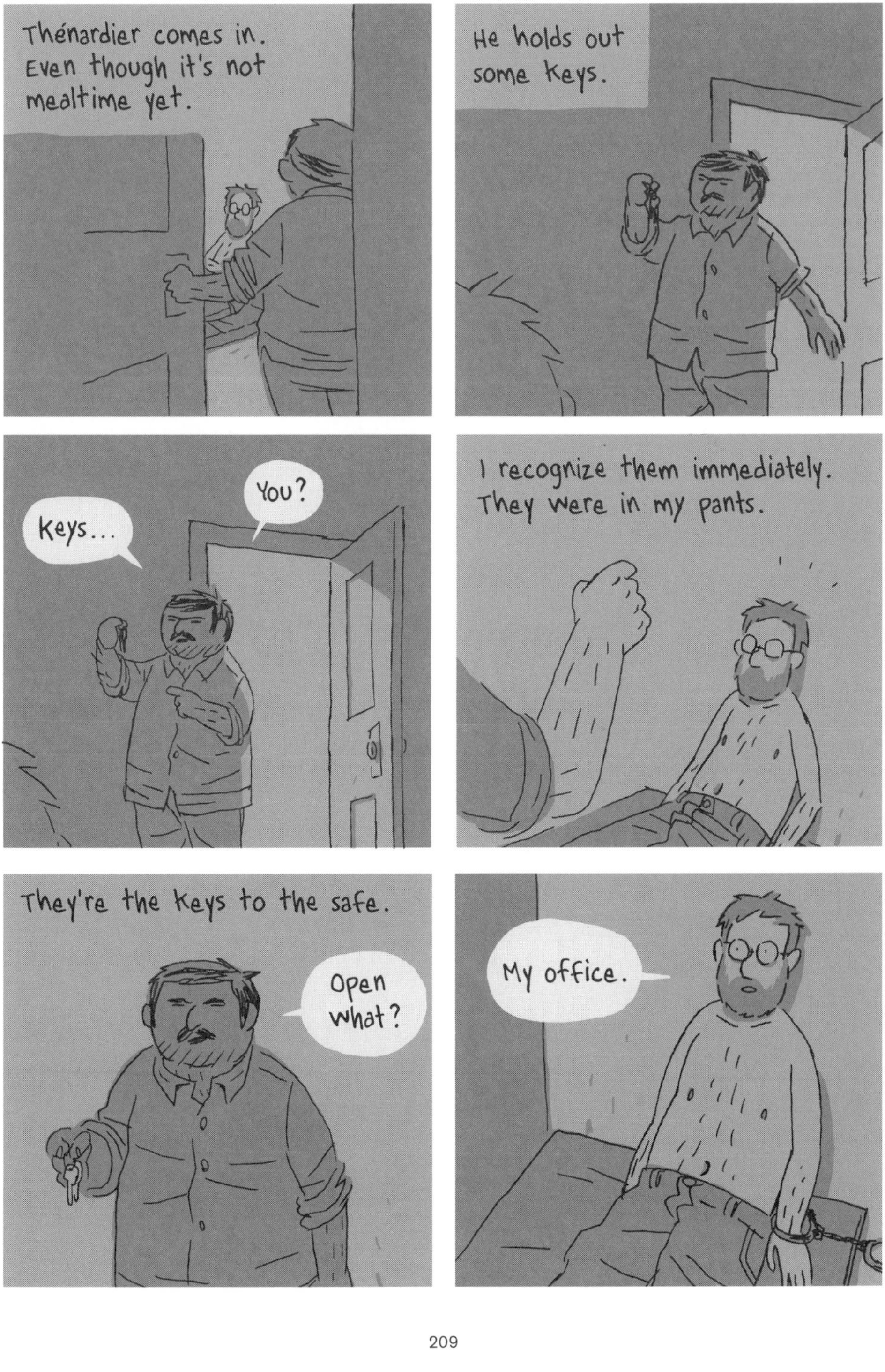
Thénardier comes in. Even though it's not mealtime yet.
He holds out some keys.
Keys...
You?
I recognize them immediately. They were in my pants.
They're the keys to the safe.
Open what?
My office.

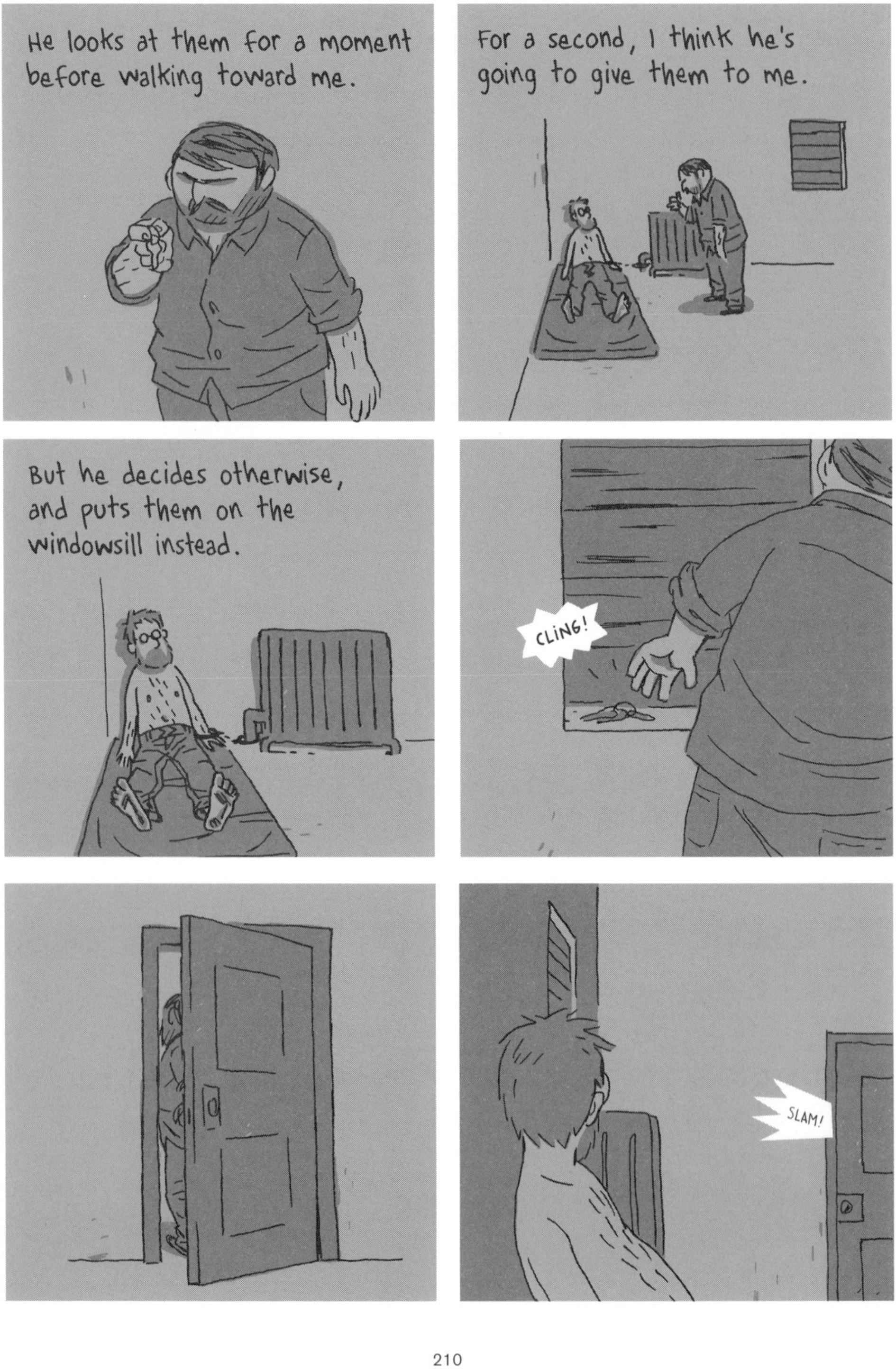

He looks at them for a moment before walking toward me.
For a second, I think he's going to give them to me.
But he decides otherwise, and puts them on the windowsill instead.
CLING!
SLAM!

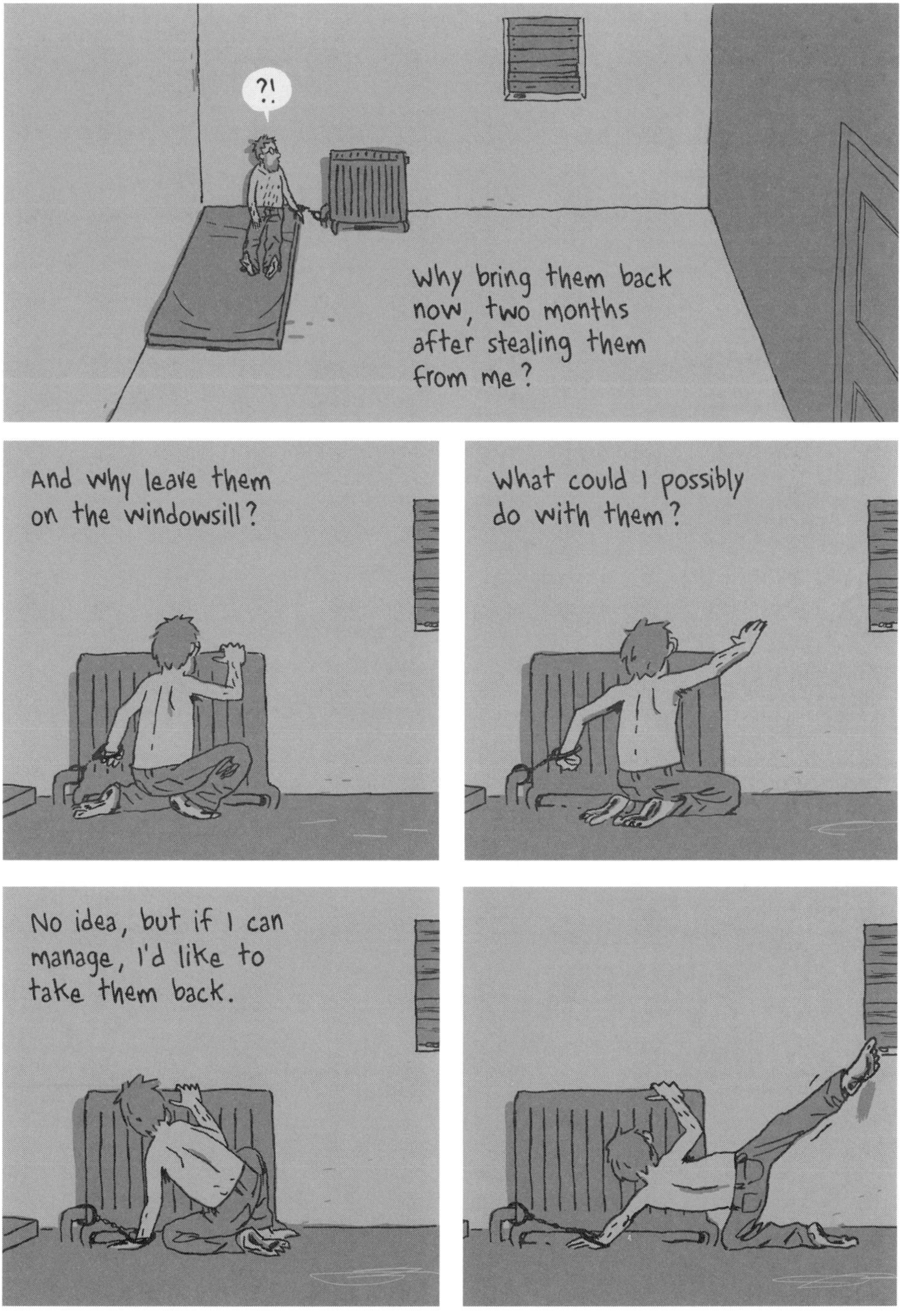
?!
Why bring them back now, two months after stealing them from me?
And why leave them on the windowsill?
What could I possibly do with them?
No idea, but if I can manage, I'd like to take them back.

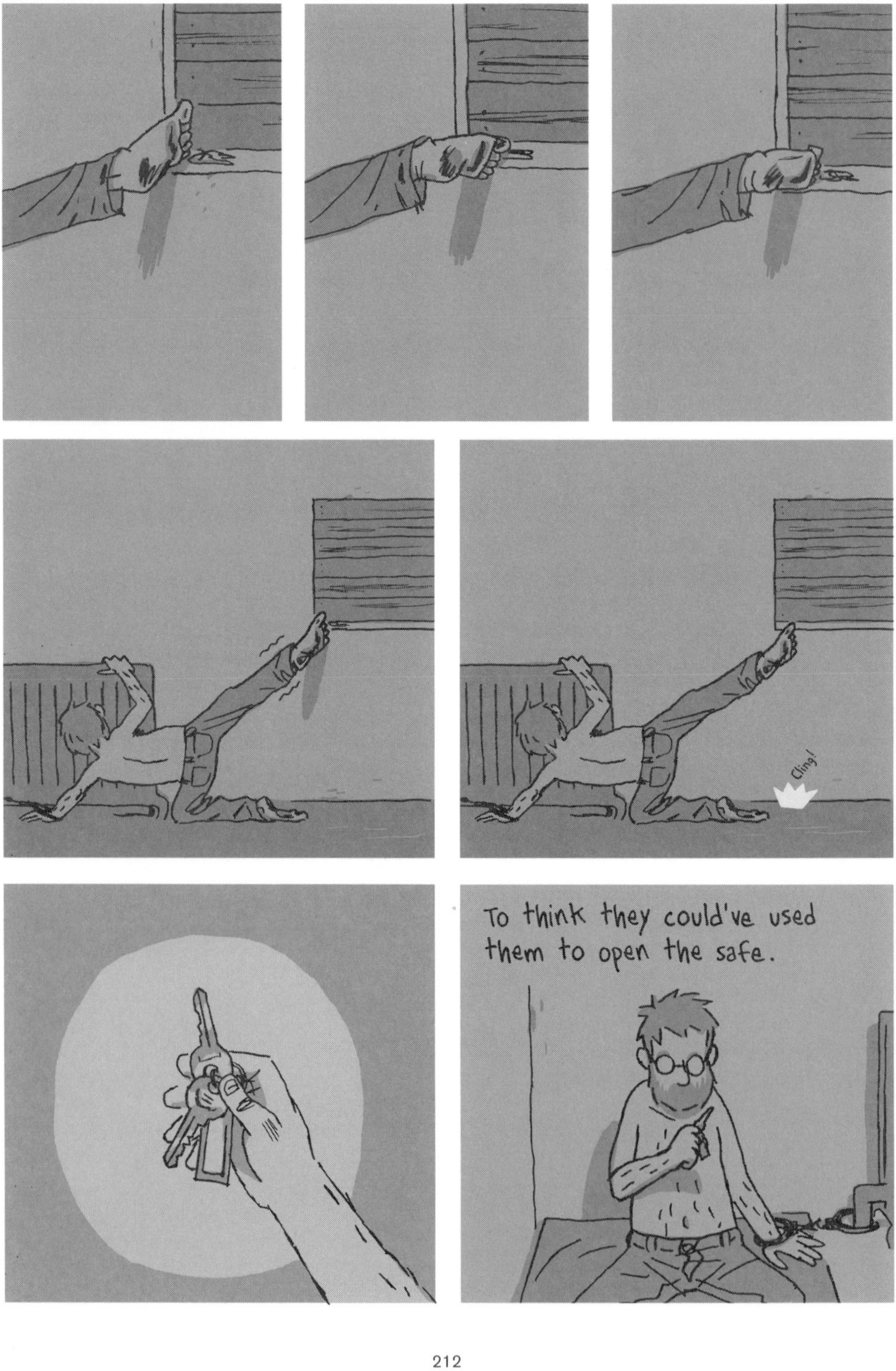
Cling!
To think they could've used them to open the safe.

I don't remember how much was in it, but it was quite a lot.

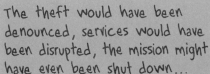

The theft would have been denounced, services would have been disrupted, the mission might have even been shut down...

But I would have been spared the hell of the past two months.

They'd have stolen a ton of money, but nobody would have been kidnapped and locked away.

Nobody would have had to go through all this.

For fuck's sake!

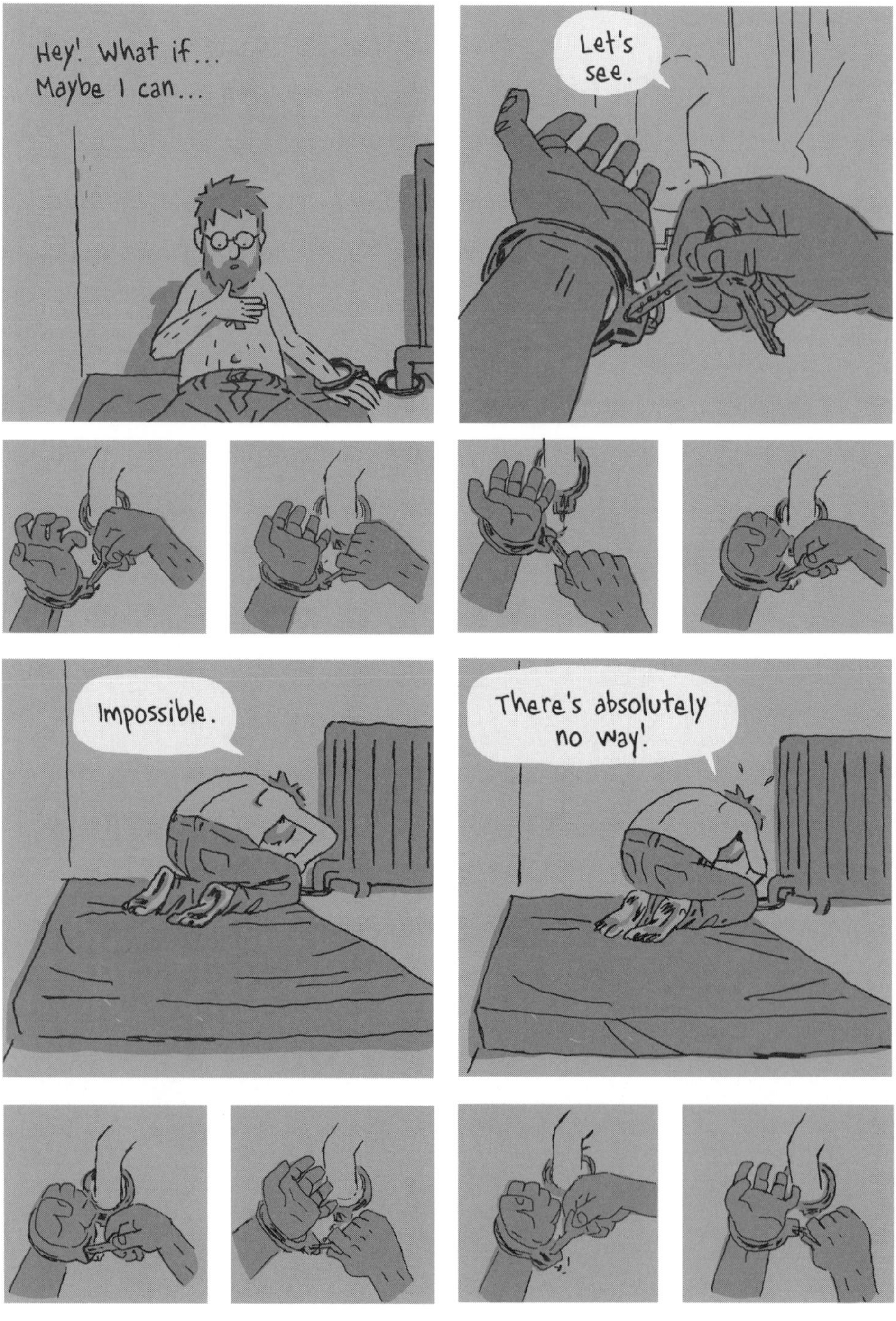
Hey! What if...
Maybe I can...
Let's see.
Impossible.
There's absolutely no way!

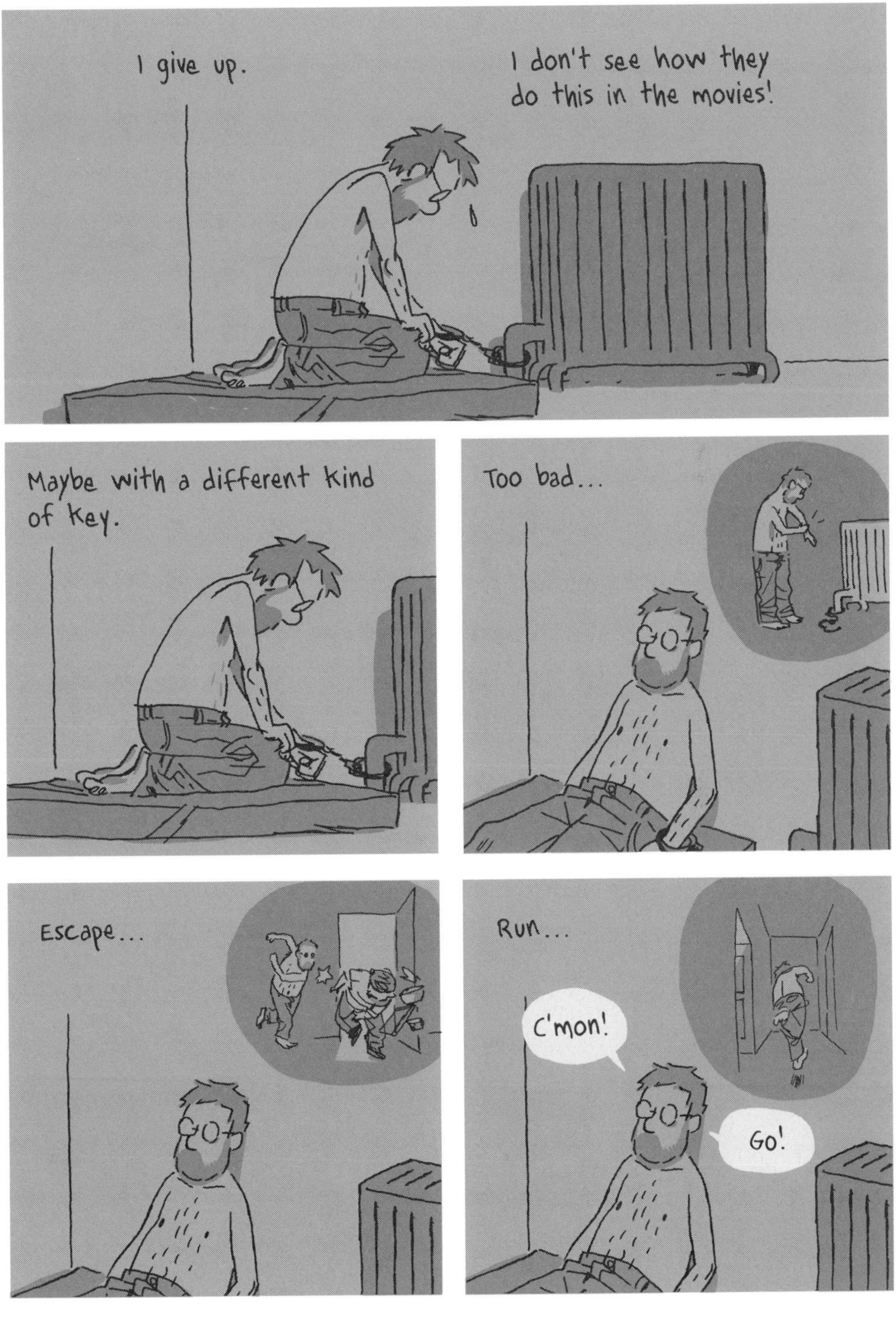
I give up.
I don't see how they do this in the movies!
Maybe with a different kind of key.
Too bad...
Escape...
Run...
C'mon!
Go!

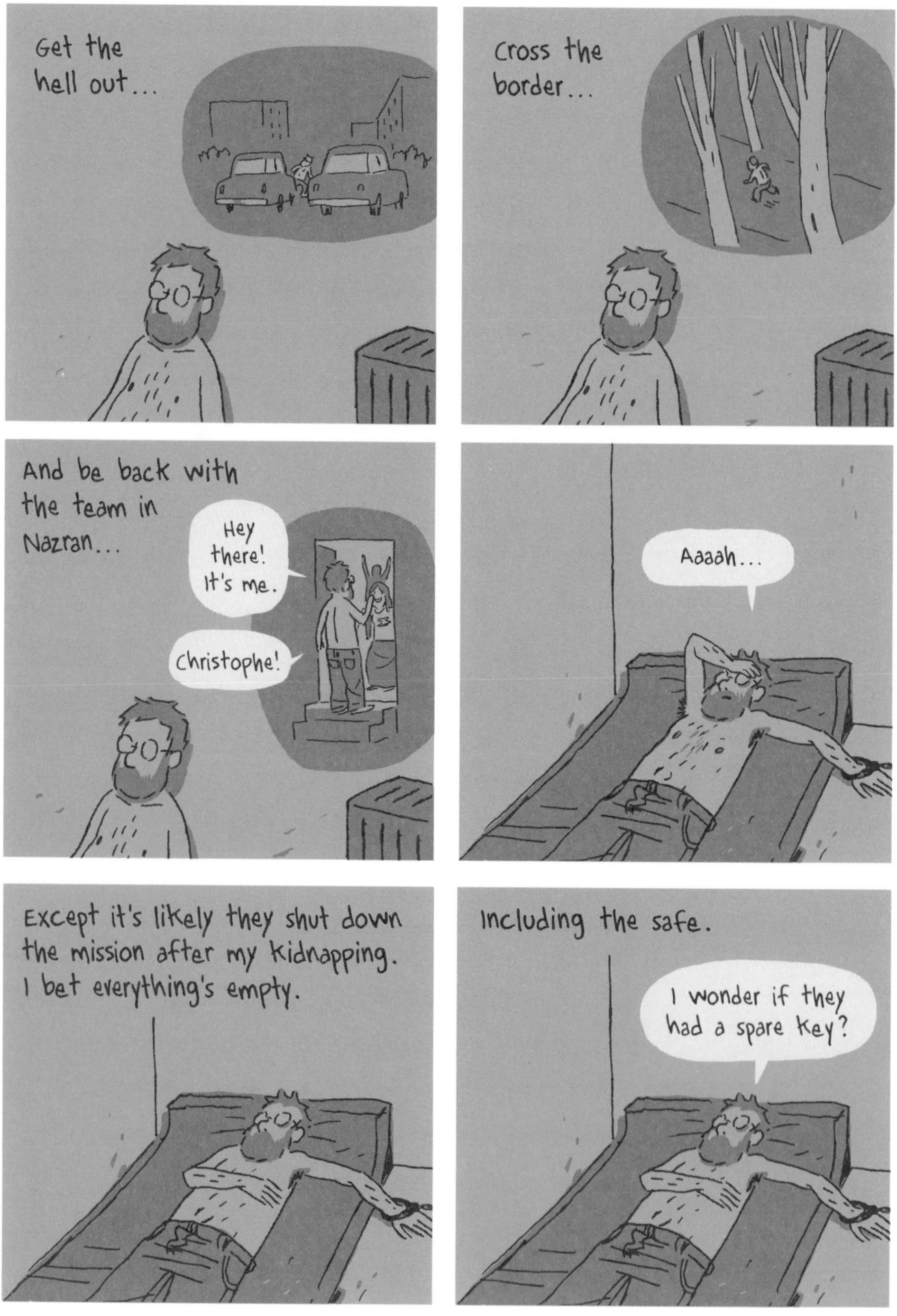
Get the hell out...
Cross the border...
And be back with the team in Nazran...
Hey there! It's me.
Christophe!
Aaaah...
Except it's likely they shut down the mission after my kidnapping. I bet everything's empty.
Including the safe.
I wonder if they had a spare key?

61

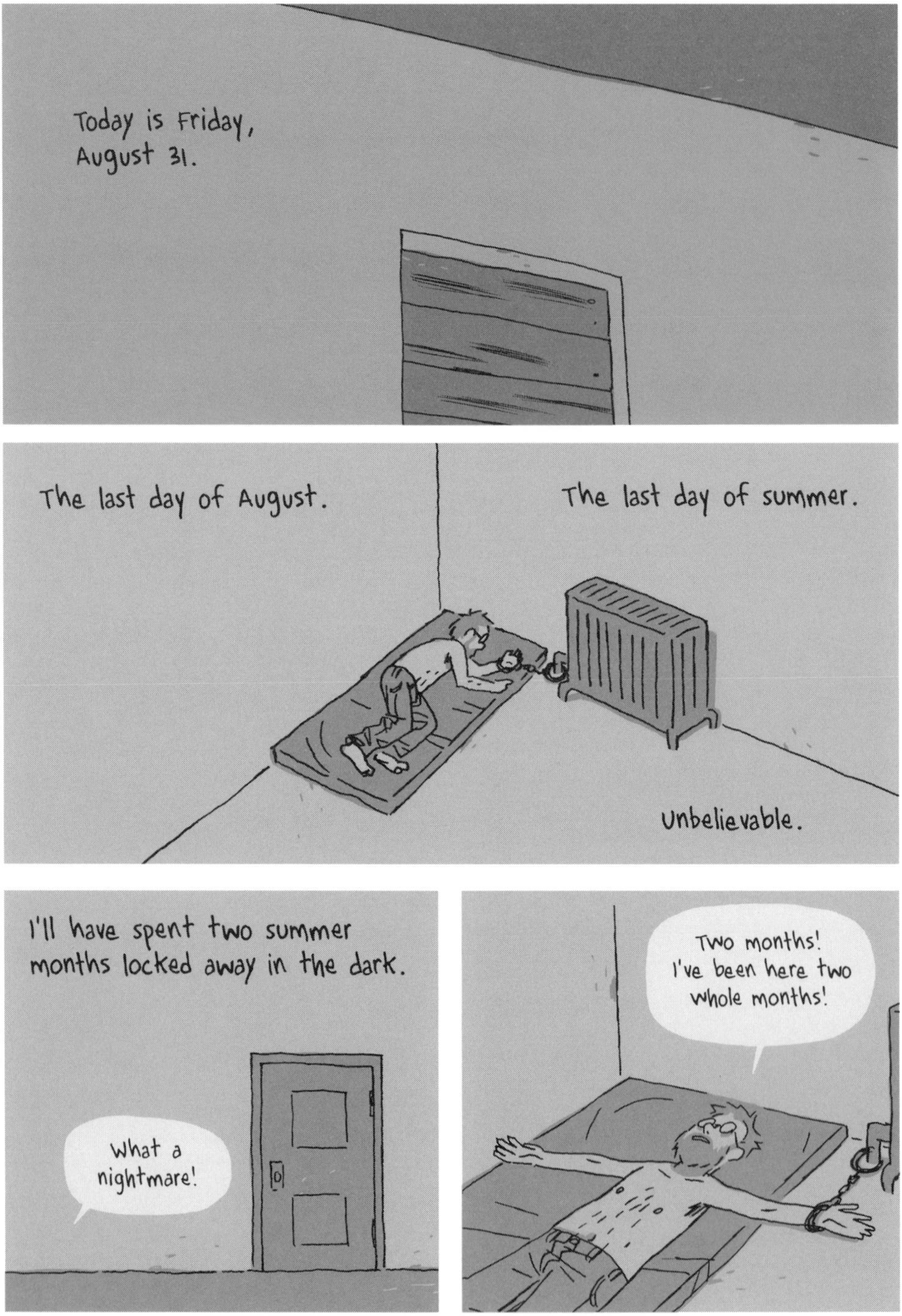
Today is Friday, August 31.
The last day of August.
The last day of summer.
Unbelievable.
I'll have spent two summer months locked away in the dark.
What a nightmare!
Two months! I've been here two whole months!

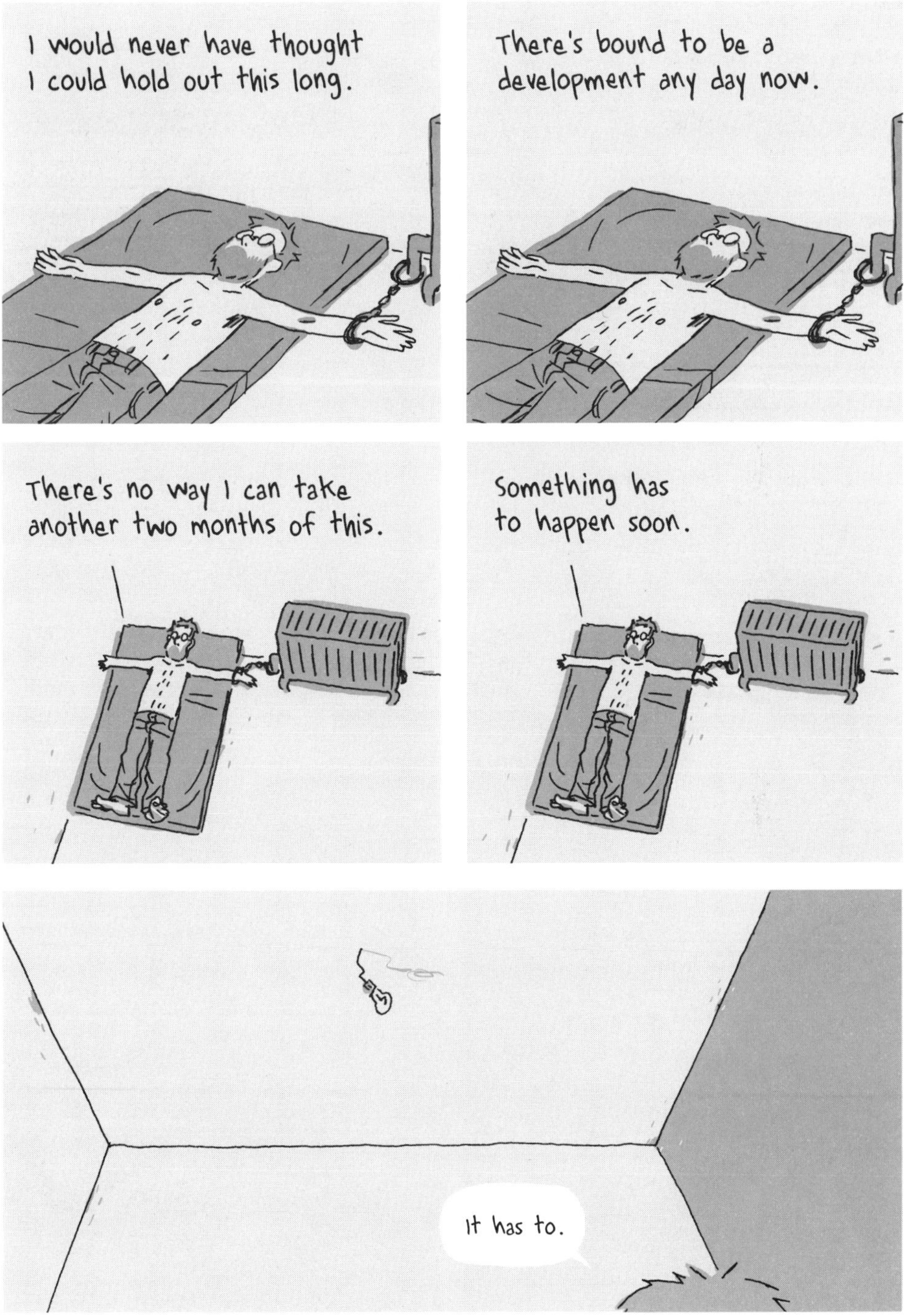
I would never have thought I could hold out this long.
There's bound to be a development any day now.
There's no way I can take another two months of this.
Something has to happen soon.
It has to.

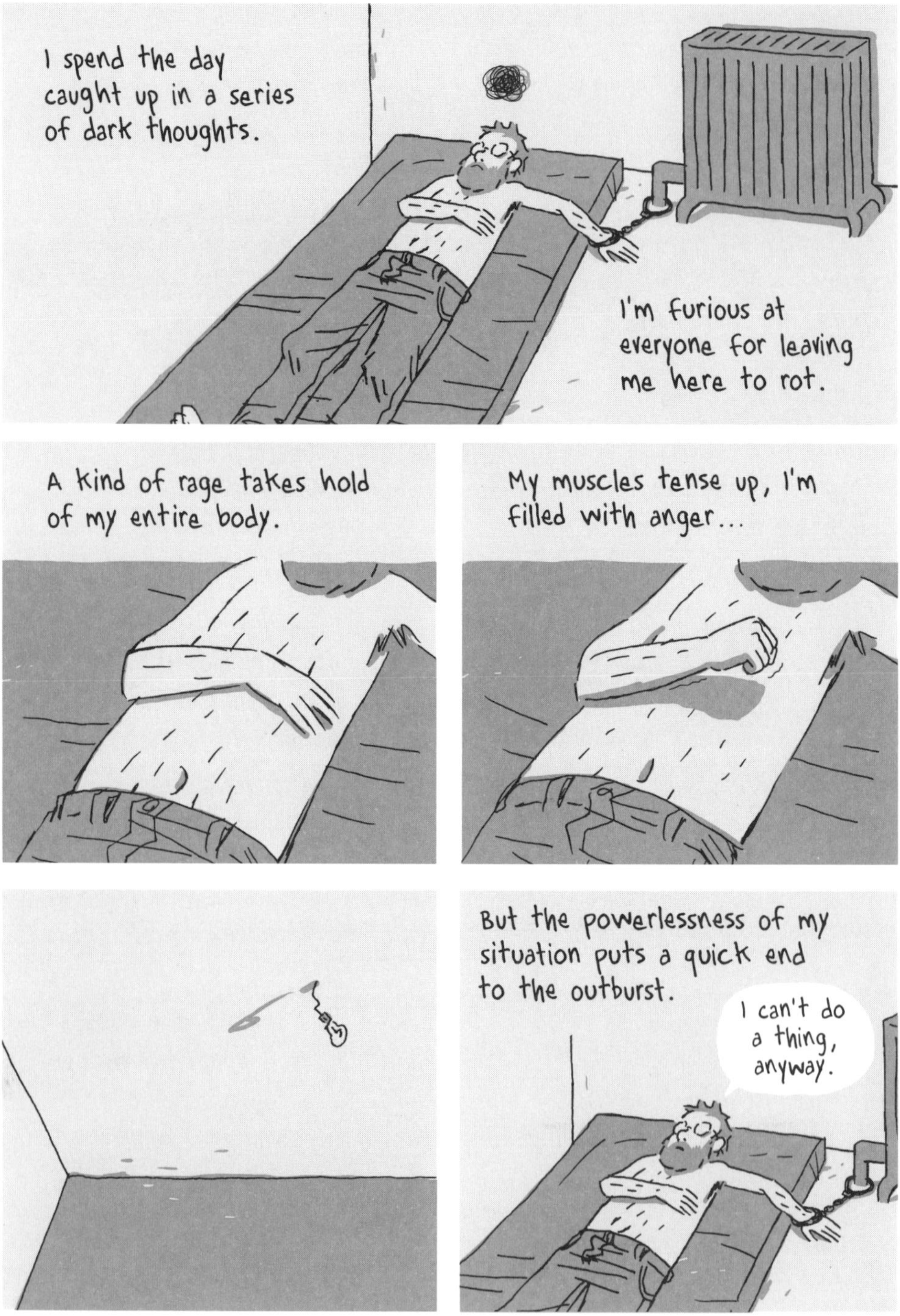
I spend the day caught up in a series of dark thoughts.
I'm furious at everyone for leaving me here to rot.
A kind of rage takes hold of my entire body.
My muscles tense up, I'm filled with anger...
But the powerlessness of my situation puts a quick end to the outburst.
I can't do a thing, anyway.

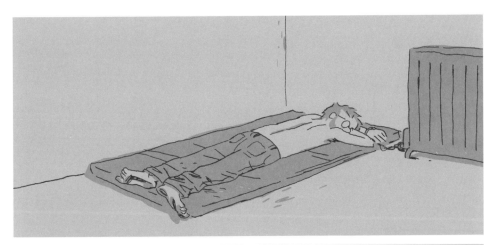

I manage to doze in the afternoon.

I feel a bit better when I wake up.

Time goes by faster when I sleep.

For a moment, I escape my condition.

And that's some-thing, at least.

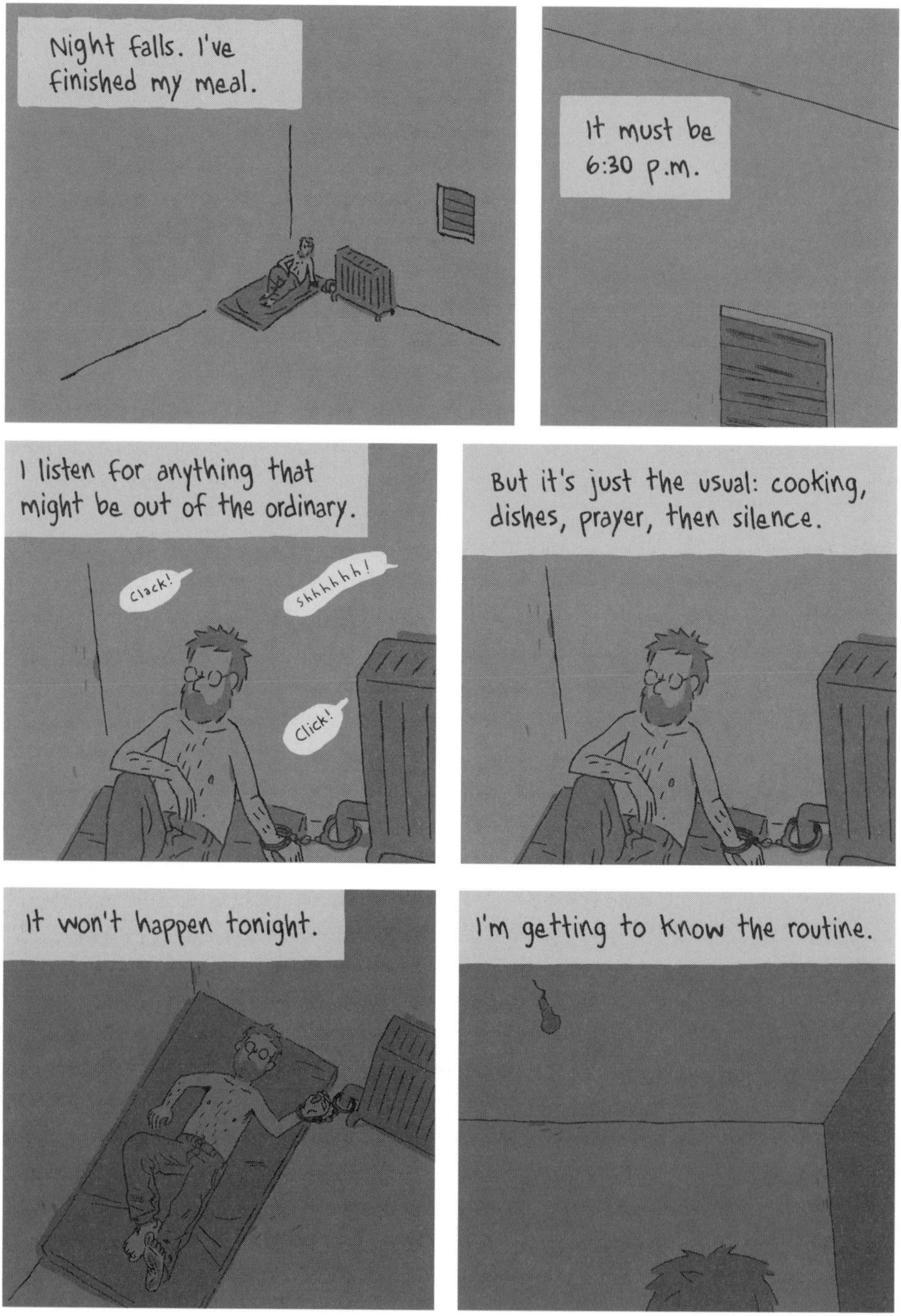
Night falls. I've finished my meal.
It must be 6:30 p.m.
I listen for anything that might be out of the ordinary.
Clack!
Shhhhhh!
Click!
But it's just the usual: cooking, dishes, prayer, then silence.
It won't happen tonight.
I'm getting to know the routine.

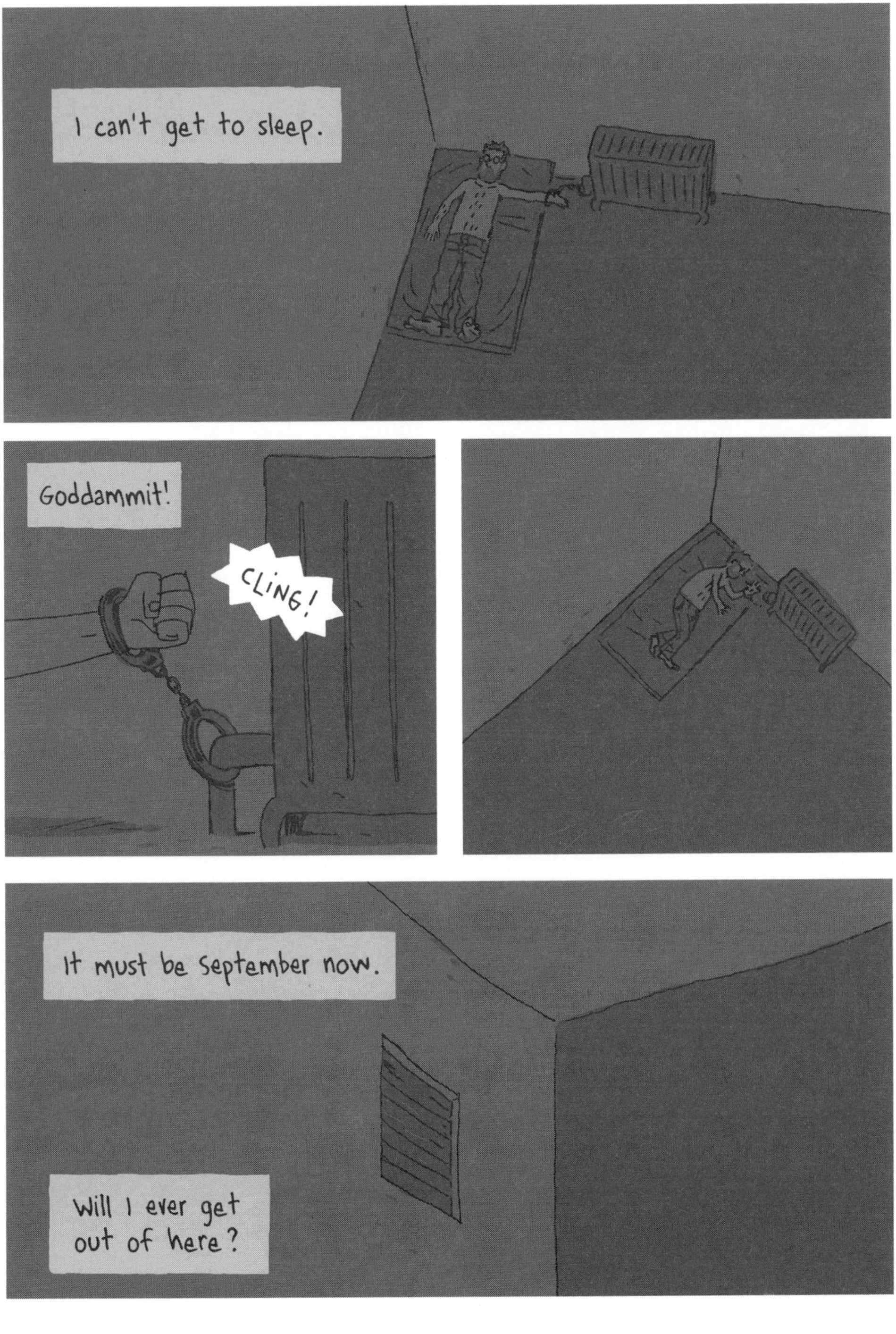
I can't get to sleep.
Goddammit!
CLING!
It must be September now.
Will I ever get out of here?

62

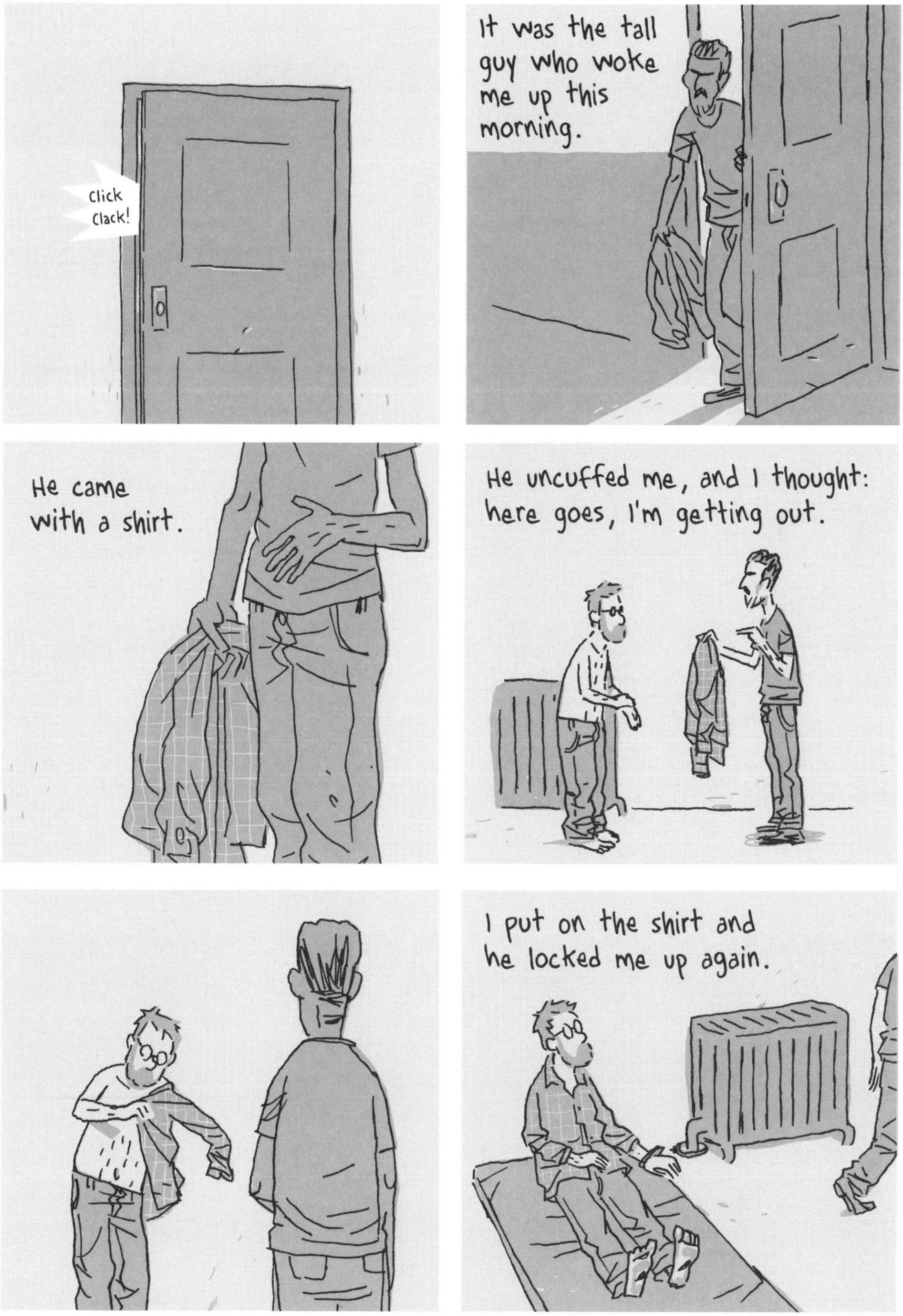
Click Clack!
It was the tall guy who woke me up this morning.
He came with a shirt.
He uncuffed me, and I thought: here goes, I'm getting out.
I put on the shirt and he locked me up again.

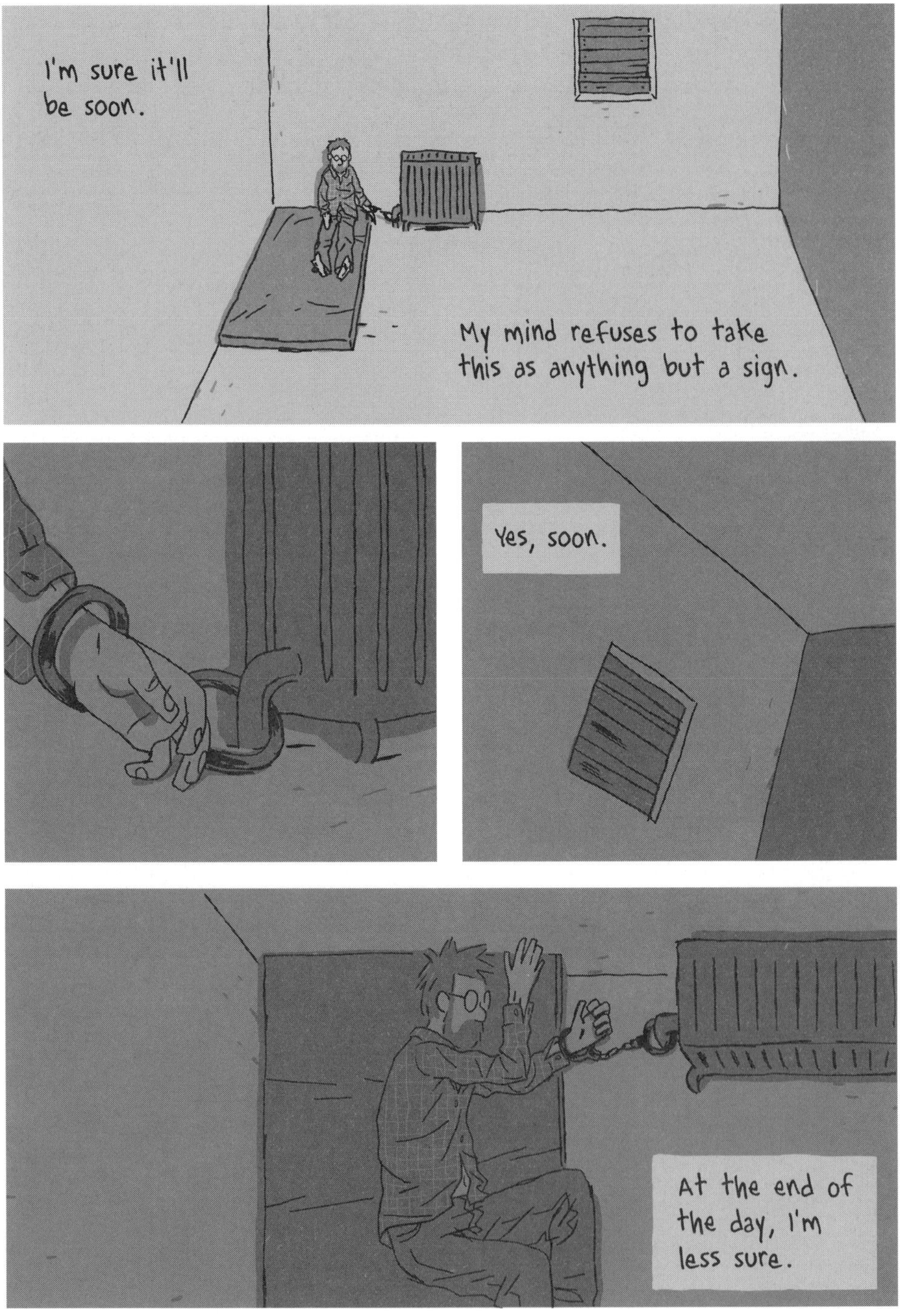
I'm sure it'll be soon.
My mind refuses to take this as anything but a sign.
Yes, soon.
At the end of the day, I'm less sure.

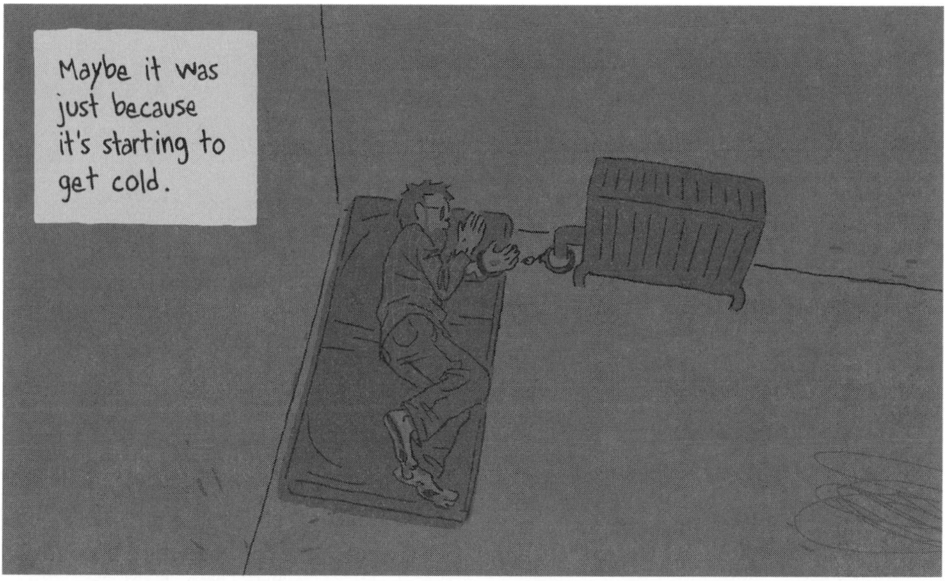
Maybe it was just because it's starting to get cold.

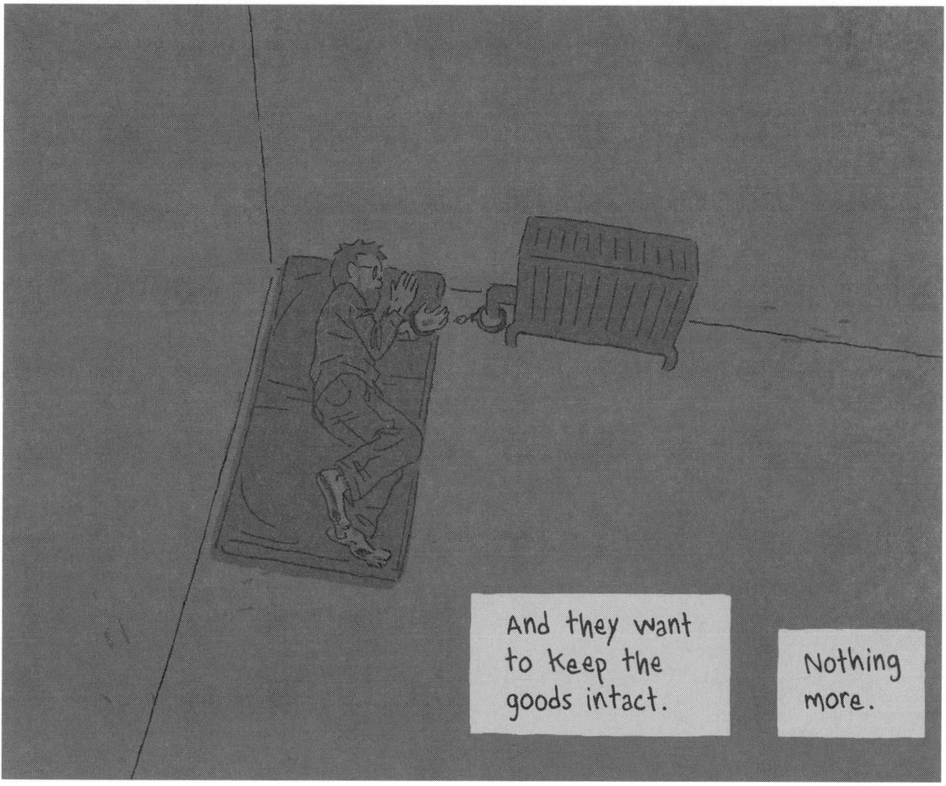
And they want to keep the goods intact.
Nothing more.

66

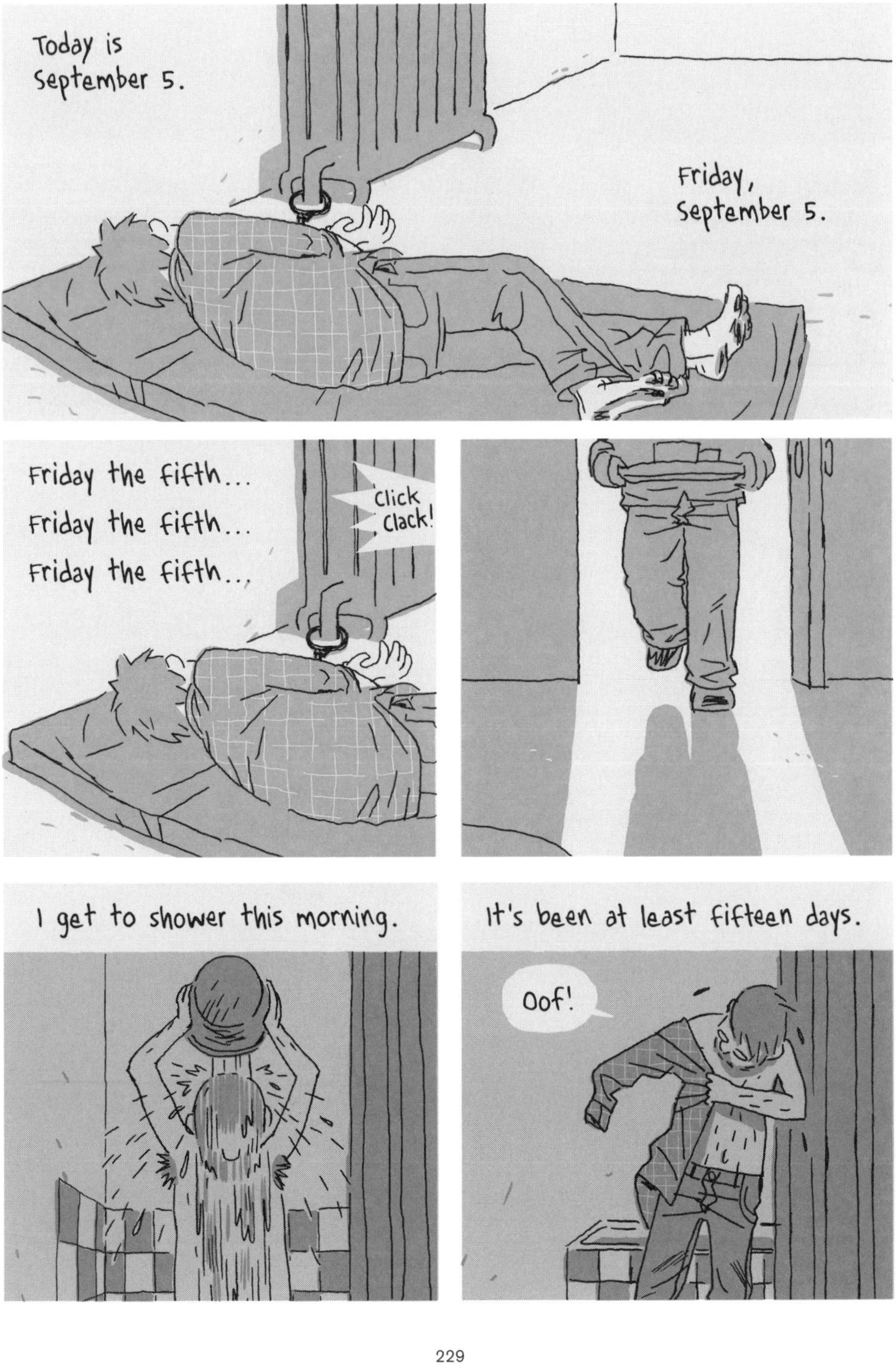
Today is September 5.
Friday, September 5.
Friday the fifth...
Friday the fifth...
Friday the fifth...
Click Clack!
I get to shower this morning.
It's been at least fifteen days.
Oof!

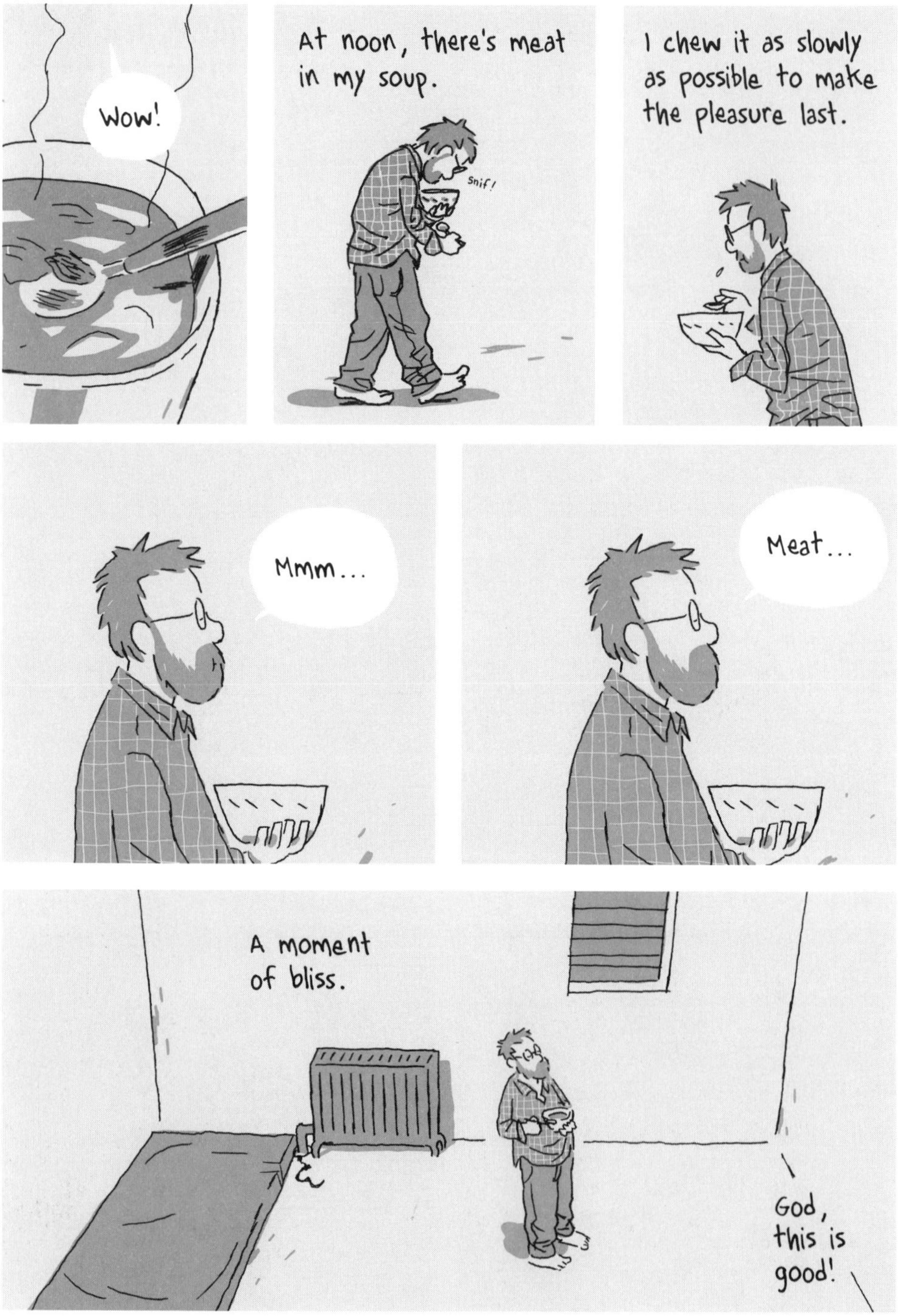
Wow!
At noon, there's meat in my soup.
Snif!
I chew it as slowly as possible to make the pleasure last.
Mmm...
Meat...
A moment of bliss.
God, this is good!

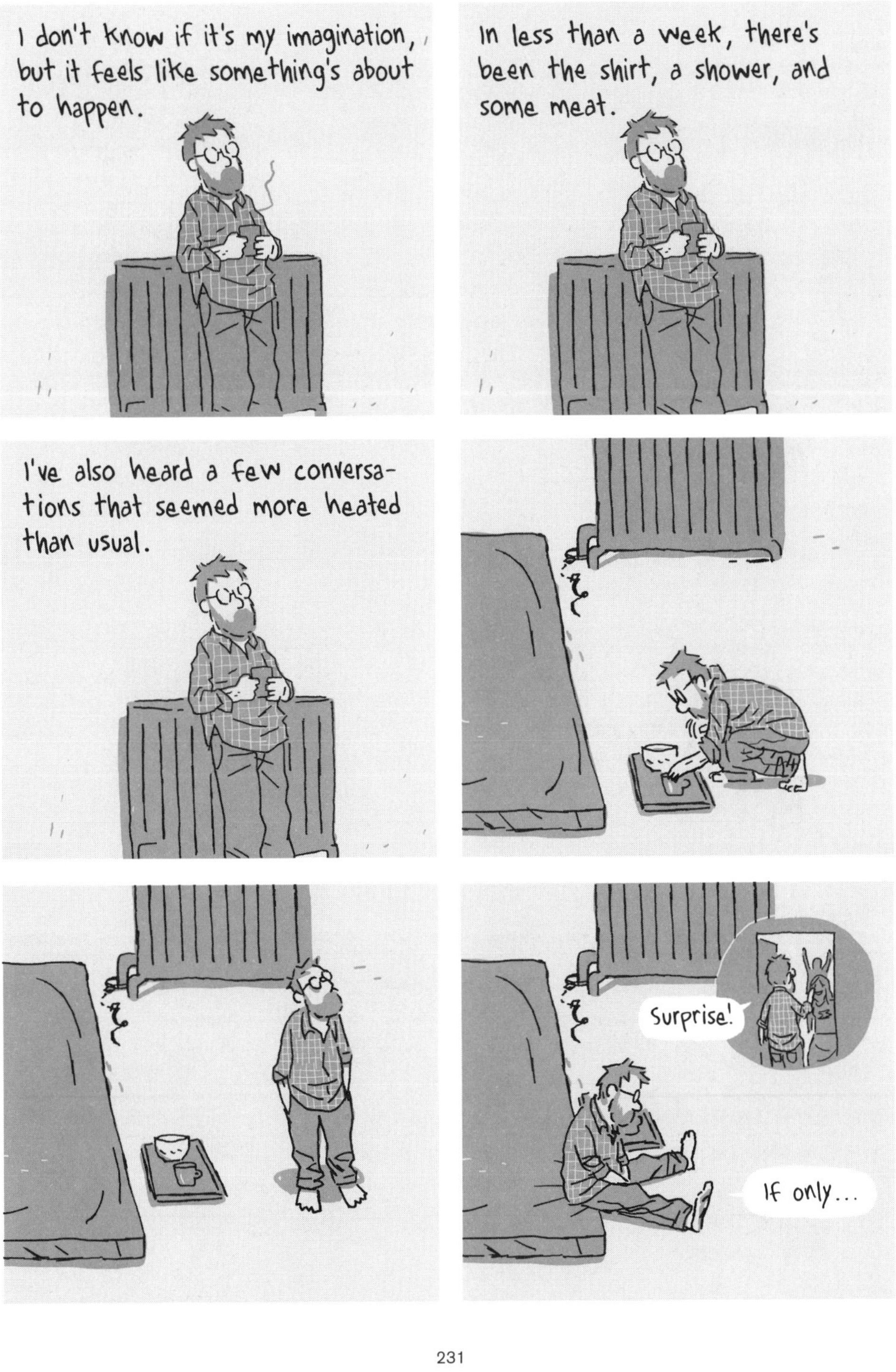

I don't know if it's my imagination, but it feels like something's about to happen.
In less than a week, there's been the shirt, a shower, and some meat.
I've also heard a few conversations that seemed more heated than usual.
Surprise!
If only...

Click
Clack!

After the evening meal, Thénardier comes back for the tray.

Even though we can't communicate, I wish he'd tell me what's going on.

Crrrrick!

Powerless, I watch him go. I see myself jumping him and strangling him with my handcuffs.

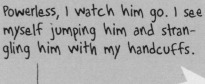

Click
Clack!

How many times have I imagined strangling this jerk?

Here!

How's that feel, asshole?

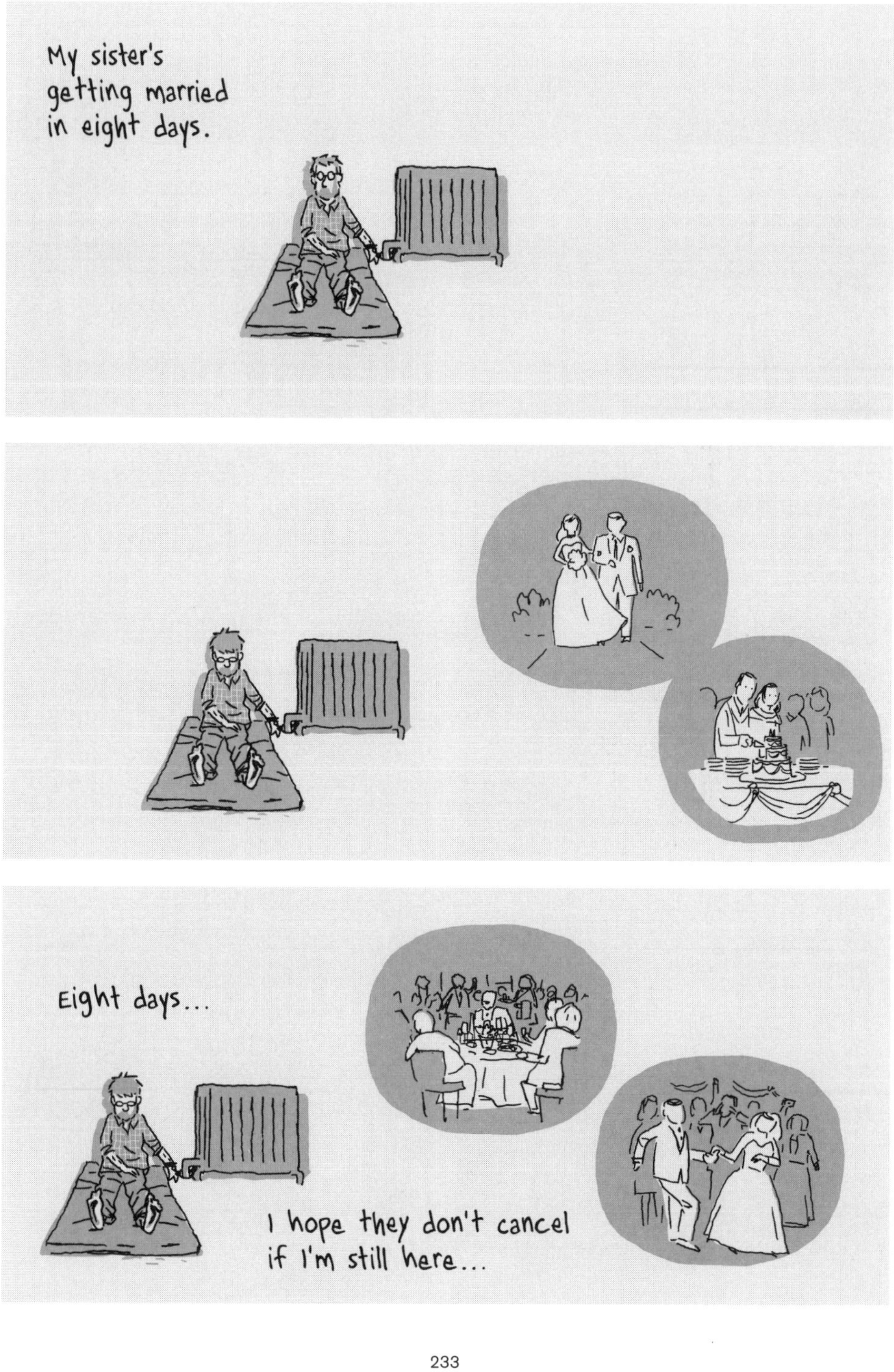
My sister's getting married in eight days.
Eight days...
I hope they don't cancel if I'm still here...

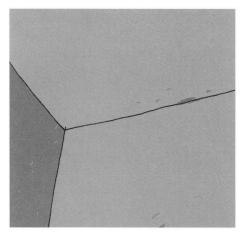

Let's see...

Where was I?

Oh, right, the letter E.

E as in...

Uh...

Ah, I know... Elchingen.

The Battle of Elchingen, October 1805. Marshal Ney attacks on the north bank of the Danube. Victory over the Austrian army.

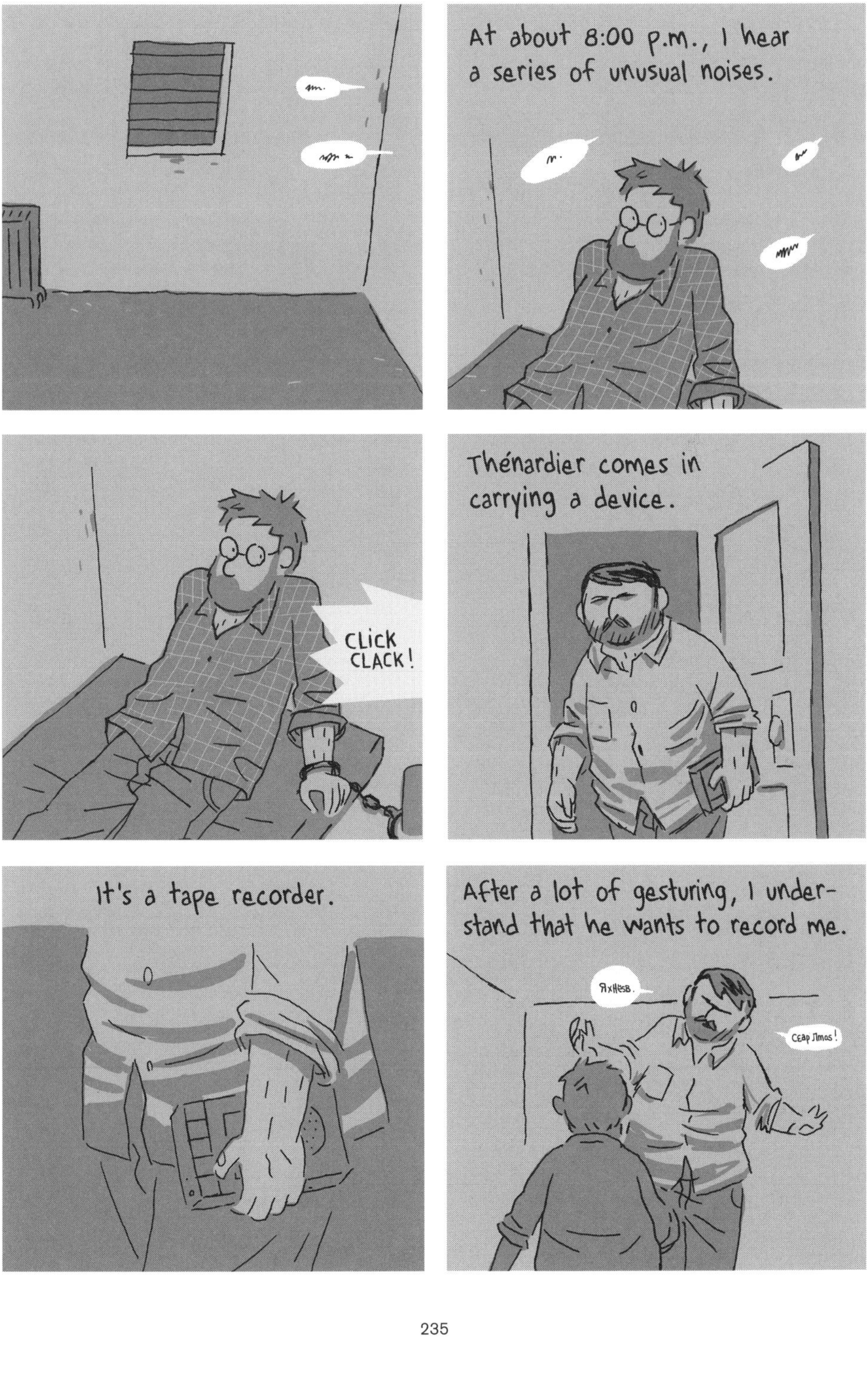
At about 8:00 p.m., I hear a series of unusual noises.
CLICK CLACK!
Thénardier comes in carrying a device.
It's a tape recorder.
After a lot of gesturing, I understand that he wants to record me.

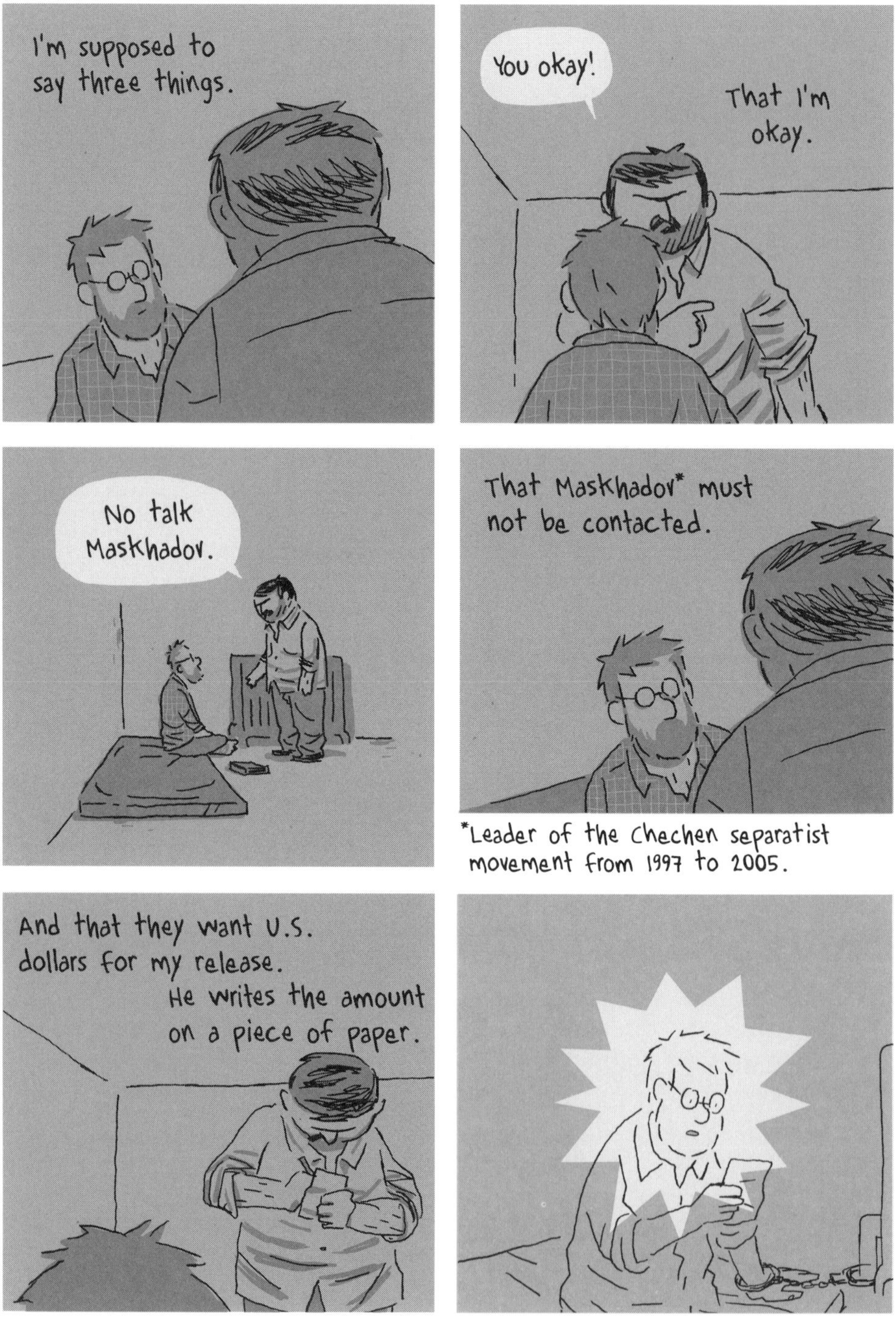
I'm supposed to say three things.
You okay!
That I'm okay.
No talk Maskhador.
That Maskhador* must not be contacted.
*Leader of the Chechen separatist movement from 1997 to 2005.
And that they want U.S. dollars for my release.
He writes the amount on a piece of paper.

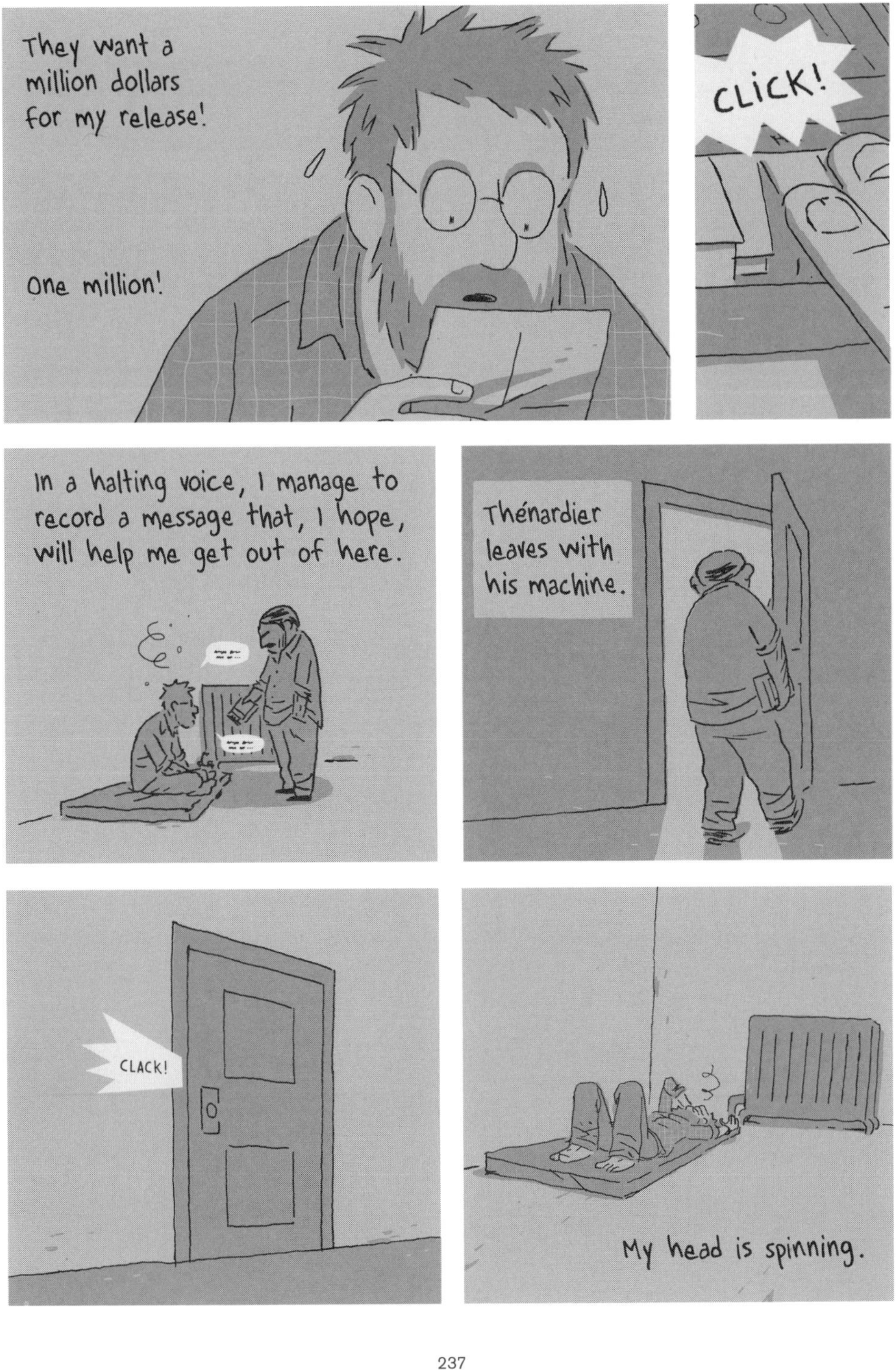
They want a million dollars for my release!
One million!
CLICK!
In a halting voice, I manage to record a message that, I hope, will help me get out of here.
Thénardier leaves with his machine.
CLACK!
My head is spinning.

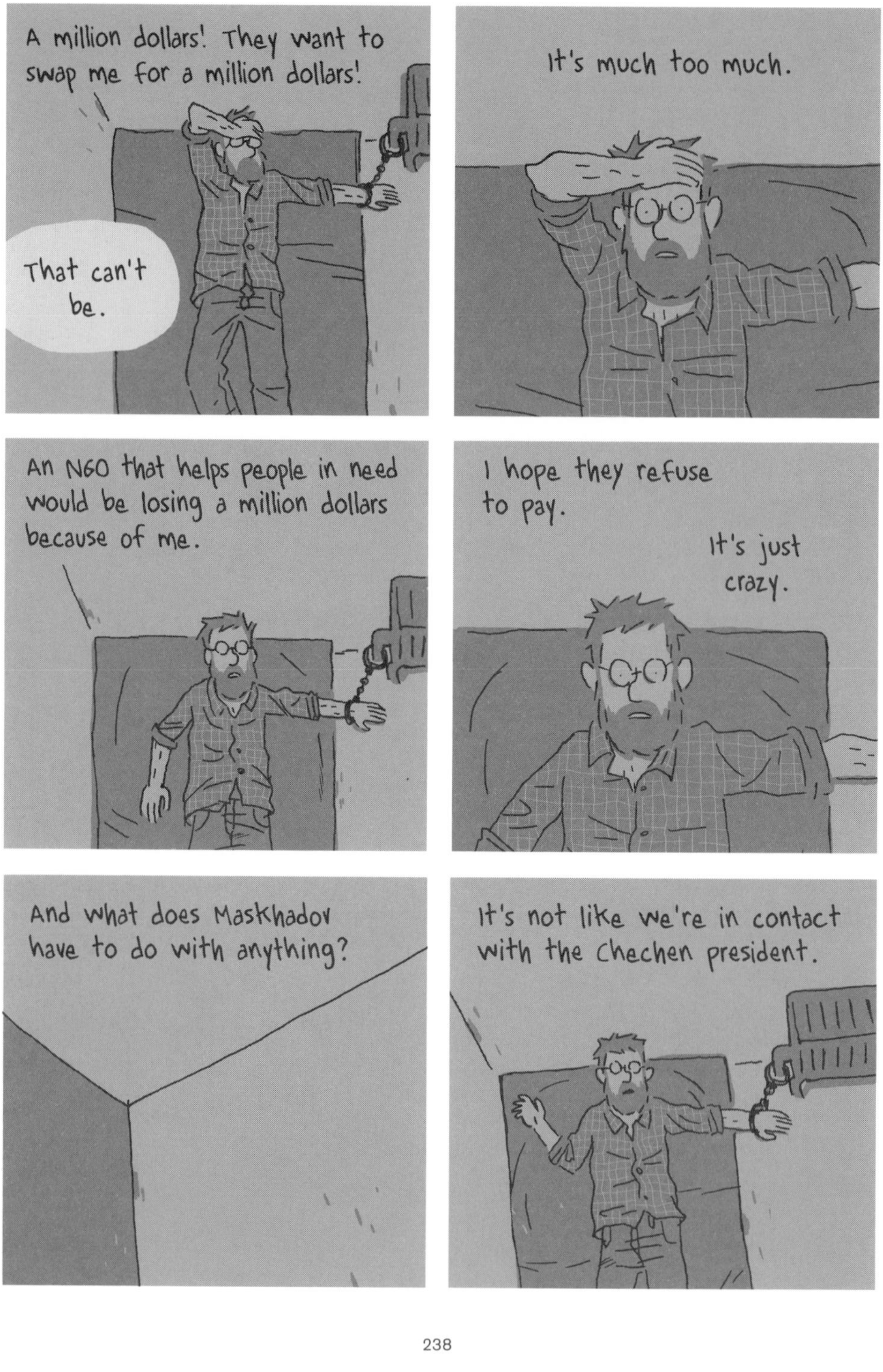
A million dollars! They want to swap me for a million dollars!
That can't be.
It's much too much.
An NGO that helps people in need would be losing a million dollars because of me.
I hope they refuse to pay.
It's just crazy.
And what does Maskhadov have to do with anything?
It's not like we're in contact with the Chechen president.

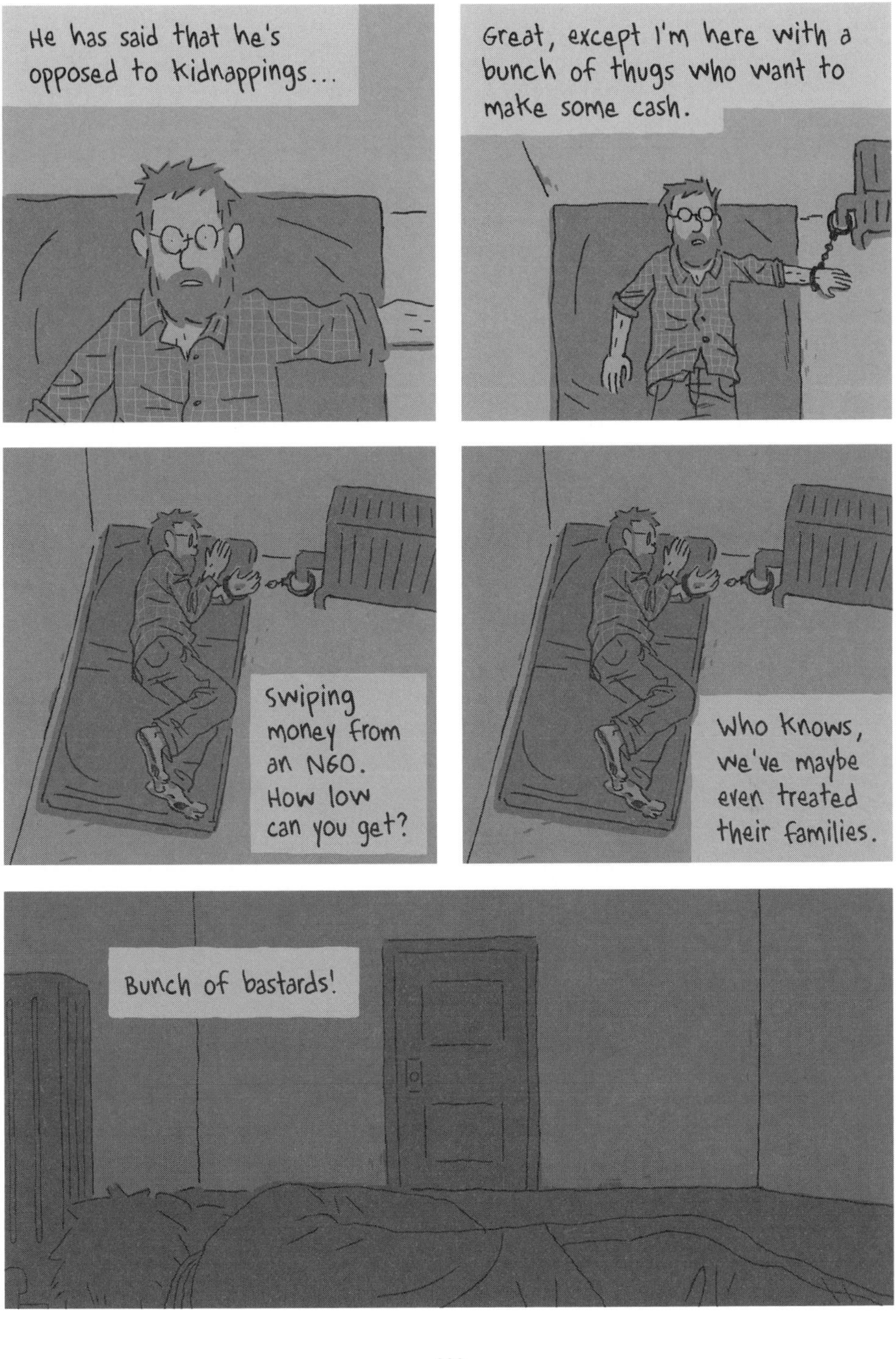

He has said that he's opposed to kidnappings...
Great, except I'm here with a bunch of thugs who want to make some cash.
Swiping money from an NGO. How low can you get?
Who knows, we've maybe even treated their families.
Bunch of bastards!

69

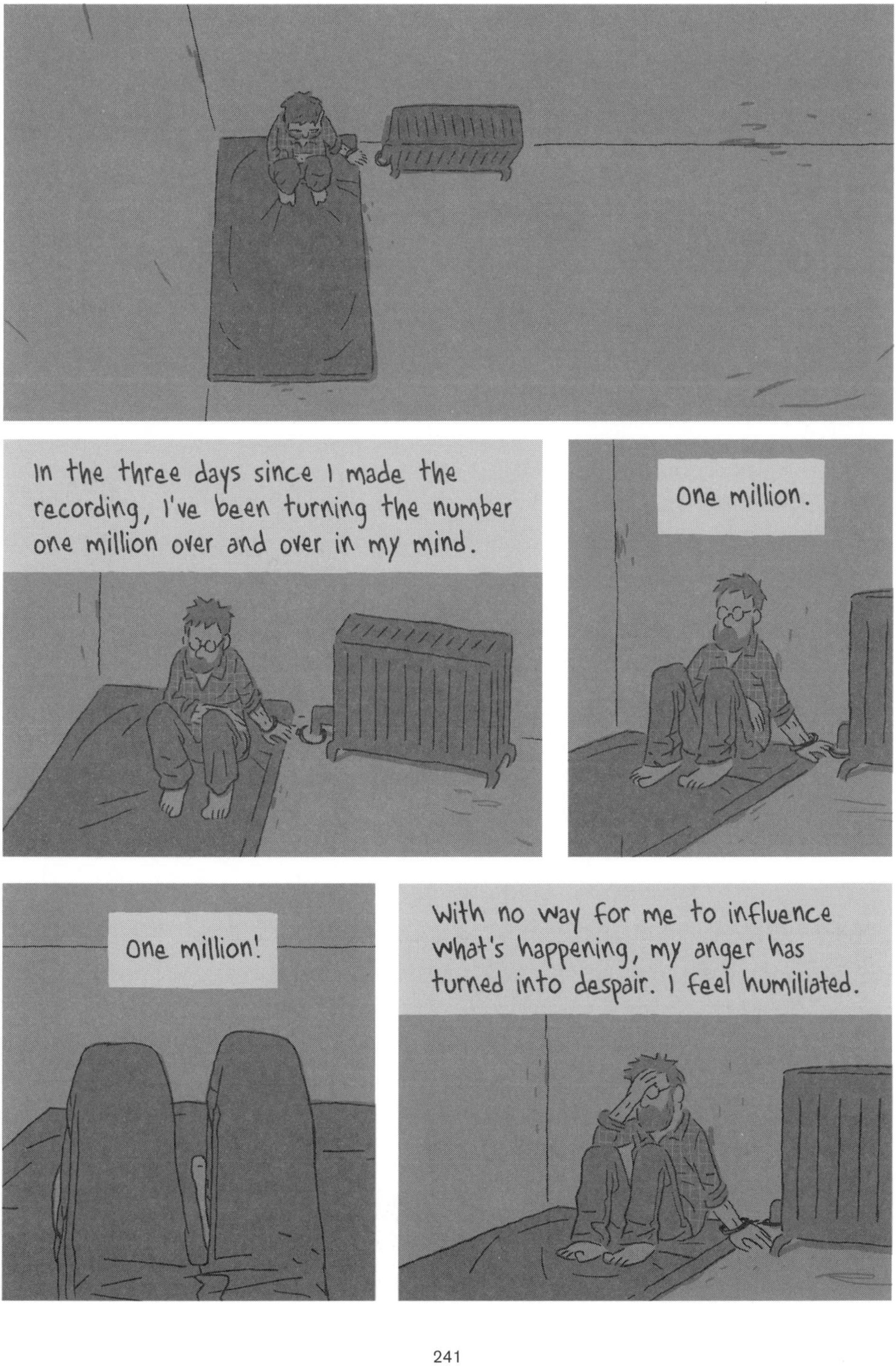
In the three days since I made the recording, I've been turning the number one million over and over in my mind.
One million.
One million!
With no way for me to influence what's happening, my anger has turned into despair. I feel humiliated.

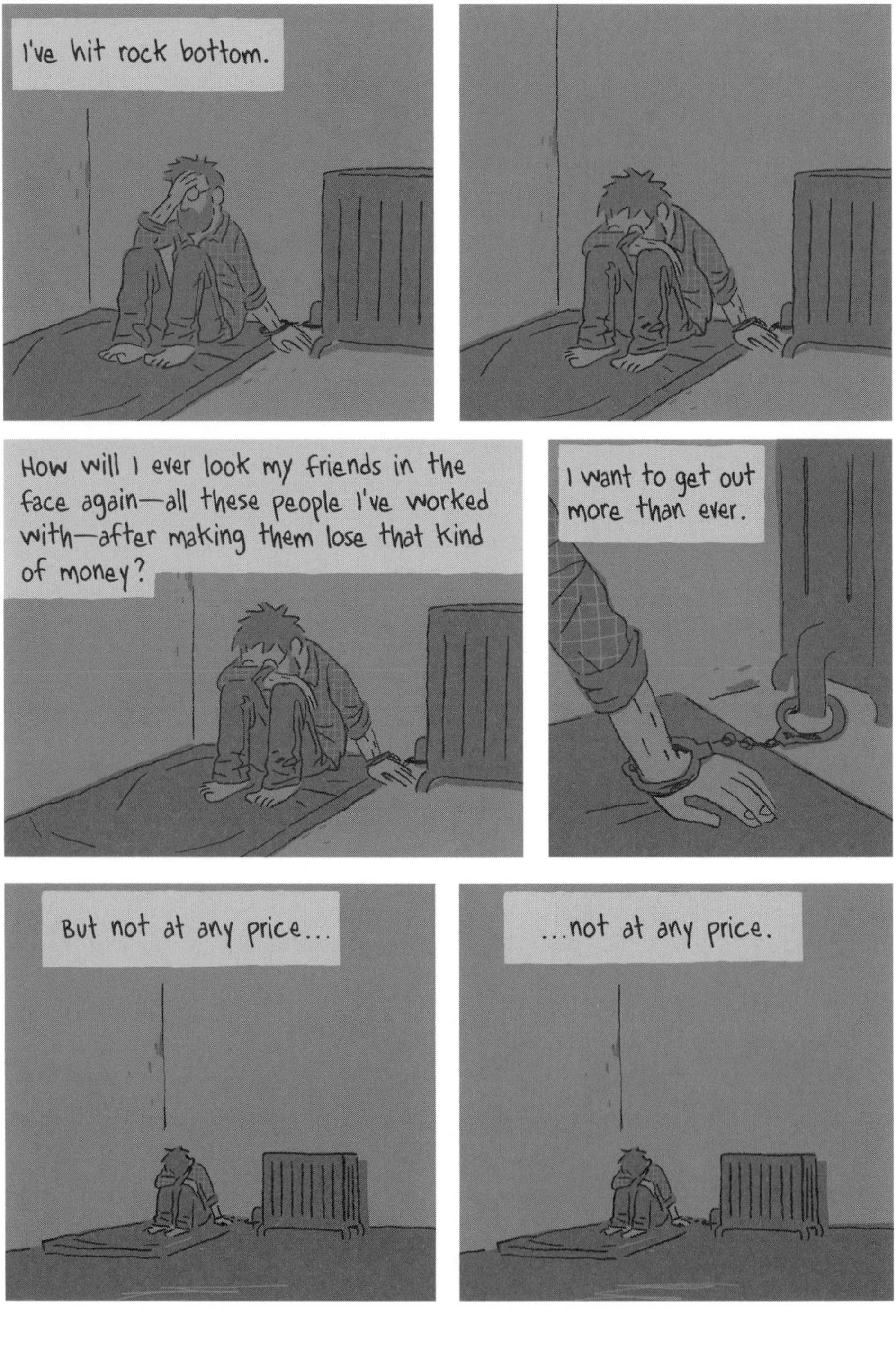
I've hit rock bottom.
How will I ever look my friends in the face again—all these people I've worked with—after making them lose that kind of money?
I want to get out more than ever.
But not at any price...
...not at any price.

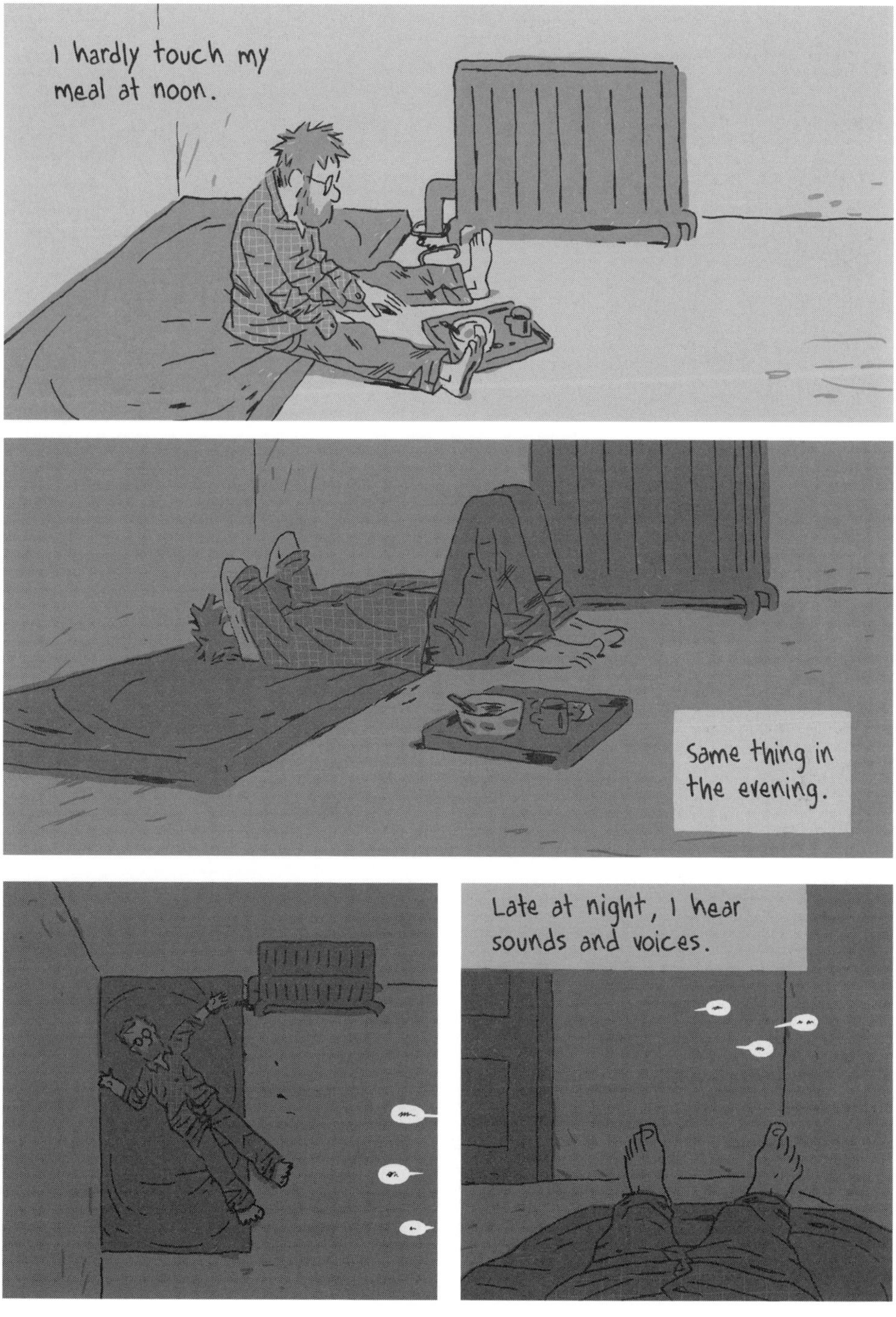
I hardly touch my meal at noon.
Same thing in the evening.
Late at night, I hear sounds and voices.

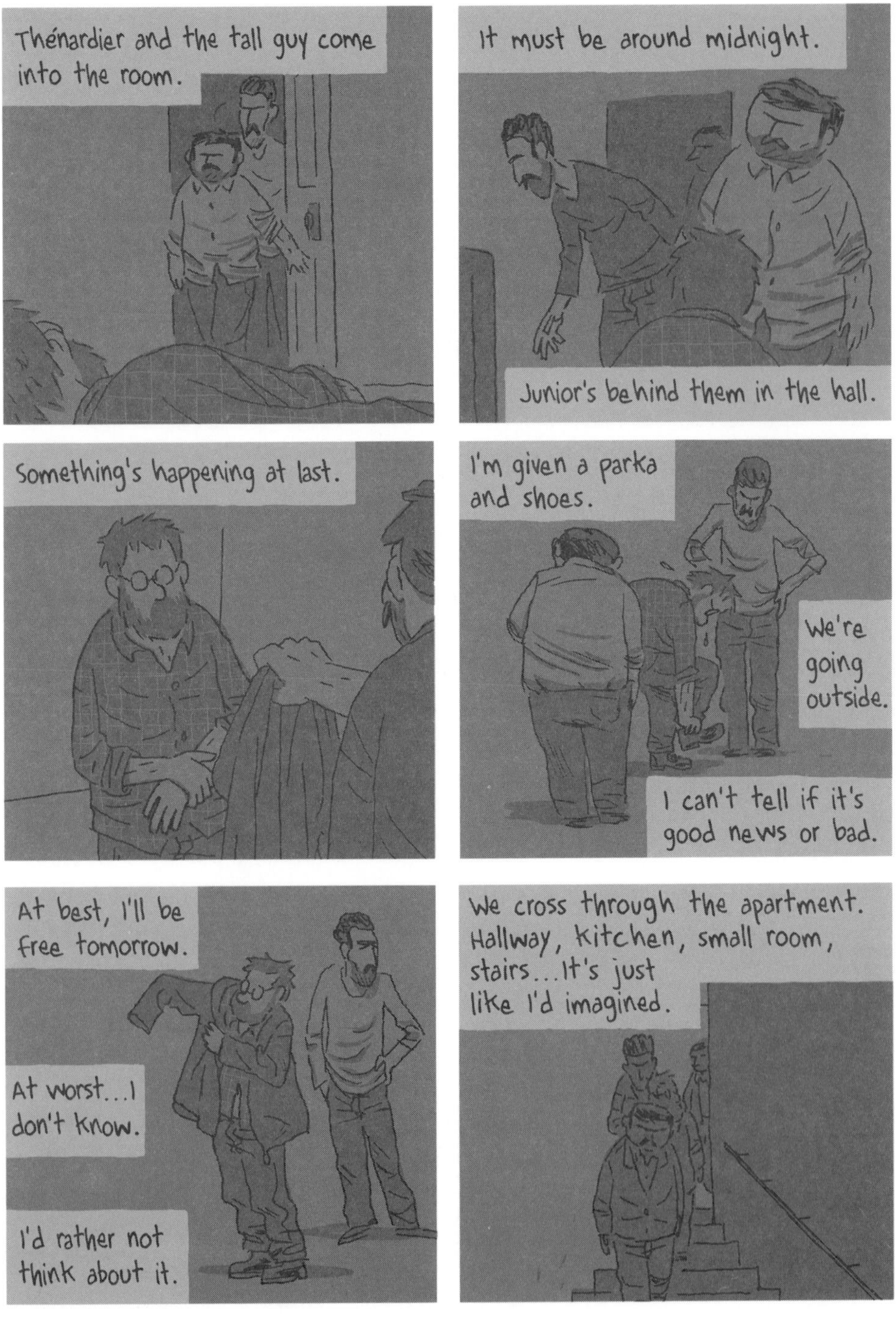
Thénardier and the tall guy come into the room.
It must be around midnight.
Junior's behind them in the hall.
Something's happening at last.
I'm given a parka and shoes.
We're going outside.
I can't tell if it's good news or bad.
At best, I'll be free tomorrow.
At worst... I don't know.
I'd rather not think about it.
We cross through the apartment. Hallway, kitchen, small room, stairs... It's just like I'd imagined.

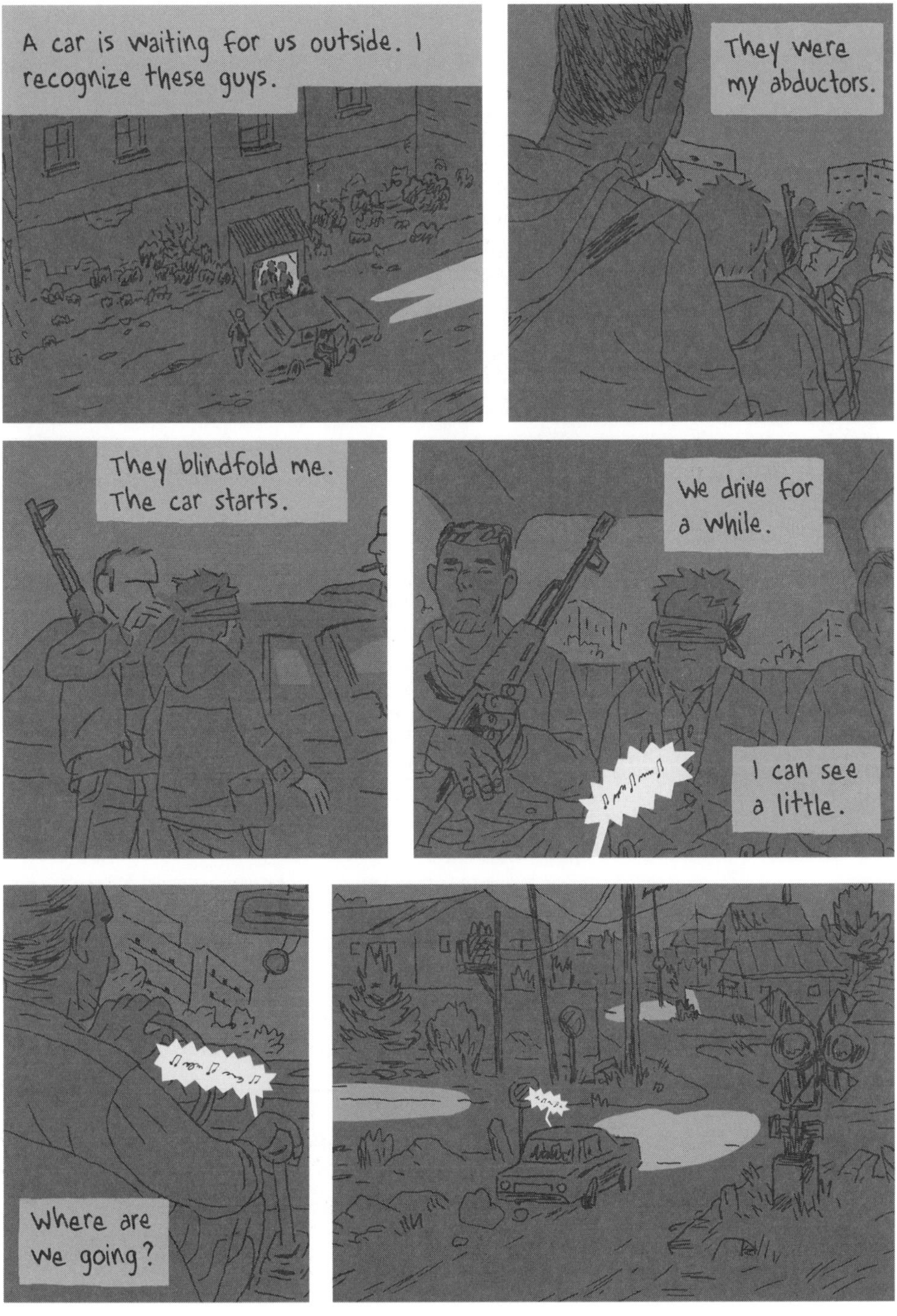
A car is waiting for us outside. I recognize these guys.
They were my abductors.
They blindfold me. The car starts.
We drive for a while.
I can see a little.
Where are we going?

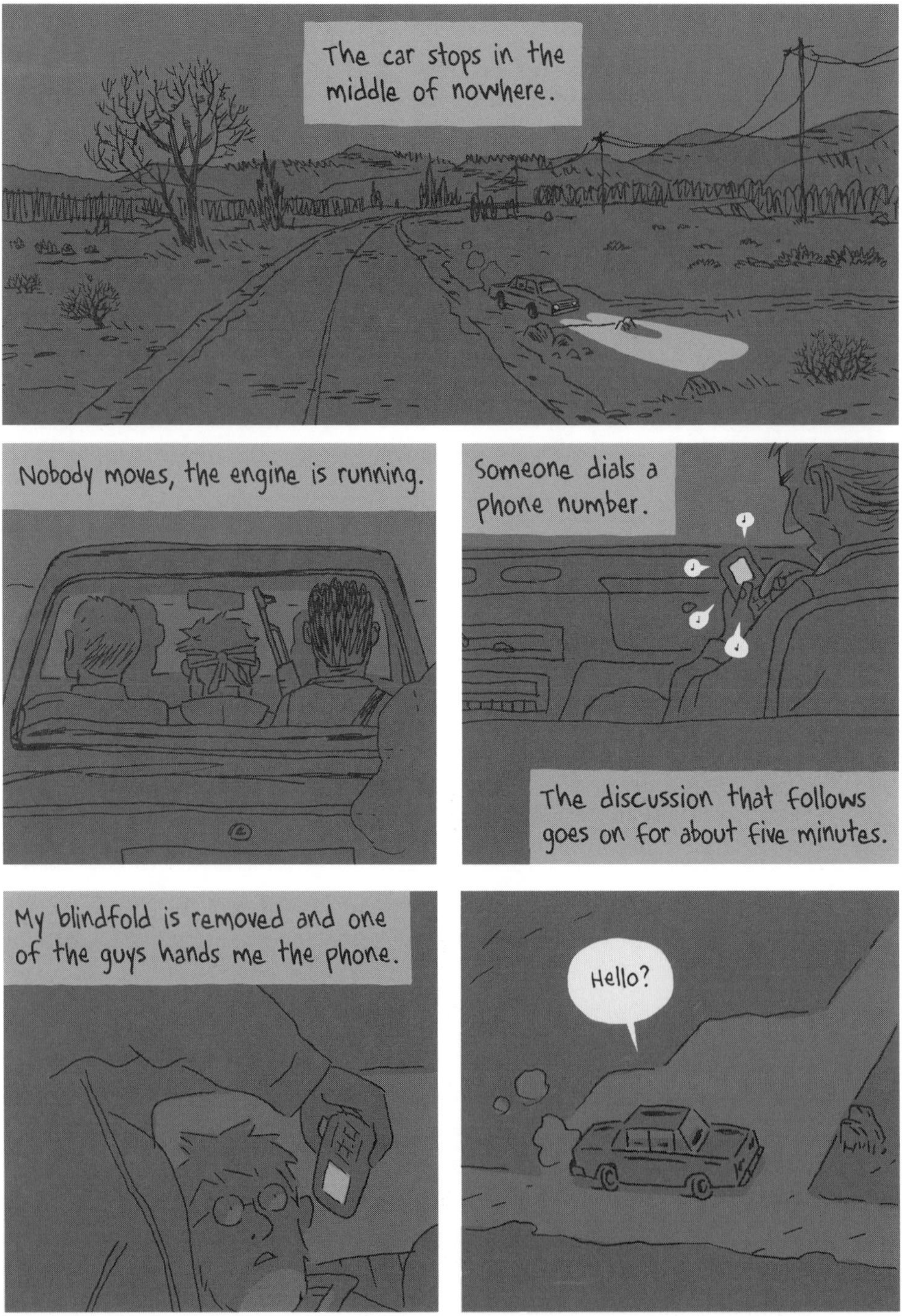
The car stops in the middle of nowhere.
Nobody moves, the engine is running.
Someone dials a phone number.
The discussion that follows goes on for about five minutes.
My blindfold is removed and one of the guys hands me the phone.
Hello?

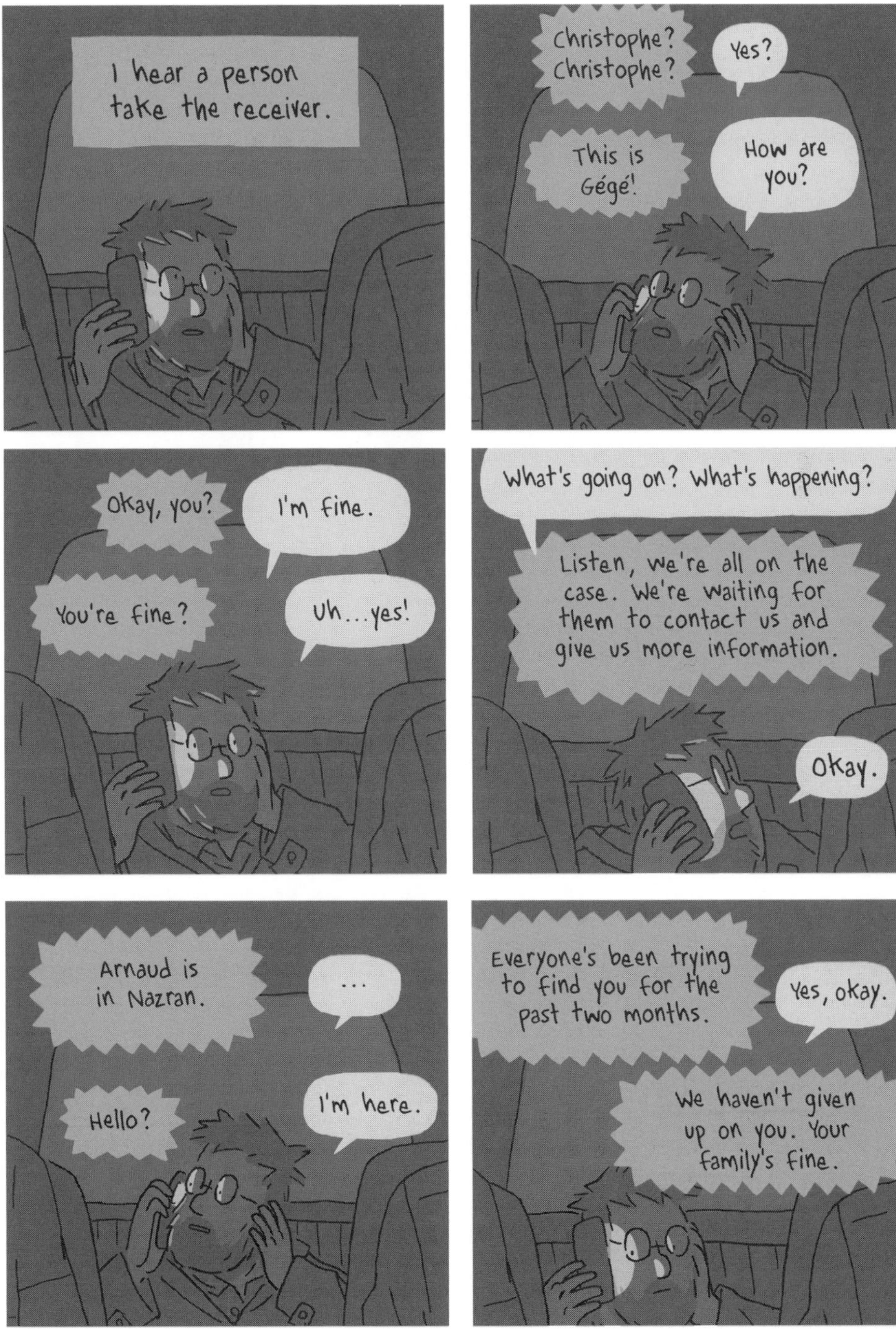

I hear a person take the receiver.
Christophe? Christophe?
Yes?
This is Gégé!
How are you?
Okay, you?
I'm fine.
You're fine?
Uh...yes!
What's going on? What's happening?
Listen, we're all on the case. We're waiting for them to contact us and give us more information.
Okay.
Arnaud is in Nazran.
...
Hello?
I'm here.
Everyone's been trying to find you for the past two months.
Yes, okay.
We haven't given up on you. Your family's fine.

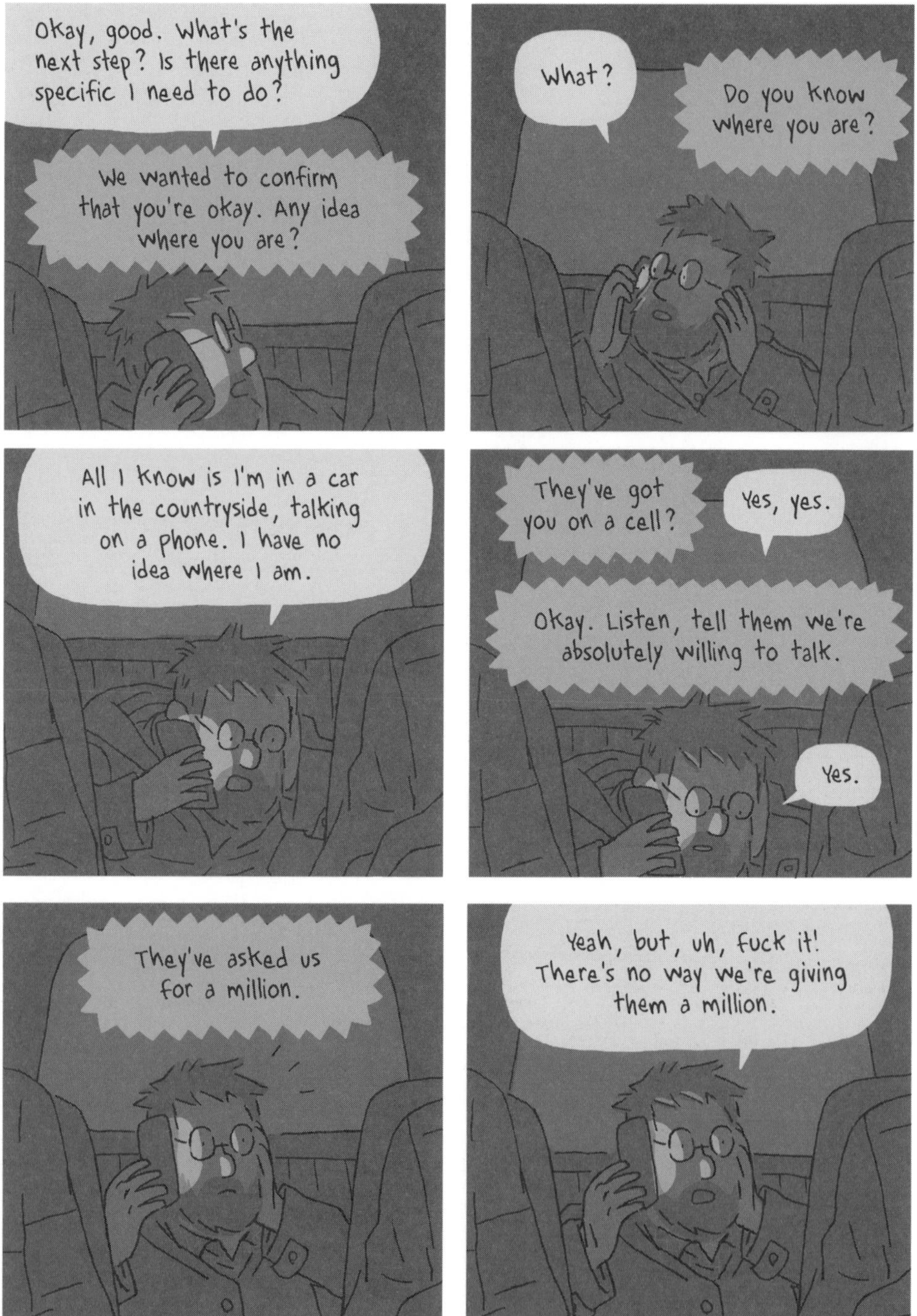
Okay, good. What's the next step? Is there anything specific I need to do?
We wanted to confirm that you're okay. Any idea where you are?
What?
Do you know where you are?
All I know is I'm in a car in the countryside, talking on a phone. I have no idea where I am.
They've got you on a cell?
Yes, yes.
Okay. Listen, tell them we're absolutely willing to talk.
Yes.
They've asked us for a million.
Yeah, but, uh, fuck it! There's no way we're giving them a million.

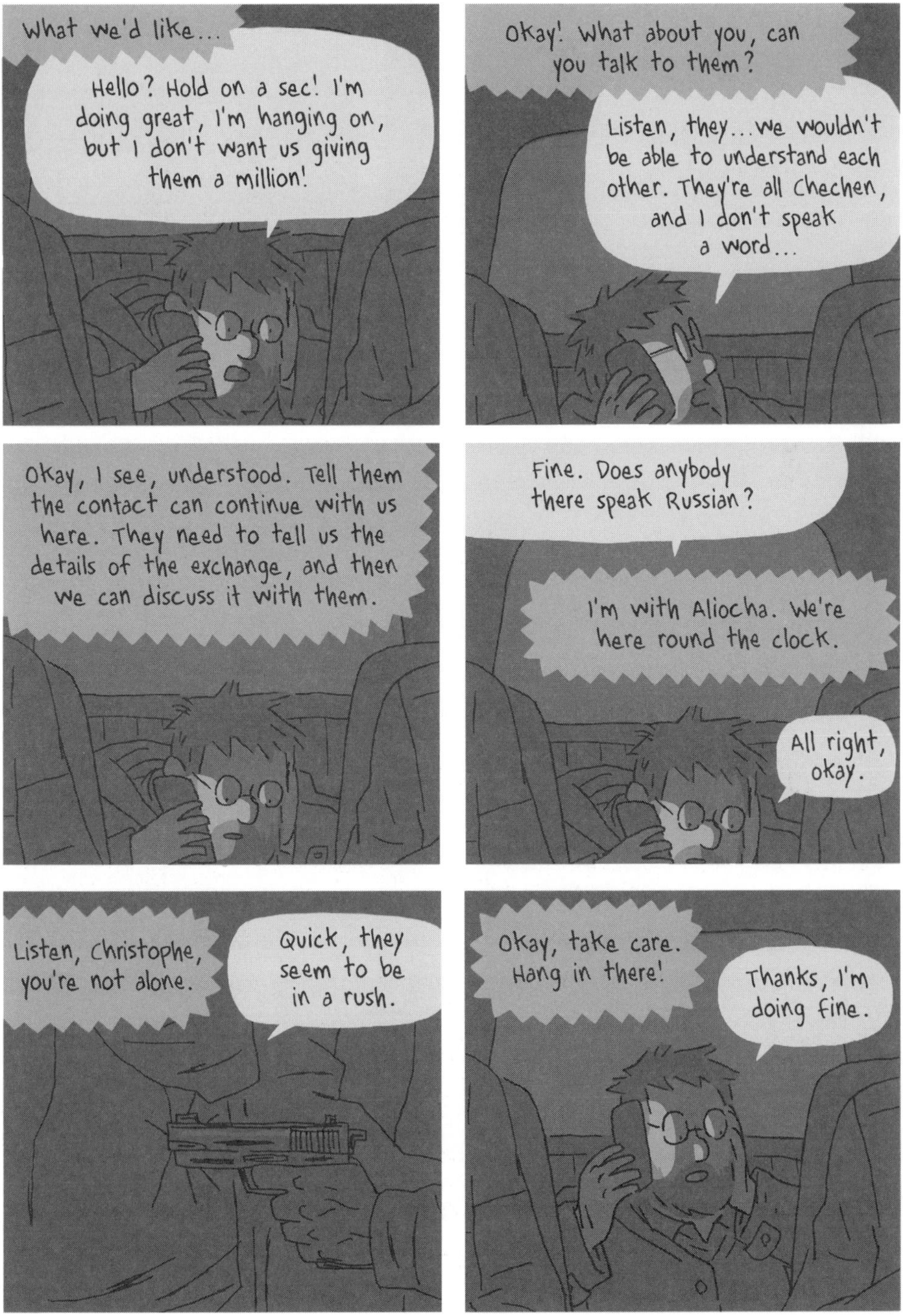
What we'd like...
Hello? Hold on a sec! I'm doing great, I'm hanging on, but I don't want us giving them a million!
Okay! What about you, can you talk to them?
Listen, they... we wouldn't be able to understand each other. They're all Chechen, and I don't speak a word...
Okay, I see, understood. Tell them the contact can continue with us here. They need to tell us the details of the exchange, and then we can discuss it with them.
Fine. Does anybody there speak Russian?
I'm with Aliocha. We're here round the clock.
All right, okay.
Listen, Christophe, you're not alone.
Quick, they seem to be in a rush.
Okay, take care. Hang in there!
Thanks, I'm doing fine.

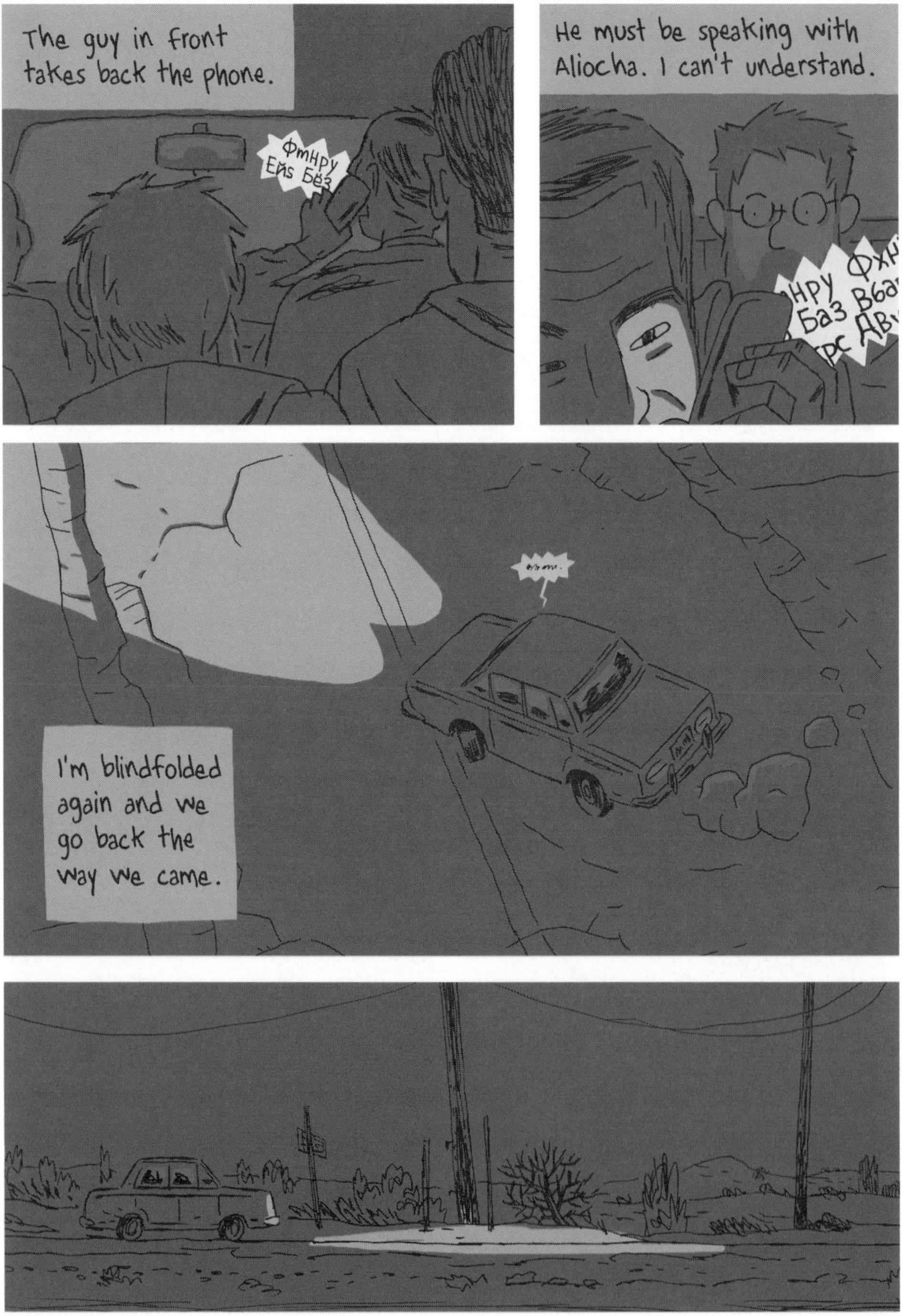
The guy in front takes back the phone.
Фmнру Ейs Бёз
He must be speaking with Aliocha. I can't understand.
I'm blindfolded again and we go back the way we came.

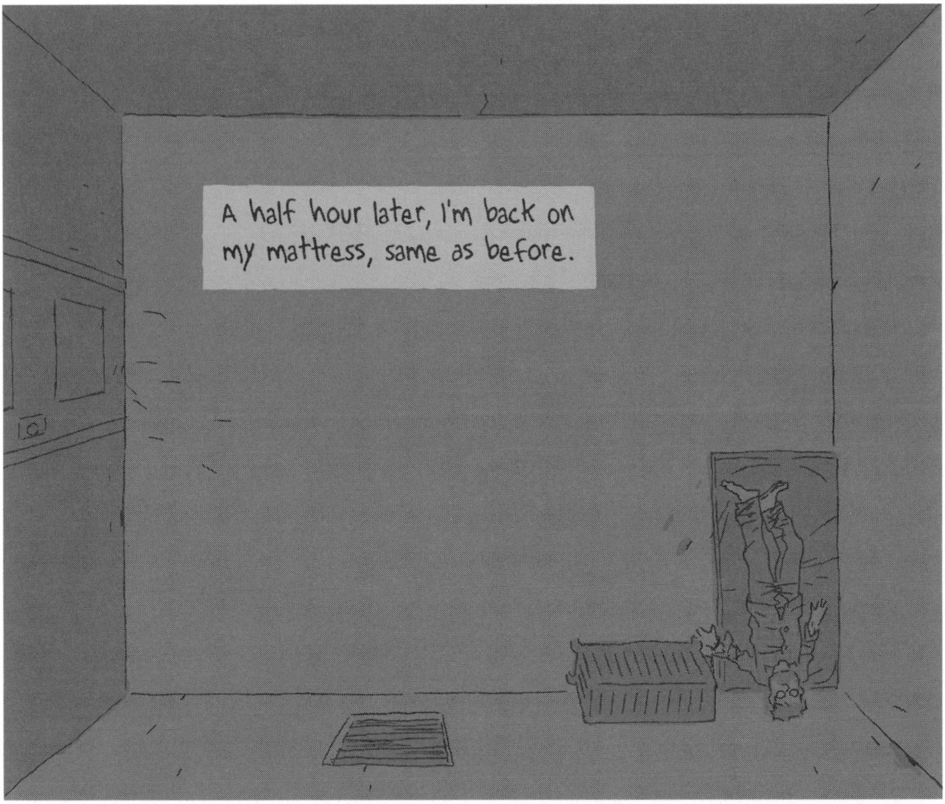
A half hour later, I'm back on my mattress, same as before.

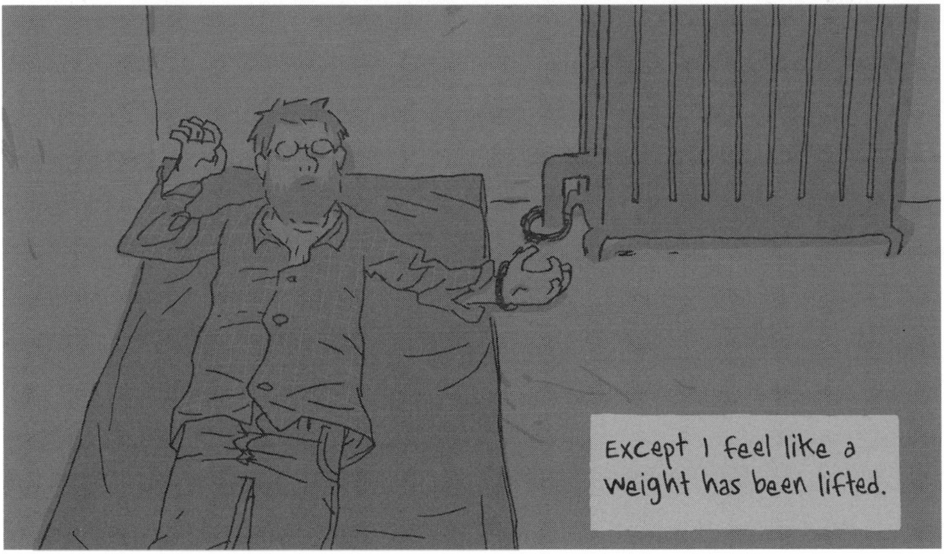
Except I feel like a weight has been lifted.

First of all, I'm not in the dark anymore. I've finally had contact with the outside.

I know for sure that people are working on my release.

I don't need to keep torturing myself with all kinds of questions.

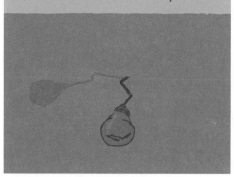

It's reassuring to know that Gérard is on it. I'm in good hands.

For the first time in two months, I've been able to act on what's happening. I told them what I think and that I don't want them paying the ransom.

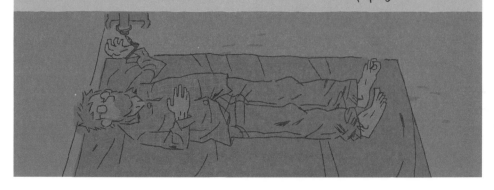

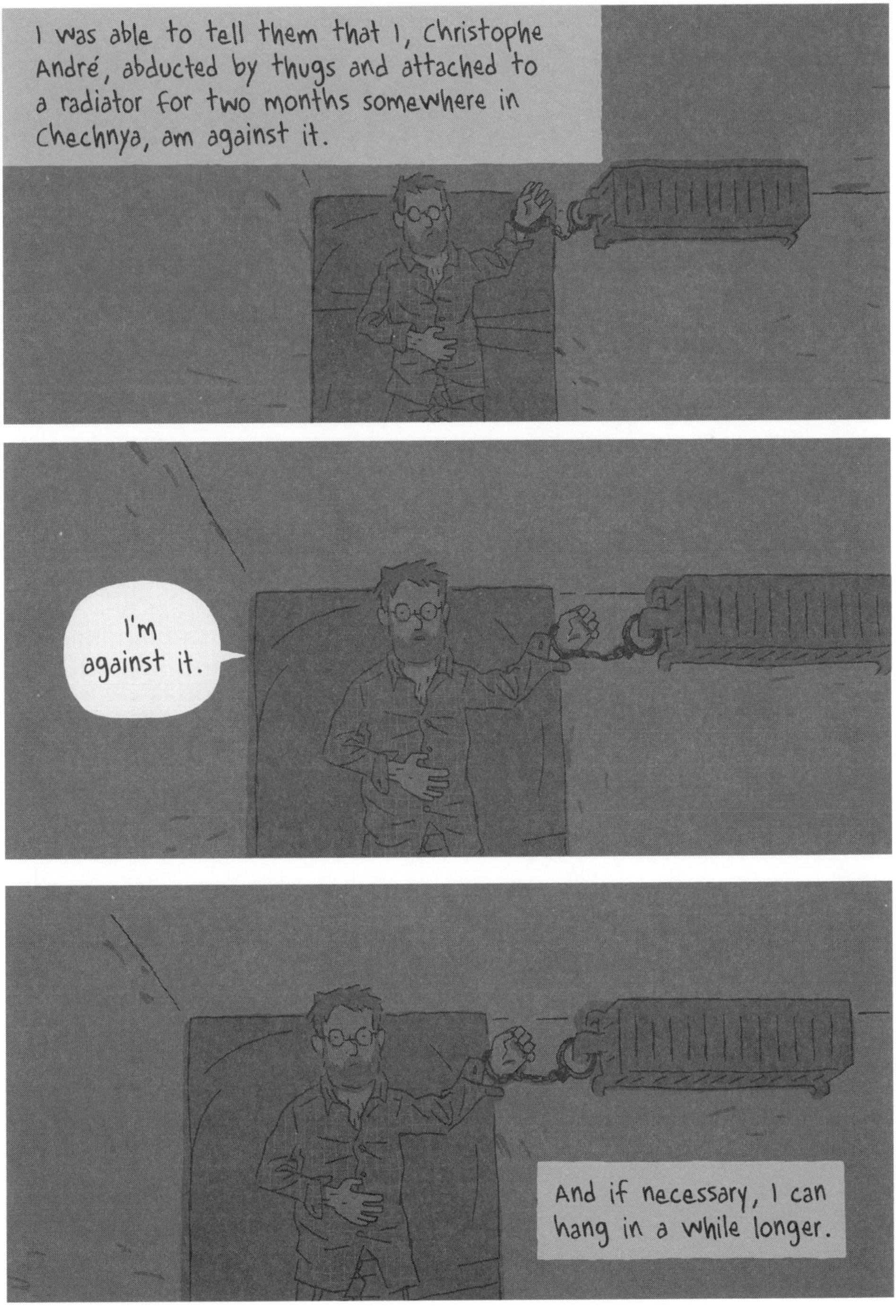
I was able to tell them that I, Christophe André, abducted by thugs and attached to a radiator for two months somewhere in Chechnya, am against it.
I'm against it.
And if necessary, I can hang in a while longer.

72

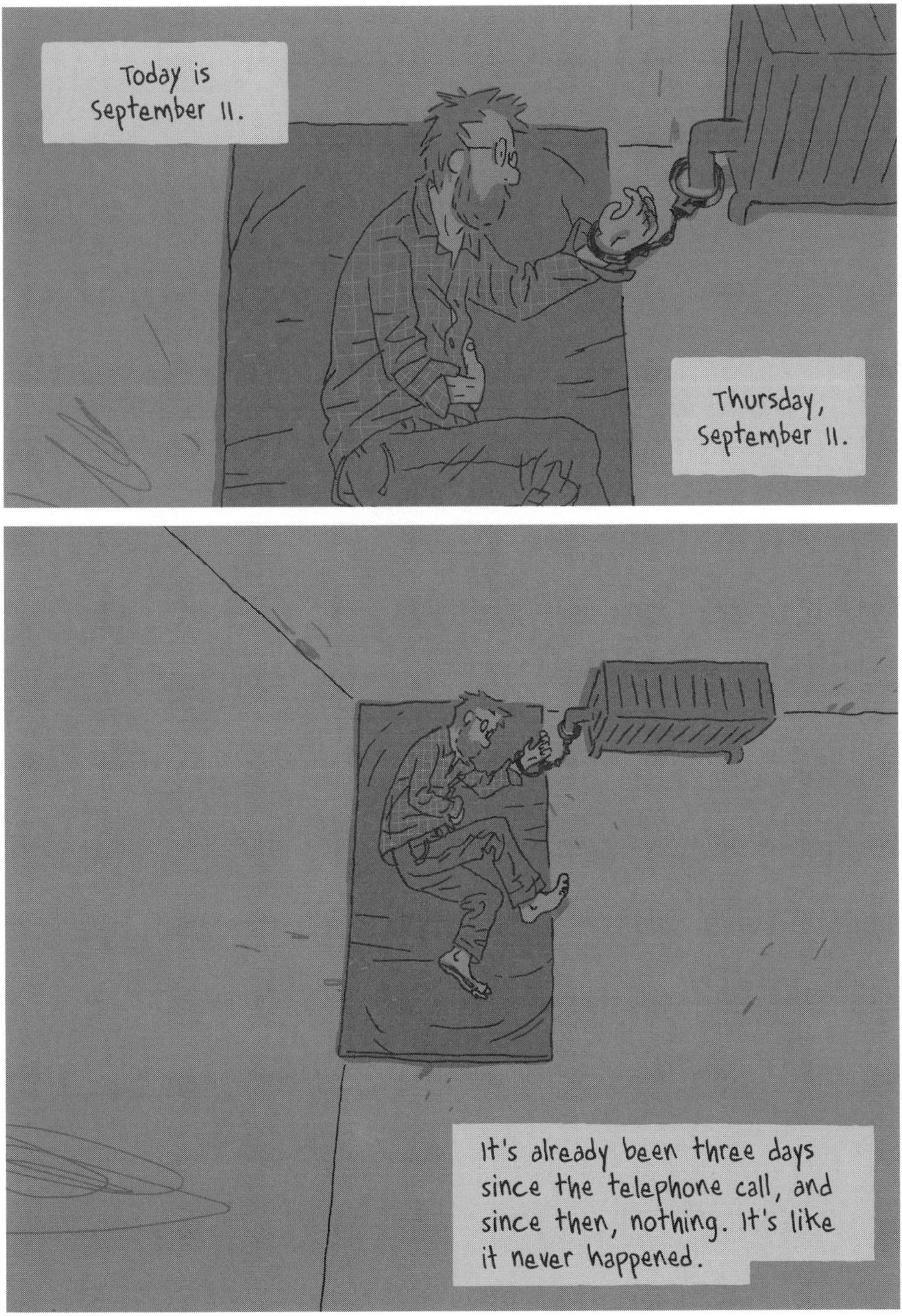
Today is September 11.
Thursday, September 11.
It's already been three days since the telephone call, and since then, nothing. It's like it never happened.

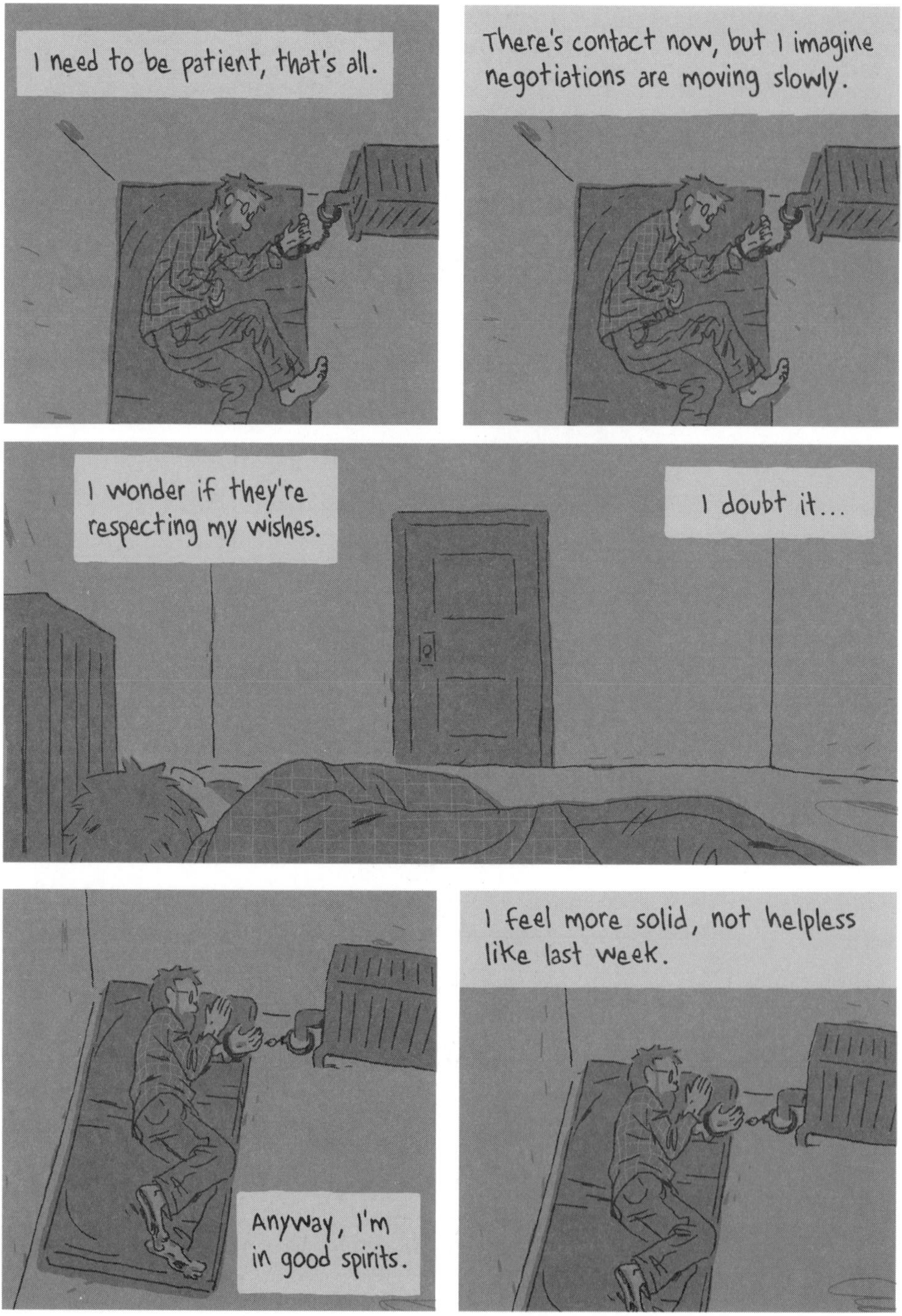
I need to be patient, that's all.
There's contact now, but I imagine negotiations are moving slowly.
I wonder if they're respecting my wishes.
I doubt it...
Anyway, I'm in good spirits.
I feel more solid, not helpless like last week.

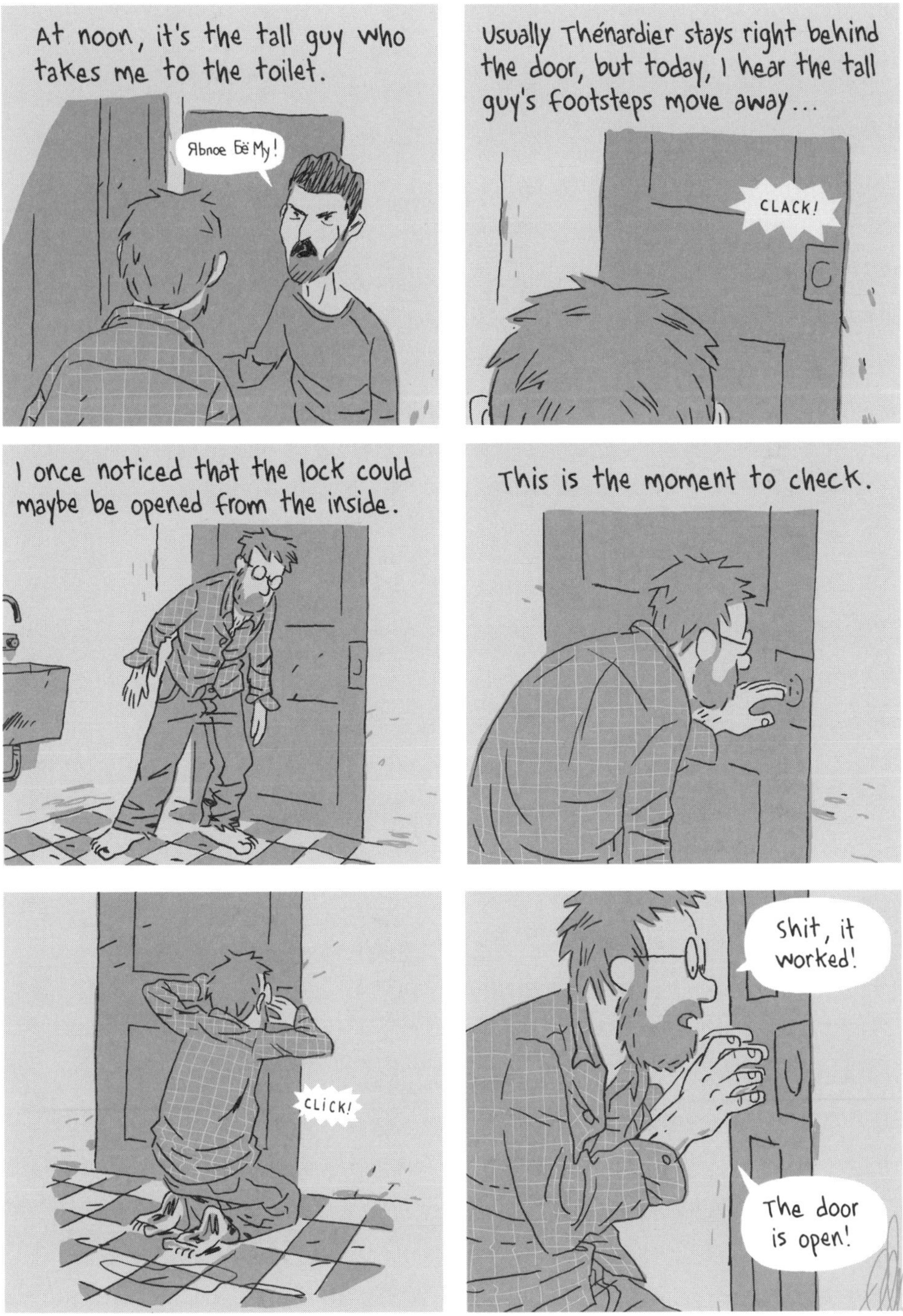

At noon, it's the tall guy who takes me to the toilet.
Яьпое Бё Му!
Usually Thénardier stays right behind the door, but today, I hear the tall guy's footsteps move away...
CLACK!
I once noticed that the lock could maybe be opened from the inside.
This is the moment to check.
CLICK!
Shit, it worked!
The door is open!

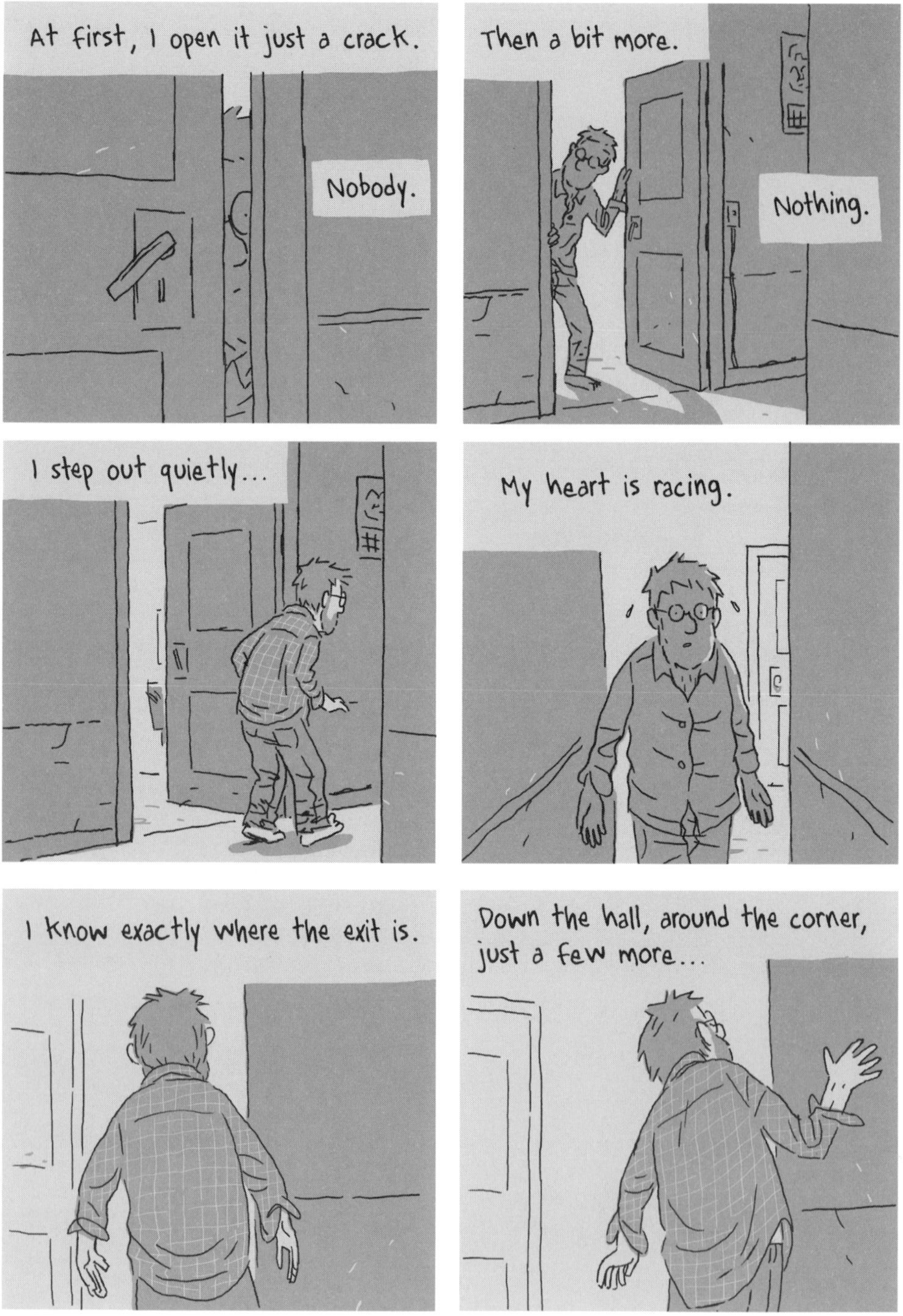
At first, I open it just a crack.
Nobody.
Then a bit more.
Nothing.
I step out quietly...
My heart is racing.
I know exactly where the exit is.
Down the hall, around the corner, just a few more...

He's there, smirking.

Ласу Дтив Вcy!

He packs me off to the back room.

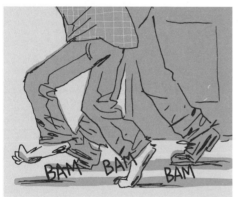

BAM BAM BAM

CRRRRRICK!

SLAM!

shit...

At least I gave it a try...

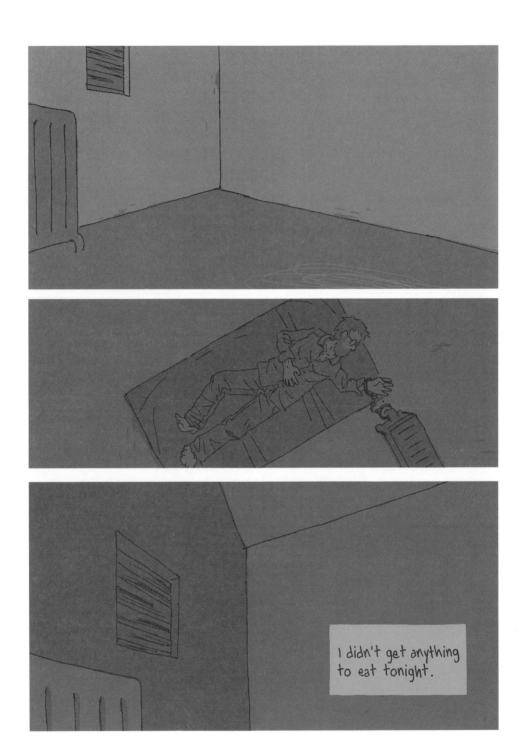

I didn't get anything to eat tonight.

74

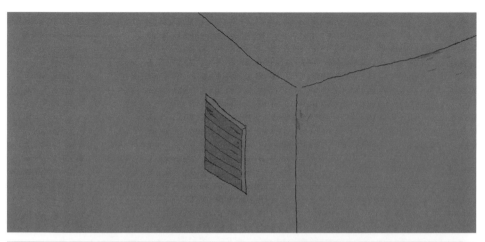

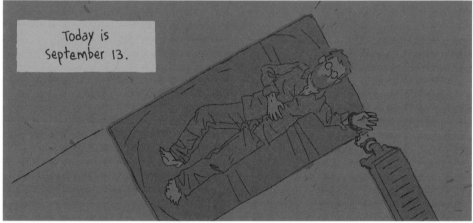

Today is
September 13.

Saturday, September 13.

It's a date
I'm not likely
to forget.

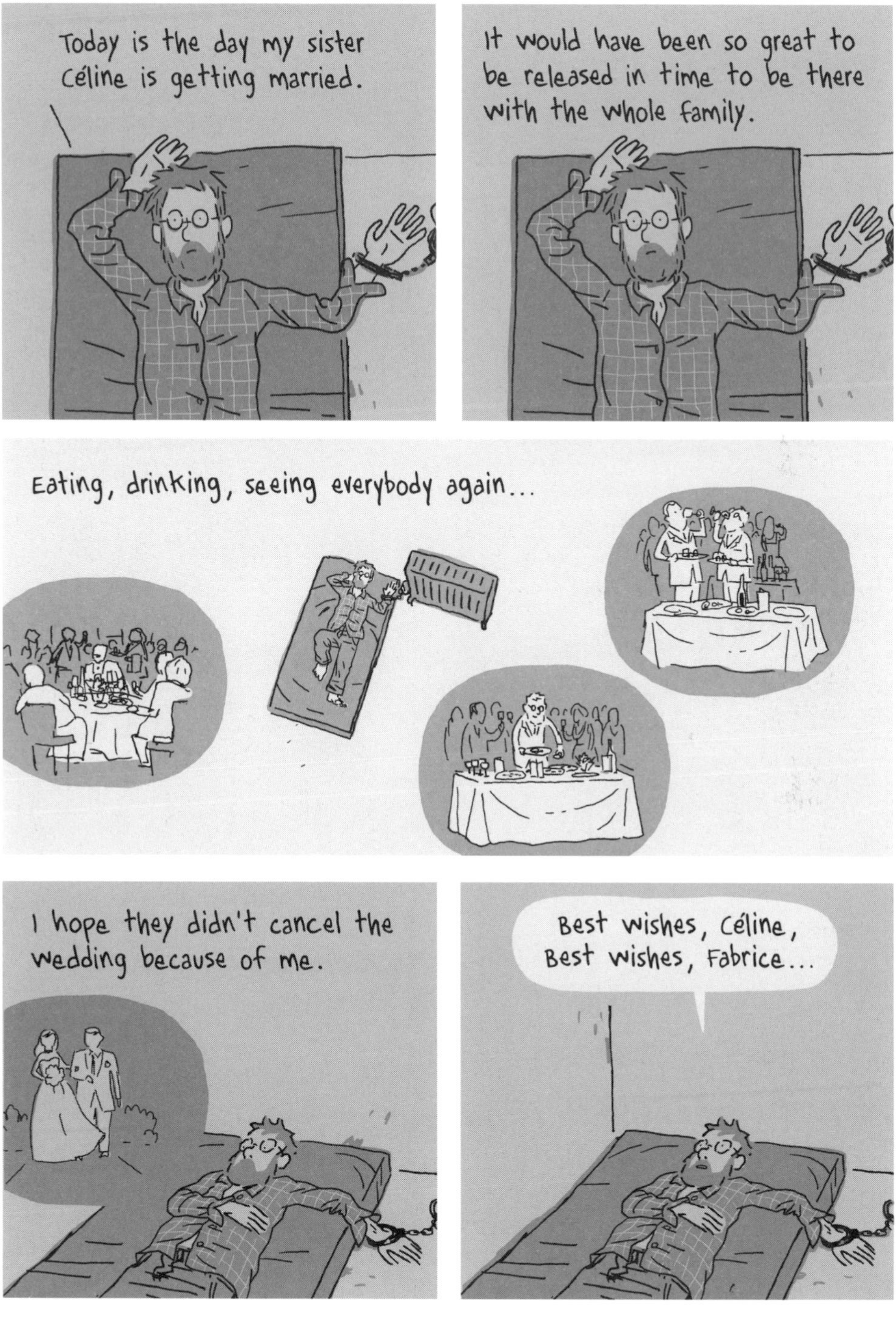
Today is the day my sister Céline is getting married.
It would have been so great to be released in time to be there with the whole family.
Eating, drinking, seeing everybody again...
I hope they didn't cancel the wedding because of me.
Best wishes, Céline, Best wishes, Fabrice...

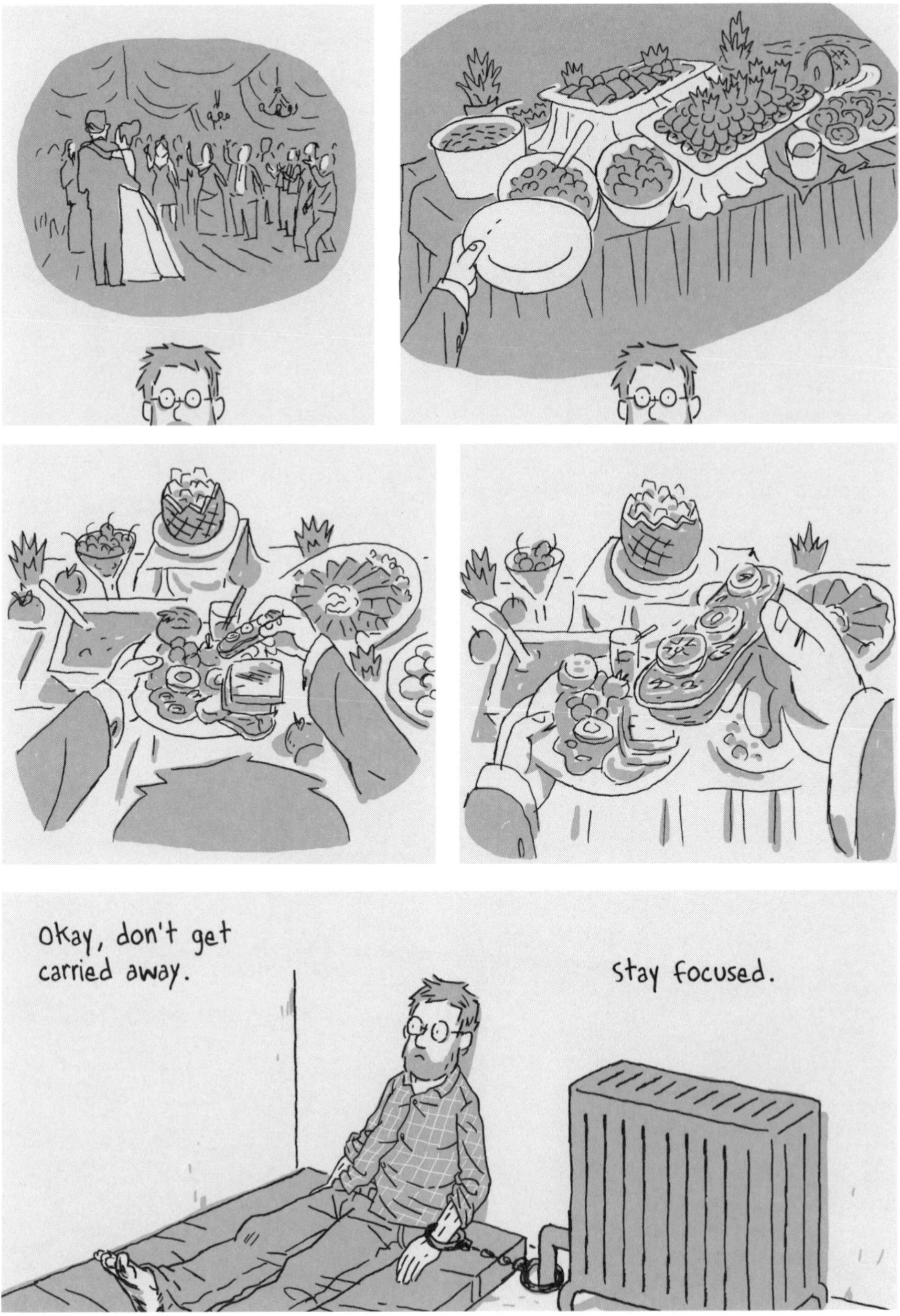
Okay, don't get
carried away.
Stay focused.

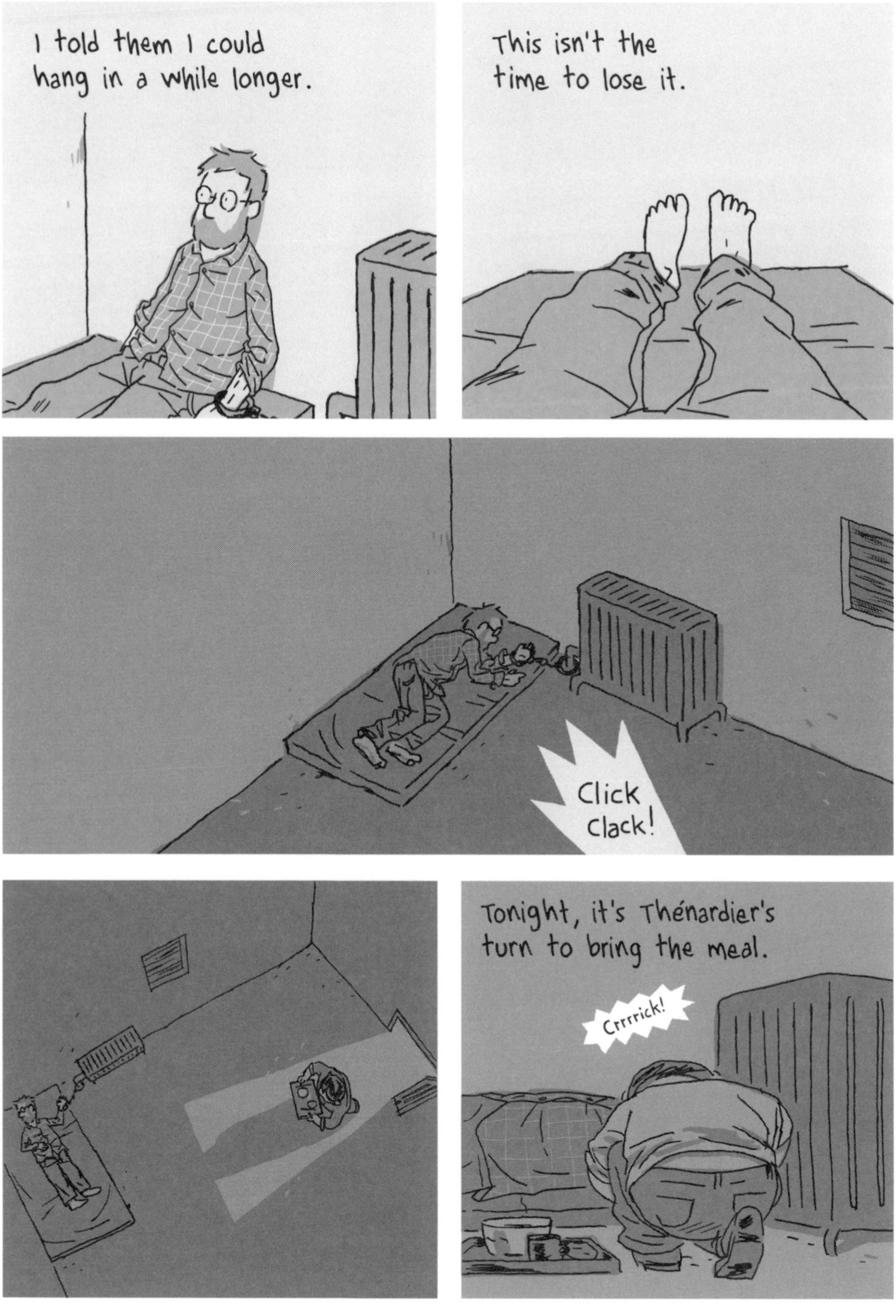
I told them I could hang in a while longer.
This isn't the time to lose it.
Click Clack!
Tonight, it's Thénardier's turn to bring the meal.
Crrrick!

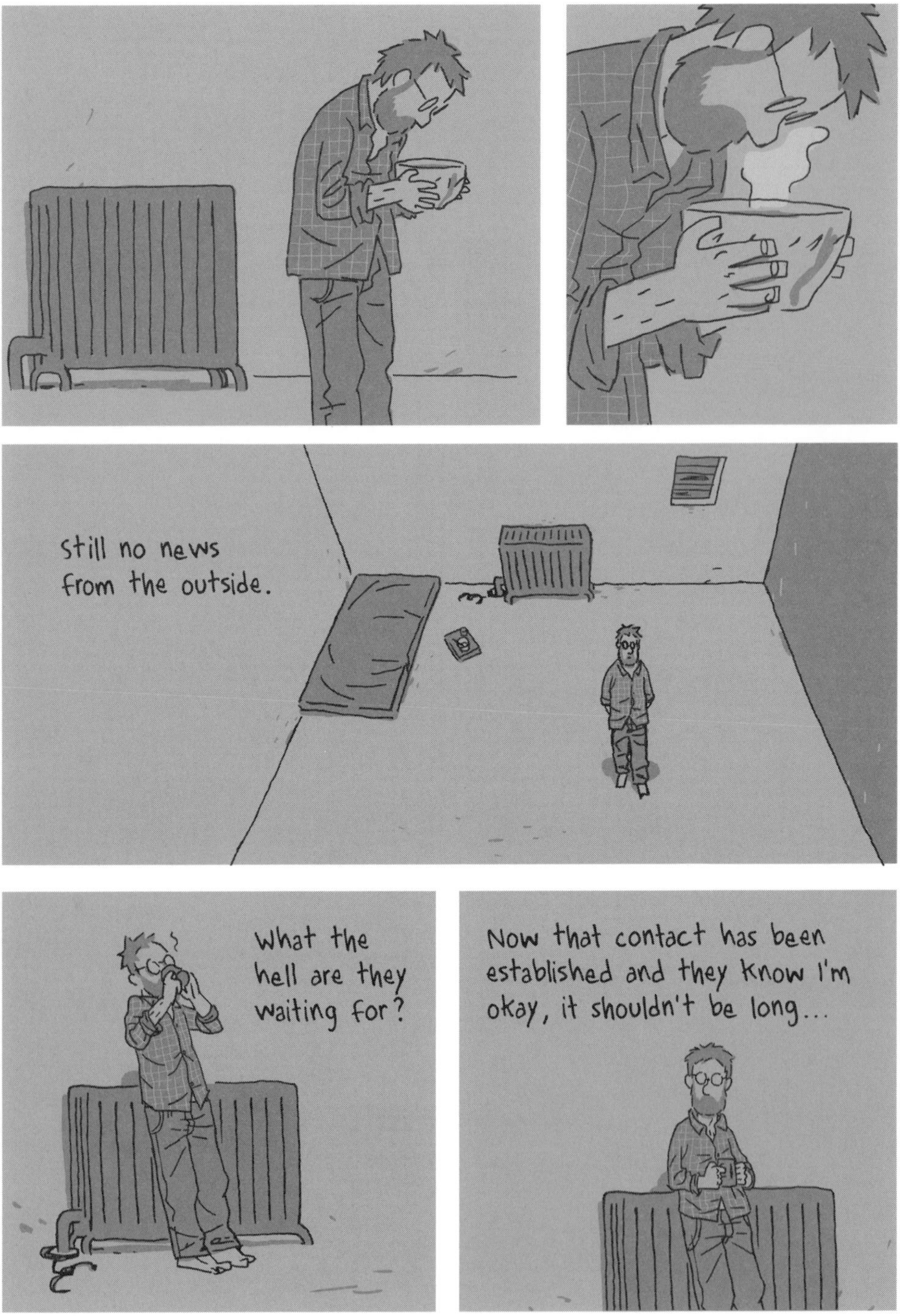
Still no news from the outside.
What the hell are they waiting for?
Now that contact has been established and they know I'm okay, it shouldn't be long...

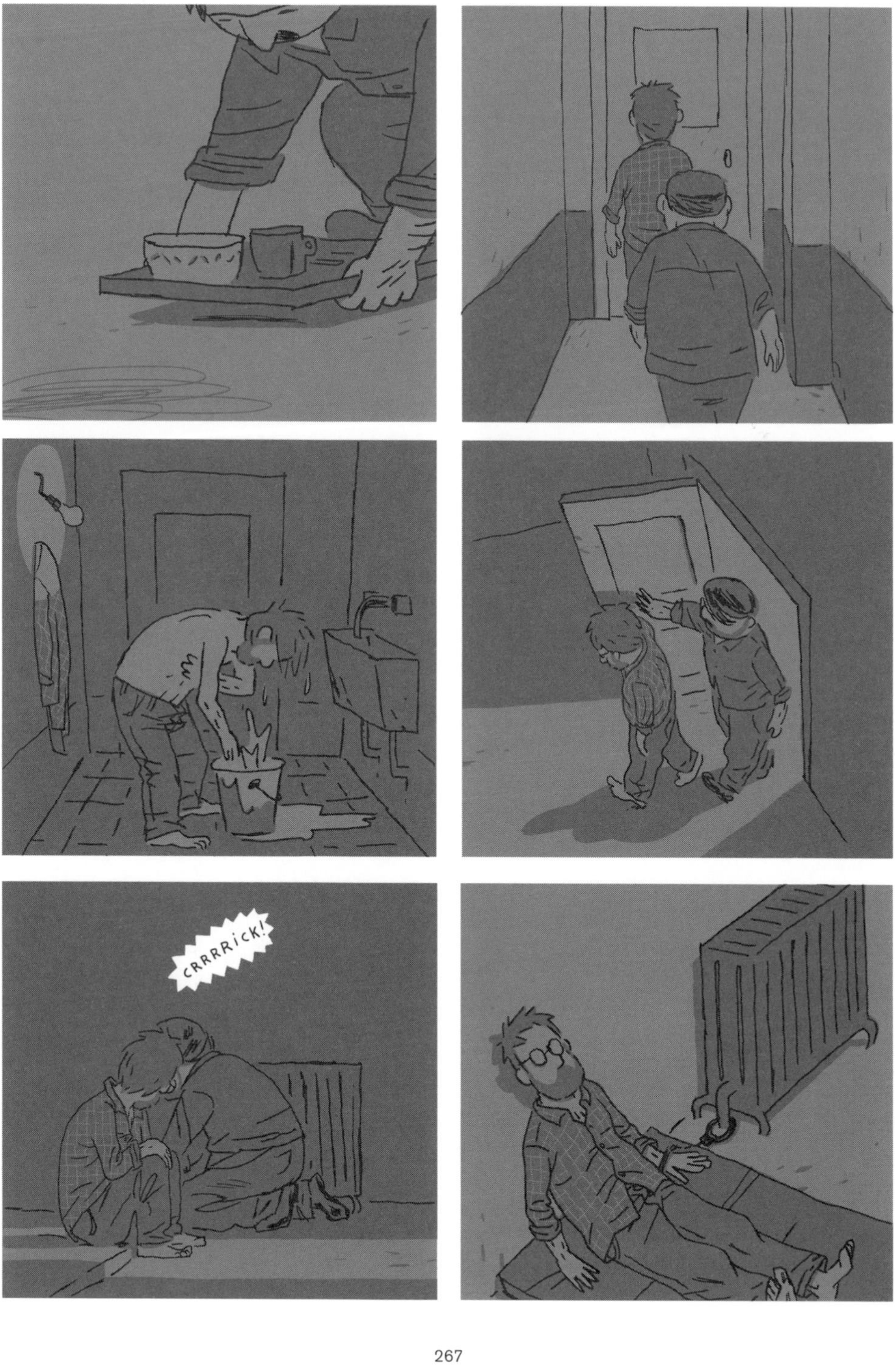
CRRRRiCK!

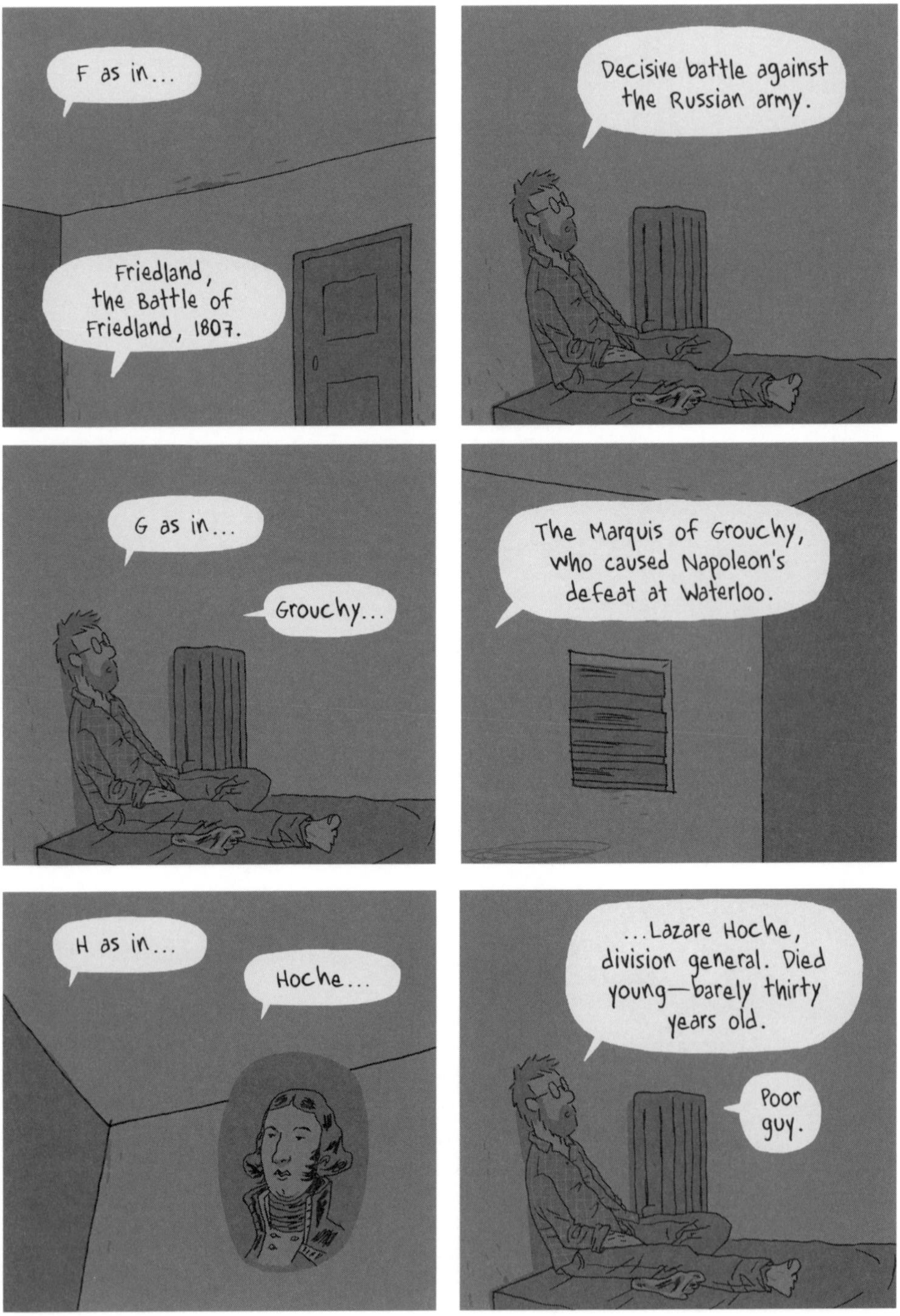
F as in...
Friedland, the Battle of Friedland, 1807.
Decisive battle against the Russian army.
G as in...
Grouchy...
The Marquis of Grouchy, who caused Napoleon's defeat at Waterloo.
H as in...
Hoche...
...Lazare Hoche, division general. Died young—barely thirty years old.
Poor guy.

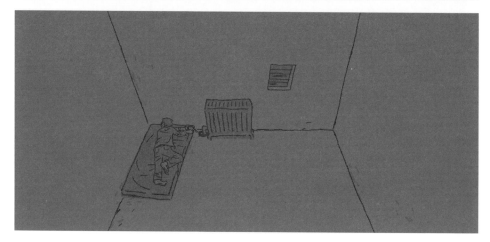

75

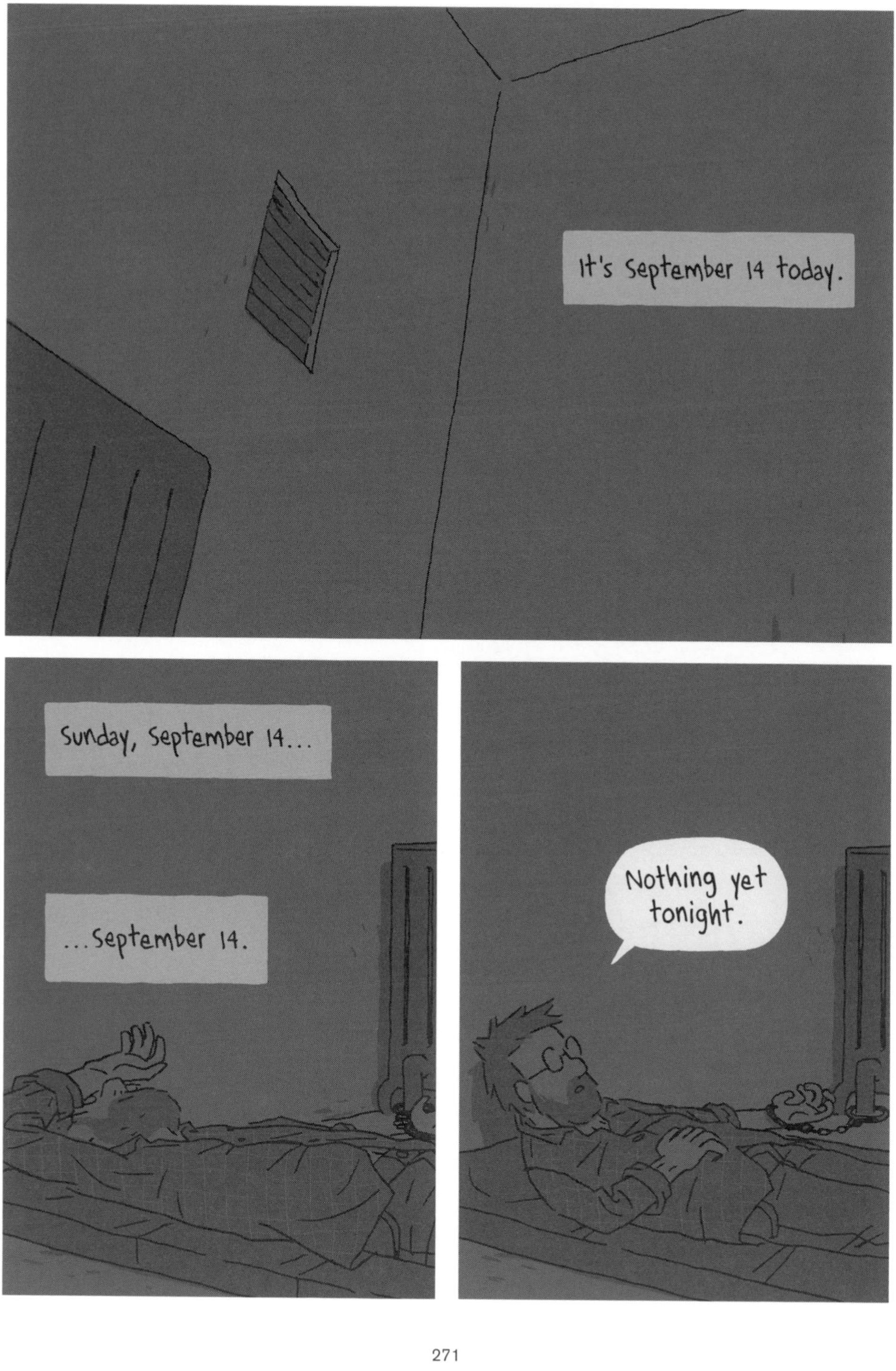
It's September 14 today.
Sunday, September 14...
...September 14.
Nothing yet tonight.

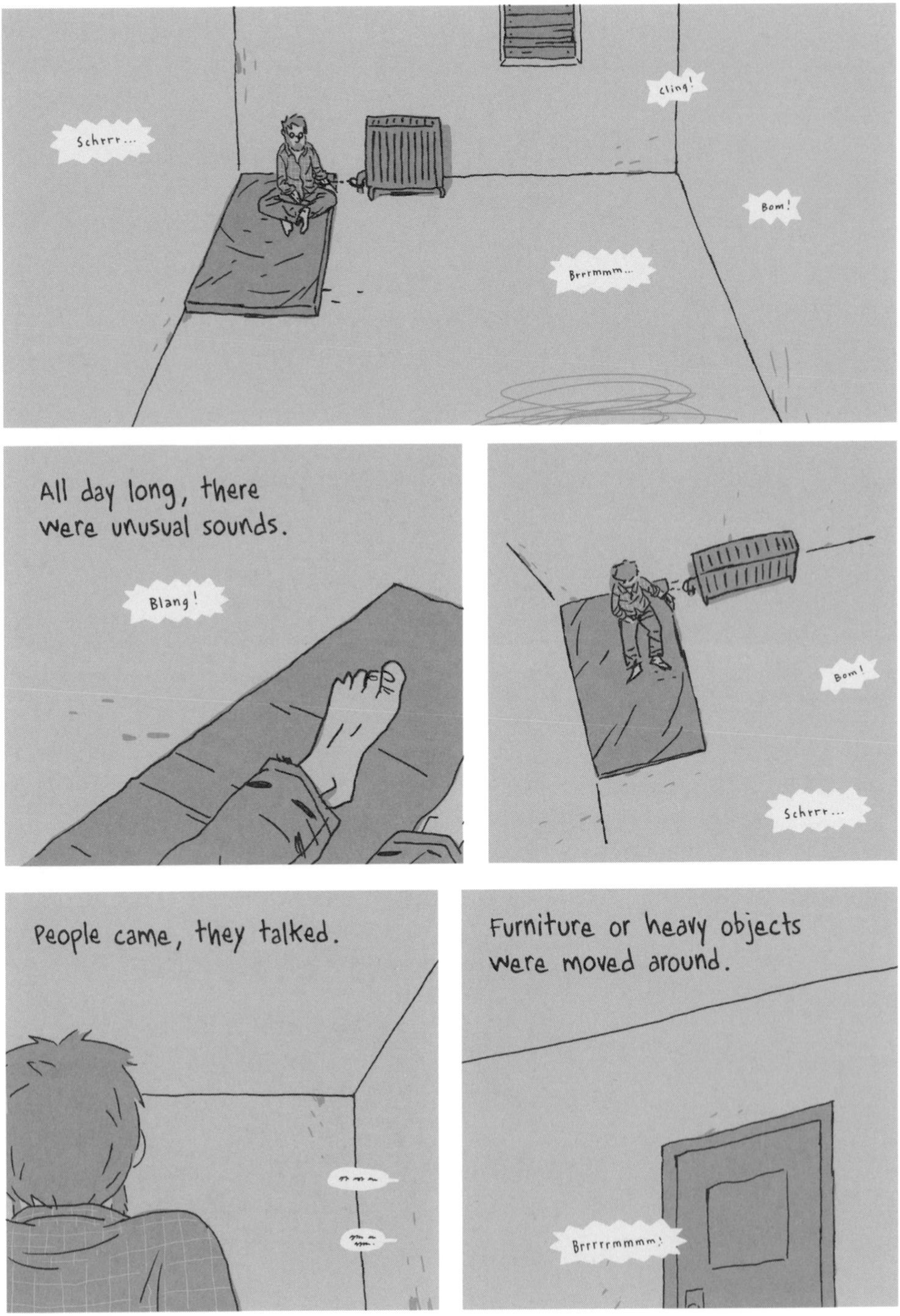
Schrrr...
cling!
Bom!
Brrrmmm...
All day long, there were unusual sounds.
Blang!
Bom!
Schrrr...
People came, they talked.
Furniture or heavy objects were moved around.
Brrrrmmmm!

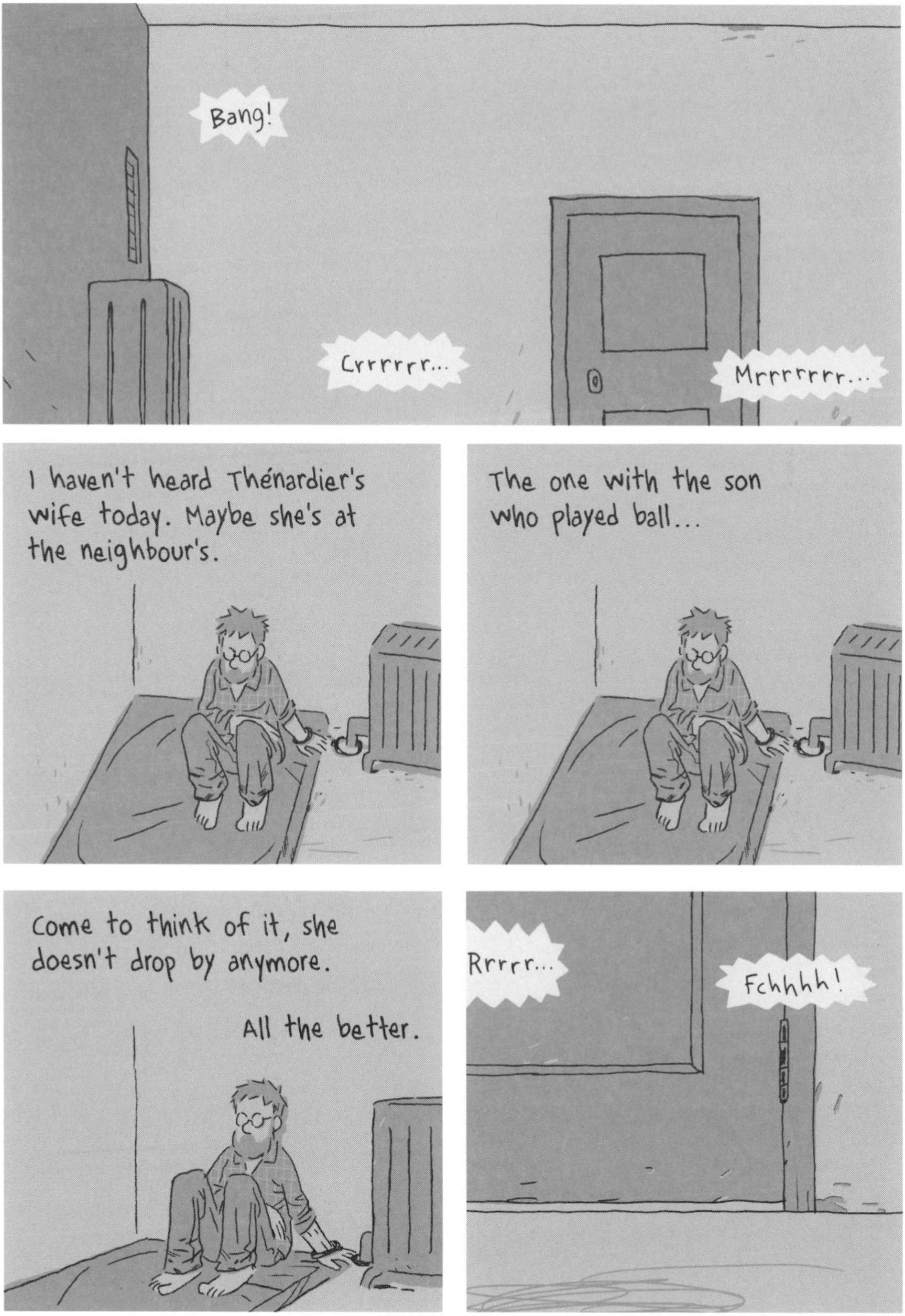
Bang!
Crrrrrr...
Mrrrrrrr...
I haven't heard Thénardier's wife today. Maybe she's at the neighbour's.
The one with the son who played ball...
Come to think of it, she doesn't drop by anymore.
All the better.
Rrrrr...
Fchhhh!

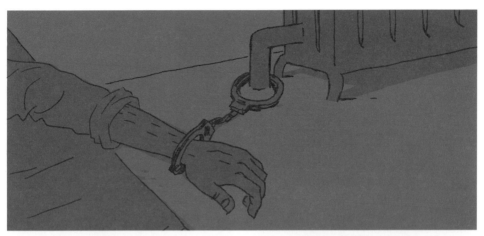

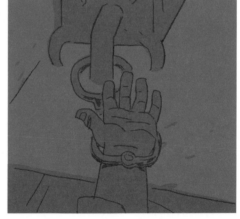

Click
Clack!

The door opens in the middle of the night.

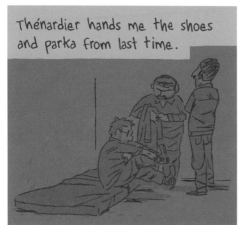

Thénardier hands me the shoes and parka from last time.

We walk through the apartment.

A car is waiting outside.

We drive for just under half an hour.

This time, I'm not blindfolded.

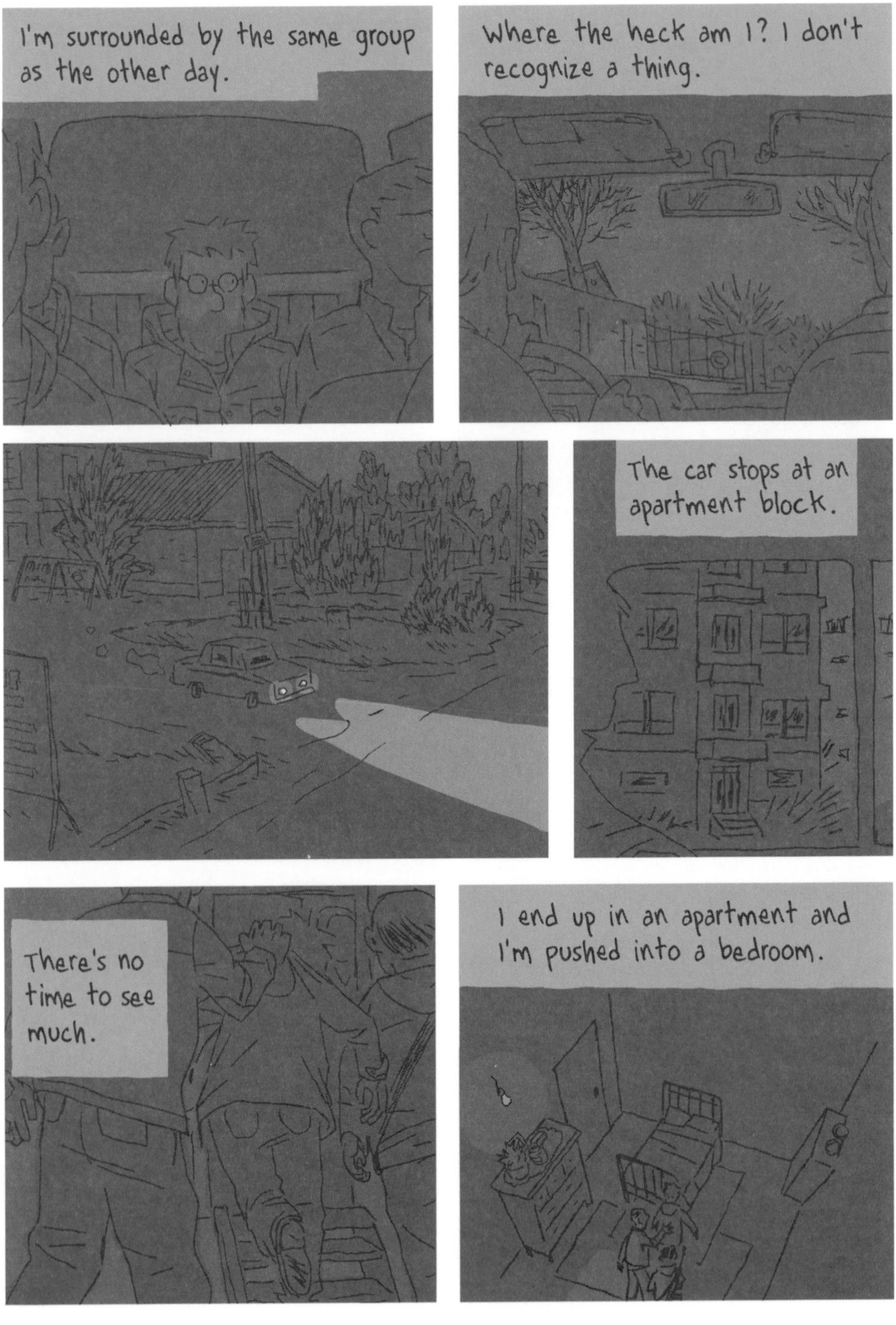
I'm surrounded by the same group as the other day.
Where the heck am I? I don't recognize a thing.
The car stops at an apartment block.
There's no time to see much.
I end up in an apartment and I'm pushed into a bedroom.

A guy I haven't seen before motions for me to sit next to the bed.

He handcuffs me with my arm up, and I find myself in a very uncomfortable position.

Crrrick!

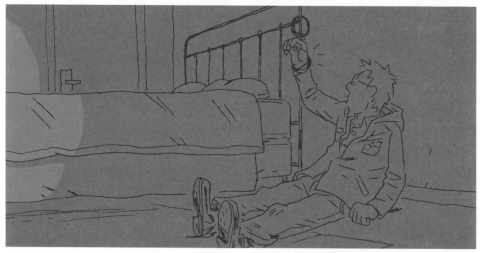

CLICK!

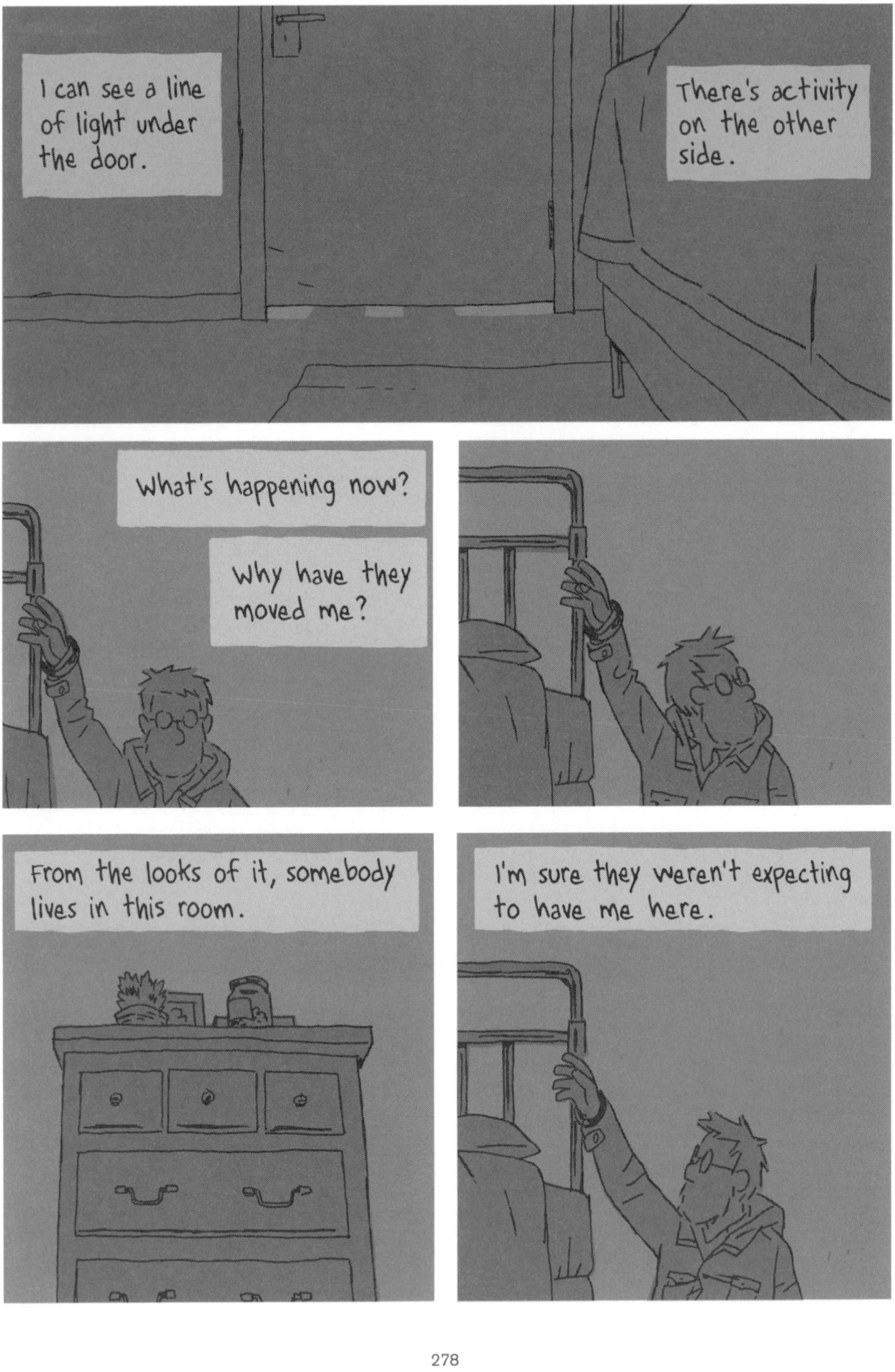
I can see a line of light under the door.
There's activity on the other side.
What's happening now?
Why have they moved me?
From the looks of it, somebody lives in this room.
I'm sure they weren't expecting to have me here.

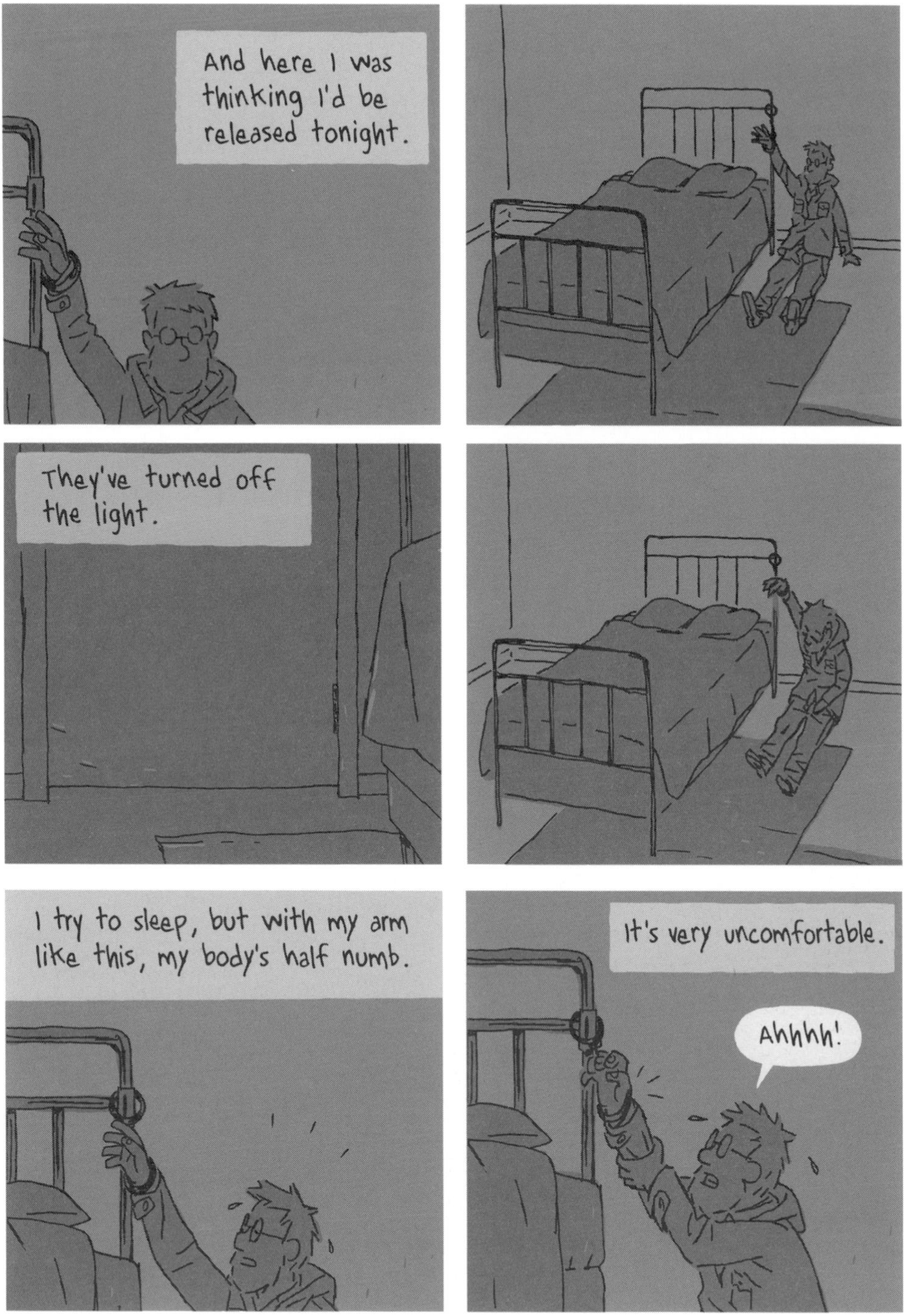
And here I was thinking I'd be released tonight.
They've turned off the light.
I try to sleep, but with my arm like this, my body's half numb.
It's very uncomfortable.
Ahhhh!

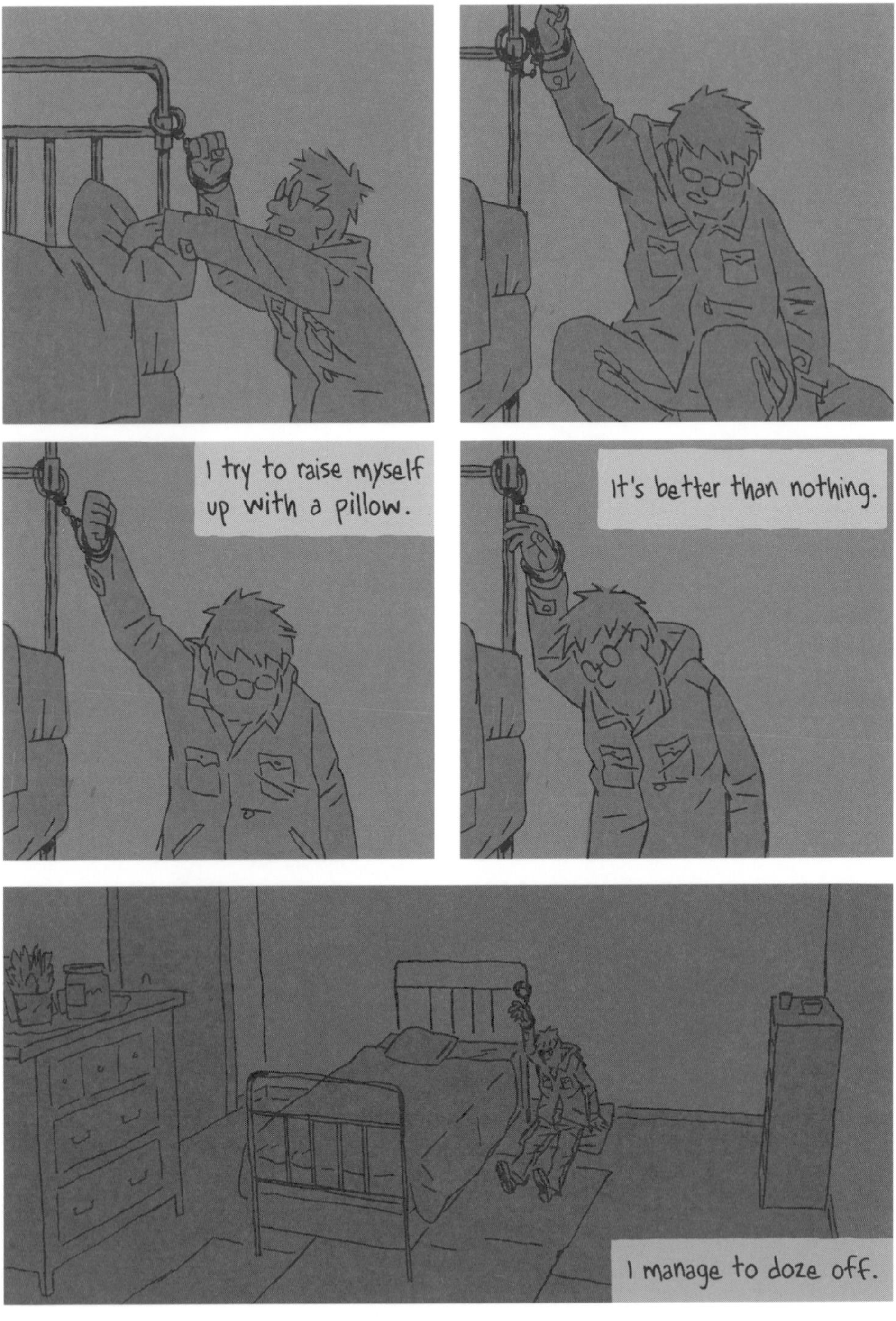
I try to raise myself up with a pillow.
It's better than nothing.
I manage to doze off.

76

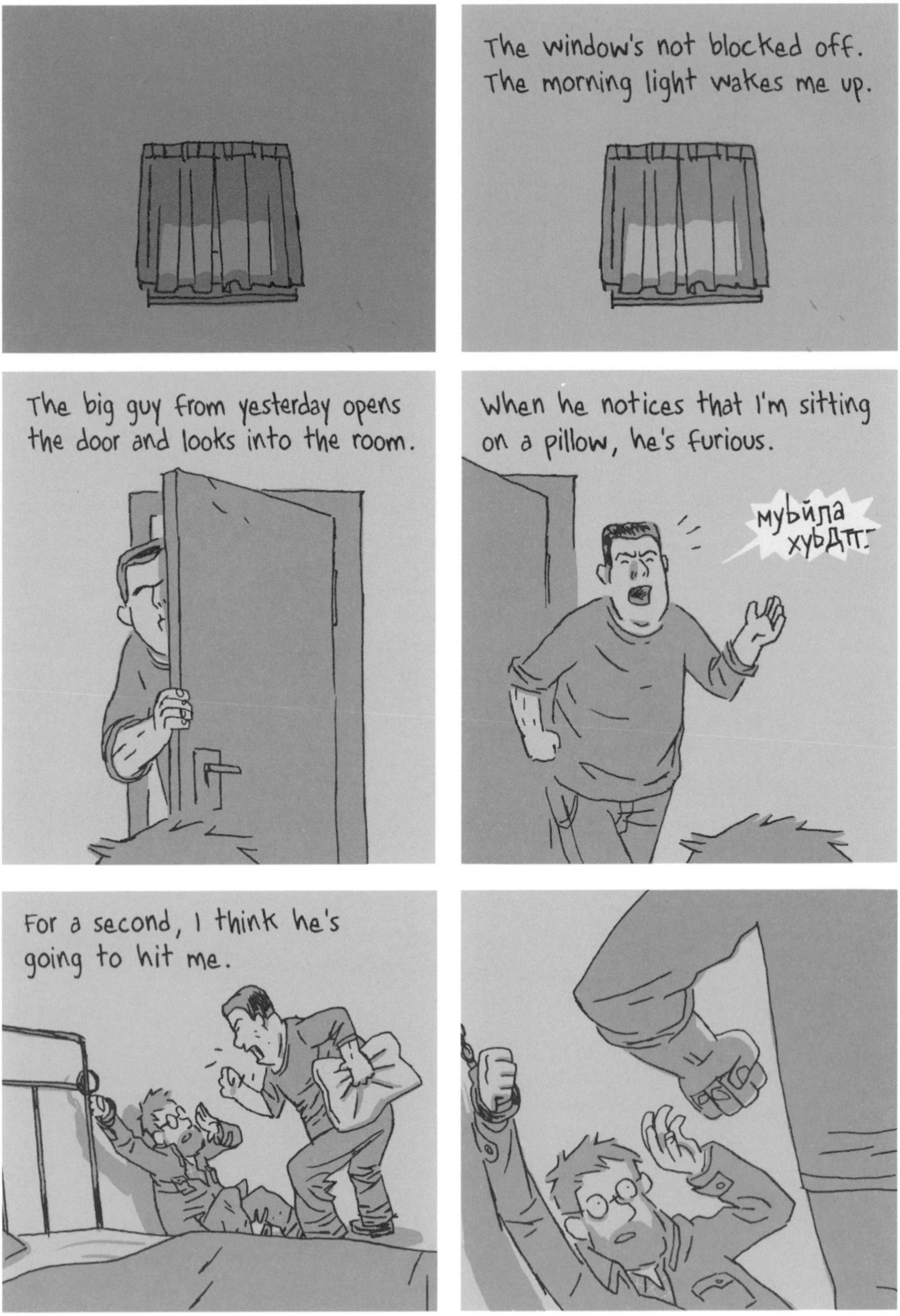
The window's not blocked off.
The morning light wakes me up.
The big guy from yesterday opens the door and looks into the room.
When he notices that I'm sitting on a pillow, he's furious.
муЬйла хуЬДПП!
For a second, I think he's going to hit me.

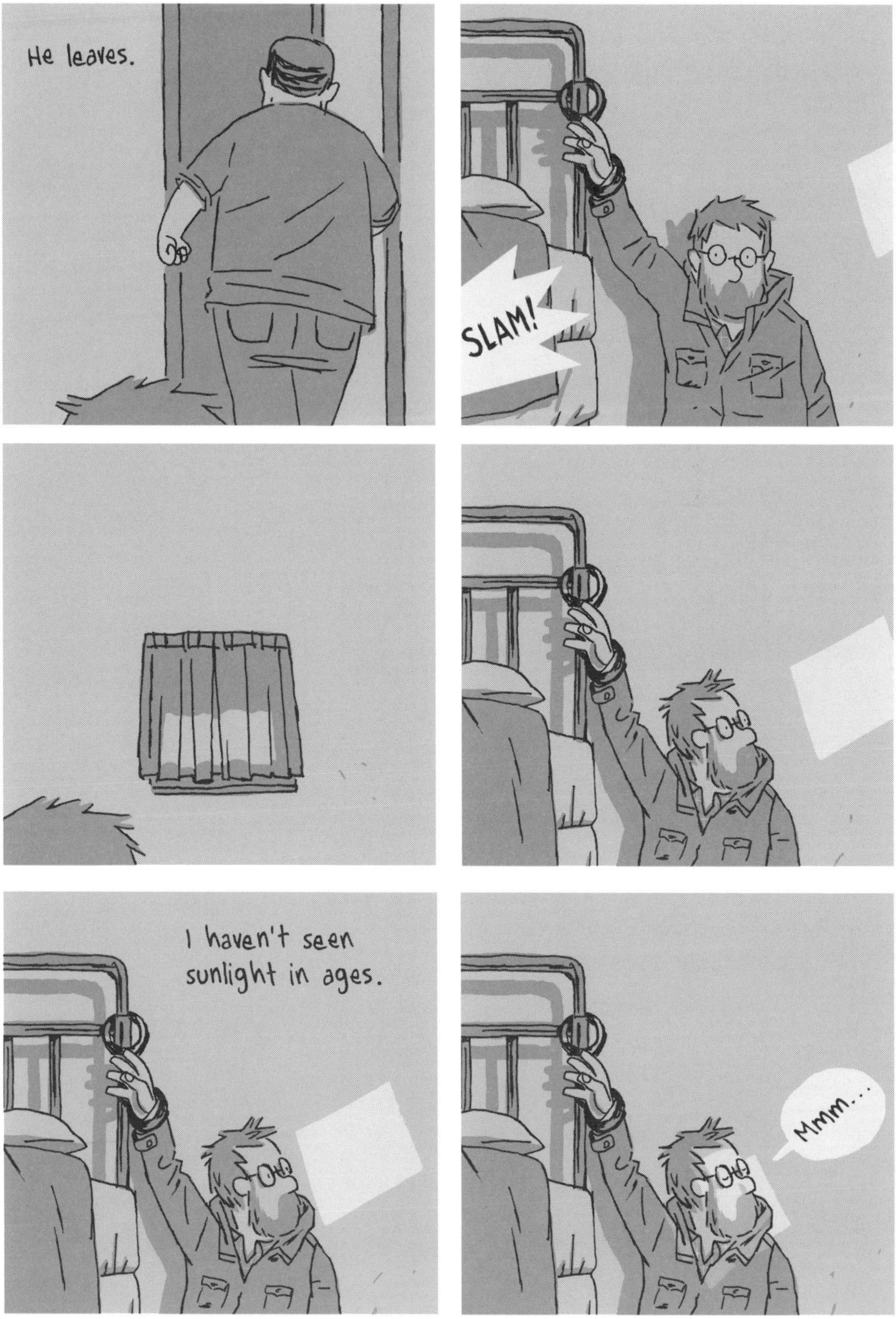
He leaves.
SLAM!
I haven't seen sunlight in ages.
Mmm...

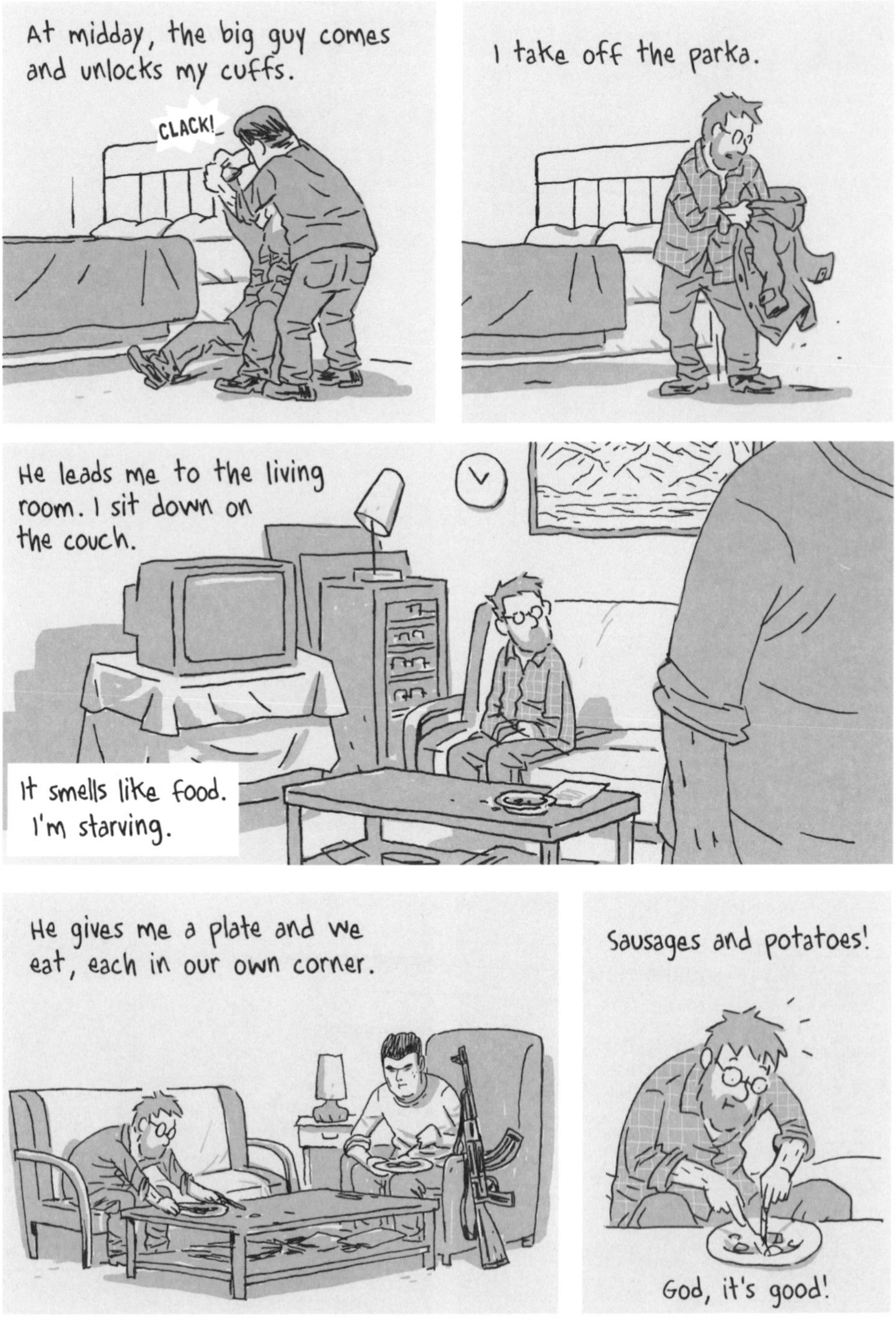
At midday, the big guy comes and unlocks my cuffs.
CLACK!
I take off the parka.
He leads me to the living room. I sit down on the couch.
It smells like food. I'm starving.
He gives me a plate and we eat, each in our own corner.
Sausages and potatoes!
God, it's good!

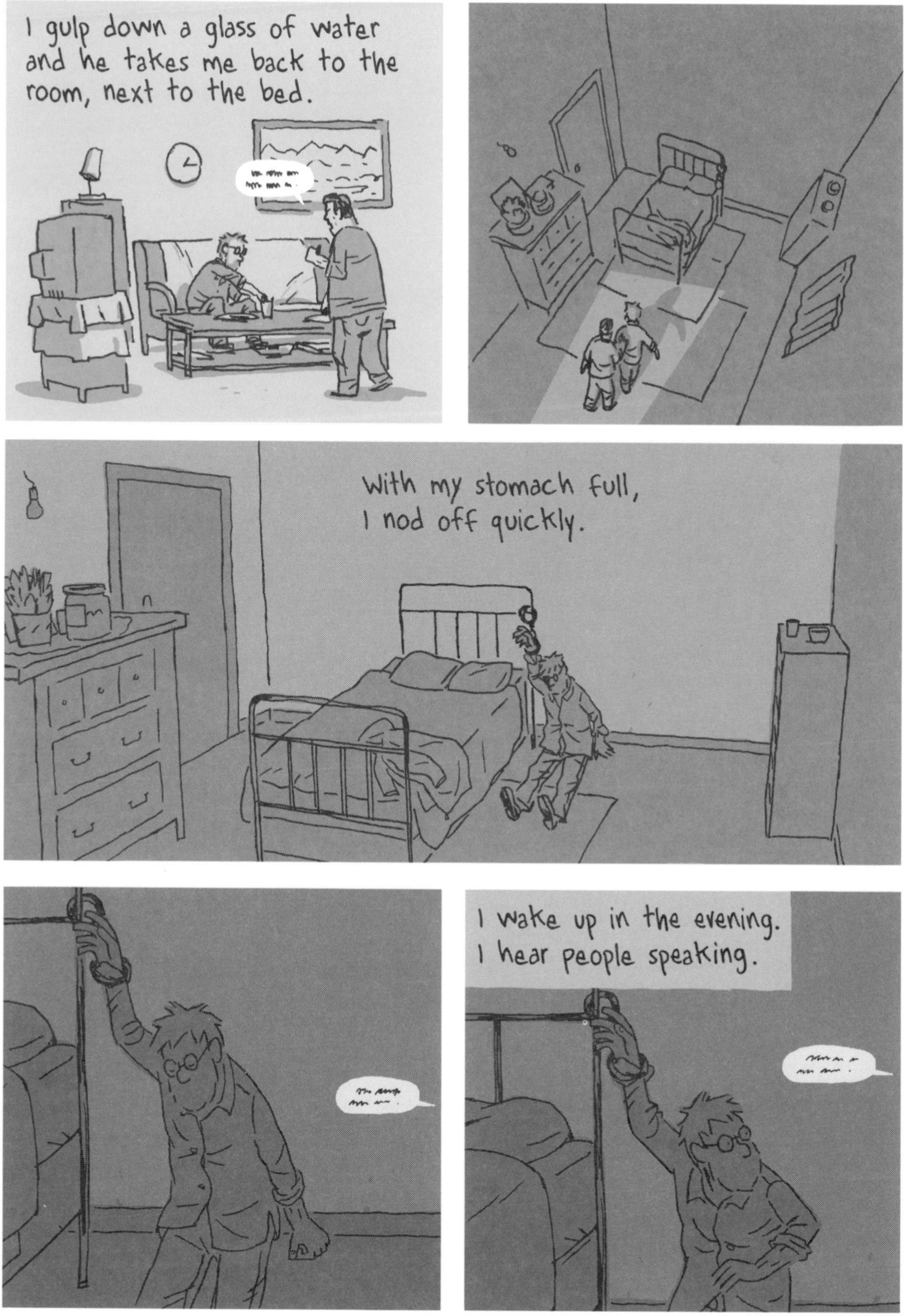
I gulp down a glass of water and he takes me back to the room, next to the bed.
With my stomach full, I nod off quickly.
I wake up in the evening. I hear people speaking.

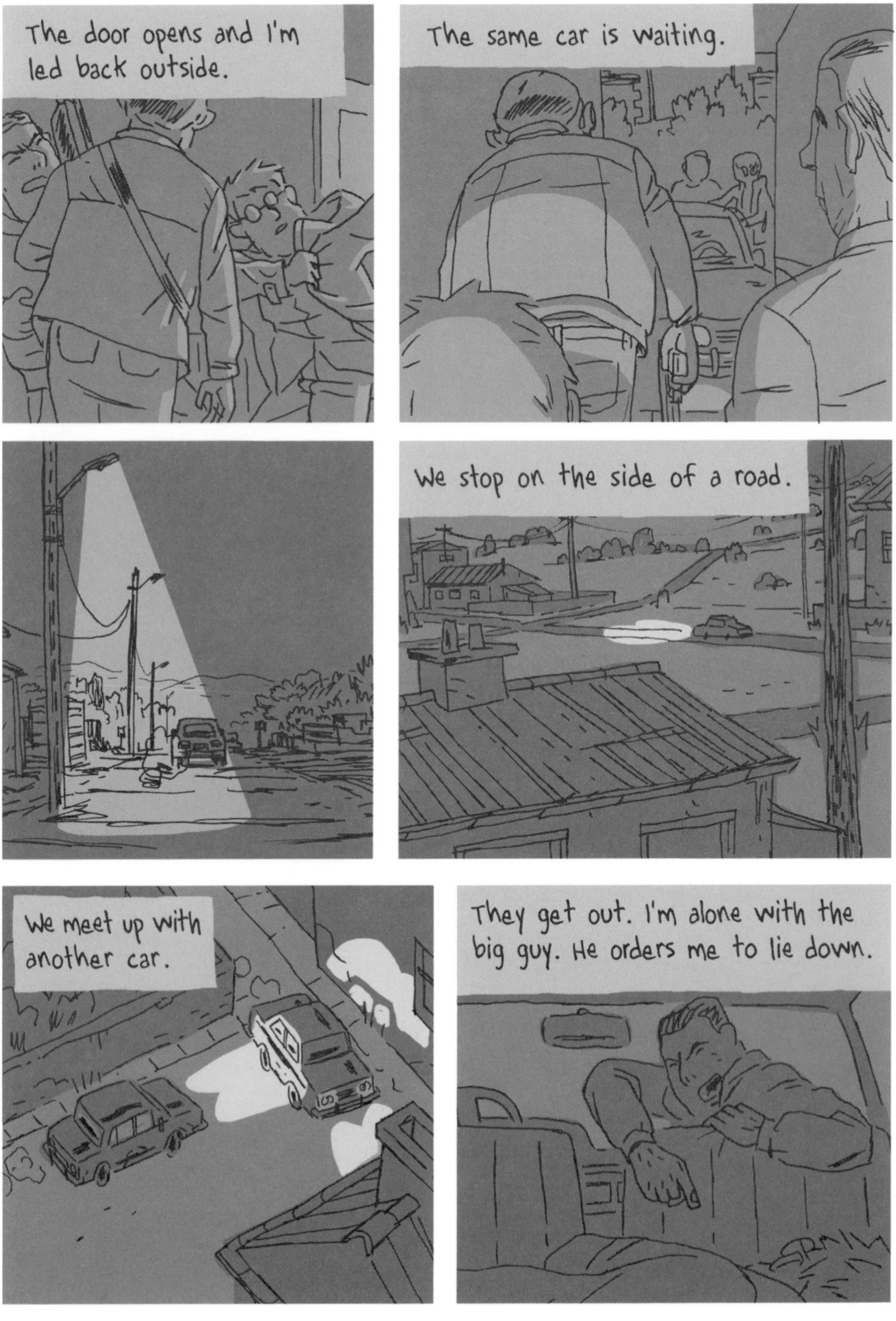
The door opens and I'm led back outside.
The same car is waiting.
We stop on the side of a road.
We meet up with another car.
They get out. I'm alone with the big guy. He orders me to lie down.

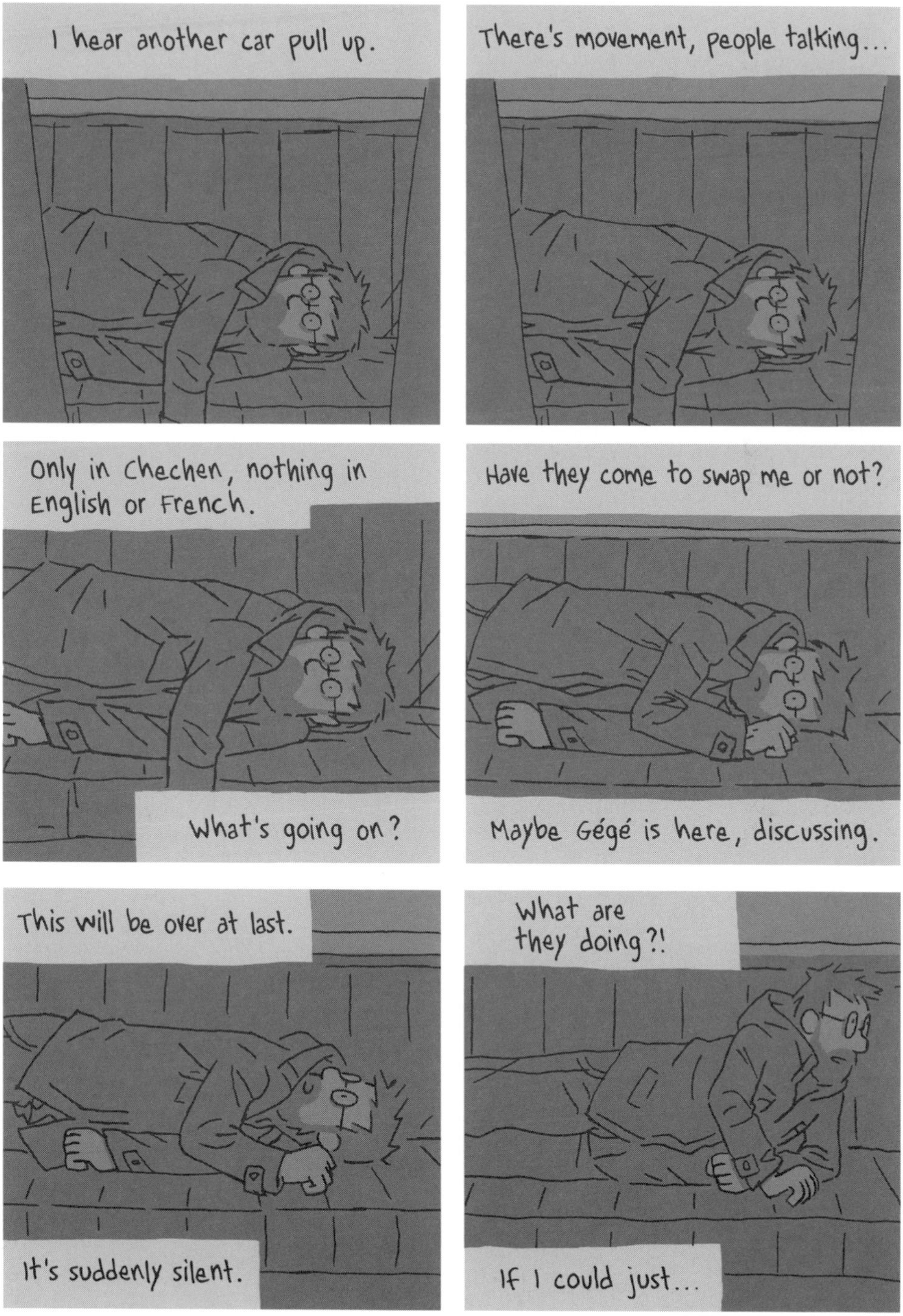
I hear another car pull up.
There's movement, people talking...
Only in Chechen, nothing in English or French.
What's going on?
Have they come to swap me or not?
Maybe Gégé is here, discussing.
This will be over at last.
It's suddenly silent.
What are they doing?!
If I could just...

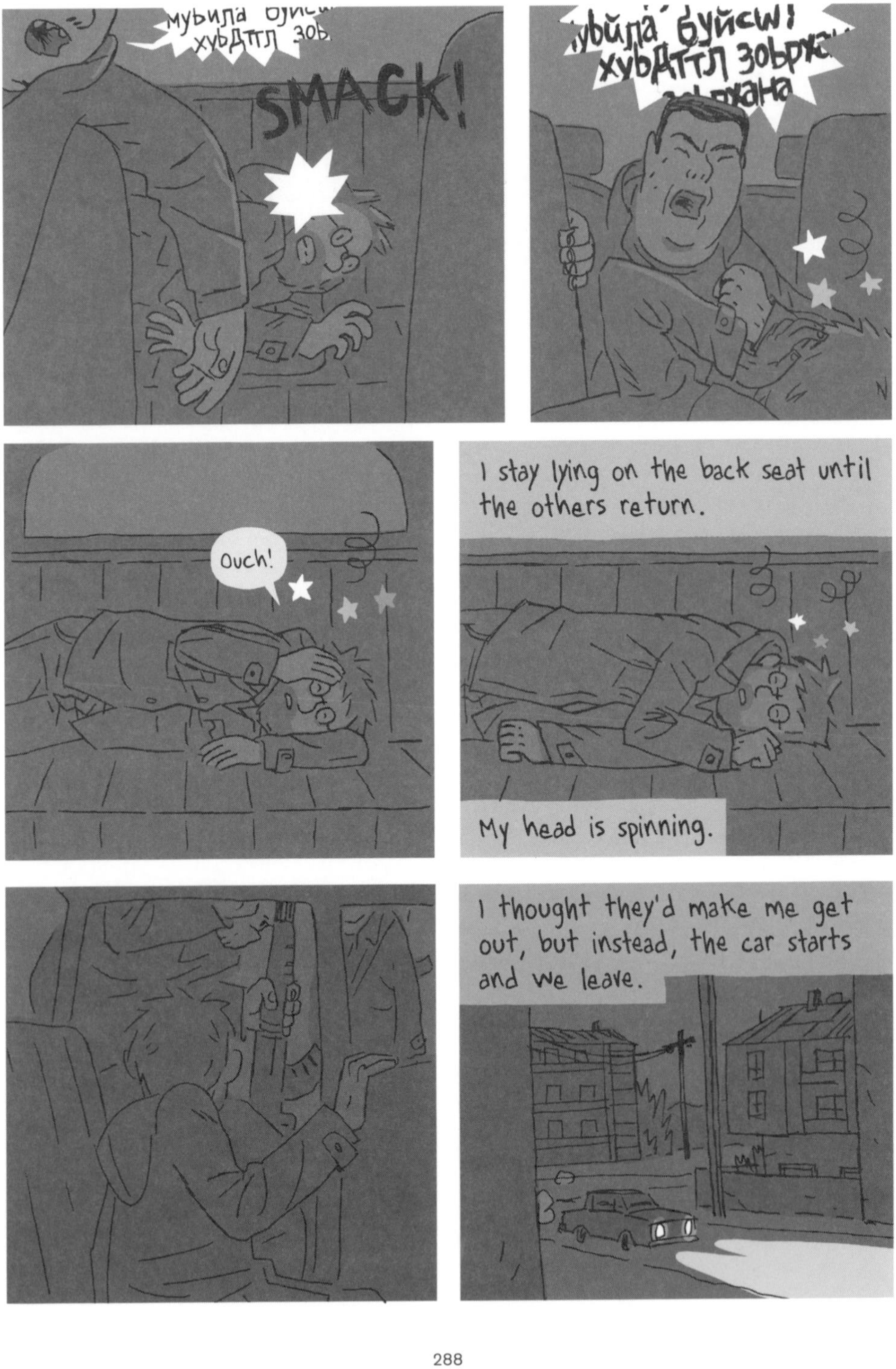
SMACK!
Ouch!
I stay lying on the back seat until the others return.
My head is spinning.
I thought they'd make me get out, but instead, the car starts and we leave.

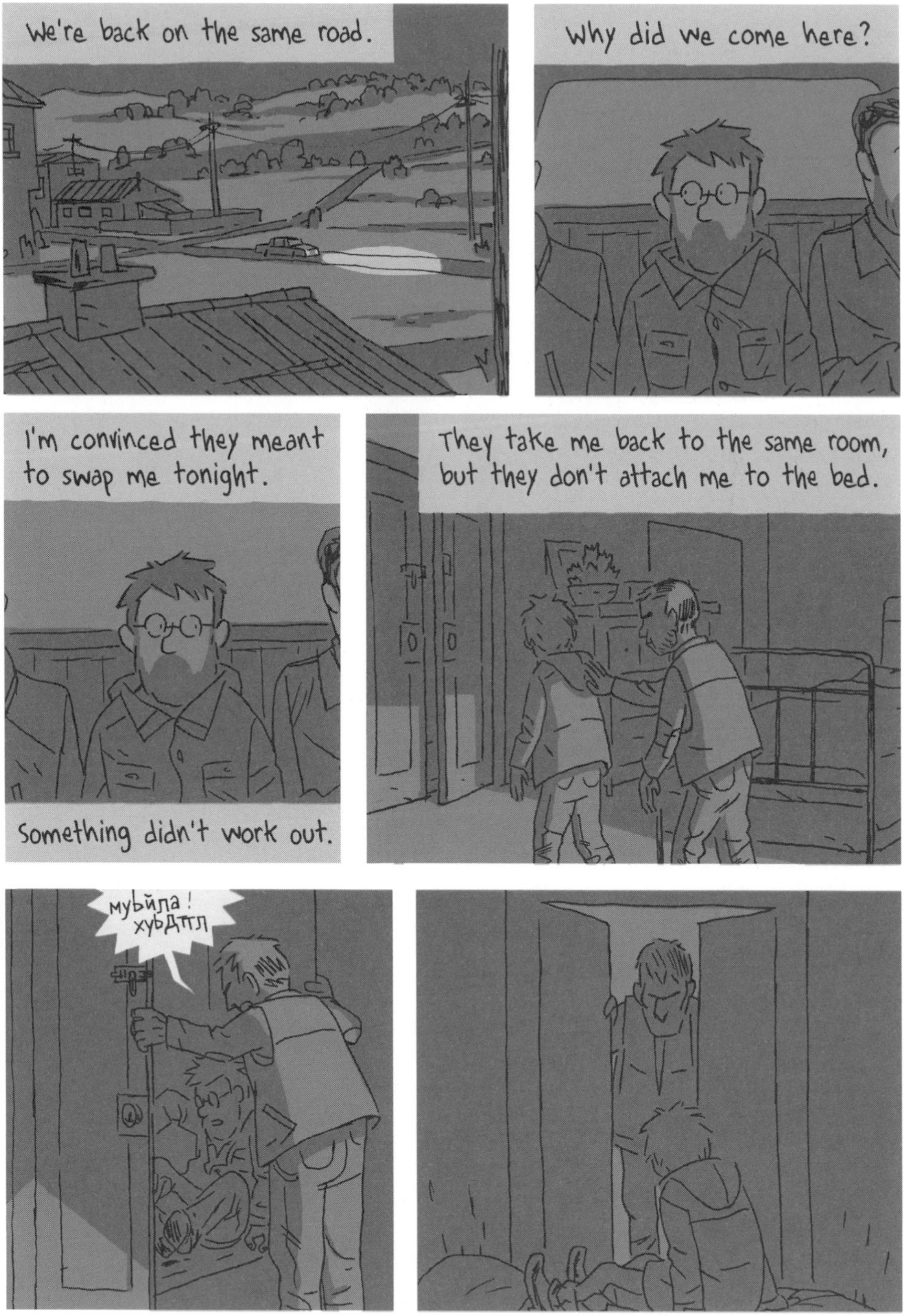
We're back on the same road.
Why did we come here?
I'm convinced they meant to swap me tonight.
Something didn't work out.
They take me back to the same room, but they don't attach me to the bed.
мубйла!
хубдпл

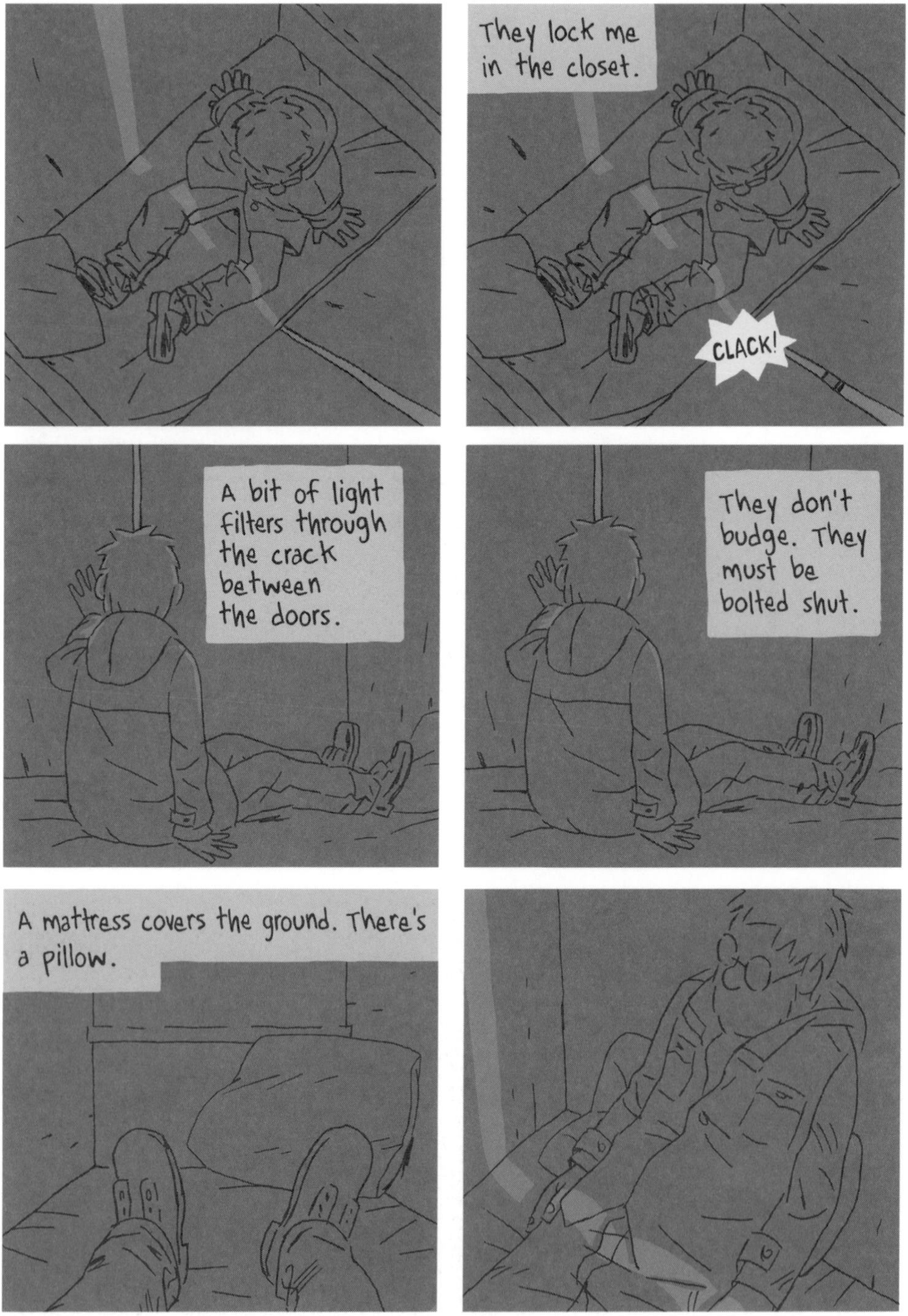
They lock me in the closet.
CLACK!
A bit of light filters through the crack between the doors.
They don't budge. They must be bolted shut.
A mattress covers the ground. There's a pillow.

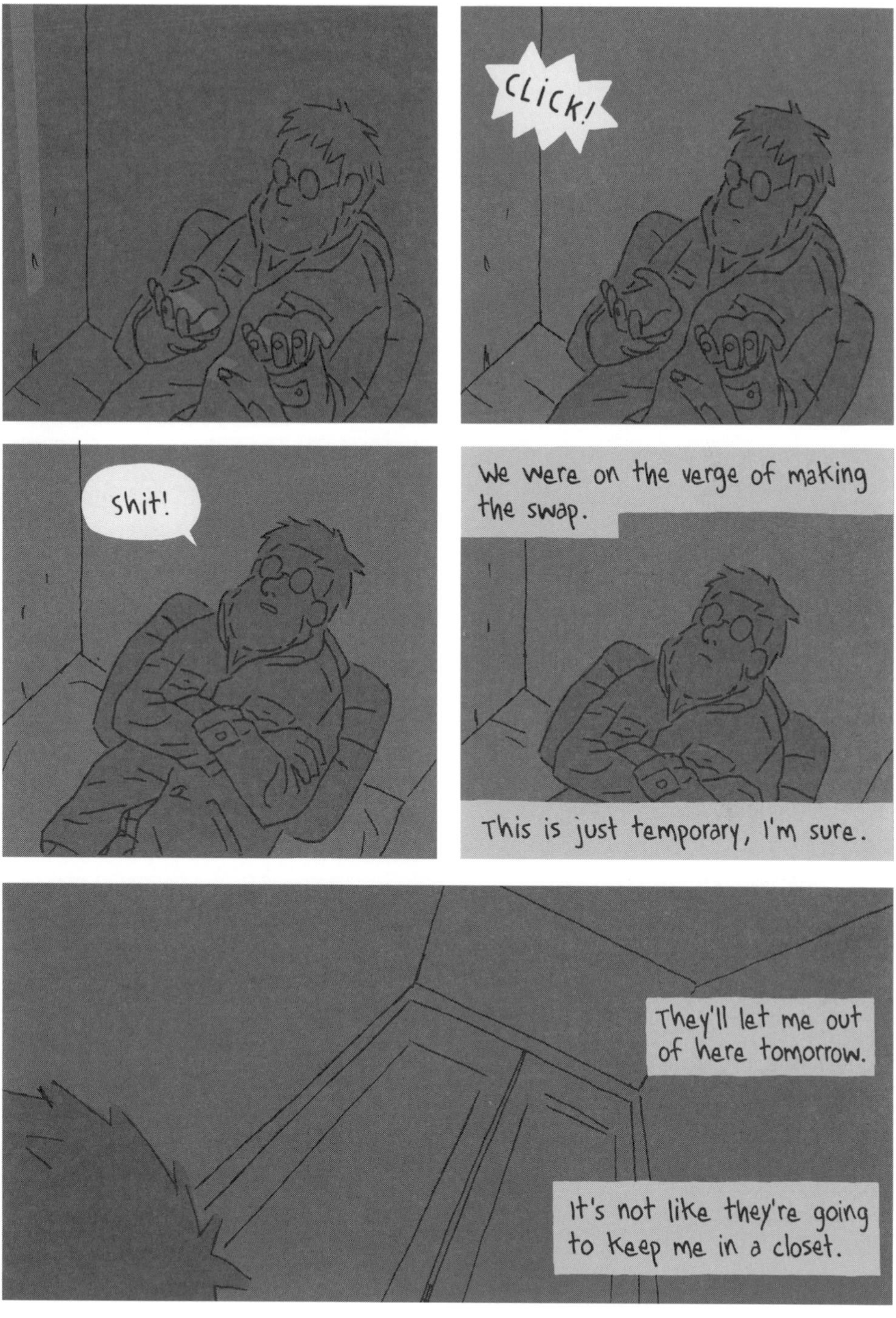
CLICK!
shit!
We were on the verge of making the swap.
This is just temporary, I'm sure.
They'll let me out of here tomorrow.
It's not like they're going to keep me in a closet.

78

It's daybreak. I can see the sunlight.

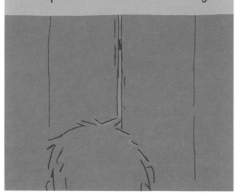

Today is...

Oh no! shit, I've lost track of the date!

Hold on, let's see...

They came to get me at night on Sunday. Monday I was next to the bed. Tuesday was the failed swap...

Uh...so...

So today must be Wednesday.

Right, the seventeenth.

Today is Wednesday, September 17.

Whew!

I've got the parka in a roll by my feet. I was too hot.

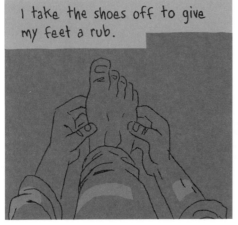

I take the shoes off to give my feet a rub.

The shoes have no laces.

294

And they have no cushioning either, so the soles of my feet press down hard against a kind of plastic grid.

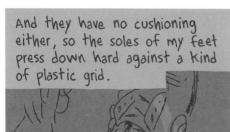

I put them back on in case I'm let out of here and we need to leave quickly.

It's been more than two months since I've had my hands free for more than half an hour a day.

Except when they forgot to lock my cuffs.

I'm locked up in a tiny space without any light, but having both hands free is really something.

I can cross my arms now.

...Cross my arms and wait.

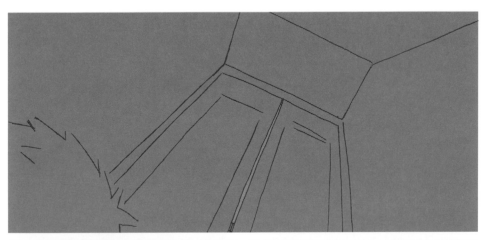

I hear the big guy moving around. It must be about noon...

Actually, it's hard to say.

I'm starting to feel a serious need to piss.

I'm hungry, too.

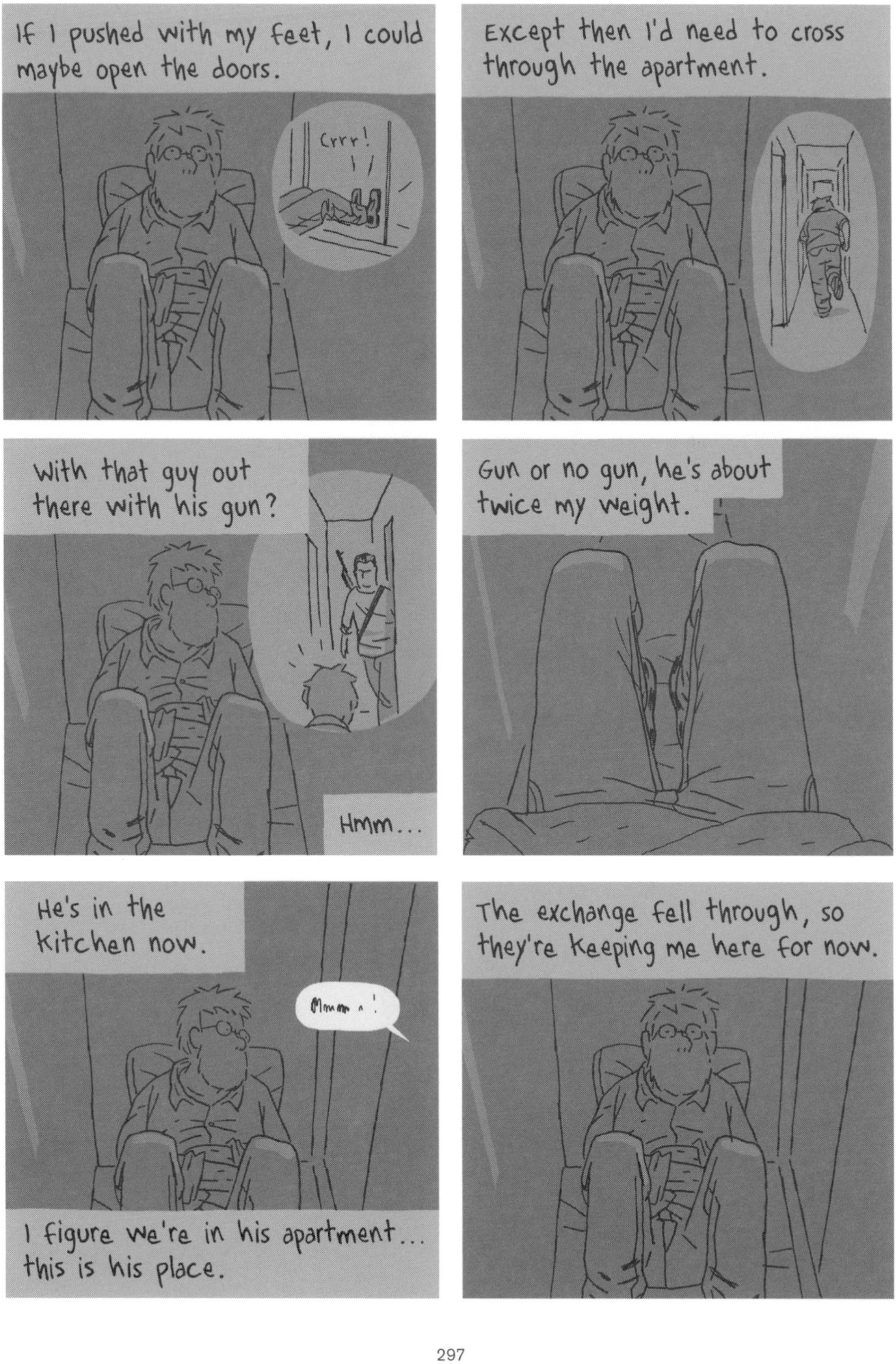
If I pushed with my feet, I could maybe open the doors.
Crrr!
Except then I'd need to cross through the apartment.
With that guy out there with his gun?
Hmm...
Gun or no gun, he's about twice my weight.
He's in the kitchen now.
I figure we're in his apartment... this is his place.
The exchange fell through, so they're keeping me here for now.

Mmm...It smells like food.

Damn! I'm starving!

I hope he comes to get me before I piss myself.

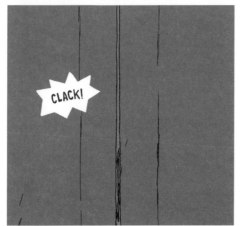

CLACK!

The doors suddenly swing open.

First he takes me to the toilet.

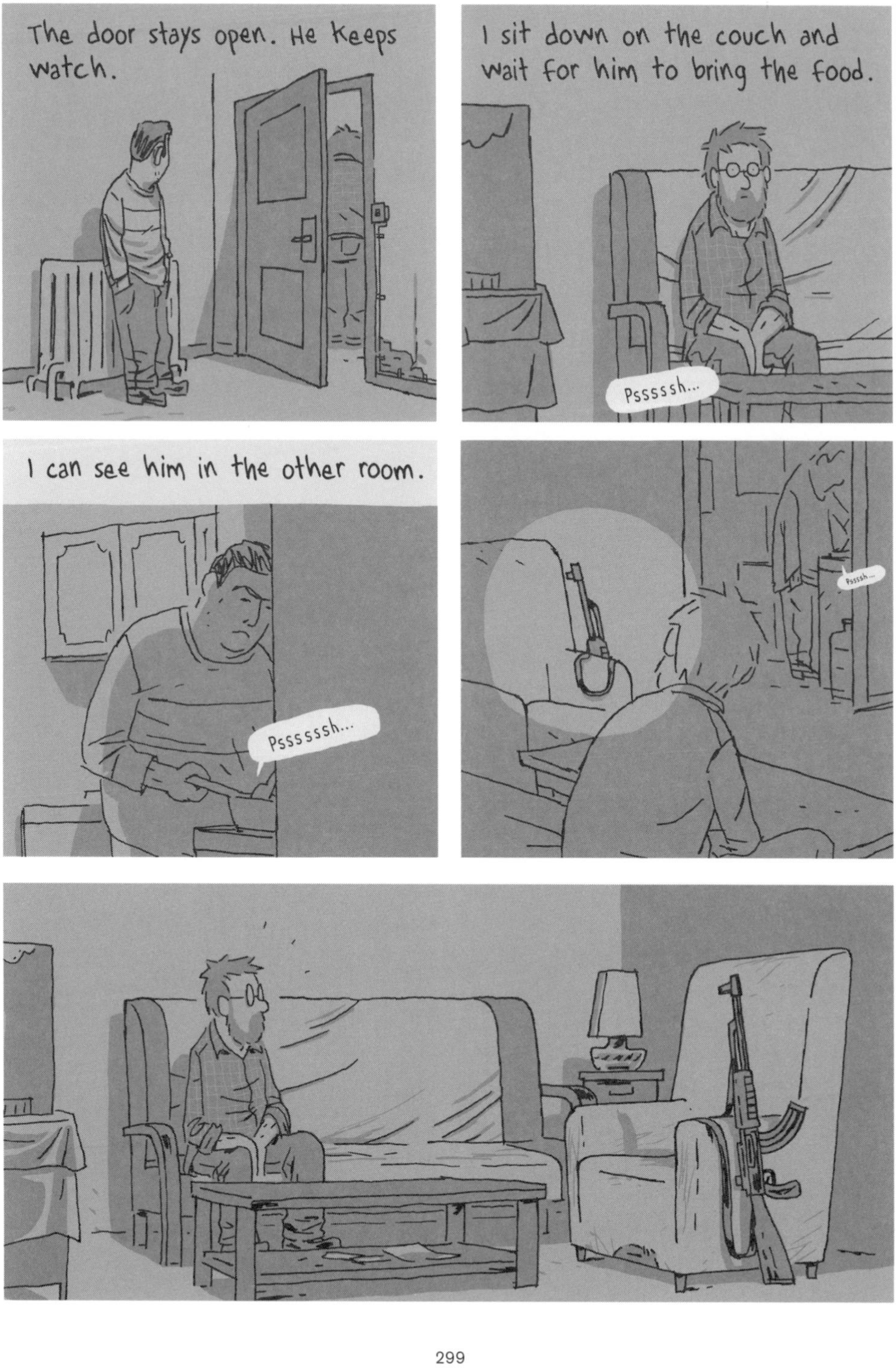
The door stays open. He keeps watch.
I sit down on the couch and wait for him to bring the food.
Pssssssh...
I can see him in the other room.
Psssssssh...
Psssh...

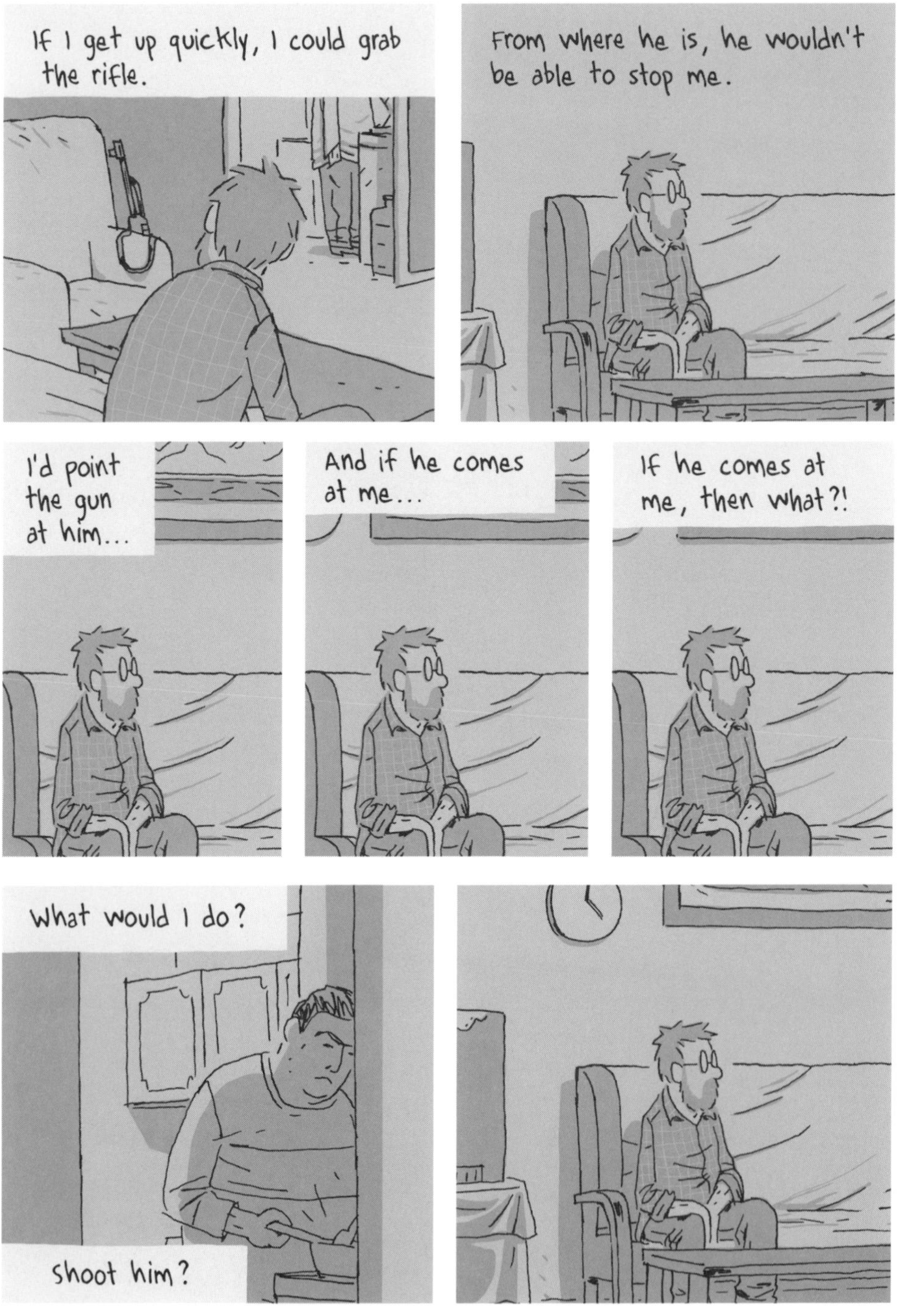
If I get up quickly, I could grab the rifle.
From where he is, he wouldn't be able to stop me.
I'd point the gun at him...
And if he comes at me...
If he comes at me, then what?!
What would I do?
Shoot him?

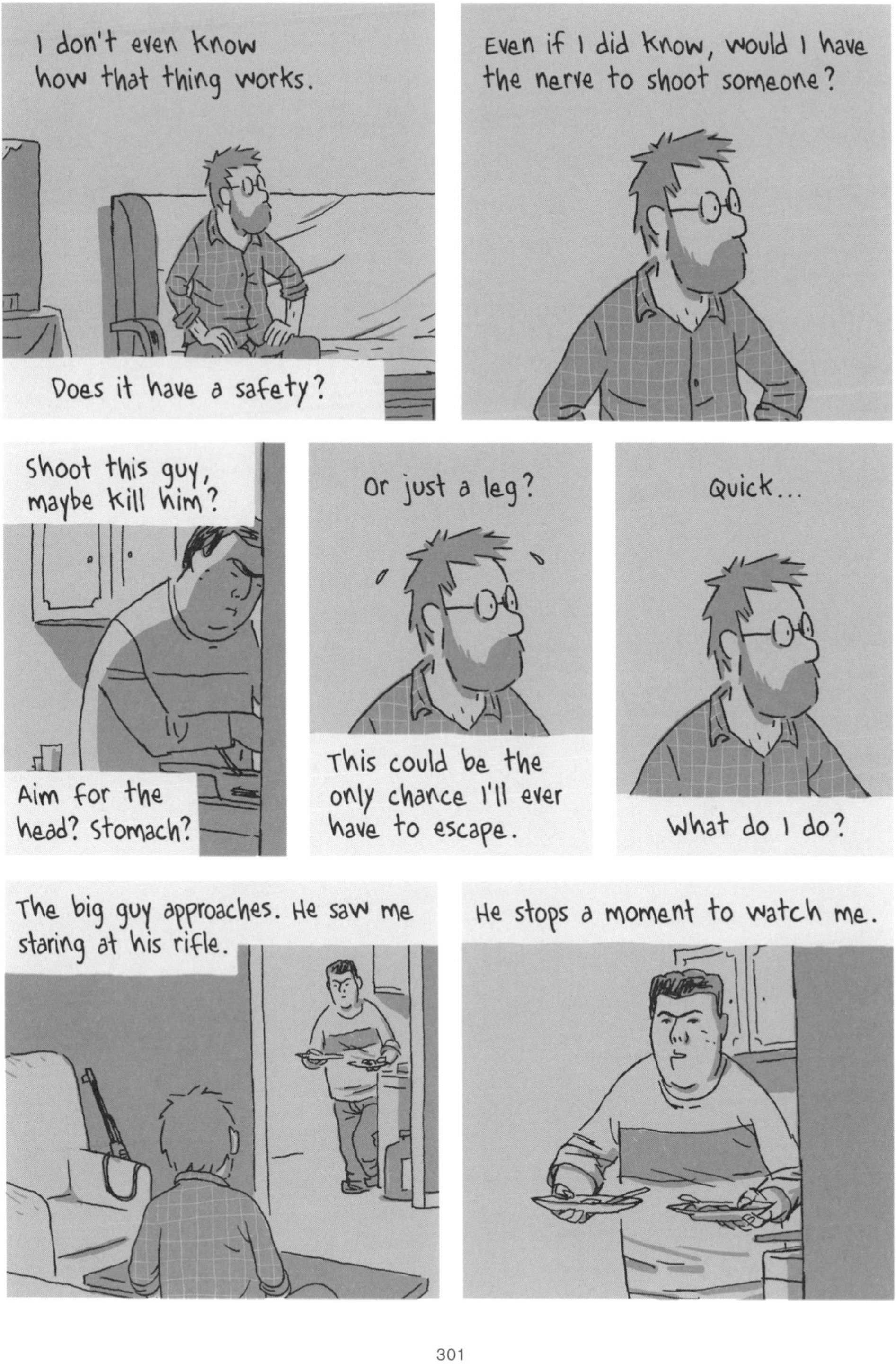

I don't even know how that thing works.
Does it have a safety?
Even if I did know, would I have the nerve to shoot someone?
Shoot this guy, maybe kill him?
Aim for the head? Stomach?
Or just a leg?
This could be the only chance I'll ever have to escape.
Quick...
What do I do?
The big guy approaches. He saw me staring at his rifle.
He stops a moment to watch me.

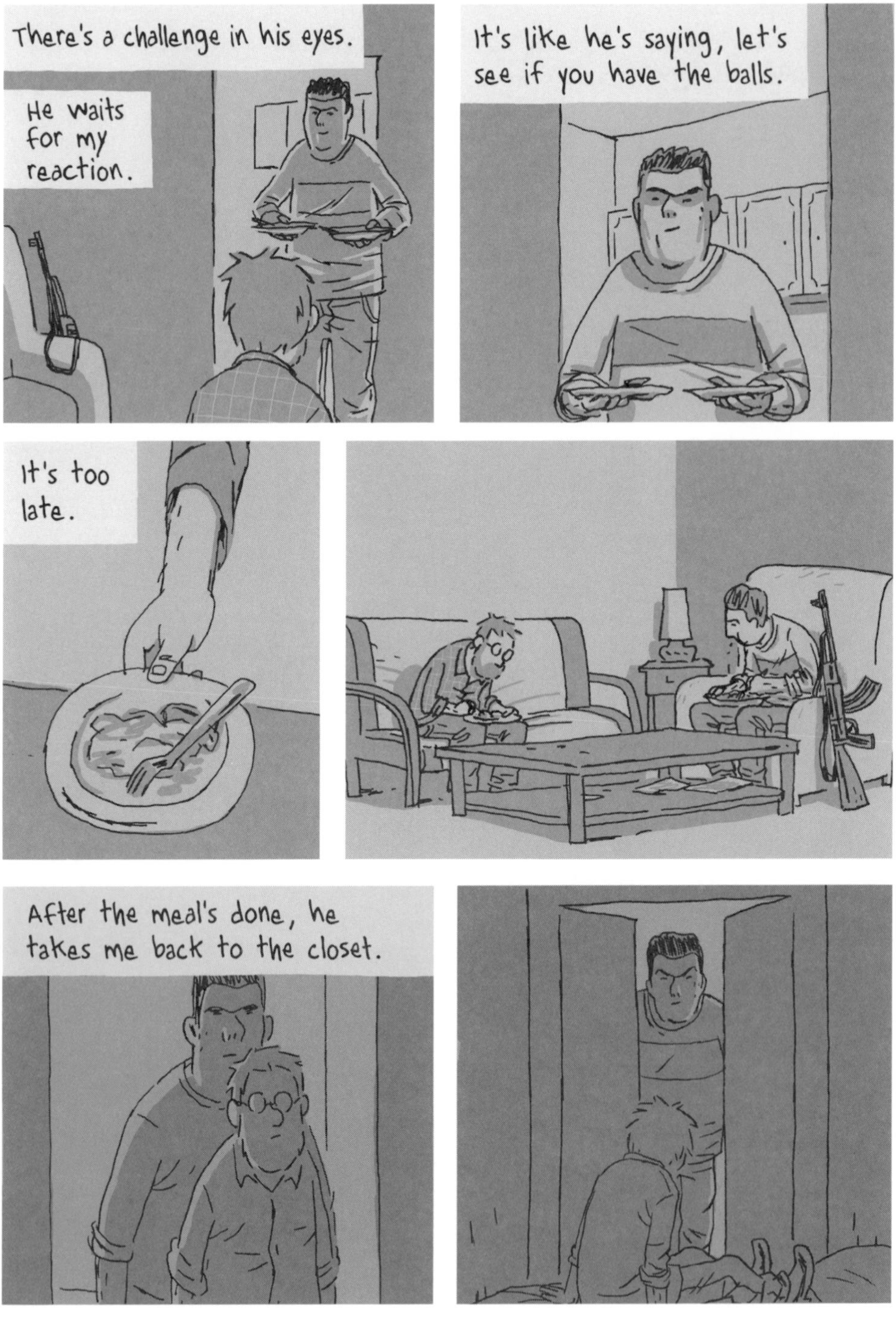
There's a challenge in his eyes.
He waits for my reaction.
It's like he's saying, let's see if you have the balls.
It's too late.
After the meal's done, he takes me back to the closet.

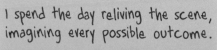
I spend the day reliving the scene, imagining every possible outcome.

Shit! I should have risked it.

I've probably missed the best chance I'll ever have to escape.

But it all happened so fast.

And how do you fire a gun?

I'd never be able to shoot someone.

But I could have tried to threaten him at least.

Under the circumstances, I did the only thing I could.

I did the right thing.

There'll never be another opportunity like it.

I try to fall asleep.

79

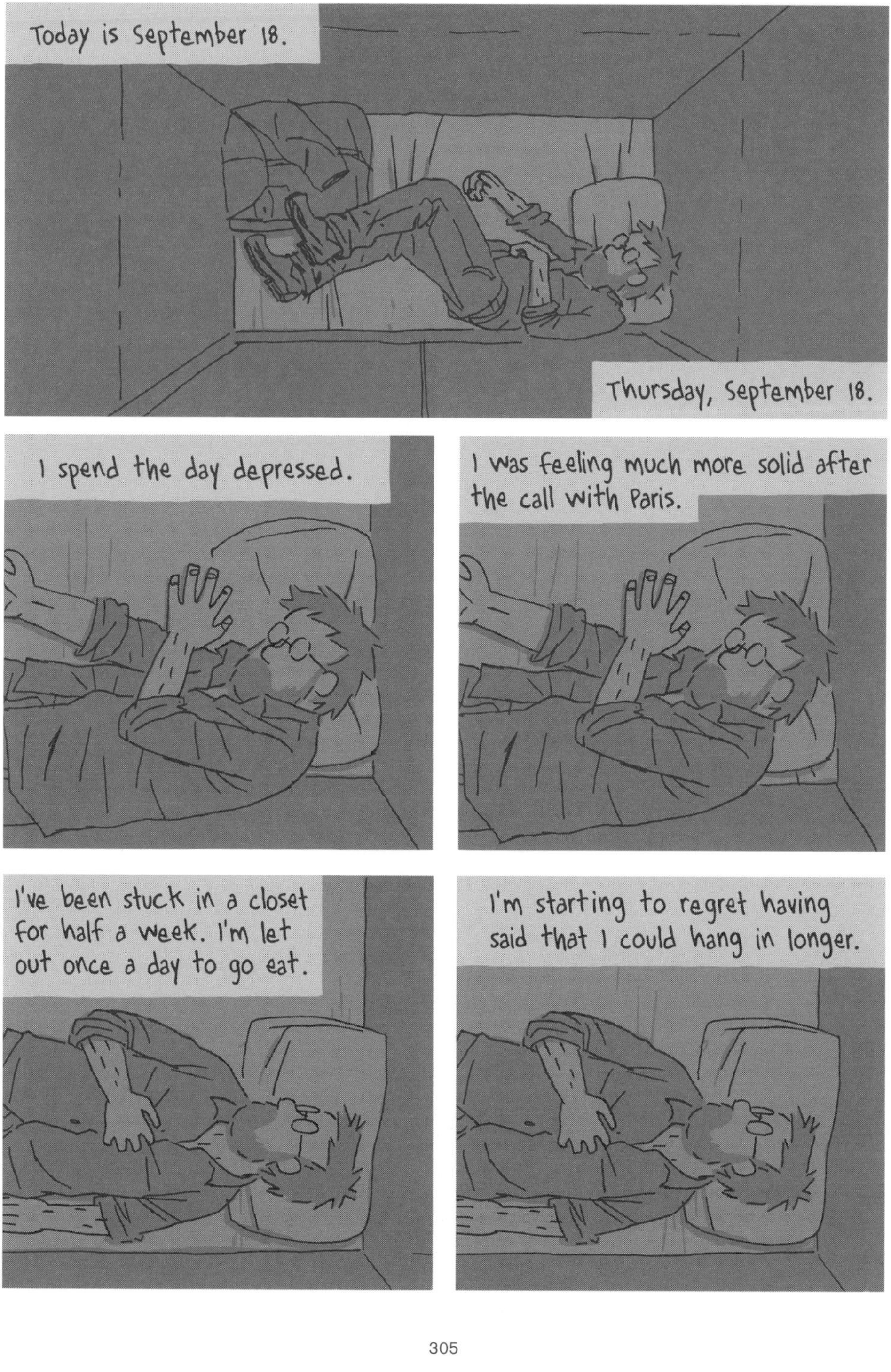
Today is September 18.
Thursday, September 18.
I spend the day depressed.
I was feeling much more solid after the call with Paris.
I've been stuck in a closet for half a week. I'm let out once a day to go eat.
I'm starting to regret having said that I could hang in longer.

It's inhuman. There's no way I can keep this up.

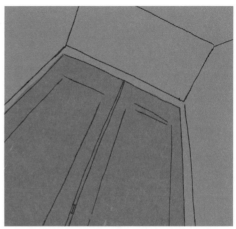

What the hell are Gégé and the rest of them doing?

Fuck, get me out of here!

306

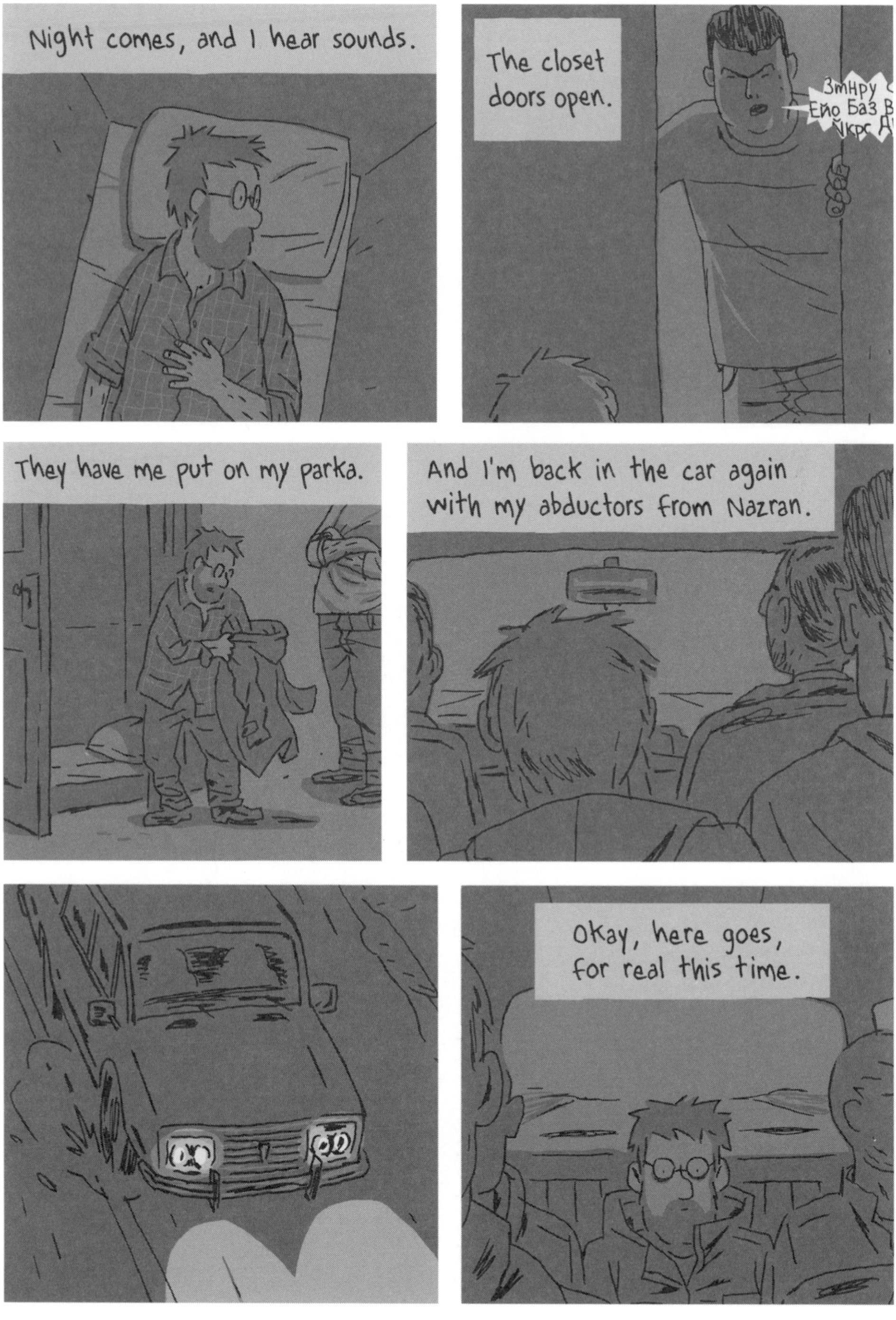
Night comes, and I hear sounds.
The closet doors open.
Зтнру
Ейо Баз
Йкрс
They have me put on my parka.
And I'm back in the car again with my abductors from Nazran.
Okay, here goes, for real this time.

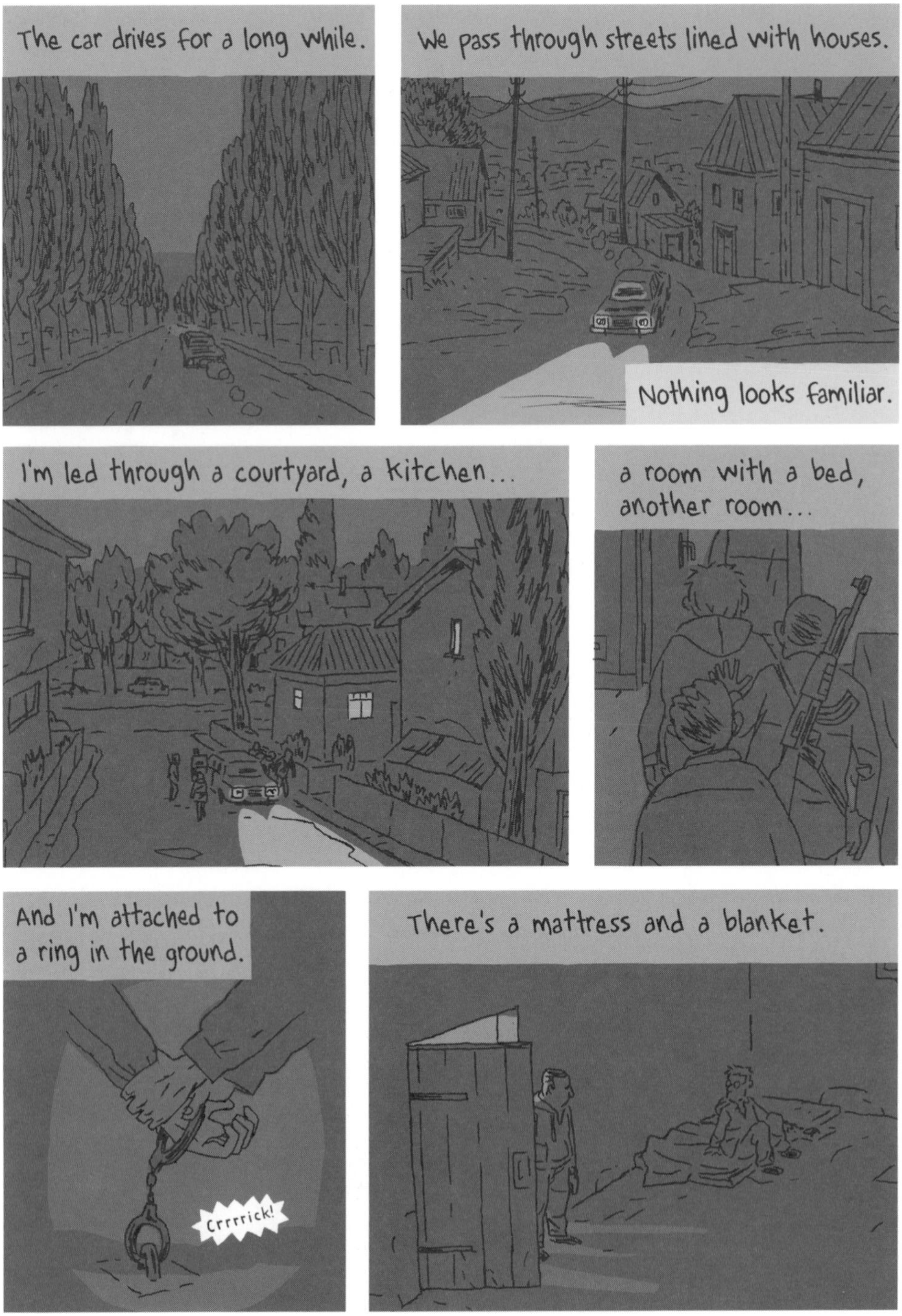
The car drives for a long while.
We pass through streets lined with houses.
Nothing looks familiar.
I'm led through a courtyard, a kitchen...
a room with a bed, another room...
And I'm attached to a ring in the ground.
Crrrrick!
There's a mattress and a blanket.

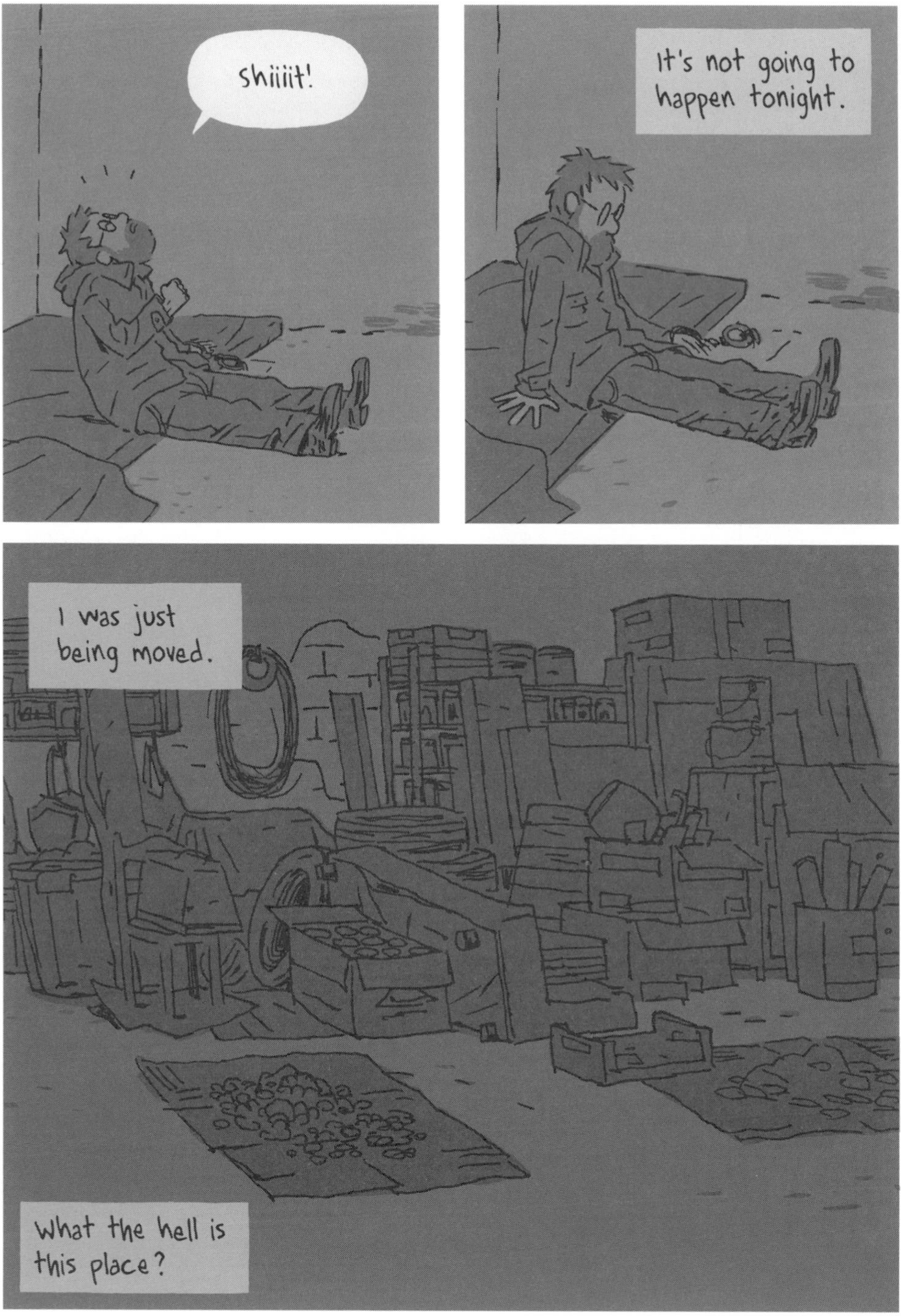
shiiiit!
It's not going to happen tonight.
I was just being moved.
What the hell is this place?

80

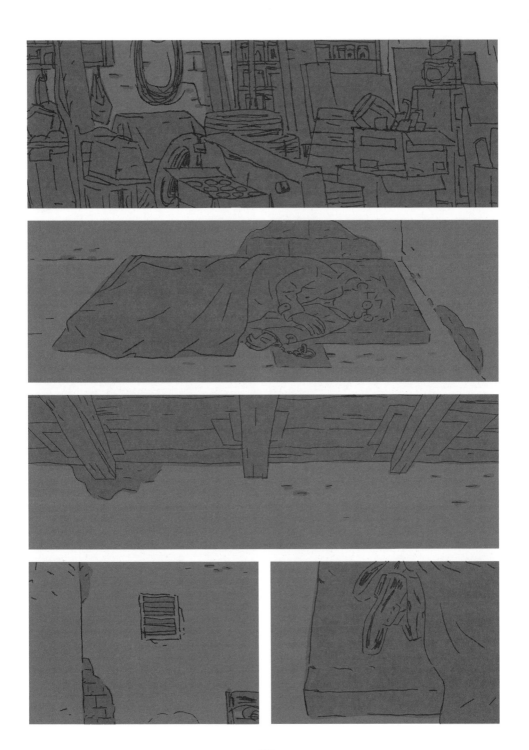

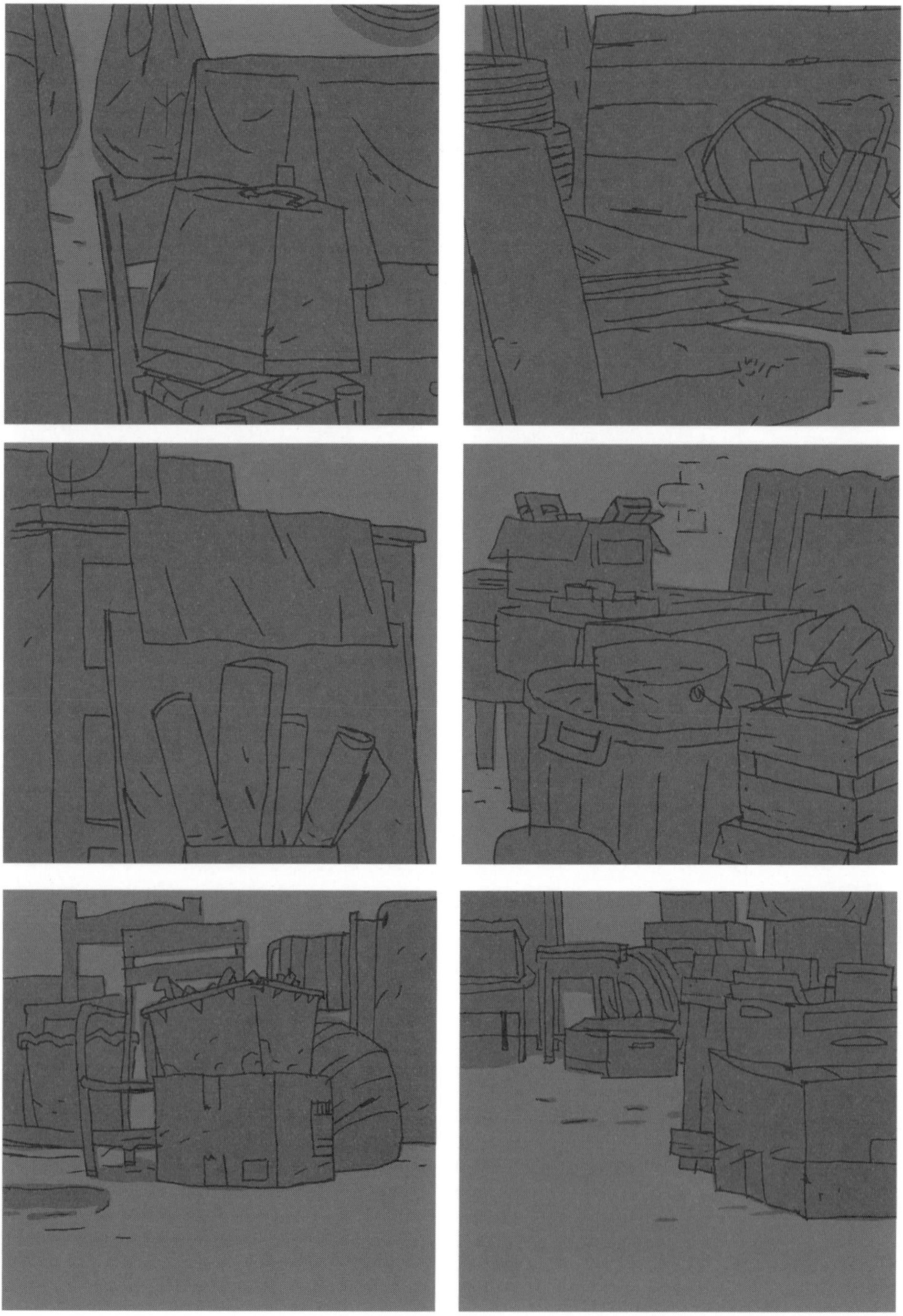

Day dawns at last. Light enters through cracks in the boarded-up window.

Where am I?

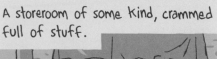

A storeroom of some kind, crammed full of stuff.

Why have they put me here?

Was the apartment compromised?

I'm still wearing the parka, and I'm getting hot.

Sound of steps...

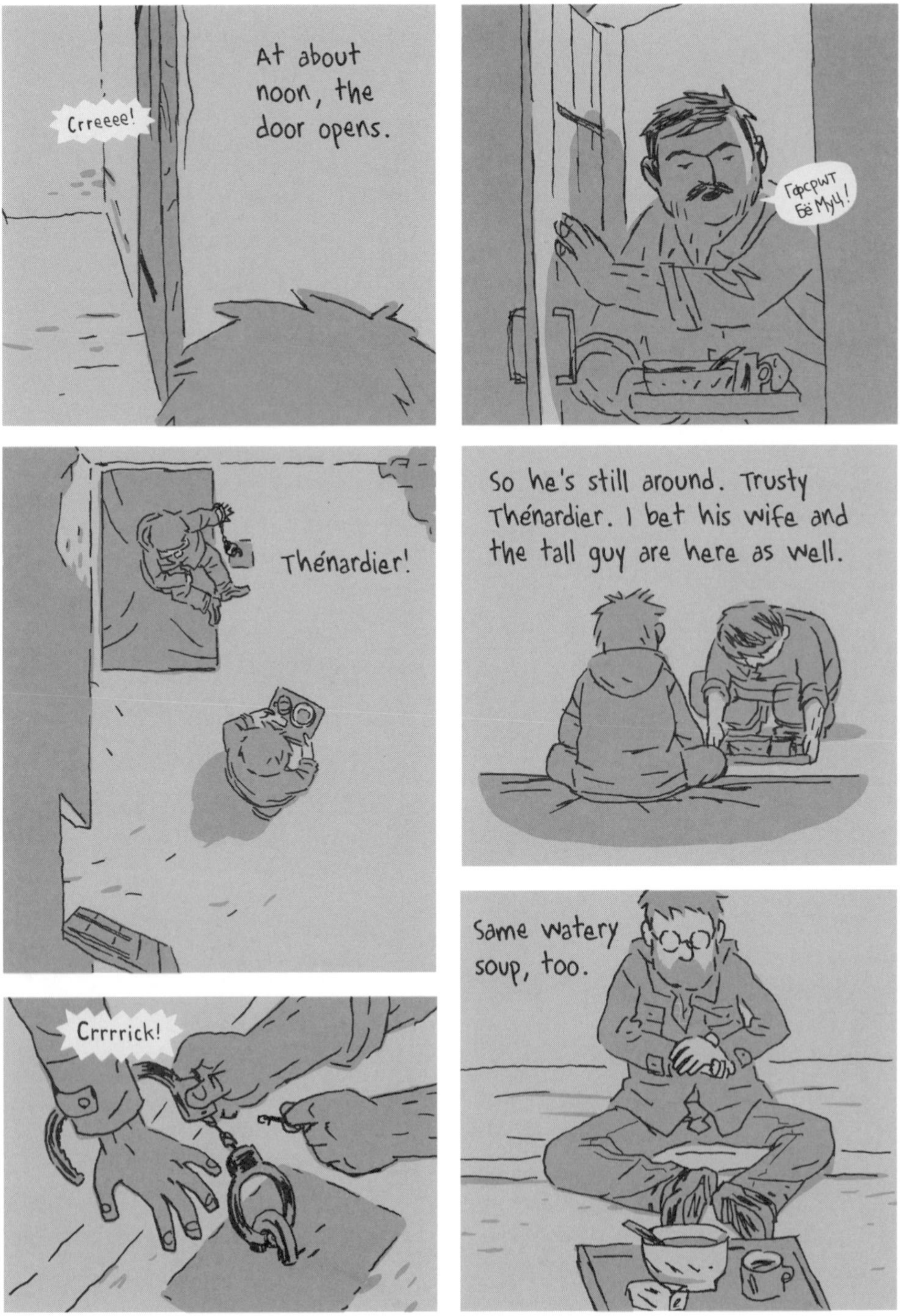
At about noon, the door opens.
Crreeee!
Гфсрwт Бё Муч!
Thénardier!
So he's still around. Trusty Thénardier. I bet his wife and the tall guy are here as well.
Crrrrick!
Same watery soup, too.

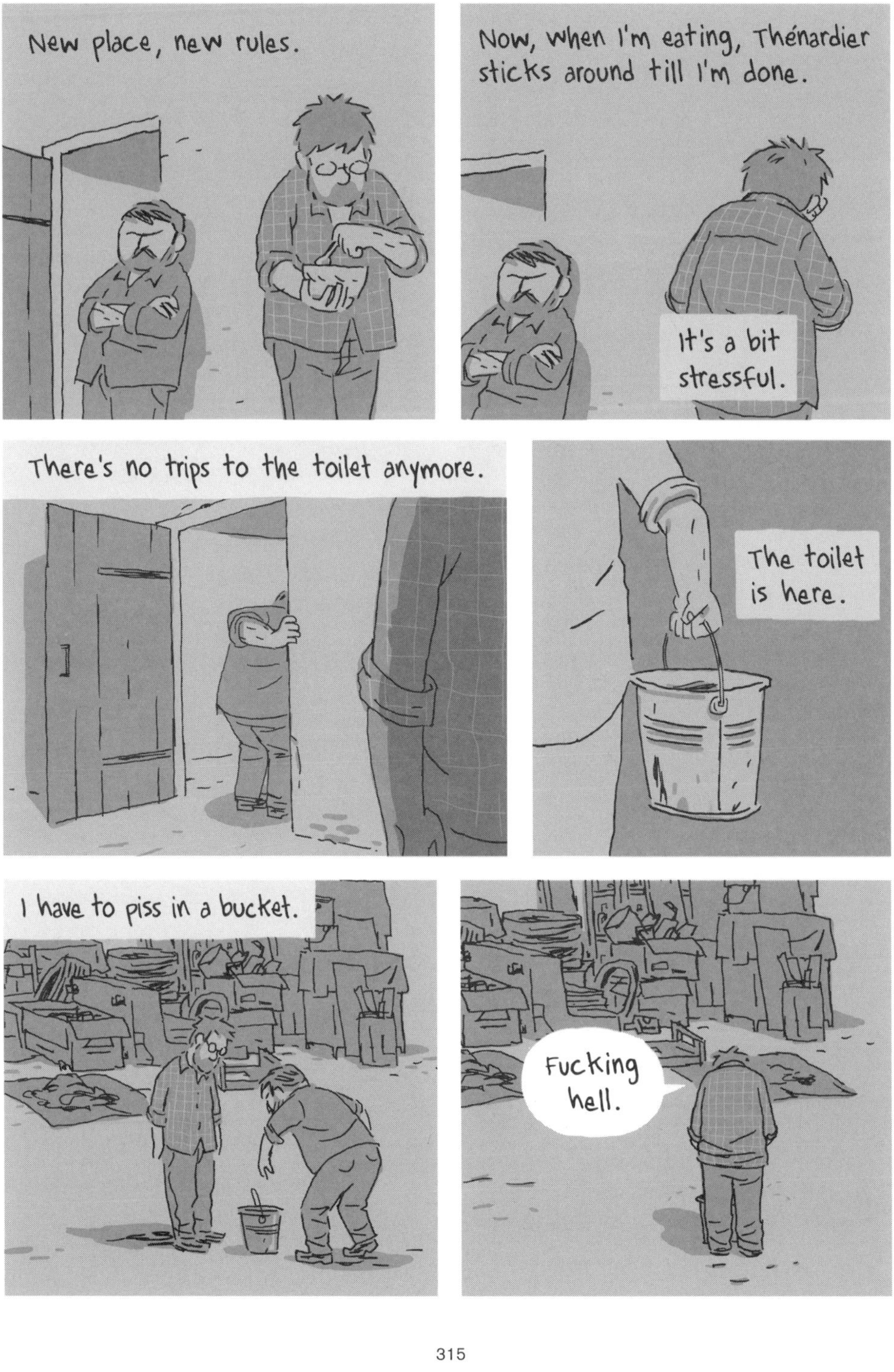
New place, new rules.
Now, when I'm eating, Thénardier sticks around till I'm done.
It's a bit stressful.
There's no trips to the toilet anymore.
The toilet is here.
I have to piss in a bucket.
Fucking hell.

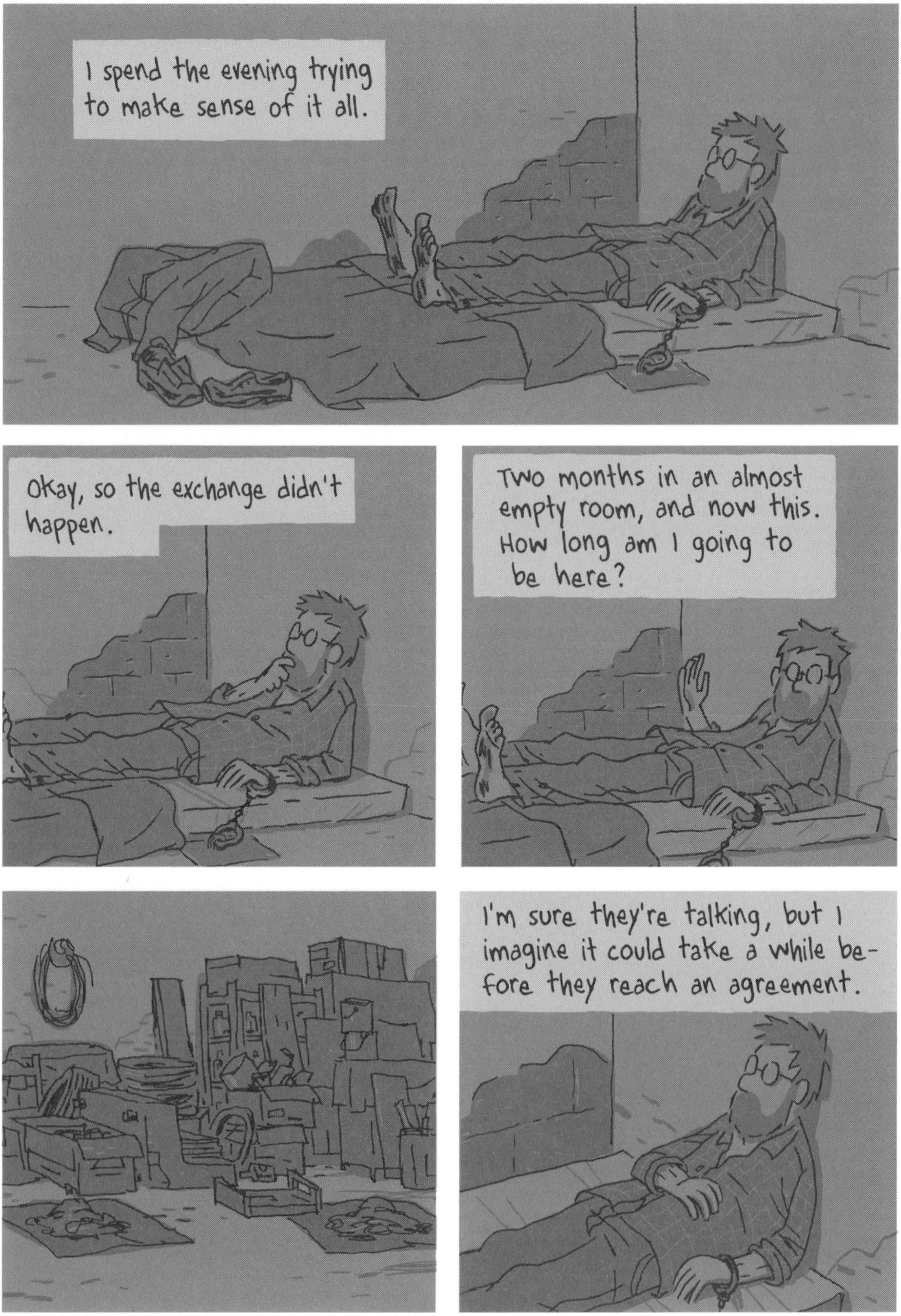

I spend the evening trying to make sense of it all.
Okay, so the exchange didn't happen.
Two months in an almost empty room, and now this. How long am I going to be here?
I'm sure they're talking, but I imagine it could take a while before they reach an agreement.

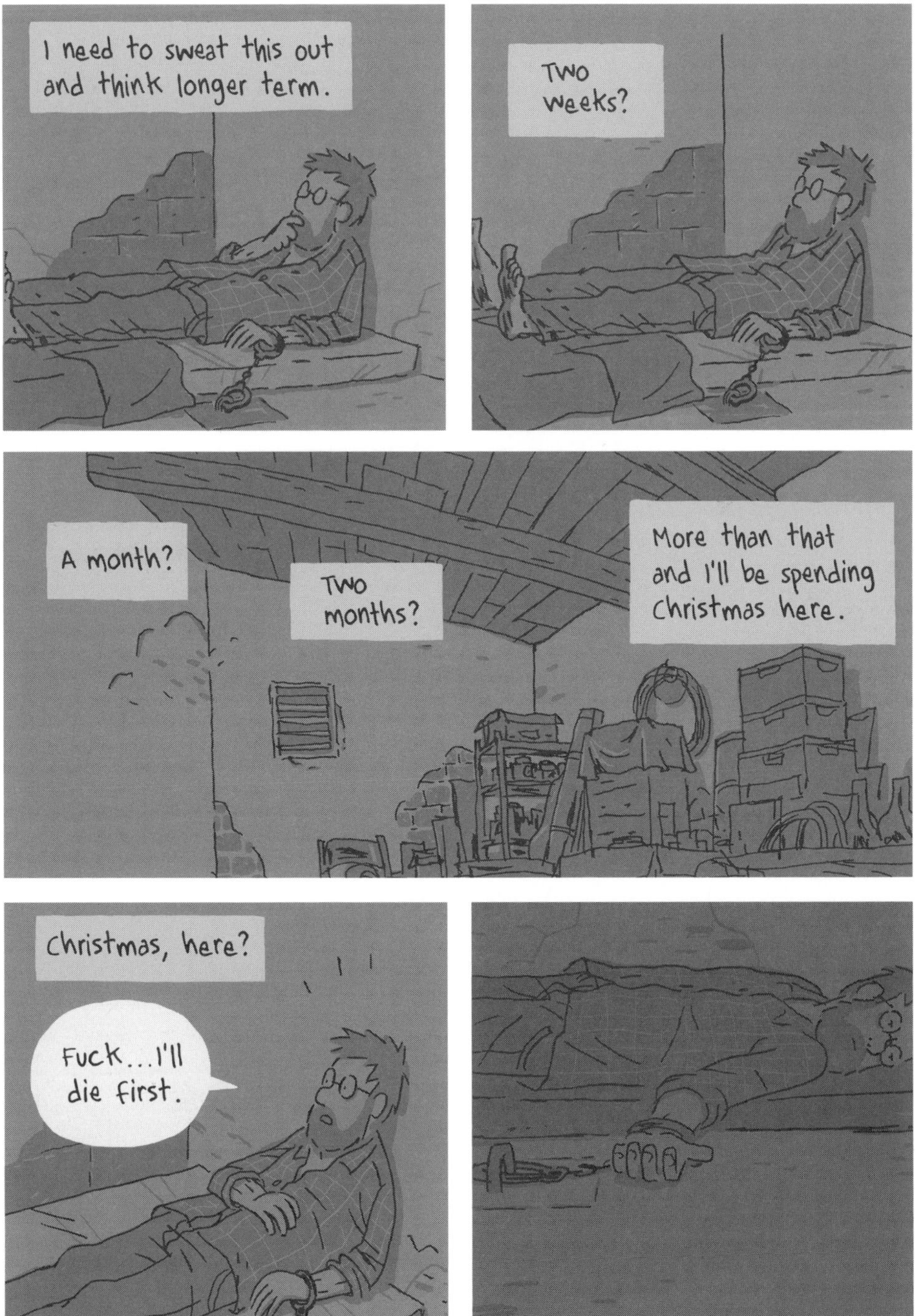
I need to sweat this out and think longer term.
Two weeks?
A month?
Two months?
More than that and I'll be spending Christmas here.
Christmas, here?
Fuck...I'll die first.

Hey!....

What is that?

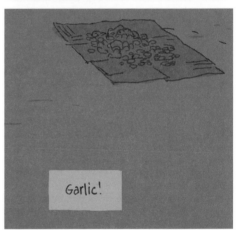

It's garlic.

And further off, maybe shallots.

Wow, if I could swipe a clove and treat myself to it over here in my corner...

Mmm ...

Garlic!

I fall asleep thinking of ways to get my hands on that treasure.

When they unlock my cuffs to let me eat, I could drop my spoon...

Or I could try grabbing one between my toes when I walk by...

The next day, it's the tall guy who opens the door.

He puts down the tray, unlocks the cuffs, and leans against the door frame.

I pace back and forth as I eat.

I try to get near the garlic, but he keeps a close eye on me.

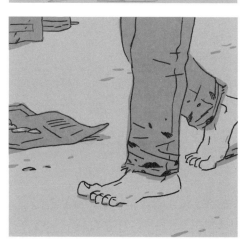

There's no way, forget it.

I stash my bread under the blanket for later.

Clack!

The tall guy leaves.

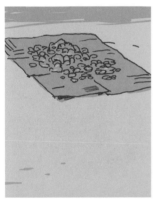

Hey! What if...

Maybe if I stretch as far as I can...

Let's see...

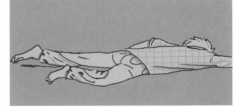

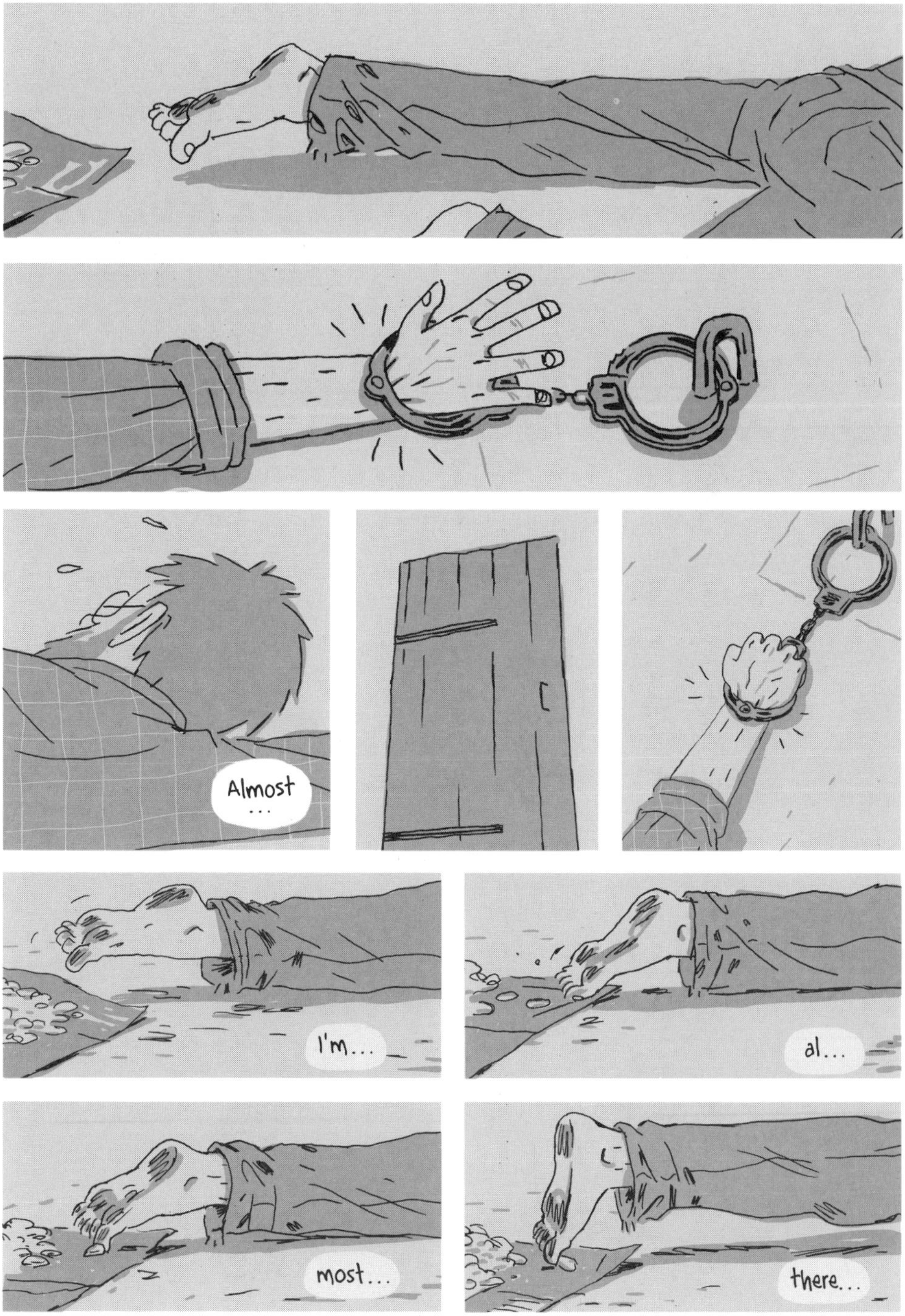
Almost
...
I'm...
al...
most...
there...

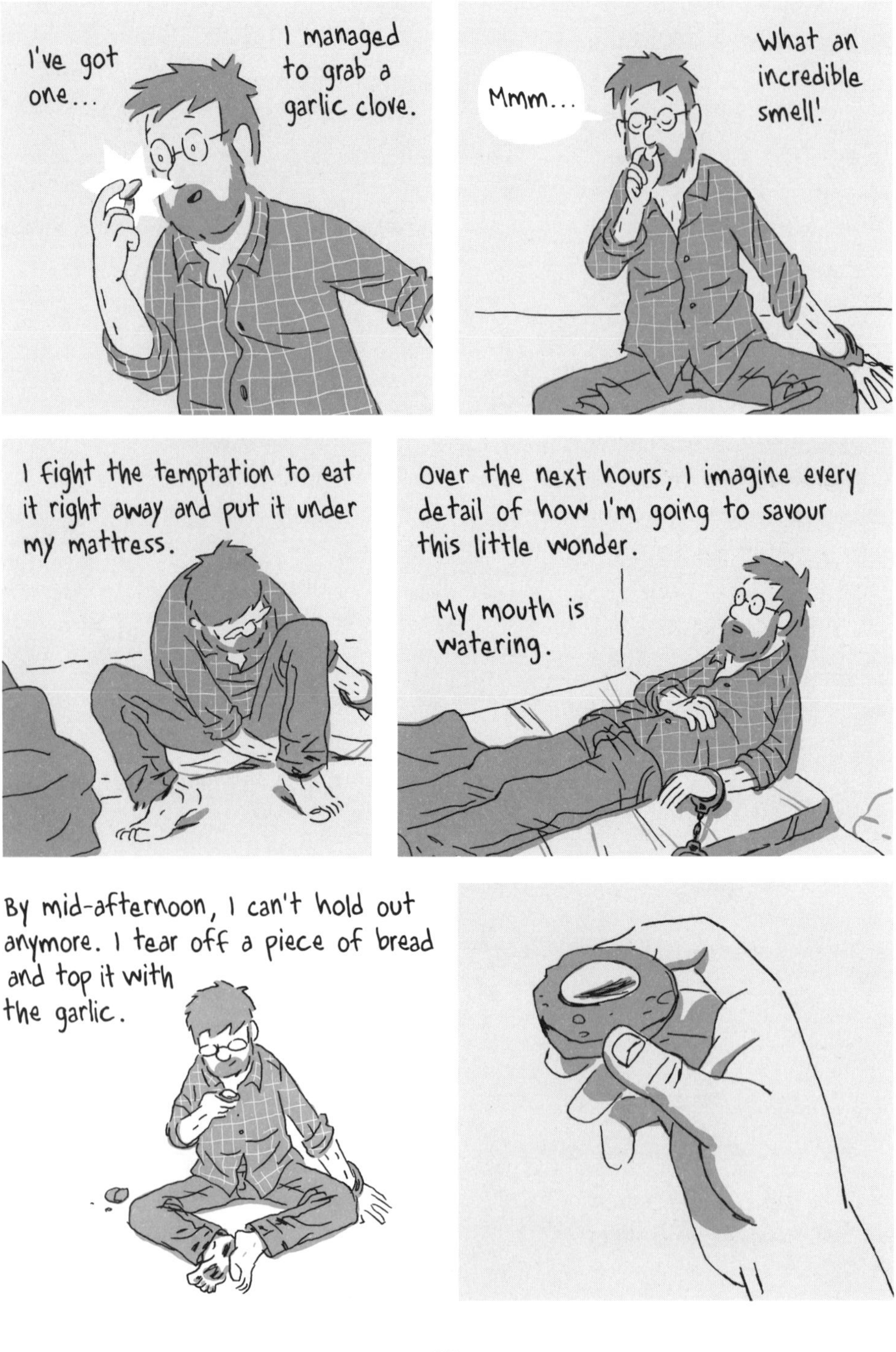
I've got one...
I managed to grab a garlic clove.
Mmm...
What an incredible smell!
I fight the temptation to eat it right away and put it under my mattress.
Over the next hours, I imagine every detail of how I'm going to savour this little wonder.
My mouth is watering.
By mid-afternoon, I can't hold out anymore. I tear off a piece of bread and top it with the garlic.

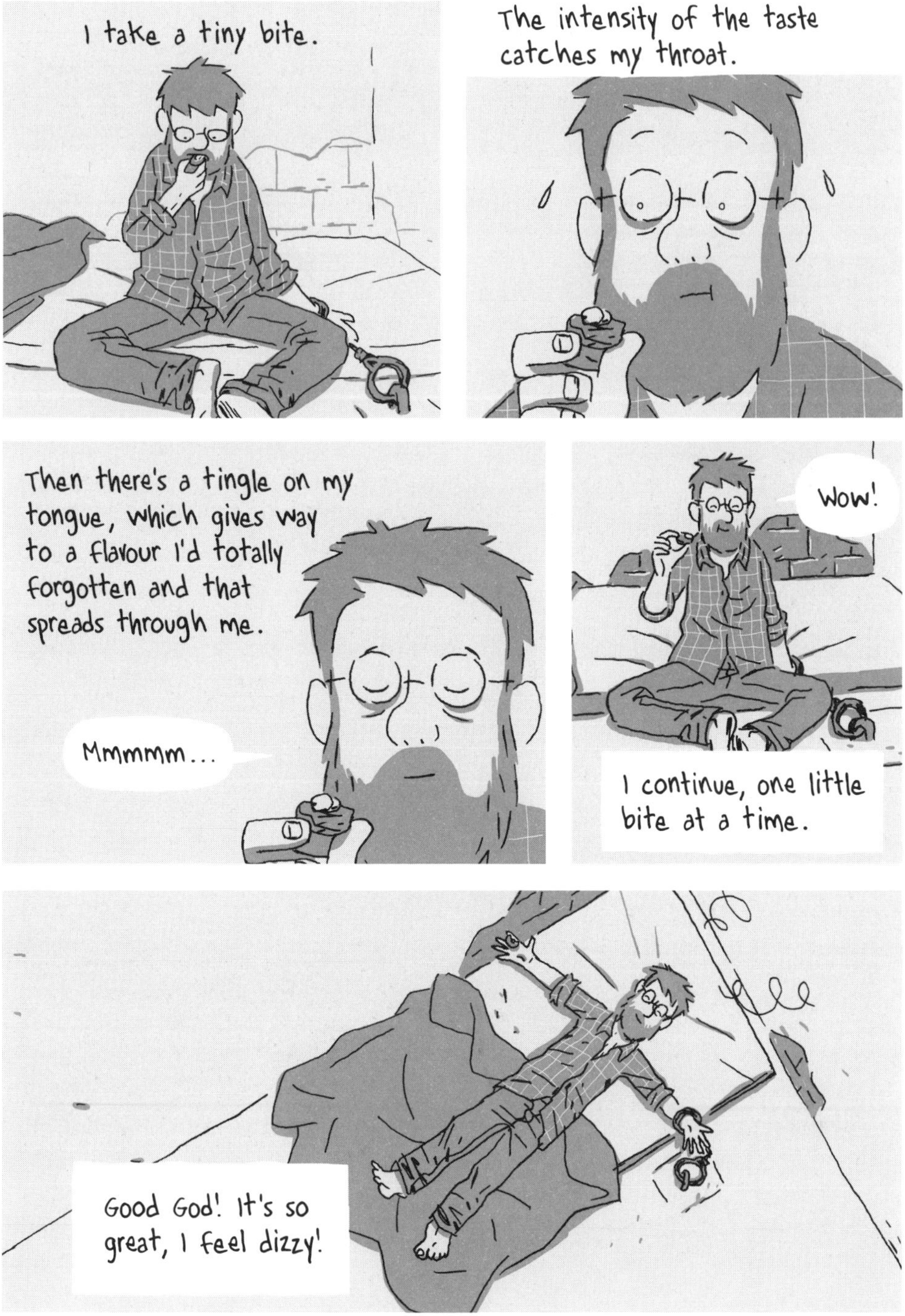

I take a tiny bite.
The intensity of the taste catches my throat.
Then there's a tingle on my tongue, which gives way to a flavour I'd totally forgotten and that spreads through me.
Mmmmm...
Wow!
I continue, one little bite at a time.
Good God! It's so great, I feel dizzy!

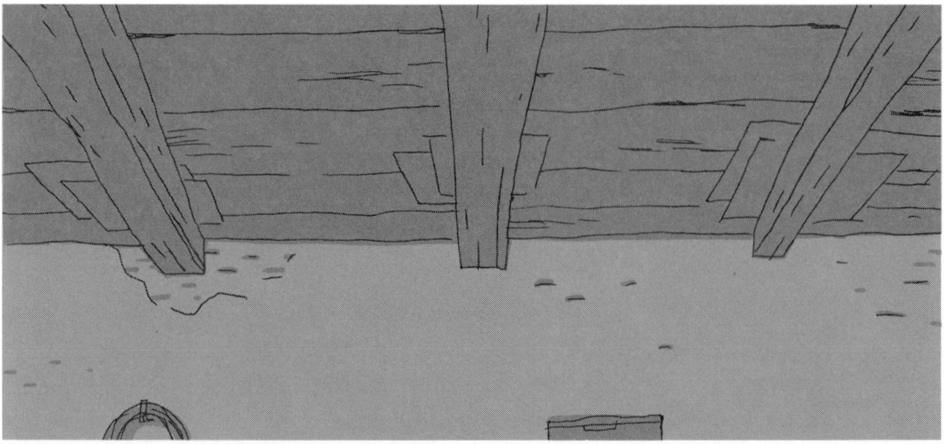

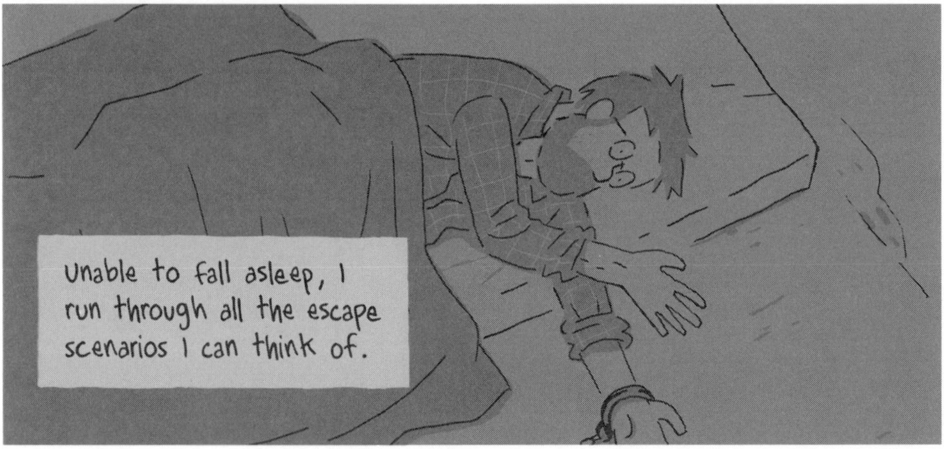
Unable to fall asleep, I run through all the escape scenarios I can think of.

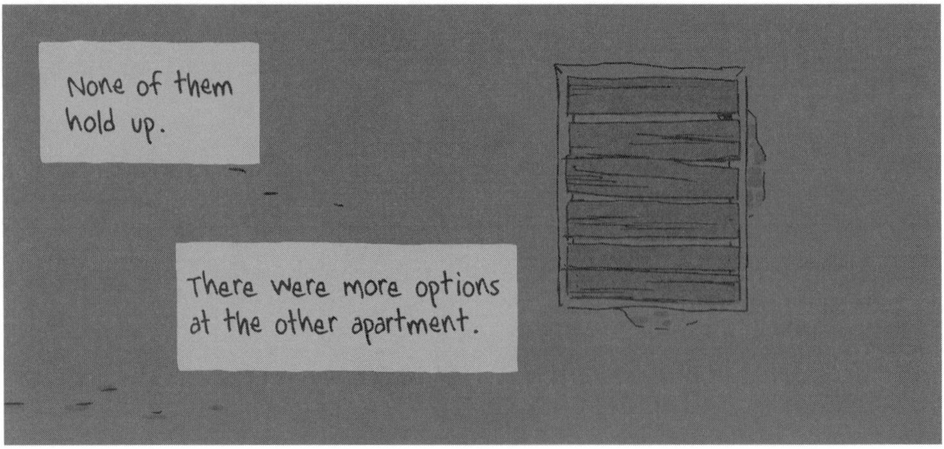
None of them hold up.
There were more options at the other apartment.

87

Today is
September 26...

Friday,
September 26.

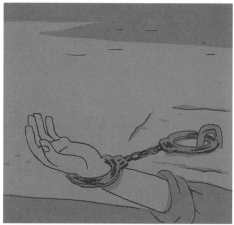

I've been in this store-
room for a week now.

The days seem to go by faster.

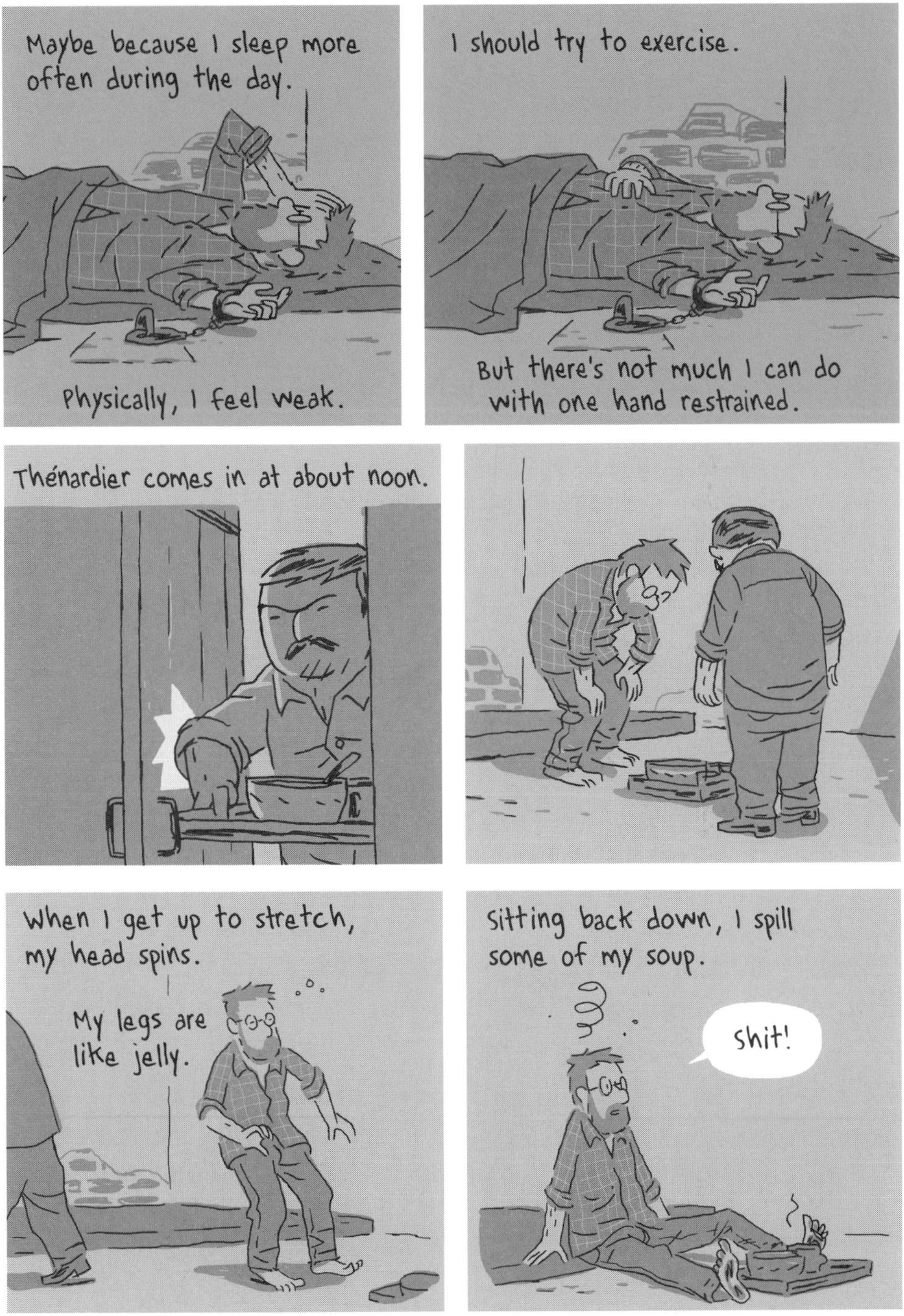
Maybe because I sleep more often during the day.
Physically, I feel weak.
I should try to exercise.
But there's not much I can do with one hand restrained.
Thénardier comes in at about noon.
When I get up to stretch, my head spins.
My legs are like jelly.
Sitting back down, I spill some of my soup.
Shit!

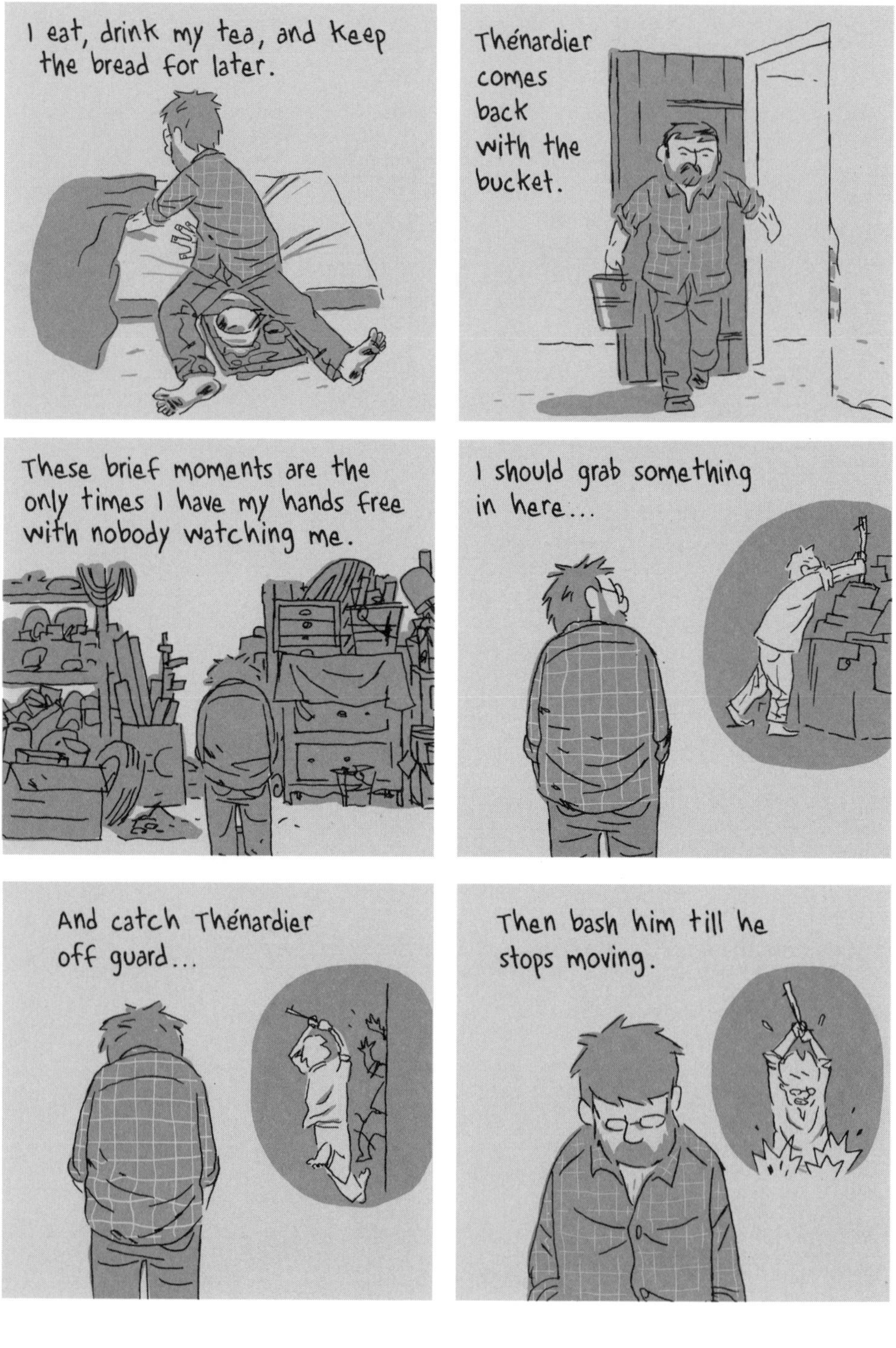
I eat, drink my tea, and keep the bread for later.
Thénardier comes back with the bucket.
These brief moments are the only times I have my hands free with nobody watching me.
I should grab something in here...
And catch Thénardier off guard...
Then bash him till he stops moving.

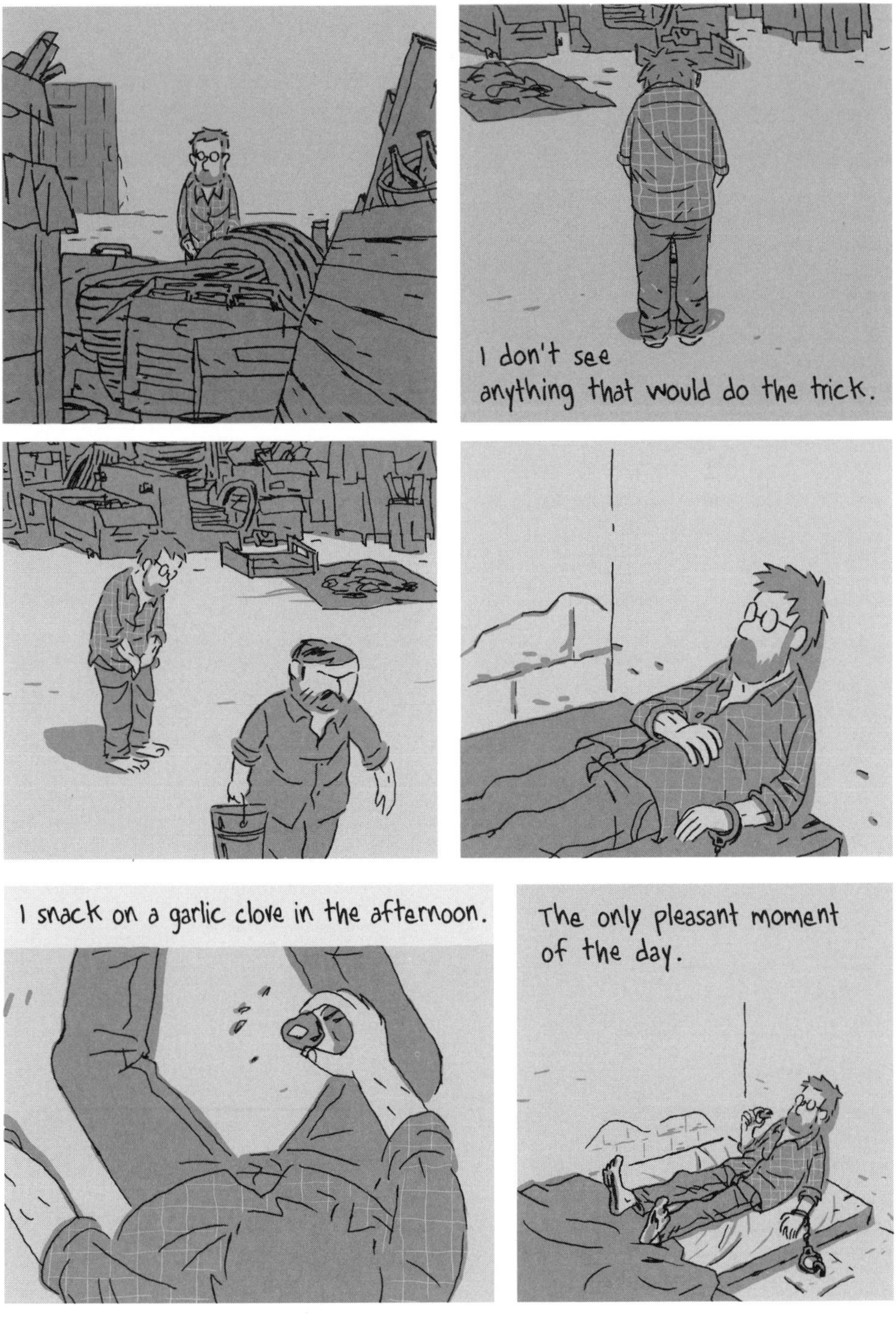
I don't see
anything that would do the trick.
I snack on a garlic clove in the afternoon.
The only pleasant moment
of the day.

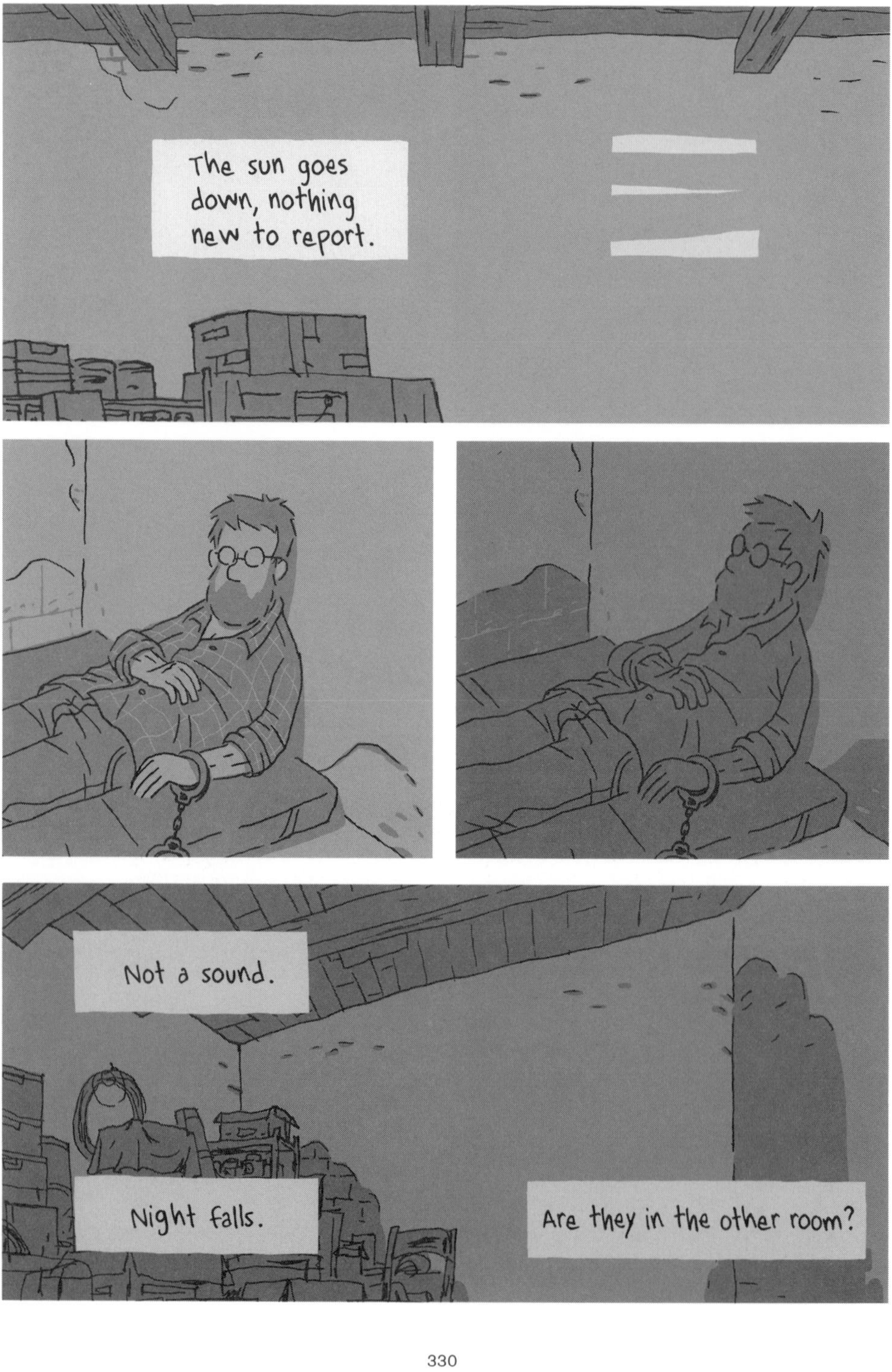
The sun goes down, nothing new to report.
Not a sound.
Night falls.
Are they in the other room?

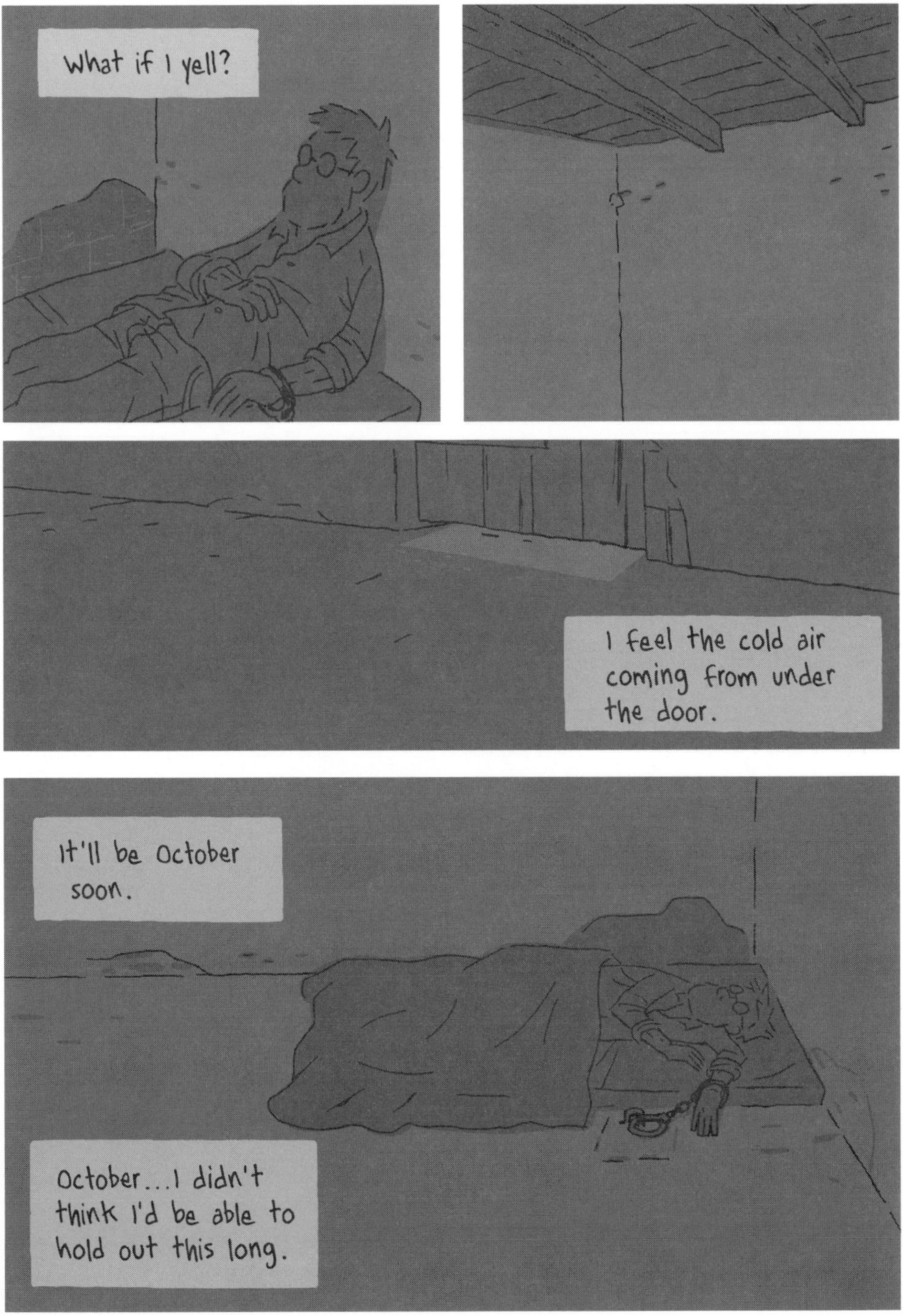
What if I yell?
I feel the cold air coming from under the door.
It'll be October soon.
October...I didn't think I'd be able to hold out this long.

92

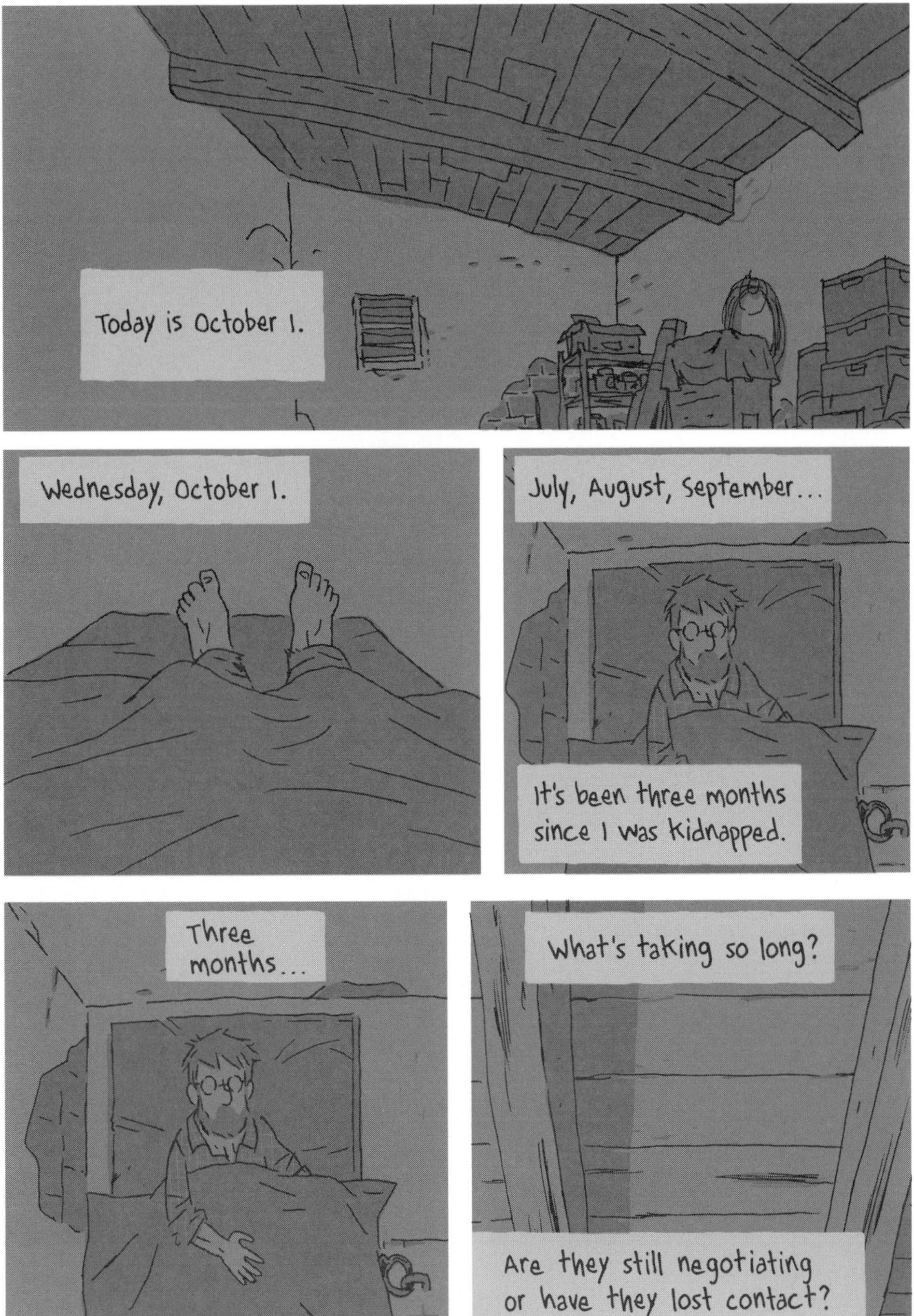
Today is October 1.
Wednesday, October 1.
July, August, September...
It's been three months since I was kidnapped.
Three months...
What's taking so long?
Are they still negotiating or have they lost contact?

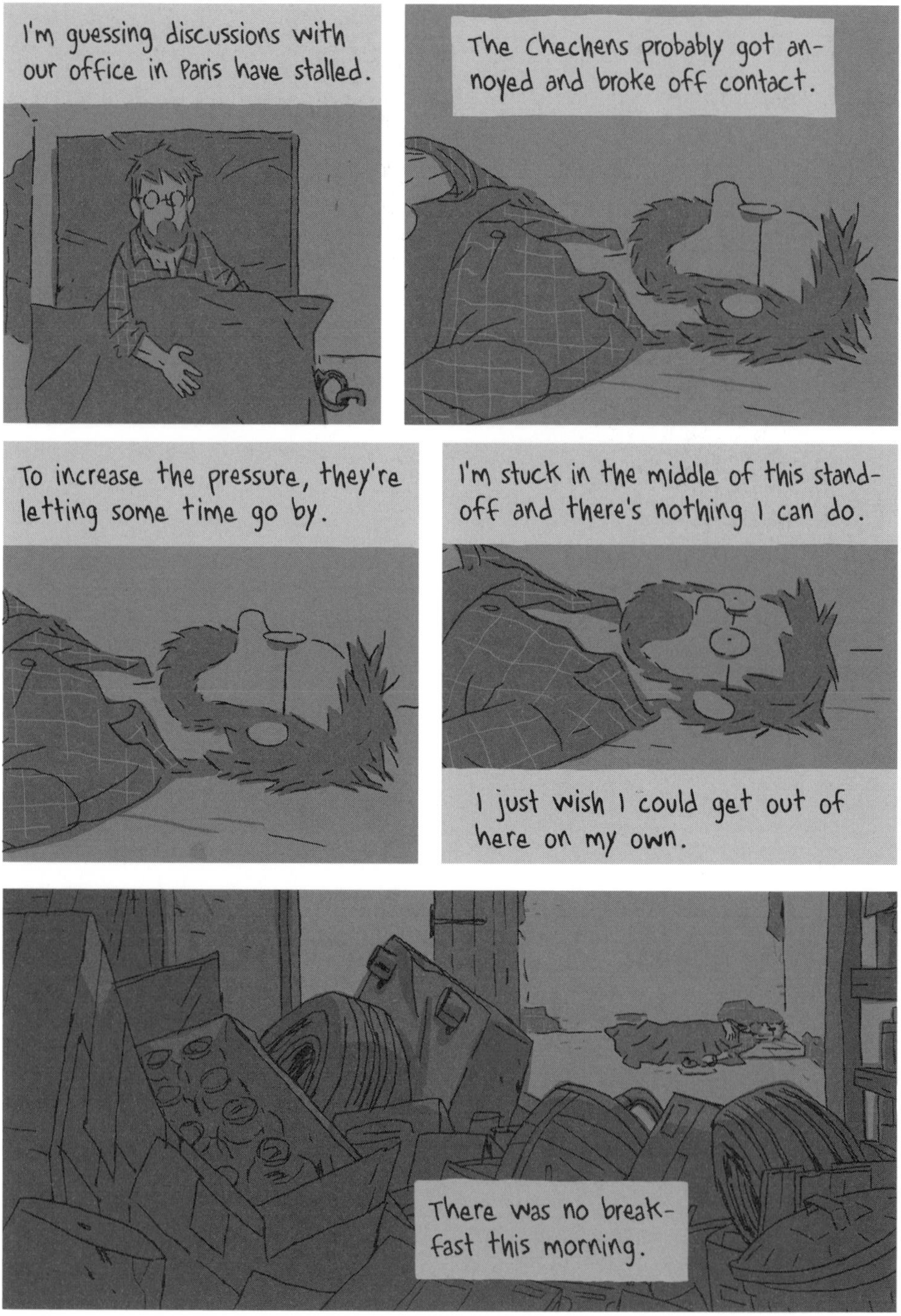
I'm guessing discussions with our office in Paris have stalled.
The Chechens probably got annoyed and broke off contact.
To increase the pressure, they're letting some time go by.
I'm stuck in the middle of this standoff and there's nothing I can do.
I just wish I could get out of here on my own.
There was no breakfast this morning.

Vroooom

Sometimes I hear cars drive by.

People coming and going... busy with their everyday activities.

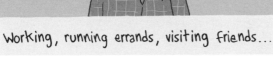

Working, running errands, visiting friends...

They pass by this house.

It's so unreal to think that life outside continues, banal as ever, while I'm locked up in here, handcuffed to the ground.

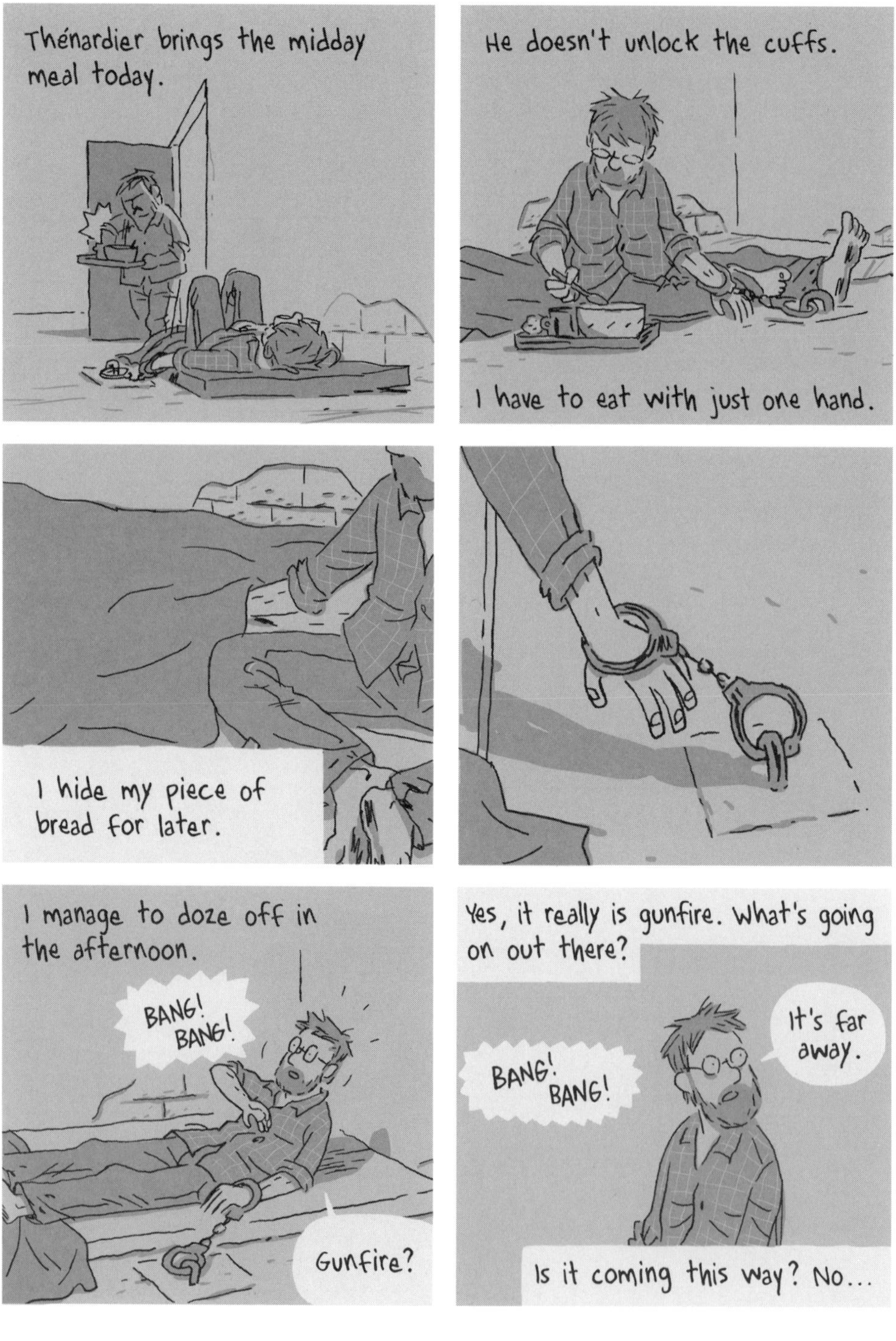
Thénardier brings the midday meal today.
He doesn't unlock the cuffs.
I have to eat with just one hand.
I hide my piece of bread for later.
I manage to doze off in the afternoon.
BANG! BANG!
Gunfire?
Yes, it really is gunfire. What's going on out there?
BANG! BANG!
It's far away.
Is it coming this way? No...

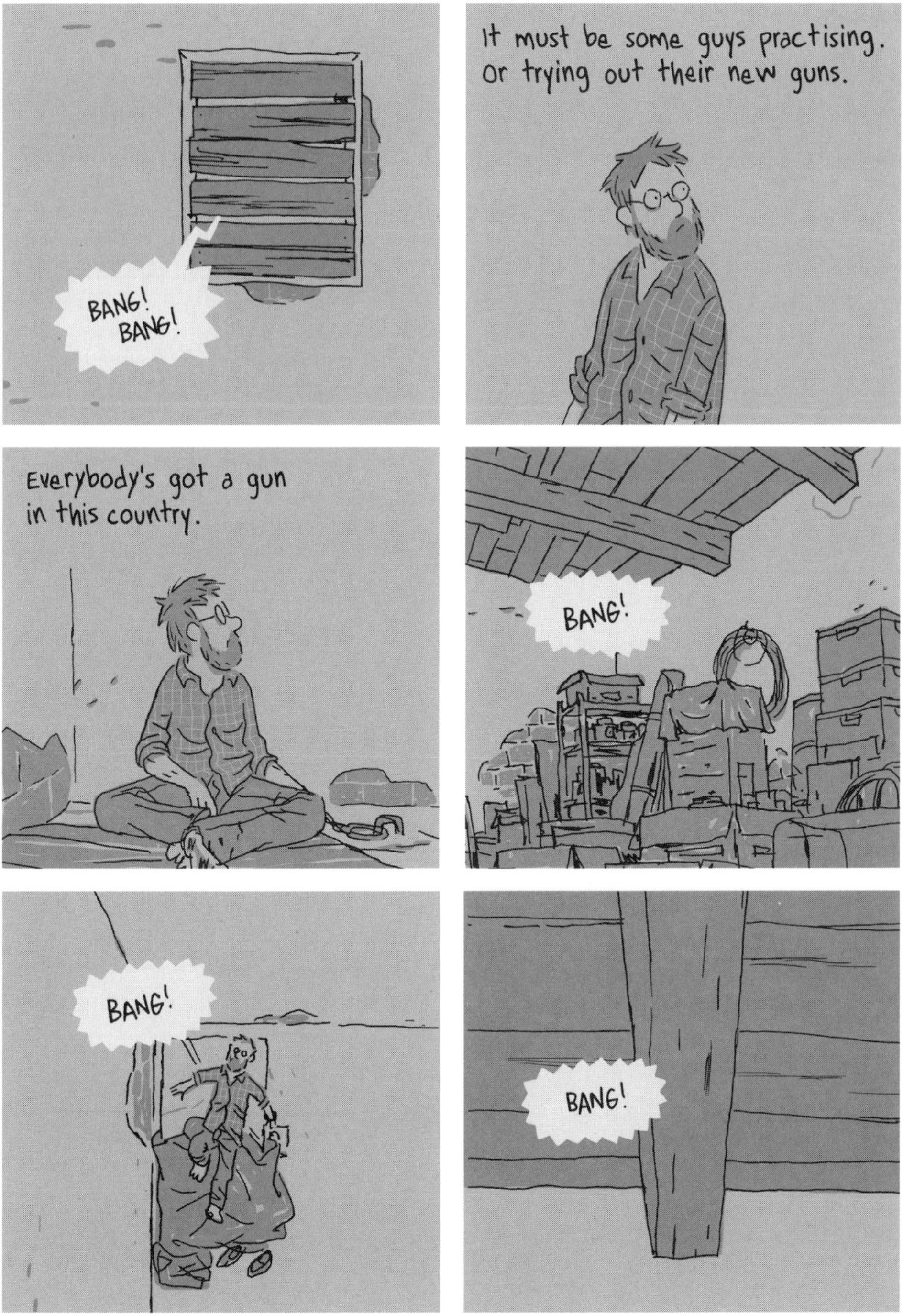
BANG! BANG!
It must be some guys practising. Or trying out their new guns.
Everybody's got a gun in this country.
BANG!
BANG!
BANG!

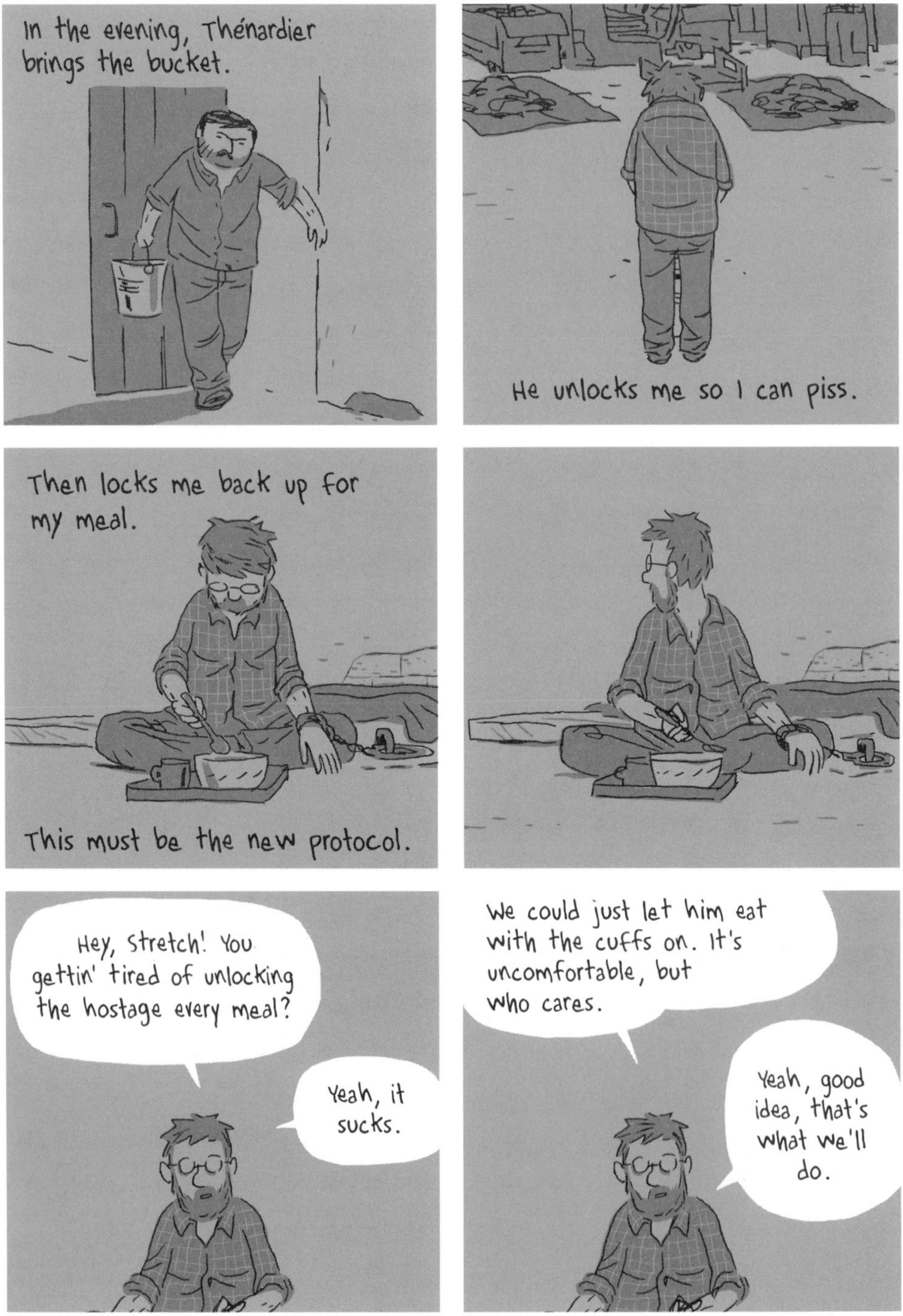
In the evening, Thénardier brings the bucket.
He unlocks me so I can piss.
Then locks me back up for my meal.
This must be the new protocol.
Hey, Stretch! You gettin' tired of unlocking the hostage every meal?
Yeah, it sucks.
We could just let him eat with the cuffs on. It's uncomfortable, but who cares.
Yeah, good idea, that's what we'll do.

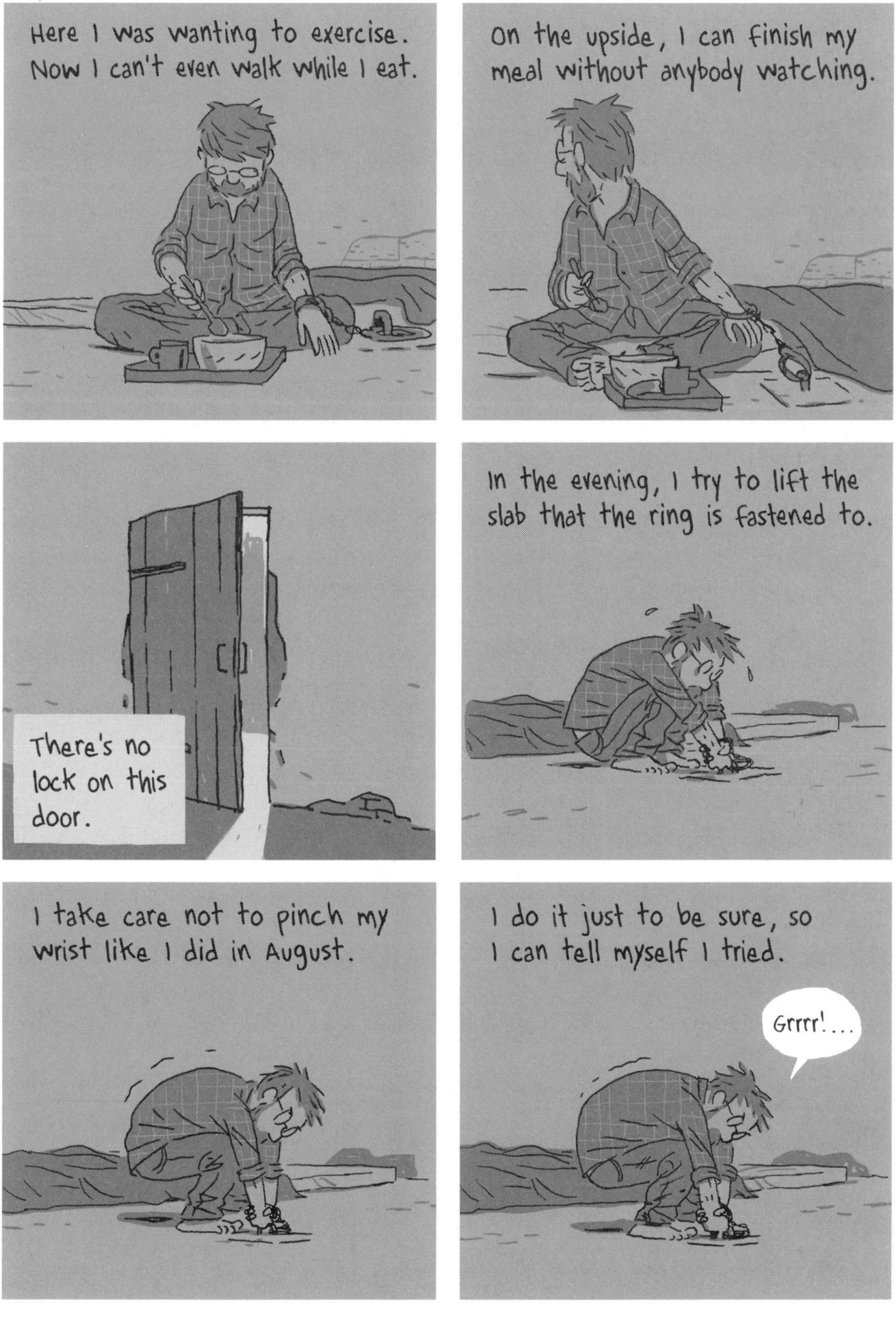
Here I was wanting to exercise. Now I can't even walk while I eat.
On the upside, I can finish my meal without anybody watching.
There's no lock on this door.
In the evening, I try to lift the slab that the ring is fastened to.
I take care not to pinch my wrist like I did in August.
I do it just to be sure, so I can tell myself I tried.
Grrrr!...

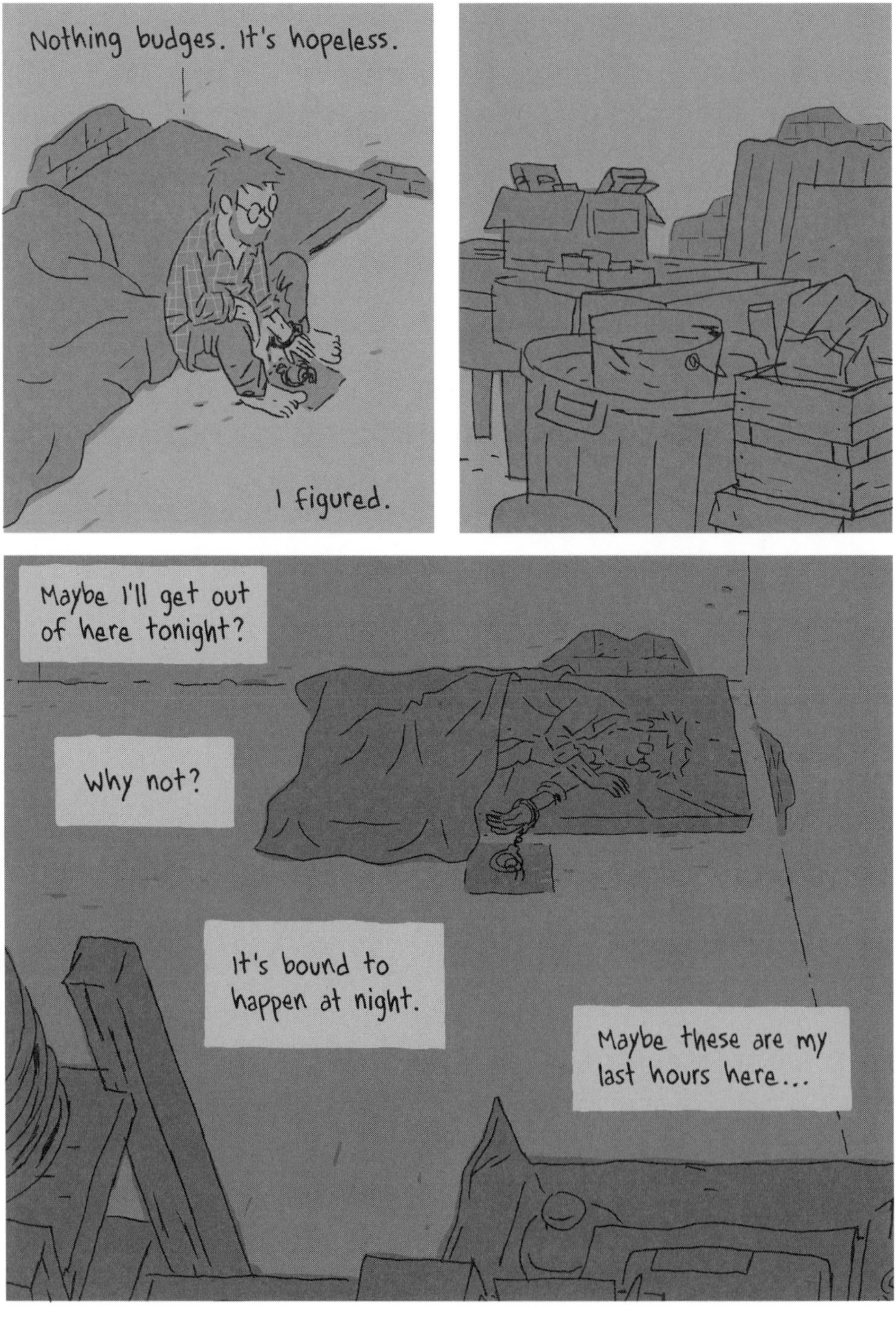
Nothing budges. It's hopeless.
I figured.
Maybe I'll get out of here tonight?
Why not?
It's bound to happen at night.
Maybe these are my last hours here...

96

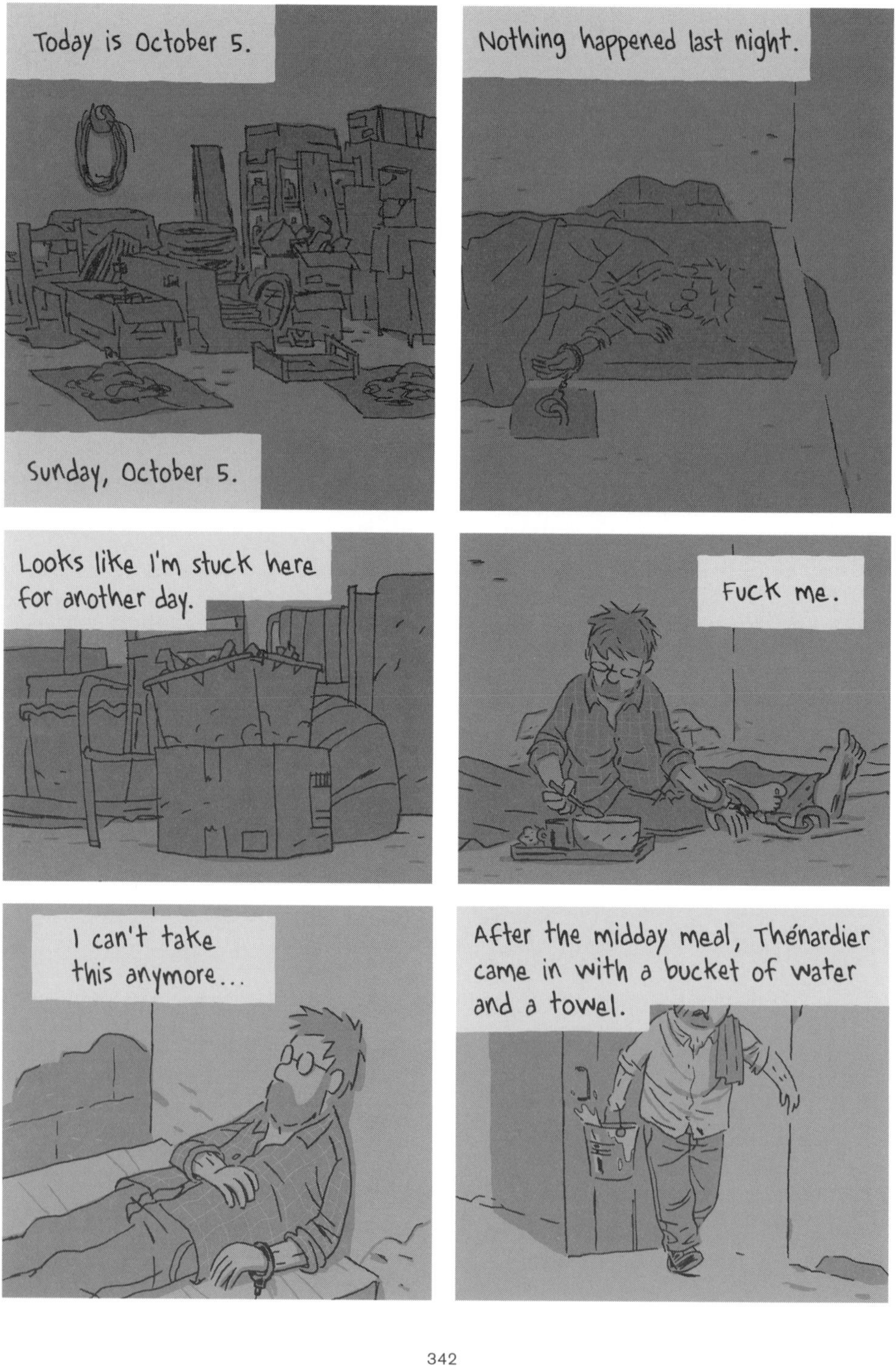
Today is October 5.
Sunday, October 5.
Nothing happened last night.
Looks like I'm stuck here for another day.
Fuck me.
I can't take this anymore...
After the midday meal, Thénardier came in with a bucket of water and a towel.

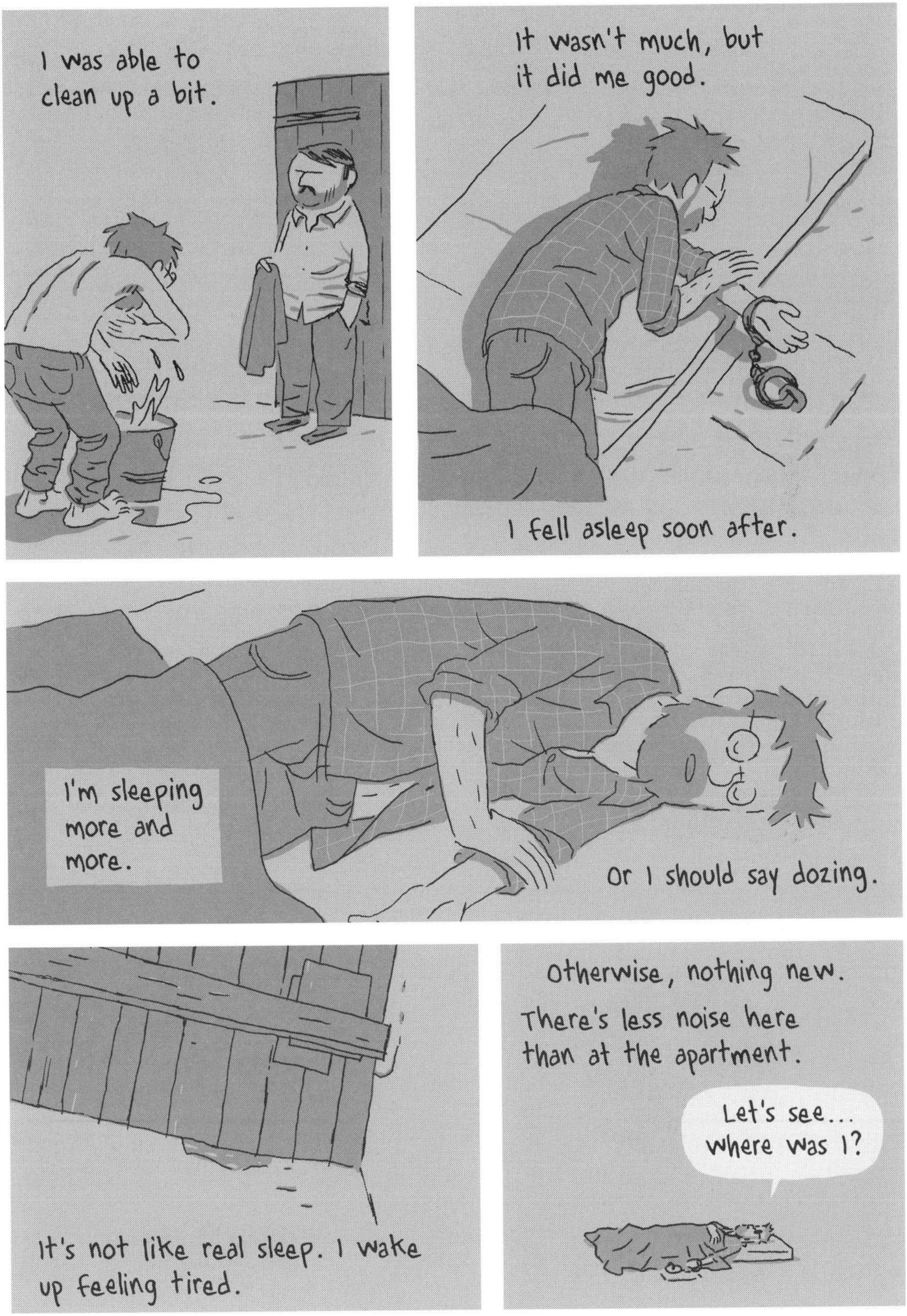
I was able to clean up a bit.
It wasn't much, but it did me good.
I fell asleep soon after.
I'm sleeping more and more.
Or I should say dozing.
It's not like real sleep. I wake up feeling tired.
Otherwise, nothing new.
There's less noise here than at the apartment.
Let's see... where was I?

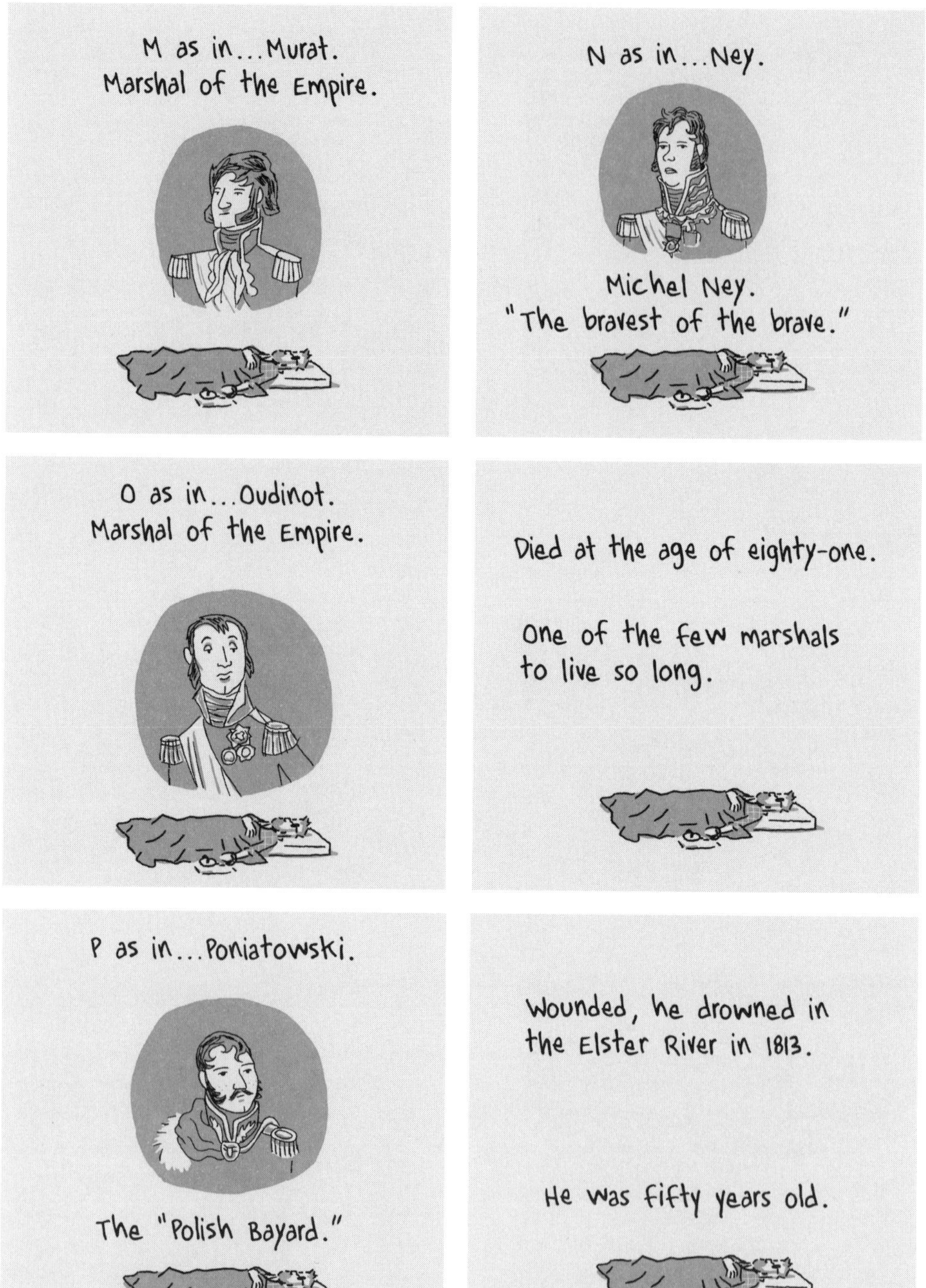
M as in... Murat.
Marshal of the Empire.
N as in... Ney.
Michel Ney.
"The bravest of the brave."
O as in... Oudinot.
Marshal of the Empire.
Died at the age of eighty-one.
One of the few marshals to live so long.
P as in... Poniatowski.
The "Polish Bayard."
Wounded, he drowned in the Elster River in 1813.
He was fifty years old.

Зтнру
Ейо Баз
The tall guy comes in. It must be about 4:00 p.m.
What's he here for?
He releases me and signals for me to follow.
ио Баз Вбар
I feel my pants slipping down as I walk.
Shit!
This is getting serious.
How much weight have I lost over the past three months?
Яьпое Бё Муц
Хюту Нкрф
Yeah, yeah.

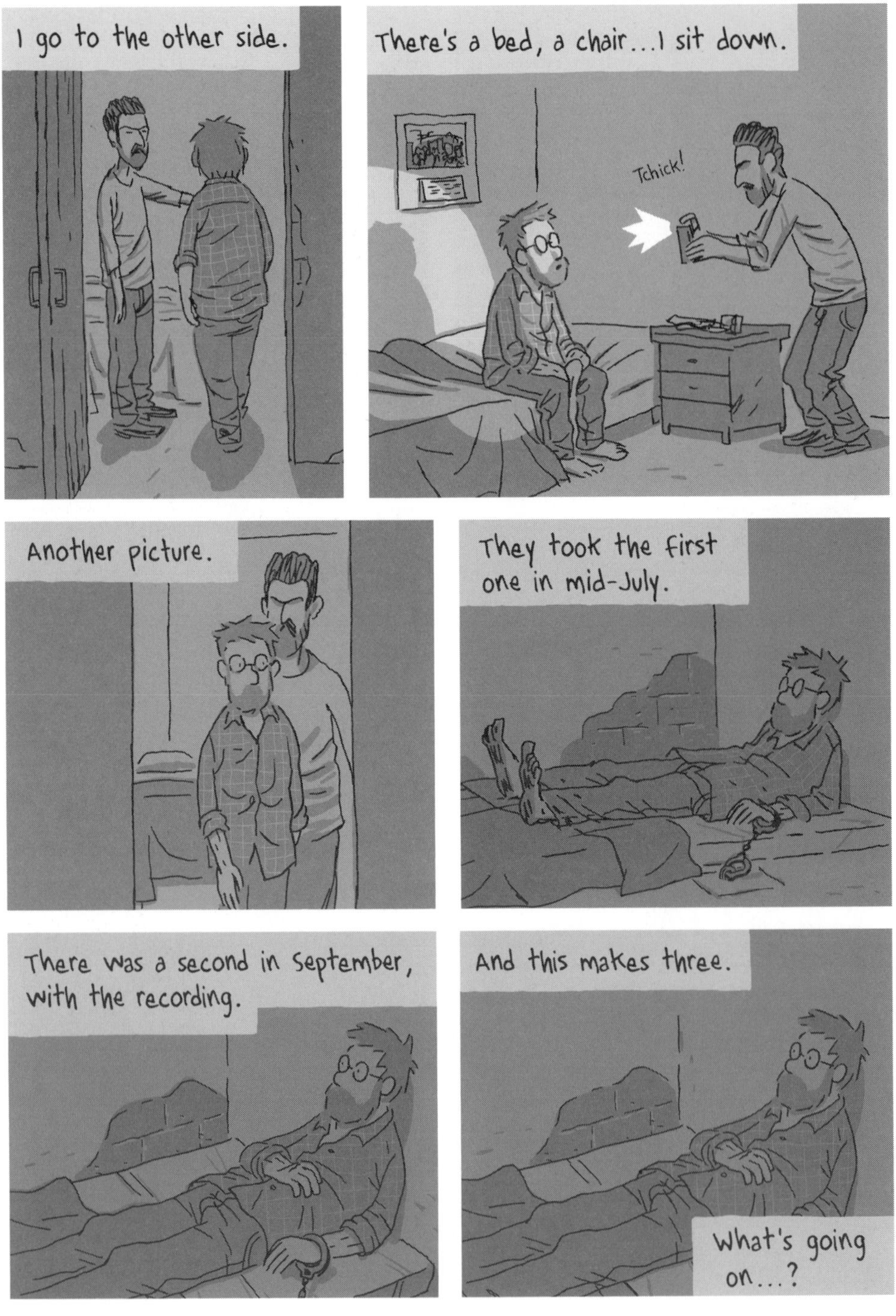
I go to the other side.
There's a bed, a chair... I sit down.
Tchick!
Another picture.
They took the first one in mid-July.
There was a second in September, with the recording.
And this makes three.
What's going on...?

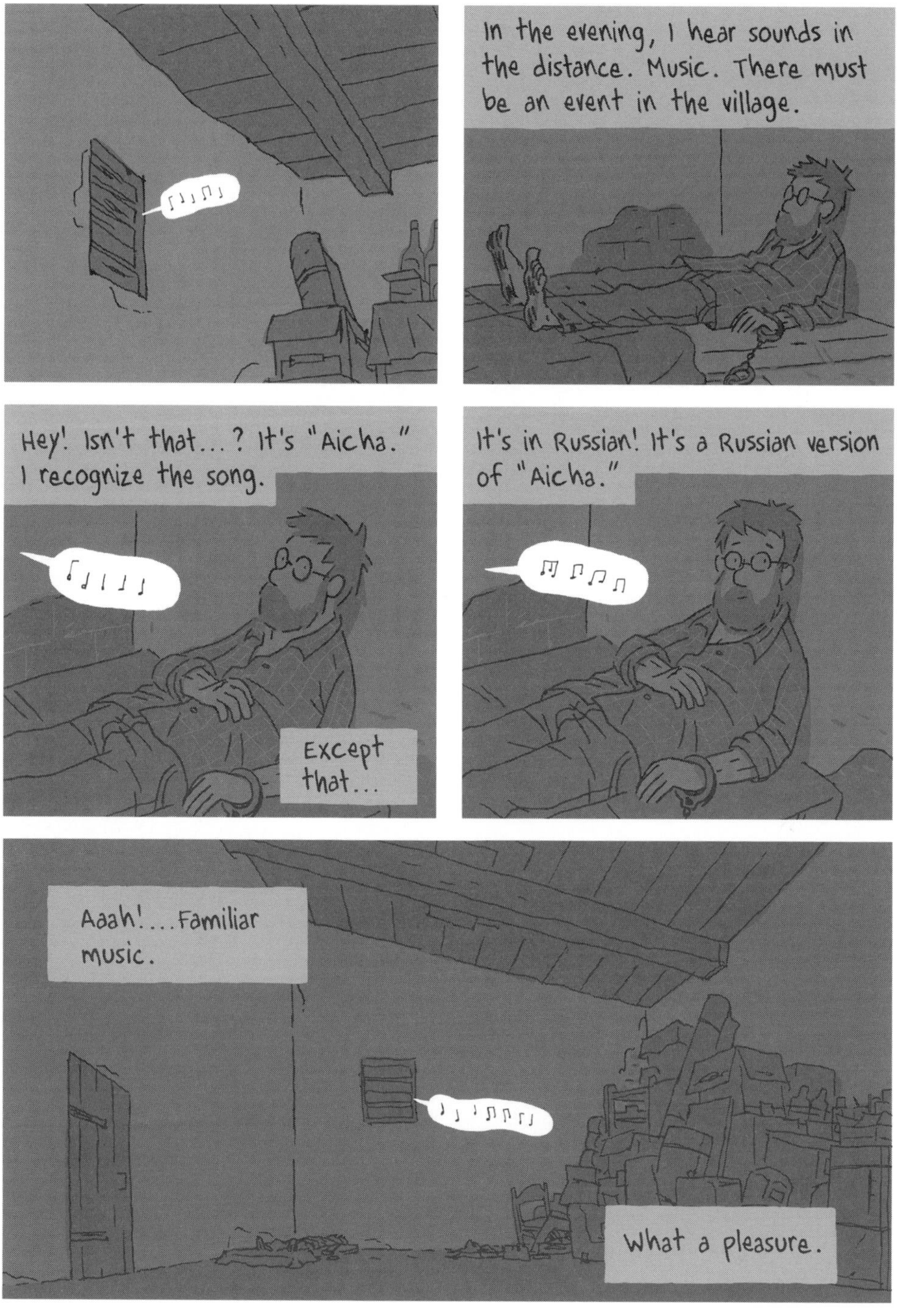
In the evening, I hear sounds in the distance. Music. There must be an event in the village.
Hey! Isn't that...? It's "Aicha." I recognize the song.
Except that...
It's in Russian! It's a Russian version of "Aicha."
Aaah!...Familiar music.
What a pleasure.

100

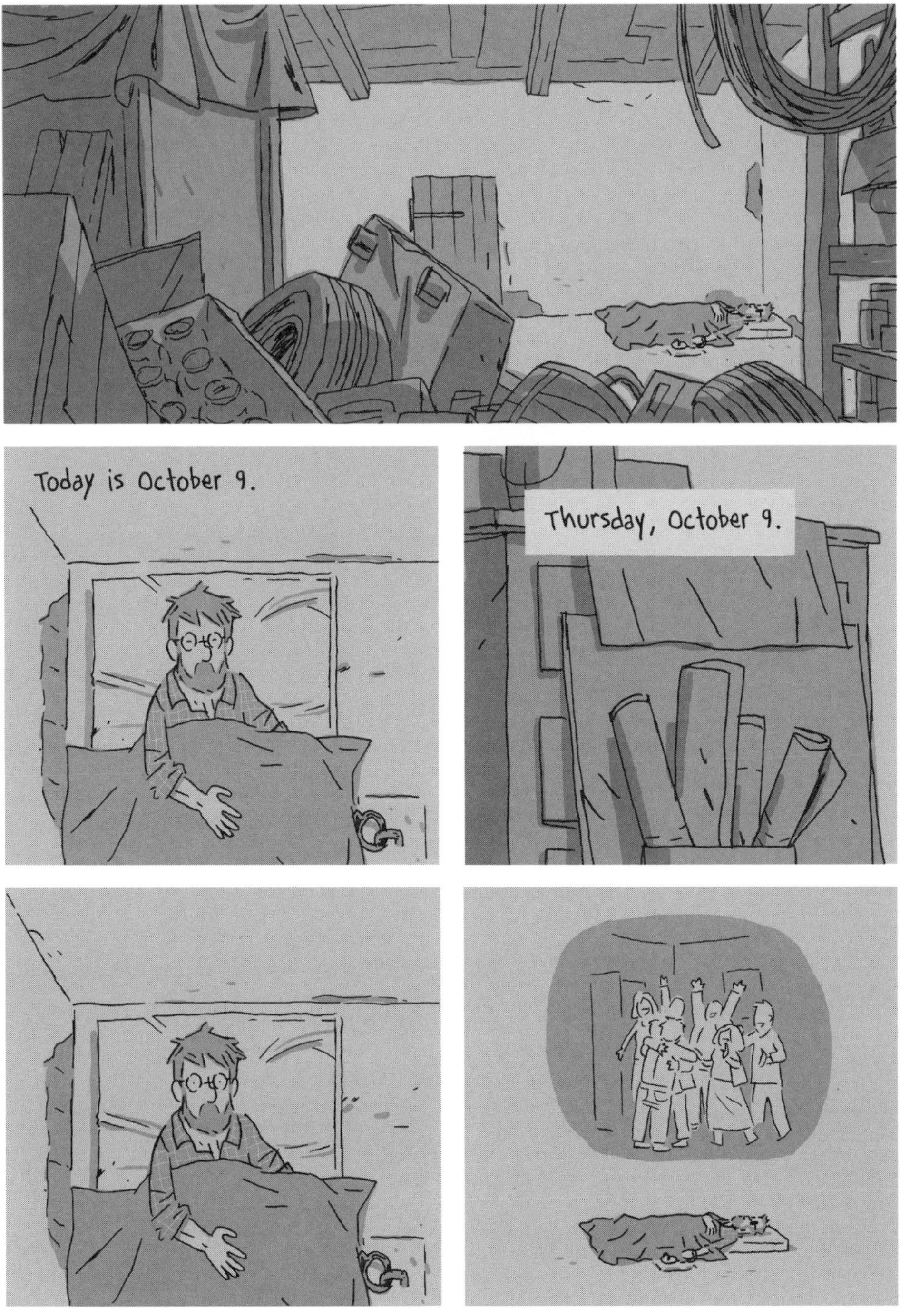
Today is October 9.
Thursday, October 9.

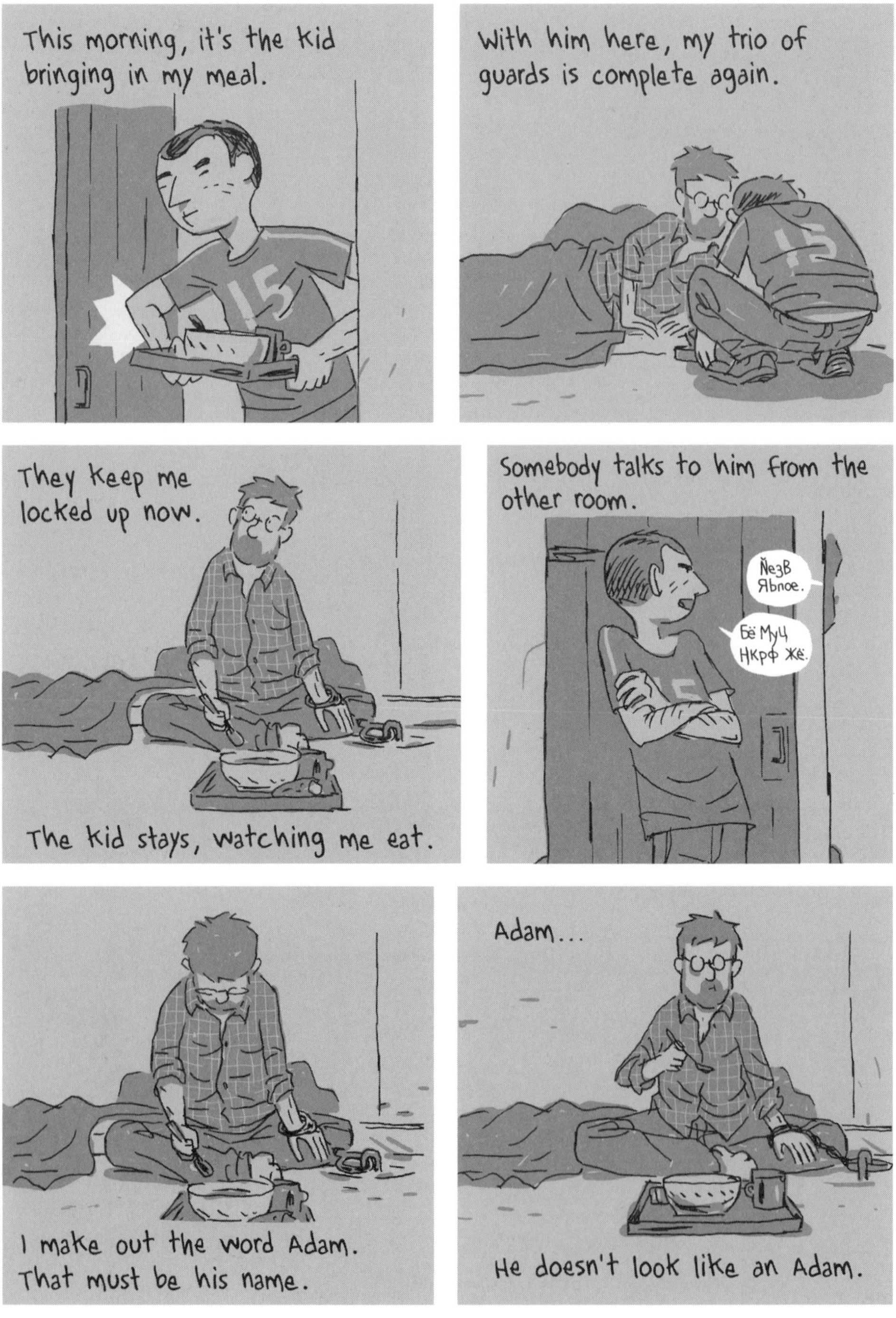
This morning, it's the kid bringing in my meal.
With him here, my trio of guards is complete again.
They keep me locked up now.
The kid stays, watching me eat.
Somebody talks to him from the other room.
N̆езв Яьпое.
Бё Муц Нкрф Жё.
I make out the word Adam. That must be his name.
Adam...
He doesn't look like an Adam.

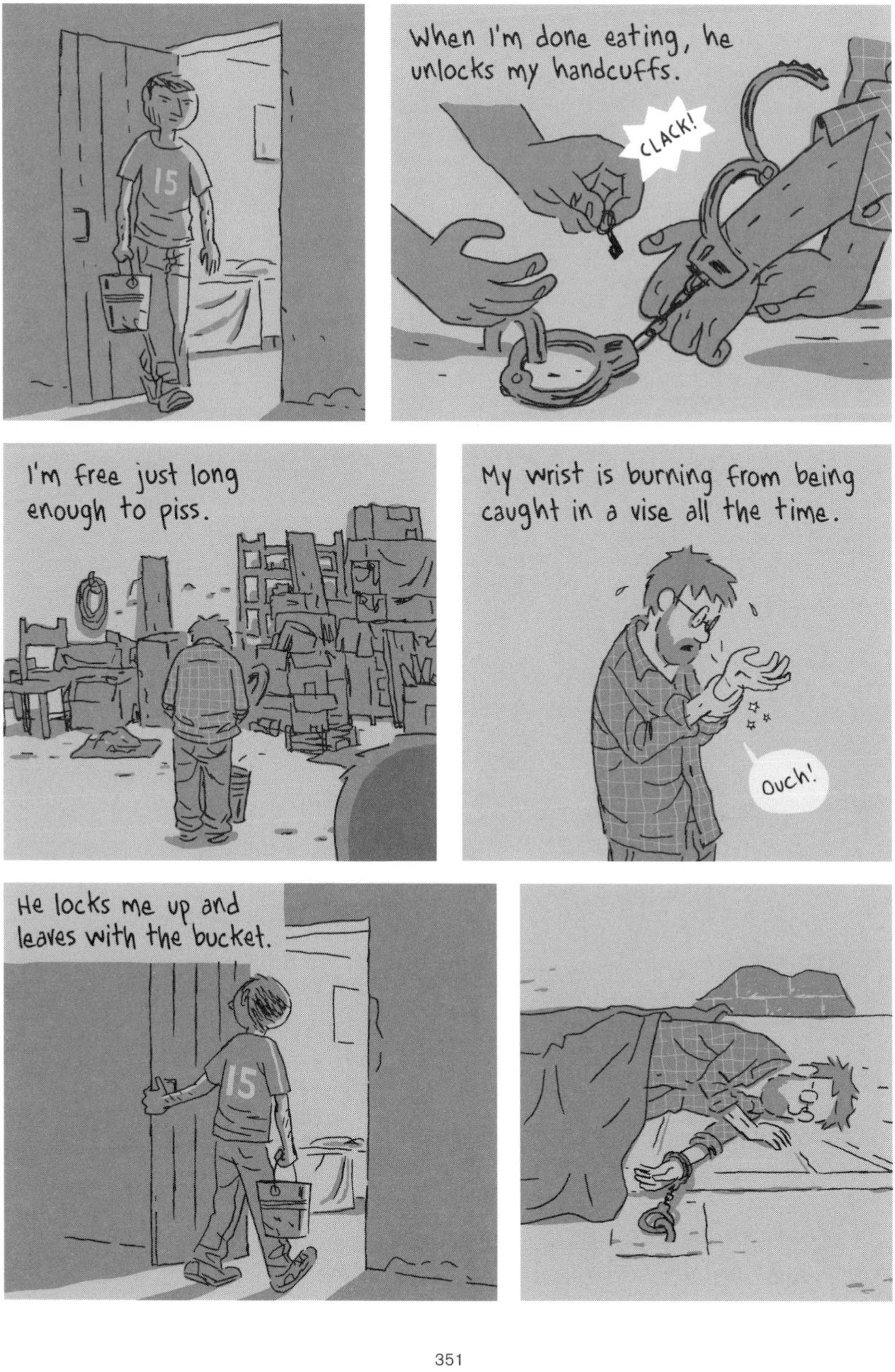
When I'm done eating, he unlocks my handcuffs.
CLACK!
I'm free just long enough to piss.
My wrist is burning from being caught in a vise all the time.
Ouch!
He locks me up and leaves with the bucket.

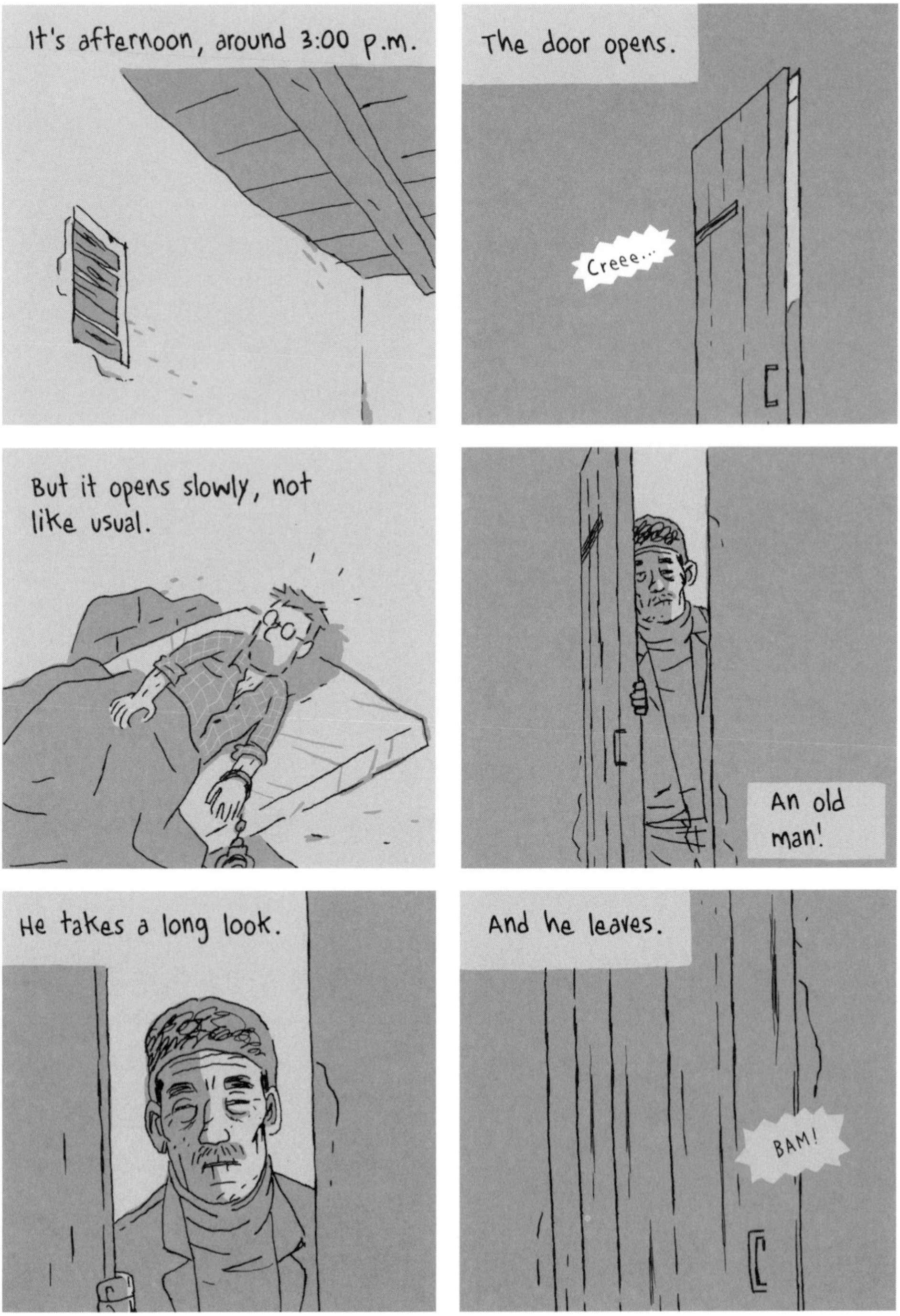
It's afternoon, around 3:00 p.m.
The door opens.
Creee...
But it opens slowly, not like usual.
An old man!
He takes a long look.
And he leaves.
BAM!

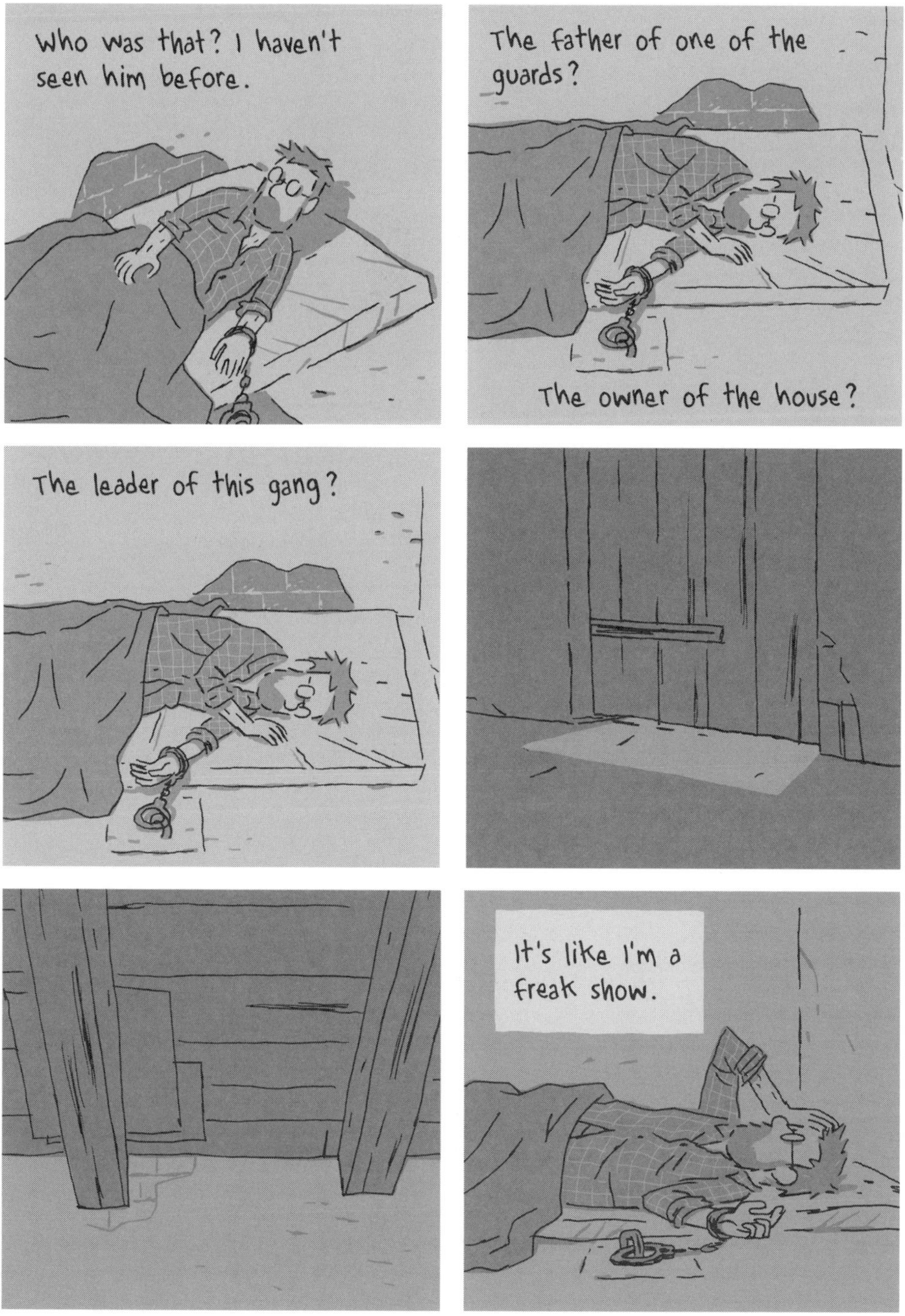
Who was that? I haven't seen him before.
The father of one of the guards?
The owner of the house?
The leader of this gang?
It's like I'm a freak show.

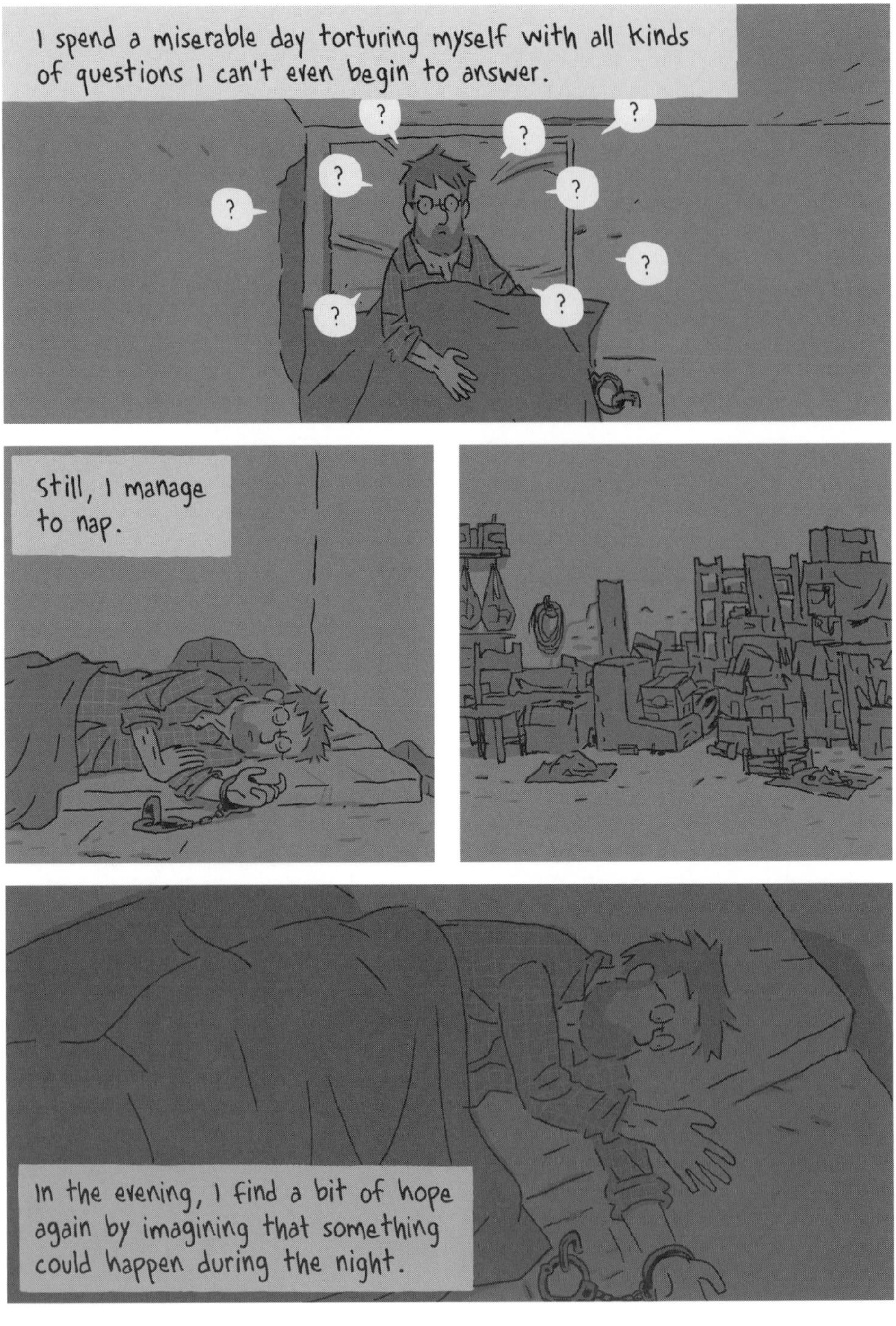
I spend a miserable day torturing myself with all kinds of questions I can't even begin to answer.
?
?
?
?
?
?
?
?
?
Still, I manage to nap.
In the evening, I find a bit of hope again by imagining that something could happen during the night.

105

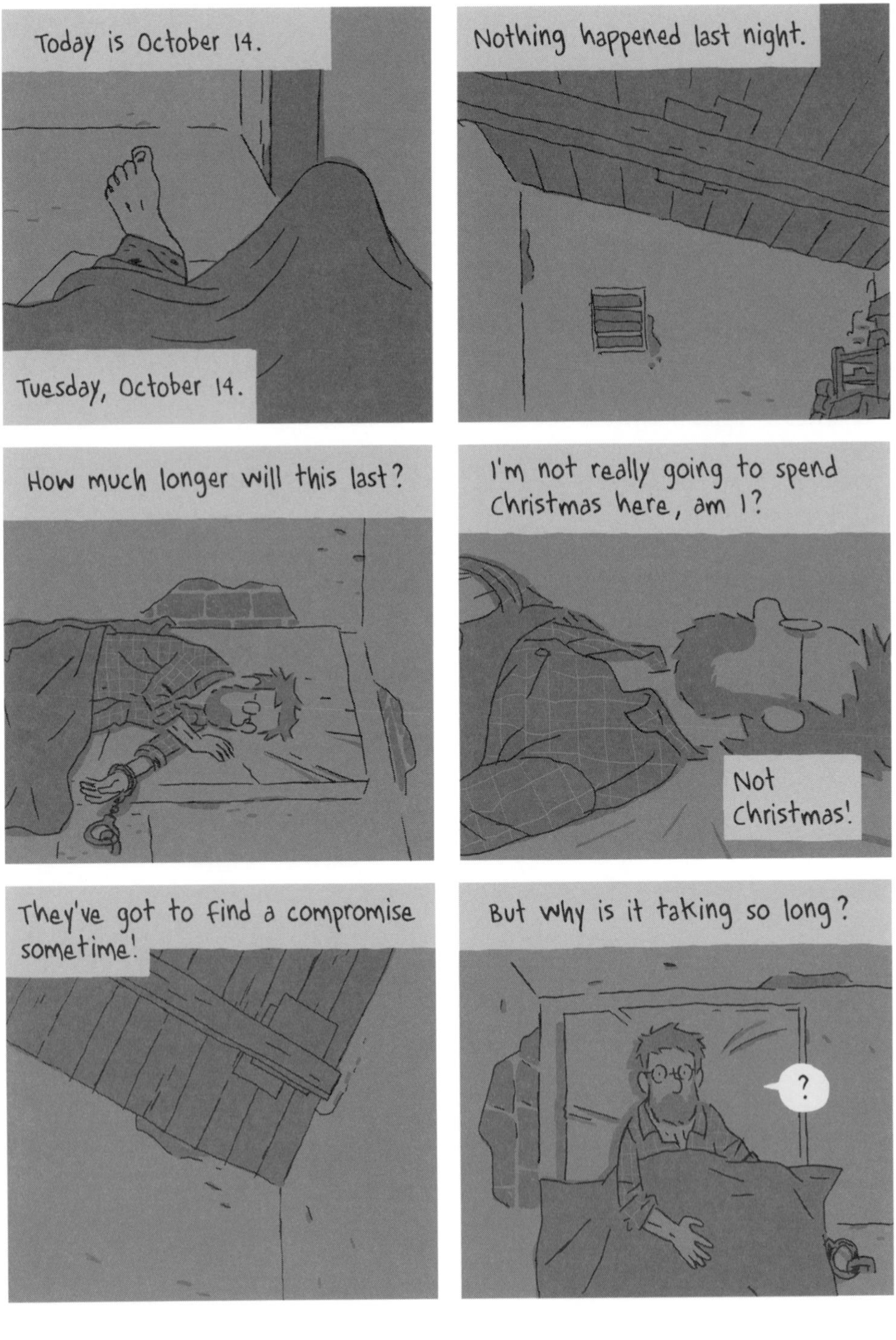
Today is October 14.
Tuesday, October 14.
Nothing happened last night.
How much longer will this last?
I'm not really going to spend Christmas here, am I?
Not Christmas!
They've got to find a compromise sometime!
But why is it taking so long?
?

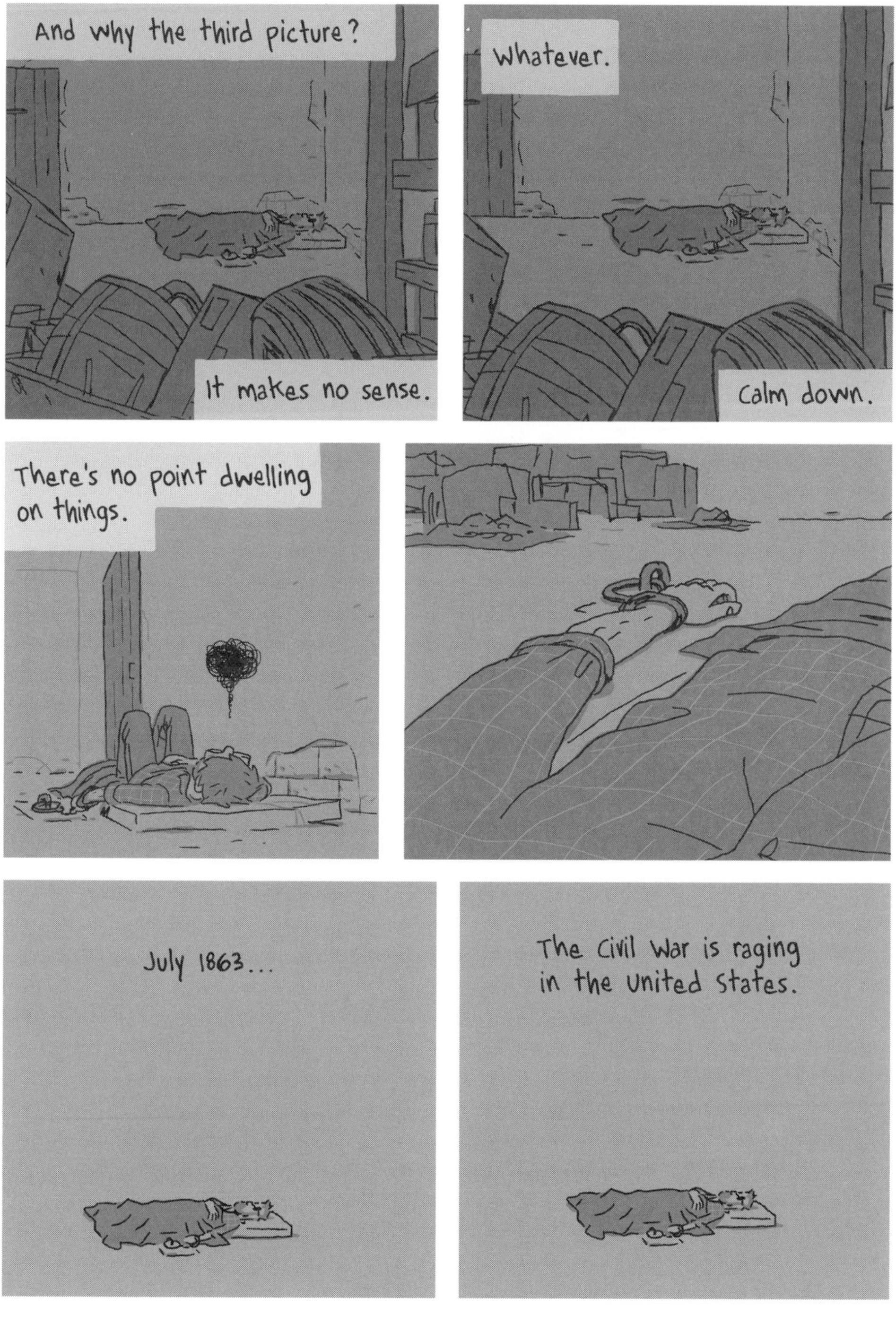
And why the third picture?
It makes no sense.
Whatever.
Calm down.
There's no point dwelling on things.
July 1863...
The Civil War is raging in the United States.

After a crushing victory two months earlier, Confederate General Robert E. Lee marches his army toward the northern states.
Robert Edward Lee
The Marble Man
His counterpart, General George Meade, needs to block his advance before he can threaten towns like Philadelphia and Washington.
George Gordon Meade
Old Snapping Turtle
On the morning of July 1, the two armies collide northwest of Gettysburg.
Hill
Ewell
Howard
Reynolds
Gettysburg
At day's end, the outnumbered Union forces retreat to the hills south of town.
Gettysburg
Ewell
Hill
Newton
Hancock
Slocum
Sickles
Sykes
Fighting ensues on July 2, and Meade's defensive line holds.
But in the afternoon, this idiot here, Sickles, dissatisfied with the terrain, takes position 800 metres ahead of the Union line.

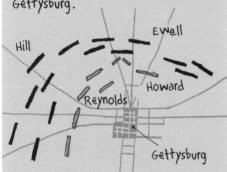

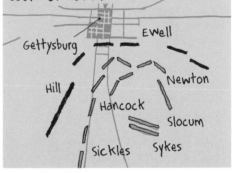

Longstreet, across from him, detects the blunder and bifurcates to the right toward Little Round Top.

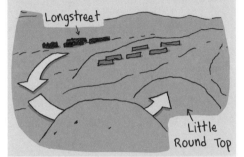

Longstreet

Little Round Top

Meade sends troops to reoccupy the space vacated by Sickles.

Control of Devil's Den changes hands three times during the day.

Follow me!

Chamberlain's men end up pushing back the Confederates with their bayonets.

On July 3, Lee sends the bulk of his troops to the left flank.

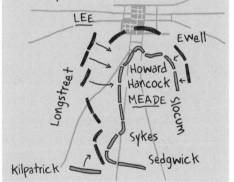

LEE

Ewell

Howard
Hancock
MEADE

Longstreet

Slocum

Sykes

Sedgwick

Kilpatrick

Across open ground, 12,500 soldiers mount a charge.

But the Union artillery, which Lee has failed to disable, decimates the Confederate ranks.

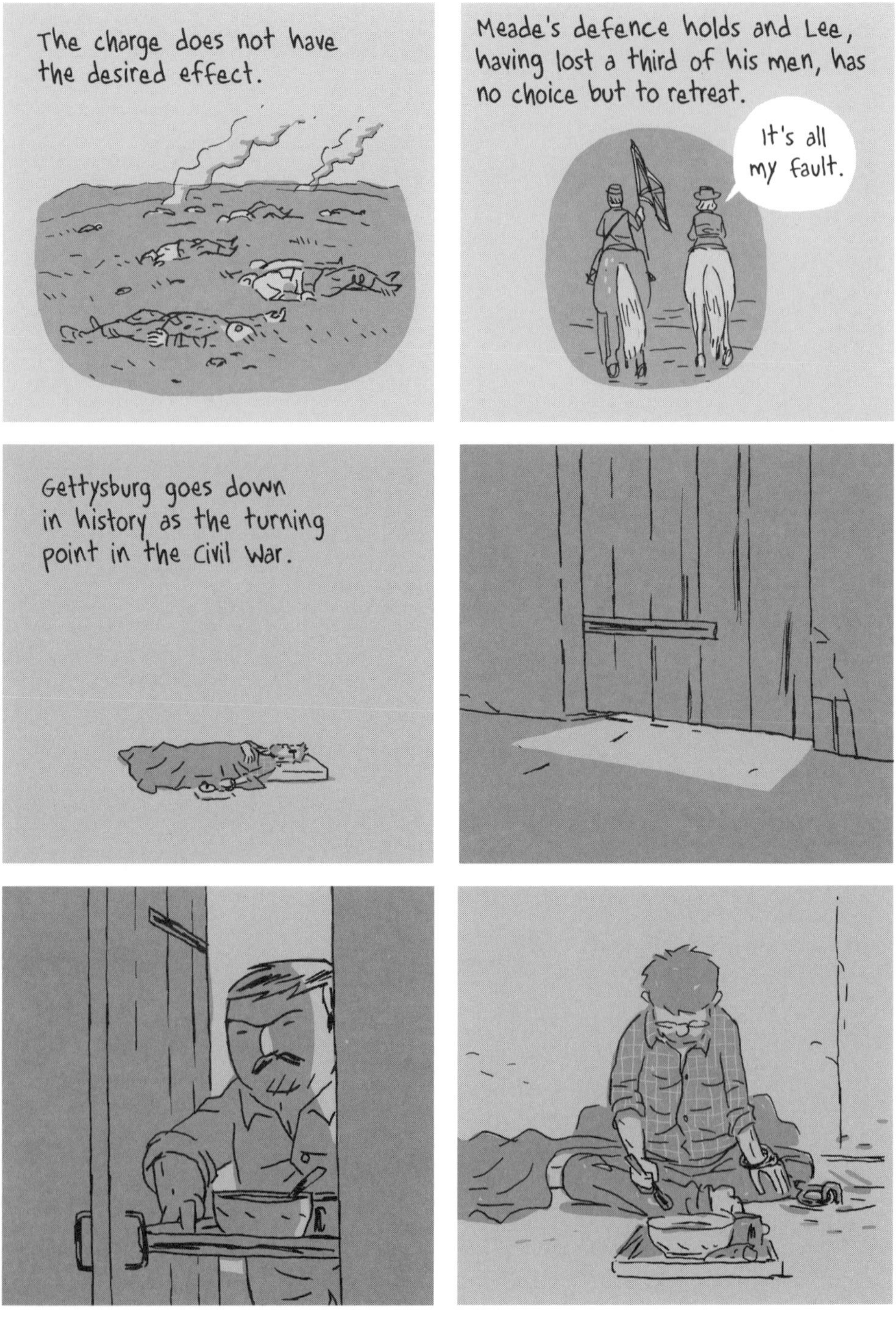
The charge does not have the desired effect.
Meade's defence holds and Lee, having lost a third of his men, has no choice but to retreat.
It's all my fault.
Gettysburg goes down in history as the turning point in the Civil War.

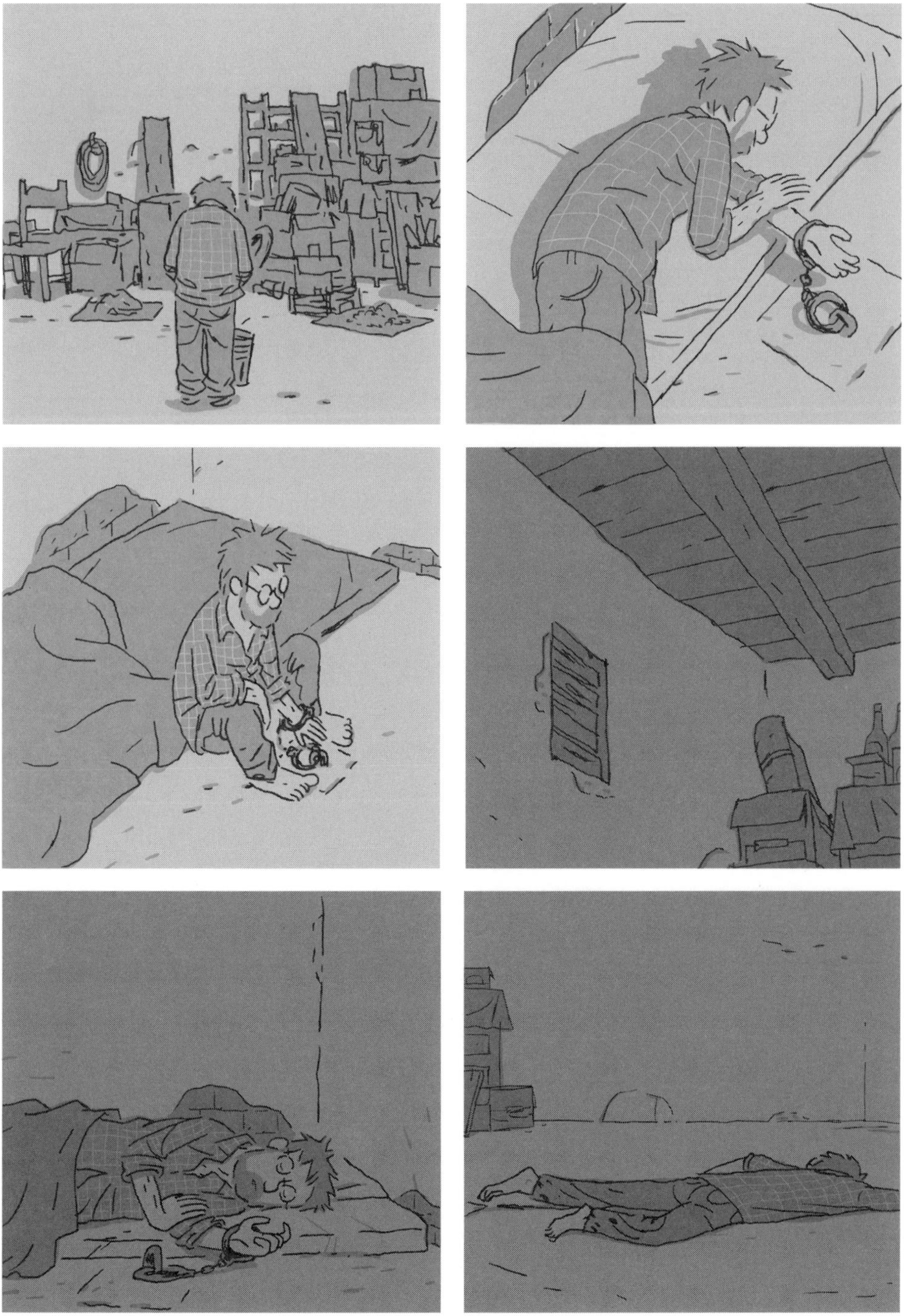

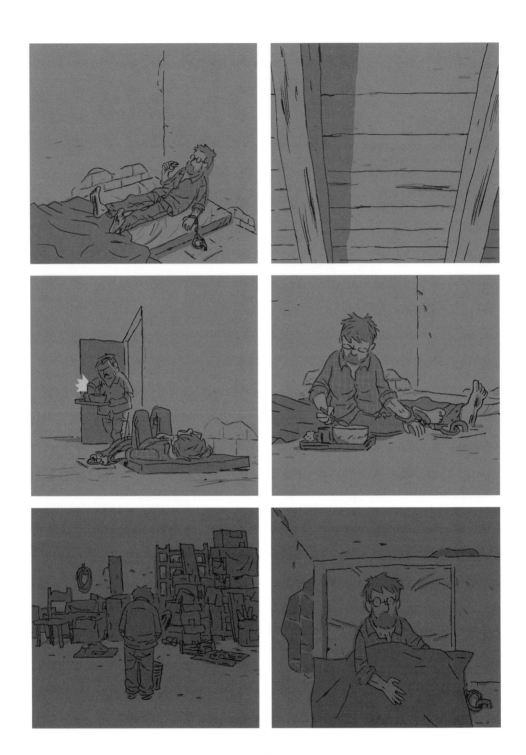

110

Today is October 19.

Sunday, October 19.

It's chilly this morning.

I put on the parka to warm up.

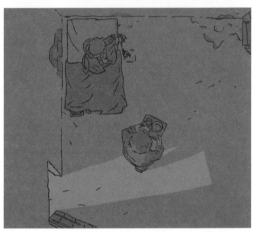

After the meal, Thénardier unlocks my cuffs and motions for me to follow.

We walk through the room with the bed in it and then a kind of kitchen with a camp stove.

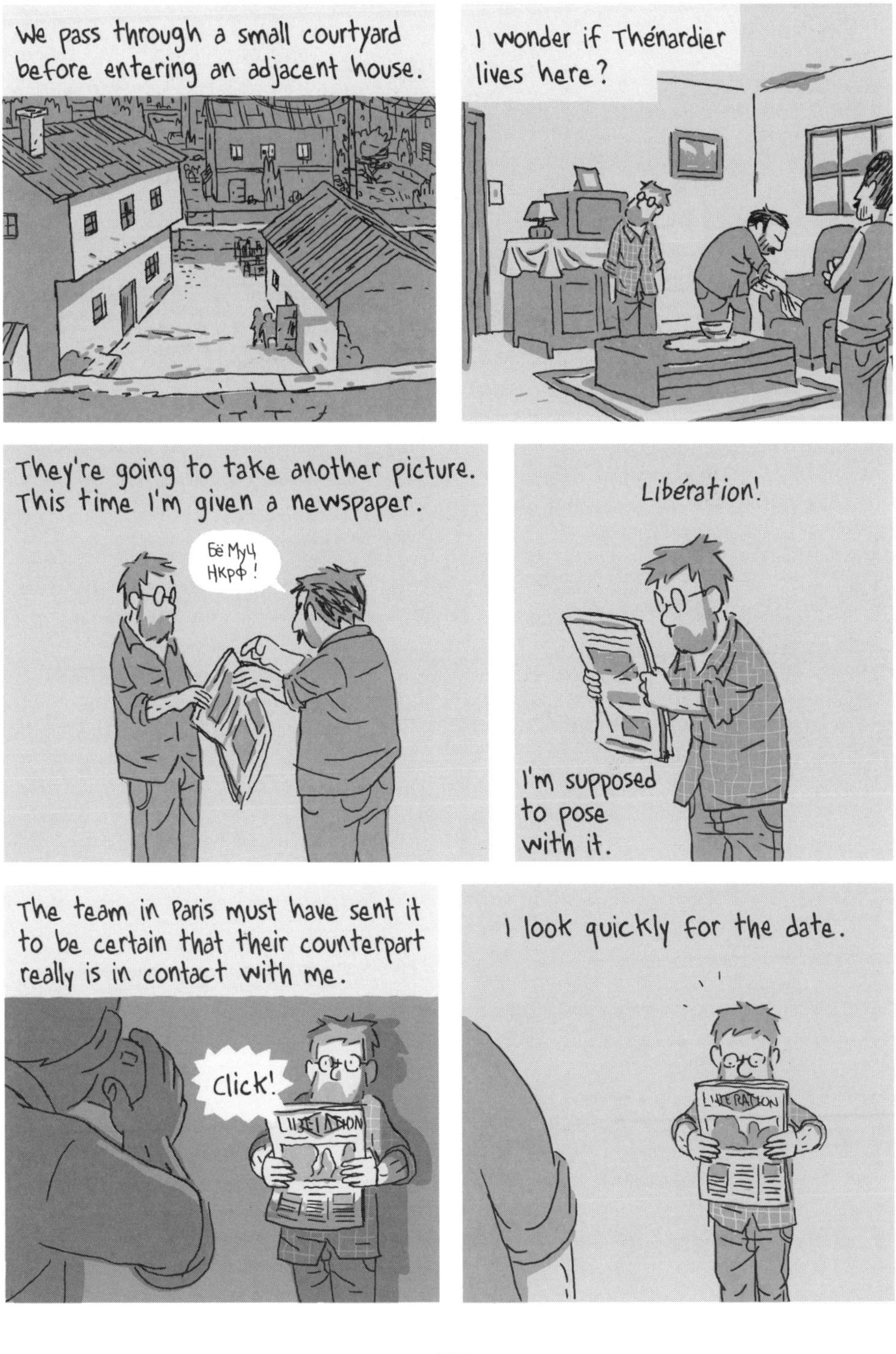
We pass through a small courtyard before entering an adjacent house.
I wonder if Thénardier lives here?
They're going to take another picture. This time I'm given a newspaper.
Бё Муц Нкрф !
Libération!
I'm supposed to pose with it.
The team in Paris must have sent it to be certain that their counterpart really is in contact with me.
Click!
I look quickly for the date.

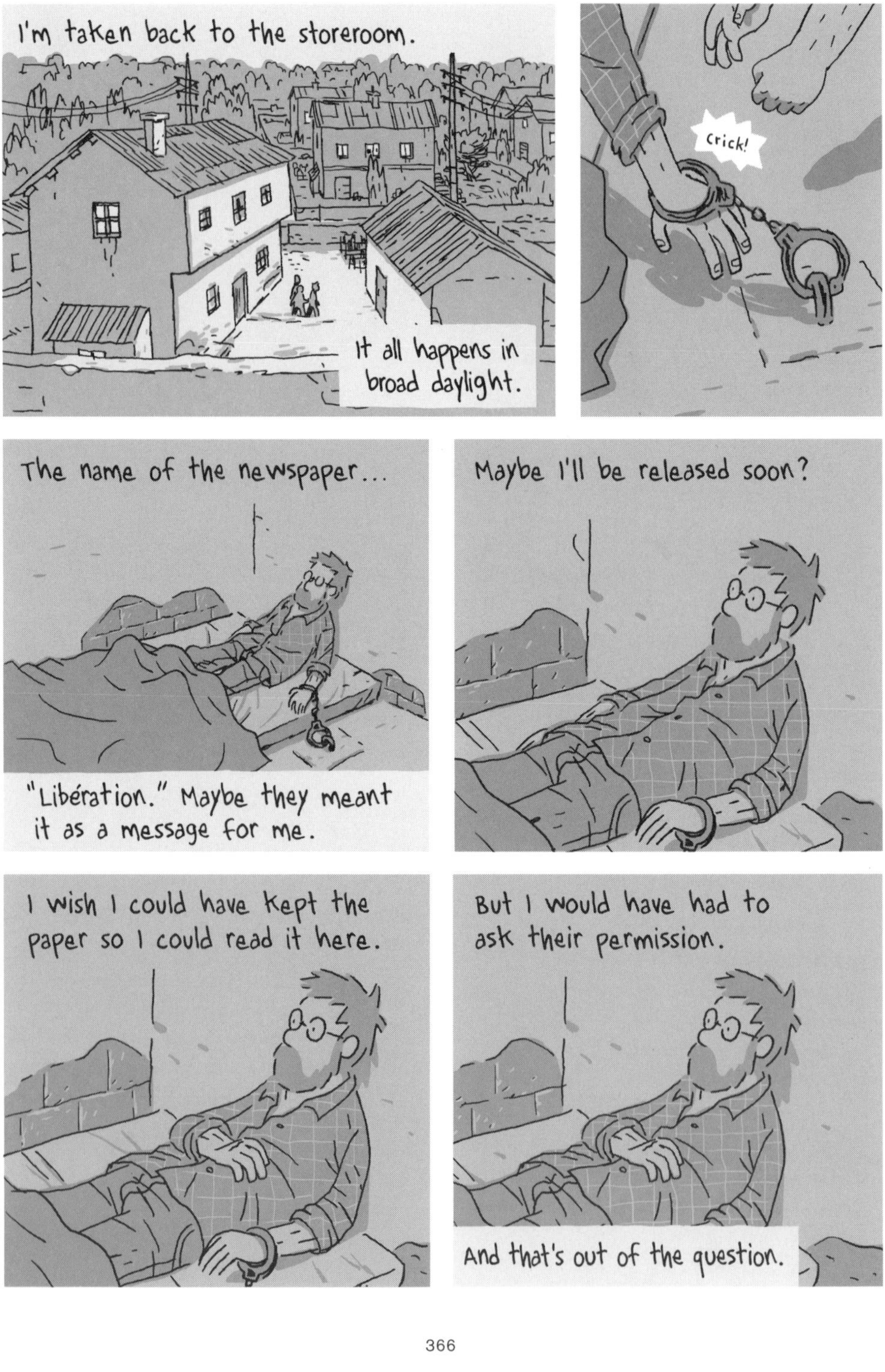
I'm taken back to the storeroom.
It all happens in broad daylight.
Crick!
The name of the newspaper...
"Libération." Maybe they meant it as a message for me.
Maybe I'll be released soon?
I wish I could have kept the paper so I could read it here.
But I would have had to ask their permission.
And that's out of the question.

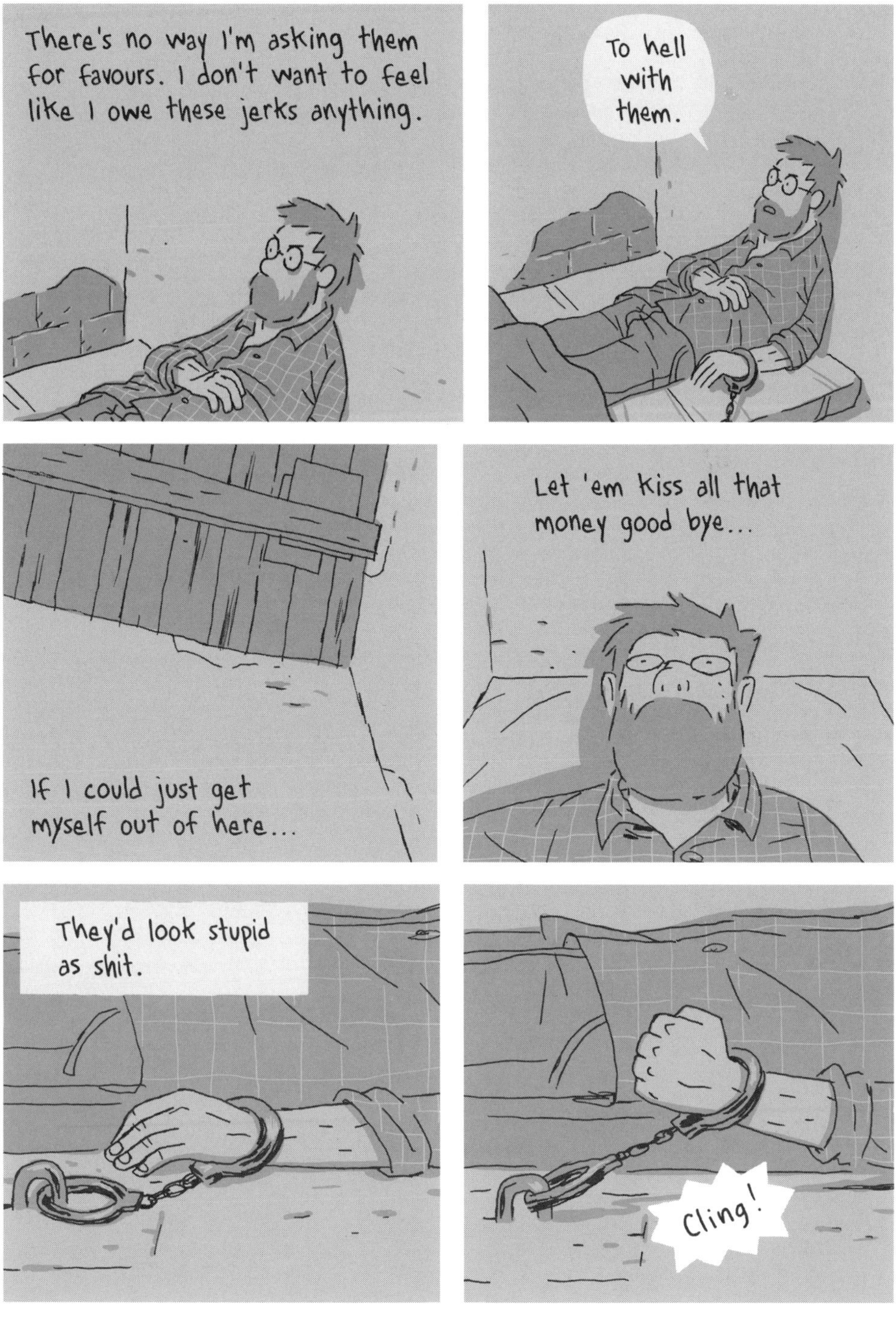
There's no way I'm asking them for favours. I don't want to feel like I owe these jerks anything.
To hell with them.
If I could just get myself out of here...
Let 'em kiss all that money good bye...
They'd look stupid as shit.
Cling!

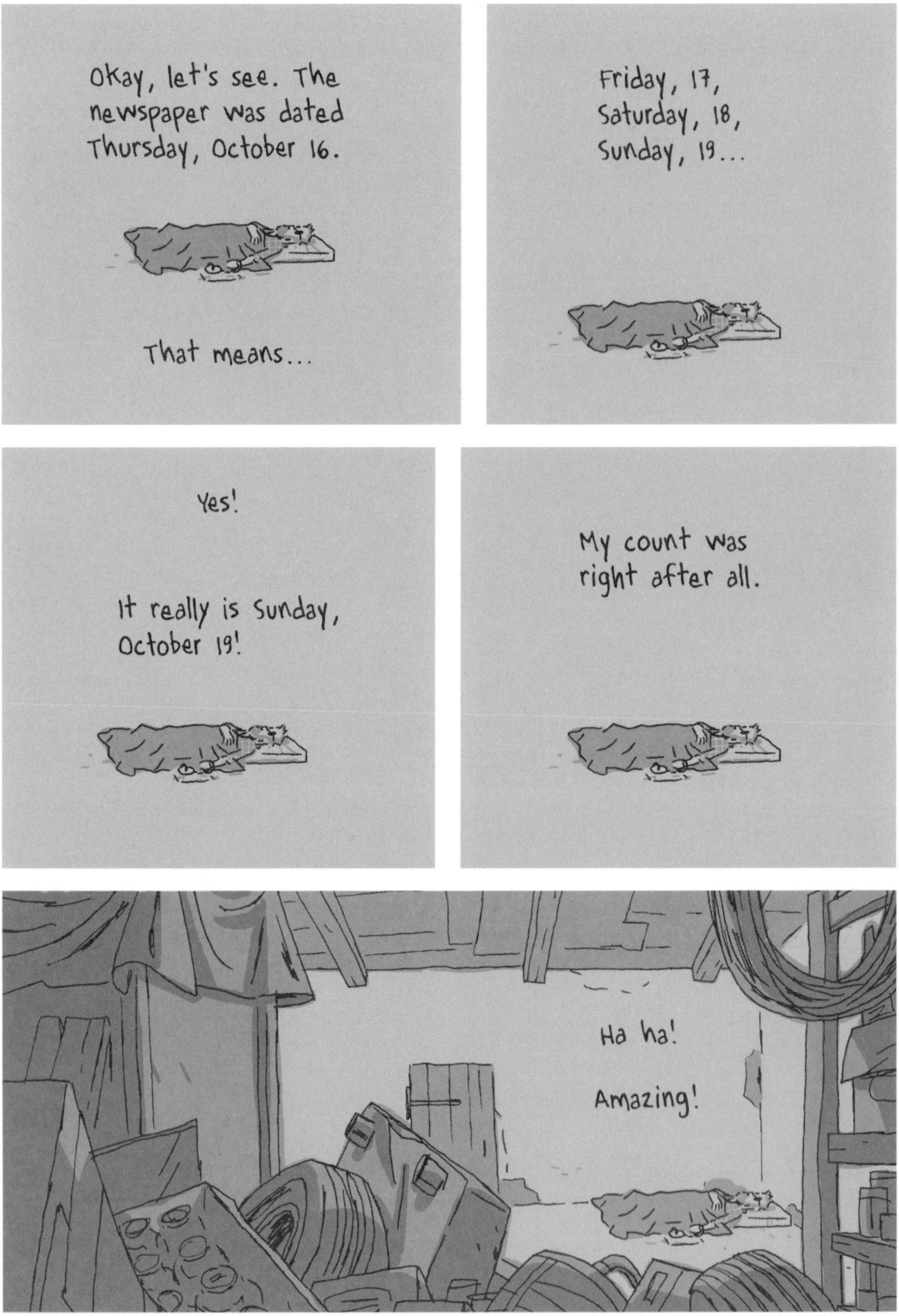
Okay, let's see. The newspaper was dated Thursday, October 16.
That means...
Friday, 17, Saturday, 18, Sunday, 19...
Yes!
It really is Sunday, October 19!
My count was right after all.
Ha ha!
Amazing!

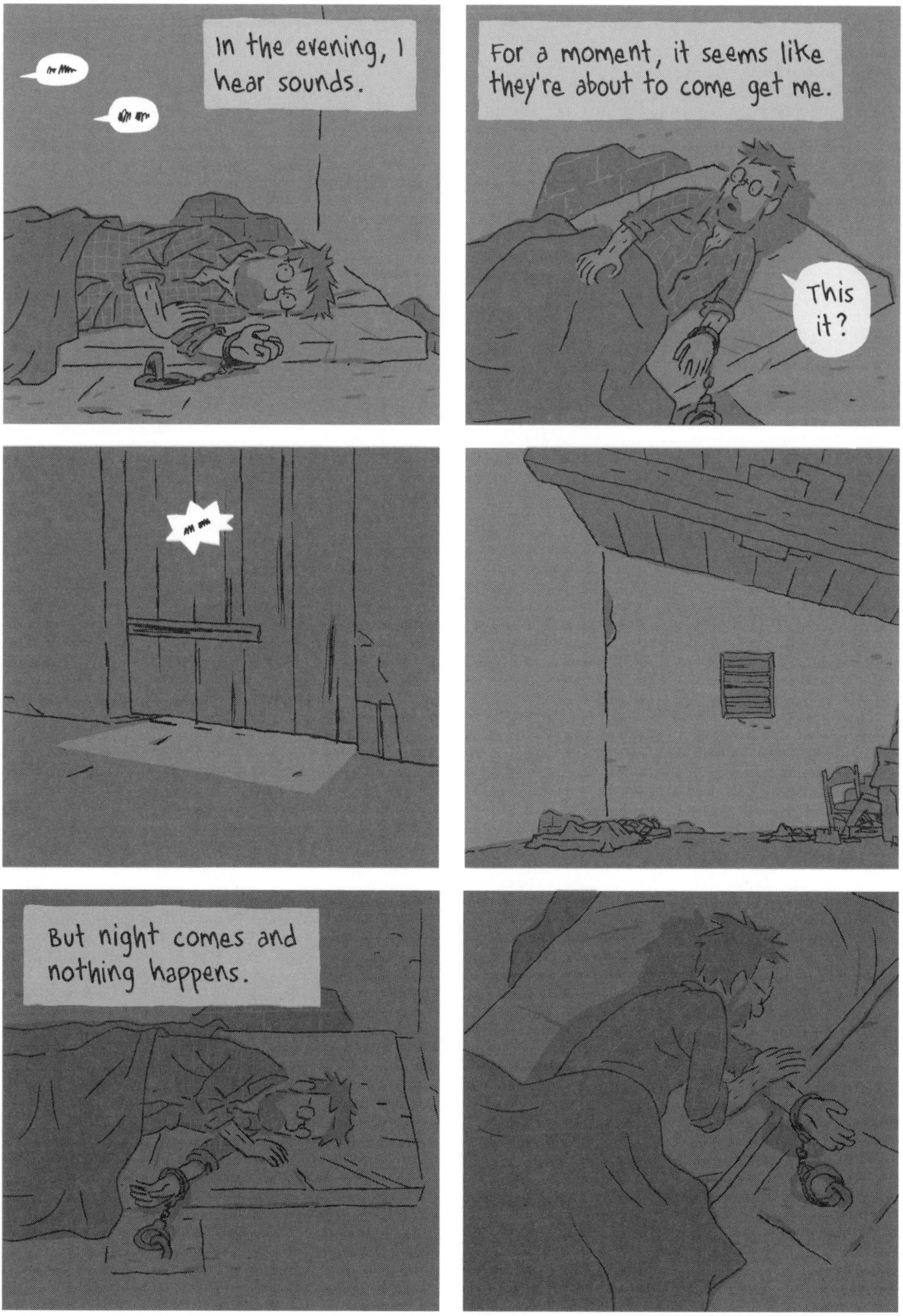
In the evening, I hear sounds.
For a moment, it seems like they're about to come get me.
This it?
But night comes and nothing happens.

III

Today is Monday, October 20.

At least I'm sure about the date again.

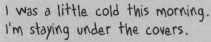

I was a little cold this morning. I'm staying under the covers.

Creeee!

The tall guy brings in the meal.

Змнру Ейо Баз!

Around noon, the room warms up. I feel better.

Still tired, but not as cold.

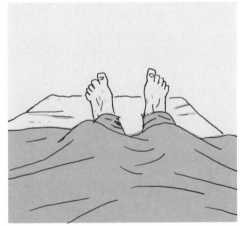

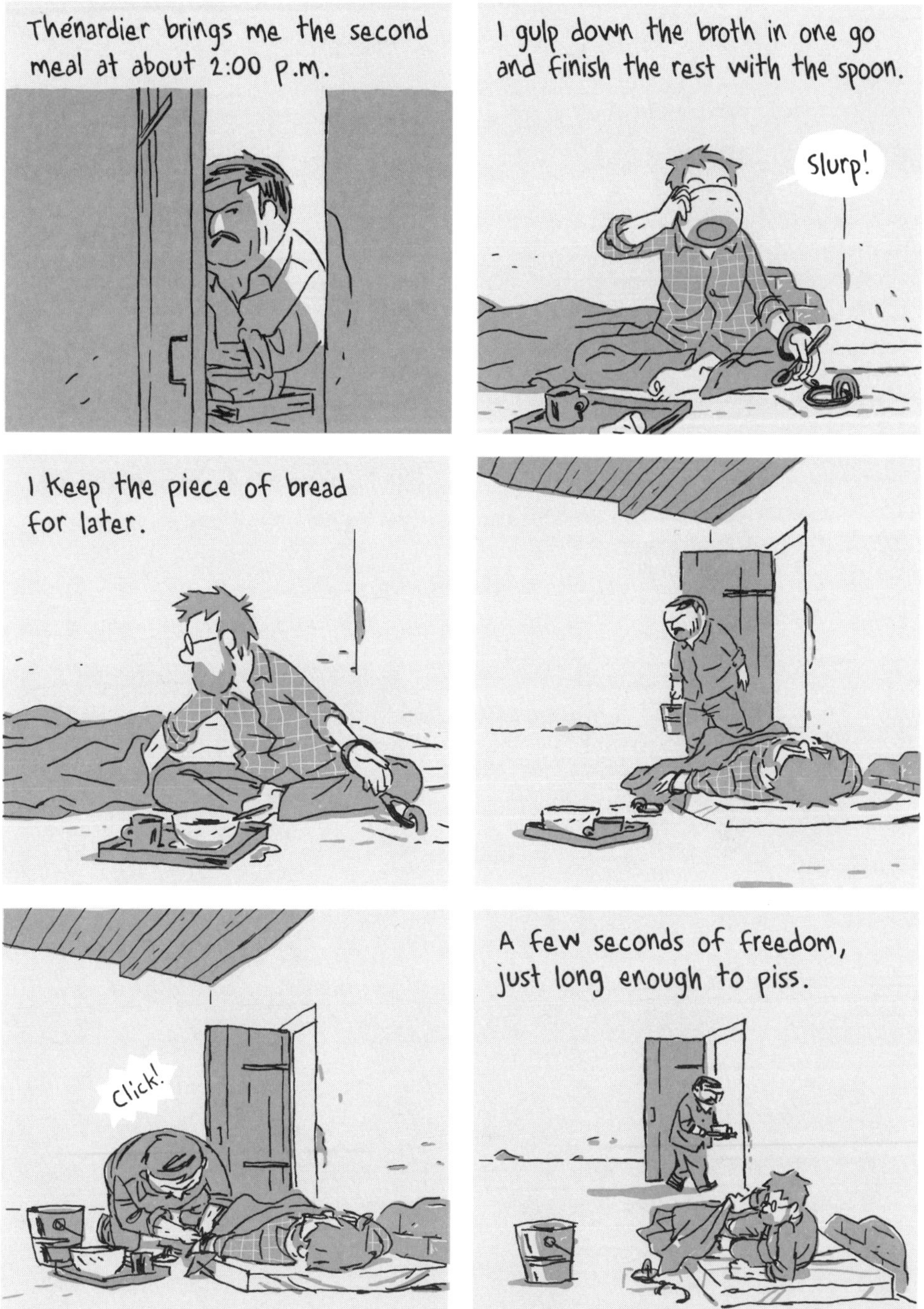
Thénardier brings me the second meal at about 2:00 p.m.
I gulp down the broth in one go and finish the rest with the spoon.
Slurp!
I keep the piece of bread for later.
Click!
A few seconds of freedom, just long enough to piss.

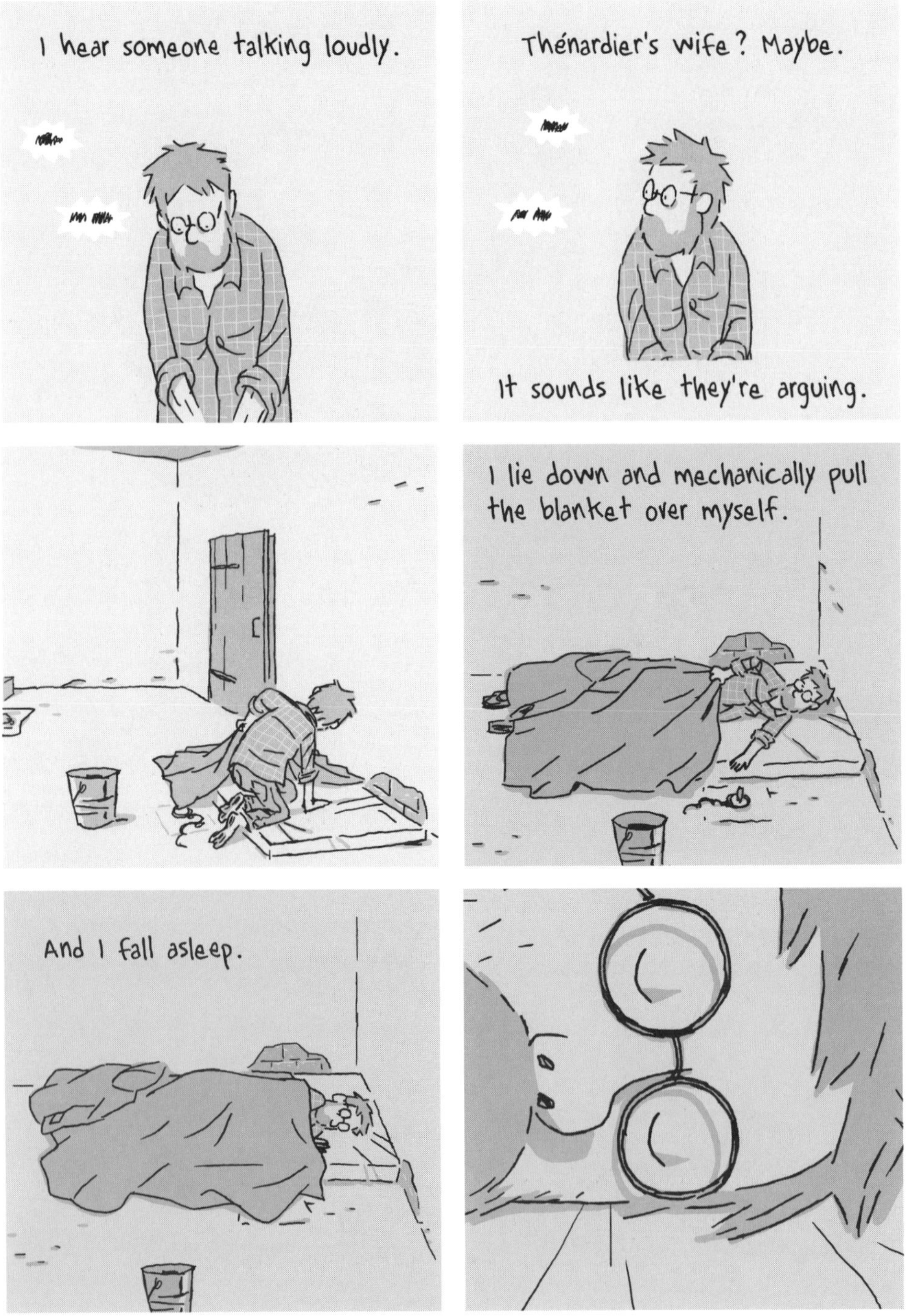
I hear someone talking loudly.
Thénardier's wife? Maybe.
It sounds like they're arguing.
I lie down and mechanically pull the blanket over myself.
And I fall asleep.

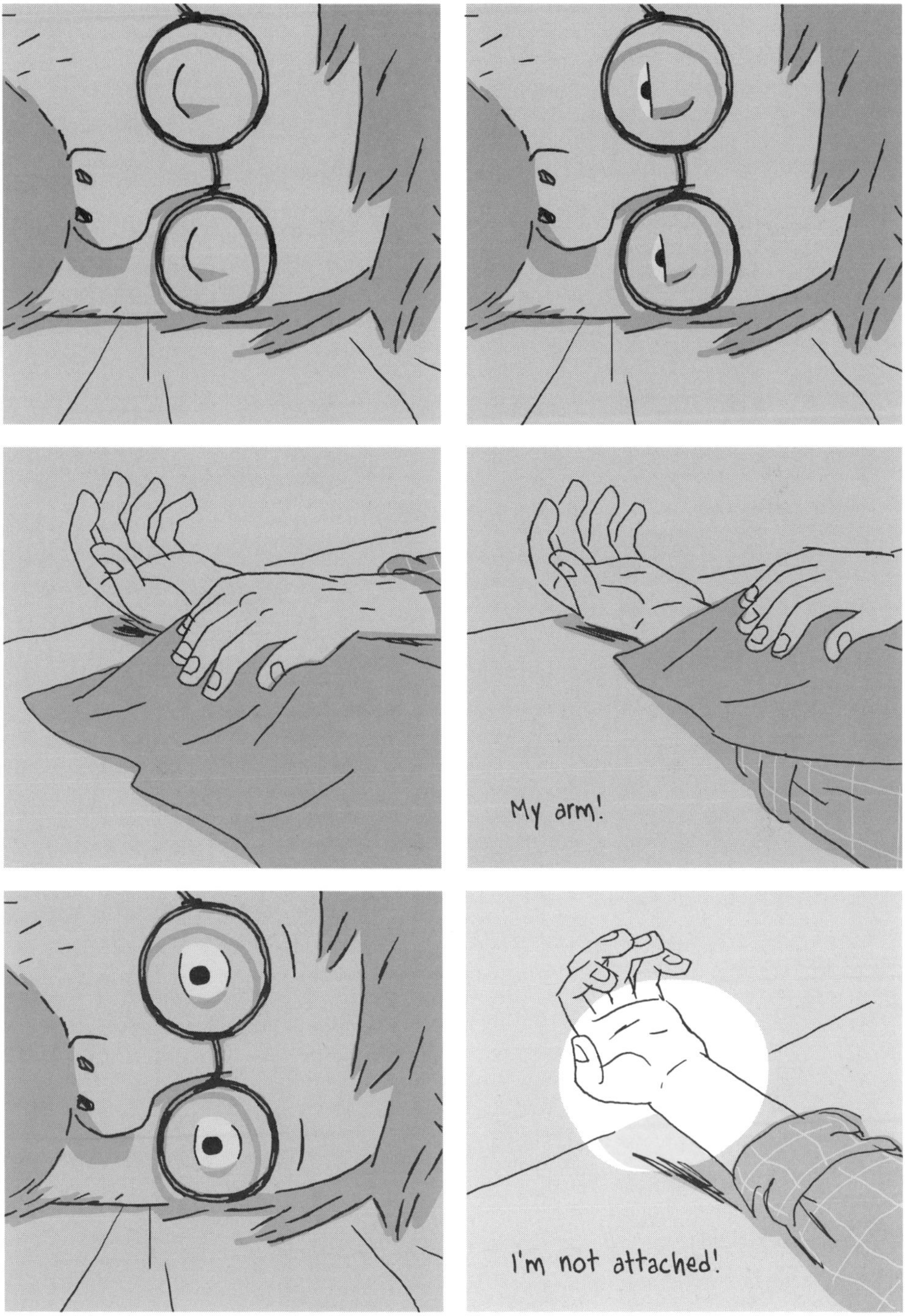
My arm!
I'm not attached!

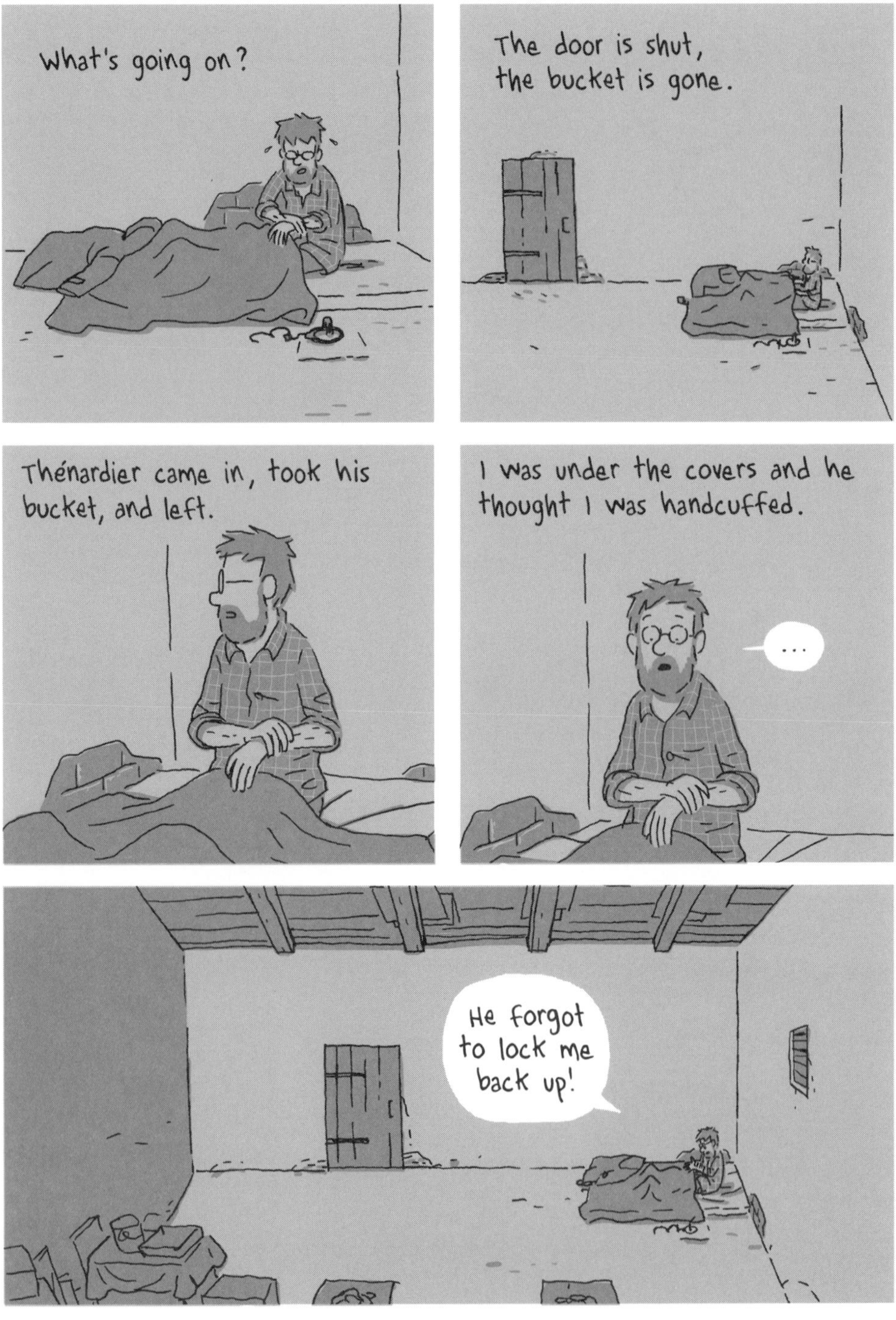

What's going on?
The door is shut, the bucket is gone.
Thénardier came in, took his bucket, and left.
I was under the covers and he thought I was handcuffed.
...
He forgot to lock me back up!

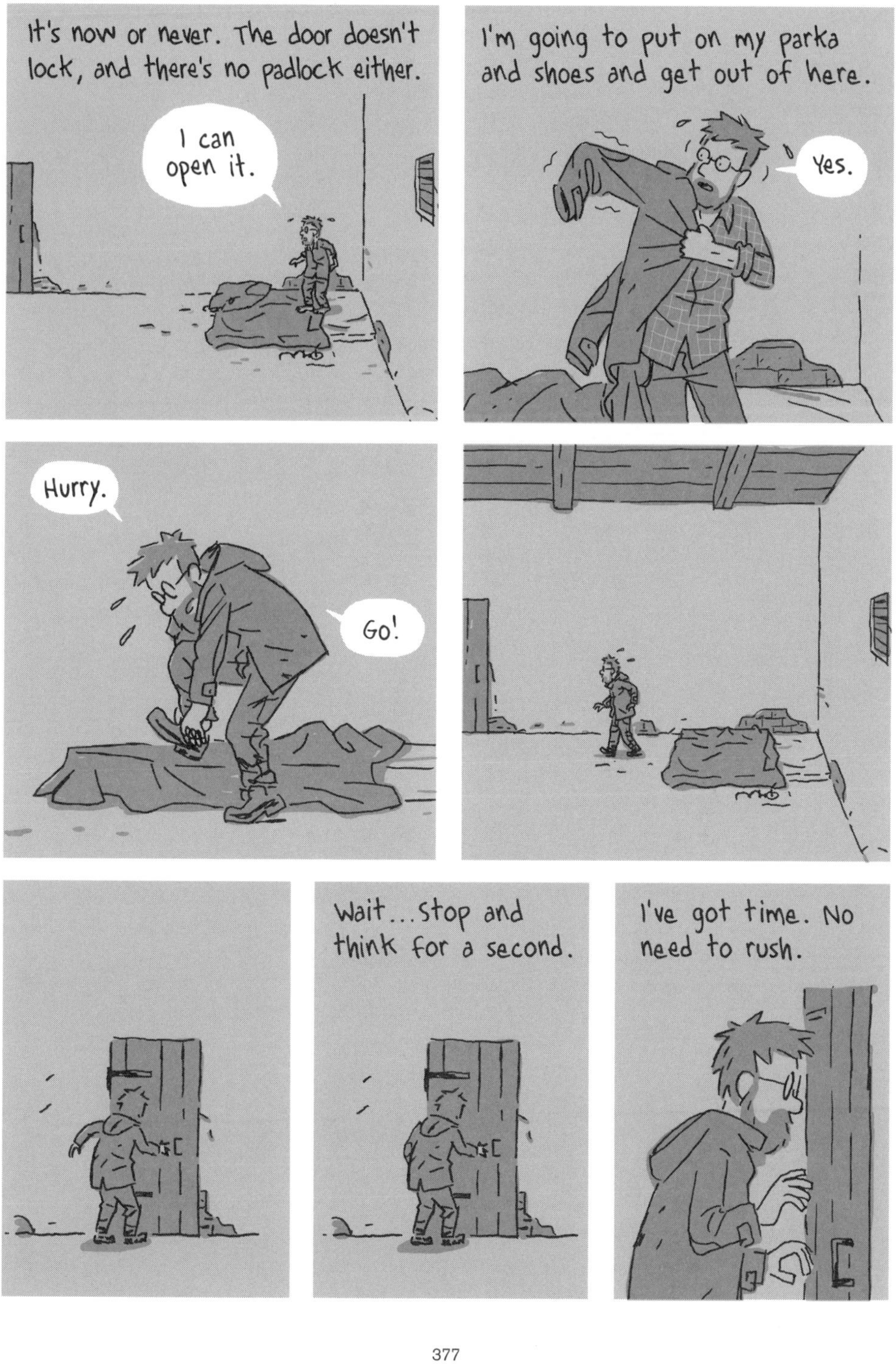
It's now or never. The door doesn't lock, and there's no padlock either.
I can open it.
I'm going to put on my parka and shoes and get out of here.
Yes.
Hurry.
Go!
Wait...stop and think for a second.
I've got time. No need to rush.

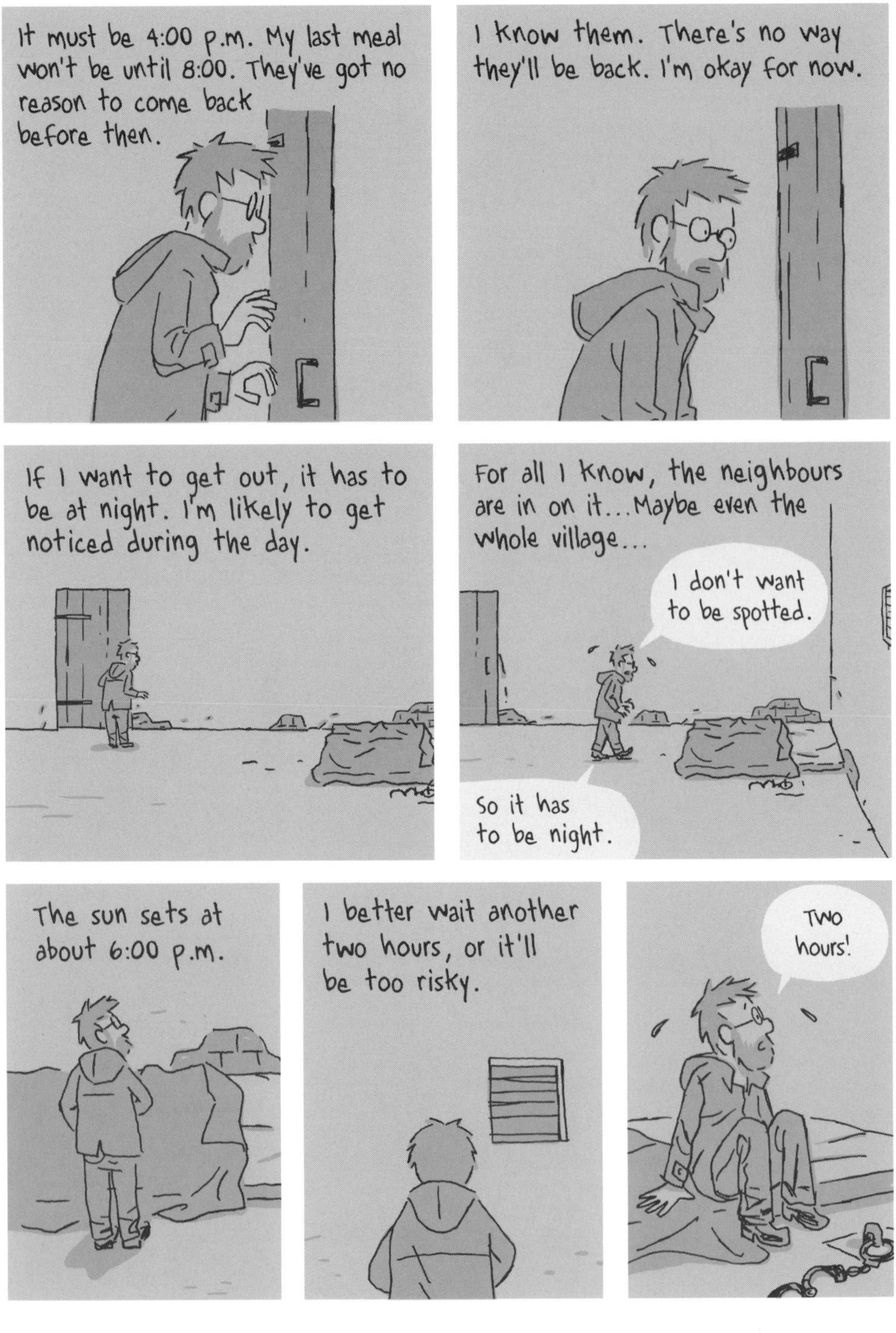
It must be 4:00 p.m. My last meal won't be until 8:00. They've got no reason to come back before then.
I know them. There's no way they'll be back. I'm okay for now.
If I want to get out, it has to be at night. I'm likely to get noticed during the day.
For all I know, the neighbours are in on it... Maybe even the whole village...
I don't want to be spotted.
So it has to be night.
The sun sets at about 6:00 p.m.
I better wait another two hours, or it'll be too risky.
Two hours!

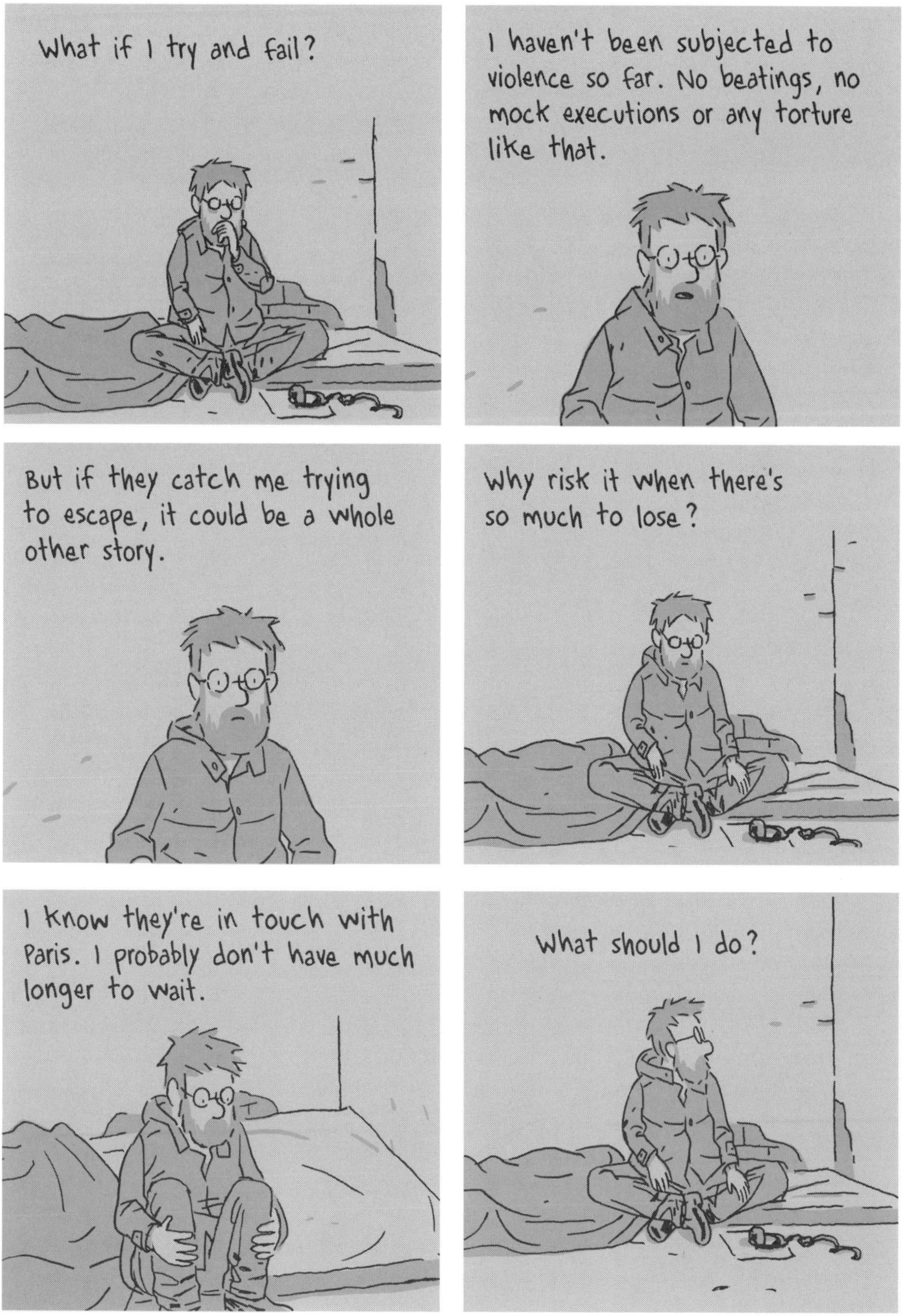
What if I try and fail?
I haven't been subjected to violence so far. No beatings, no mock executions or any torture like that.
But if they catch me trying to escape, it could be a whole other story.
Why risk it when there's so much to lose?
I know they're in touch with Paris. I probably don't have much longer to wait.
What should I do?

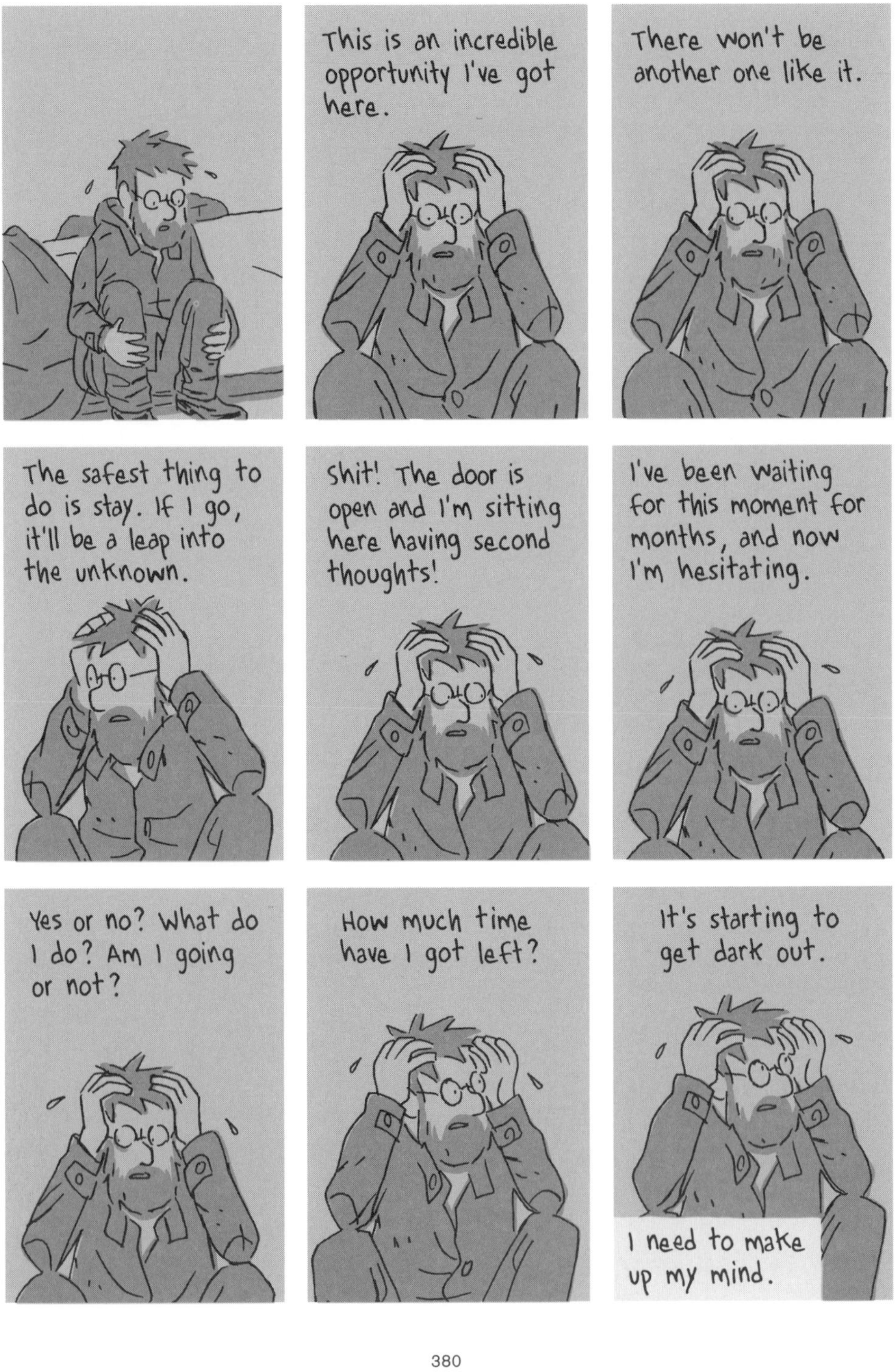
This is an incredible opportunity I've got here.
There won't be another one like it.
The safest thing to do is stay. If I go, it'll be a leap into the unknown.
Shit! The door is open and I'm sitting here having second thoughts!
I've been waiting for this moment for months, and now I'm hesitating.
Yes or no? What do I do? Am I going or not?
How much time have I got left?
It's starting to get dark out.
I need to make up my mind.

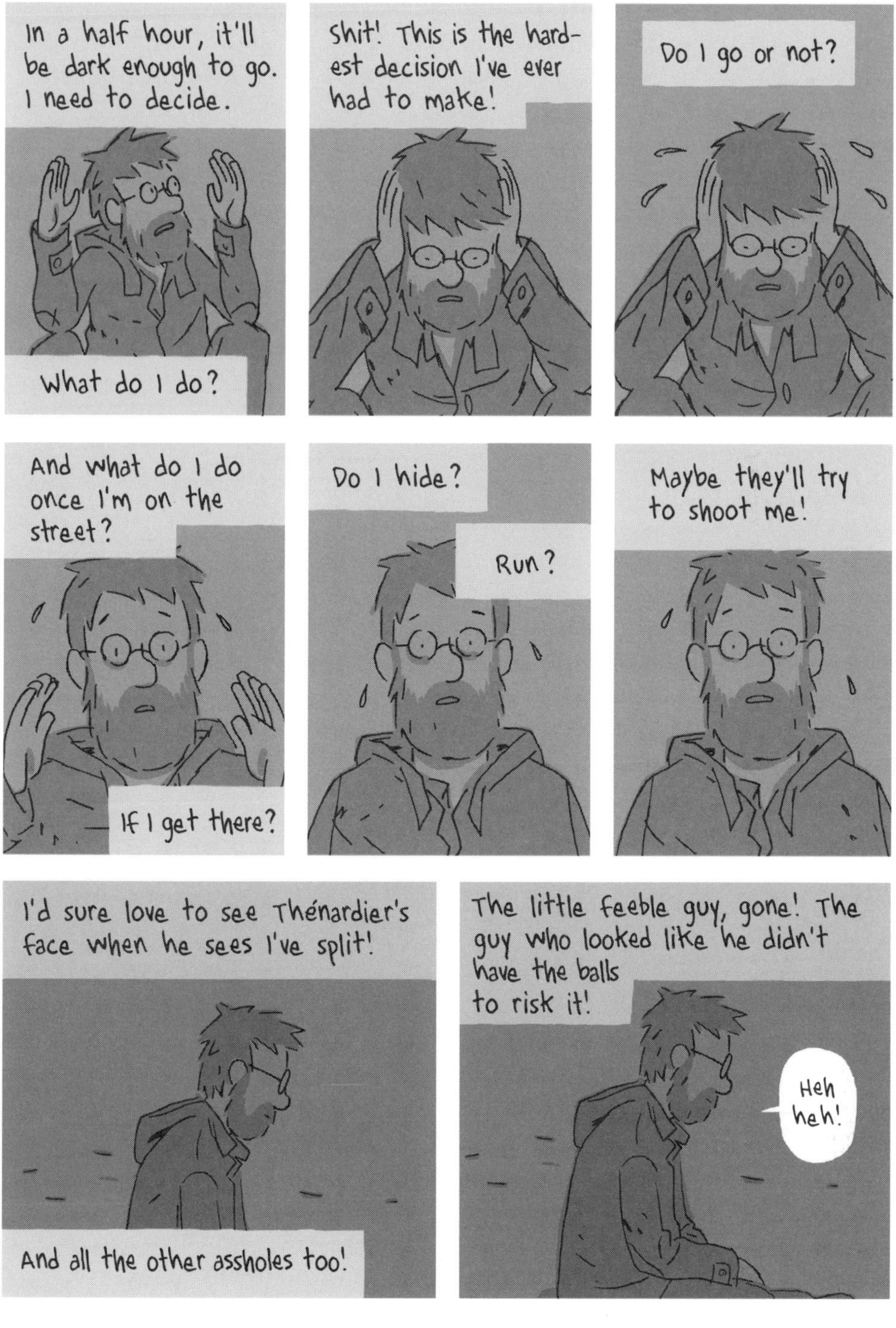
In a half hour, it'll be dark enough to go. I need to decide.
What do I do?
Shit! This is the hardest decision I've ever had to make!
Do I go or not?
And what do I do once I'm on the street?
If I get there?
Do I hide?
Run?
Maybe they'll try to shoot me!
I'd sure love to see Thénardier's face when he sees I've split!
And all the other assholes too!
The little feeble guy, gone! The guy who looked like he didn't have the balls to risk it!
Heh heh!

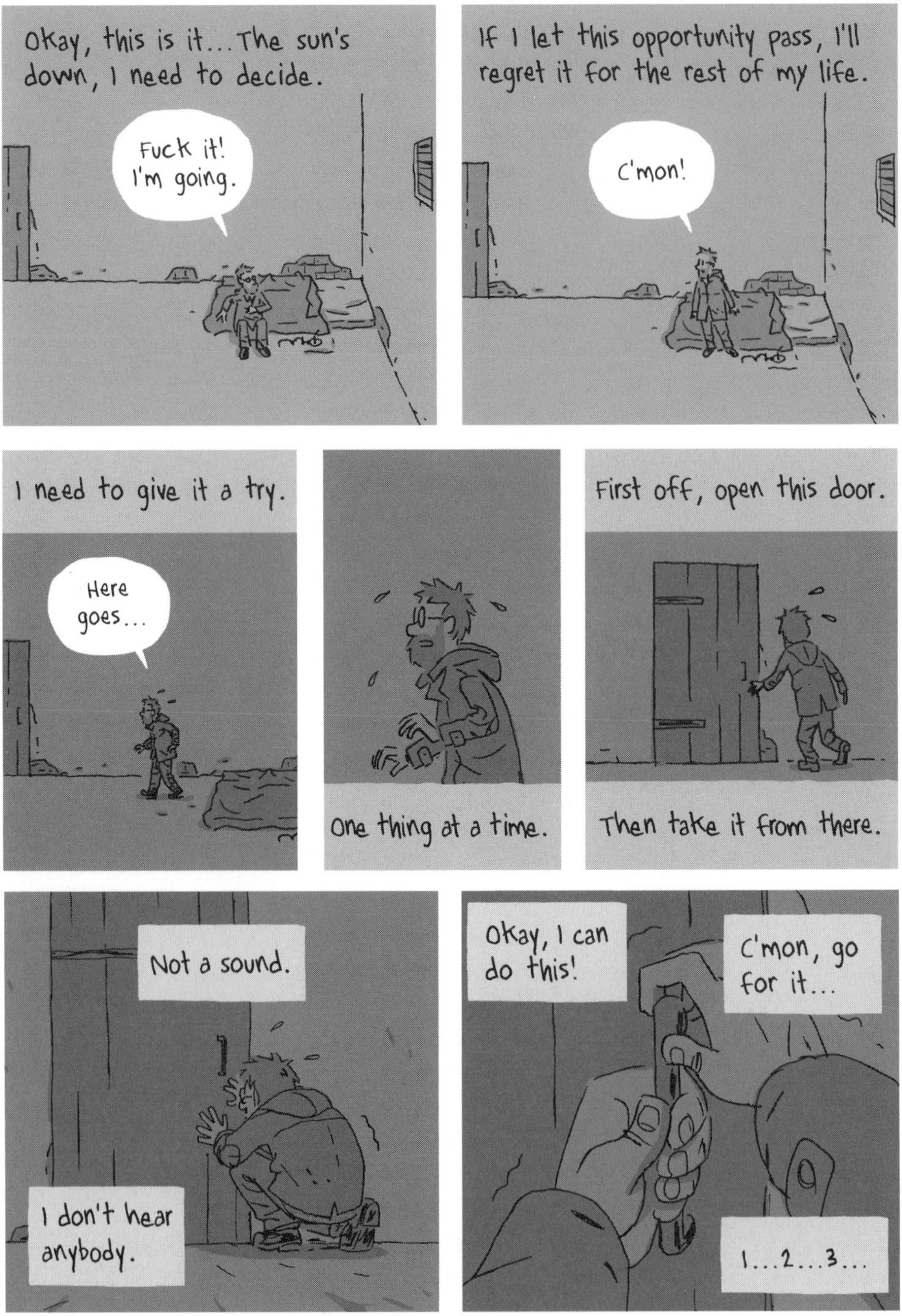
Okay, this is it... The sun's down, I need to decide.
Fuck it! I'm going.
If I let this opportunity pass, I'll regret it for the rest of my life.
C'mon!
I need to give it a try.
Here goes...
One thing at a time.
First off, open this door.
Then take it from there.
Not a sound.
I don't hear anybody.
Okay, I can do this!
C'mon, go for it...
1...2...3...

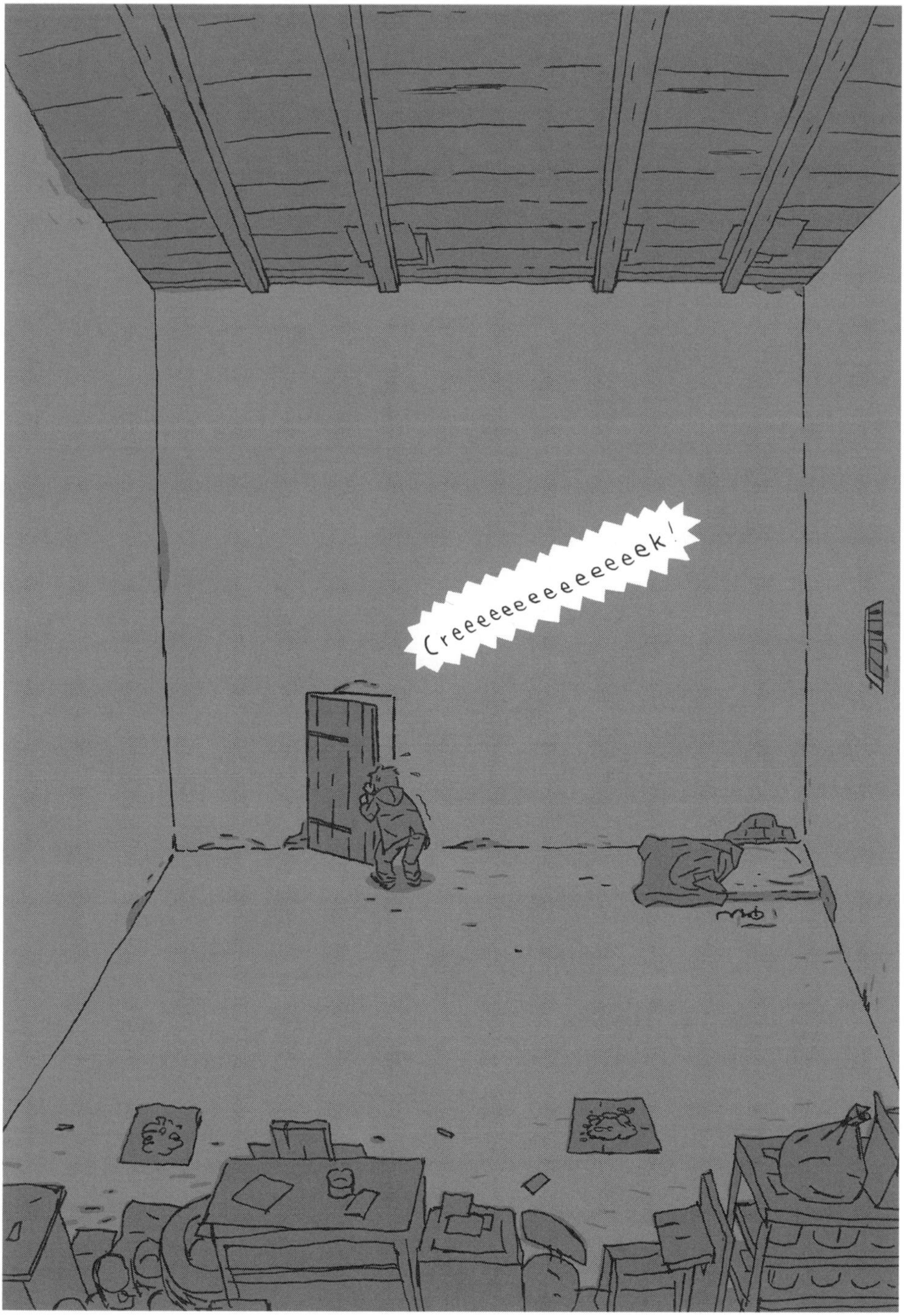
Creeeeeeeeeeeeeeek!

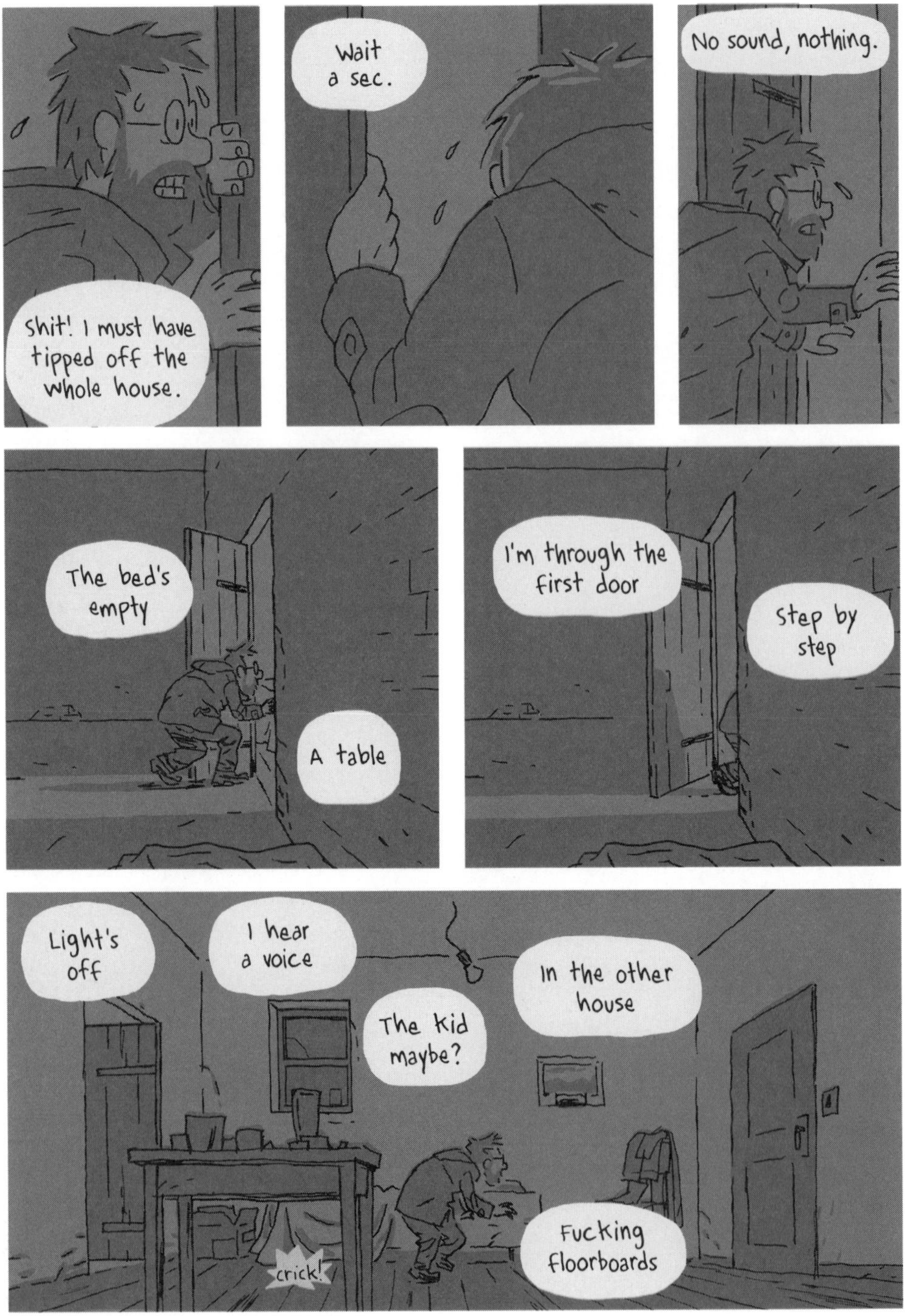
Shit! I must have tipped off the whole house.
Wait a sec.
No sound, nothing.
The bed's empty
A table
I'm through the first door
Step by step
Light's off
I hear a voice
The kid maybe?
In the other house
crick!
Fucking floorboards

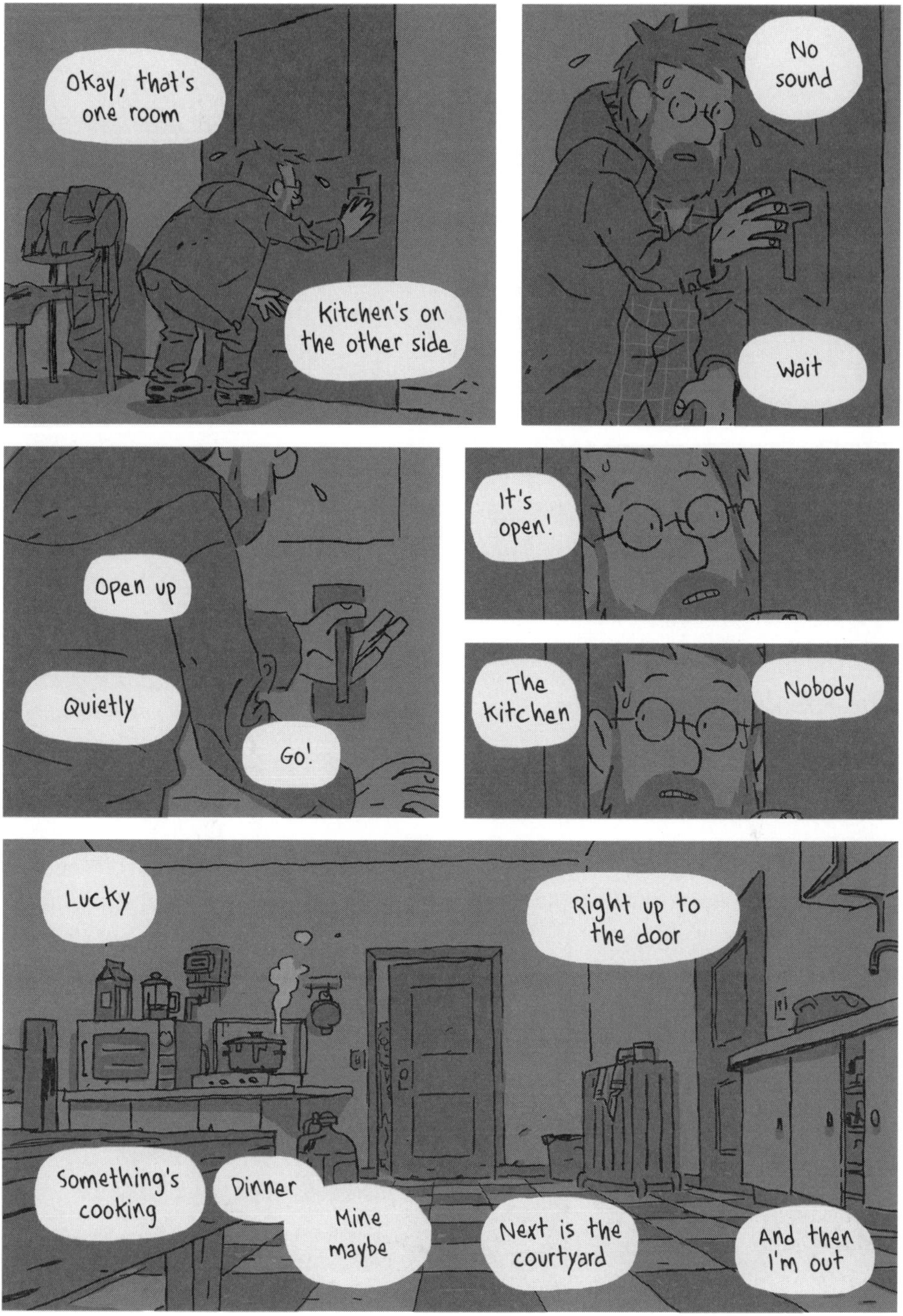
Okay, that's one room
Kitchen's on the other side
No sound
Wait
Open up
Quietly
Go!
It's open!
The kitchen
Nobody
Lucky
Right up to the door
Something's cooking
Dinner
Mine maybe
Next is the courtyard
And then I'm out

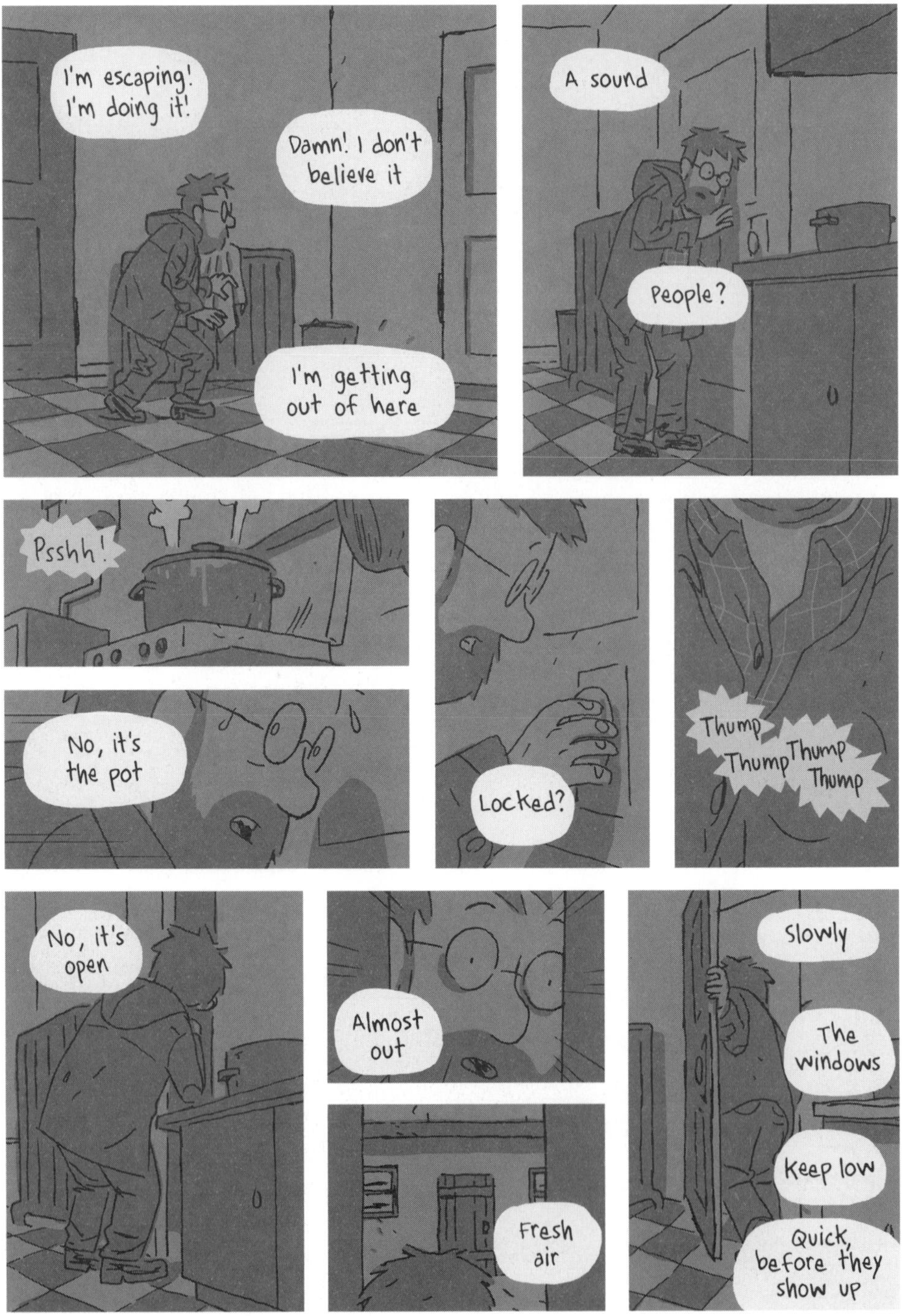
I'm escaping! I'm doing it!
Damn! I don't believe it
I'm getting out of here
A sound
People?
Psshh!
No, it's the pot
Locked?
Thump
Thump
Thump
Thump
No, it's open
Almost out
Fresh air
Slowly
The windows
Keep low
Quick, before they show up

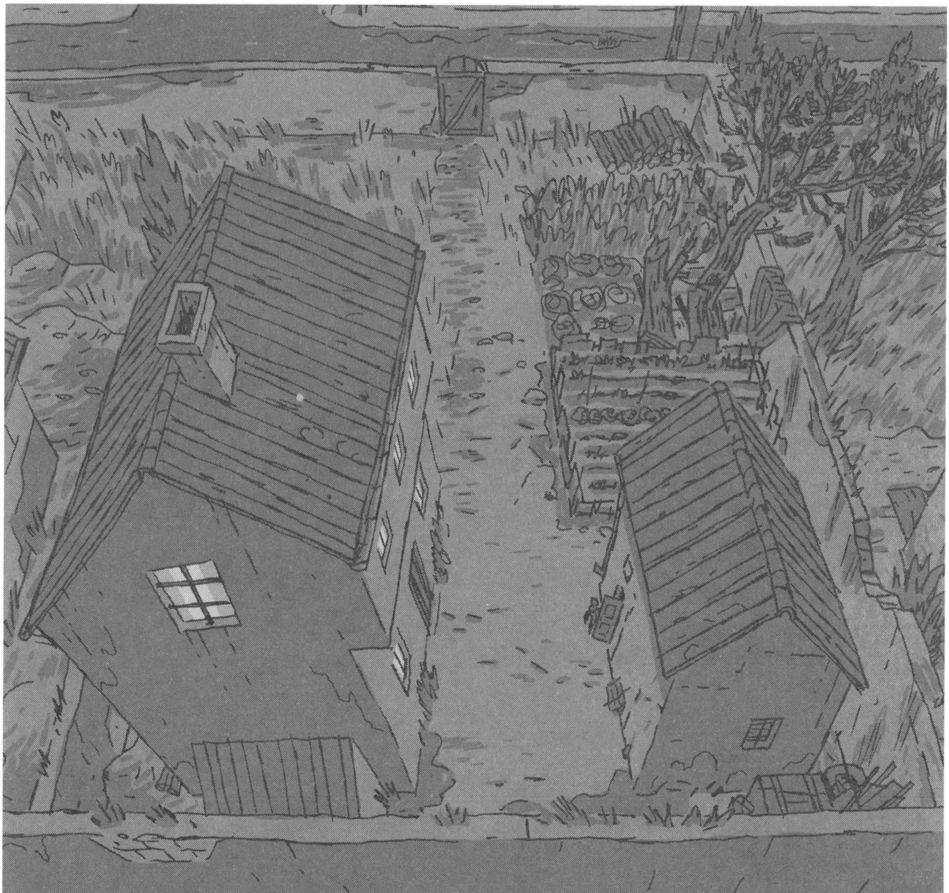

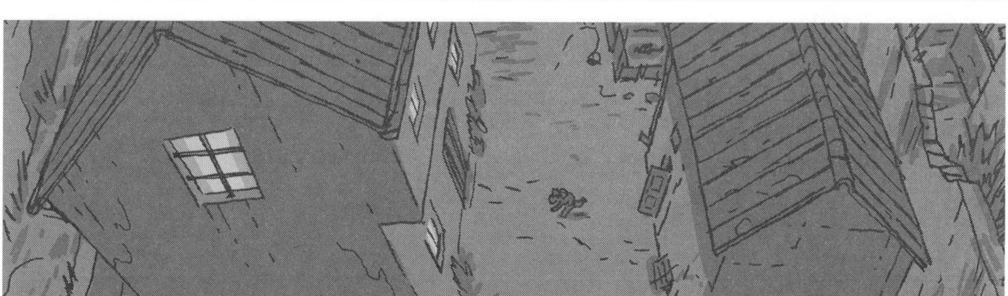

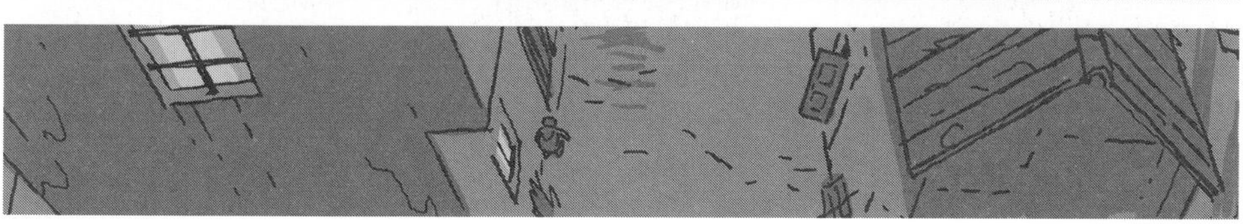

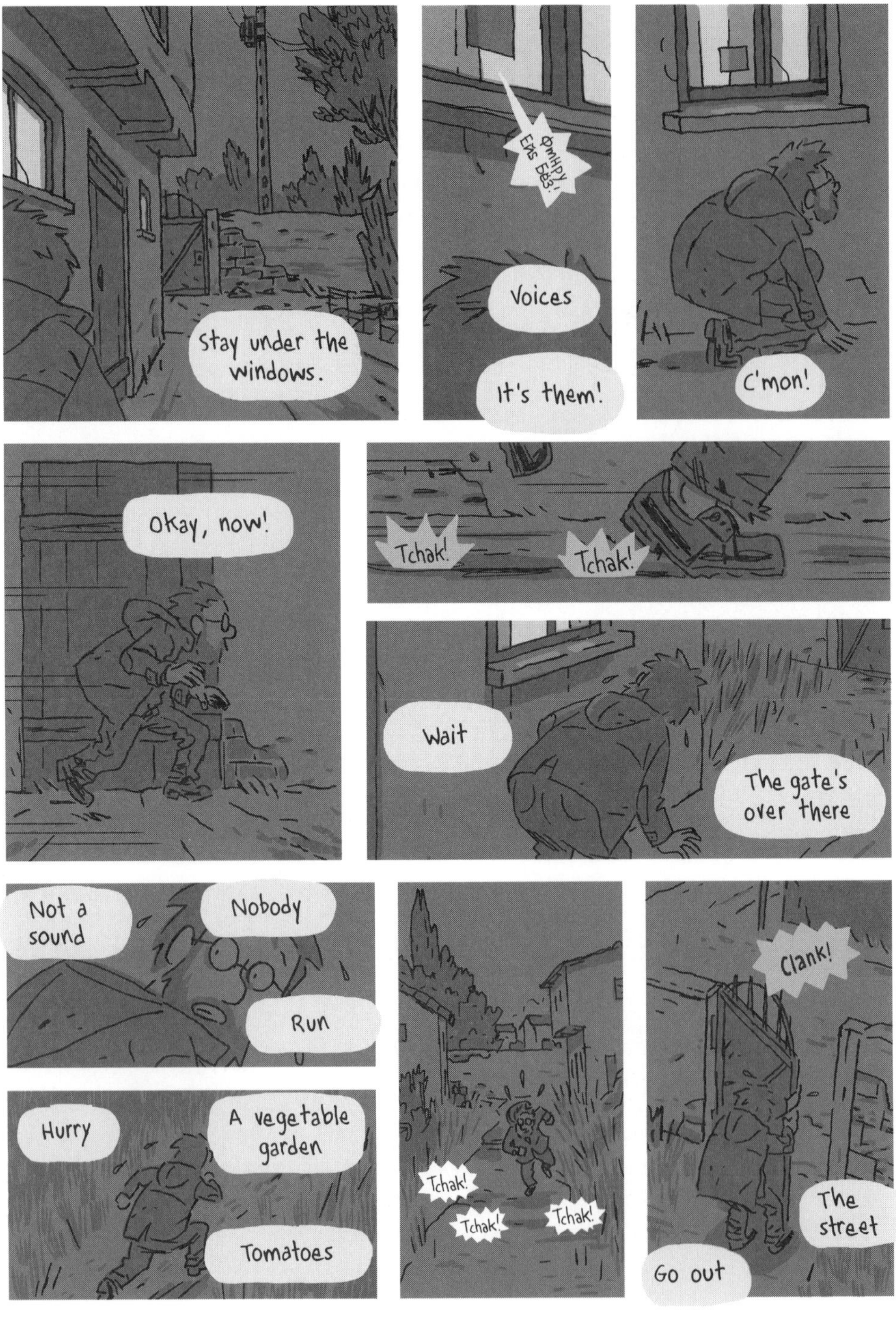
Stay under the windows.
Voices
It's them!
C'mon!
Okay, now!
Tchak!
Tchak!
Wait
The gate's over there
Not a sound
Nobody
Run
Hurry
A vegetable garden
Tomatoes
Tchak!
Tchak!
Tchak!
Clank!
The street
Go out

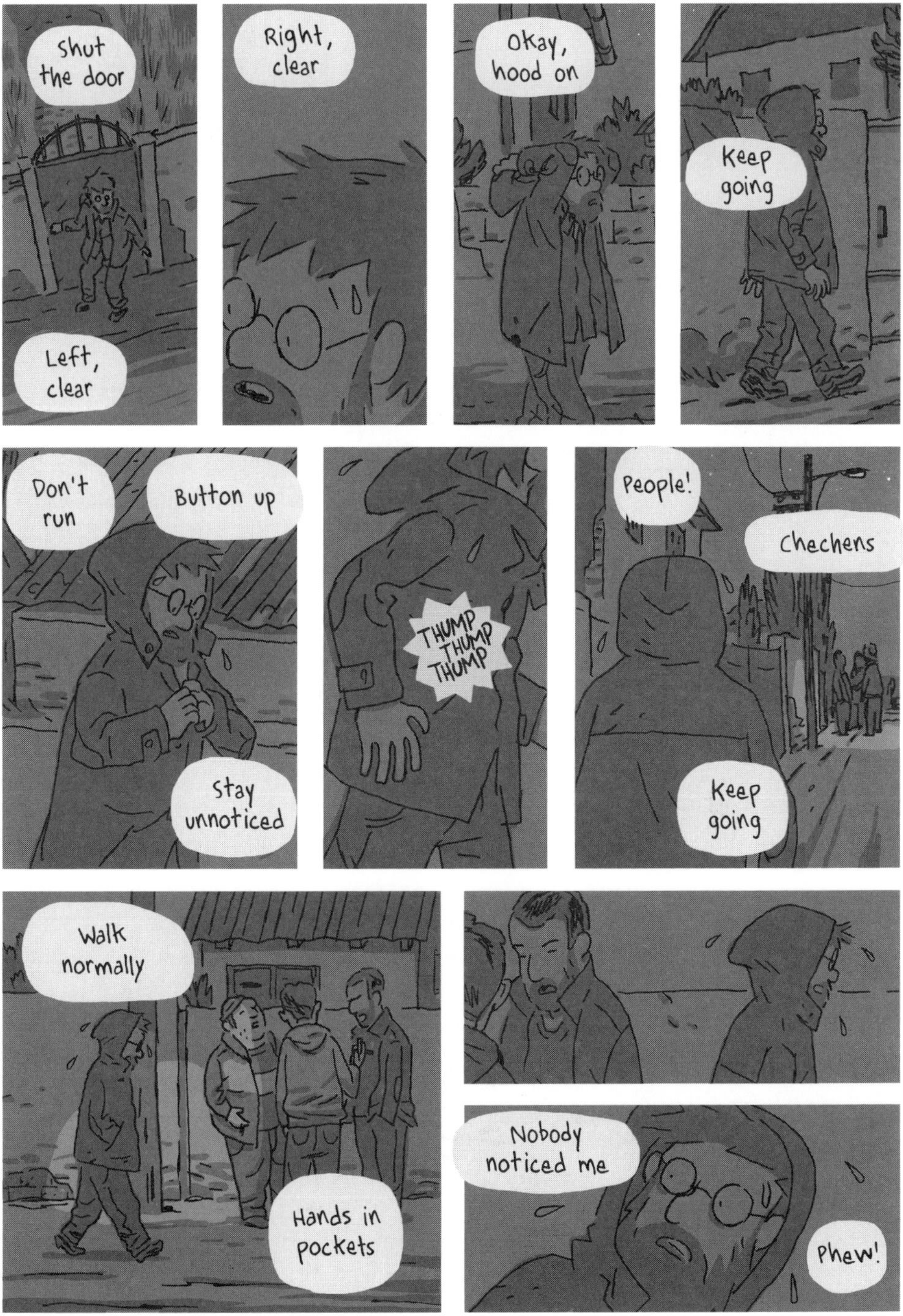
Shut the door
Left, clear
Right, clear
Okay, hood on
Keep going
Don't run
Button up
Stay unnoticed
THUMP THUMP THUMP
People!
Chechens
Keep going
Walk normally
Hands in pockets
Nobody noticed me
Phew!

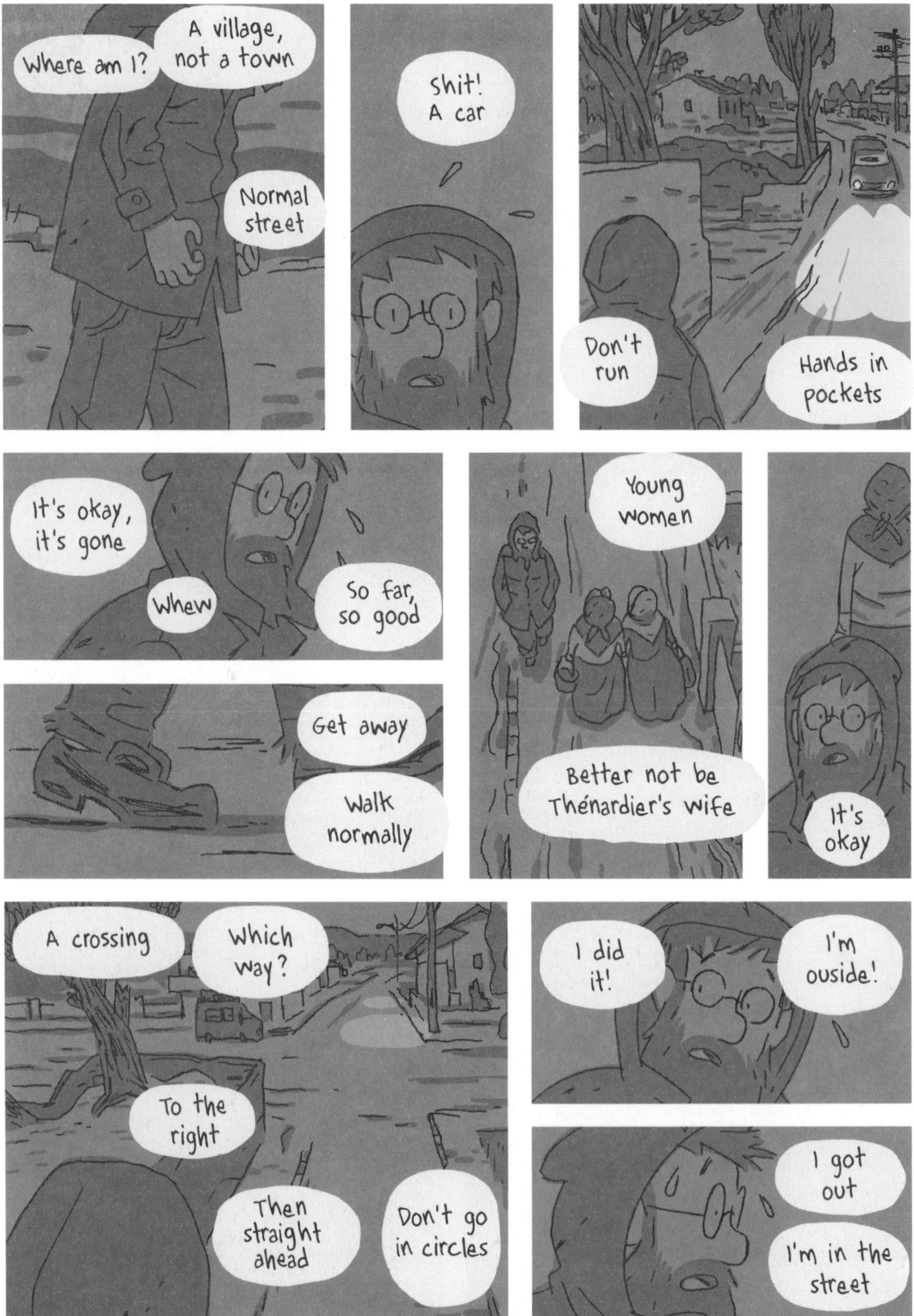
Where am I?
A village, not a town
Normal street
Shit! A car
Don't run
Hands in pockets
It's okay, it's gone
Whew
So far, so good
Get away
Walk normally
Young women
Better not be Thénardier's wife
It's okay
A crossing
Which way?
To the right
Then straight ahead
Don't go in circles
I did it!
I'm ouside!
I got out
I'm in the street

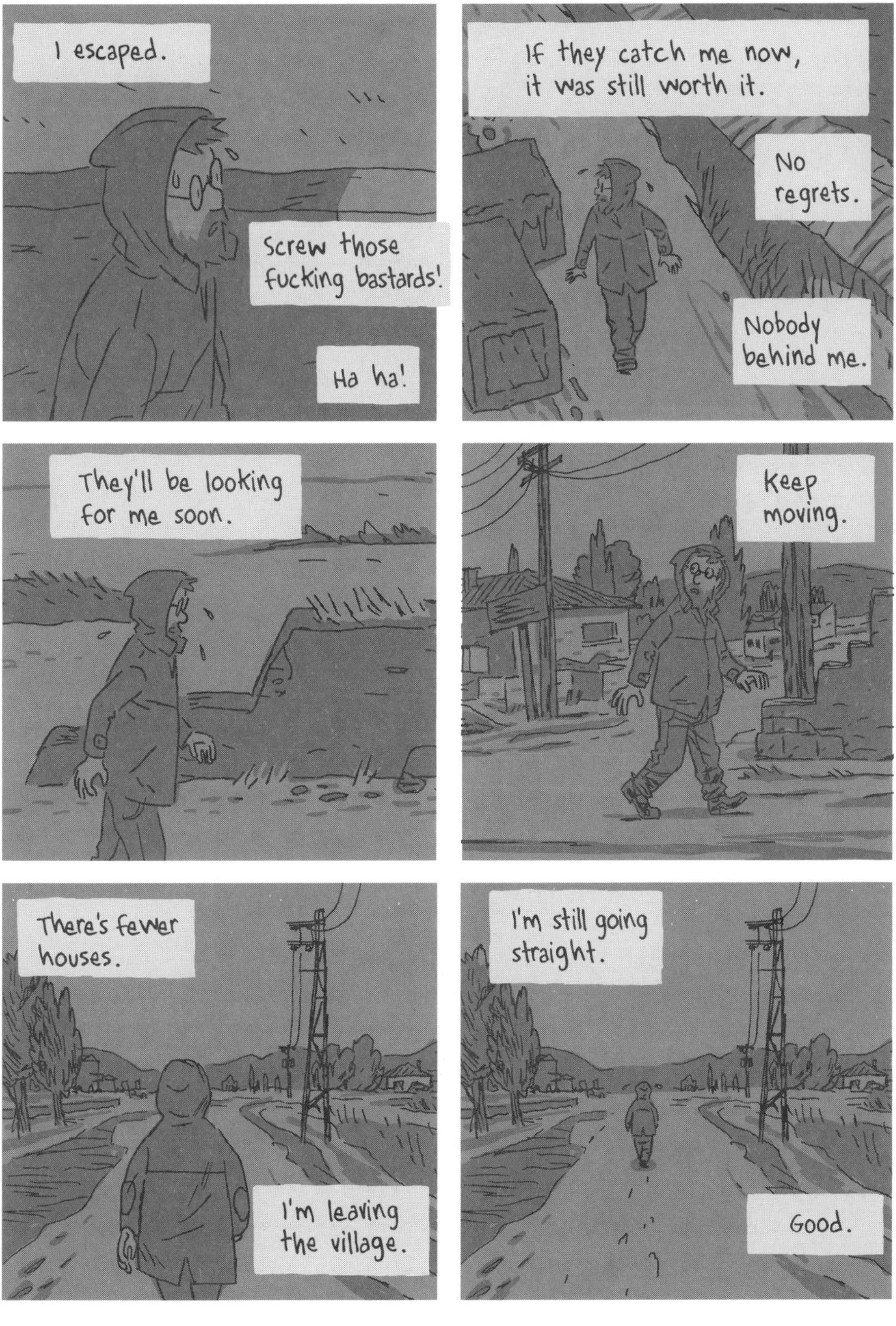
I escaped.
Screw those fucking bastards!
Ha ha!
If they catch me now, it was still worth it.
No regrets.
Nobody behind me.
They'll be looking for me soon.
Keep moving.
There's fewer houses.
I'm leaving the village.
I'm still going straight.
Good.

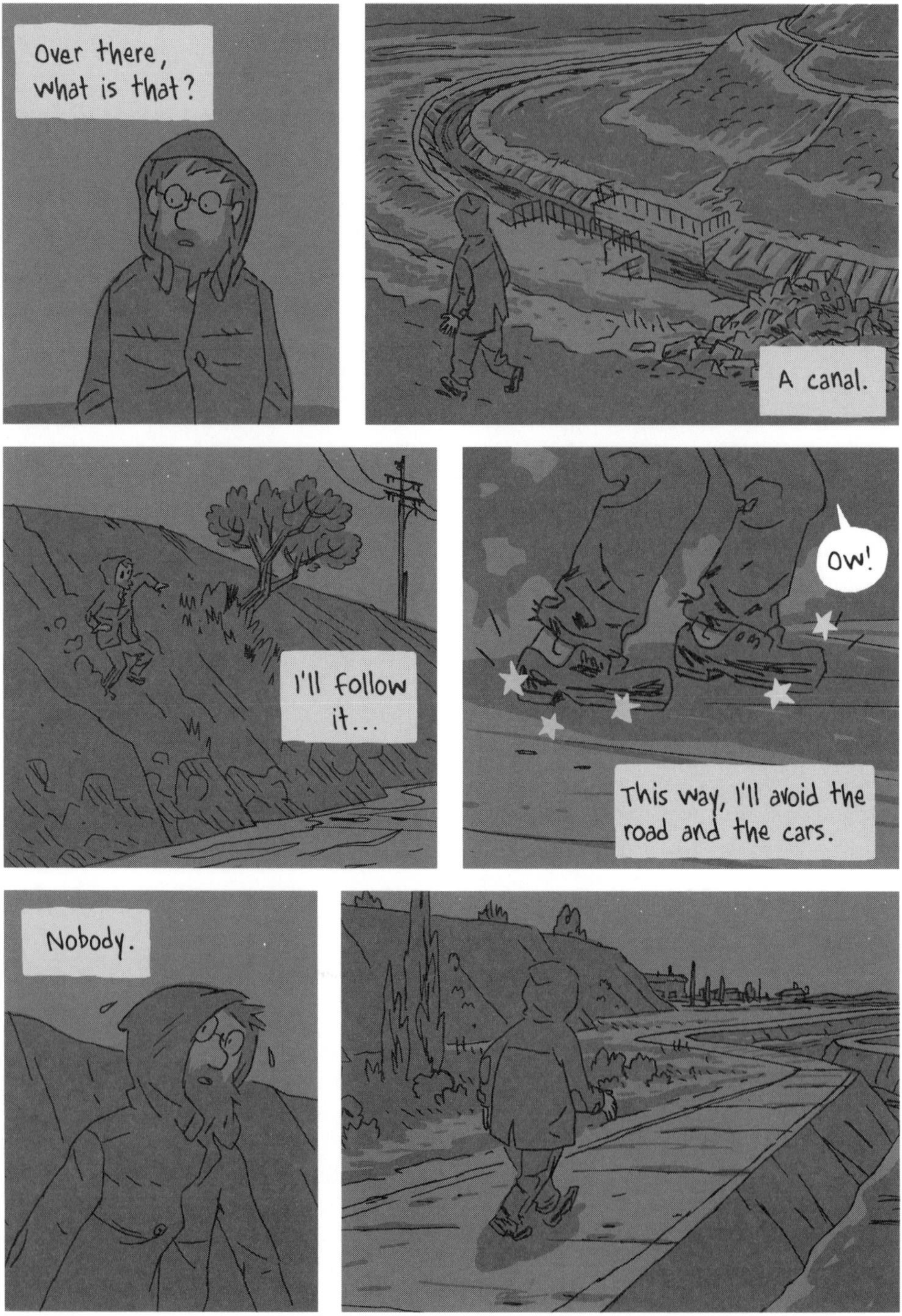
Over there, what is that?
A canal.
I'll follow it...
Ow!
This way, I'll avoid the road and the cars.
Nobody.

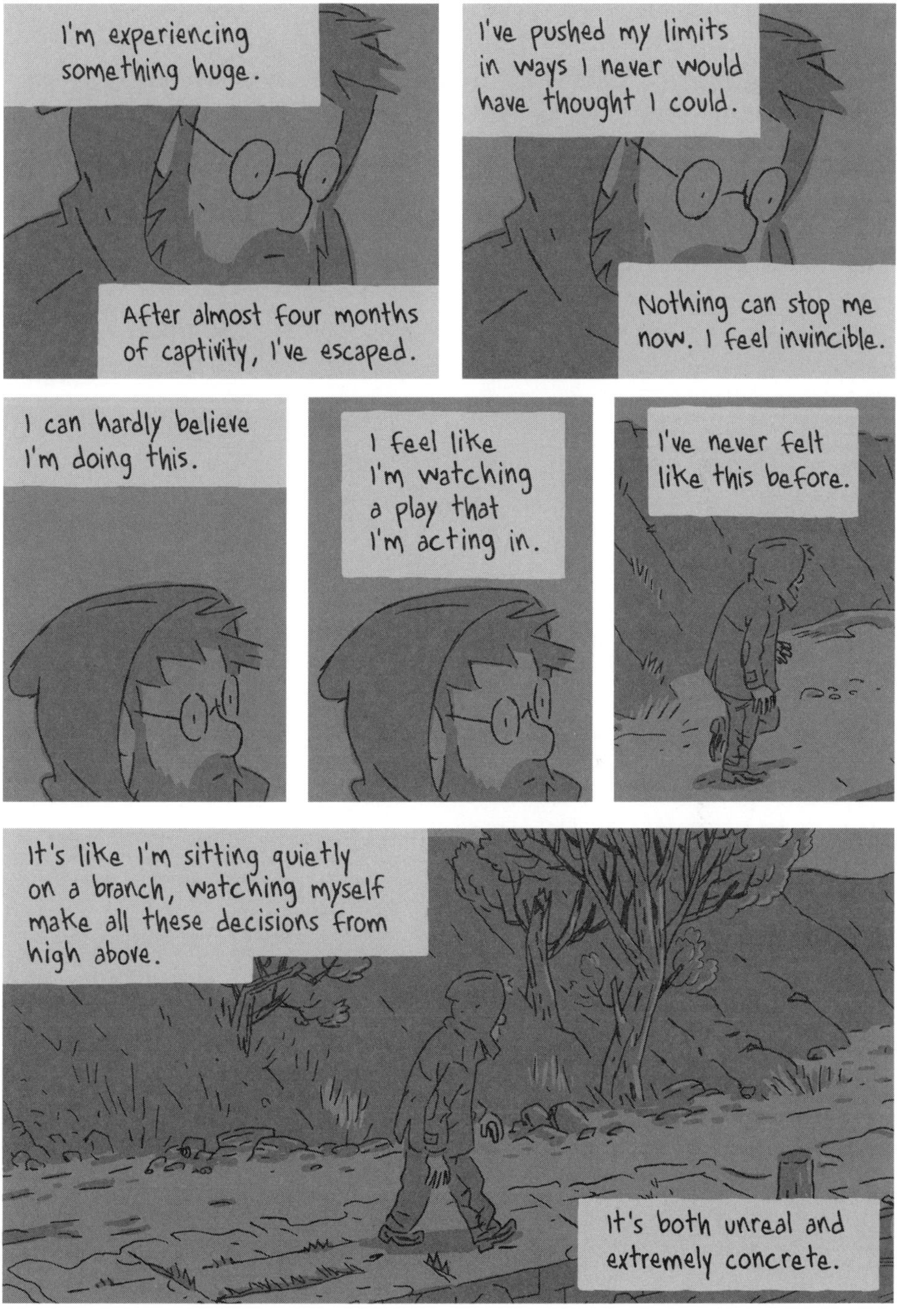
I'm experiencing something huge.
After almost four months of captivity, I've escaped.
I've pushed my limits in ways I never would have thought I could.
Nothing can stop me now. I feel invincible.
I can hardly believe I'm doing this.
I feel like I'm watching a play that I'm acting in.
I've never felt like this before.
It's like I'm sitting quietly on a branch, watching myself make all these decisions from high above.
It's both unreal and extremely concrete.

After walking for a kilometre, I feel the pressure subside a bit.

That's when I notice that my feet are in excruciating pain.

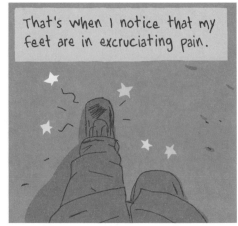

I stop to have a look.

Aauugh!

My feet are bloody.

shit, that hurts!

It's the grid in the soles of the shoes that's been digging into my feet.

I tear the collar off my parka to use as cushioning.

Crack!

Ow!

It's bearable. I continue.

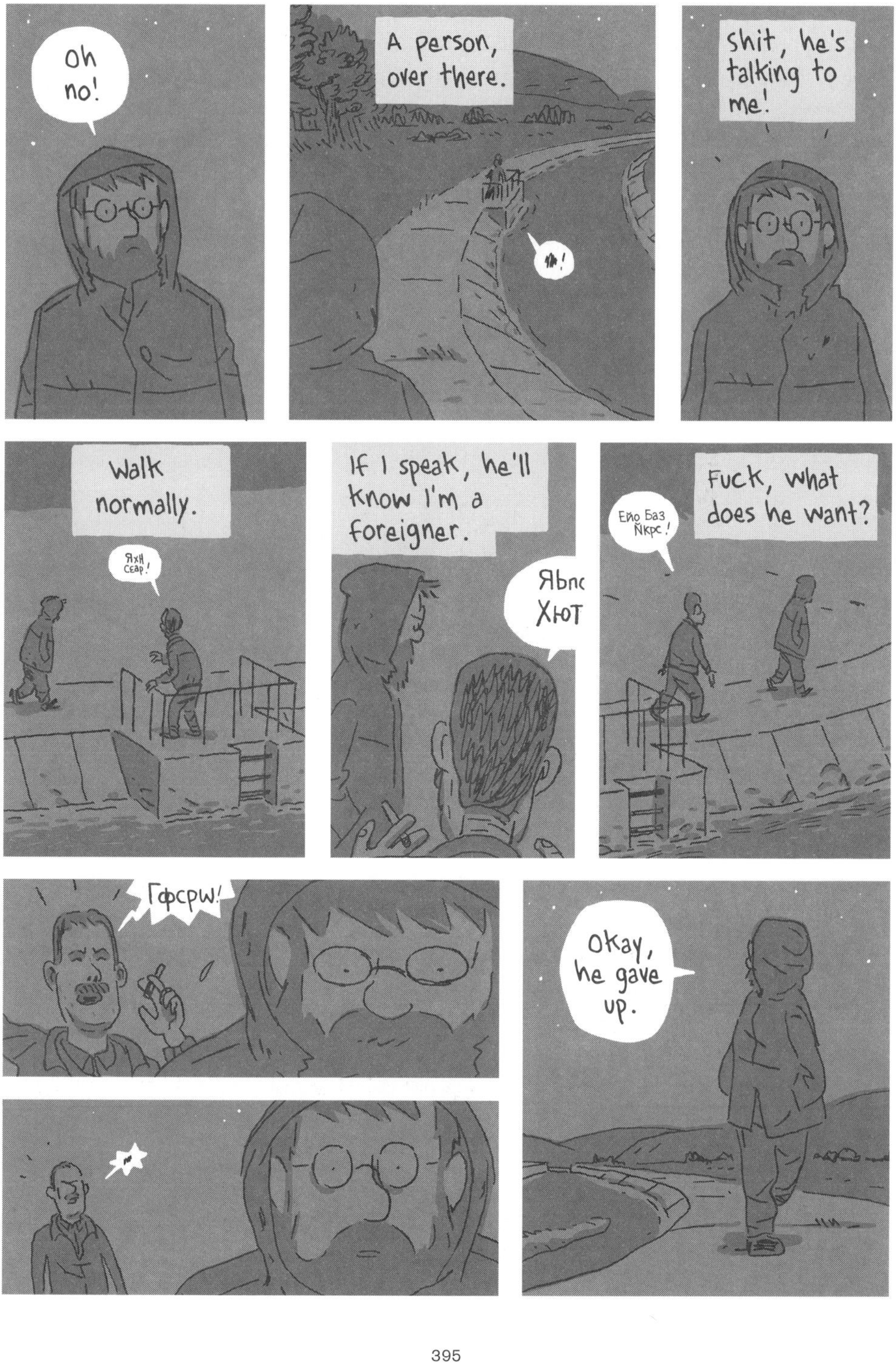
Oh no!
A person, over there.
Shit, he's talking to me!
Walk normally.
Яхн Сеар!
If I speak, he'll know I'm a foreigner.
Ябпс Хют
Fuck, what does he want?
Ейо Баз Ӣкрс!
Гфсрw!
Okay, he gave up.

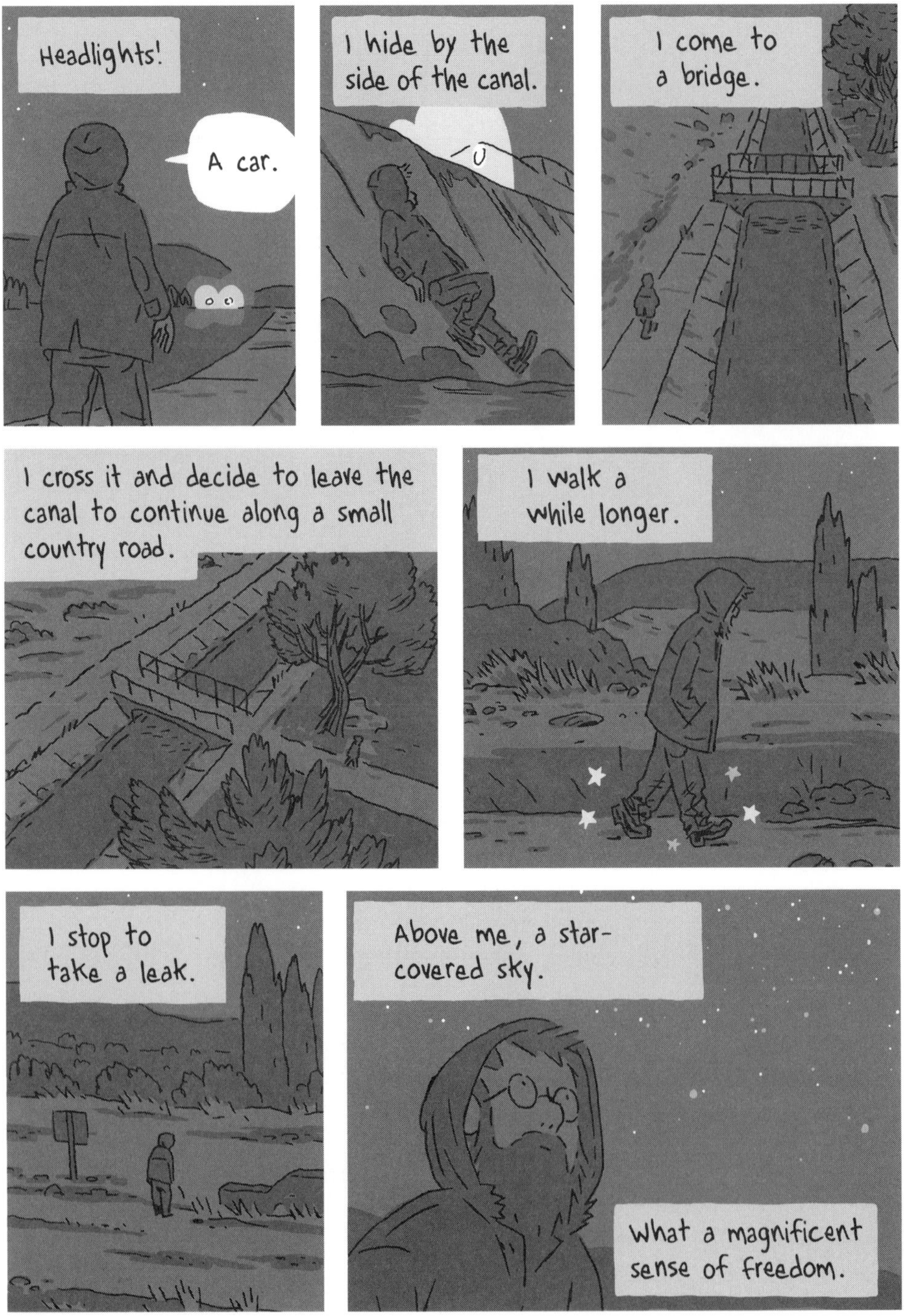
Headlights!
A car.
I hide by the side of the canal.
I come to a bridge.
I cross it and decide to leave the canal to continue along a small country road.
I walk a while longer.
I stop to take a leak.
Above me, a star-covered sky.
What a magnificent sense of freedom.

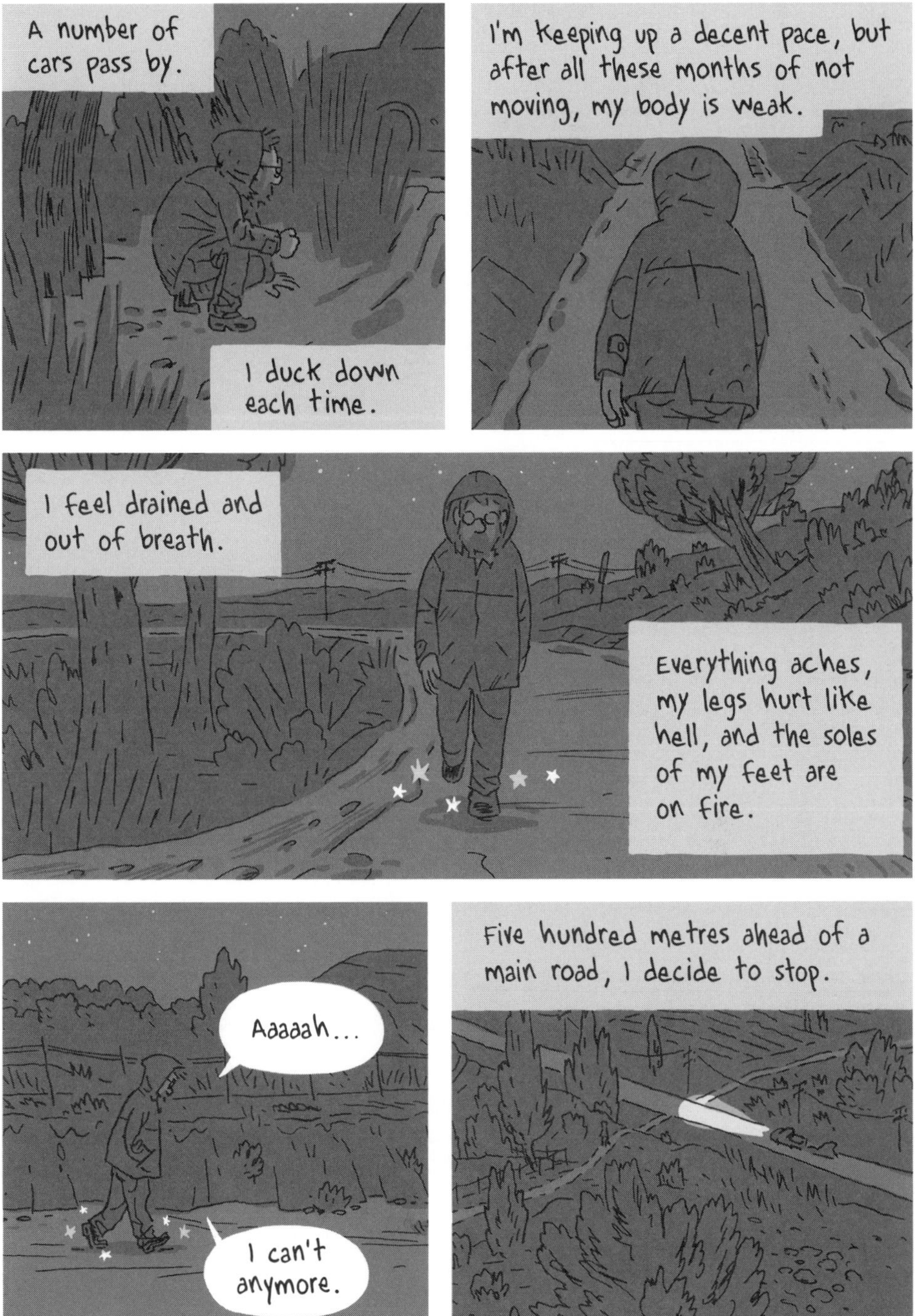
A number of cars pass by.
I duck down each time.
I'm keeping up a decent pace, but after all these months of not moving, my body is weak.
I feel drained and out of breath.
Everything aches, my legs hurt like hell, and the soles of my feet are on fire.
Aaaaah...
I can't anymore.
Five hundred metres ahead of a main road, I decide to stop.

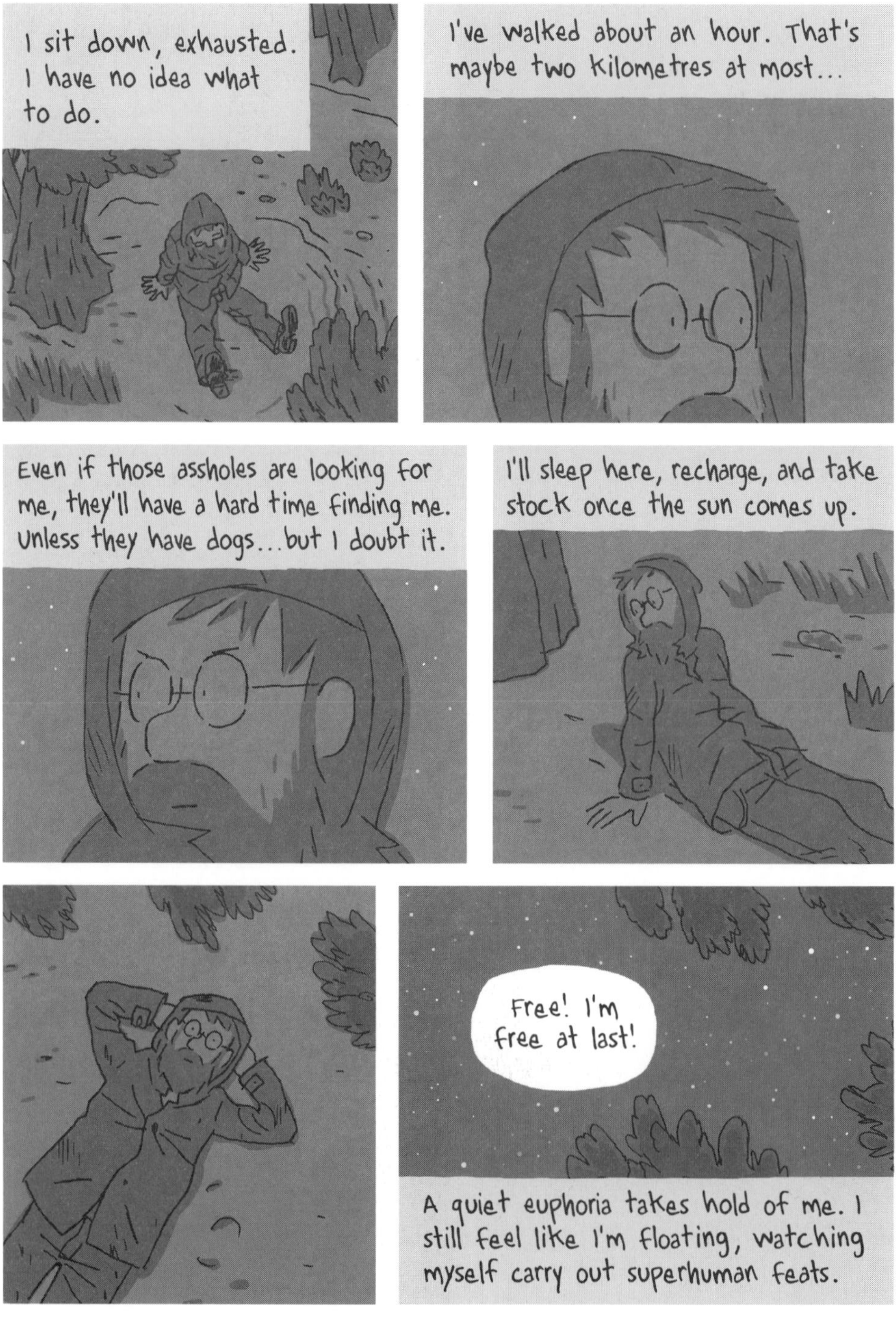
I sit down, exhausted. I have no idea what to do.
I've walked about an hour. That's maybe two kilometres at most...
Even if those assholes are looking for me, they'll have a hard time finding me. Unless they have dogs... but I doubt it.
I'll sleep here, recharge, and take stock once the sun comes up.
Free! I'm free at last!
A quiet euphoria takes hold of me. I still feel like I'm floating, watching myself carry out superhuman feats.

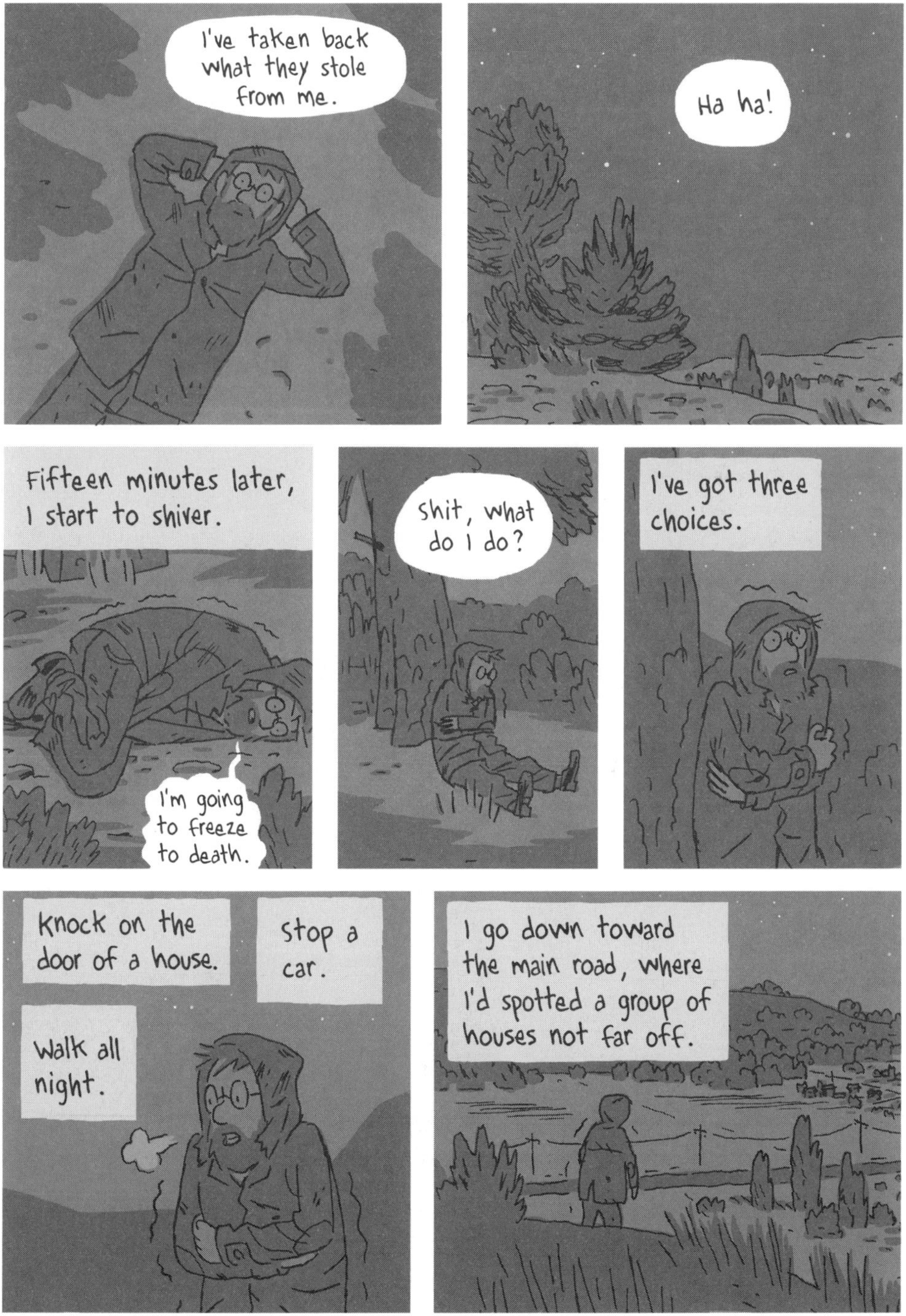
I've taken back what they stole from me.
Ha ha!
Fifteen minutes later, I start to shiver.
I'm going to freeze to death.
Shit, what do I do?
I've got three choices.
Knock on the door of a house.
Stop a car.
Walk all night.
I go down toward the main road, where I'd spotted a group of houses not far off.

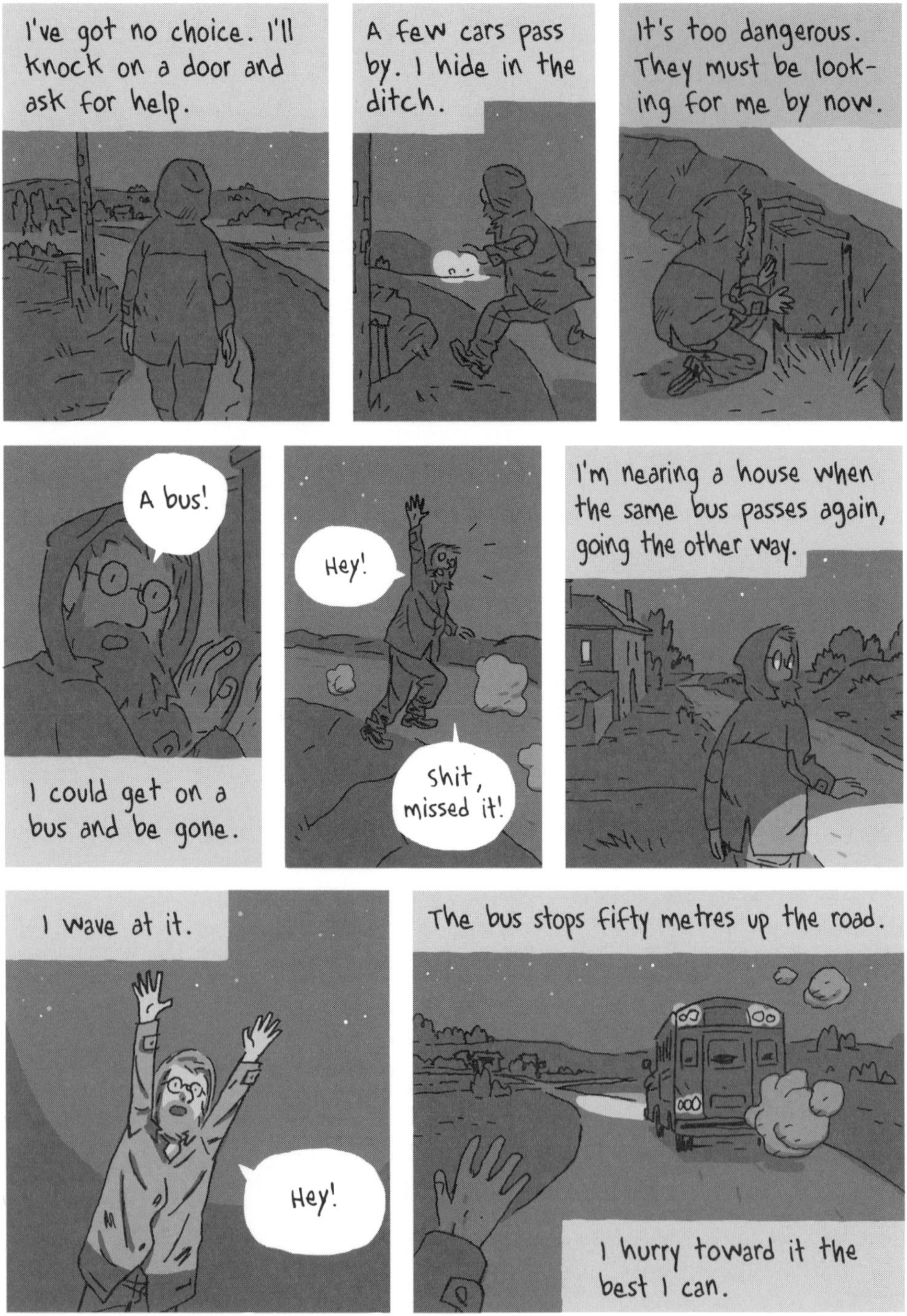

I've got no choice. I'll knock on a door and ask for help.
A few cars pass by. I hide in the ditch.
It's too dangerous. They must be looking for me by now.
A bus!
I could get on a bus and be gone.
Hey!
Shit, missed it!
I'm nearing a house when the same bus passes again, going the other way.
I wave at it.
Hey!
The bus stops fifty metres up the road.
I hurry toward it the best I can.

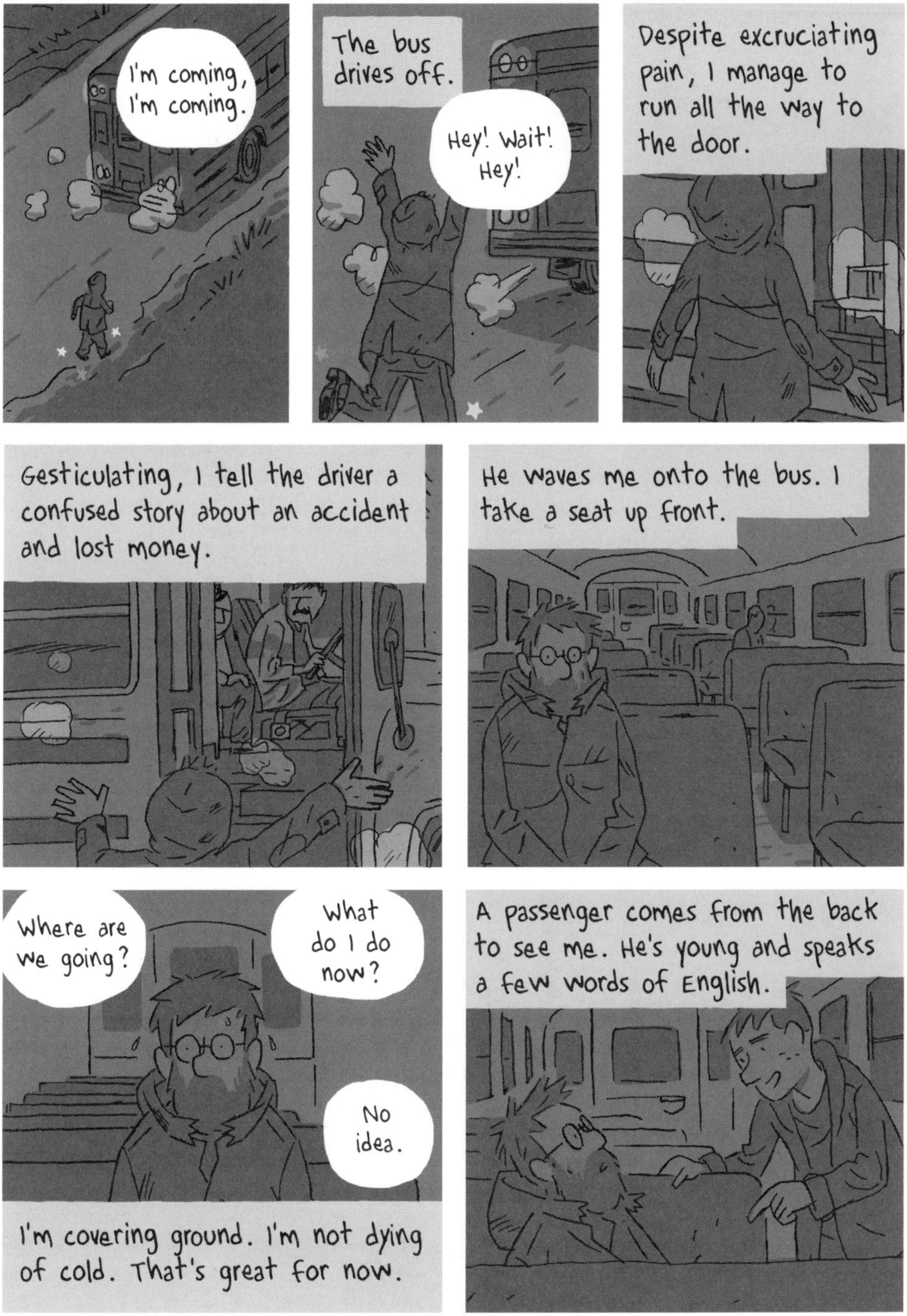
I'm coming, I'm coming.
The bus drives off.
Hey! Wait! Hey!
Despite excruciating pain, I manage to run all the way to the door.
Gesticulating, I tell the driver a confused story about an accident and lost money.
He waves me onto the bus. I take a seat up front.
Where are we going?
What do I do now?
No idea.
I'm covering ground. I'm not dying of cold. That's great for now.
A passenger comes from the back to see me. He's young and speaks a few words of English.

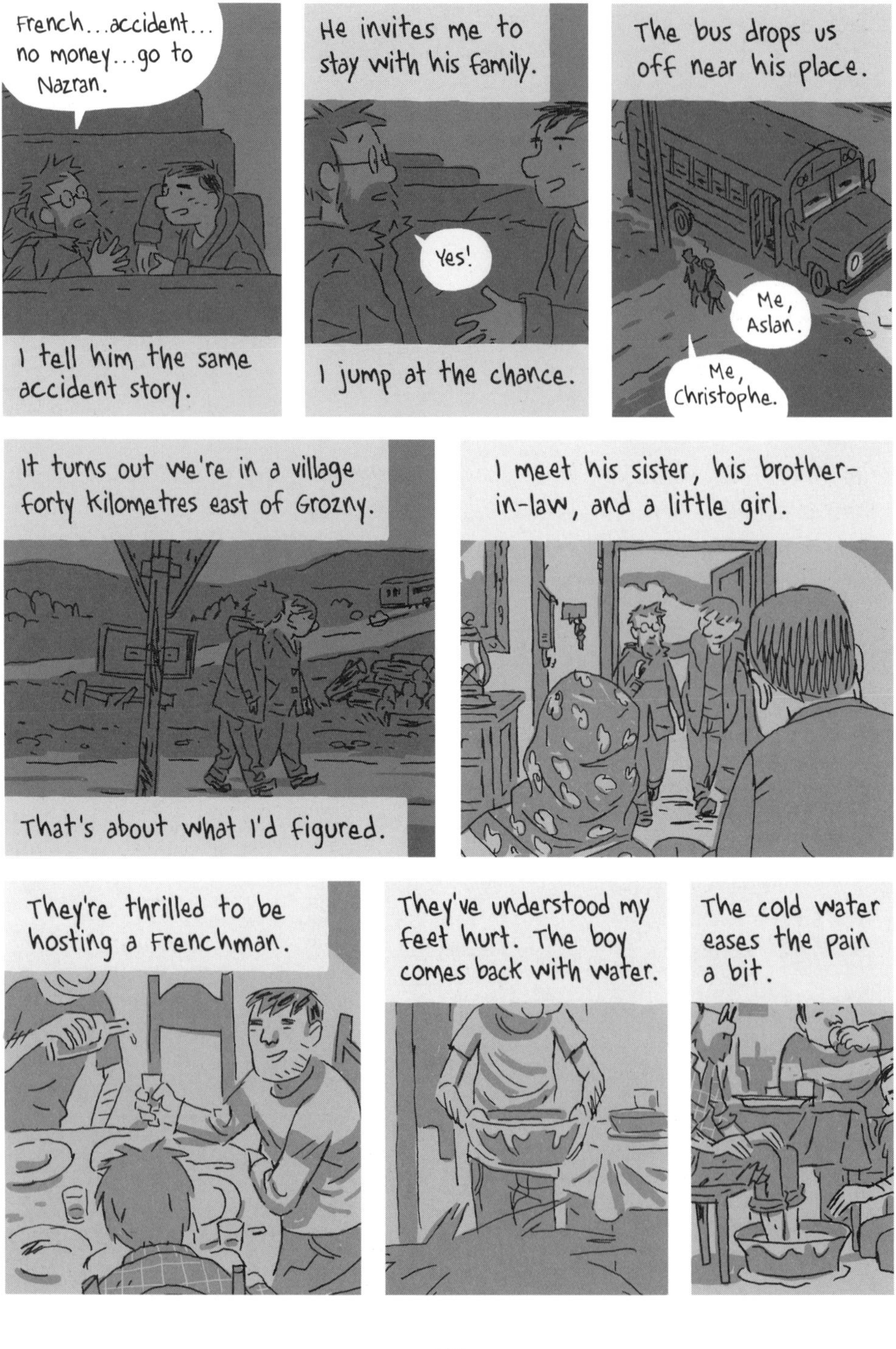
French...accident... no money...go to Nazran.
I tell him the same accident story.
He invites me to stay with his family.
Yes!
I jump at the chance.
The bus drops us off near his place.
Me, Aslan.
Me, Christophe.
It turns out we're in a village forty kilometres east of Grozny.
That's about what I'd figured.
I meet his sister, his brother-in-law, and a little girl.
They're thrilled to be hosting a Frenchman.
They've understood my feet hurt. The boy comes back with water.
The cold water eases the pain a bit.

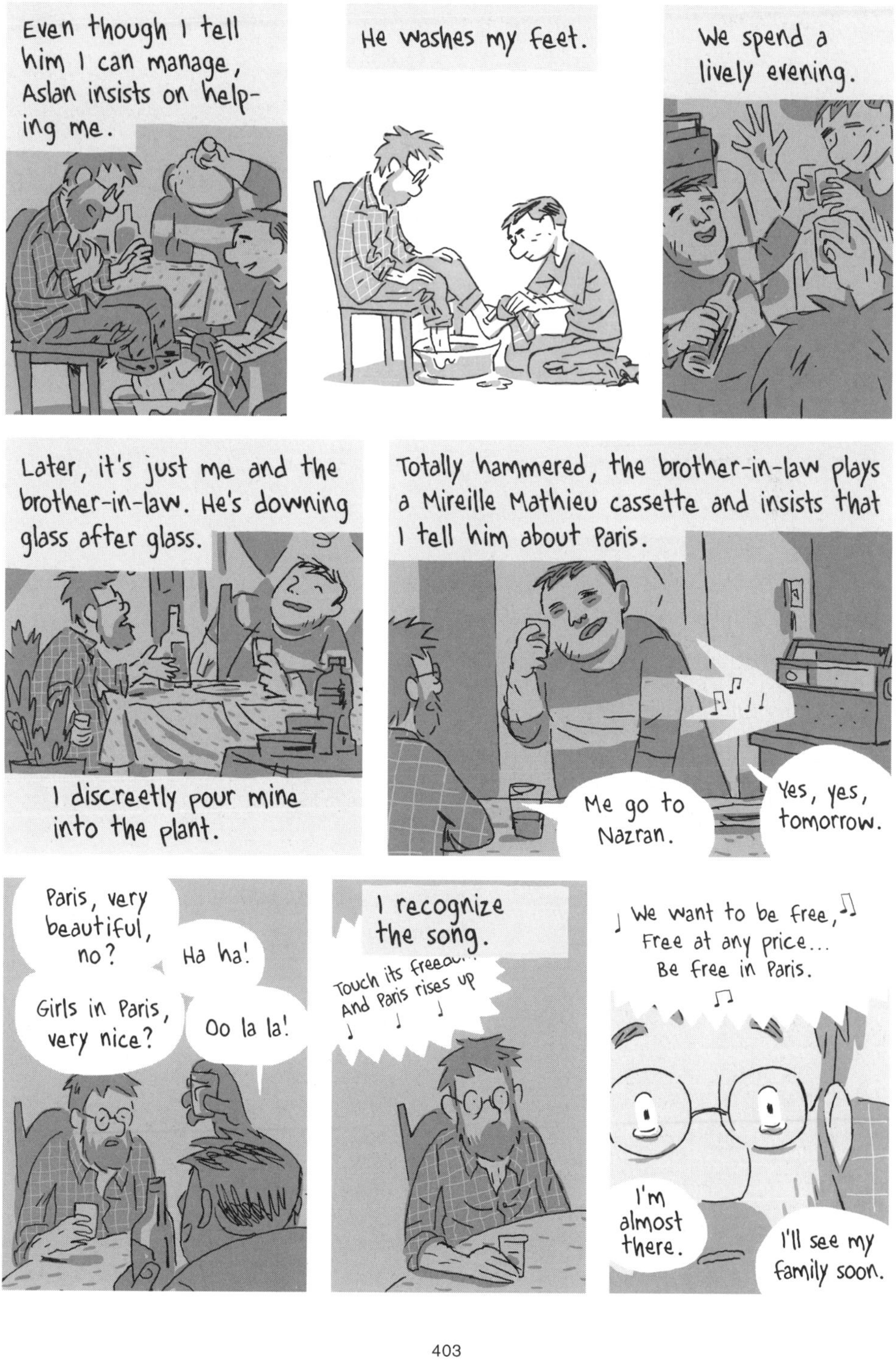
Even though I tell him I can manage, Aslan insists on help-ing me.
He washes my feet.
We spend a lively evening.
Later, it's just me and the brother-in-law. He's downing glass after glass.
I discreetly pour mine into the plant.
Totally hammered, the brother-in-law plays a Mireille Mathieu cassette and insists that I tell him about Paris.
Me go to Nazran.
Yes, yes, tomorrow.
Paris, very beautiful, no?
Ha ha!
Girls in Paris, very nice?
Oo la la!
I recognize the song.
Touch its
And Paris rises up
We want to be free,
Free at any price...
Be free in Paris.
I'm almost there.
I'll see my family soon.

It's 4:00 a.m. I'm worn out. He asks me to help him go outside.

I walk with him to the street.

To think I was handcuffed to the floor this morning...

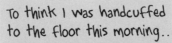

Christ, what a day!

He heads off to bed and points at a room I can sleep in.

It has a straw mattress like I've used for more than three months now. Except tonight I can sleep in whatever position I want.

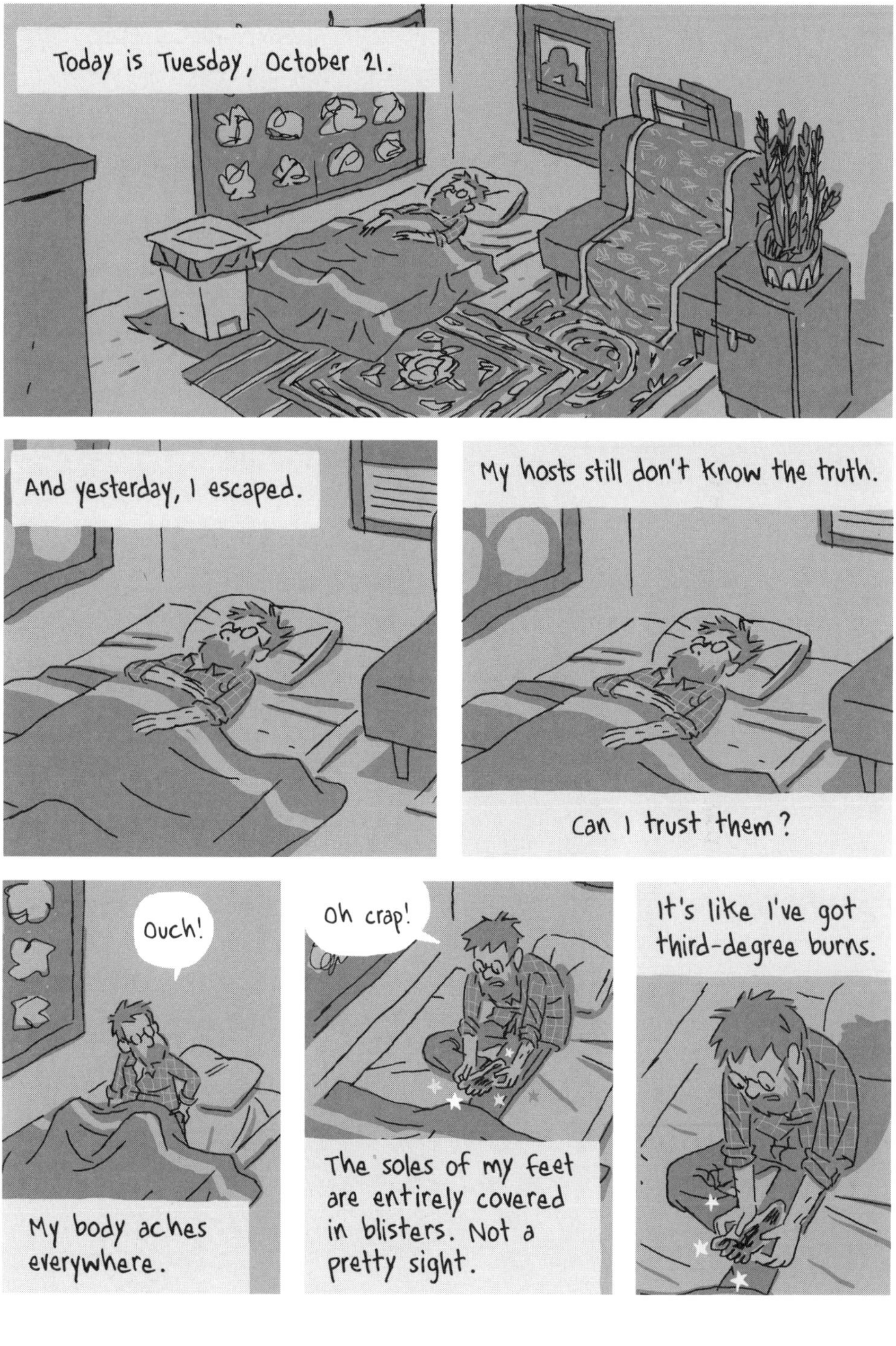
Today is Tuesday, October 21.
And yesterday, I escaped.
My hosts still don't know the truth.
Can I trust them?
Ouch!
My body aches everywhere.
Oh crap!
The soles of my feet are entirely covered in blisters. Not a pretty sight.
It's like I've got third-degree burns.

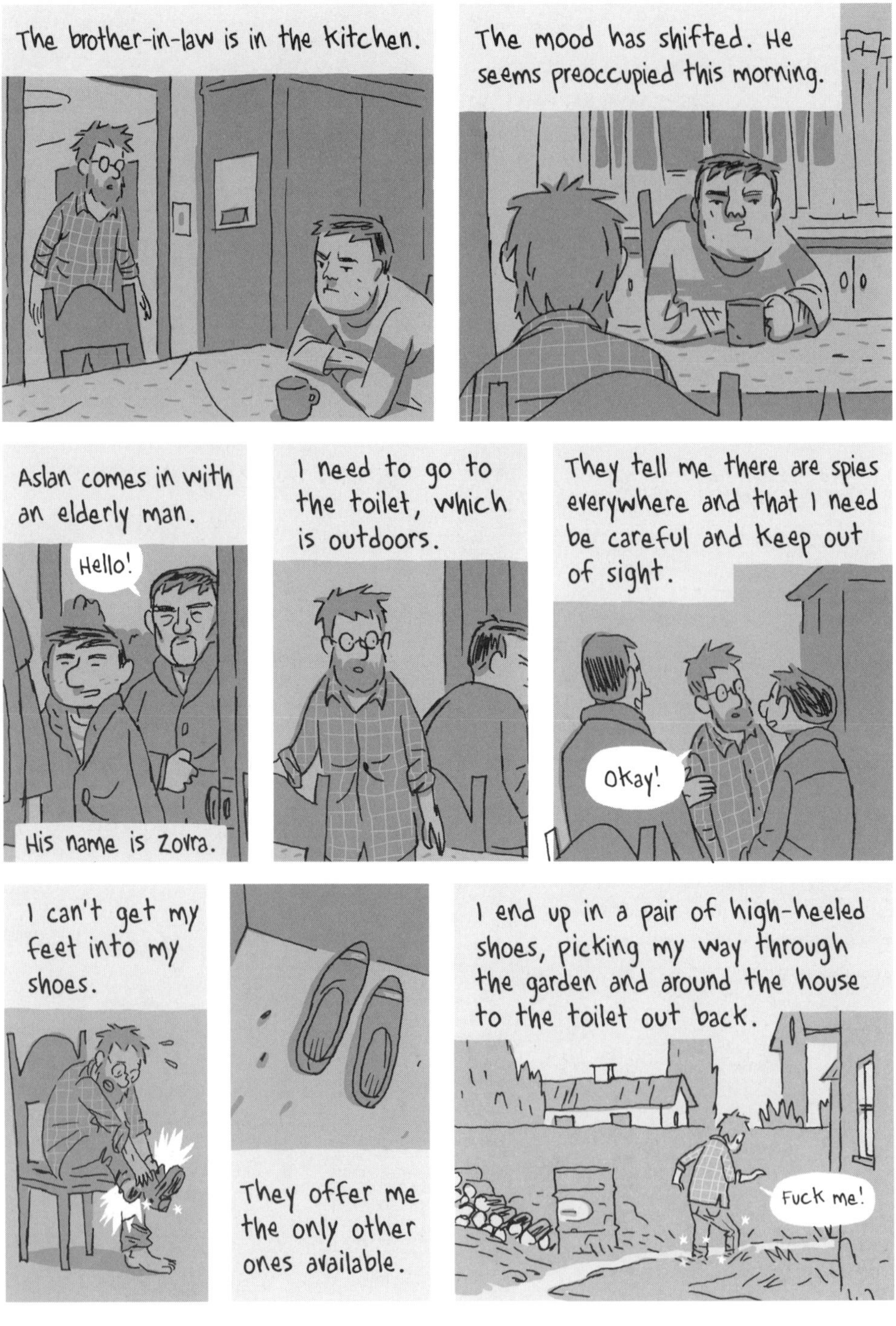
The brother-in-law is in the kitchen.
The mood has shifted. He seems preoccupied this morning.
Aslan comes in with an elderly man.
Hello!
His name is Zovra.
I need to go to the toilet, which is outdoors.
They tell me there are spies everywhere and that I need be careful and keep out of sight.
Okay!
I can't get my feet into my shoes.
They offer me the only other ones available.
I end up in a pair of high-heeled shoes, picking my way through the garden and around the house to the toilet out back.
Fuck me!

When I return, I decide to trust them.

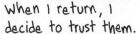

No accident.

I'd know by now if they'd contacted my abductors.

I tell them the whole story.

It takes a while to get it across with the little English, Russian, and German I know.

Kidnapped

NGO

Everyone listens attentively and the mood becomes very heavy.

I give Zorra a telephone number.

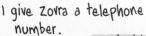

Wait here.

He's going into town.

I spend some time with Aslan who wants to practise his English.

Morning.

Mo-r-ning.

I'm still on a cloud. The simple fact of being in this kitchen with Aslan has me feeling quietly elated.

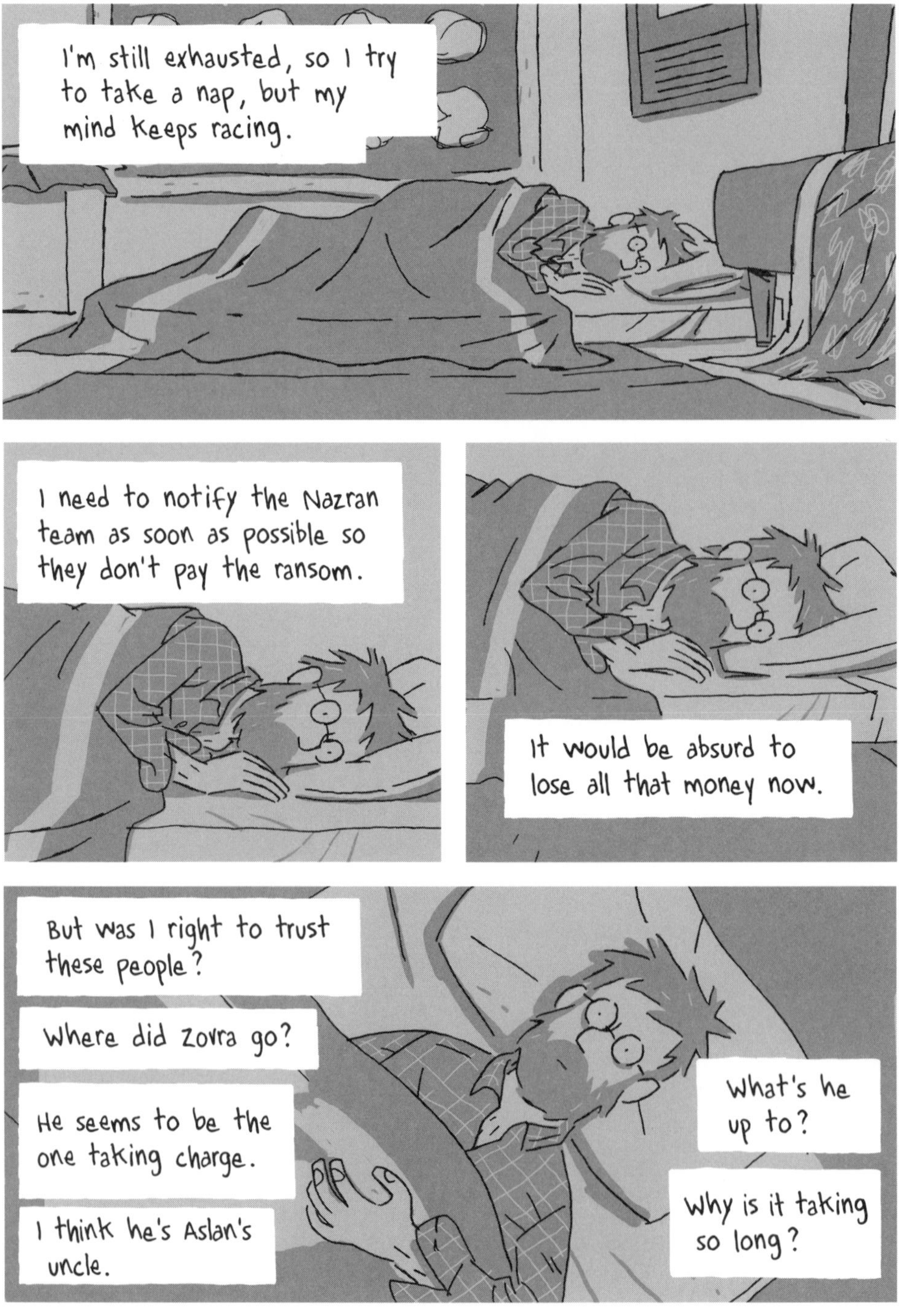
I'm still exhausted, so I try to take a nap, but my mind keeps racing.
I need to notify the Nazran team as soon as possible so they don't pay the ransom.
It would be absurd to lose all that money now.
But was I right to trust these people?
Where did Zovra go?
He seems to be the one taking charge.
I think he's Aslan's uncle.
What's he up to?
Why is it taking so long?

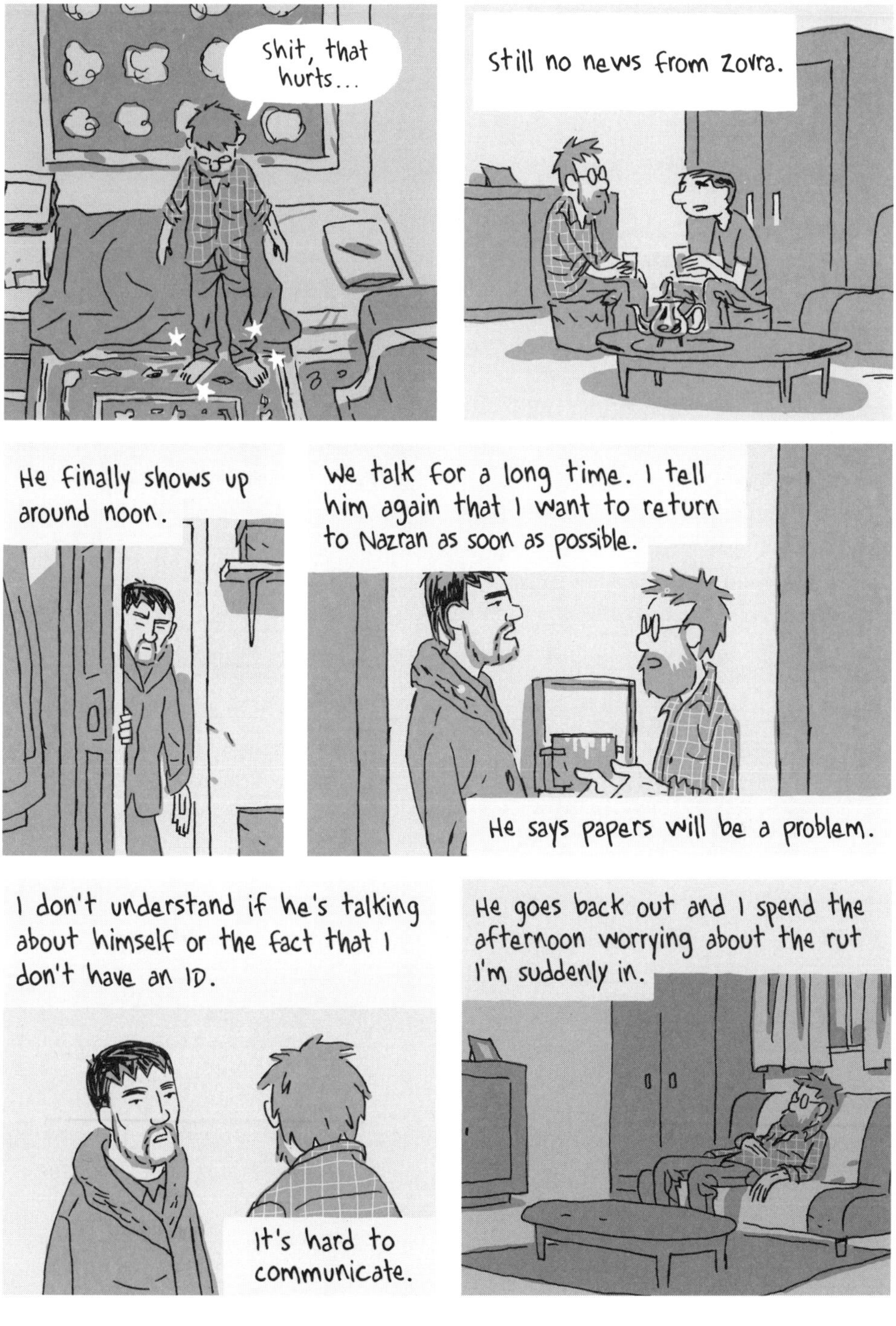
Shit, that hurts...
Still no news from Zovra.
He finally shows up around noon.
We talk for a long time. I tell him again that I want to return to Nazran as soon as possible.
He says papers will be a problem.
I don't understand if he's talking about himself or the fact that I don't have an ID.
It's hard to communicate.
He goes back out and I spend the afternoon worrying about the rut I'm suddenly in.

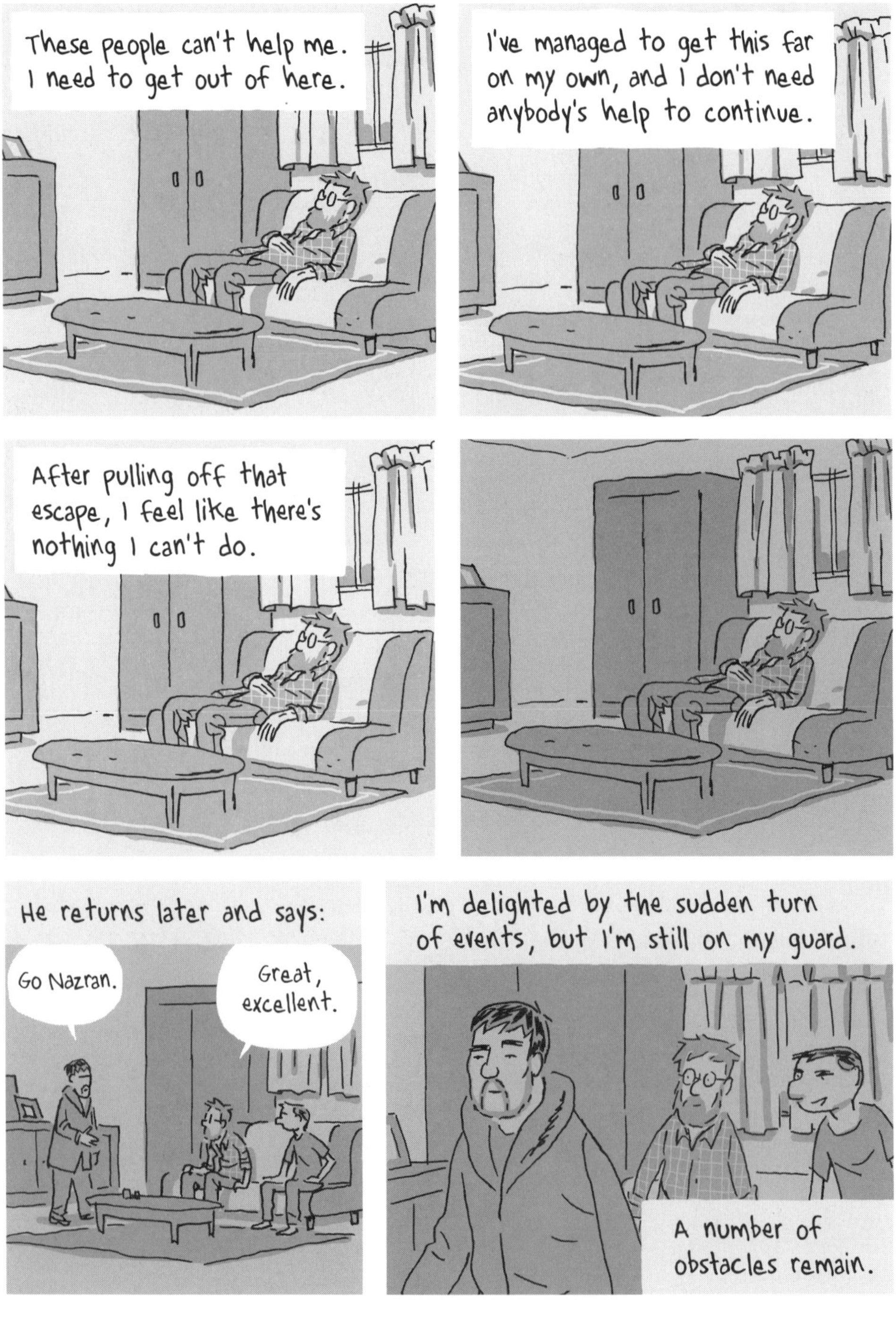

These people can't help me. I need to get out of here.
I've managed to get this far on my own, and I don't need anybody's help to continue.
After pulling off that escape, I feel like there's nothing I can't do.
He returns later and says:
Go Nazran.
Great, excellent.
I'm delighted by the sudden turn of events, but I'm still on my guard.
A number of obstacles remain.

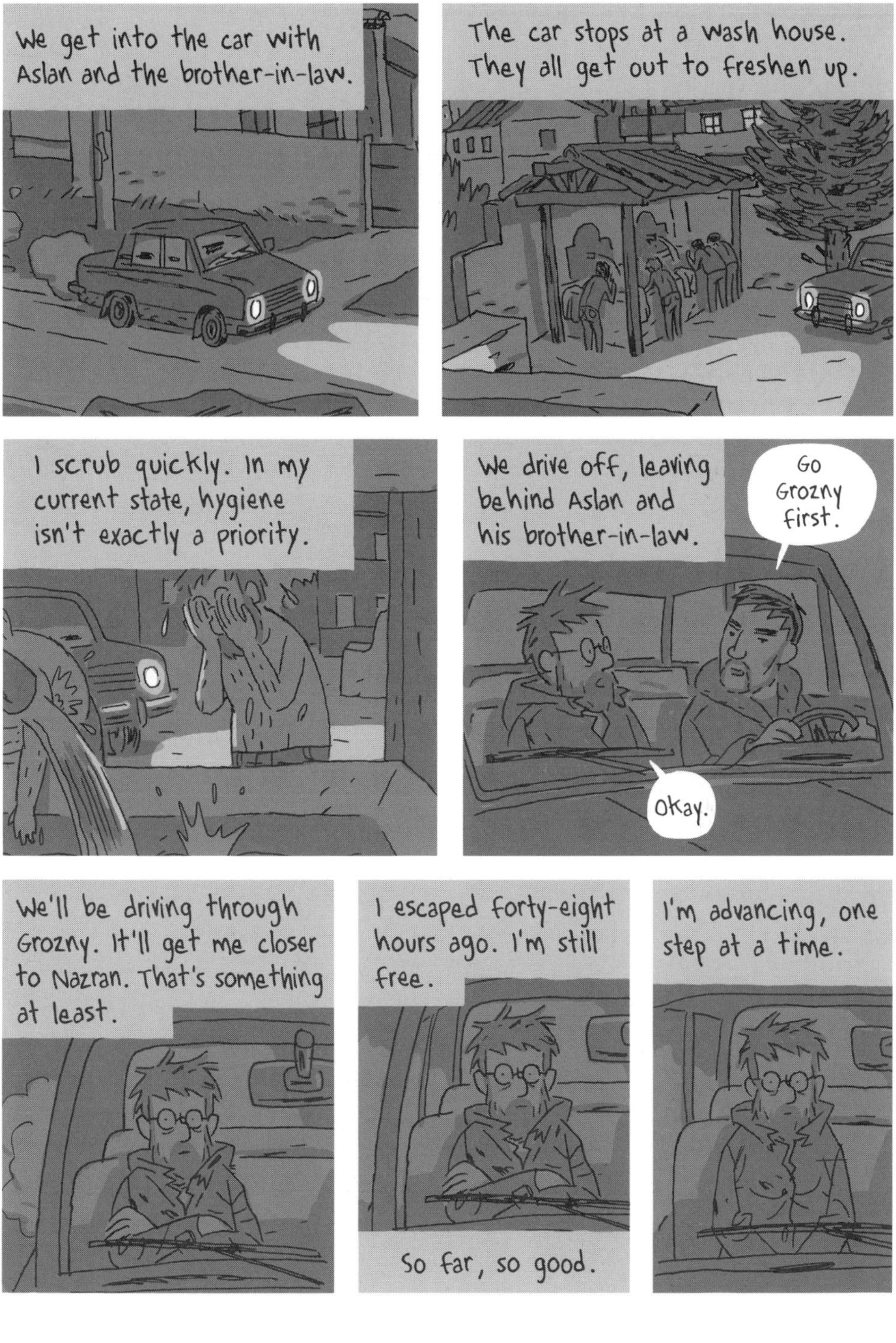
We get into the car with Aslan and the brother-in-law.
The car stops at a wash house. They all get out to freshen up.
I scrub quickly. In my current state, hygiene isn't exactly a priority.
We drive off, leaving behind Aslan and his brother-in-law.
Go Grozny first.
Okay.
We'll be driving through Grozny. It'll get me closer to Nazran. That's something at least.
I escaped forty-eight hours ago. I'm still free.
So far, so good.
I'm advancing, one step at a time.

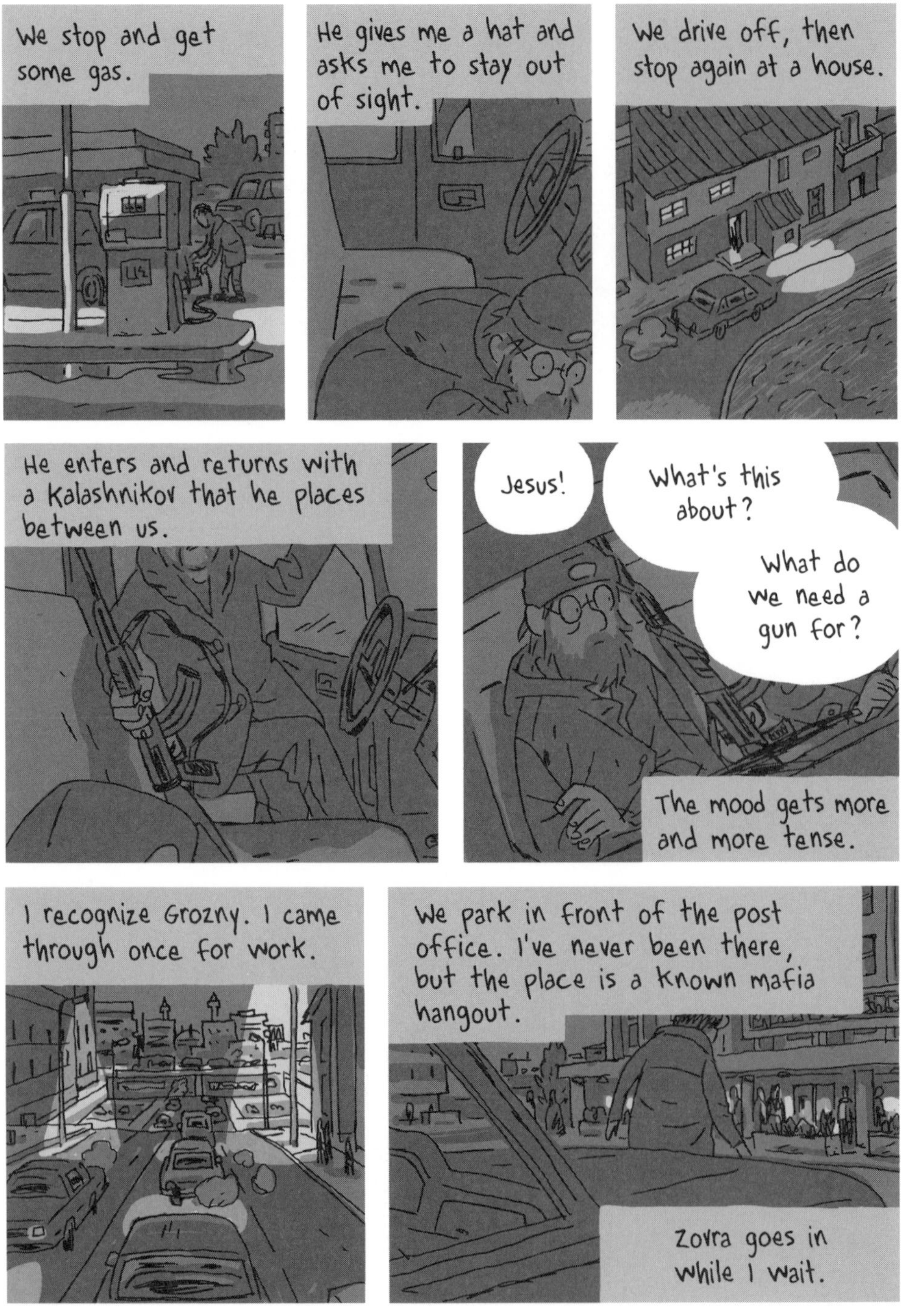

We stop and get some gas.
He gives me a hat and asks me to stay out of sight.
We drive off, then stop again at a house.
He enters and returns with a Kalashnikov that he places between us.
Jesus!
What's this about?
What do we need a gun for?
The mood gets more and more tense.
I recognize Grozny. I came through once for work.
We park in front of the post office. I've never been there, but the place is a known mafia hangout.
Zovra goes in while I wait.

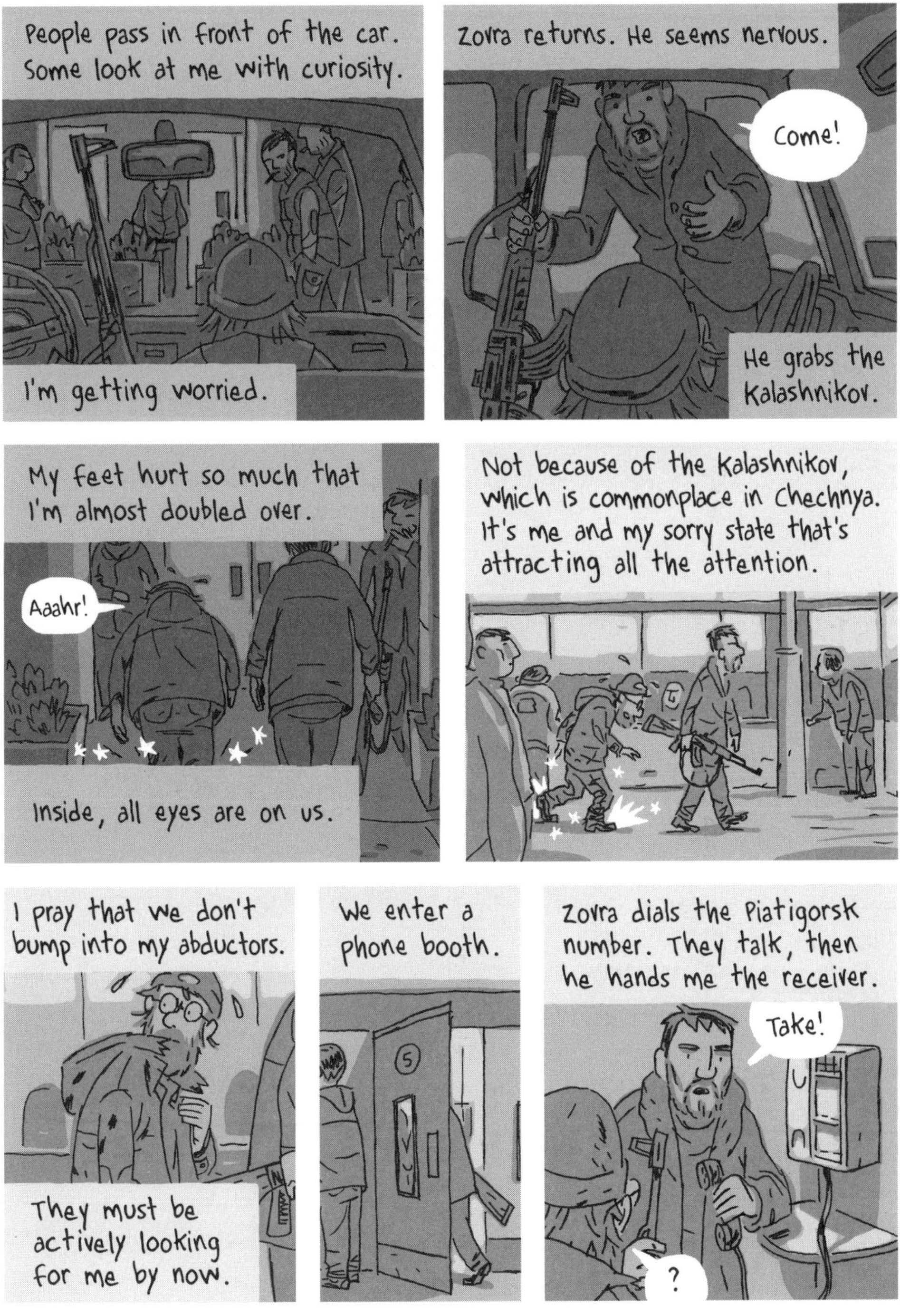
People pass in front of the car. Some look at me with curiosity.
I'm getting worried.
Zovra returns. He seems nervous.
Come!
He grabs the Kalashnikov.
My feet hurt so much that I'm almost doubled over.
Aaahr!
Inside, all eyes are on us.
Not because of the Kalashnikov, which is commonplace in Chechnya. It's me and my sorry state that's attracting all the attention.
I pray that we don't bump into my abductors.
They must be actively looking for me by now.
We enter a phone booth.
5
Zovra dials the Piatigorsk number. They talk, then he hands me the receiver.
Take!
?

Hello?

Christophe?

I'm on line with someone from the NGO in Nazran who speaks French.
I don't know him.

Yes, it's me.

He's as surprised about the call as I am.

Are you okay?

Yes, I'm fine.

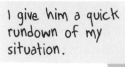

I give him a quick rundown of my situation.

I met some people...

I got away...

I'm on my way to Nazran...

Just be sure you don't give them the money!

Yes, okay.

Zovra takes back the receiver and talks for a moment before hanging up.

ЗмНру Еño Баз ÑКрс.

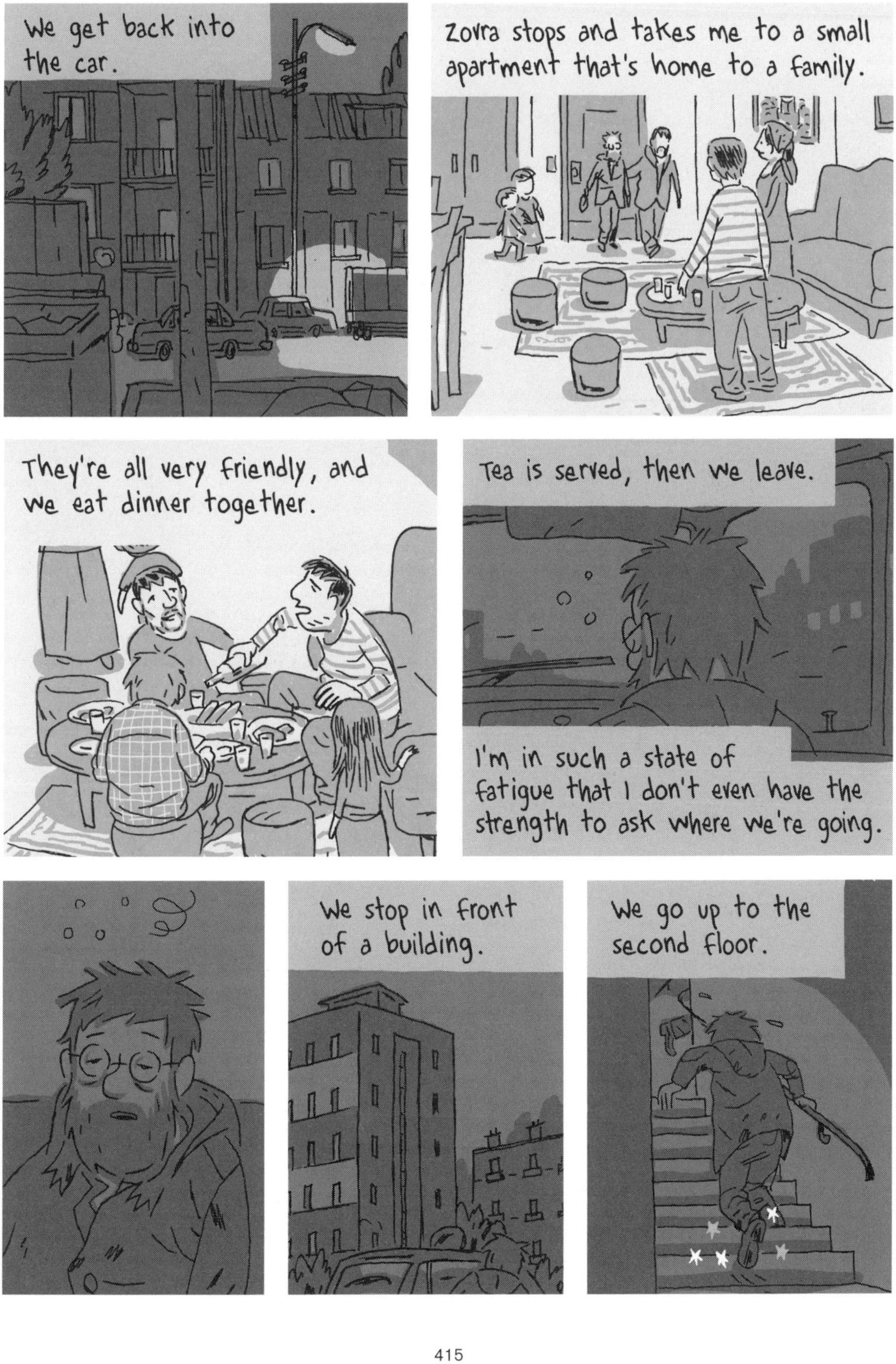
We get back into the car.
Zovra stops and takes me to a small apartment that's home to a family.
They're all very friendly, and we eat dinner together.
Tea is served, then we leave.
I'm in such a state of fatigue that I don't even have the strength to ask where we're going.
We stop in front of a building.
We go up to the second floor.

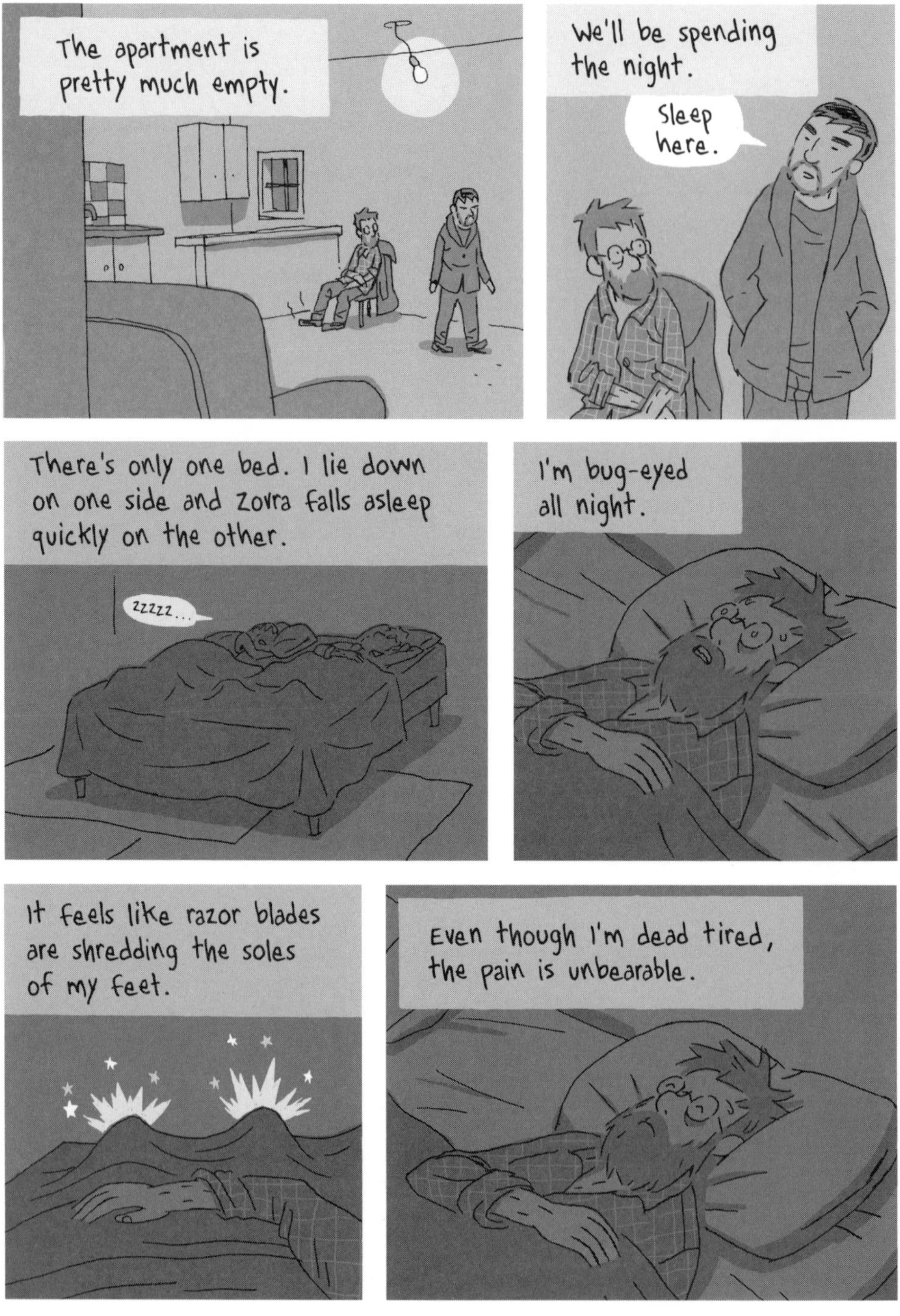
The apartment is pretty much empty.
We'll be spending the night.
Sleep here.
There's only one bed. I lie down on one side and Zovra falls asleep quickly on the other.
zzzzz...
I'm bug-eyed all night.
It feels like razor blades are shredding the soles of my feet.
Even though I'm dead tired, the pain is unbearable.

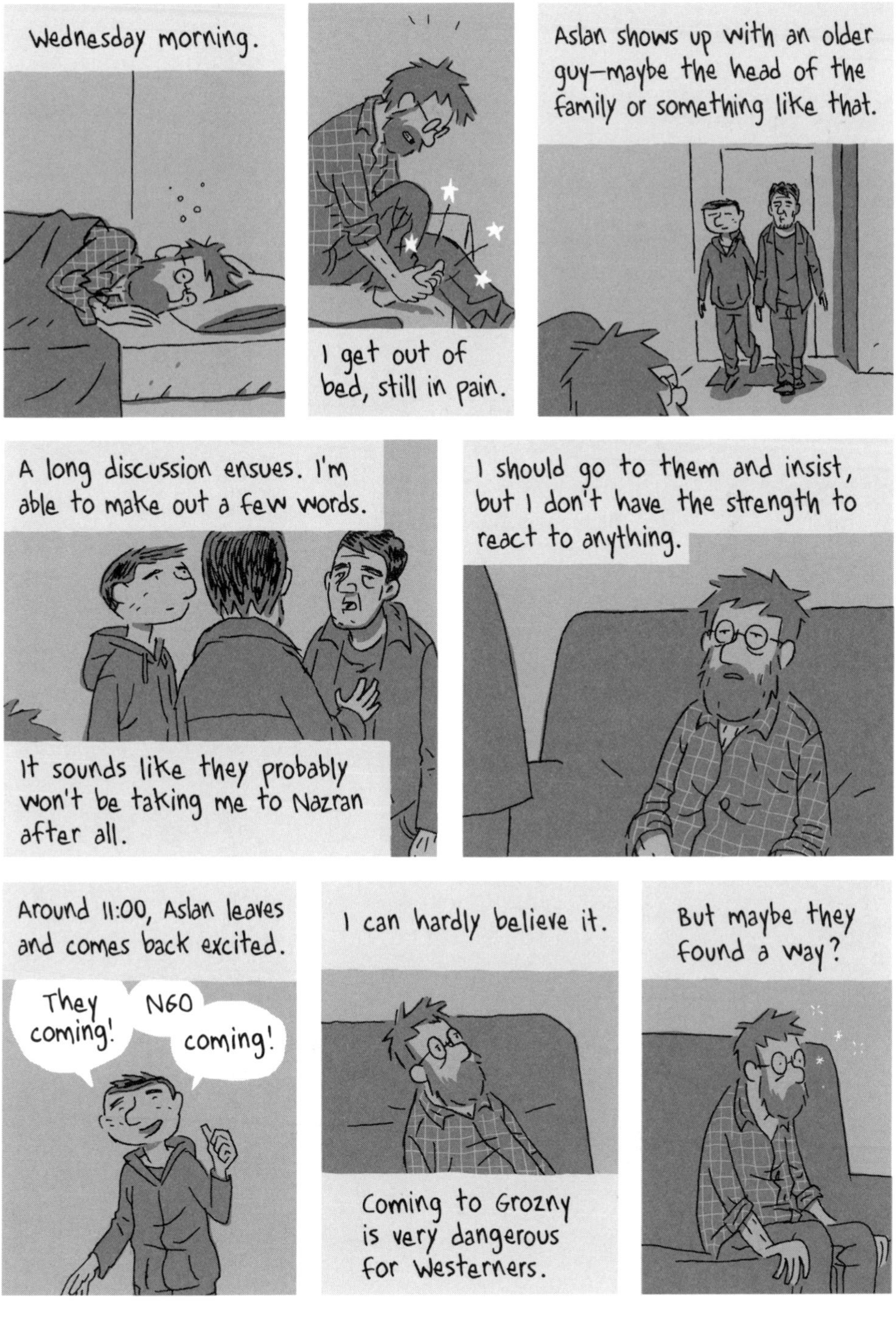
Wednesday morning.
I get out of bed, still in pain.
Aslan shows up with an older guy—maybe the head of the family or something like that.
A long discussion ensues. I'm able to make out a few words.
It sounds like they probably won't be taking me to Nazran after all.
I should go to them and insist, but I don't have the strength to react to anything.
Around 11:00, Aslan leaves and comes back excited.
They coming!
NGO coming!
I can hardly believe it.
Coming to Grozny is very dangerous for Westerners.
But maybe they found a way?

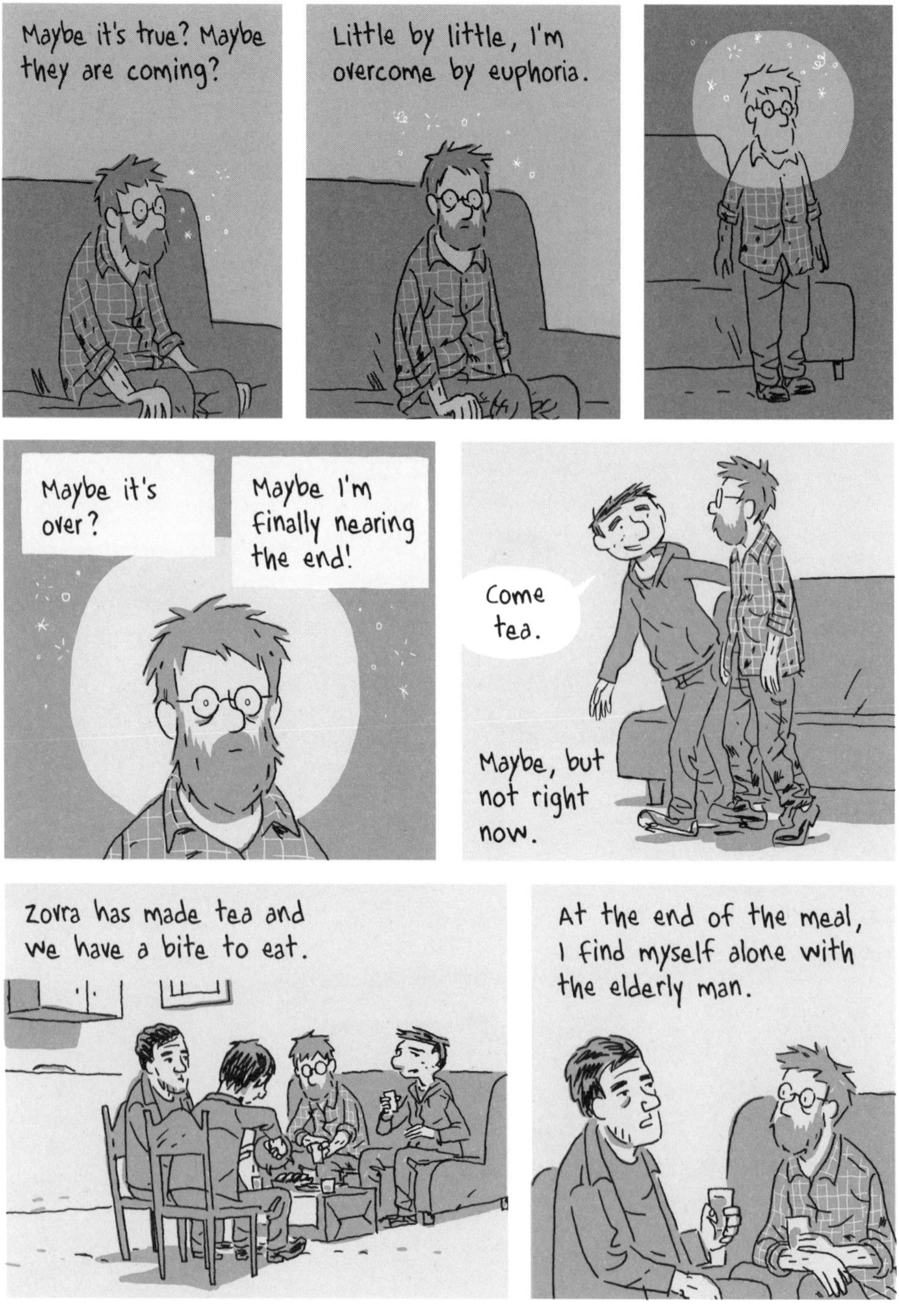
Maybe it's true? Maybe they are coming?
Little by little, I'm overcome by euphoria.
Maybe it's over?
Maybe I'm finally nearing the end!
Come tea.
Maybe, but not right now.
Zovra has made tea and we have a bite to eat.
At the end of the meal, I find myself alone with the elderly man.

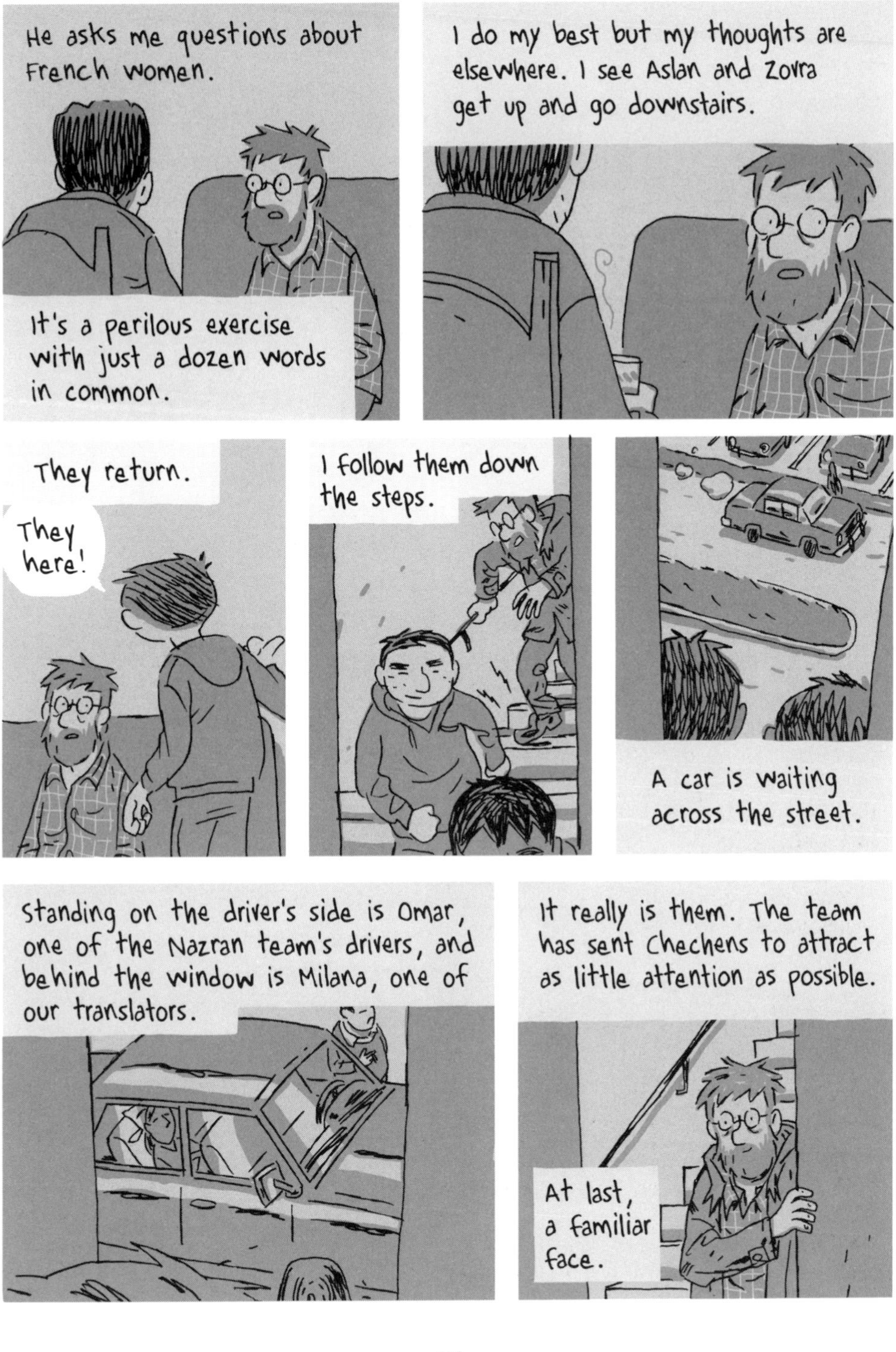
He asks me questions about French women.
It's a perilous exercise with just a dozen words in common.
I do my best but my thoughts are elsewhere. I see Aslan and Zovra get up and go downstairs.
They return.
They here!
I follow them down the steps.
A car is waiting across the street.
Standing on the driver's side is Omar, one of the Nazran team's drivers, and behind the window is Milana, one of our translators.
It really is them. The team has sent Chechens to attract as little attention as possible.
At last, a familiar face.

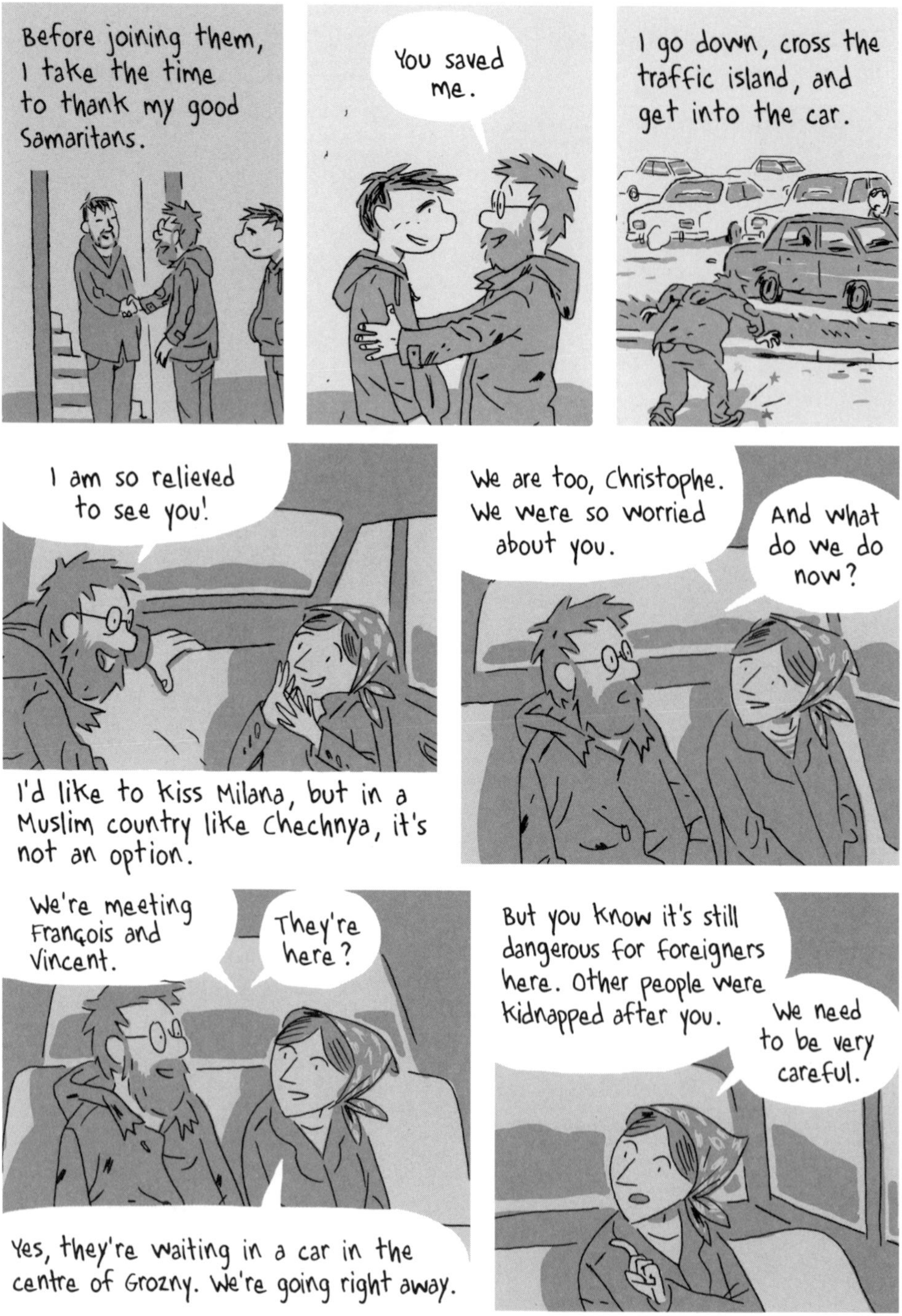
Before joining them, I take the time to thank my good Samaritans.
You saved me.
I go down, cross the traffic island, and get into the car.
I am so relieved to see you!
I'd like to kiss Milana, but in a Muslim country like Chechnya, it's not an option.
We are too, Christophe. We were so worried about you.
And what do we do now?
We're meeting François and Vincent.
They're here?
Yes, they're waiting in a car in the centre of Grozny. We're going right away.
But you know it's still dangerous for foreigners here. Other people were kidnapped after you.
We need to be very careful.

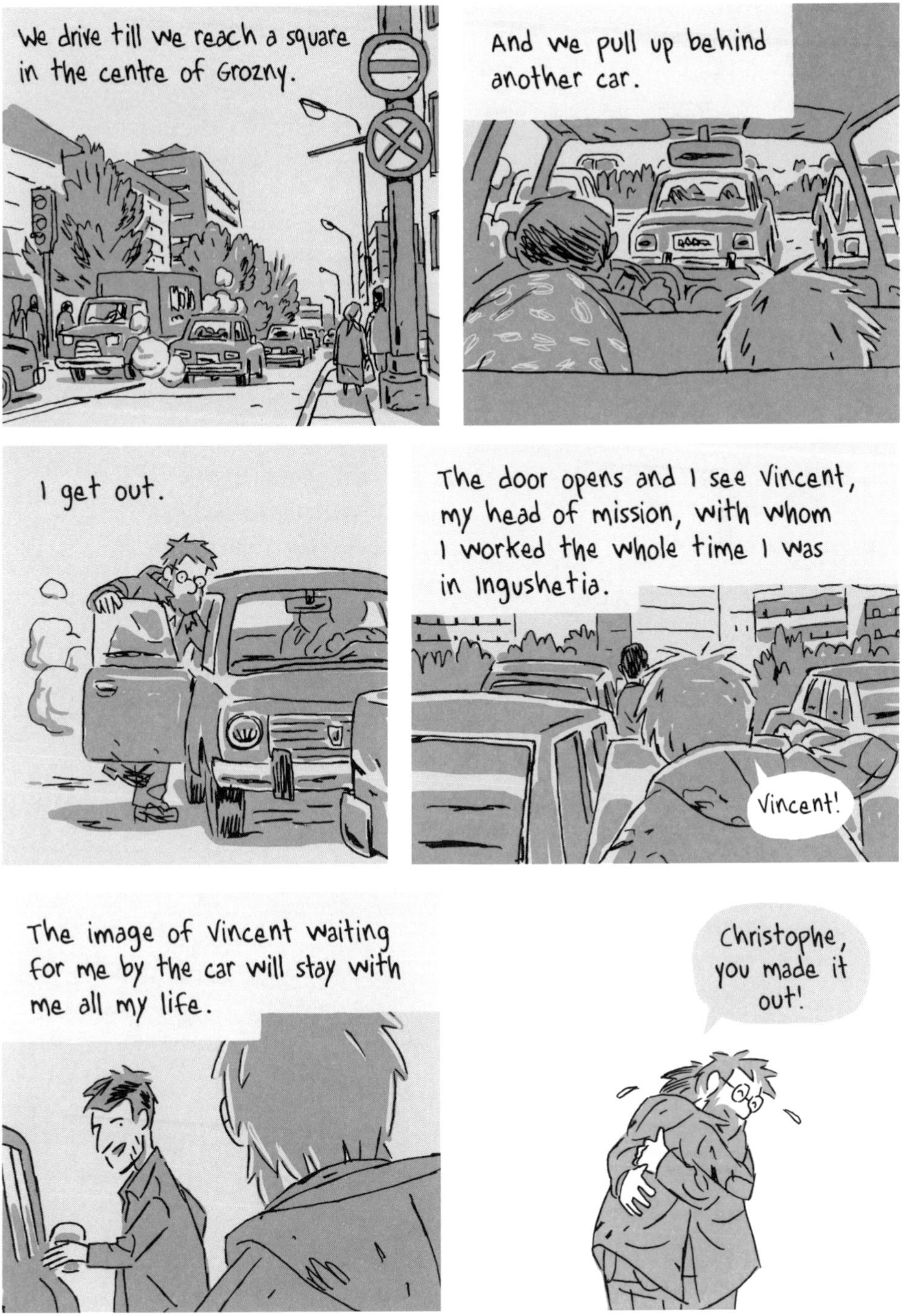
We drive till we reach a square in the centre of Grozny.
And we pull up behind another car.
I get out.
The door opens and I see Vincent, my head of mission, with whom I worked the whole time I was in Ingushetia.
Vincent!
The image of Vincent waiting for me by the car will stay with me all my life.
Christophe, you made it out!

François, a Caucasus specialist and a key members of the crisis unit that was working on my release, has come along as well.

What a relief to see you!

But it's no time to linger, and we continue on to the OSCE,* the only European organization still present in Chechnya.

It turns out my transfer was organized right down to the smallest detail after Zovra called.

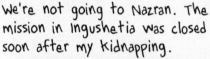

We're not going to Nazran. The mission in Ingushetia was closed soon after my kidnapping.

In the end, shutting down the mission is the only thing those bastards managed to do.

The OSCE is a real fortress. The place is surrounded by fences and armed guards.

*Organization for Security and Cooperation in Europe

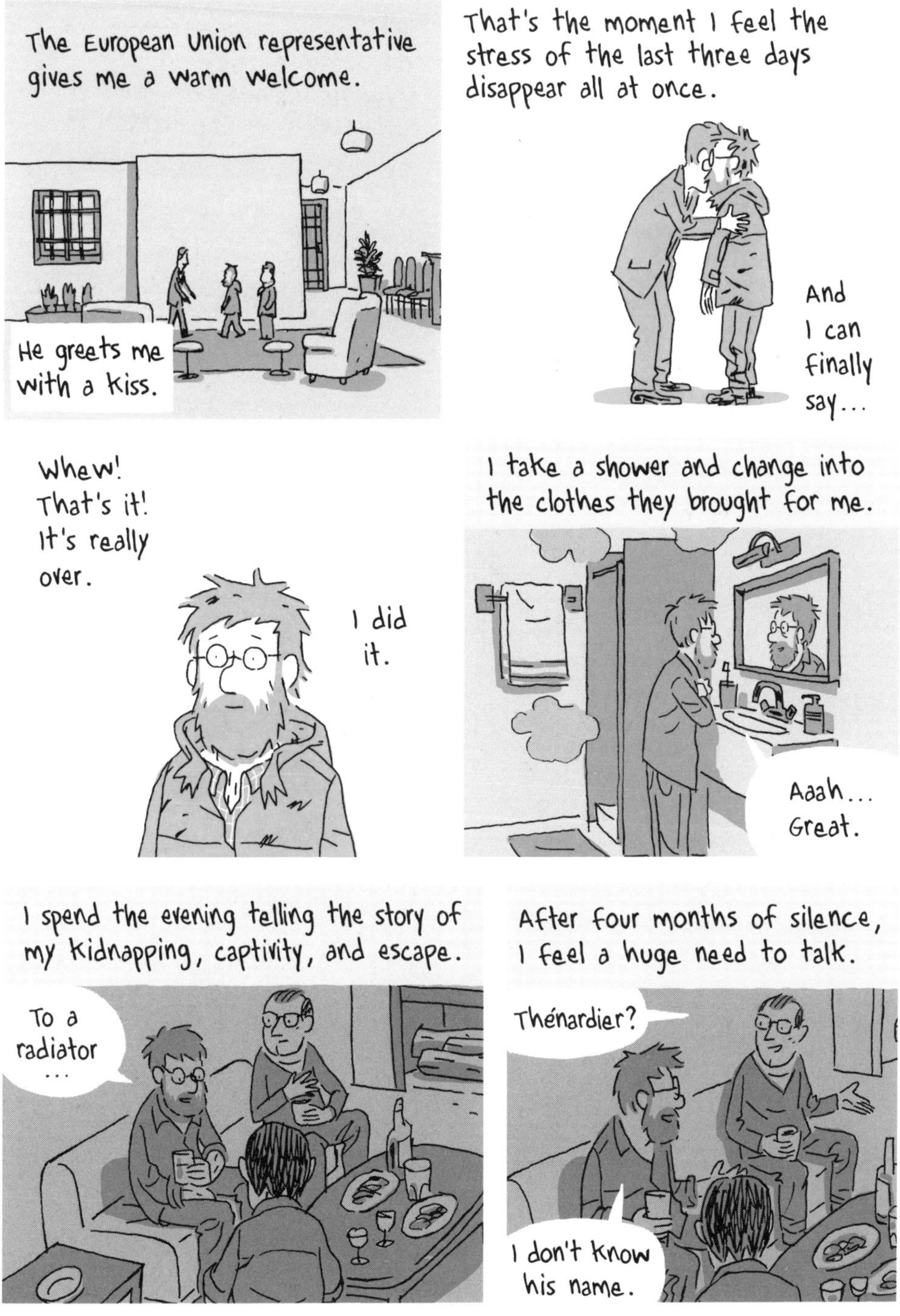

The European Union representative gives me a warm welcome.
He greets me with a kiss.
That's the moment I feel the stress of the last three days disappear all at once.
And I can finally say...
Whew! That's it! It's really over.
I did it.
I take a shower and change into the clothes they brought for me.
Aaah... Great.
I spend the evening telling the story of my kidnapping, captivity, and escape.
To a radiator ...
After four months of silence, I feel a huge need to talk.
Thénardier?
I don't know his name.

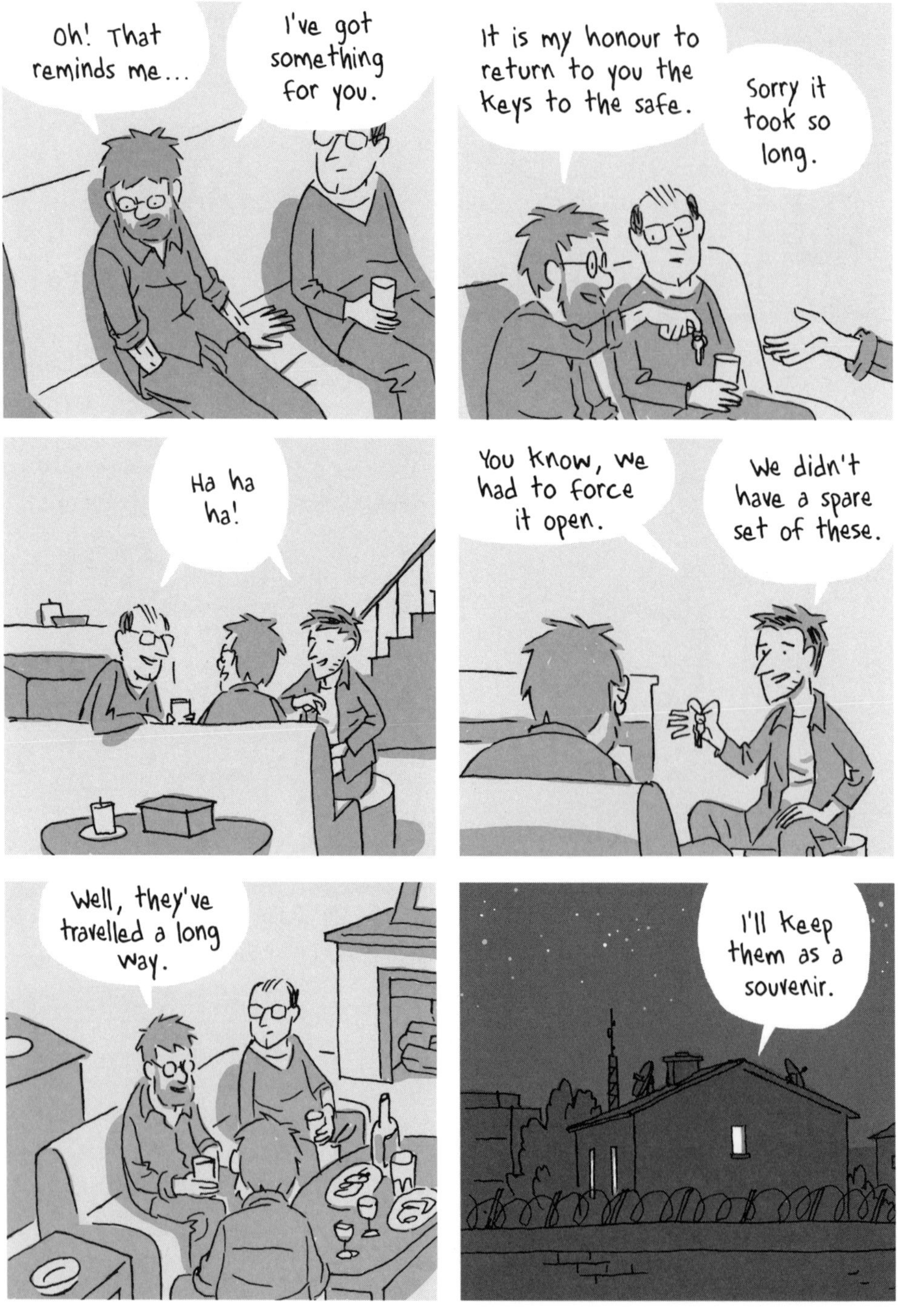
Oh! That reminds me...
I've got something for you.
It is my honour to return to you the keys to the safe.
Sorry it took so long.
Ha ha ha!
You know, we had to force it open.
We didn't have a spare set of these.
Well, they've travelled a long way.
I'll keep them as a souvenir.

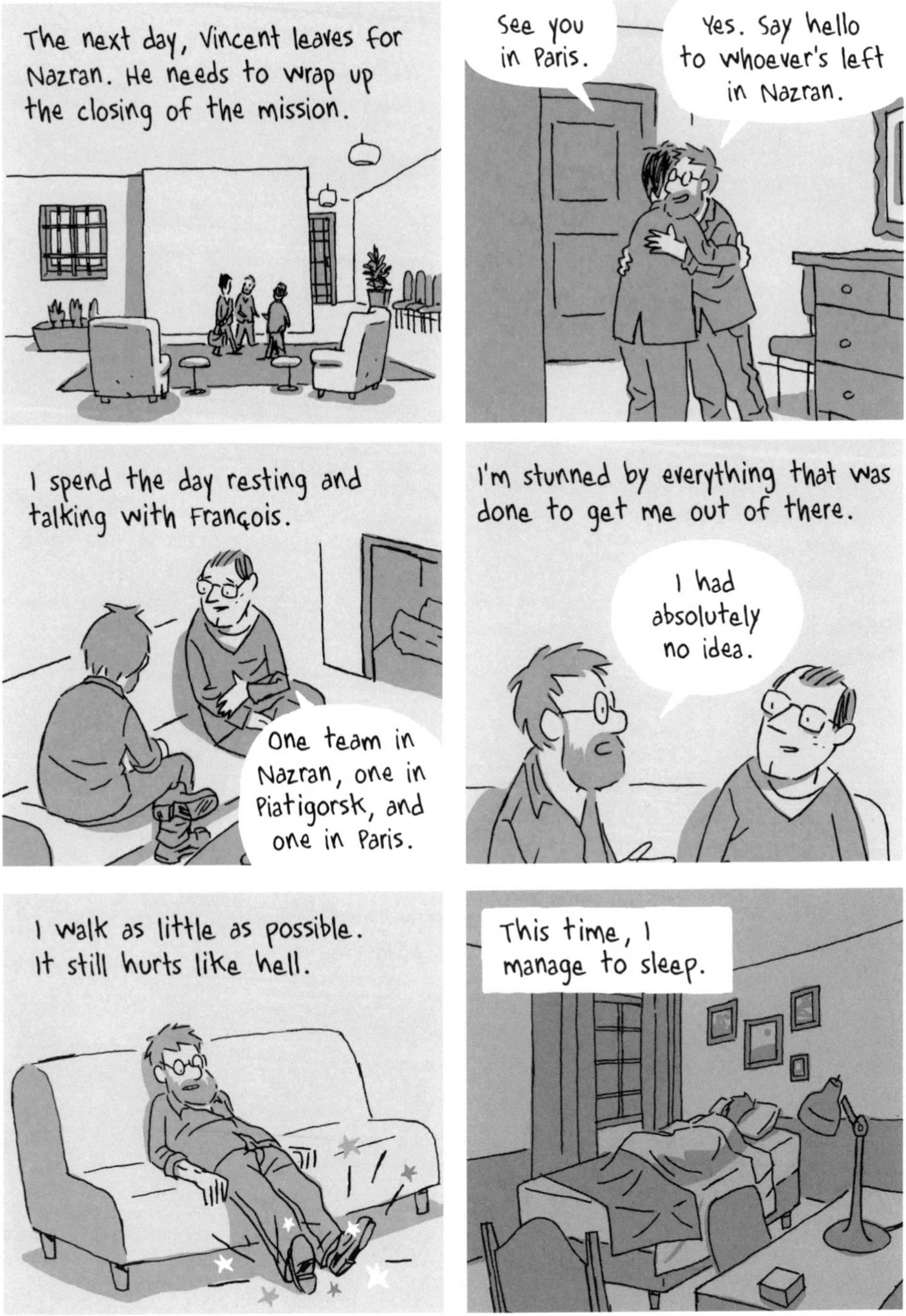
The next day, Vincent leaves for Nazran. He needs to wrap up the closing of the mission.
See you in Paris.
Yes. Say hello to whoever's left in Nazran.
I spend the day resting and talking with François.
One team in Nazran, one in Piatigorsk, and one in Paris.
I'm stunned by everything that was done to get me out of there.
I had absolutely no idea.
I walk as little as possible. It still hurts like hell.
This time, I manage to sleep.

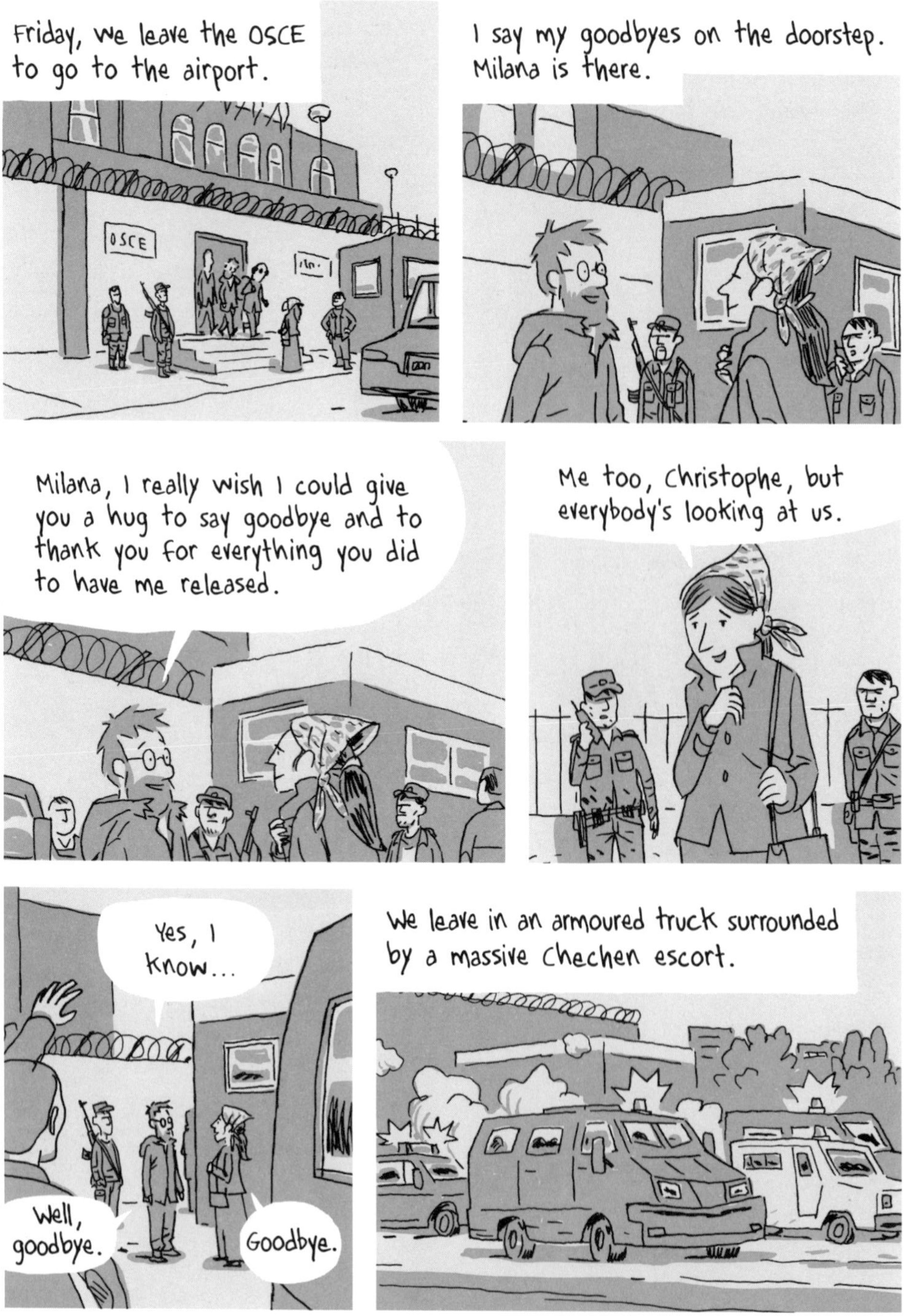
Friday, we leave the OSCE to go to the airport.
OSCE
I say my goodbyes on the doorstep. Milana is there.
Milana, I really wish I could give you a hug to say goodbye and to thank you for everything you did to have me released.
Me too, Christophe, but everybody's looking at us.
Yes, I know...
Well, goodbye.
Goodbye.
We leave in an armoured truck surrounded by a massive Chechen escort.

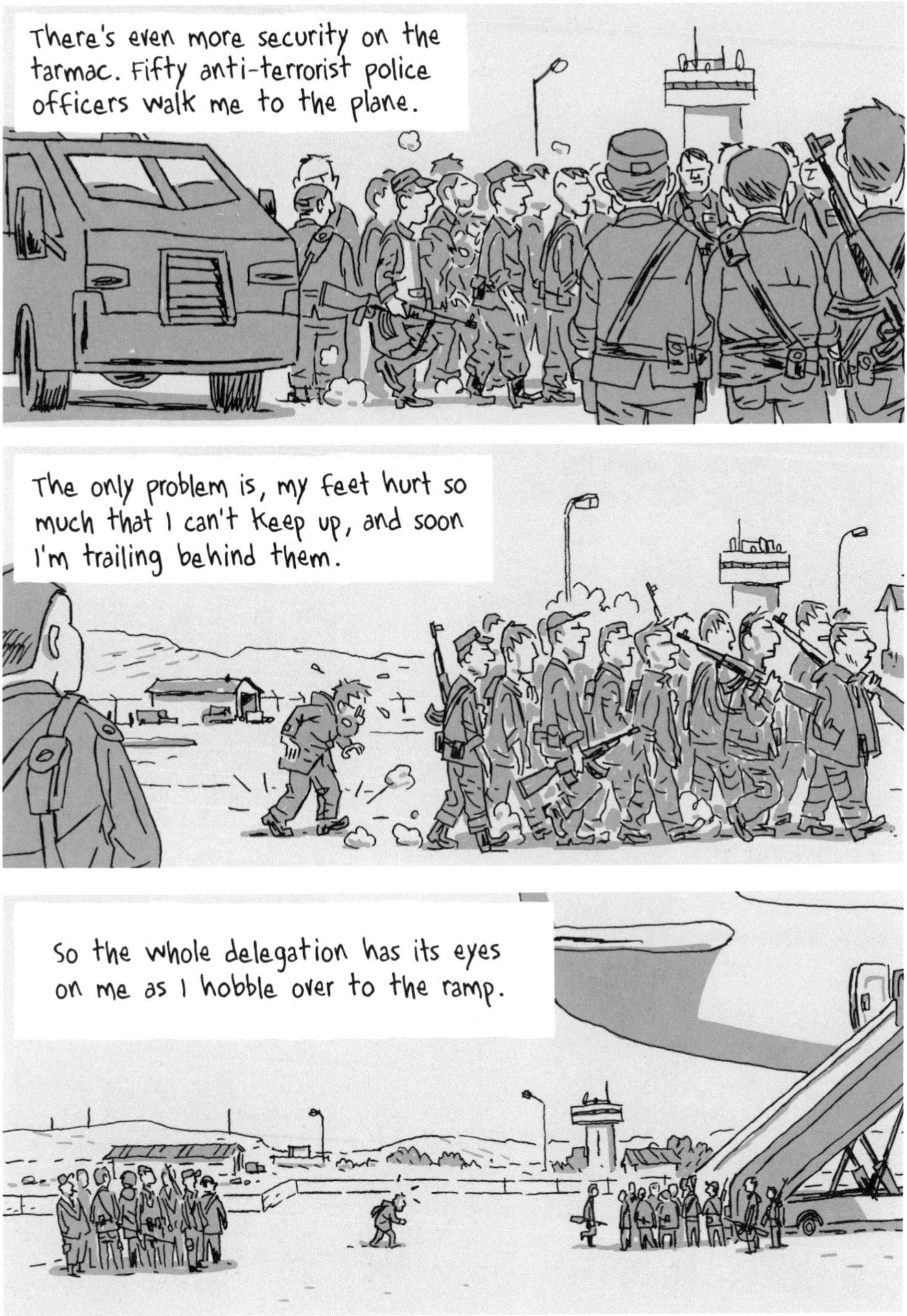
There's even more security on the tarmac. Fifty anti-terrorist police officers walk me to the plane.
The only problem is, my feet hurt so much that I can't keep up, and soon I'm trailing behind them.
So the whole delegation has its eyes on me as I hobble over to the ramp.

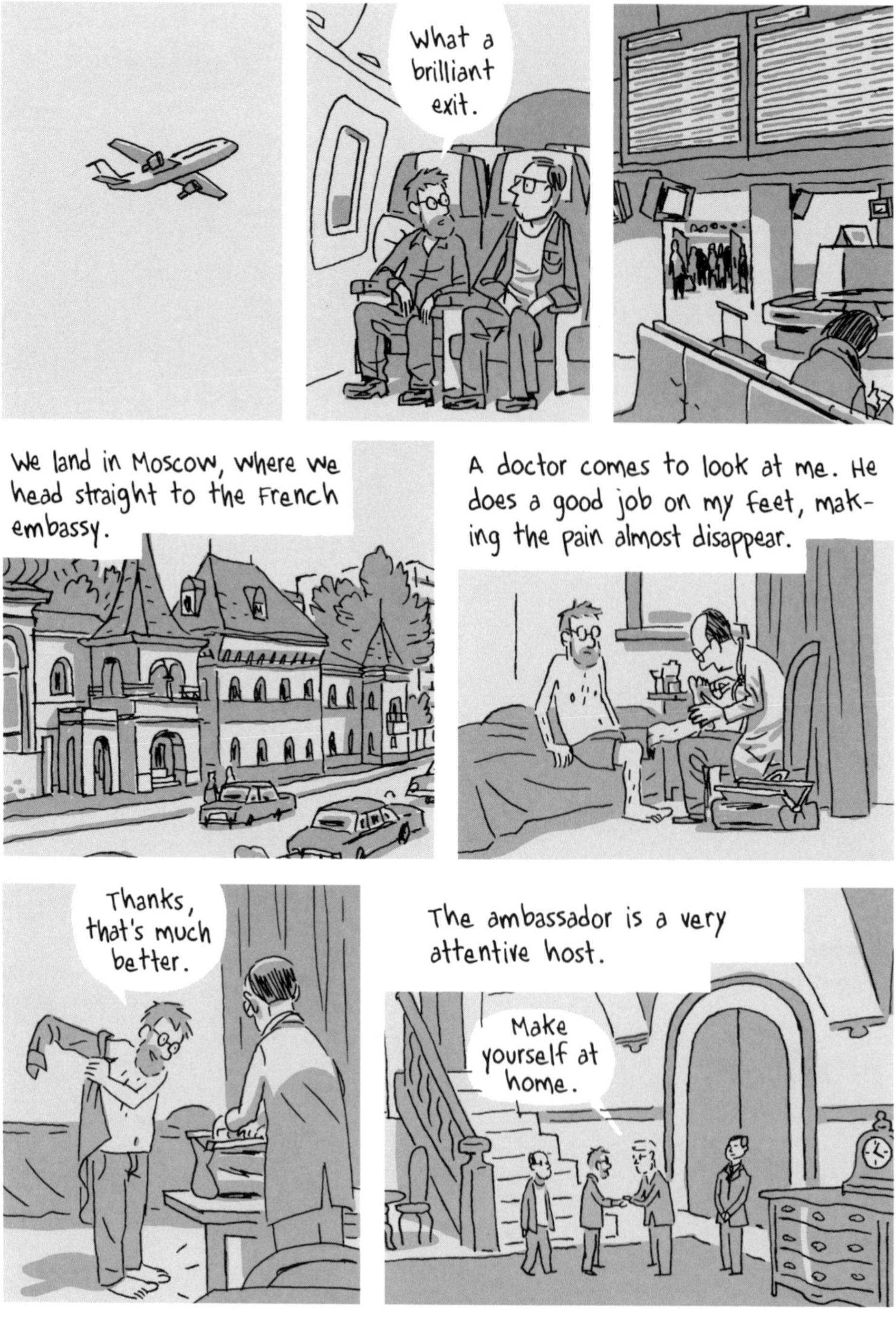
What a brilliant exit.
We land in Moscow, where we head straight to the French embassy.
A doctor comes to look at me. He does a good job on my feet, making the pain almost disappear.
Thanks, that's much better.
The ambassador is a very attentive host.
Make yourself at home.

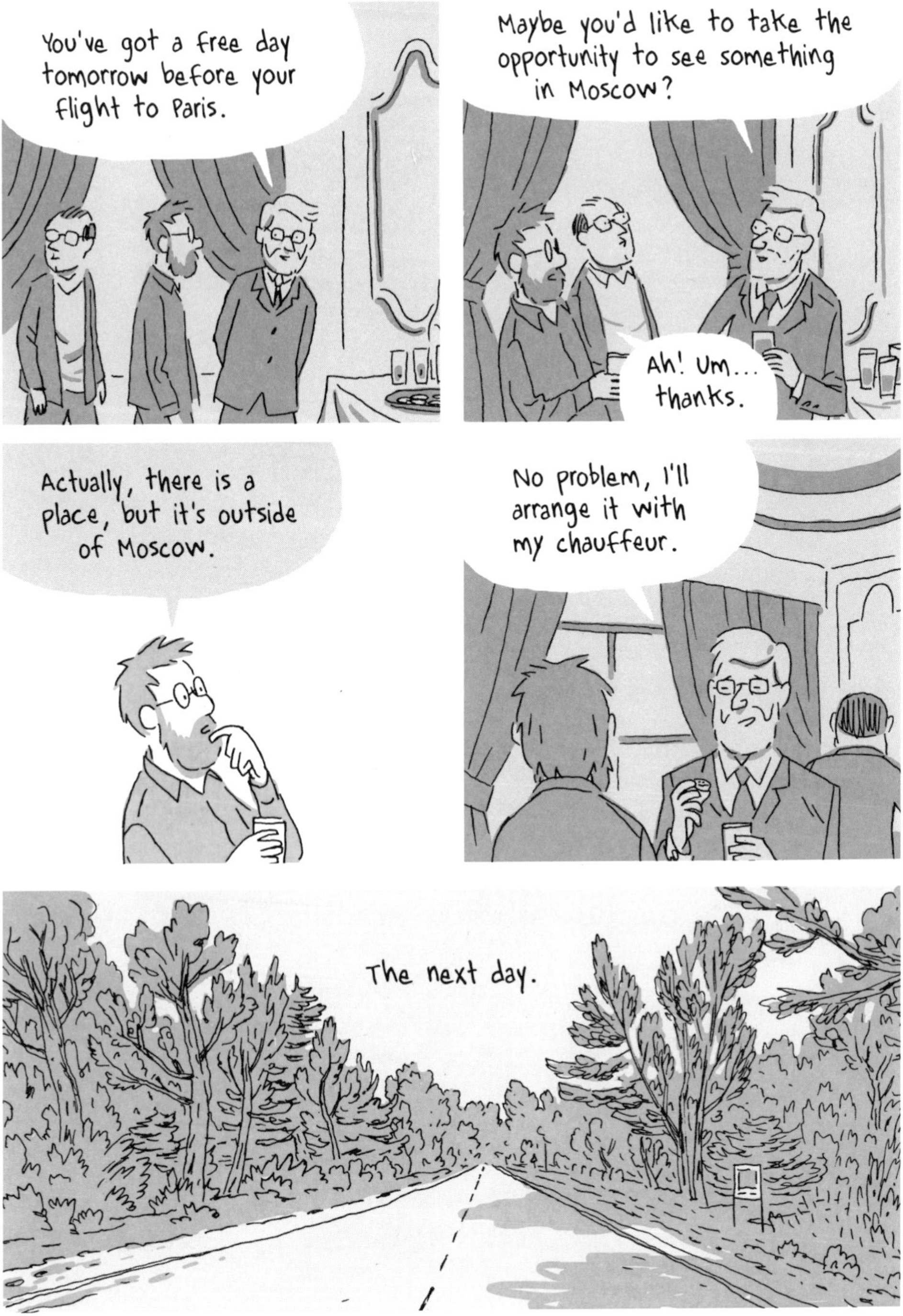
You've got a free day tomorrow before your flight to Paris.
Maybe you'd like to take the opportunity to see something in Moscow?
Ah! Um... thanks.
Actually, there is a place, but it's outside of Moscow.
No problem, I'll arrange it with my chauffeur.
The next day.

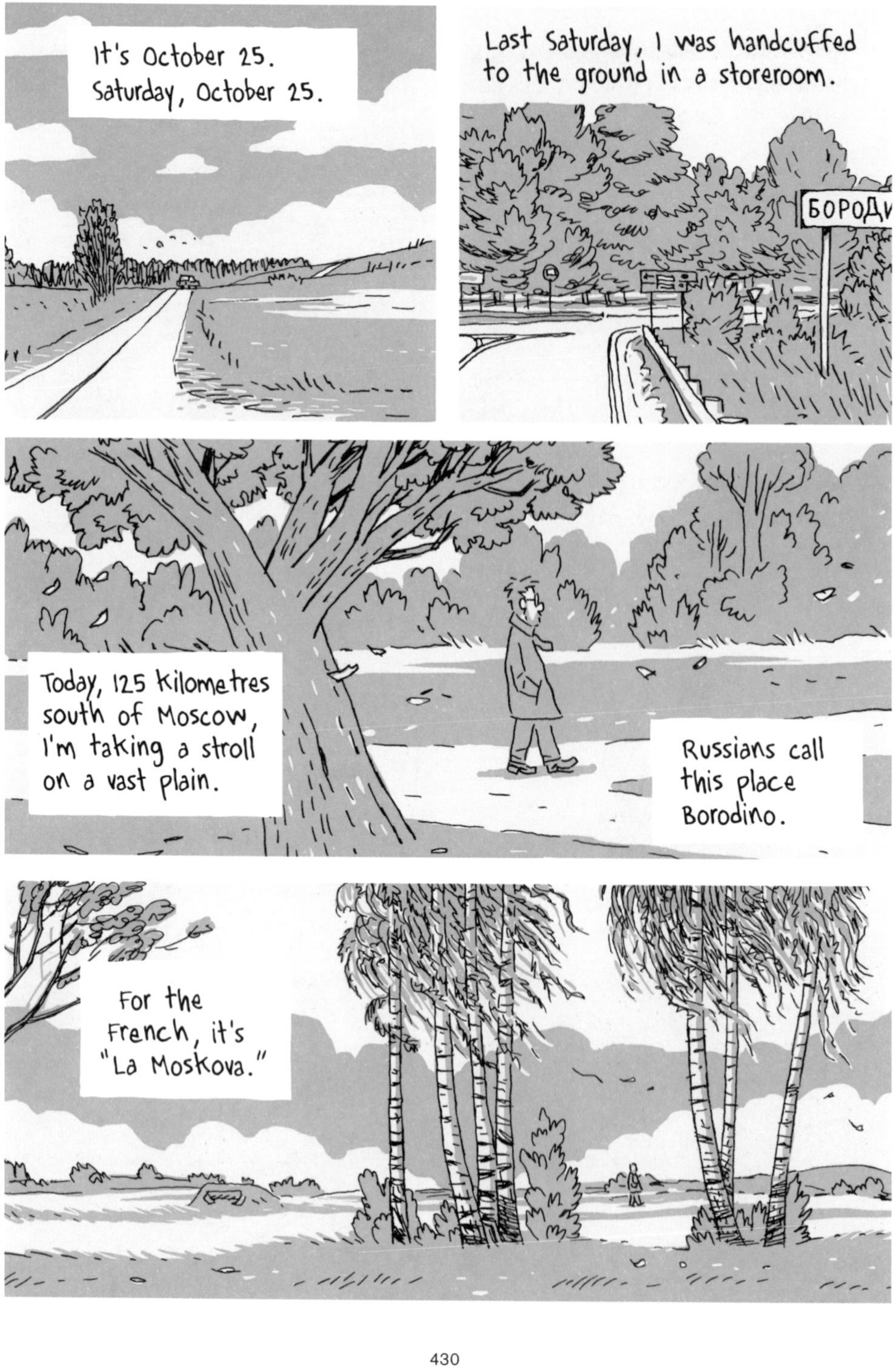
It's October 25. Saturday, October 25.
Last Saturday, I was handcuffed to the ground in a storeroom.
БОРОДИ
Today, 125 kilometres south of Moscow, I'm taking a stroll on a vast plain.
Russians call this place Borodino.
For the French, it's "La Moskova."

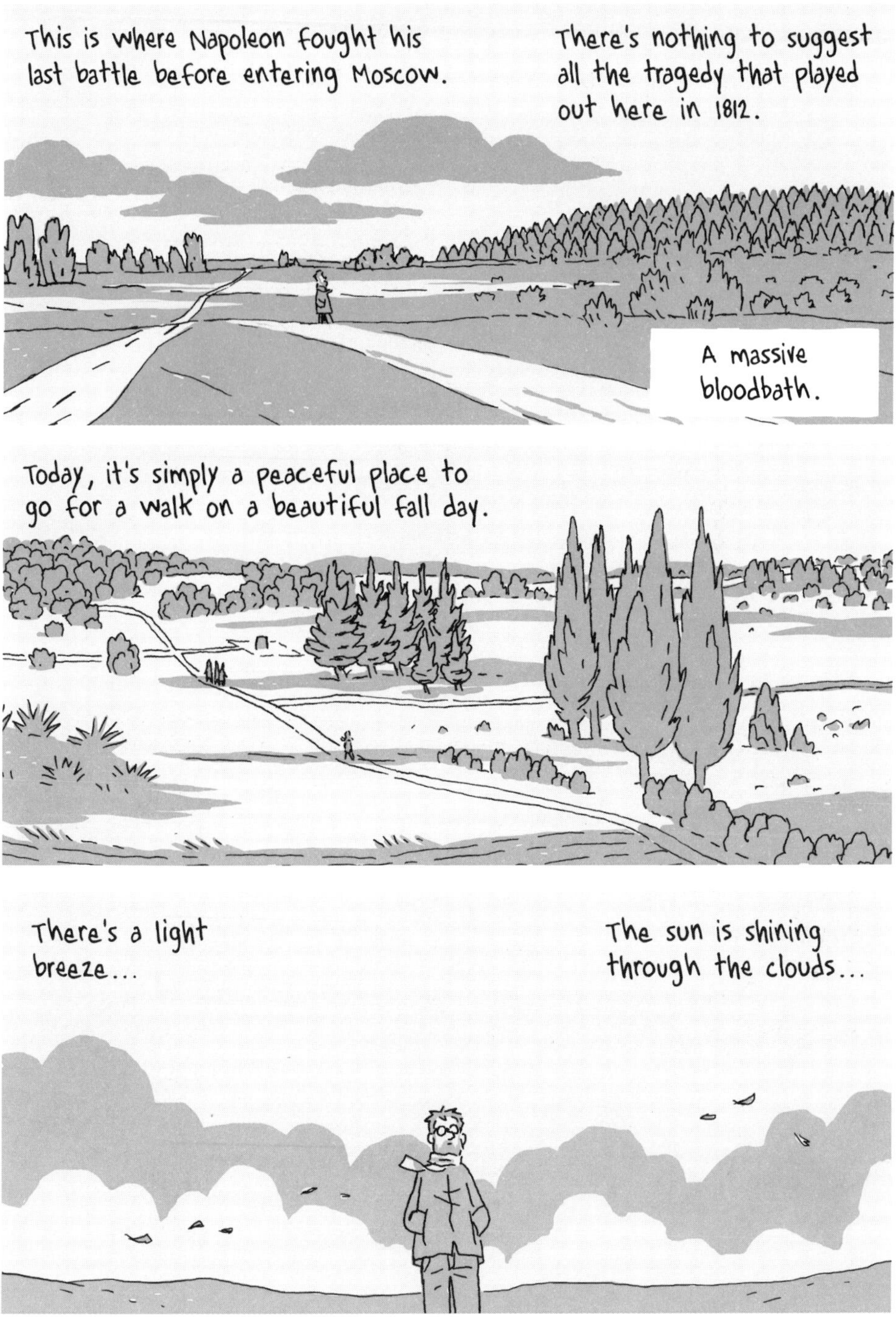
This is where Napoleon fought his last battle before entering Moscow.
There's nothing to suggest all the tragedy that played out here in 1812.
A massive bloodbath.
Today, it's simply a peaceful place to go for a walk on a beautiful fall day.
There's a light breeze...
The sun is shining through the clouds...

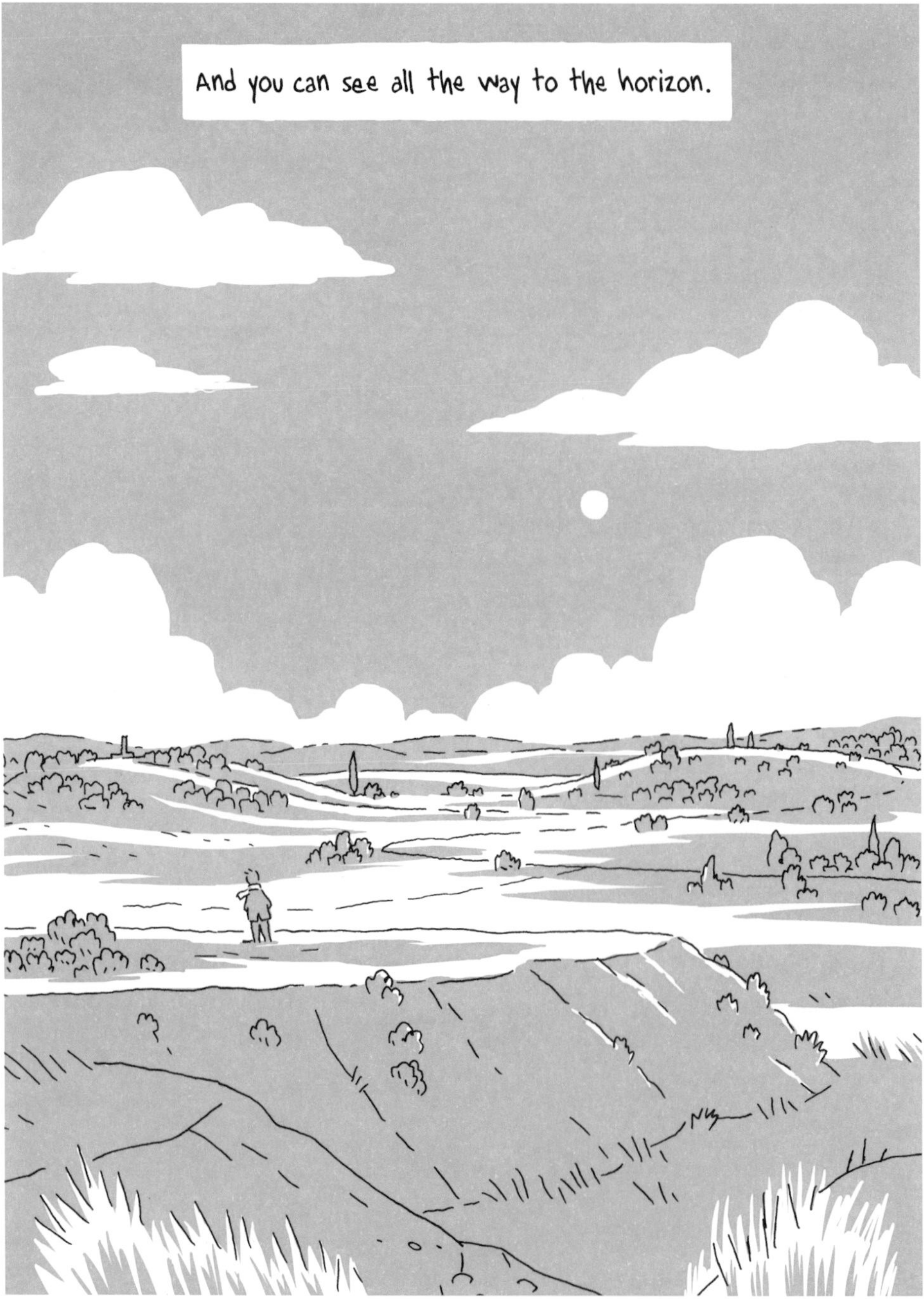
And you can see all the way to the horizon.

Delisle 2016

Epilogue

Christophe André was on a mission with Médecins Sans Frontières (Doctors Without Borders) when he was kidnapped in Nazran on July 2, 1997. Despite this harrowing experience, he remained committed to humanitarian work. After six months of well-deserved rest, he returned on a mission for MSF and continued to work for the organization for another eighteen years.

Aslan and Zovra experienced serious difficulties as a result of this incident, including death threats from Christophe's abductors. With the help of MSF and Christophe, they were able to come to France, where they were granted asylum by French authorities.

Christophe's sister Céline did not cancel her wedding after all. An empty chair and plate at the table of honour symbolized her brother's absence.

Thank you to Christophe for his trust, patience, and availability during the fifteen years it took to make this book. And thank you to Lewis.